P9-CNE-629

SHAKESPEARE SURVEY

ADVISORY BOARD

1 Shakespeare and his Stage
2 Shakespearian Production
3 The Man and the Writer
4 Interpretation
5 Textual Criticism
6 The Histories
7 Style and Language
8 The Comedies
9 *Hamlet*
10 The Roman Plays
11 The Last Plays (with an index to *Surveys 1–10*)
12 The Elizabethan Theatre
13 *King Lear*
14 Shakespeare and his Contemporaries
15 The Poems and Music
16 Shakespeare in the Modern World
17 Shakespeare in his Own Age
18 Shakespeare Then Till Now
19 *Macbeth*
20 Shakespearian and Other Tragedy
21 *Othello* (with an index to *Surveys 11–20*)
22 Aspects of Shakespearian Comedy
23 Shakespeare's Language
24 Shakespeare: Theatre Poet
25 Shakespeare's Problem Plays
26 Shakespeare's Jacobean Tragedies
27 Shakespeare's Early Tragedies
28 Shakespeare and the Ideas of his Time
29 Shakespeare's Last Plays
30 *Henry IV* to *Hamlet*
31 Shakespeare and the Classical World (with an index to *Surveys 21–30*)
32 The Middle Comedies
33 *King Lear*
34 Characterization in Shakespeare
35 Shakespeare in the Nineteenth Century
36 Shakespeare in the Twentieth Century
37 Shakespeare's Earlier Comedies
38 Shakespeare and History
39 Shakespeare on Film and Television
40 Current Approaches to Shakespeare through Language, Text and Theatre
41 Shakespearian Stages and Staging (with an index to *Surveys 31–40*)
42 Shakespeare and the Elizabethans
43 *The Tempest* and After
44 Shakespeare and Politics
45 *Hamlet* and its Afterlife
46 Shakespeare and Sexuality
47 Playing Places for Shakespeare
48 Shakespeare and Cultural Exchange
49 *Romeo and Juliet* and its Afterlife
50 Shakespeare and Language

Aspects of *Macbeth*
Aspects of *Othello*
Aspects of *Hamlet*
Aspects of *King Lear*
Aspects of Shakespeare's 'Problem Plays'

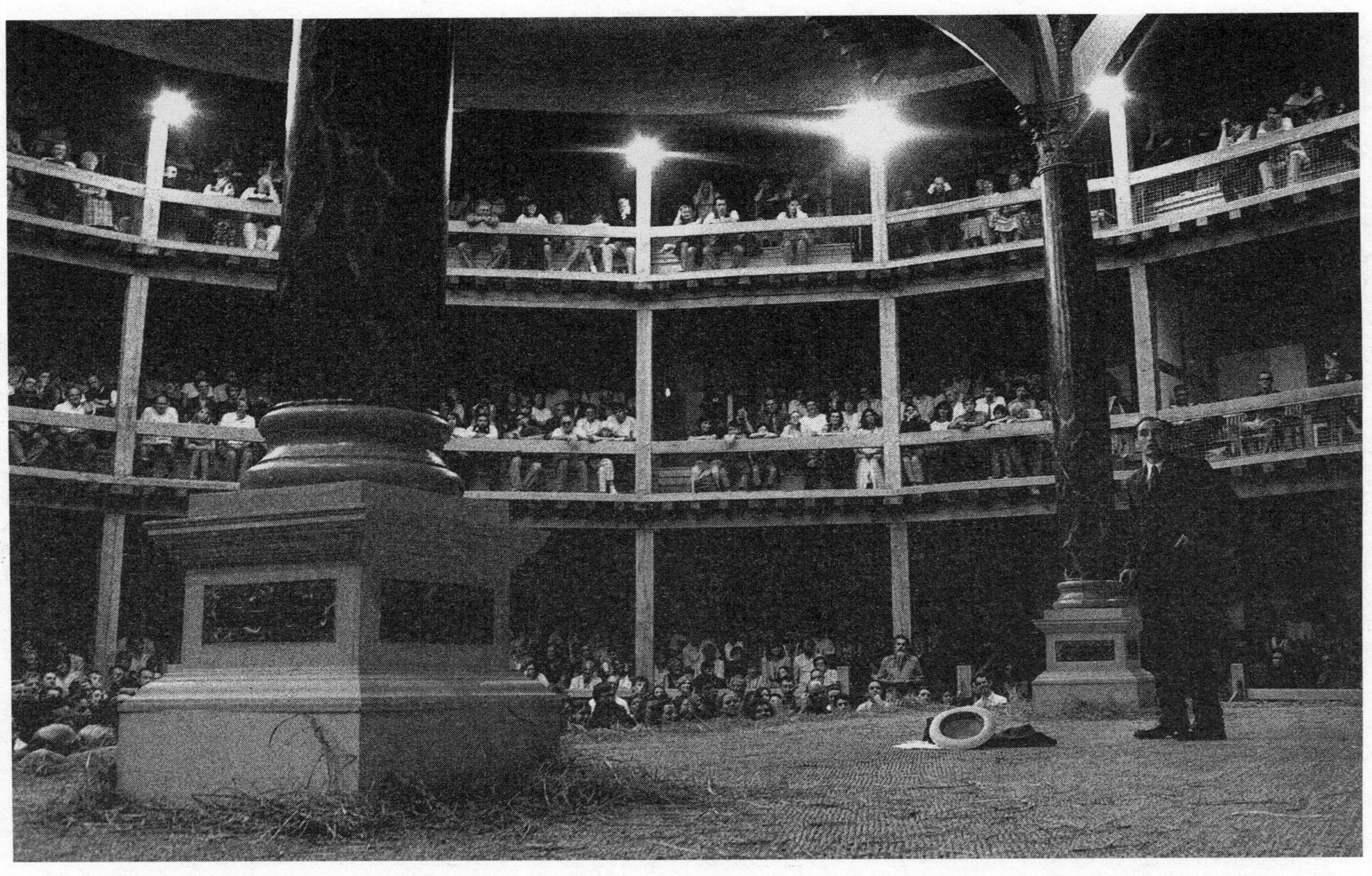

Frontispiece: From the Prologue Season at the Globe Theatre on Bankside – Mark Rylance as Proteus in *The Two Gentlemen of Verona*.

SHAKESPEARE SURVEY

AN ANNUAL SURVEY OF

SHAKESPEARE STUDIES AND PRODUCTION

50

Shakespeare and Language

EDITED BY

STANLEY WELLS

PUBLISHED BY THE PRESS SYNDICATE OF THE UNIVERSITY OF CAMBRIDGE
The Pitt Building, Trumpington Street, Cambridge CB2 1RP, United Kingdom

CAMBRIDGE UNIVERSITY PRESS
The Edinburgh Building, Cambridge CB2 2RU, United Kingdom
40 West 20th Street, New York, NY 10011–4211, USA
10 Stamford Road, Oakleigh, Melbourne 3166, Australia

First published 1997

Printed in Great Britain at the University Press, Cambridge

Typeset in Bembo 10/12pt

A catalogue record for this book is available from the British Library

Shakespeare Survey was first published in 1948. Its first eighteen volumes were edited by Allardyce Nicoll. Kenneth Muir edited volumes 19 to 33.

ISBN 0 521 59135 X hardback

CE

EDITOR'S NOTE

We have the privilege of printing in this volume Kenneth Muir's last conference paper, read in his presence during the 27th International Shakespeare Conference on 19 August 1996. At the opening reception of the Conference, sponsored by Cambridge University Press, he had cut the first slice of a cake celebrating fifty years of *Shakespeare Survey*. He died on 30 September at the age of 89. His editorship of *Shakespeare Survey* from Volume 19 to Volume 33 was only one among his innumerable services to Shakespeare scholarship over a long lifetime of distinguished achievement. He was a friend to scholars all over the world, and is greatly mourned.

Volume 51 of *Shakespeare Survey*, which will be at press by the time this volume appears, is to be on 'Shakespeare in the Eighteenth Century'. Volume 52, on 'Shakespeare and the Globe', will include papers from the 1998 International Shakespeare Conference. The theme of Volume 53 will be 'Shakespeare and Narrative'.

Submissions should be addressed to the Editor at The Shakespeare Centre, Henley Street, Stratford-upon-Avon, Warwickshire CV37 6QW, to arrive at the latest by 1 September 1998 for Volume 52 and 1 September 1999 for Volume 53. Pressures on space are heavy; priority is given to articles related to the theme of a particular volume. Please either enclose postage (overseas, in International Reply Coupons) or send a copy you do not wish to be returned. All articles submitted are read by the Editor and at least one member of the Editorial Board, whose indispensable assistance the Editor gratefully acknowledges.

Unless otherwise indicated, Shakespeare quotations and references are keyed to the modern-spelling Complete Oxford Shakespeare (1986).

Review copies of books should be addressed to the Editor, as above. In attempting to survey the ever-increasing bulk of Shakespeare publications our reviewers inevitably have to exercise some selection. We are pleased to receive offprints of articles which help to draw our reviewers' attention to relevant material.

S. W. W.

CONTRIBUTORS

JOHN ASTINGTON, *University of Toronto*
PHILIPPA BERRY, *King's College, Cambridge*
STEPHEN BOOTH, *University of California, Berkeley*
MARK THORNTON BURNETT, *The Queen's University, Belfast*
JEAN-MICHEL DÉPRATS, *University of Paris – Nanterre*
JANETTE DILLON, *University of Nottingham*
KEIR ELAM, *University of Florence*
BRIAN GIBBONS, *University of Münster*
PETER HOLBROOK, *University of Queensland*
LISA HOPKINS, *Sheffield Hallam University*
JOHN JOWETT, *The Shakespeare Institute, University of Birmingham*
DENNIS KENNEDY, *Trinity College, Dublin*
JOHN KERRIGAN, *St. John's College, Cambridge*
LYNNE MAGNUSSON, *University of Waterloo, Ontario*
KENNETH MUIR, *University of Liverpool*
NIKY RATHBONE, *Birmingham Shakespeare Library*
MEREDITH SKURA, *Rice University, Texas*
ROBERT SMALLWOOD, *Shakespeare Birthplace Trust*
A. B. TAYLOR, *The Swansea Institute*
MARION TROUSDALE, *University of Maryland*

CONTENTS

ILLUSTRATIONS

Frontispiece: From the Prologue Season at the Globe Theatre on Bankside – Mark Rylance as Proteus in *The Two Gentlemen of Verona* [Courtesy of Shakespeare's Globe]

LIST OF ILLUSTRATIONS

SHAKESPEARE'S LANGUAGE AND THE LANGUAGE OF SHAKESPEARE'S TIME

STEPHEN BOOTH

> 'Many things are true which only the commonest minds observe.'
> 'Then I think the commonest minds must be rather useful.'
>
> *Middlemarch*, Book 1, chapter 5

Shakespeare is our most underrated poet. It should not be necessary to say that, but it is. We generally acknowledge Shakespeare's poetic superiority to other candidates for greatest poet in English, but doing that is comparable to saying that King Kong is bigger than other monkeys. The difference between Shakespeare's abilities with language and those even of Milton, Chaucer, or Ben Jonson is immense. The densities of his harmonies – phonic and ideational both – are beyond comfortable calculation, are so great that the act of analysing them is self-defeating, uncovers nests of coherence that make the physics of analysed lines less rather than more comprehensible.

The reason it is necessary to point out Shakespeare's poetic superiority to competing poets is, I think, that we have so long, so industriously ignored the qualities in literature that drew us to it in the first place. As a result, we – or, at any rate, the scholarly books and essays we write and read – and our students treat a Shakespeare play or *Paradise Lost* or *Huckleberry Finn* or even 'Kubla Khan' as if we valued it for its paraphrasable content or as a source of information about the time and society that spawned it or about its author. When I talk about what 'we' do, I speak not just of the 'us' of the last several years of sociology, sentimental anthropology, and crusading sanctimony in literary criticism but of the cultural residue of a trend that goes back in Western culture at least to Horace and Philip Sidney and their intellectually casual conclusion that value in literature resides in its supposed, rarely witnessed capacity as an agent of moral improvement.

In 1990 I published an essay in *Shakespeare Quarterly* called 'The Function of Criticism at the Present Time and All Others' (*Shakespeare Quarterly*, 41 (1990), 262–8). At its core were (1) the idea that what the kind of literary criticism we call 'academic' does for us is offer plausible, but so far always insufficient excuses for the improbably high value society places on literature and (2) an appeal to the academic community (a), to admit that we have no good reason – that is that we have no philosophically dignified reason – for valuing the ultimately frivolous commodity that literature is when weighed against the things human beings value only slightly more – things like food, shelter, children, parents, gods, honour, and such; and (b), to admit also that we can and will and should cheerfully go on valuing art as we always have whether we have dignified excuse for it or not.

This paper continues in the vein of the essay. And my first ambition for it is that it remind you that there is good reason why the word 'poetry' has for so long seemed to be a simple synonym for the word 'verse' and that it remind you too just what the qualities are that differentiate verse from prose.

When we recognize something as verse, we recognize it as being organized in at least one non-substantive system, one system – traditionally a phonic one – other than the one composed of syntactic and semantic signals. Often a piece of verse will present several substantively extraneous phonic organizations, for instance, systematic rhythmic patterning, a rhyme scheme, and alliterative patterning or pattern in assonance or pattern in consonance or pattern in all three.

The key fact about verse is the irrelevance of its defining, non-substantive organizations to the matter of the sentences and paragraphs in which the extra organizations sport themselves. The qualities of verse that define it are ones that – if anything is frivolous – are frivolous. As I have implied, we are beings uncomfortable with ourselves as creatures who care about what does not matter. We want to believe that what is immaterial to what is being said doesn't matter. Witness the pathetic tradition by which apologists for poetry still sometimes attempt to comfort themselves and us with pious assertions that *s* sounds make us hear snakes and that rhythms imitate the substance conveyed by rhythmic lines (several generations of American high school students were regularly submitted to John Masefield's rhythmically purposeful 'Sea Fever', a poem called forward by English teachers under stress and a poem that thus caused several generations of Americans to grow up thinking that the purpose of rhythm in verse is to simulate seasickness in stay-at-homes).

Concentration on intellectually dignified, philosophically defensible elements in literature has left us so comfortably and so thoroughly self-deluded that we hear – and accept the underlying assumptions of – the phrase 'redeeming social value' without blushing – or even giggling. Moreover, concern with what sentences, speeches, poems, plays, and writers *say* (or can be said to say or once to have said) encourages attention to the kind of coherence that derives from *logical* relationships among elements and inattention to orderly relationships based in common factors comparable to colours and shapes, relationships that can matter to us though they convey none.

By way of exemplification, I want now to talk about the editorial glosses that we are used to seeing as adjuncts to Shakespeare texts. They are a product of the assumption that only signification signifies – that only the paraphrasable matter of a sentence or paragraph or speech matters in our experience of a work. They are also prime culprits in that assumption's preservation and perseverance. Glosses in footnotes give students the impression that Shakespeare's language and the language of Shakespeare's time are the same thing. And they encourage the widespread student belief that their purpose in reading a Shakespeare play is to show a teacher that they can find in it the slim little narrative it was before 400 years got in the way. Such notes also encourage the belief that a Shakespeare play is an obstacle course, encourage the assumption that the clarified, modernized versions of the plays that footnotes embody is the real thing and that simple substitution for Shakespeare's words (and some pruning of action and assertion that make the plot hard to figure or hard to take) is desirable.

The notion that Shakespeare's language is merely a screen to penetrate on the way to something simple is a close relative of the kind of commentary that recommends Shakespeare plays to students as essentially comparable in value to modern fictions that treat of similar situations – the kind of commentary that attempts to engender enthusiasm for the great literature of the past by insisting on the likenesses between – for example – Romeo and Juliet, on the one hand, and, on the other, the comic-book teenagers Archie and Veronica. I once heard a surprisingly reputable Shakespeare scholar tell a graduate seminar that the greatness of Shakespeare was evident from the fact that, four centuries after *Romeo and Juliet* was first performed, newly pubescent boys and girls still like to fondle one another. No wonder students think the value of Shakespeare is as an obstacle course and a source of stuff to test them on.

Anyway, Shakespeare's language and the language of Shakespeare's time were not the same – any more than the music of Beethoven is the same as the music of Beethoven's time or Vermeer's paintings are typical of the work of his contemporaries or the simple prose of Abraham Lincoln is typical of the simple prose of Lincoln's time.

Shakespeare's language really is as special as people say it is.

It is special in two ways.

(1) Shakespeare's sentences don't always make sense.

(2) Shakespeare's language is exciting to the minds that hear it – exciting to minds because what is being said in a Shakespearian sentence often comes to us in a soup of possibilities, possibilities engendered by substantively negligible, substantively irrelevant relationships among elements in a syntax to which those relationships do not pertain and by which those relationships are filtered from consciousness.

Number 1 is hard to take. Nonetheless, it is true that, when one hears a Shakespearian sentence or speech and understands what it is saying, one is often led to understanding by situation and by connotations of the words used – not by the demonstrable content signalled by syntax and the probabilities of the diction.

That is, one is hearing sense in nonsense.

And, when we do that, we do what we want to do: understand what we do not understand, what we still don't understand.

The best example I know of both kinds of specialness is the following passage from *Othello*; Desdemona, momentarily alone on stage, soliloquizes on Othello's abusive behaviour towards her:

> 'Tis meet I should be used so, very meet.
> How have I been behaved, that he might stick
> The small'st opinion on my least misuse?
> (4.2.110–12)

In the third of those three lines, editors who gloss 'opinion' ordinarily gloss it as 'censure' (or 'suspicion' or something similar and similarly improbable in a context other than this one). The Riverside Shakespeare says simply: 'opinion: censure'; so does David Bevington's 1992 complete works; the revised Pelican of 1964 glosses 'small'st opinion' as 'least suspicion'. What such glosses report is true, but the manner of the report distorts the truth. Such glosses casually, benevolently give readers the impression that 'opinion' once meant 'ill opinion'. M. R. Ridley's 1958 Arden edition of *Othello* is unusual in noting the anomaly by which context thrusts a sense upon the word 'opinion' that that word is not known ever to have had elsewhere; Ridley says '*opinion* must here, unusually, mean unfavourable opinion'.

Ridley's use of 'must here . . . mean' points in passing to a truth about the lines that is vital to an understanding, not of the lines, but of the way they work. 'Must mean' acknowledges the fact that a scholarly gloss on 'opinion' in *Othello* 4.2.112 is as unnecessary as it is unavailable: context tells one – tells anyone capable of getting the general drift of the scene – that '*opinion* must here, unusually, mean unfavourable opinion'. The New Folger editors, Barbara Mowat and Paul Werstine, did not gloss – evidently saw no need to gloss – 'opinion' at all. The same was apparently true for Kenneth Muir; he too sensibly leaves Desdemona's use of 'opinion' unglossed in his New Penguin edition. Although I have not attempted a full survey, I expect that those three editors have had a lot of company in their omission. That is because editorial glosses on words that act as 'opinion' does in *Othello* 4.2.112 mean to say only 'You, reader, are right: context does indeed demand that this word be understood as if it were "———".'

The same is true of all editorial glosses that begin 'i.e.'; glosses headed by 'i.e.' acknowledge that the sense both editor and readers take from some unlikely linguistic unit is determined by context not the syntactic and semantic signals that ordinarily govern and direct understanding.

What I care about in *Othello* 4.2.110–12 is what it is about these particular lines that makes the anomalous use of 'opinion' seem so commonplace, so usual, so *right* that one can read across the lines without pause and hear them in the theatre without even so much as a flicker of puzzlement.

When I say that the use of 'opinion' sounds right, the rightness I refer to is of the sort one feels in music where, at least in my purely amateur experience, one's mind regularly hears a given note or chord in a piece of unfamiliar music as if one had predicted it ahead of time.

One possible source of the rightness of 'opinion' in Desdemona's soliloquy – one possible sustainer of the word 'opinion' as a synonym for 'blame' – is a bit of unstated trick logic – a logic probably generated in Shakespeare's unconscious and, I assume, ordinarily available only to the unconsciousnesses of listeners and readers. In the case of 'opinion' in the present passage, the logic would run this way: since 'censure' is a synonym for 'opinion' (as it is when Leontes says 'How blest am I / In my just censure, in my true opinion!' (*The Winter's Tale* 2.1.38–9), and since 'censure' and 'blame' are synonyms (as in 'the fault / Would not scape censure' (*King Lear* 1.4.203–4), 'opinion' and 'blame' must be synonyms too.[1]

Most of the other sources of overpowering rightness in the 'opinion' passage in *Othello* are much more ordinary in literary constructs than the subterranean chop logic by which 'opinion' is confusable with 'blame', but they are presumably just as distant – just as inevitably, just as eternally, distant – from the consciousnesses of audiences and readers. For one thing, a dusting of *m* sounds lies over the whole three-line passage. Only slightly more complex in its assurances of quasi-organic rightness is the recurrence of the third, and fifth syllables of line 110 – 'I' and 'be' – as the third and fifth syllables of line 111 – where, though nearly identical with the corresponding pair of sounds in the previous line, the syllables figure in a syntax entirely foreign to the one they echo ('I should be used' / 'I been behaved'). Moreover, in each of those two lines the sixth syllable concludes in a *d* sound; and '-haved', the sixth syllable of line 111 repeats the *v* of 'have' but in combination with what in any dialect at any time must have been a different kind of *a* sound. In the line that actually harbours the nonce synonym for 'blame', 'opinion' is not only supported on either side by the simultaneously paired and contrasted 'small'st' and 'least', but – by virtue of its second syllable,

[1] Compare the subscription of the Maria-Olivia letter in *Twelfth Night*: 'She that would alter services with thee' (2.5.153). The otherwise unheard-of use there of 'alter' to mean 'exchange' is made meaningful by accidents of its location. It is informed by a context relevant to 'an altar' – an altar in a church, sustained by the relevance of both the liturgical and sexual senses of 'service', and smoothed over by an implied logic that says that – since 'to exchange' and 'to change' are synonyms, and since 'to alter' and 'to change' are synonyms – 'to exchange' and 'to alter' must also be synonyms. For similarly casual nonce logic in the same play, consider Feste's use of the word 'welkin' – 'sky' – to mean 'proper sphere of action': 'Who you are and what you would are out of my welkin – I might say "element", but the word is over-worn' (3.1.56–8); 'element' can mean 'air' and can therefore replace 'welkin', but that does not make 'welkin' a universally available substitute for all senses of 'element'. The phenomenon occurs earlier when Toby commends Feste's singing voice by calling it 'a contagious breath' (2.3.53). 'Contagious', which is not known elsewhere as a synonym for 'attractive', *is* a synonym for 'catching', and 'catching' was presumably already capable of saying 'attractive' (*OED*'s first example of the adjective in that sense is from 1654, but 'to catch' meaning 'to charm', 'to attract', 'to captivate' goes back at least to Chaucer). In a typically Shakespearian skitter, Toby proceeds in his next speech to propose that he and his companions sing a *catch*.

'-pin', the fourth of the line – rhymes with 'been' the fourth syllable of the line it follows. The last word of the soliloquy also vouches mutely for the integrity of the whole: 'misuse' – there referring to impropriety committed *by* Desdemona, not against her – is also, is entirely incidentally, an echo of 'used' in ''Tis meet I should be used so' in the first line of the speech where 'used' said what 'misused' might have.

The phenomenon that led me to lead with Desdemona's 'opinion' speech here is of a kind to which I will devote the bulk of my paper: 'stick the small'st o*pin*ion on' enfolds within it the stuff of the familiar, here irrelevant, idea of sticking a pin (in fact sticking the 'small'st' pin: pins were already proverbial for both literal and metaphorical smallness – as in 'not worth a pin').

I contend that substantively incidental irrelevant relationships like 'stick the small'st . . . pin . . . on' in Desdemona's speech are worth attention. They are the sort of typically Shakespearian phenomena that prompted me to say that Shakespeare's language is exciting to listening minds – that is, minds that listen casually the way we all do, not minds poised to pounce on the sorts of non-signifying organizations I pounce on here. Things like the locally irrelevant 'stick' / 'pin' relationship in Desdemona's soliloquy are the spiciest ingredients of the soup of possibilities in which the paraphrasable substance, the matter, of Shakespeare's sentences floats.

Such relationships are ordinarily and properly as completely overlooked by readers and listeners as the unostentatious extra organizations inherent in blank verse or in gentle consonance and assonance among syllables that perform their overt tasks without any substantive enhancement from the extra patterning. I suggest that, where they occur, substantively insignificant semantic relationships like 'stick' / 'pin' in *Othello* 4.2.111–12 are like alliteration, assonance, consonance, rhythm and rhyme in being persuasive contributors to our sense of the organism-like coherence of Shakespearian sentences, paragraphs, and speeches.

The submerged 'stick' / 'pin' pair in Desdemona's soliloquy would do what it does even if it were the only such pair in the canon, but, as champion of the aesthetic value and efficacy of this pair and of shadow locutions similarly submerged but unrelated to sticks or pins, I am encouraged to note other places in the plays where Shakespeare's mind appears to toy casually with one or another of the particulars of Desdemona's stick and pin speech. For instance, *Measure for Measure* 1.3.23–7: lines that play casually, gracefully, and without any demand for audience applause or acknowledgement on the verb 'to stick', meaning 'to affix' and the noun 'stick' meaning something akin to 'twig' and to 'rod':

Now, as fond fathers,
Having bound up the threat'ning twigs of birch
Only to stick it in their children's sight
For terror, not to use, in time the rod
More mocked becomes than feared . . .

For a final kind of casual 'stick' relationship, consider the incidental 'drumsticks' in *All's Well That Ends Well* 3.6.45–6: 'This drum sticks sorely in your disposition.'

Now I want to look at a succession of Shakespearian passages similarly enhanced by substantively extra patterning. Attention to that patterning should seem less frivolous, more reasonable than it otherwise might if you remember that I am not for a minute suggesting that there is any meaning to be squeezed out of these patterns and into the passages in which they lurk. You will be less uncomfortable than you might otherwise be, if you remember too that I do not mean for a second to imply that conscious perception of such patterning ought properly be part of your conscious experiences of Shakespeare plays.

All I do suggest is that such patterns contribute largely to the *eventfulness* of the passages. Indeed, my principal purpose in this paper is to argue that Shakespeare's language is more *eventful* than anybody else's appears to be, that Shakespeare's language all but bursts with activity generated by incidental relationships among its elements.

The following sentence is *Macbeth* 1.4.33–5. Duncan, overwhelmed with gratitude to his victorious generals, comments on his response:

> My plenteous joys,
> Wanton in fullness, seek to hide themselves
> In drops of sorrow.

The sentence is overtly witty, hinged on the familiar irony in which tears, signs of grief, register joy; Miranda remarks on the same stock paradox in *The Tempest*: 'I am a fool / To weep at what I am glad of' (3.1.73–4). But Duncan's sentence is also full to overflowing with relationships that could have been exploited, could have been pointed up and pointed out, but are not. A Biondello or a Grumio could have leapt upon the contextually irrelevant – and therefore contextually hidden – opposition of the paired words 'seek' and 'hide' and/or upon the irony by which the embarrassed joys attempt to *hide* in tears: agents of *display*. A pun-hungry Shakespearian clown might also be imagined to pick up on the contrasting pair that 'fullness' makes with 'want', the first syllable of 'wanton'. On the other hand, no responsible comic character would try to make something of the two uses of 'in' in the sentence. The 'in' of 'wanton in' says 'with respect to'; the 'in' of 'in drops of sorrow' is literal: it indicates location. The pair of non-identical twins that the two *ins* present is of a sort so common in everyday speech that not even the most desperate of Shakespeare's clowns would be likely to pick up on it, but – commonplace or not – the two *ins* in Duncan's sentence give it one more charge of incidental energy. An effect need not be unusual to be.

I just used the word 'energy' as a critical term, and I will use it several times more in the next few pages. Before going on to other Shakespearian passages, I should acknowledge some uneasiness about my terminology. I worry that I will seem to be generating a jargon, a special, especially imprecise language that behaves as if compensating for its vagueness were the responsibility of consumers. I worry in particular about my use of the word 'energy'. I would use a more precise word if I could find it. What I wish 'energy' better labelled is the product of a substantively incidental organization that coexists with the syntactic organization of a sentence or paragraph or speech. I call that product energy because it resembles the heat generated by the interaction of two bodies that rub or jar against one another.

I want now to look at *As You Like It* 4.1.191–4, a speech occasioned by a display of traditional, knee-jerk antifeminism by Rosalind in her role as Ganymede, boy physician to the lovesick. Orlando takes his leave, and Celia accuses Rosalind:

> You have simply misused our sex in your love-prate. We must have your doublet and hose plucked over your head, and show the world what the bird hath done to her own nest.

The passage is prose, but it has extra energy comparable to the energy that derives from phonic patterning in verse.

It gets that energy first – and most obviously, given the specialized context of this paper – from the ordinarily non-obvious conjunction of 'bird' with the word 'plucked' – a word that has a specialized sense in context of birds and feathers but is here used – used in a context still ten syllables short of concern for birds – to mean simply 'pulled'.

Secondly and just as unostentatiously, the speech gets energy from the multiple physics it conflates and makes easy for us. For one thing, the passage lets us believe ourselves able to imagine a doublet and hose as capable of being lifted over the wearer's head like a skirt; what is described is presumably not what a listener imagines: the action the words describe would at best result in pain to the wearer and destruction of the garment. One's mind has to behave – and easily does behave – as if it had imagined a doublet and hose as a skirt. Interestingly then, what the passage invites one to imagine includes an incidental assertion of the femininity the speaker wants to expose.

The passage rests heavily and obviously on the idea that 'it is a foul bird that defiles its own nest' (a time-honoured proverb to which, by the way, two details give just the sort of incidental energy that concerns me here: (1) the unexploited pun on 'foul' meaning 'evil' and 'fowl', a synonym for 'bird' and (2) the presence of 'defiles' doing a job that 'fouls' might have done: *it is a foul fowl that fouls its own nest*). The proverb feels straightforwardly pertinent to Celia's speech – feels so and therefore is so, even though, if one gives the speech the sort of thought it does not invite, one would be hard put to explain its application.

Two mutually exclusive thought patterns meet when Celia introduces the proverb. The two might be expected to collide, but they do not; instead they do something vaguely comparable to blending together and passing through one another. Each of the two thought processes relates to the same general private area of Rosalind's anatomy. Given the dramatized situation in which Celia speaks, the proverb refers to Rosalind's hidden identity as a female, but in the terms of the proverb itself what is hidden by clothes and discernible in demesnes adjacent to her telltale genitalia would be that Rosalind has fouled herself.

Let me insist once again that my point about Celia's speech is a variation on the points I have made about the passages I talked about earlier: Celia's speech makes its listeners effortlessly capable of an experience so complicated as to seem impossible to a mechanism as limited as the human mind. The several intertwined intricacies I have laboured to describe in Celia's speech come into our minds as smoothly as butter. They are ideational counterparts of the phonic complexities we handle with equal ease when we hear verse or rhythmically elegant prose.

The next thing I want to talk about is Antonio's big speech from the courtroom scene in *The Merchant of Venice*. I want to spend more time on that passage than any other – not because it is richer than the others or even because it is longer, but because it is at once so showy about its rhetorical flourishing *and* alive with unobtrusive patterning that makes no call at all for our attention. The speech, I contend, is thus like the other pieces that concern me here in letting us feel more capable mentally than human beings can be or can imagine being – lets us feel an orderliness beyond our capacities to comprehend and lets us feel capable of doing what in fact we never do – cannot do: cope with unmediated experience.

These lines are openly, insistently artificial – brittle and brittly witty in the 'hard' (difficult)/'hard' (rock-like) play in 77–9: 'You may as well do any thing most hard / As seek to soften that – than which what's harder? – / His Jewish heart':

I pray you think you question with the Jew.
You may as well go stand upon the beach
And bid the main flood bate his usual height;
You may as well use question with the wolf
Why he hath made the ewe bleak for the lamb;
You may as well forbid the mountain pines
To wag their high tops and to make no noise
When they are fretten with the gusts of heaven,
You may as well do any thing most hard
As seek to soften that – than which what's harder? –
His Jewish heart. Therefore, I do beseech you,
Make no more offers, use no further means,
But with all brief and plain conveniency
Let me have judgement and the Jew his will.
(*The Merchant of Venice* 4.1.69–82)[2]

The open play on kinds of hardness has lots of equally showy company here. Whatever else it may be, the parallelism of 'question with the Jew' in line 69 and 'question with the wolf' in line 72 is also brazen in its artifice. The speech is also openly artful in its organization. The standard anaphora by which one repeated

[2] In following the quarto and giving 'bleak for the lamb' in line 73, I deviate from the Oxford text, which follows the Folio and gives 'bleat'.

phrase, 'You may as well', begins lines 70, 72, 74 and 77 is similarly palpable and similarly gross as an effect.

At the same time, however, the speech is full of unobserved echoes and repetitions and substantively irrelevant articulations. For a simple first example, note that the play on kinds of hardness is at once enriched and rendered less openly artful by the unassertive phonic echo that 'heart' in line 80 is of 'hard' and 'harder' in lines 78 and 79. Similarly simple are the pattern in prominent *b* sounds in lines 70–4 (in 'beach', 'bid', 'bate', 'bleak', and 'forbid') and the accidental-sounding echoes of 'may' from the 'you may as well' formula audible in 'main' (71), 'made' (73), and 'make' (75). And, at the end of the speech, the 'Make no' construction in 'Make no more offers' in line 80 is at once urgently like and urgently unlike the 'Make no' construction in 'Make no noise' back in line 75. I suggest that each of those unobtrusive patterns gives extra, non-purposeful (and thus less artificial-seeming) unity to the lines over which they spread.

Consider too the casually complex, deeply uninteresting patterning that results when the fifth syllable of line 76, the *en* sound in 'fretten', is casually echoed by the fifth syllable of line 78, the *en* sound in 'soften'. A similarly quiet harmony occurs earlier, within line 76 itself, when the last word of the line, 'heaven', echoes 'fretten' from its middle. The harmonies in which 'fretten', 'heaven', and 'soften' participate are only specialized variations on more pervasive, even less obtrusive patterning in final *n* sounds in the speech. All three words chime almost as precisely with 'mountain' in line 74 as with one another. And better than one in ten of the speech's 143 syllables ends in an *n* sound (four of them in line 81 in 'plain conveniency' alone).

Listen too to the final harmonious note the last word of the passage strikes when 'will' casually, quietly echoes 'well' from the repeated formula 'You may as well' (the echo would presumably have been even more audible in Shakespeare's time than in ours because vowels like the one in 'well' were apparently pronounced West Texas style: 'You may as will').

The speech, a very forest of quiet, substantively insignificant relational harmonies, is unusual not only in the density of its patterning but in the complexity of some of the patterns. However, such accounts of patterns in minutiae as I give here are hard to read about. I fear that my accounts will already have become a mere drone. Moreover, I have a strong impression that – hurrying toward a critic's conclusion and the chance to judge that conclusion as convenient or inconvenient to their own thinking – readers of literary criticism regularly skip across the details on which the critic's conclusion depends – even details inherently much more interesting than the muted patterns I present here. So, lest my accounts of the further harmonies nested within Antonio's 'question with the Jew' speech get overlooked, I want to mark some of the patterns out with arbitrary uses of italics and small capitals. For instance, quoted below are the first lines of the speech in a typography designed to call attention to what is perhaps the most delicate, least effect-like effect in the whole passage. That effect occurs when the fourth line – 'You may as well use question with the wolf' – echoes first the first four words of the speech's second line ('You may as well go stand upon the beach') and then the last five words of the first ('I pray you think you question with the Jew'):

I pray you think **YOU** QUESTION WITH THE JEW
You may as well go stand upon the beach
And bid the main flood bate his usual height;
You may as well **USE** QUESTION WITH THE WOLF
Why he hath made the ewe bleak for the lamb . . .

In addition to its bold italics and small capitals, the foregoing copy of *The Merchant of Venice* 4.1.69–73 uses large, bold capitals to take special notice of 'you' in the first line and 'use' in the fourth. It thereby accentuates (and thus makes cruder than it is as heard or read) the most elegant of the relationships within the complex of asymmetrical pairs that compose lines 69–72. 'Use' – the sixth syllable of line 72 ('You may as well *use* question with the wolf') – is the non-identical phonic twin of 'you' – the sixth syllable of line 69 ('I pray you think *you* question with the Jew'). Similarly delicate and similarly elegant is the interaction of the word 'question' in line 72 with the word it so ostentatiously repeats from line 69. The rhetorically crude equation of 'wolf' and 'Jew' that the variation in line 72 of the 'question with' construction induces is made less crude by the semantic non-identity of the grammatical functions of the two otherwise identical uses of the word 'question', a verb in line 69 and a noun in line 72.

This next typographically distressed copy of the speech notices unactivated potential in the speech for general play on the pronoun 'you', the verb 'use', the idea of what is usual, and female sheep – all of which occur in context of the topic of usury, and each of which echoes and is echoed in the vowel sound of the word 'Jew'.[3]

I pray **YOU** think **YOU** question with the Jew.
YOU may as well go stand upon the beach
And bid the main flood bate his **USUAL** height;
YOU may as well **USE** question with the wolf
Why he hath made the **EWE** bleak for the lamb;
YOU may as well forbid the mountain pines
To wag their high tops and to make no noise
When they are fretten with the gusts of heaven,
YOU may as well do any thing most hard
As seek to soften that – than which what's harder? –
His Jewish heart. Therefore, I do beseech **YOU**,
Make no more offers, **USE** no further means,
But with all brief and plain conveniency
Let me have judgement and the Jew his will.

And here are lines 72–6 of the 'You may as well' speech, the lines that immediately precede the flat-footed but complexly contorted wit of the 'hard/difficult' – 'hard/rock-like' pair. A lot happens in lines 72–6:

You may as well use question with the wolf
Why he hath made the ewe **BLEAK FOR** the lamb;
You may as well forbid the mountain **PINES**
To wag their high tops and to make no noise
When they are fretten with the gusts of heaven . . .

The mountain pines that wag their high tops in lines 74–5 arrive in context of the line about the ewe bleaking for her lost lamb – arrive in context of the *idea* of pining for the lost lamb. Note also (1) that for reasons obvious to anyone who has seen the rear end of a lamb, the verb 'to wag' and the noun 'lamb' have a traditional association in the language at large – even though they are disassociated in the syntax in which we hear them in lines 73 and 75 – and (2) that the syllable 'bleak' (here possibly a dialect synonym for the verb 'to bleat' or – as the Folio printers apparently guessed – a mistranscription of 'bleat' itself), pertains – as the contextually impertinent adjective meaning

---

[3] A variant configuration takes shape early in the play at the first interview between Antonio and Shylock (1.3). There, however, the topic of usury, the topic of what is customary (usual), and the various words that sound like the pronoun 'you' are joined by the idea of sexual 'use':

ANTONIO: Shylock, albeit I neither lend nor borrow
By taking nor by giving of excess,
Yet to supply the ripe wants of my friend
I'll break a *custom* . . . (59–62)

SHYLOCK: Well then, your bond; and let me see – but hear you.
Methoughts you said you neither lend nor borrow
Upon advantage.
ANTONIO: I do never *use* it.
SHYLOCK: When Jacob . . . (67–70)

ANTONIO: And what of him? did he take interest?
SHYLOCK:
No, not take interest, not as *you* would say,
Directly int'rest. Mark what Jacob did . . . (74–7)

SHYLOCK: . . . the *ewes*, being rank,
In end of autumn turnèd to the rams . . . (79–80)

ANTONIO: . . . Was this inserted to make interest good,
Or is **your** gold and silver **ewes** and rams?
SHYLOCK: I cannot tell. I make it breed as fast. (93–5)

(Note, by the way, the metallurgic potential the conjunction 'or' gets in line 94 from the company of 'gold and silver'.)

'cold and barren' – to windswept mountains like the ones where these pines grow.

That brings me at last to the proposition to which this long analysis has built: I submit that the swirl of substantively irrelevant coherences overrides our ability to see that 'forbid the mountain pines ... To make no noise' in lines 75 and 76 is absolute nonsense:

You may as well **FORBID THE MOUNTAIN PINES**
To wag their high tops and **TO MAKE NO NOISE** ...

I want now to talk about a number of similarly eventful Shakespearian passages. It matters that there be many. I want to give you reason to believe me when I say that passages pulsating with substantively irrelevant energy are very common in Shakespeare, reason to believe me when I suggest that a look at virtually any page in Shakespeare will yield several phenomena like the ones incidental to the passages I bring up here. Now that I have shown you the kinds of extra organization that concern me and why I bother with them, I should be able to move quickly from one passage to the next.

At the first appearance in *Cymbeline* of the king's lost sons Guiderius and Arviragus, their foster father regales them with some stoic posturing:

A goodly day not to keep house with such
Whose roof's as low as ours. Stoop, boys, this gate
Instructs you how t'adore the heavens, and bows you
To a morning's holy office. (*Cymbeline* 3.3.1–4)

In the words 'this gate / Instructs you how t'adore', the sound of the word 'adore' casually echoes the sense of the word 'gate'.

This is Cleopatra pretending to rant in the third scene of *Antony and Cleopatra*:

O, never was there queen
So mightily betrayed! Yet at the first
I saw the treasons planted. (1.3.24–6)

The phrase 'treasons planted' embodies an entirely irrelevant arboreal reminiscence that presumably goes unobserved – or is at best dismissed from a listener's consciousness.

In an unrelated speech, much later in the play, Cleopatra lists the indignities that await her and her women if they are taken captive to Rome:

Saucy lictors
Will catch at us like strumpets, and scald rhymers
Ballad's out a' tune. (5.2.210–12)

Although 'tune' is a workable synonym for a sense of 'catch', a sense of which the verb in the preceding line is entirely innocent, the major incidental mental event of this passage is generated by 'saucy lictors'. 'Saucy': 'ill-mannered', 'presumptuous'. Sure. But why lictors? As one may or may not remember from Latin class, lictors were minor Roman functionaries who carried the fasces before a magistrate. Why lictors? My guess is that Shakespeare was drawn to the word by its first syllable, 'lick', a word intimately related with 'saucy' in its literal sense. (Note, by the way, that Shakespeare took up the topic of finger licking in the opening lines of *Romeo and Juliet* 4.2 and that in *Twelfth Night* 3.4.141–3 he revivifies the long dead literal sense of 'saucy'.)[4]

For a final instance of eventful language in *Antony and Cleopatra*, consider this exchange from act 3; Octavius and his sister are discussing her wayward husband, Antony:

CAESAR ... Where is he now?

[4] The 'saucy lictors' sentence is additionally crowded with energy because of all-but-inconsequential potential demonstrated in the Folio's 'Ballads vs out a Tune' by the emended version I quote here: 'Ballad's out a' tune'. The emendation is G. B. Evans's and appears in his *Riverside Shakespeare* (Boston, 1974). 'Ballad's out a' tune' approximates, I think, what would have been heard from the stage. Riverside's 'Ballad's' ('ballad us') repairs both syntax and metre. And 'a'' acknowledges the conflation of senses the spoken sound makes and thus lets the phrase say both 'sing a tune' (sing what the rhymers will ballad out for them) and 'sing out 'uh' tune' ('sing about us out of tune': 'slander us in song' and/or 'sing out of tune – that is sing unskilfully, unmusically – about us').

OCTAVIA My lord, in Athens.
CAESAR No, my most wrongèd sister. Cleopatra
Hath nodded him to her. (3.6.64–6)

Antony is not in Athens. Octavia is *wrong*. The first syllable of 'wrongèd' says so. The word then goes on to say quite another thing – another thing that is also true.

These next four brief passages are from *Julius Caesar*.

In the scene where the conspirators meet at Brutus's house and debate their coming action, Brutus rejects the suggestion that Antony be killed as well as Caesar:

Our course will seem too bloody, Caius Cassius,
To cut the head off and then hack the limbs . . .
(2.1.162–3)

As Brutus uses the word, 'course' means 'proceeding', 'course of action' and nothing else, but 'course' is homonym to the word we now spell and pronounce 'corpse', and corpses are urgent to the topic under discussion.

Later in the same scene, Portia kneels to Brutus:

BRUTUS Kneel not, gentle Portia.
PORTIA I should not need if you were gentle
Brutus. (2.1.277–8)

One's experience of that altogether straightforward, seemingly prosaic exchange is one where the verb 'to need' occurs in context of 'kneel' and thus of knees.[5]

In the next scene, where Caesar notes that 'Antony that revels long a-nights / Is notwithstanding up' (2.2.116–17), the words that say that Antony is no longer lying in bed contain the sounds of the phrase 'standing up'.

And in 5.1.110–11 the words Brutus uses to say that he will not allow himself to be taken in bondage to Rome include the phrase 'bound to Rome': 'No, Cassius, no. Think not, thou noble Roman, / That ever Brutus will go bound to Rome . . .' (compare 'bound to Persia' – *The Comedy of Errors* 4.1.3–4 – and 'bound to Tripolis' – *The Merchant of Venice* 1.3.18).

I am again worried that you will fear that, in presenting such demonstrations of ideational static as I have just pointed out and in presenting them as elements that matter in our experience of the speeches that harbour them, you will carelessly assume that I present them as elements that once were or should henceforth be active elements in one's conscious experience of the passages in which they innocently lurk, that I present them as truths that should henceforth be part of the paraphrasable substance of those passages. Let me say in one more way why I think ideational static, irrelevant to analysis of a passage's substantive content, is worth taking analytic account of in considering the value of a passage. Let me again give reasons why Shakespeare's language is admirable for more than its sense and sounds.

What things like, for another example, the sound of 'piled high' in Biron's pious rejection of 'three-piled hyperboles' (*Love's Labour's Lost* 5.2.407), do for audiences presumably and properly inattentive to them is just sit there in the air, sit there as available material for puns the scripts never make. Biron's 'piled high' occurs in a context that restricts the syllable 'piled' from any signification but the one that derives from its ancestor, one of the several Latin words for 'hair'. 'Three-piled' has nothing at all to do with heaps or heaping, but the static-like shadow presence of the idea of piling high can create an exciting situation for the minds that read *Love's Labour's Lost* or hear Biron's line spoken.

Actual puns, however, have nothing like that

[5] Spoken in the theatre and thus relatively free of punctuational persuaders, the 'kneel'/'need' exchange gets further density of texture from the simultaneous parallelism and non-parallelism of 'gentle Portia' (indicating the person addressed), and 'gentle Brutus' (that is, 'your ordinarily gentle self') – or, alternatively, what punctuation would limit as 'gentle, Brutus' (where 'gentle' is again a predicate adjective, and 'Brutus' indicates the person addressed; 'Brutus' is thus parallel with 'gentle Portia' and, because its attendant 'gentle' is doing other work, is not). Moreover, there is, of course, fleeting but inevitable oxymoronic energy in the mere conjunction of the word 'gentle' and the first syllable of 'Brutus'.

sort of effect upon their hearers. Consider, for example, the overt pun on two senses of 'boot' with which Hotspur goads Glendower in *1 Henry IV*. Glendower boasts that King Henry has 'three times . . . made head' against him and that he, Glendower, has thrice sent the King 'bootless home, and weather-beaten back'. Hotspur's response is 'Home without boots, and in foul weather too! / How scapes he agues, in the devil's name?' (3.1.61–6). Contrast that with this exchange from the first scene of *Richard II*:

KING RICHARD Norfolk, throw down! We bid; there is no boot.
MOWBRAY Myself I throw, dread sovereign, at thy foot . . . (1.1.164–5)

'Boot' in King Richard's command and 'foot' in Mowbray's answer relate to one another via a sense that 'boot' ('advantage', 'profit') does not carry in this context. That connection is based in exactly the accident of the English language from which Hotspur harvests his pun. Where, for us as audience, hearing Hotspur make his pun is merely to be a bystander, to be in the company of 'foot' and 'boot' in the Richard/Mowbray exchange is to be in a place made rich – made rich by the mere availability of a pun.

The difference between hearing an actual pun and being on ground where there is one to be made is very like the difference between being the maker of a pun and being its groaning audience. Why do people on whom puns are inflicted groan at them? Because the culture has taught them that groaning is expected? I think not. There is great joy to be had from puns, but all of it ordinarily belongs to the person who senses opportunity in a linguistic situation. The joy, I suggest, is in sensing the availability of a simultaneously likely and unlikely connection, an unexpected opportunity for articulating two contexts that are and remain essentially unconnected. When the pun maker snatches at the hidden thread by which the two contexts can be joined, brings the connection to consciousness, and triumphantly blurts it out, he or she reveals the insubstantiality, the triviality of a relation that, until realized, might have turned out to have been profound and profoundly illuminating. What the pun's audience hears is a mere gimcrack, a toy, something entirely irrelevant to the natures of the things so suddenly linked. What the punster feels in the air before he/she brings it forth and exposes it for the mouse a pun inevitably turns out to be is thrilling, is a sense of a previously unsuspected new order to things. A comparable feel of limitless mental possibility, I suggest, derives to us from the presence of substantively irrelevant organizations in the literary constructs we value best and longest.

The passages I trot out here are in no particular order. That is because I see no reasonable basis for one. I would like to organize them by kind, and I toyed briefly with doing so, but, like most categorization projects, the attempt to organize quickly became an end rather than a means and thus proved a diversion and a waste of time. Left with no reasonable criterion for dealing with any one passage in the company of any particular other one, I will settle for an illusion of rational order and talk now about a group of passages relatable as frivolously and casually as the components of the shadow phrases I have been pointing out. I will talk about three passages that relate to one another only as they relate to the sound 'rain'.

In the third of the following lines 'bridal' means 'wedding', and 'arraigning' two lines later means 'accusing'. But, since reins are a part of every bridle, the sound of 'bridal' and the sound of the second and third syllables of 'arraigning' have an extra, substantively irrelevant affinity as terms in horsemanship:

Nay, we must think men are not gods,
Nor of them look for such observancy
As fits the bridal. Beshrew me much, Emilia,
I was – unhandsome warrior as I am –
Arraigning his unkindness with my soul . . .
(*Othello* 3.4.146–50)

This next is a sentence from *The Winter's Tale*: 'Now he thanks the old shepherd, which stands by like a weather-bitten conduit of many kings' reigns' (5.2.54–6). 'Conduit' comes very close there to triggering an overt play on 'reigns' meaning 'terms in office' and the same sound as it refers to meteorological precipitation, but – if the silence of most editors is the guide I take it to be – the pun never quite emerges. The same appears to be true of essentially the same potential pun in the song Autolycus sings earlier as he makes his first entrance into the play:

When daffodils begin to peer,
  With heigh, the doxy over the dale!
Why then comes in the sweet o' the year,
  For the red blood reigns in the winter's pale.
(*The Winter's Tale* 4.3.1–4)

Context says that 'pale' in the last of those four lines means only 'enclosure', 'preserve'. The sound of 'pale', however, is a sound capable elsewhere of labelling a receptacle for liquids. As a result, 'pale' there yearns after 'reigns', a sound elsewhere capable of labelling liquid that, like 'blood', is capable of containment in pails. Moreover, because of its conjunction with 'red', the word 'pale' figures in a shadowy conflation of the idea of paleness with the idea of enclosure. (Compare the activity of the word 'pale' in the following speech from *King John*. Austria swears that he will not go home until all the lands in dispute acknowledge Prince Arthur as their king:

... to my home I will no more return
Till Angers, and the right thou hast in France,
Together with that pale, that white-faced shore,
Whose foot spurns back the ocean's roaring tides
And coops from other lands her islanders,
Even till that England, hedged in with the main,
That water-wallèd bulwark ...
Salute thee for her king ...
(*King John* 2.1.21–7, 30)

If in the third of these lines the phrase 'that white-faced shore' did not intervene to gloss 'pale' and insist that it be understood as an adjective akin in its sense to 'white', 'pale' would remain a noun meaning 'fence': 'that pale whose foot spurns back the ocean's roaring tides and coops from other lands her islanders'.)

Consciously or unconsciously, Shakespeare appears to have heard and responded to the sound 'pence' and its potential as the plural for the word 'penny'. The word 'recompense' (in which '-pense' derives from Latin *pensare*, 'to weigh', and has no etymological kinship with 'penny' at all), recommends itself semantically to contexts of payment and debt, but Shakespeare's uses of the word sometimes seem to me right on the edge of overt play on 'pence'. For example, consider the suggestions of coins evoked by 'purse' when Viola rejects a proffered tip from Olivia: 'I am no fee'd post, lady. Keep your purse. / My master, not myself, lacks recompense' (*Twelfth Night* 1.5.274–5). 'Pence' – pennies, money that could be 'paid down' – is and isn't part of the experience of lines 3 and 4 of this next speech, lines casually complicated by ideational fluidity well before there is any whisper of coins. The speech is the first of 5.1 of *The Winter's Tale*, the scene in which Leontes' courtiers urge him to remarry:

Sir, you have done enough, and have performed
A saint-like sorrow. No fault could you make
Which you have not redeemed, indeed paid down
More penitence than done trespass. (5.1.1–4)

At the point in the third of those lines where we hear 'redeemed' (literally 'bought back'), context limits its meaning to the common metaphoric one: 'atoned for'. At the end of the line, however, 'paid down' takes the line into the ideational area to which the literal sense of 'to redeem' belongs. 'Penitence', the word that removes the assertion from the newly invaded realm of finance – the word that makes 'paid down' a metaphor – *also* contains the sound of 'pence'. The first syllable of 'penitence', being the first of the metaphor-invited word 'pennies', confirms the context of finance. The next syllable undoes that confirmation. And the final sibilant of the third completes the (now alien) word 'pence' that, given the context established by 'paid down', the first syllable promised.

For a simpler, but distantly similar, exercise in syllabic shuffling, consider this sentence of Cleopatra's: 'Think on me, / That am with Phoebus' amorous pinches black, / And wrinkled deep in time' (*Antony and Cleopatra* 1.5.27–9). The sentence approaches – but never quite reaches – play on 'blackamoor' in '*amor*ous pinches *black*'.

Some of Shakespeare's limpest wit is made less so by inherent potential that lies unharnessed beside it. For instance, the following passage from *The Comedy of Errors* sweats to delight its audiences with sudden, minimally provoked reference to a baroque legal fiction called 'fine and recovery'. Challenged to do so, Dromio of Syracuse provides the rule by which he rejects the proverbial truth that 'there's a time for all things':

DROMIO Marry, sir, by a rule as plain as the plain bald pate of Father Time himself.
ANTIPHOLUS Let's hear it.
DROMIO There's no time for a man to recover his hair that grows bald by nature.
ANTIPHOLUS May he not do it by fine and recovery?
DROMIO Yes, to pay a fine for a periwig, and recover the lost hair of another man.
(*The Comedy of Errors* 2.2.69–77)

The passage was presumably stillborn and has stayed that way – even after suffering scholarly CPR from Helge Kökeritz, who declared play in the passage between 'fine' and the word 'foin': 'fur used as trim on garments' (*Shakespeare's Pronunciation* (New Haven, CT, 1953), 107). I doubt that even an Inns of Court audience could have mustered more than a smirk of recognition for the 'fine and recovery' joke. My reason for bothering with it here is to say that – however dead the overt joking – the passage is livelier than it would otherwise be for the presence of available, entirely unexploited play on the relevant sense of 'recover' by which it means 'cover again' (a wig recovers a bald scalp), and by the equally inviting, equally dormant potential inherent in the conjunction of 'to pay' and 'periwig' (*OED*'s first citation for the English word 'toupee' is from 1731, but the French word *toupet*, 'a tuft of hair', goes way back).

In this next passage poor spurned Helena concludes the first scene of *A Midsummer Night's Dream* by resolving to tell Demetrius about Lysander's and Hermia's intention to run away.

If I have thanks, it is a dear expense.
But herein mean I to enrich my pain,
To have his sight thither and back again.
(*A Midsummer Night's Dream* 1.1.249–51)

The last syllable's pronunciation, distorted for rhyme (other Shakespearian rhymes suggest that the more usual pronunciation was already 'agen'), occurs in context of what the speaker will *gain*.

This is *Macbeth* 1.2.59–62: 'Sweno, the Norways' king, craves composition; / Nor would we deign him burial of his men / Till ...' 'Deign' is and – sixteenth- and seventeenth-century spellings and rhymes suggest – was akin to 'Norways' king' in the preceding line: its sound is the sound that labels a native of another area of Scandinavia: Denmark.[6]

Just before the Battle of Agincourt, King Henry prays:

O God of battles, steel my soldiers' hearts.
Possess them not with fear. Take from them now
The sense of reck'ning, ere th'opposèd numbers
Pluck their hearts from them. Not today, O Lord,
O not today, think not upon the fault
My father made in compassing the crown.
I Richard's body have interrèd new,
And on it have bestowed more contrite tears,

[6] Note, for what it's worth, that Shakespeare's ear may have been tempted towards the verb 'to deign' by his source: Holinshed repeatedly refers to the army led by 'Sueno king of Norway' as 'the Danes'; in the time of Hector Boece (Holinshed's source for the history behind *Macbeth*), of Holinshed himself, and of Shakespeare, Norway was little more than a province of Denmark.

Than from it issued forcèd drops of blood.
Five hundred poor I have in yearly pay
Who twice a day their withered hands hold up
Toward heaven to pardon blood . . . (4.1.286–97)

Context makes it impossible for audiences to hear reference to theft in the sound of 'steal' in 'steel my soldiers' hearts'. In asking God to 'take from' his soldiers, however, the next line asks him to do something ideationally akin to stealing. And, two lines further on, a non-imperative, non-parallel construction presents a precise echo of the contextually impossible sense that 'steel my soldiers' hearts' does not convey at the beginning of the speech: 'Pluck their hearts from them.' Note, moreover, that that unspectacular verbal event occurs in company with even less spectacular give and take between the negated 'give' of 'Possess them not' and the effectively positive 'take' of 'Take from them now / The sense of reck'ning'. When the prayer continues, its topic shifts and also does not: 'Not today, O Lord, / O not today, think not upon the fault / My father made in compassing the crown' (289–91). The new topic, Lancastrian guilt, maintains and makes overt the shadow topic of the first lines, theft: Henry Bolingbroke's fault was stealing the crown.

The larcenous strain in the speech runs out at that point, but careless, submerged play on giving and taking continues momentarily in 'bestowed more contrite tears, / Than from it' (293–4). But the potential 'give and take' construction that begins in 'bestowed' and continues in 'from' turns out otherwise. Instead of referring to the expense of tears exacted upon Shakespeare's luxuriously lachrymose Richard II by Bolingbroke's rebellion, the lines turn to his murder and his bleeding corpse: 'more contrite tears, / Than from it issued forcèd drops of blood' (293–4). Consider 'than from it issued for-': 'issued for-' – which is momentarily on its way to the probable idiom 'issued forth' – arrives instead at another, equally appropriate locution: 'issued forcèd drops of blood'. The next line begins 'Five hundred poor'; its first syllable, 'five', presents the ear with a sound casually akin to the sound of the number 'four' in the sound of 'for', the sound that yearned for completion as 'forth' but that in fact came to ideational rest in 'forcèd'.

This next passage is also from *Henry V*. In a speech generally infused with variations on the idea of fathers and the idea of offspring, the French king warns his nobles against overconfidence and recalls reasons to fear the English:

Witness our too-much-memorable shame
When Crécy battle fatally was struck,
And all our princes captived by the hand
Of that black name, Edward, Black Prince of Wales;
Whiles that his mountant sire, on mountain standing,
Up in the air, crowned with the golden sun,
Saw his heroical seed and smiled to see him,
Mangle the work of nature, and deface
The patterns that by God and by French fathers
Had twenty years been made. (2.4.53–62)

The words 'air' and 'sun' in 'Up in the air, crowned with the golden sun' (line 58) present a pair of sounds – 'son' and 'heir' – that relate to one another in syntaxes entirely foreign to the one in which they occur here but that relate to the substantive context, one in which Edward III watches the exploits of his son and heir. The next line – the line that reports that Edward III 'saw his heroical seed, and smiled to see him' – substitutes for the relevant sound in the preceding line, uses 'his . . . seed' to say 'his son'. The word 'seed' is itself in a shadowy extra relationship with two forms of the verb 'to see': 'see' in 'smiled to see him' is in obvious phonic relationship to 'seed', and, if the verb 'to see' were a so-called weak verb rather than a strong one, its past tense would presumably be what it is in some vulgar dialects, not 'saw' but 'seed'.

This is the rhetorical flourish with which Othello concludes protestation that he will do his duty to Venice, even if his wife goes with him to the wars:

Let housewives make a skillet of my helm,
And all indign and base adversities

Make head against my estimation.
(*Othello* 1.3.272–4)

The two 'make' constructions in the passage are superficially alike and emphasized as such by the recurrence of 'my' in the second clause. The 'make' constructions are just as obviously different. In the first, 'make' says 'fashion', 'manufacture'. The second 'make' means 'gather' and functions in the idiom 'make head', meaning 'gather an army'. The word 'head' in 'make head' is an ideational echo of 'helm' in the first of the three lines – *and* – because its metaphoric root in the body part housed in a helmet was already long atrophied when Shakespeare's first audiences heard it – is not. On the other hand, since helmets and armies are so closely related conceptually, 'make head' does indeed efficiently relate to 'helm' – albeit in a dimension distant from the one in which 'head' is an anatomical label.

In the next passage Polixenes and the Old Shepherd are watching '*a dance of Shepherds and Shepherdesses*'.

POLIXENES Pray, good shepherd, what fair swain is this
Which dances with your daughter?
SHEPHERD They call him Doricles, and boasts himself
To have a worthy feeding; but I have it
Upon his own report, and I believe it.
He looks like sooth. He says he loves my daughter.
I think so, too; for never gazed the moon
Upon the water as he'll stand and read,
As 'twere, my daughter's eyes; and to be plain,
I think there is not half a kiss to choose
Who loves another best.
POLIXENES She dances featly.
SHEPHERD So she does anything, though I report it
That should be silent. If young Doricles
Do light upon her, she shall bring him that
Which he not dreams of. (4.4.167–81)

Because the moon is a light – and *only* because the moon is a light – 'light upon' in line 180 (where 'light upon her' means 'get her for wife') does and does not echo 'moon upon' in 173–4. 'Light upon' also relates to 'featly' in 'She dances featly'. 'Feet' are at play in that assertion anyway (because dancing is done with feet; for the actual pun, see *The Tempest* 1.2.381, 'Foot it featly here and there'). And, in context of a discussion of dancing, there is pressure upon 'light upon her' from a sense 'light upon' could have in a sentence about weight, a sentence that said Perdita was 'light of foot', 'light on her feet'. Note, moreover, that, since he is dancing, Florizel might well light upon Perdita's foot.

Finally, three sentences from *Romeo and Juliet*:

If I profane with my unworthiest hand
This holy shrine, the gentler sin is this:
My lips, two blushing pilgrims, ready stand
To smooth that rough touch with a tender kiss.
(1.5.92–5)

But soft, what light through yonder window breaks?
(2.1.44)

O Romeo, Romeo, wherefore art thou Romeo?
(2.1.75)

The first of the three sentences is here because of the incidental pertinence of 'red', the first syllable of 'ready', to blushing lips: 'My lips, two blushing pilgrims, ready stand'. The next two are from what traditionally has been called the balcony scene and are among the most famous lines in English. I strongly suspect that the ideational companionship of glass windows and breakage is one of the sources of the popularity of 'But soft, what light through yonder window breaks?' The quiet crash between 'soft' and 'breaks' may contribute something too. As for 'O Romeo, Romeo, wherefore art thou Romeo?' – many twentieth-century English speakers who in other contexts have no trouble recognizing 'wherefore' as a synonym for 'why', take it to mean 'where' in Juliet's line – take 'wherefore art thou Romeo?' to be an inquiry as to Romeo's whereabouts – and in so mistaking bring joy to

English teachers who get to correct their obvious error. Not only do we all know what 'wherefore' means, but Juliet's next lines make it evident that her concern is with Romeo's name and not his location. What *follows* the 'where' of 'wherefore' does indeed define the function of the word. But what the word 'wherefore' *itself* follows are forty-two lines occasioned by Mercutio's and Benvolio's efforts to find Romeo, to find out *where* Romeo is. 'Wherefore art thou Romeo', I suggest, is an instance of just the sort of submerged, demonstrably irrelevant, dismissable content in Shakespearian locutions that I am concerned with here; it is anomalous only in having risen to the surface of popular imagination.

'I'LL PLAGUE THEE FOR THAT WORD': LANGUAGE, PERFORMANCE, AND COMMUNICABLE DISEASE

KEIR ELAM

FOREIGN BODIES

Jacobean drama begins – like a Beckett or Pinter play *ante litteram* – with a pause. In his patent creating the company of the King's Servants, on 19 May 1603, the as yet uncrowned King James I was obliged to insert a holding clause, putting off his players' dramatic displays to more propitious times: 'and the said comedies, tragedies, histories, interludes, morals, pastorals, stage plays, and such like to show and exercise publicly to their best commodity when the infection of the plague shall cease.'[1] Now James may appear, in his diligent cataloguing of the postponed dramatic genres, to be echoing Polonius, but for the first months of the new reign it was not pastoral or pastoral-comical or tragical-comical-historical pastoral that dominated the stage, but tragical-historical *pastuerella pestis*,[2] the bacillus of the bubonic plague, in its most virulent visitation since the Middle Ages.

This was an inauspicious start not only for the King's Men but also for the King's person, whose ceremonial progress from the north, conducted by horses, was upstaged by the triumphal entry from the east of another powerful foreign body, conducted by rats. The two rival bodies, Rex Britanniae and Rattus rattus, or rather the pathogenic micro-organisms carried by the parasitic riders of the unwitting rodent, first crossed paths in North London in the month of April.[3] Even the superstitious James might have preferred to have his path crossed by a black cat than by a black rat, had he had the epidemiological know-how to know why.

Among the new king's first public pronouncements, his opening royal speech acts, were two performative, or self-enacting,[4] rites of nomination – the nominating or, better, renominating of the theatre company that from then on bore his royal title, and the official naming of the epidemic itself. As Cindy Patton has observed with reference to the performativity of the AIDS crisis, 'Epidemiology ... is performative: by separating pathogens from the body, epidemiology enables itself to declare "disease".'[5] 'I name this infection HIV, or BSE.'

[1] *Malone Society Collections* (Oxford, 1907), 1.3, pp. 264–5.

[2] This was the name first given by epidemiologists to the plague bacillus, later renamed *Yersinia Pestis*.

[3] See J. Leeds Barroll, *Politics, Plague, and Shakespeare's Theater: The Stuart Years* (Ithaca, 1991), p. 103. On the plague in Early Modern England, see also Charles Creighton, *A History of Epidemics in Britain* (London, 1965, first edition Cambridge 1891); Charles F. Mullett, *Bubonic Plague and England: An Essay in the History of Preventive Medicine* (Lexington, 1956); F. P. Wilson, *The Plague in Shakespeare's London* (London, 1963); Philip Ziegler, *The Black Death* (London, 1969); J. F. D. Shrewsbury, *A History of Bubonic Plague in the British Isles* (London, 1970); Graham Twigg, *The Black Death: A Biological Reappraisal* (London, 1984); Paul Slack, *The Impact of Plague in Tudor and Stuart England* (London, 1985).

[4] On performative utterances, see J. L. Austin, *How to Do Things with Words*, second edition, ed. J. O. Urmson and Marina Sbisà (Oxford, 1975).

[5] Cindy Patton, 'Performativity and Spatial Distinction:

James's diagnostic decrees, separating the pestilential pathogens from the supposedly healthy body politic, brought the epidemic into institutional being: 'We name this malady bubonic plague'; or, as Thomas Lodge puts it in his *Treatise of the Plague* of 1603, 'The Plague ... is a pernicious and dangerous *Epidermy* (that is to say a general, or popular sickness)';[6] or as James himself phrases it in his proclamation of 23 June, affirming the epidemic proportions of the crisis and consequently adjourning Trinity Term, 'the infection of the Plague is at this present greatly increased and dispersed as well in the Cities of London and Westminster, as also in the suburbs thereof'.[7]

James's third performative act places the first two into direct relationship, instituting such preventive measures against the disease as the suspending of stage performance. Thus, if the royal word affirmed its institutional ability to create the epidemic as social fact, it also asserted its own powers of immunogenic prophylaxis in forestalling further contagion, for example by performatively naming performance itself as agency of infection: 'to show and exercise publicly ... when the infection of plague shall cease'. So much so that the King does not hesitate to put off his own public show and exercise, the performance of the coronation itself, in a proclamation of 6 July, setting out from the premise that the 'great concourse of people' is 'a means not only of increasing the infection within our City, but of dispersing it into all places of this Realm'. His Majesty nobly forgoes the ceremonial displaying of his royal self to the assembled masses: 'we had rather forbear some part of our ornament and custom, which is due to the honour and solemnity of our Coronation, than by having the uttermost thereof performed, be the occasion of so great an evil to our people, as is the spreading of infection amongst them'.[8]

These early Jacobean pronouncements set up a triangular relationship between speech act, performance and epidemic. My aim in this paper is to explore this three-way pathogenetic dialectic as it is worked out in some of Shakespeare's texts, especially his early Jacobean drama. It is my (possibly pathological) thesis that not only is the relationship between discourse and plague of primary importance to these texts, but that indeed bubonic contagion comes to constitute for Shakespearian drama a paradigm for language itself, especially in performance. What I will attempt here, therefore, is a brief reflection on the historicity of Shakespeare's discourse, even if in one of its lousier or rattier guises.

'AND LANGUAGE END': OF DISCOURSE EPIDEMIC, EPIDEICTIC, APOCALYPTIC

'More man? Plague, plague!' This apocalyptic outburst, equating the human with the pestiferous, and so, as it were, bubonizing the world at large, is issued not by James of Britain but by Timon of Athens, at the sight of Alcibiades. And indeed *Timon*, which may well have been written during or shortly after the bubonic hiatus of 1603–4, is by a long way the most pestilential of Shakespeare's plays, both lexically – with its fourteen occurrences of the word 'plague' or its derivatives – and in its theatrical destiny, since it seems to have remained long unperformed, as if in dutiful obeisance to His Majesty's decree of adjournment,[9] besides

The End of Aids Epidemiology', in Andrew Parker and Eve Kosofsky Sedgwick, eds., *Performativity and Performance* (New York and London, 1995), 173–97; p. 186.

6 Thomas Lodge, *A Treatise of the Plague* (London, 1603), sig. Bv.

7 'A Proclamation for the adjournment of part of Trinities Terme', 23 June 1603, in *A booke of Proclamations* (London, 1609), p. 25.

8 King James I, 'A Proclamation signifying the Kings Maiesties pleasure, touching the resort of people to his Coronation', 6 July 1603, in *Proclamations*, p. 33.

9 On the probable non-performance of *Timon of Athens* in Shakespeare's day, due in part to the incompleteness of the text as we have received it, see H. J. Oliver's introduction and appendix to the Arden edition of the play (London, 1959), pp. xxv–xxviii, 149–50.

being probably a 'contaminated' or collaborative text.[10] It is also of its unhappy performative, or theatrically non-performative, early Jacobean moment in that its plaguey discourse takes the predominant form of the solemn optative proclamation, whereby Timon, in the latter half of the tragedy, wills pandemic catastrophe on his fellows.

Timon of Athens gives us an altogether darker and less reassuring version of the epidemic-creating performative power of language than James's decrees. Among Timon's proclamatory speech acts, the chief verbal symptom of both the desire and the anxiety of infection, is what we might call the contagious curse, that infests or infects the play's later scenes, beginning with the awesome world-destroying soliloquy with which Timon opens Act 4:

> And let confusion live! Plagues incident to men,
> Your potent and infectious fevers heap
> On Athens, ripe for stroke! Thou cold sciatica,
> Cripple our senators, that their limbs may halt
> As lamely as their manners! Lust and liberty,
> Creep in the minds and marrows of our youth,
> That 'gainst the stream of virtue they may strive
> And drown themselves in riot! Itches, blains,
> Sow all th' Athenian bosoms, and their crop
> Be general leprosy! Breath infect breath,
> That their society, as their friendship, may
> Be merely poison! (4.1.21–32)

Timon figures the Athenian *polis* as precisely the kind of disease-spreading 'great concourse of people' feared by James, the concourse, for example, of spectators at a coronation or at a stage performance. And he produces, moreover, a plausible epidemiological rationale for the workings of such mass contamination, the kind of rationale that lay behind the preventive measures of the Crown and the Cities of London and Westminster. 'Breath infect breath': Timon's vision of mortal halitosis discloses one of the two main rival medical theories concerning the transmission of the epidemic, namely the theory of direct respiratory contagion. The notion that the plague might be passed on through the breath, like TB in more recent times, enjoyed, as Leeds Barroll has shown,[11] considerable currency in the early modern period. Jehan Goevrot's *Regiment of Life* expounds the theory with negative Timon-like emphasis: 'the venomous air itself is not half so vehement to infect as is the conversation or breath of them that are infected already'.[12] The theory survives in Defoe's *Journal of the Plague Year* (1722), whose narrator blames what he terms 'the fatal Breath' for the devastating 1665 outbreak: 'This put it out of Question to me, that the Calamity was spread by Infection, that is to say, by some certain Steams, or Fumes, which the Physicians call *Effluvia*, by the Breath, or by the Sweat, or by the Stench of the Sores of the sick Persons.'[13]

Timon's 'breath infect breath' imperative is not mere misanthropic wishful thinking, since respiratory contagion was indeed responsible for the spreading of at least the pneumonic form of the plague. And if his epidemic desire has its own medical plausibility, it also has its own Shakespearian pedigree. Shakespeare's narrative poems, the product of an earlier bubonic pause – the theatre-closing visitation of 1592–3 – first introduce the symptoms or referential traces of epidemic in his texts. *Venus and Adonis* appears at first reading to introject the plague as fanciful Petrarchan conceit, as in Venus' invocation to Cynthia to mingle Adonis' beauty with infirmity, making his very loveliness the cause of his own malady, a malady which she rhetorically amplifies with arch pseudo-medical redundancy, spinning out the sickly synonyms:

> As burning fevers, agues pale and faint,
> Life-poisoning pestilence, and frenzies wood,
> The marrow-eating sickness whose attaint
> Disorder breeds by heating of the blood;

---

10 The Complete Oxford Shakespeare, as well as much current scholarly opinion, attributes the play to Shakespeare and Middleton.

11 Barroll, *Politics*, pp. 95–6.

12 Jehan Goevrot, *The Regiment of Life*, tr. Thomas Phayre, quoted in Barroll, *Politics*, p. 94.

13 Daniel Defoe, *Journal of the Plague Year*, ed. Louis Landa (Oxford, 1990), p. 74.

Surfeits, impostumes, grief, and damned despair
Swear nature's death for framing thee so fair.
(739–44)

Or in her pretty allegory pitching love against death and electing Adonis instead as antidote to the disease:

Long may they [thy lips] kiss each other, for this cure!
O, never let their crimson liveries wear,
And as they last, their verdure still endure
To drive infection from the dangerous year,
That the star-gazers, having writ on death,
May say the plague is banished by thy breath!
(505–10)

But Venus' amorous, or perhaps venereal, hyperboles have, on closer inspection, a cryptic referentiality that brings them closer than one might suspect to the epidemiological moment of the poem's composition, to the 'dangerous year' as she calls it. Encoded in her assertion that 'the plague is banished by thy breath' is a playfully inverted version of the respiratory contagion theory, whereby Adonis becomes paradoxically or homeopathically curative, since it is his very state of amorous infectiveness – his adored body being chillingly metonymized as 'but a swallowing grave' – that allows him to emit sickness-banishing effluvia. Venus' breathless rhapsodizing on Adonis' 'breath perfumed' alludes, furthermore, to the optimistic early modern prophylactic practice of sweetening the breath and the body in order to keep the pest at bay. 'It is good also', advises Lodge, 'to wear sweet savors and perfumes about us', 'for such an odour and of so wholesome a quality vehemently repulseth the venom that assaileth the heart, and altereth the pestilence of the air'.[14] Shakespeare revisits both the practice and the trope in Orsino's eulogy to Olivia in the opening scene of *Twelfth Night* – 'O, when mine eyes did see Olivia first / Methought she purged the air of pestilence' (1.1.18–19) – where the beloved's body becomes one of the air fresheners used in times of visitation in order to disperse the noxiousness of the atmosphere.[15]

Timon's vision of a mutually infecting great concourse or intercourse of breaths is not particularly flattering towards his imaginary playhouse audience, from which, however, he was probably saved by the play's nonperformance. One is reminded of the Epistle to the reader appended to another eminently pestilential text, the 1609 Quarto of *Troilus and Cressida*, which makes a bogus claim to similar non-performance and thus to analogous non-contamination: 'nor like this the less, for not being sullied, with the smoky breath of the multitude'.[16] A view of the audience not far removed from that of the puritan enemies of the stage: William Prynne, for example, describes playgoers as 'contagious in quality, more apt to poison, to infect all those who dare approach them, than one who is full of plague-sores'.[17]

The respiratory contagion theory justifies not only suspicions regarding crowds or theatre audiences but also suspicions regarding language itself as a contaminated and contaminating medium. The logical or epidemiological step from bad breath to bad speech is short. Jehan Goevrot yokes them unceremoniously together in his already quoted warning to avoid 'the conversation or breath of them that are infected already'. As Eric Mallin notes in his recent essay on word and plague in *Hamlet*: 'The bubonic plague always activated fears and metaphors of communicability ... In a pestilent culture, all conversation carries risk: intimate spaces of encounter hold the greater dangers.'[18] Such fears have a respectable literary ancestry: Boccaccio

14 Thomas Lodge, *Treatise*, sig. C^{r}.

15 See Barroll, *Politics*, p. 94; see also my essay '"In What Chapter of his Bosom?": Reading Shakespeare's Bodies', in *Alternative Shakespeares Volume 2*, ed. Terence Hawkes (London, 1996), p. 156.

16 Quoted in *Troilus and Cressida*, ed. Kenneth Palmer (Arden edition, London, 1982), p. 95.

17 William Prynne, *Histrio-Mastix* (London, 1633), p. 152.

18 Eric S. Mallin, 'Word and Plague in the Second Quarto *Hamlet*', in *Inscribing the Time: Shakespeare and the End of Elizabethan England* (Berkeley, 1995), 62–105; pp. 80–1.

explains in the First Day of *The Decameron* how, in the Florence of 1348, everyday conversational exchange contributed to the rapid spread of the epidemic: 'And the plague gathered strength as it was transmitted from the sick to the healthy through normal intercourse ["lo comunicare insieme"], ... by talking to or keeping company with the sick ['il parlare e l'usare con gl'infermi"]'.[19] The plague, therefore, is not only a communicable but above all a communicational disease, although if *The Decameron* represents an escape from the talking disease, it also represents a talking or narrating cure, since Boccaccio upholds the talismanic efficacy of 'cheerful banter' ('piacevoli motti') in keeping the illness at bay.[20]

In willing destruction on the audience and on the world, however, Timon hedges his medical and rhetorical bets. On his next appearance, and in his next great optative soliloquy, he abandons the respiratory theory in favour of the rival explanation of the epidemic, presumably in the hope that it might embody greater prognostic powers:

> O blessèd breeding sun, draw from the earth
> Rotten humidity; below thy sister's orb
> Infect the air. (4.3.1–3)

Here Timon's dream of universal contamination rests not so much on respiratory as on ecological infection, through the agency of environmental breath or earthly vapours. What Timon's second would-be performative appears to embody is the so-called miasmic theory of transmission, according to which the prime cause of the disease lay in a sort of mortal air pollution provoked by unwholesome effluvia emanating from the earth. This is the theory, derived from Galen, that Lodge espouses in his *Treatise*: 'all pestilential sicknesses, as from a proper cause, are engendered, by a certain vicious mixture of corrupted and strange vapours, contrary to the life of man, and corrupting the vital spirit: which unkindly excretion, sowed into the air, and infecting the same, communicateth unto us by our continual alteration of the same, the venom which poisoneth us ... because men having a necessity to suck in the air, together with the same suck in the infection and venome'.[21] The miasma theory opposes to the notion of contagious exhalation, poisonous outbreathing, that of infectious inhalation, the 'in-breathing of the air' as Lodge puts it. The plague remains nonetheless a communicational disease: indeed, the key word in Lodge's exposition is precisely 'communicateth'. Language sucks disease into itself: it is no longer the word that infects the world, but the world that infects the word by means of pneumonic contamination.

Timon's version of the bubonic miasma has the earth materially participating in the moral and linguistic corruption of its inhabitants. Shakespeare alludes to the theory in an analogous ethical as well as venereal mode in his second 'dangerous year' poem, *The Rape of Lucrece*, in the heroine's invocation to night to infect Sextus the Sexual Molester:

> O hateful, vaporous, and foggy night ...
> With rotten damps ravish the morning air,
> Let their exhaled unwholesome breaths make sick
> The life of purity, the supreme fair,
> Ere he arrive his weary noon-tide prick ... (771–81)

Lucrece's moral appeal to exhaled unwholesome breaths, interpreting the miasma as divine or diabolical scourge, is famously echoed by Hamlet in another imagined scene of infectious nocturnal emission, prior to his bedchamber encounter with Gertrude:

> 'Tis now the very witching time of night,

[19] Giovanni Boccaccio, *The Decameron*, tr. Guido Waldman (Oxford, 1993), p. 7. The Italian quotations are taken from *Decamerone*, ed. Mario Marti (Milan, 1994), p. 11.

[20] Boccaccio, *Decameron*, p. 22; *Decamerone*, p. 25. On the history of literary representations of the plague, see David Steel, 'Plague Writing: From Boccaccio to Camus', *Journal of European Studies*, xi (1981), 88–110. On the plague in non-Shakespearian Jacobean drama, see Cheryl Lynn Ross, 'The Plague of *The Alchemist*', *Renaissance Quarterly*, 41:3 (1988), pp. 439–58.

[21] Thomas Lodge, *A Treatise of the Plague*, sigs. B3^{v}–B4^{r}.

When churchyards yawn, and hell itself breathes out
Contagion to this world. (3.2.377–9)

Lucrece's 'make sick the life of purity', like Timon's 'draw . . . rotten humidity' suggests the influence of a kind of sociolinguistic miasma or habitus, whereby Shakespeare's discourse is, as it were, referentially contaminated by the corrupted and strange vapours of the historical contexts or dangerous years of the poem's and play's respective conceptions. At the same time Lucrece's invocation to the contagious powers of night anticipates Timon and his discourse in claiming its own would-be performative force, the bubonic capacity of the speech act itself to bring about direct infection through the agency of the contagious curse, a rhetorical mode that becomes a staple of Shakespearian drama, most notoriously in Mercutio's 'a plague a' both your houses', and most self-consciously in the ritual insult-exchanges of the first tetralogy, as, for example, in the pestiferous ping-pong of *3 Henry VI*, whose participants compete in the search for the most infectious *bon*, or perhaps *mauvais, mot*:

PRINCE EDWARD His currish riddles sorts not with this place.
RICHARD OF GLOUCESTER By heaven, brat, I'll plague ye for that word.
QUEEN MARGARET Ay, thou wast born to be a plague to men. (5.5.26–8)

'I'll plague ye for that word': here language becomes both source and object of contagion, a referentially self-infecting artefact. This intimate association between, on the one hand, the curse as a primary modality of speech and, on the other, the prospect of bubonic infection is similarly the point of Caliban's celebrated imprecation to Prospero, importer and imposer of language, and possibly of diseases:

You taught me language, and my profit on't
Is I know how to curse. The red plague rid you
For learning me your language!
(*The Tempest* 1.2.365–7)

It might be noted, with regard to Caliban's curse, that the plague has its own sociolinguistic as well as intertextual history. As Geoffrey Hughes has shown in his social history of swearing, the sixteenth and early seventeenth centuries saw a notable increase in the purely imprecatory use of 'plague', 'pestilence' and their derivatives, together with 'pox' and its cognates, even though they had been introduced into the language centuries earlier. Indeed, terms such as 'plaguey', which Shakespeare employs in the 'pox'-ridden *Troilus and Cressida*,[22] and 'pestiferous', which crops up in *All's Well that Ends Well*,[23] actually begin their lexical life as imprecations and are only later literalized as descriptive 'medical' terms.[24]

Timon brings this linguistic and dramaturgic history to a rhetorical climax by making the pestilence his lexical home and the curse his illocutionary norm. Timon's own plaguey imprecations translate the epidemic into the epideictic, giving rise to a series of formidable oratorical performances, ironically replete with a contagious theatricality of their own. What ought to be the culminating moment in this bubonic display is represented by Timon's last dying, or rather suicidal, words, the spectacular self-contaminating performative with which he successfully wills himself to pestilential death:

Thither come,
And let my gravestone be your oracle.
Lips, let four words go by, and language end.
What is amiss, plague and infection mend.
Graves only be men's works, and death their gain.
Sun, hide thy beams. Timon hath done his reign.
(5.2.103–8)

Timon puts an end to himself by fatally infecting his own speech in and through the act of uttering it. His language implodes, like the

22 'ULYSSES What should I say? / He [Achilles] is so plaguy proud that the death tokens of it / Cry "No recovery"' (2.3.174–6).

23 'INTERPRETER The general says that you [Parolles] have . . . made such pestiferous reports of men very nobly held' (4.3.306–8).

24 Geoffrey Hughes, *Swearing: A Social History of Foul Language, Oaths and Profanity in English* (Oxford, 1991), p. 190.

self-devouring and silenced bodies of victims described in the plague treatises: 'Many one is so strait-winded', observes Goevrot, 'that he cannot speak'.[25] His final self-fulfilling 'Timon hath done' seems to answer Judith Butler's question regarding the effects of injurious speech: 'what would it mean', asks Butler, 'for a thing to be "done by" a word or, for that matter, for a thing to be "done in by" a word?'[26]

But in fact Timon's dying words are not his last word. He saves his best or worst till after the end, producing what may be the most uncanny post-mortem *côup de théâtre* in the history of drama, namely the virulent posthumous curse on the community of his fellows, e.g. the audience, that constitutes his characteristically ill-wishing will and testament, inscribed in his Epitaph:

> Here lies a wretched corpse,
> Of wretched soul bereft.
> Seek not my name. A plague consume
> You wicked caitiffs left! (5.5.71–4)

Caveat spectator: having seen Timon do himself in so effectively with words, let the audience look to its own state of health.

'THE LORD'S TOKENS': SYMPTOMS AND SIGNS

Timon's identification of speech with infection goes beyond the contingencies of the situation of utterance, the fatal contaminating of the word by respiratory or environmental vapours, and touches the very constitution of language as semiotic system. In the scene of Timon's Epitaph, Alcibiades, who has the thankless task of reading the curse and of defending the deceased old imprecator before his enemies, is challenged by one of the victims of the curse itself, the Second Senator:

> SECOND SENATOR [*to Alcibiades*] Throw thy glove,
> Or any token of thine honour else. (5.4.49–50)

This is an innocent and conventional enough challenge, but in the pestilent context of the scene and of the tragedy as a whole, one should not overlook the irony of the Senator's choice of terminology: 'token', in addition to its general meaning of 'sign', had the specific symptomatological or semeiotic meaning of symptom of the plague: buboes and the rest. Thomas Lodge's definition is as vividly unpleasant as any: 'wherein usually there appear certain Tumours, Carbuncles, or spots, which the common people call Gods tokens ... These be the signs and tokens by which you may gather a sure and unfeigned judgement of that which shall befall him that is attainted with the Plague'.[27] The emphasis in Lodge's definition is on the unambiguous hermeneutic certainty – 'a sure and unfeigned judgement' – of the plague symptom, popularly known as God's token because, being a dubious gift from above, it leaves no room either for doubt or for remedy. The Second Senator, therefore, in asking for a token from Alcibiades, wants a sure and unambiguous signifier – he gets a glove – but at the same time risks inviting Alcibiades to show or maybe even pass on the symptoms wished on him by Timon.

Shakespeare introduces the term 'token' in its symptomatological sense in *The Rape of Lucrece* in a striking medical excursus on the separation of the blood clot from the serum as tell-tale facial signifier:

> And ever since, as pitying Lucrece' woes,
> Corrupted blood some watery token shows;
> And blood untainted still doth red abide,
> Blushing at that which is so putrefied.
> (1747–50)[28]

---

25 Jehan Goevrot, *Regiment*, quoted in Barroll, *Politics*, p. 76.

26 Judith Butler 'Burning Acts – Injurious Speech', in Parker and Kosofsky Sedgwick, *Performativity*, 197–227, p. 198.

27 Thomas Lodge, *Treatise*, sigs. B2^v, C3^v.

28 See also the reference in *Antony and Cleopatra*, which emphasizes the interpretative absoluteness of the bubonic token: 'ENOBARBUS How appears the fight? / SCARUS On our side like the tokened pestilence, / Where death is sure.' (3.10.8–10).

Here the separated serum becomes an unmistakable symptom of putrefaction but also an emblem of ethical and rhetorical duplicity of the kind displayed by Lucrece's rapist. This is the terrain on which language itself is most at risk. The issue is elaborately worked out in the finale of *Love's Labour's Lost*, with Berowne's maladroit attempt to save the day and the play by exercising his persuasive or infectious powers over the ladies. Berowne's unconvincing *mea culpa* ends with a confession of contagion that has less than courteous implications for the women, playfully accused of being the carriers of deadly pathogens:

BEROWNE They are infected, in their hearts it lies.
They have the plague, and caught it of your eyes.
These lords are visited, you are not free;
For the Lord's tokens on you do I see.
(5.2.420–3)

Berowne's semantic tergiversation transforms God's tokens from deadly symptoms to erotic signifiers, but in the light of the recent news of the death – presumably not from the plague – of the King of France, his unhappy choice of semeiotic terminology takes on greater significance than he desires, as the Princess of France is quick to point out: 'No, they are free that gave these tokens to us.' (5.2.424). The Princess out-Berownes Berowne in further transforming his 'tokens' from bodily signifiers to ambiguous objects of symbolic exchange (the men's rings), just as she semantically overturns Berowne's 'free' from the self-justifying sense of 'uninfected' to the accusatory sense of 'insincere'. Here the association between language and infection becomes quite intricate. On the one hand, linguistic tokens cease to be signifiers and become direct symptoms of pathology, that is, of the very ethical and political 'freedom' or superficiality of which the Princess complains. 'Thus pour the stars down plagues for perjury' admits Berowne at the outset of his suspect renunciation of rhetoric (394ff.), which concludes with his confessional plea 'Bear with me, I am sick' (417). At the same time, the etiology of language is in direct contrast to the symptomatology of the plague, since it is the very hermeneutic and moral ambiguity of linguistic tokens, as opposed to the univocal absoluteness of bubonic tokens, that characterizes their pathological potential.

Berowne's debacle at the hands of the Princess poses the question of the performativity of language in quite different terms from those implied by James's proclamations and Timon's imprecations. The bubonic quality of language has to do here not with the efficacy of the speech act but on the contrary with its performative emptiness and lack of consequentiality. What is at stake in the Princess's accusation is the men's repeated failure to keep their word. It is curious to note that J. L. Austin, father of the performative, in defining what he calls the 'infelicities' of speech acts – empty and especially insincere verbal undertakings – uses precisely the same tropes of disease and contagion employed by Shakespeare: 'as *utterances* our performatives are . . . heir to certain . . . kinds of ill which infect all utterances'.[29] All language may become contaminated if not kept under strict ethical control. Notoriously, Austin goes on to give as prime example of unhappy or infected discourse a speech act uttered on stage: 'a performative utterance will, for example, be *in a peculiar way* hollow or void if said by an actor on the stage, or if introduced in a poem, or spoken in a soliloquy . . . language in such circumstances is in special ways – intelligibly – used not seriously, but in ways *parasitic* upon its normal use – ways which fall under the doctrine of the *etiolations* of language.'[30] 'Parasitic', 'etiolations': we are back to the sickness-inducing parasite-borne bacilli of epidemic, and are likewise back to the peculiar pathogeny of dramatic performance, or at least of dramatic performatives.

This is Timon's predicament, caught between the ills of the performative and the

29 Austin, *How to Do Things*, p. 21.
30 *Ibid.*

infelicities of performance. Betrayed by his erstwhile friends who have absented themselves from felicity through flattery and insincere undertakings, Timon admonishes Alcibiades: 'Promise me friendship, but perform none. If thou wilt not promise, the gods plague thee, for thou art a man! If thou dost perform, confound thee, for thou art a man!' (4.3.74–7).[31] The gods plague thee: there is no way out of the great Bubonia Triangle, language-performance-disease triad that defines 'a man'. If you fail to promise, you elude your social responsibilities and are thus contaminated. If you promise and fail to perform, you betray your undertaking, and are thus contaminated. But if you promise *and* perform, confound you, you are doubly contaminated, especially if you perform on the stage or in a poem or in a soliloquy. The tricky rapport between performatives and dramatic performance is raised directly in the play by the presence of the poet. Even if he solemnly promises 'No levelled malice / Infects one comma in the course I hold' (1.1.47–8), he is accused nonetheless of etiolated or hollow discourse:

APEMANTUS Art not a poet?
POET Yes.
APEMANTUS Then thou liest. Look in thy work, where thou hast feigned him a worthy fellow ... He that loves to be flattered is worthy o' th' flatterer. (1.1.223–30)

Timon endeavours to distance himself from the poet's feigning flattery by sarcastically pointing out its insincerity:

[*To Poet*] And, for thy fiction,
Why, thy verse swells with stuff so fine and smooth
That thou art even natural in thine art. (5.1.81–3)

But to no avail: it is Timon's speech that is determined and appropriated by the discourse of the poet, who has indeed feigned him a worthy fellow, and so Timon's every utterance is subject to the laws of the fine and smooth fiction he tries to refute. Even his precious pestilential proclamations are hollow and void because feigned or fictional, and thus as sick as the world they are launched against. All that remains for Timon to do is let language end, but this is another empty fiction. Language does not end with his death. And indeed the tragedy closes with Alcibiades' obituary feigning him a worthy fellow: 'Dead is noble Timon,' etc., just the kind of flattering discourse the protagonist most abhorred. More words? Plague, plague!

---

[31] This is the Folio version of the passage, which is often emended to 'Promise me friendship, but perform none. If thou wilt promise, the gods plague thee, for thou art a man! If thou dost not perform, confound thee, for thou art a man!', as in the Complete Oxford Shakespeare. The emendation reverses the terms of the question, although the problem remains that of the performance or otherwise of verbal undertakings.

THE LANGUAGE OF THE SPECTATOR

DENNIS KENNEDY

RECONSTRUCTING THE BARD

Since the end of the Second World War the number of Shakespeare performances has increased remarkably. The English national poet is also the world's most popular dramatist, produced in an amazement of versions and with a frequency that is next to alarming. Because they are performed so often, and on something approaching a global scale, the most popular plays are arenas of impassioned scrutiny, sites of intense cultural gaze. Why did this happen?

On a material level Shakespeare's burgeoning is directly related to the rise in public subsidy for the theatre in the twentieth century. In the English-speaking countries this is exclusively a postwar phenomenon: the theatres that dominate the Shake-scene are products of a state sponsorship that began in the 1950s. But subsidy alone is not sufficient explanation, for public or private funding for the arts operates inside a larger cultural system that enables it. I suggest that in the Anglo-American examples, and in numerous European cases as well, the reason for funding and the reason for Shakespeare were intertwined: after the war the theatre was seen as a site for the recovery of the past, Shakespeare an opportunity to preserve a dying European memory.

The movement is first registered in the founding and development of international arts festivals. Though a few models existed before the war, in the late 1940s and early 1950s new types of festivals appeared over much of Europe, and their rapid development was tied from the start to a sense of reconstruction. The earliest major example, the Edinburgh International Festival of Music and Drama, opened in August 1947. It was founded and led by Austrian-born Rudolph Bing, then the general manager of the Glyndebourne Opera Festival, whose work in Britain, and as the long-lived manager of the Metropolitan Opera in New York, was characterized by a sense of aesthetic preservation. The Edinburgh Festival's opening flourish was an enactment of power politics: *Richard II*, in a production by the Old Vic starring Alec Guinness and directed by Ralph Richardson. The clash between a medieval and a modern political theory dramatized in that play, or between a theologic and a pragmatic version of rule, might be seen to parallel questions about contemporary European governance. Thus the Festival implicitly connected Shakespeare to the sense of international recovery and universal peace Bing wished to promote.

A more potent example of the theme of reconstruction can be found at the Avignon Festival, which was inaugurated in September 1947, only weeks after Edinburgh. It was founded by Jean Vilar, who saw theatre, in his own phrase, as a 'public service', a place where class barriers could be transcended, political differences set aside, and a new community celebrated around timeless dramatic themes.[1]

[1] See Vilar's *Le théâtre, service public*, ed. Armand Delcampe (Paris, 1975).

Vilar's utopian project took seriously the warning that civilization as he understood it might have been destroyed, and that French culture might still be destroyed in the aftermath of war. In this light the Avignon Festival, taking advantage of the warm nights of Provence, was a scheme for the maintenance of memory, a re-creation of European past.

And what play would most exemplify that past in France? Vilar's first production in September 1947 was *Richard II*. The venue was significant: outdoors in the Court of Honour of the Papal Palace, with more than 3,000 seats in front of the monumental walls of the fourteenth-century palace. In such an environment the performance depended on large-scale vocal delivery and gesture, rich period costumes, and a sense of ritual that resembled High Mass. The opulence and ceremony on stage could be reassuring to an audience aware of themselves as survivors in a ruined world. The Papal Palace, recalling the greatest period of a long-decayed Avignon, contextualized a play about a royal history from the same era, collapsing the past upon the past in an uncertain present. *Richard II* reappeared every year at Avignon through 1953.

Vilar's lead in staging in ancient surroundings plays with historical settings was followed in the 1950s all over France and in Germany as well. *Coriolanus* was mounted by Jean Renoir at the Roman amphitheatre in Nîmes, *Richard III* in the amphitheatre in Arles, *Julius Caesar* in the ruins of Jupiter's temple at Baalbeck, *Hamlet* in the courtyard of the Château d'Annecy, *King John* at the Château d'Angers. In Germany a number of cities recently filled with rubble put Shakespeare in ancient sites, like the festival at Bad Hersfeld in Hesse set in the Gothic ruins of a former convent.[2]

Even where Shakespeare had never been institutionalized there was a trend immediately after the war to use the plays in a spirit of recovery. In Italy, for instance, a number of revealing productions fitted into the general pattern of asking Shakespeare to assist with the reconstruction of European culture. In April 1948 Giorgio Strehler opened the first full season of the Piccolo Teatro in Milan with *Richard II*. Perhaps the choice had been cued by Vilar, as it was the first time the play had been performed in Italy; a cast of ninety jammed the small stage. In the summer of 1949 Luchino Visconti staged *Troilus and Cressida* in the Boboli Gardens in Florence, designed by Franco Zeffirelli with 'unparalleled magnificence of costumes and circus-like pageantry'.[3] The island in the middle of the lake was transformed into a walled Troy, all in white, accessible only by a drawbridge. It seems almost grotesque to have spent 30 million lire to stage an extravagant operatic spectacle, complete with actors on horseback, for this war play so soon after the war, with much of Italy still lying in ruins, but the prodigal staging stood as vicarious richness for a devastated bourgeoisie. When taken with the other examples the case shows how crucial Shakespeare was in reviving European memory.

The major Shakespeare festivals might profitably be seen in the same light. The vitalization of Stratford immediately after the war, accomplished by the hiring of Barry Jackson as director and his bringing along the young Peter Brook and Paul Scofield, marked a clear turning from the undistinguished past of The Shakespeare Memorial Theatre to new claims for Shakespeare's centrality, developed in the following two decades by Anthony Quayle and Peter Hall. In case you are wondering, *Richard II* had already appeared at Stratford in 1947,

[2] See Jean Jacquot, *Shakespeare en France: mises en scène d'hier et d'aujourd'hui* (Paris, 1964), pp. 112–17; Robert Speaight, *Shakespeare on the Stage* (London, 1973), p. 260; and Wilhelm Hortmann, *Shakespeare on the German Stage: The Twentieth Century* (Cambridge, forthcoming).

[3] Mario Praz, *Shakespeare Survey 3* (1950), p. 118. I discuss these productions in *Looking at Shakespeare: A Visual History of Twentieth-Century Performance* (Cambridge, 1993), pp. 195–9; details can also be found in entries for some of them in Samuel L. Leiter (ed.), *Shakespeare Around the Globe: A Guide to Notable Postwar Revivals* (New York, 1986).

some two months before its staging at Edinburgh and Avignon. In Canada, Tyrone Guthrie's creation of the Stratford Shakespearian Festival in 1953 transported the spirit of postwar recovery to North America. It is significant that an undistinguished railway town in a remote part of Ontario contextualized Shakespeare with the prerogative of the past through the construction of a stage with assertions of Elizabethan authenticity. The New York Shakespeare Festival, established in 1954, and the one in Stratford, Connecticut, that opened the next year, were followed by a number of Shakespeare festivals that brought similar perceptions to the United States.

An intriguing connection may be drawn between festival performance and the desire to frame it in ancient surroundings, or with the antiquity of the town in Stratford, or with the building of Elizabethanist stages and Old Globe replicas. In productions in English – despite the separate passion for contemporizing the meaning of Shakespeare – there has been a striking tendency since the war to have the text spoken in architectural environments that claim to match its authenticity and obsolescence. In these cases Shakespeare's language as spoken on stage more or less equals the quality of pastness of the structure, but is quite consciously *not* the language of the spectator. Outside of the theatre we are likely to hear such speech, or any archaic form of English, only momentarily in classrooms or in a few reformation churches, primarily the Church of England. (In this regard the theatre, the school, and the church stand as ramparts of custom, suggesting an unbroken line with a common anglican past.) Ironically in most foreign production of Shakespeare, even when performed in ancient sites, the language of the spectator is the same as that spoken on stage – but of course it is not Shakespeare's language. That may explain why the lure of authenticity for Shakespearian spaces has not been as strong outside the English-speaking theatre, even though the open stage movement began in Germany in the nineteenth century, well before William Poel.

BABEL IN DISNEYLAND

Bloomsday. On 16 June every year celebrations occur across Dublin to recreate a history that never happened. 'We encourage participants in Bloomstime events to dress in period style', says the 1996 brochure from the James Joyce Centre. The Centre defines itself in an admirably democratic manner: 'We are constituted to assist both the Joycean scholar and those who have a developing interest in Joyce, whether they have read none or all of his work.' The Joyce Summer School, the Yeats Summer School, the Synge Summer School, the Shaw Summer School, the Wilde Autumn School, nightly literary pub crawls with actors impersonating writers: at times all of Ireland seems a site for the performance of modernism. Ireland is hardly alone. Jack-the-Ripper tours in London, visits to artists' houses and to stately homes, the costumed adventures of Williamsburg in Virginia or of Plimouth Plantation in Massachusetts – the entire heritage industry commodifies history as a site-specific cultural theme park. The past becomes a universal Disneyland.

Disneyland does not have to be understood as a convenient scapegoat but rather as the most available and logical model of how to present the culture of pastness in a global economy at the end of the century. We assume that 'higher' cultural transactions, sojourns to museums or to Shakespeare, normally involve an intellectual or emotional complexity that a theme park lacks. But even in this realm the Walt Disney Company knows how to respond to a growing market in cultural leisure. The company has opened the Disney Institute in Orlando where conferences in a number of fields take place, and holiday-makers who want to use their time profitably can enrol in a range of classes from cooking to film-making. Visits from celebrities add lustre – including actors from the RSC.

Disney calls this 'edutainment' and also has a scientific word for the study of consumer behaviour in theme parks: 'guestology'.[4]

In the section of the edutainment trade marked Shakespeare, the most obvious example of a cultural theme park is the International Shakespeare Globe Centre in London, predicated upon concepts of cultural tourism analogous to those of Bloomsday or Disney. Its key concepts are its most problematic issues: authenticity versus simulation, art versus antiquarianism, instruction versus tourism. The sociologist Adolf Ehrentrant has remarked that 'any authenticity claimed for a heritage structure' is a social construction of its assessors 'rather than the intrinsic property of the object'. Thus the crucial issue for the visitor is not the structure itself but, as Erik Cohen says, 'the manner of the negotiation of its meaning' provided in the experience.[5] David Harvey puts it another way when he notes that a characteristic of the simulacra created in the Disney Worlds is an almost perfect concealment of 'any trace of origin, of the labour processes that produced them, or the social relations implicated in their production'.[6] Despite widespread criticism the Globe Centre operates under a kindred camouflage, erasing the conservative ideology that underpins it and concealing alternative perspectives on its historical virtue. Whatever its ultimate successes or failures, the Globe Centre pinpoints the dilemma that faces all traffic in Shakespeare in the postmodern age, what Terence Hawkes calls 'Bardbiz'.[7]

There are elements of the same intellectual quandary in many Shakespeare festivals, whether or not they have mandates based on Elizabethanist architecture. The RSC, which used to advertise itself as the largest theatre company in the world, despite state funding and non-profit status is in the strictest sense an entrepreneurial venture, and in Stratford, by geographical necessity, unremittingly dependent upon cultural tourists. The postwar international festivals in general are now forced to operate as large-scale business enterprises, using the marketing strategies of global capitalism. I don't mean that they are money-making machines, but rather that they must compete for consumers in the same way as an airline or a manufacturer of big-screen televisions.

It is a multinational traffic: Bardbiz is implicated in global tourism in an intriguing way. The rapidity and ease of jet transport brings spectators from around the world to theatrical centres: major theatre events now are sites on the large map of intellectual safari. The festivals have as a result assumed the affliction of postmodernity, moving away from the spirit of recovery and communal enterprise that marked their foundations. The postwar urge to re-create a European purpose drew on the modernist reclaiming of theatre as a social and religious force and operated on both sides of the Iron Curtain during the height of the Cold War. In the theatres built under Guthrie's influence the open stage carried an architectural ideology of inclusion, the suggestion of spectator participation in the event. This form of theatre tended to be nationalist, celebrating in many cases singularity and tribal identity. But now in the major festivals the ideal of communion has given way to self-conscious and competitive marketing strategies as the spectator's options for art and edutainment increase. This is hardly surprising in a world where Coca-Cola sponsors the Olympics, where *Pravda* has become a tabloid newspaper, and where the Vatican has

---

[4] A conference report by Turgut Var, *Annals of Tourism Research* 20.2 (1993), p. 376.

[5] Adolf Ehrentrant, 'Heritage Authenticity and Domestic Tourism in Japan', *Annals of Tourism Research* 20.2 (1993), 262–78; p. 270. Erik Cohen, 'Authenticity and Commoditization in Tourism', *Annals of Tourism Research* 15 (1988), 371–86; p. 374.

[6] David Harvey, *The Condition of Postmodernity: An Enquiry into the Origins of Cultural Change* (Oxford, 1990), p. 300.

[7] Terence Hawkes, *Meaning by Shakespeare* (London, 1992), pp. 141–53.

licensed for sale reproductions of the Papal throne.[8]

One guestologic response in the theatre to the dense ecology of entertainment has been the creation of large-scale sentimental work like the Lloyd Webber megamusicals. Another has been a kind of shotgun approach, with the provider securing so many choices that something is bound to appeal to a potential ticket-buyer. The Edinburgh Festival, fifty years after its founding, offers almost a thousand events in three weeks and Avignon has one hundred presentations a day for more than a month. Equally prodigious have been the marathon performances of classics like Brook's nine-hour *Mahabharata* or Ariane Mnouchkine's eight-hour *Les Atrides*. As early as 1977 Peter Zadek's *Hamlet* in Bochum and Peter Stein's *As You Like It* in Berlin created monumental performance for Shakespeare in specially constructed non-theatre spaces. Mnouchkine's production of three Shakespeare plays in 1980s, the English Shakespeare Company's eight-play marathon of the histories, and the occasional scheduling of thematic cycles at Stratford have continued this trend with a vengeance. In 1994 I witnessed a landmark in marathon Bardbiz: Stuart Seide's three parts of *Henry VI* in French at Avignon, performed in the same courtyard that Vilar used. Starting at ten in the evening when it was sufficiently dark outdoors, we got to the rise of Gloucester by dawn and finished with the exiling of Margaret at 6.30 in the morning. Café et croissants avec Edward IV.

The consumers of culture at such festivals are as international as the consumers of material goods targeted by multinational corporations, and as likely to respond to non-linguistic signals. The major characteristic of global product promotion is its reliance on icon and image in a pop culture context, backed by music. It is not necessary to speak Chinese, as a clever TV commercial reminds us, to buy a Coke in China. International Shakespeare performance, though inevitably focussed on locution, has in the past fifteen years or so moved into translinguistic areas of signification, corresponding to the move away from nationalist ideology. Even Anglophones who supposedly speak Shakespeare's language can have difficulty in comprehending the archaism of the text, and no circumstance points more to the unpredictability of reception than the prospect that spectators may not completely construe the dialogue. If the language of the international spectator is less connected with normalized linguistic competence, we have moved into a pomo no-man's-land where signifiers remain conventional but are drained of conventional meaning. Paradox: a non-logocentric Shakespeare is still called Shakespeare.

THE IDEOLOGY OF LANGUAGE

In most foreign-language performances of Shakespeare, where the text has been translated into a modern vernacular, the losses in the poetic subtlety of the original are compensated by ease of understanding. That is why *Hamlet* in English sounds like a series of quotations while in foreign environments it can sound like a new play. The visual inventiveness of Shakespeare performance outside of English in this century is due in part to freedom from the demands of tradition imposed by the renaissance text in the home countries. Peter Zadek, for example, one of the most successful and outrageous of the German directors of Shakespeare in our time, has been motivated toward travesty productions by his deep knowledge of the original text. Raised in England as the son of German exiles, he began his career in London before returning to Germany; when he turned to Shakespeare he recognized that no translation can hope to indicate the full value of Shakespeare's language. His effrontery in the realms of staging

[8] Rajeev Syal, 'Vatican enterprises puts its faith in soft furnishings', *Sunday Times*, 4 August 1996. I discuss the implications of global capitalism on Shakespeare performance in 'Shakespeare and the Global Spectator', *Shakespeare Jahrbuch* 131 (1995), 50–64.

and design has been an attempt to reveal 'Shakespeare's nonverbal dramatic potential',[9] to make up for the loss of Shakespeare's language.

Zadek's *Antony and Cleopatra* for the Berliner Ensemble, a rather tame production by his standards, played at the Edinburgh Festival in 1994. The critics complained most about the three and three-quarters hours without an interval; what I found intriguing, however, was the language of the spectator. As is his habit, Zadek commissioned a new translation, a highly colloquial and informal prose that suited the proletarian acting style of the Berliner Ensemble. It was a casual, anti-heroic performance notably contemporary in body, gesture, and vocal delivery – but spectators at Edinburgh were reading the original text projected above the stage. This extra-dramatic circumstance created classes of reception: German-speakers heard a translated text in complete accord with the acting, non-German-speakers read a text whose archaism and formality made a severe disjunction with the relaxed stage events. And the sporadic, even optional, experience of reading surtitles fragmented the audience further. If Zadek approached this production with a sense of the inadequacy of translation, in crossing borders it undermined any hope of an uncontested reception.

The problematics of foreign-language performance in Shakespeare's own country were brought home that same year by the reactions of London critics to the RSC's 'Everybody's Shakespeare' Festival. In this adventurous project the language of the spectator became paramount. Karin Beier's zestful production of *Romeo and Juliet* from Düsseldorf, hailed and awarded throughout Germany, was savaged by some critics for its lack of English. Michael Ratcliffe noted that the text was cut with the zeal of those who are not 'compatriots of the playwright', conveniently forgetting how frequently the playwright's compatriots cut the plays. 'They come without the poetry', complained Jeremy Kingston of the actors, 'and must fall back on plot and fancy dress'. Charles Spencer made the most straightforward case:

> Although it is stimulating to be exposed to different views of Shakespeare, there is something coals-to-Newcastle-ish about importing foreign-language productions to England: there we sit, following an edited version of the script in surtitles while listening to the performers delivering matchless poetry in an incomprehensible tongue.[10]

Other productions fared even worse. Tadashi Suzuki's *The Tale of Lear* had already achieved wide international success, but Benedict Nightingale found it painful to listen to actors 'standing very still, and speaking an edited version of the original in very loud, abrupt Japanese'. And as for Peter Sellars' *Merchant of Venice*, which was in English but spoken by multicultural American actors, Nicholas de Jongh thought the speech so slurred that he wanted surtitles anyway, effectively appealing for Shakespeare to remain the property of trueborn Englishmen. Though some critics thought it darkly disturbing, Sheridan Morley used the opportunity to sum up: 'this whole RSC Shakespeare Festival is clearly a plot to make us aware of how much better the home team is than any of the visitors they have chosen'. The general reaction was so egregiously xenophobic that Michael Kustow, the producer of Everybody's Shakespeare, took the unusual step of reproaching the critics in print. They were behaving, he charged, with 'fury and betrayal at foreign fingerprints on the family heirlooms':

> This festival is the first time Britain has invited foreign companies to show their versions of our greatest playwright – and the challenge of these productions, and the resistance to them, has been extreme. The cries of outrage have revealed some not very attractive aspects of our beleaguered na-

[9] Volker Canaris, 'Peter Zadek and *Hamlet*', *The Drama Review* 24.1 (1980), p. 56.

[10] I quote the reviews from *Theatre Record* for 5–18 November 1994. In order they come from *Observer* of 30 October, *Times* of 1 November, and *Daily Telegraph* of the same date.

tional psyche. 'Everything else is turning to dust,' says the collective voice, 'can't they at least leave our Shakespeare alone?'[11]

The sense of national violation had been even more noticeable in the critical response to Robert Lepage's multicultural *A Midsummer Night's Dream* at the Royal National Theatre in 1992. This was not an import but a British production directed by a French-Canadian, yet it was treated in the press as a colonial annoyance. I admit that there were difficulties with this performance, which, because of the pool of water in the centre of the stage, was called 'A Mudsummer Night's Dream' or 'the wet Dream'. But in their complaints the critics often went beyond judgement to reveal deep unease about a foreign approach by a foreigner.

The same year Lepage directed a cycle of *Coriolanus*, *Macbeth*, and *The Tempest* in new Québécois translations which toured across Europe and in Japan. Lepage acknowledges that, like Zadek, he is 'preoccupied with Shakespeare's original texts' and when working in French nonetheless spends a great deal of rehearsal time with actors on the English text.[12] As with Beier, however, Lepage's background and high reputation were ignored in London, where he was seen as a 'show-off Canadian'. The Québécoise Angela Laurier, who played Puck as a genderless acrobat, was heavily berated for her non-native speech: 'She isn't Puck, what with her funny accent and one breast hanging out, but she's a cute act'; and 'she negotiates English verse with all the nimbleness of Inspector Clouseau'.[13] In a recent essay on the critical response, Barbara Hodgdon notes that though Laurier was actually the 'only non-British citizen in the cast', many of the other multiracial actors 'had their passports revoked and were constructed as colonials'. In the same vein the mudpool in the centre of the stage was imagined by some reviews as African and colonial.[14] Thus the attacks on speech were at base again attacks on an imagined invasion by dramatic immigrants, interlopers to the swelling scene. 'The company plays the full Shakespeare text, if not the verse', said Malcolm Rutherford, 'but any other connection with the original is tenuous.'[15]

PENTECOST

Enough critic bashing, it's too easy a way out. Instead let's turn to two multilingual productions by Lepage and Beier that demonstrate just how complex the language of the spectator can be. A history of multilingual Shakespeare could be extensive, starting perhaps with *The Spanish Tragedy*, the bilingual scenes in *Henry V*, and the travelling English Comedians on the Continent in the early seventeenth century. Such a history would include the great touring actors of the end of the nineteenth century like Tommaso Salvini and Ernesto Rossi, who when playing in Britain or America emoted Italian in the leading roles while the remainder of the cast performed in English. Politically more intriguing was the case of Jacob P. Adler, star of the New York Yiddish stage, who took his Shylock to Broadway in 1903; he continued to speak Yiddish while his supporting actors delivered Shakespeare's lines in English.[16]

A century later this kind of intertextual performance has new resonances. My first

---

[11] *Times* of 11 November 1994, *Evening Standard* of 17 November, *Spectator* of 26 November, *Independent* of 19 November.

[12] Denis Salter, 'Borderlines: An Interview with Robert Lepage and Le Théâtre Repère', *Theater* 24.3 (1993), 71–9; p. 71.

[13] Kenneth Hurren, *Mail on Sunday*, 12 July 1992; Paul Taylor, *Independent*, 11 July, both quoted from *Theatre Record*, 1–14 July 1992.

[14] Barbara Hodgdon, 'Looking for Mr Shakespeare after "the Revolution": Robert Lepage's Intercultural *Dream* Machine', *Shakespeare, Theory, and Performance*, ed. James C. Bulman (London, 1996), 68–91; p. 80.

[15] *Financial Times*, 11 July 1992.

[16] See Marvin Carlson, *The Italian Shakespearians* (Washington, 1985); and Joel Berkowitz, '"A True Jewish Jew": Three Yiddish Shylocks', *Theatre Survey* 37 (May 1996), 79–81.

example was an experiment in Canadian bilingualism from 1990 called *Romeo and Juliette*, initiated by Gordon McCall of the Shakespeare on the Saskatchewan Company. He invited Lepage to join him as co-director in transferring Verona to the Canadian plains, the setting 'a stretch of the Trans-Canada Highway passing through a contemporary Saskatchewan farming community'.[17] The two families entered from opposite directions, the Montagues presented as Anglophones, the Capulets as Francophones from the Métis culture. The dialogue of the Capulets, which amounts to about twenty per cent of the text, was translated into a pastiche archaic French meant to approximate Shakespeare's diction. In a highly unusual move, McCall directed the English-speaking actors, Lepage the French. As Lepage remembers, '*Romeo and Juliette* was an intercultural exchange from the start. The idea was to get English and French actors together and to work on the problems of translation, mainly with Shakespeare.'[18]

But McCall's agenda was more complex. Requesting funding from the federal Canadian government, he noted the undertaking would demonstrate that 'bilingualism in Western Canada is viable within the arts and that this type of nation[al] artist collaboration is enhanced not hindered by the use of and promotion of linguistic duality'.[19] For most English-speakers in Canada bilingualism is a myth, but the summer of 1990 was a tense moment for the nation; the Meech Lake Accord, which would guarantee a degree of autonomy for Québec if it ratified the repatriated constitution, was under severe attack by Québécois nationalists. The production of *Romeo and Juliette* was intended to strike advantage from the political moment. Though its ideology was cloudy, it hoped to use the two languages to underline the need for understanding and forgiveness.

In the end the production's bilingualism replicated the divided country, for its final performances outside Ottawa occurred as the Meech Lake Accord broke down, and it never played in Québec. Lepage remembers that the rehearsal process itself was marked by wariness. The working methods of the two groups of actors, their habits of preparation and thought, proved substantially different; they even had separate unions. Though the directors had agreed to collaborate with both groups, McCall became suspicious, refused to direct the Francophone players, and insisted on being present when Lepage worked with the English-speakers.[20] The exercise in co-existence served to reinforce cultural mistrust. (A similar approach was taken to the play in Jerusalem in 1993 in a co-production by the Khan Theatre and a Palestinian company from the West Bank, in which the Montagues spoke Arabic and the Capulets spoke Hebrew.)[21]

Karin Beier's *A Midsummer Night's Dream* of 1995 also had a political backdrop but was a different story altogether. Whether you think a united Europe is a reality, an ideal or a post-industrial fable, Shakespeare holds a unique place in the new (semi-)borderless EU, and this production put the language of the spectator to the severest test. Now only thirty, Beier had formed a theatre company called Countercheck Quarrelsome while studying English at the University of Cologne, for which she directed nine Shakespeare plays in English with German actors. 'Shakespeare', she has said, 'is the man in my life.' Her professional career began at Düsseldorf, where she mounted the *Romeo and Juliet* already mentioned. In January 1995 she

17 Denis Salter, 'Acting Shakespeare in Postcolonial Space', *Shakespeare, Theory, and Performance*, 113–32; p. 127.

18 Interview with Lepage by Christie Carson, 'Collaboration, Translation, Interpretation', *New Theatre Quarterly* 9 (February 1993), 31–6; p. 31.

19 Gordon McCall in a letter to Francis Landry of the Office of the Secretary of the State of the Government of Canada. I am grateful to Moira Day for this quotation and for other information on the production. Denis Salter and Sheila Stowell have also been most cooperative in providing details.

20 Carson, 'Collaboration', p. 32.

21 I thank Avraham Oz for this example.

participated in a workshop for young directors organized by the Union of European Theatres, led by Andrej Wajda, Ingmar Bergman, and Giorgio Strehler. From this she created an immediate project for 'a European Shakespeare'. In August fourteen actors from nine countries started work in the south of Italy, then moved to Düsseldorf for rehearsals on *A Midsummer Night's Dream*. The production opened in October.[22]

The consequential aspect of the project was the actors' lack of a common language. They overcame this rather forbidding difficulty, it seems, by speaking their own tongues loudly and relying on gestures, like stubborn monolingual tourists, adapting various national methods of rehearsal under Beier's leadership. If the Canadian bilingual *Romeo and Juliette* was fraught with cross-cultural mistrust, this European Shakespeare was designed to take profit from difference. Intercultural work in European theatre has for the most part imposed a pastiche or Orientalist style on Western actors as with Mnouchkine, or submitted multiracial actors to an overarching aesthetic master as with Brook. With those and other directors the language spoken in performance has been the language of the audience, regardless of the native language of the actors. In Beier's production, however, the point was to maintain division: the actors would speak Shakespeare's text in their own tongues. Though Beier herself is bilingual, she wished to rise above language, or, paradoxically, to use language as a non-linguistic signifier.

The performance opened with a stunning image: a naked, black Hippolyta, long hair covering her breasts, shot an arrow in dim light. Then bright white light on Theseus' assembled court, dressed in formal men's clothing, all except Hippolyta, centre stage, still naked, cowering. The smiling Theseus, an elegant practical joker and no-nonsense dictator, delivered his opening speech in upbeat Italian. When Hippolyta did not respond, Philostrate handed her a white shirt, formal trousers and shoes as Theseus prompted her speech line by line. Dressing, she repeated the words in Italian, but hesitantly, as the actress was British – an intriguing idea, suggesting that Hippolyta must learn the language of her conqueror.

But Italian was not the universal language of the court after all. Seven actors (later they would become the mechanicals and the fairies) entered together and spoke 'Happy be Theseus, our renownèd Duke' chorally in English. Thereafter Egeus' lines were delivered individually by the members of this cluster in their own languages, German, Bulgarian, Polish, Italian, French, Russian, and German again; while the end of the speech was given once more in unison in English: 'As she is mine, I may dispose of her ...' Philostrate, handling Hermia roughly, gave interpolated commands in Hungarian. At last she responded in English. Whether the characters or the actors understood one other was unclear, but they unashamedly continued to speak their own languages. Left alone with Hermia, Lysander, wearing a yamalke, beat his breast and prayed ritualistically. Unable to speak English to her, he gave instructions about their meeting in Hebrew with charade gestures, which Hermia enthusiastically translated into Shakespeare's words. Helena, convinced that Demetrius loves Hermia because she is English, near the end of the first scene broke the script to recite 'Shall I compare thee to a summer's day' to prove her linguistic equality. But she returned to the dialogue in her native Italian.

[22] I rely here on a profile article by Eva Pfister, 'Shakespeares Schwester', *Die Deutsche Bühne, Das Theatermagazin*, January 1996, 18–21; a review essay by Reinhard Kill, *Rheinische Post*, 3 November 1995; details printed in the Düsseldorf programme; a report by Marvin Carlson, 'Karin Beier's *Midsummer Night's Dream* and *The Chairs*', *Western European Stages* 7.3 (1995–6), 71–6; and the TV version of the performance at the Schiller Theater, Berlin, broadcast on the German channel Sat 3 in 1996. 'Shakespeare is the man in my life' is quoted in a number of these sources. My thanks to Wilhelm Hortmann for locating much valuable information.

The court officers doubled as the chief fairies, as in Brook's famous production, and their physical transformations were wonderful to watch. Oberon kept Theseus' black tailcoat but removed his shirt and added a latex bald cap; Titania took off Hippolyta's long wig to reveal a shaved head; the tall and stalwart Philostrate mussed up his hair, stripped down to tight toreador trousers and put on high heels to become an androgynous Puck. But they stuck to their Italian, English, and Hungarian speech. The old confusions of the wood provided a thematic background for Beier's new confusions of language, and as the linguistic chaos grew a spectator might well wonder how concord could ever come from such intertextual discord. Titania delivered her crucial speeches about the disturbances of nature ('These are the forgeries of jealousy') in English and with intense gestural disturbance, marking the passages as indicative of theme for even the most lexically challenged spectator.

Occasionally the Babel provided metatheatrical comic advantage. At one point in 2.1 Oberon did not understand Puck; 'non capito', said Paolo Calabresi. So Zoltán Mucsi helped him out by translating the line: 'I'll put a girdle au tout le monde in vierzig minuten.' When Oberon still didn't get it, Puck commented in Hungarian, 'These Italians – never have been any good at languages.' Similarly, in their rehearsal in the wood the mechanicals argued ad lib about the most appropriate acting technique for their play. Each selfishly proposed a national tradition in a national language: Peter Quince – here turned into Petra Squenz and played by Margherita di Rauso from Milan – insisted on an Italian operatic style appropriate to her impresario manner, while Jost Grix, the Flute from Düsseldorf, offered a Thisbe with a sweater over his head, a Brechtian 'alienation effect', he called it. Snug (Mladen Vasary from Paris) asked for classical 'delicatesse' and gave a balletic example; Starveling (Anastasia Bousyguina from the Moscow Art Theatre) invoked Stanislavsky and gave a deeply emotional speech from Chekhov, ending downstage with 'V Mosva, V Mosva'. Bottom would not be outdone: Jacek Poniedzialek from Cracow believed only Grotowski would serve and performed a show-stopping parody of physical acting, complete with a kicking fit on his back on the floor.[23]

The tensions of post-cold war Europe also broke through the cacophony of utterance and action, especially when the Hungarian Demetrius called the Israeli Lysander, in English, a 'fucking Jew'. Ludic anger easily spilled over into racial hatred, and Lysander in turn tagged his rival a 'fucking gypsy'. Not for the first time, the metaphoric brawls of the play became earnestly physicalized in a fight. In the final scene Philostrate, insistently recommending against allowing Pyramus and Thisbe, informed the Duke that the players were Eurotrash: 'International mechanicals – Auslander – Poland – Russian – Germany – Bulgarian – French – Italian – Italian very stupid – but all crazy.'

International mechanicals: not a bad name for the enterprise as a whole. The multilingual confusion evoked, of course, the chaos of self in Shakespeare's play, and emphasized the disorderly theme of sex and violence familiar from Jan Kott, who was quoted in the programme along with Camille Paglia. But the onstage Babel was a complex sign: of the new Europe, of the problems of independence and sovereignty within union, of the mixed styles of acting, of differing national traditions of Shakespeare, of the need for and the difficulty of translinguistic communication. Though performed for a German audience, neither German nor English was dominant on stage. Indeed the occasional lines in English delivered by non-native speakers served chiefly to remind the hearers of what was absent. Wilhelm Hortmann, in his comprehensive history of Shakespeare on the German stage in the twentieth

[23] Carlson, 'Karin Beier', p. 73.

century, takes this production as his final example. Noting the losses Beier's approach entailed, he holds that 'the play as a poetic cosmos dropped out of sight. The words were there, but only as a reminder that they once, and in a different language, carried meaning.'[24]

Yet the production carried great meaning, and some of it derived from Shakespeare. To convey meaning, however, whether literal or thematic, the actors could not rely on literary signifiers. Physical action substituted for speech, or was abundantly required to support speech: it was no accident that half of the players were selected from companies preoccupied with physical theatre.[25] Beier's European Shakespeare was necessarily a gestural Shakespeare, a Shakespeare with so many languages as to render language unimportant. Or rather, the company provided a corporeal template of the play and the audience was asked to provide a memory of language, a memory of Shakespeare, who was and was not present. Repeatedly told that Shakespeare is important because of his language, we here discovered the opposite; the normalized assumption of a language shared by actors and listeners was subverted, the position of the auditors undermined. This Euro-Shakespeare demanded a Euro-spectator, preferably one more linguistically competent than the actors themselves.

A character in one of Michael Dibdin's novels says that Europe is becoming 'like an airport terminal where every language is spoken badly'.[26] Though English is lingua franca in airports and in resorts, in business and in international soccer matches, it has not become Esperanto for Shakespeare: production outside English is often noteworthy to Anglophones for its alien features. Yet the most interesting movement in Shakespeare production is deliberately crossing boundaries, connecting with intercultural and post-colonial politics, using the bodies and voices of multiracial and multicultural actors as signifiers of a world which is now covered indiscriminately by satellite TV transmission. There has been some resistance to this movement in Britain, where Shakespeare production lately has often been dulled by the patterns of the routine and the absence of political or social urgency. But the movement is gaining force nonetheless, drawing on the protean cultural array of our confusing time, mixing high and low culture, crossing races and nations, transgressing linguistic frontiers.

It seems significant that Peter Brook, who reinvented Shakespeare at Stratford a couple of times since the war, has done his most radical work on the plays in French. He once told his translator, Jean-Claude Carrière, that his ideal text for Paris would be 'a new play, written in French, and written by Shakespeare'.[27] Brook's latest venture, a 'mosaic' of exercises and scenes from *Hamlet* called *Qui est là?*, has his two chief African actors, Bakary Sangré and Sotigui Kouyaté, playing Hamlet and the Ghost. In the 1990 *Tempest* in Paris they spoke French like the rest of Brook's international troupe; in 1996 they took the next step and spoke Shakespeare's lines in Bambara, their native tongue.[28]

Directors like Brook and Zadek, Lepage and Beier, who are immersed in Shakespeare's original but stage him in accents strange, have forged a performative language that combines the probity of the archaic text with the liberty of contemporary translation. Haunted by the elusive spectre of textual authenticity, they have nonetheless begun to come to textual terms with the human and cultural migration that marks the millennium's edge. In their

[24] Hortmann, *Shakespeare on the German Stage.*

[25] Josette Bushell-Mingo (Hippolyta/Titania) from Théâtre de la Complicité; Vasary from the Jacques Lecoq School; Poniedzialek from the Stary Theatre; Calabresi, Rauso, and Giorgia Senesi (Helena) from the Piccolo Teatro di Milano.

[26] Michael Dibdin, *Dead Lagoon* (London, 1994), p. 311.

[27] Reported by Jean-Claude Carrière, in a talk in Los Angeles in 1991. See the introduction to my edition *Foreign Shakespeare: Contemporary Performance* (Cambridge, 1993), p. 15.

[28] Rosette C. Lamont, 'Letter from Paris: 1995–1996', *Western European Stages* 8.2 (1996), 11–16; p. 15.

intercultural and interlingual instances, Shakespeare once again becomes Johannes Factotum: with or without his original language, in the theatre it now seems possible to use him to create what Barbara Hodgdon calls 'the other's dream'.[29]

In times of change cultural production has ridden on Shakespeare's back before. Will he, as Beier proposes, become a symbol of the new Europe, a strange sign of unity in a diverse and fractional world? Whatever the answer, in the theatre and in film his plays can no longer be considered simply English words on pages with fixed meanings and settled dramatic styles. They have become an international art enterprise, various and ungoverned, a construct of history, icon, idea, and many languages. Perhaps they will someday escape English entirely and descend over spectators like tongues of fire.

---

[29] Hodgdon, 'Looking for Mr Shakespeare', p. 86.

MARLOWE'S *EDWARD II*: PENETRATING LANGUAGE IN SHAKESPEARE'S *RICHARD II*

MEREDITH SKURA

In an often-quoted judgement, Charles Lamb noted that Shakespeare's *Richard II* took hints from, but 'scarce improved' on, 'the reluctant pangs of abdicating Royalty' in Marlowe's *Edward II*. But was Shakespeare in fact trying to 'improve' on Marlowe when he created his own 'weak king' in *Richard II*?[1] Or was he doing something else? This paper re-examines Shakespeare's play as a more complicated response to *Edward II* that reveals dynamic tensions between the two playwrights. Bertolt Brecht's modern response to Marlowe in his 1922 *Edward II* provides a useful introductory comparison. Brecht seems to have been drawn to Marlowe's play not so much for its political as for its personal relevance, in particular for its portrayal of the doomed bond between Edward and Gaveston – the kind of bond Brecht had just written about in *The Jungle*. Brecht was indeed trying to improve on, or at least to outdo, Marlowe's bleak play. With a 'savage pessimism', he rewrote Marlowe to create a world where, as his Edward says, 'There is nothing in life besides the touch of men's bodies, and even that is minimal and vain.'[2] What interests me about Brecht's play however is that it is not only about the difficult closeness between two men but – as adaptation, collaboration, and partly cribbed translation – it is also the product of such closeness. *Edward II* was the first of the collaborative ventures that were to serve Brecht so effectively as catalysts for creativity throughout his career.

On the face of it, Shakespeare's response to Marlowe seems to have been quite different from Brecht's. He was interested in the politics of *Richard II*, not the touch of men's bodies in *Edward II*; and, even politically, the difference between Shakespeare's and Marlowe's plays has always seemed far more striking than the similarity. Where Marlowe reduces politics to personal appetite and a struggle for power, Shakespeare transcends the personal, contextualizing abdication in a universe that makes moral and political sense. Where Marlowe's play is full of sex and violence, Shakespeare's is almost devoid of both. For one thing, Edward II's passion for Gaveston seems to have left no trace on Richard's relationships. Edward's

[1] On Lamb and critical discussion since Lamb, see Charles Forker's introduction to *Edward the Second*: The Revel Plays (Manchester and New York, Manchester University Press, 1994), pp. 36–41; on Michael Manheim, 'The Weak King Dilemma in Plays of the 1590s', *Renaissance Drama*, n.s. 2 (1969), 71–80.

[2] 'Savage pessimism' is Richard Beckley's phrase, in 'Adaptation as a Feature of Brecht's Dramatic Technique', *German Life and Letters*, n.s. 15 (1962), pp. 274–84, 277. On the play's political implications and its place in Brecht's political career, see John Willett and Ralph Manheim, eds., introduction to *Bertolt Brecht Collected Plays* (London, Methuen, 1970), pp. xii–xiii; and John Fuegi, *The Essential Brecht* (Los Angeles, Hennessy and Ingalls, 1972), pp. 26ff. On the importance of Edward and Gaveston's relationship to Brecht, see Louise J. Laboulle, 'A Note on Bertolt Brecht's Adaptation of Marlowe's *Edward II*', *Modern Language Review*, 54 (1959), pp. 214–20; and Eric Bentley, introduction to *The Works of Bertolt Brecht* (New York, Grove Press, 1966), p. vii and passim.

favourites (and Richard's favourites in the anonymous *Woodstock* (*c.* 1592), which Shakespeare also knew), all but disappear in *Richard II.*[3] For another, Edward's extraordinary pain at losing Gaveston is paralleled only by Richard's regret that his roan Barbary now serves the new king Bolingbroke so willingly and by his abstract complaint that 'love to Richard / Is a strange brooch in this all-hating world' (5.5.65–6). As for violence, no one has found any trace of Edward's appalling murder in *Richard II.* In fact Shakespeare, offered a choice of deaths in Holinshed, could have scripted a passive starvation or even suffocation for Richard; but instead he chose to make his king die fighting. Edward's death is devastatingly physical as the world bears in on him in the form of a burning spit thrust up his fundament; but Richard's death allows him to escape the world of bodies altogether ('Mount, mount, my soul ... / Whilst my gross flesh sinks downward' [5.5.111–12]).

I shall argue, however, that Shakespeare was more influenced than we have realized by the erotic passion and erotic violence associated with male friendship and male rivalry in Marlowe. Both Edward's love for Gaveston and his erotically suggestive death affect the portrayal of Richard, his friends, and his (often premature) visions of death. Marlowe's love and death have been ousted from Shakespeare's plot by the more languid 'pangs' of abdication, but they return in Shakespeare's language, or rather in what Ruth Nevo has called Shakespeare's 'other language', the unconscious effects that words and verbal images create as they circulate between Marlowe and Shakespeare.[4] They imply less about Richard's sexuality than about his subjectivity – less about whom he loves than about who he is – but their quiet presence is particularly important in *Richard II*, because it helps fill in the gaps of a plot that is so undermotivated in places that critics have had to postulate a missing 'part 1' in order to understand why Richard attacks Bolingbroke at the beginning of the play, and they have had to postulate neurosis in order to understand why Richard abdicates even before Bolingbroke claims the throne at the end of the play. In what follows, I will first single out aspects of Marlowe's *Edward II* that were important to Shakespeare insofar as they left their mark on his other plays; and then I will suggest how such material might fill in the missing gaps of *Richard II* as well, even though it is supposed to have been eliminated from that play. Finally, I will suggest that Shakespeare's response to *Edward II* may help us understand new dimensions of dramatic collaboration on the early modern stage.

WHAT SHAKESPEARE SAW IN MARLOWE'S *EDWARD II*: TWINS AND RIVAL TWINS

Sex and violence per se have hardly been neglected in Marlowe's play. Critics no longer either discreetly ignore Edward's homosexuality or mention it only to condemn it; indeed, the erotic implications of Edward's death have become increasingly important to our understanding of the play.[5] And yet I am not sure that we appreciate the range of fantasies in this

[3] Glynne Wickham, 'Shakespeare's *King Richard II* and Marlowe's *King Edward II*', in *Shakespeare's Dramatic Heritage: Critical Studies in Medieval, Tudor, and Shakespearean Drama* (London, Routledge & Kegan Paul, 1969). Quotations from *Richard II* and other Shakespeare plays which follow are from the Arden editions.

[4] Ruth Nevo, *Shakespeare's Other Language* (New York, Methuen, 1987).

[5] In the 1970s critics talked about gender identity in the play; recent discussion is more often devoted to sexual orientation and object choice in the play, and to early modern attitudes toward same-sex love. For discussion of gender identity in the play, see, e.g., Barbara J. Bains, 'Sexual Polarity in the Plays of Christopher Marlowe', *Ball State University Forum*, 23 (1982), 317; and Sara Munson Deats, '*Edward II*; A Study of Androgyny', *Ball State University Forum*, 22 (1981), 30–41; for discussion of sexual orientation, see, e.g., Purvis Boyette, 'Wanton Humor and Wanton Poets: Homosexuality in Marlowe's *Edward II*', *TSE*, 12 (1977), 33–50; and Wickham, 'Shakespeare's *King Richard*'.

play if we stop short after specifying the gender of Edward's lover or the particular orifice implicated in their coupling. One can certainly see why Edward's Queen Isabel refers to him and Gaveston bitterly as 'Jove and Ganymede' (or why the barons cite as models Hylas and Hercules, and other famous male lovers). But Edward and Gaveston also compare themselves to the heterosexual Hero and Leander, Jupiter and Danae, and Actaeon and Diana. In fact, Edward and Gaveston in this play are very different from the Jupiter and Ganymede whom Marlowe had actually staged in his earlier *Dido, Queen of Carthage*. The difference is important: in *Dido*, Jupiter and Ganymede are canny, in control – and comically unequal. The couple in this play are tragic. Edward's dotage is far more serious than Jupiter's; and even Gaveston, opportunistic as he is, loves Edward. Edward's love for Gaveston is actually like the heterosexual dotage Marlowe portrays in the rest of *Dido*, between Dido and Aeneas, or like the dotage he draws on for Edward II's lines[6] – like Margaret and Suffolk's love in Shakespeare's *Henry VI, Part One*, or like Andrea's love for Bel-Imperia in Kyd's *Spanish Tragedy*. In any case, more than its classification as 'homosexual' or 'heterosexual',[7] what matters in Marlowe's play is not only the actual 'object' of Edward's love but Edward's – and Marlowe's – narratives (or fantasies) about that object and about love.

Marlowe's narrative of love involves not only love but friendship – and even rivalry. It needs to be read in the context, not only of Jupiter and Ganymede or Hero and Leander, but also of the twinning that Bacon, Montaigne, and Elyot see as prerequisite for ideal friendship. (A friend is 'another I', Elyot writes; 'another himself', says Bacon; they 'entermixe and confound themselves one in the other', says Montaigne.)[8] Gaveston, Edward says, 'loves me more than all the world' (1.4.164); but instead of simply loving back, Edward responds with an 'almost manic desire'[9] to be 'another Gaveston' (1.1.142–3) and to 'knit' his soul to Gaveston.[10] In addition, Edward's love is defined partly by its difference from his other relationships – to his father and the barons, and

---

6 Forker, 34. Shakespeare may have drawn on Marlowe's portrayal of Edward and Gaveston, reappropriating them for heterosexuality in *Richard II* (for Richard and Isabel) and in *Antony and Cleopatra*. Jonathan Goldberg argues strongly against reducing homosexuality to a form of or substitute for heterosexuality (*Sodometries. Renaissance Texts and Renaissance Sexualities* (Stanford, Calif., 1992), p. 121). But the echoes across the gap between the two playwrights – and the two orientations – are certainly there.

7 Or 'presexual', like love between parent and child. Shakespeare, for example, may have heard Edward's lament for Gaveston as parental; it later provided him with a voice for two famous bereaved parents – for Constance in Shakespeare's *King John*, when her son Arthur dies, and for Lear in *King Lear* when he loses Cordelia. Edward: 'I shall never see / My lovely Pierce, my Gaveston again.' Constance: 'Never, never / Must I behold my pretty Arthur more.' Lear's familiar words hardly need quoting: 'Never, never, never, never, never.'

8 Sir Thomas Elyot, *Boke Named the Governour (1531)*, 'Amity or Friendship', ed. Croft (London, 1880), p. 119. (Elyot goes on to tell about 'Titus and Gisippius', who were 'one in form in personage', as well as in affection, will, and appetites, and had 'so confederated themselves, that it seemed none other, when their names were declared, but that they had only changed their places, issuing (as I might say) out of the one body, and entering in to the other' (134). Bacon, *Essays* (1857), p. 265; Montaigne, tr. Florio, vol I, p. 202.)

9 Josie Slaughter Shumake, *The Sources of Marlowe's Edward II* (Ph.D. diss., University of South Carolina, 1984), p. cxiii.

10 Edward's tragedy, in fact, is that he found himself not by being King but by being Gaveston. David H. Thurn speaks of the couple's imaginary 'unity, identity and totality in a structure of reflection', 'Sovereignty, Disorder, and Fetishism in Marlowe's *Edward II*', *Renaissance Drama*, 21 (1990), 115–41. Claude J. Summers says that Gaveston is 'a mirror in which the king sees reflected his own possibilities of selfhood', and identifies a pattern of sight imagery associated with mirroring in the play ('Sex, Politics, and Self-Realization in *Edward II*', in *'A Poet and a Filthy Play-Maker': New Essays on Christopher Marlowe* (New York, 1988), p. 233). Forker expands this argument with telling details from the text, observing for example that Edward defines his existence in terms of attachments ('take my heart in rescue of my friends' (4.7.66–7)).

to his rival Mortimer. Edward II is not only a 'weak king' but also a bad boy, one of the Elizabethan prodigals whom Richard Helgerson saw moving out of the old school plays and into Elizabethan prose fiction, and who had leapt up onto the contemporary stage with Prince Hal in *The Famous Victories*.[11] Like all prodigals, Edward is matched against a straight man or 'good' son' and Mortimer plays this role in Edward's story. If Gaveston is Edward's mirror, Mortimer is his reversal; if Gaveston is his twin, Mortimer is his 'rival twin'. Edward is thus defined not only by his twin, the man he wants to be, but also by his rival, the man who wants to be him and take his place.

We might see in this doubling a Girardian structure of rivalry between Edward and Mortimer, that is, a social truth about division between competitors trying to create difference between them in order to avoid the terrible truth of similarity.[12] In this reading Mortimer seems to be defined by sheer difference from Edward – rational where Edward is passionate, macho where Edward is effeminate – but the two men turn out after all to be alike, two versions of egocentric wilfulness, undistinguished twins who take turns being 'good' or 'bad', but who are finally defined simply by being on opposite sides and competing for the same place. Similarly, we might see a political structure in the subsequent rivalry between Gaveston and Mortimer, whereby each calls forth one of 'the king's two bodies' in Tudor doctrine, or one side of 'the king's twin nature', as Anne Barton calls it, the vulnerable human king versus the divinely protected warrior king.[13] But for the moment I want to focus on the psychological rather than the political or social repercussions of the fact that Marlowe's Edward has both a twin and rival twin, so that he himself is split into two: Gaveston's Edward and Mortimer's Edward, lover's Edward and rival's. The presence of *both* pairings situates *Edward II* among examples of what Bruce Smith calls 'the myth of combatants and comrades', which, he argues, shaped so many early modern texts.[14] Read this way, Gaveston and Mortimer, twin and enemy twin, can be seen as two different faces of Edward's relationships to other men, possibly even to the one other man who counts most, Gaveston. Edward's death at Mortimer's hands, in fact, *has* been read as a nightmare version of Edward's love for Gaveston, in which the twin (Gaveston) is not only replaced by the enemy twin (Mortimer) but metamorphosed into a satanic version of the enemy (Mortimer's tool, Lightbourne) who promises to 'comfort' but comes to kill (5.5.2) – and whose attack transforms sodomy into rape.[15] Passionate love calls forth passionate hatred; hatred, if it is strong enough, ignites a kind of love. Edward's death can be read as punishment – a homophobic society's idea of poetic justice – but it may also be an inevitable fulfilment, just as Romeo's and Juliet's deaths were. This kind of self-consuming love is death.

In this reading, what Marlowe portrays is not only a kind of sexuality but a divided subjectivity inseparable from it, one construed

---

11 Edward's youth in Holinshed actually has much in common with Hal's. Both are wanton, self-indulgent, and misled by minions as well as harlots; both were warned by venerable fathers about their companions. The difference is that Edward never reforms.

12 On Girard's 'mimetic desire', see his *Violence and the Sacred* (1977). See also Joel Fineman's Girardian reading of Shakespeare, 'Fratricide and Cuckoldry: Shakespeare's Doubles', in *Representing Shakespeare: New Psychoanalytic Essays*, ed. Murray M. Schwartz and Coppélia Kahn (Baltimore and London, 1980), pp. 70–109.

13 Ernst Kantorowicz, *The King's Two Bodies* (1957); Anne Barton, 'The King Disguised: Shakespeare's *Henry V* and the Comical History' (1975), in *Essays, Mainly Shakespearean* (Cambridge, 1994), p. 220.

14 Bruce R. Smith, *Homosexual Desire in Shakespeare's England* (Chicago and London, 1991).

15 The merging of sexuality and aggression in Edward's murder is paralleled by a similar mix in Gaveston's response to Edward's love: 'I think myself as great / As Caesar riding in the Roman street / With captive kings at his triumphant car' (1.1.171–3). Here 'Tamburlaine's sadism returns as love', says Schumake (cxxii).

differently from any in Marlowe's earlier plays. Marlowe's earlier heroes, Tamburlaine, Barabas, and Faustus, were singular. Giants in a world of undifferentiated pygmies, they may have had friends, like Tamburlaine's Theridimas, though none as important as Edward's Gaveston; or they may have had rivals, like Faustus' Mephistopheles, though none with his own story like Mortimer's. But none of the earlier protagonists shared his plot with both friend and rival. It has been suggested that Marlowe learned the new balance in *Edward II* from Shakespeare's multiply heroed *Henry VI* histories; but in his play Marlowe makes the leap from mono-hero, not all the way to multitude, nor even just to doubleness, but to *double* doubleness. Marlowe could have found single pairs of opposing rivals elsewhere in Tudor theatre, where not only prodigal and thrifty sons but good and bad kings often acted out conflicting moral principles onstage. And he could have found single pairs of mirroring friends – perhaps even in Shakespeare's *Two Gentlemen of Verona*. But when Marlowe gave Edward not only a rival twin but a mirroring twin, he multiplied and internalized division. He crossed moral ambiguity with emotional ambivalence and made drama a newly subtle instrument for exploring both social and psychological complexity.

This is where Shakespeare's earlier borrowing is relevant. Doubleness and twinship are precisely what's at stake in Shakespeare's very first response to *Edward II*. Two verbal echoes of Marlowe's play had turned up before *Richard II* in the unlikely setting of *The Comedy of Errors*,[16] which is close to *Edward II* in time (*c.* 1592) but seemingly in nothing else – although Marie Axton provides a connection when she argues that *The Comedy of Errors* was also an exploration of the theme of the king's two bodies.[17] The echoes indicate still deeper affinities, however, once we read Marlowe's play as a twin play about two men who loved one another so well that Edward could say, 'I am Gaveston' and call Gaveston his brother, and once we remember that Shakespeare's play is about an identical twin separated since birth and longing to be reunited with his brother.

Marlowe shows the darker side of twinship when Edward's rival, Mortimer, steals his identity as king and husband. In Shakespeare's play, twin and rival are located in the same person, but the dark rivalry is still present. If Antipholus longs for his lost brother, he also steals that brother's identity as citizen and husband, ensuring, however inadvertently, that the ghoulish Dr. Pinch, his wife's 'minion', attacks him. As Pinch arrives to capture Antipholus, Antipholus cries out, 'What, will you murder me?' (*Errors* 4.4.107) – just as Edward II does when his murderer arrives in Marlowe's play. Though Harold Brooks, who pointed out this echo, did not, he could have argued for Marlowe's further influence here in the fact that what Pinch wants to do is to have Antipholus 'bound and laid in some dark room' (*Errors* 4.4.92), which turns out to be 'a dark and dankish vault' (*Errors* 5.1.246), the sort of 'room' one would find in Edward II's medieval castle rather than in Antipholus' bourgeois home. Later, in a second Marlovian echo, Antipholus gets back at Pinch by throwing 'puddled' mire on him (5.1.173), that is, by inflicting on him one of the humiliations that Edward had suffered in Marlowe's play. Shakespeare's allusion to Edward's torture, though inappropriate to describe what is really happening to Antipholus, does convey his fearful fantasy about what's happening to him. Apropos of what is frightening about twinning, it is interesting to note that Pinch not only questions Antipholus' identity by confusing him with another man but goes even further to tie him to another man, leaving

---

16 Harold F. Brooks, 'Marlowe and the Early Shakespeare', in *Christopher Marlowe*, ed. Brian Morris (New York, Hill and Wang, 1968), pp. 178–9.

17 Marie Axton, *The Queen's Two Bodies: Drama and the Elizabethan Succession* (London, Royal Historical Society, 1977), pp. 101–2.

... me and my man, both *bound together,*
Till, gnawing with my teeth my bonds in sunder,
I gain'd my freedom. (5.1.249–51)[18]

For Antipholus, in other words, losing your identity and being thrown into a vault is associated with being so closely – and literally – tied to another man that you have to gnaw your way free. Once before, Antipholus had been literally tied to his servant, when both were bound as infants to the mast that floated them to safety. That earlier tie saved his life (*Errors* 1.1.79–82); but Shakespeare is never certain about whether it is good or bad to be so closely tied to someone that he is your 'glass' (your spatial double (*Errors* 5.1.417)), as Dromio calls his brother, or your 'almanac' (your temporal double (*Errors* 1.2.41)), as Antipholus calls Dromio.

The violent images from Marlowe's *Edward II* left traces elsewhere in the Shakespeare canon. An echo of Mortimer's threat to Edward crops up, for example, in *Henry IV, Part One*, when Hotspur rages at King Henry IV for refusing to ransom Mortimer:

He said he would not ransom Mortimer ...
But I will find him where he lies asleep
And in his ear I'll holla "Mortimer!"
(*1 Henry IV* 1.3.217–20)

As Edmond Malone pointed out, Hotspur's lines echo Mortimer's rate at Edward's similar refusal to ransom Mortimer Senior in Marlowe's play:

If he [Edward] will not ransom him
I'll thunder such a peal into his ears
As never subject did unto a king.[19]
(*Edward II* 2.2.127)

It might be argued that Shakespeare remembered the Marlovian lines here simply because he too was writing about 'ransoming Mortimer'.[20] But perhaps it was more than Mortimer's name Shakespeare recalled from Marlowe, and Mortimer's assault specifically on Edward's ears may also have caught the playwright's attention. In any case Marlowe's villain turns up again in what is perhaps the most famous of all Shakespearian lines about ears. It appears in *Hamlet*, another story about brothers who were rival twins, though not actual twins.[21] There, Old Hamlet's Ghost describes his own death in an attack that had first been conjured up by Mortimer's hired assassin, Lightbourne, in *Edward II.* As the Ghost tells it, while he was sleeping in his orchard Claudius stole

With juice of cursed hebenon in a vial,
And in the porches of my ear did pour
The leperous distilment, whose effect
Holds such an enmity with blood of man
That swift as quicksilver it courses through
The natural gates and alleys of the body.
(*Hamlet* 1.5.62–7)

In Marlowe's play, Lightbourne boasts:

'Tis not the first time I have kill'd a man.
I learn'd in Naples how to poison flowers;
To strangle with a lawn thrust down the throat
Or pierce the windpipe with a needle's point;
Or whilst one is asleep, to take a quill
And blow a little powder in his ears;
Or open his mouth and pour quicksilver down.
And yet I have a braver way than these.
(5.4.29–36)[22]

---

18 Cf. Kent's view of adulterers as rats that 'bite the holy cords a-twain / Which are t'intrise t'unloose' (2.2.75).

19 Richard S. M. Hirsch points out a second Marlovian echo just a few lines later in the same scene of *Henry IV*, taken from the same scene in *Edward II.* This time it is a nasty wish on Edward's part toward his enemies:

EDWARD II Would Lancaster and he had both carous'd
A bowl of poison to each other's health.
(*Ed II* 1.3.230–3)

Hotspur takes up the wish for his own enemy twin, Hal: 'I would have poison'd him with a pot of ale' (*1 Henry IV* 1.3.233). ('A Second Echo of *Edward II* in 1.iii of *'I Henry Four'*, *N&Q*, 22 (1975), 168.)

20 Although he had to confuse his Mortimers before the threat could make any sense in the context of Henry IV and Hotspur.

21 Fineman describes them in these terms in 'Fratricide'.

22 William Dinsmore Briggs, *Marlowe's Edward II* (1914), p. 194; John Bakeless, *The Tragical History of Christopher Marlowe* (Cambridge, Mass., 1942), pp. 11, 209.

Here Lightbourne lists six kinds of undetectable penetration through four orifices, and tantalizes us with hints of yet a 'braver' one. Shakespeare condenses Lightbourne's last two possibilities in Claudius' similarly deadly-but-undetectable attack on Old Hamlet.

Marlowe's play is present elsewhere in *Hamlet* as well, in the prince's famous 'To be – or not to be' soliloquy. What calls Hamlet's thoughts back from suicide in that speech is the sudden thought of the 'undiscover'd country, from whose bourn / No traveller returns' (*Hamlet* 3.1.79–80), the same territory ('countries yet unknown') which Mortimer defiantly claims he is going to 'discover', just before he is hanged for killing King Edward (*Edward II* 2.6.24). Hamlet has little in common with Mortimer, but perhaps Shakespeare associated the two men because he associated the two versions of death by penetration, which the one revenged and the other perpetrated.

In other words, both Edward's passion for Gaveston and his death had already left traces in Shakespearian plays before *Richard II* and they would do so again afterwards.

EDWARD II: IN *RICHARD II*

It may seem nonetheless that neither Edward's passion nor his violent death by penetration has any part in *Richard II*. Richard's trio of minions is unimportant and erotically neutral compared to Edward's Gaveston – it is hard to imagine Richard wishing to be 'another Bushy' or 'another Bagot', for example. Unlike Gaveston, these friends are just friends, although Bolingbroke nonetheless accuses them of coming between Richard and his Queen in bed.[23] Yet these friends are far more important to Richard than would first appear. In fact, it is the thought of his friends' betrayal and news of their death that marks the turning point of Shakespeare's play – the moment at which Richard first collapses and gives up all hope. As Richard Harrier puts it, 'The impact of their deaths seems to penetrate Richard as no other event has as yet been able to do . . . some secret depth of the King has been sounded.'[24] In his speech at this point – which Harrier calls Richard's 'real abdication' – the words Richard chooses are extremely revealing.[25] To signal his defeat, Richard gives the first of Shakespeare's 'kings-are-just-people-after-all' speeches. It is like King Henry V's claim that 'the king is but a man, as I am' (*Henry V* 4.1.101–2) or King Lear's recognition that he is not 'ague-proof', or even like the related claims made by outsiders like Jewish Shylock ('Hath not a Jew eyes?') or female Emilia in *Othello* ('And have we not affections? / Desire for sport? and frailty, as men have?' 4.3.101–2). But the specific evidence that Richard cites to prove his common humanity is unusual and none of the others cites it. While they invoke the five senses and the affections that make them human, Richard invokes as well his need for friends:

> For you have but mistook me all this while.
> I live with bread like you, feel want,
> Taste grief, *need friends* – subjected thus,
> How can you say to me, I am a king?
> (*Richard II* 3.2.174–7; italics added)

The need for friends, which thus 'subjects' Richard, is precisely the need he tries to deny in a brief moment of bravado when he first comes face to face with Bolingbroke: You think that 'we are barren and bereft of friends', he says,

---

23 Some editors dismiss Bolingbroke's accusation as a thoughtless carry-over from *Edward II* – the archetypical 'mere verbal echo'; others take it as evidence for a sexual relation between Richard and his flatterers. Forker sees it as Bolingbroke's Machiavellian invention to help justify his murder of the flatterers (38–9).

24 Harrier, 'Ceremony and Politics in *Richard II*', *Shakespeare: Text, Language, Criticism; Essays in Honor of Marvin Spevack*, ed. Bernhard Fabien and Kurt Tetzeli von Rosador (Hildesheim, Zurich, and New York, Olms-Weidman, 1987), pp. 80–97.

25 Richard has three soliloquies of defeat: here when he returns from Ireland to deal with the rebels, then *during* the official abdication at Flint, and finally in prison in the tower.

Yet know, my master, God omnipotent,
Is mustering in his clouds, on our behalf,
Armies of pestilence (3.3.84–7)

By 'friend', Richard may simply mean an ally or supporter, as Burleigh did in the list of Edward II's friends and enemies that he drew up at about the same time Shakespeare was writing *Richard II.* But 'friend' was a many-faceted word, and so was the relation it designated: Jonson used it to refer to men he cared about deeply, and Marlowe used it to refer to Gaveston. I think that Richard's newly recognized need for friends is personal as well as political. He cannot think of himself as a king unless, unlike Henry V banishing Falstaff, he needs no friends – or unless he has friends who will never leave him needy, who love him more than all the world, as if they were another Richard. I don't want to claim that Richard's friends are his doubles, as Gaveston was for Edward. But like Gaveston they do serve as Richard's flattering mirror; and their subterranean role in his life may give yet another meaning to the literal mirror that intrudes into Richard's abdication scene. There, bereft of all friends, Richard has to call for a mirror to see 'what a face I have / Since it is bankrupt of his majesty' (4.1.266–7). And when it reflects his face unchanged, he thinks immediately of those false friends:

O flatt'ring glass,
Like to my followers in prosperity,
Thou dost beguile me.
(*Richard II* 4.1.279–81; italics added)

Here Richard, like the poet in Shakespeare's Sonnet 62, compares the mirror's literal reflection of his face to the very different 'self' he had seen reflected in the glass of his friend's face.[26] When he shatters the mirror[27] he shatters the fantasy of perfect friendship as well as shattering the image of himself. Richard's famous echo of Marlowe's *Doctor Faustus* in this speech – with himself playing Helen's face as well as Faustus asking, 'Was this the face . . ?' – bears out the importance of male devotion to Richard's sense of himself. 'Was this face the face', he asks, 'That every day under his household roof / Did keep ten thousand men?' (4.1.281–3).[28] If Helen's face could send forth a thousand men, Richard's had power to keep ten times that number with him.[29] Finally, in a

26 But when my glass shows me myself indeed
Beated and chopped with tanned antiquity,
Mine own self-love quite contrary I read . . .
'Tis thee, myself, that for myself I praise,
Painting my age with beauty of thy days.
(Son. 62, 9–11, 13–14)

27 At the equivalent moment in Marlowe's play, Edward tears up Mortimer's written name. Edward, that is, attacks his enemy and holds on to his faith in his friends. Richard is more cynical.

28 Ure notes that Richard's speech probably echoes Holinshed's account of Richard's 'noble housekeeping' ('For there resorted dailie to his court above ten thousand persons that had meat and drink there allowed them' (508/1/8)). But this rational connection is supplemented by the Faustus echo, which suggests that the tie between Richard and the men he kept was also like the erotic tie between Helen and the men she 'launched'. The allusion to Helen may also lead back indirectly to Marlowe's Gaveston, who, as Forker reminds us, was called a 'Greekish strumpet' (39).

29 What has not been noticed is that Richard may already have put himself into a well-known woman's position even earlier in the mirror scene, when he offers to 'submit' to Bolingbroke:

I'll give my jewels for a set of beads,
My gorgeous palace for a hermitage;
My gay apparel for an almsman's gown;
My figur'd goblets for a dish of wood;
My sceptre for a palmer's walking staff;
My subjects for a pair of carved saints.
(3.3.146–52)

In the old *King Leir* play Cordella meets the Gallican king disguised as a Palmer and offers to give up her royal estate to marry him:

My mind is low ynough to love a Palmer,
Rather then any King upon the earth . . .
Ile hold thy Palmers staffe within my hand,
And think it is the Scepter of a Queene.
Sometime Ile set thy Bonnet on my head,
And thinke I weare a riche imperiall Crowne,
Sometime Ile help thee in thy holy prayers,
And thinke I am with thee in Paradise.
(692–3, 698–703)

There is something of Cordella in Richard's perversely loving submission to Bolingbroke.

last reversal of his feeling about friends, when Richard does begin to accept his defeat, he sweetens it by embracing it as a 'sworn brother'; 'The truth of what we are shows us but this', he tells the Queen,

> . . . I am sworn brother, sweet,
> To grim Necessity, and he and I
> Will keep a league till death. Hie thee to France
> And cloister thee in some religious house.
> (5.1.20–3)

This is the truth of 'what we are': Richard banishes the Queen to a solitary cloister, but he imagines his own death as a transcendent brotherhood.

Marlowe's Edward is not only passionate about his friend and sworn brother Gaveston but is also engaged in a passionate as well as political rivalry with Mortimer for Queen Isabel. By contrast there seems to be no overt sexual rivalry in Shakespeare's plot; Bolingbroke is simply Richard's political enemy. Nonetheless, a more personal rivalry is suggested when we hear, for example, that one way in which Richard has alienated Bolingbroke was by preventing Bolingbroke's French marriage (*Richard II* 2.1.167–8), or that Richard resents Bolingbroke for having made a divorce between Richard and his queen (*Richard II* 5.1.72–3).[30] More strikingly, the England for which the two men compete is herself a woman, 'a teeming womb of royal kings' (*Richard II* 2.1.51),[31] whom both men image as their own with a passion that has helped make this play seem so much more universal and profoundly patriotic than Marlowe's. In one sense they fight over the Queen as well, insofar as she figures England when she appears in a real, if allegorical, bit of England's green garden, strangely prescient about 'some unborn sorrow ripe in Fortune's womb' (2.2.10). Assimilating the womb to herself, she calls Greene 'the midwife to my woe', herself 'a gasping new-deliver'd mother', and Bolingbroke 'my sorrow's dismal heir' (2.2.62, 65). Not only has England's 'teeming womb of royal kings' produced Bolingbroke as well as Richard, but the human Queen too has Bolingbroke in her womb. In the Queen's prophecy, Bolingbroke and Richard are not only cousins but rival twins, as Murray Schwartz calls them,[32] two brothers fighting for space in the same womb.[33] John Barton's famous production of the play emphasized this twinning between Richard and Bolingbroke by having Richard Pasco and Ian Richardson alternating as Richard and Bolingbroke – and by having Richard stare through the empty frame of his shattered mirror at Bolingbroke's face.[34] But any production reveals the similarity between Richard's and Bolingbroke's will to power and shows each to be similarly possessive of the motherland each sees as his birthright.

Richard's opening attack on Bolingbroke also suggests a more passionately personal rivalry between these enemies than he admits. It becomes clear, for example, that something else is going on besides judicial process or even power politics in the 'chivalrous design of

---

30 Wangh, 'A Psychoanalytic Commentary on Shakespeare's *The Tragedie of Richard the Second*', *Psychoanalytic Quarterly*, 37 (1968), 212–38.

31 Murray Schwartz, 'Anger, Wounds, and the Forms of Theater in *King Richard II*: Notes for a Psychoanalytic Interpretation', *Assays*, 2 (1982), 115–29.

32 Schwartz, 'Anger, Wounds', 120. Richard's entire struggle with Bolingbroke is framed by Bolingbroke's two references to the rival brothers Cain and Abel, in connection first with Richard's murder of Gloucester and then with Bolingbroke's murder of Richard (1.1.104; 5.6.43).

33 As did the unborn twins in Plautus' *Amphytruo*, one of Shakespeare's sources for *The Comedy of Errors*. Wayne Koestenbaum's *Double Talk: The Erotics of Male Literary Collaboration* (New York and London, 1989, p. 11) notes images of a shared womb among twentieth-century collaborators, and cites as an example *Dead Ringers*, the film about twin gynaecologists sharing the single womb of a patient-lover who thinks there is only one of them.

34 See Miriam Gilbert's review essay, '*Richard II* at Stratford: Role-Playing as Metaphor', in *Shakespeare: The Theatrical Dimension*, ed. Philip C. McGuire and David A. Samuelson (New York, 1979), pp. 85–102.

knightly trial' (1.1.81) that Richard stages in the opening scenes of the play. That 'something else' emerges as soon as the trial is over, when Richard, alone with Aumerle, for the first time drops his royal mask. With a 'threatening sneer', as Peter Ure calls it, he tells Aumerle what he really intended by banishing his kinsman Bolingbroke:

He is our cousin, cousin, but 'tis doubt,
When time shall call him home from banishment,
Whether our kinsman come to see his friends.
(1.4.20–2)

Editors disagree about what Richard is referring to in the line about 'friends'. No 'friends' have been mentioned before, nor any merely personal antipathy to Bolingbroke. But I think we may hear in Richard's lines a whisper of Iago's malignity in the opening scene of *Othello*, when he hints to Roderigo about his plan to ruin both Othello's marriage and Othello's new alliance with Cassio. In any case, only now do we begin to suspect that getting rid of Bolingbroke may have been Richard's 'darker purpose' in staging the tournament in the first place. Then, within a few lines, Richard goes on to sneer at Bolingbroke's courtship of 'an oyster wench' and the common people, 'as were our England in reversion his' (1.4.35),[35] and his motives become still clearer: Richard is not just worried that Bolingbroke wants to steal the crown; he is afraid that the English want him to do so. He is jealous of Bolingbroke's popularity, of his 'friends', perhaps of his father, Gaunt, who would rather have Bolingbroke in England than support Richard by banishing him.

Not only is Richard jealous of what others feel about Bolingbroke; he may feel it himself. Deborah Warner's recent production made more, perhaps, of the erotic tie between Richard and Bolingbroke than the text does,[36] but some of Richard's lines suggest a masochistic attraction between them. Especially after his defeat, Richard sounds at times as if he were embracing Bolingbroke like his sworn brother Necessity – as if Bolingbroke's triumph over Richard was as erotically tinged as Lightbourne's triumph over Edward in Marlowe's play. At the end of the play, for example, in an exchange paralleling his earlier remarks to Aumerle about Bolingbroke's banishment, Richard tells his one loyal groom what he feels about Bolingbroke's return. When the Groom talks about Richard's fickle roan Barbary, whose back Bolingbroke had so easily usurped at the coronation, Richard makes the horse into a symbol of fickle England. Then he bitterly interrupts himself mid-simile to unfold a more personal and erotic metaphor. The horse, he realizes, 'Wast born to bear', but

I was not made a horse,
And yet I bear a burthen like an ass,
Spurr'd, gall'd, and tir'd by jauncing Bolingbroke.
(5.5.92–5)

Shakespeare usually associates horses with heterosexual dominance – Petruchio taming Kate ('Women are made to bear and so are you' (2.1.200)), Iago telling Brabantio that his daughter is 'cover'd with a Barbary horse' (1.1.11), or even Cleopatra's longing ('O happy horse, to bear the weight of Antony' (1.5.21)). But Edward II's fate in Marlowe's play may help explain where Richard found this equine image of male humiliation and sexual submission (it is not in Holinshed). Edward had had to bear the real burden of Lightbourne smothering him, and he was spitted rather than being merely 'spurr'd, gall'd, and jaded';[37] but the resemblance is there.

---

35 Perhaps Richard here is recalling Bolingbroke's parting dig, when banished, with his pious but quietly overweening farewell: 'Then, England's ground, farewell; sweet soil, adieu, / My mother and my nurse that bears me yet' (1.3.306–7).

36 See, e.g., Alan Riding's review, 'A Female Richard II Captivates the French', *New York Times*, 27 January 1996.

37 Perhaps Shakespeare was also recalling some scabrous horseplay in the morality plays when the devil carried the Vice off to hell on his back. 'Now here's a courteous devil, that for to pleasure his friend, will not stick to make a jade of himself', as Miles says of a similar devil come to take him away (*Friar Bacon* 15.53–5).

The groom who brings Richard news about the roan Barbary, the one loyal follower left, may also derive partly from Marlowe's play. Holinshed and Daniel had briefly mentioned a loyal Gascoigne, Jenicho, who wore Richard's badge (the symbolic 'hart') long after other men had defected; but that Jenicho had come and gone much earlier in the story. Shakespeare makes his version of Jenicho more important by sending him to Richard just before he dies – just at the point when Marlowe had sent Lightbourne to Edward. In other words, Shakespeare uses the true friend, Jenicho, who comes 'to look upon my sometime royal master's face' (5.5.75), to counter Marlowe's false friend, Lightbourne, who comes to spur, gall, and jade for real.

I think that Shakespeare may have recalled Edward's death even earlier than in Richard's speech about his roan Barbary, as early in fact as when Richard's friends first betray him. Consider the famous speech where Richard fantasizes about his own death by a different sort of penetration:

> ... for within the hollow crown
> That rounds the mortal temples of a king
> Keeps Death his court, and there the antic sits,
> Scoffing his state and grinning at his pomp,
> Allowing him a breath, a little scene,
> To monarchize, be fear'd, and kill with looks;
> Infusing him with self and vain conceit,
> As if this flesh which walls about our life
> Were brass impregnable; and, humour'd thus,
> Comes at the last, *and with a little pin,*
> *Bores through his castle wall, and farewell king!*
> (*Richard II* 3.2.160–70; italics added)

To be sure, Edward's death is not the primary source for this fantasy.[38] There were many visual and verbal emblems of Death lurking behind a king, or behind a lady looking into her glass, which could have served as models. Here, too, Death makes the foolish king think *he* can kill with looks before he discovers that death is not only already inside him – the skull beneath the skin – but outside too, looking on contemptuously, waiting to kill him when he is least ready. But M. M. Mahood suggests also a dramatic source for this speech, in the morality plays when Death enters with his dart and taunts the king before finally striking.[39] It was Marlowe who had probably provided Shakespeare with the most recent version of a morality play Death, when Lightbourne came to kill the king in *Edward II*.[40] Though Lightbourne had a spit rather than Death's dart, what Richard imagines Death doing in Shakespeare's play is exactly what Edward saw Lightbourne doing in Marlowe's play: teasingly promising comfort but really waiting 'to kill with looks': 'These looks of thine can harbour naught but death; / I see my murder written in thy brows', says Edward (*Edward II* 5.5.72–3).

It may seem a long way from Lightbourne's spit to Richard's little pin. Today we think of a pin as a trivial thing, and Shakespeare usually did too, as in Queen Isabel's offer in *Richard II* to change 'My wretchedness unto a row of pins' (*Richard II* 3.4.26). In fact, Richard's pin may seem more like Lightbourne's insidious 'needle's point' to pierce a windpipe than like Lightbourne's spit. But Richard's pin is not so trivial as he teasingly encourages us to think. For in one line the 'little' pin changes into something much more formidable when it 'bores through [the king's] castle wall'. The 'castle wall' refers literally to what Richard has just called 'this flesh which walls about our life' (3.2.167), and what Bolingbroke in a similarly depressed moment had called 'this frail sepulchre of our flesh' (1.3.196). But the figuration of body as castle wall also evokes the solid

38 Nineteenth-century commenters identified the origins of this passage in 'the spirit of the numerous medieval paintings and designs on the subject of death'. Matthew W. Black, note to line 3.2.163–73, *The Life and Death of King Richard the Second*, New Variorum Edition, ed. Matthew W. Black (Philadelphia and London, 1955).

39 M. M. Mahood, *Shakespeare's Wordplay* (London: Methuen, 1957), p. 85.

40 See David Bevington, *From Mankind to Marlowe*, on *Edward II*'s morality play structure.

mortar or timber of real castle walls, through which no little pin could bore. *This* little pin in other words is not only an inconsequential sewing implement but also a hefty 'pynne auger' or ax (*OED* 5), a carpenter's tool as listed in Warwickshire inventories.[41] When Death 'bores through' the castle wall, therefore, he is not merely sticking a pin into it – as, for example, Supervacuo threatens to do when he tells his ambitious brother, 'here is a pin / Should quickly prick your bladder' (*Revenger's Tragedy* 3.1.14–15).[42] Instead, Death is drilling the pin or screwing it in.

Is there any evidence in Shakespeare's play that the sexual implications of Death's 'pin' are being activated here as were the implications of Lightbourne's spit? That, as Venus puts it when the bore's tusk gores Adonis in Shakespeare's poem, 'death's ebon dart' has been mistook for 'love's golden arrow'? (*Venus and Adonis* lines 931–3). Elsewhere on the early modern stage the pin offers many possibilities for sexual innuendo. Autolycus knows this in *The Winter's Tale* when he offers the country lovers 'pins and poking sticks' for sale, hawking them with a song that has 'dildo' for its burthen. Marston knows it when he refers to the 'itch allaying pin'.[43] But the pin in this play is more than a fleeting anatomical metaphor, because it joins a network of potentially erotic penetrations – of bodies, castles, and country – all of which converge to convey the fragility of Richard's world.

In the play's opening scene, for example, when Bolingbroke attacks Mowbray verbally, and again at the lists, the language transforms verbal gestures into physical penetrations:

BOLINGBROKE With a foul traitor's name stuff I thy throat. (1.1.44)

MOWBRAY [I return] These terms of treason doubled down his throat (1.1.57)

and

Now swallow down that lie (1.1.132)

Far from eroticizing it, Richard has an almost phobic response to such offered violence, which he repeatedly invites only to frustrate. Bolingbroke accuses Mowbray of sluicing out Gloucester's 'innocent soul through streams of blood' (*Richard II* 1.1.103); but Richard avoids such violence at all costs. Instead, he wants to do the impossible, to kill the spirit but not the body:[44]

Let's purge this choler without letting blood –
This we prescribe though no physician:
Deep malice makes too deep incision . . .
Our doctors say this is no month to bleed.
(*Richard II* 1.1.153–7)

Later in the play the Gardeners' words will recall Richard's fatal refusal to 'let blood', when they describe Richard's bad government in similar terms, as a refusal to 'trim . . . and dress . . . his land' as they do their garden:

. . . We at time of year
Do wound the bark, the skin of our fruit-trees,
Lest, being over-proud in sap and blood,
With too much riches it confound itself.
(3.4.57–60)

Of course, as Freud said famously of cigars, sometimes an incision is just an incision; but

[41] Hilda Hulme, *Explorations in Shakespeare's Language*. It was powerful but small. Cf. Coriolanus downplaying his wound as something that could fit into an 'auger's bore' (*Cor.* 4.6.87). Janet Adelman suggests that Richard's attitude toward death's pin in fact depends on its ambiguous size – on the way in which a seemingly little thing can be strong enough to do such damage.

[42] Black compares Shakespeare's 'little pin' with the possibly derivative lines in *The Faithful Friends* (1620), which return the pin to its traditional role by likening 'the King's intrancet' to 'a bag / Blown with the breath of greatness', so that 'a little pin / Prick but the windy outside, down falls all / And leaves naught but emptiness' (2542–8).

[43] Frankie Rubinstein cites several instances of sexually charged pins in *A Dictionary of Shakespeare's Sexual Puns and Their Significance* (London and Basingstoke, 1984, p. 194), and there are others. See, e.g., Heywood's *4 P's* for jokes about a wife's pincushion, wide pincase, and so on.

[44] Like Brutus trying to deal with his love/hate relationship to his rival Caesar.

with such repugnance for incisions and wounds, such a need for wholeness, such inability to see that any good can come from violation of the walled self either in battling or in breeding, no wonder Richard images himself as a besieged castle, like the female Virtues in *The Castle of Perseverance*, or like a heroine in medieval romance.

Richard's death fantasy is realized, in a fashion, at Flint Castle, to which he withdraws in defeat after his death soliloquy. When Bolingbroke marches on Flint and hears that 'The castle royally is mann'd' by Richard against his entrance, he corporalizes the castle (and perhaps also *un*mans or 'womans' it) and makes it into a displacement of the fearful body hiding inside. Demanding entrance, Bolingbroke tells Northumberland to

> Go to the rude ribs of that ancient castle,
> Through brazen trumpet send the breath of parle
> Into his ruin'd ears. (*Richard II* 3.3.31–4)[45]

The ears here are important, but a lower orifice is suggested when Richard is forced to let Bolingbroke into his 'base court'.

Richard's actual death takes place in Pomfret castle, which is also – though only for a moment – corporealized. In Pomfret's prison Richard finds himself alone as the Duchess of Gloucester had been earlier, when she withdrew desolate to die in her home, Plashy, with its 'unpeopled offices, untrodden stones' (1.2.69). It is a measure of Richard's growth by this point that not only does he try, unlike the Duchess, to 'people' his prison with his thoughts (5.5.9); he even imagines tearing a passage out through Pomfret's 'flinty ribs' (5.5.20), as he would never have imagined doing when Bolingbroke marched on Flint Castle's 'rude ribs' earlier.[46]

The besieged castles associated with Richard are part of a larger pattern in which England too is besieged. At the imagistic centre of the play is Gaunt's emotional figuration of England walled in by the sea,[47] a 'fortress built by Nature for herself', a 'blessed plot' which is now threatened by both internal and external violation: internal because leased out to tenants and overrun with 'caterpillars', and external because invaded by the Irish from the north and by Bolingbroke from the south. Whether coded male or female or both or neither, these multiple images of enclosures ruptured create a sense not only of England and her castles but also of the human subject as a besieged structure, bounded but always vulnerable to eruptions from inside as well as to penetration from without. And sometimes, disturbingly, it is hard to tell the difference – as with Bolingbroke himself, who both invades from the outside, from France, and from the inside, from the Queen's womb; or, even more insidious, as with Richard's flattering friends who are so close, Gaunt says, they 'sit within thy crown' (2.1.100). Or with Death, whom Richard imagines both inside the hollow crown that rounds the temples of a mortal king, and outside, waiting to bore through with his pin.

45 When he first returned to England from Ireland, Richard had imagined himself the attacker ferreting out a hidden Bolingbroke, as does the sun 'dart[ing] his light through every guilty hole' (*Richard II* 3.2.43); but the roles are now reversed.

46 If Bolingbroke and Richard corporealize castles, Isabel performs the reverse transformation when she architecturalizes her body by speaking of it as a house for a 'guest of grief' (*Richard II* 2.2.7) instead of 'so sweet a guest / As my sweet Richard' (8–9); and later of Richard's body as a 'beauteous inn' where grief is lodged, while triumph is become an 'ale-house' guest, in the vulgar house of Bolingbroke (5.1.13–15). Richard similarly describes himself as a container for grief ('an unseen grief that swells with silence in the tortur'd soul' (4.1.295)); and the Duchess of Gloucester reduces Edward II's sons to seven fragile 'vials of his sacred blood' (*Richard II* 1.2.12) – one of which Richard broke, and another of which will be broken when 'Richard's sacred blood is spilt' at the end.

47 The ideal of an England bound in by walls was not just Shakespeare's; it appears as one of the magical achievements sought – unwisely – in both Marlowe's *Dr Faustus* ('I'll have them wall all Germany with walls of brass' (B Text, 1.1.88)), and Greene's *Friar Bacon and Friar Bungay* (ii. 30).

Finally, the Marlovian reverberations of Death's pin recall Edward's death not only in Richard's death fantasies but perhaps also in Richard's strikingly odd reference to love in prison just before his loyal Groom arrives: 'love to Richard,' he says meditatively, 'is a strange brooch in this all-hating world' (*Richard II* 5.5.65–6). Richard may simply mean here that love is a strange 'breach' or 'break' in the normally loveless routine of things.[48] But most editors think Richard means that love is a rich 'brooch' or jewel worn usually in one's hat.[49] As such, the brooch is an appropriate emblem for the only remnant Richard has left of Gaunt's England, that 'precious stone set in the silver sea' (*Richard II* 2.1.46), the only equivalent he has ever had to the 'jewels', or friends, whom Bolingbroke had grieved to leave behind when he was banished (1.3.267, 270). But there is more to Richard's brooch. A brooch can also be a 'badge' of livery, like Richard's badge which the loyal Jenicho kept wearing in Holinshed and which Richard's loyal Groom perhaps wore as well. And, I would add, by mentioning love as 'a strange brooch' Shakespeare may have been thinking of the brooches that were commonly offered as love-gifts, like the brooch Ganymede demands from Jupiter instead of Juno's wedding necklace in Marlowe's *Dido, Queen of Carthage*:

> I would have a jewel for mine ear,
> And a fine brooch to put in my hat, [he says]
> And then I'll hug with you a hundred times.
>
> (*Dido* 1.1.46–8)

Marlowe's Edward, you remember, having showered jewels on Gaveston, offers Lightbourne a jewel (though not a brooch) to save his life – the very jewel that Isabel had sent to him in prison. And finally, if I may speculate on one last implication of Richard's metaphor, a brooch was of course fastened with a pin. For Richard, in other words, Death comes with a little pin and bores through your skull, but love is a strange brooch pinned in your hat.

Ultimately, in *Richard II* the violation of a safely bounded subject, along with the broken mirror, the broken ceremony, and the broken word are all made more significant by being associated with the mythic fall of Edward III's demi-paradise. They transcend the merely physical violation in Marlowe's play. But my point in the comparison with Marlowe is that they could not be so powerful if they did not also reproduce the sheer physicality of Edward's relation to Gaveston and its violation at the end of Marlowe's play.

The Marlovian echoes suggest that *Richard II*, otherwise so focused on kingship and on the relation between providence and politics, language and power, is also about the lesser concerns that Shakespeare – unlike Marlowe – is supposed to have ignored. It is also about bodies and emotions, about needing friends, about friends turning into enemies, and about the darker pleasures of enmity. This is not the whole truth about *Richard II*, by any means; but, like the offstage murder of Gloucester, we need to know about it in order to understand the rest.

I think, however, that the Marlovian echoes – and the fact that they are so muffled – tell us not so much about the play as about Shakespeare and the way he saw his rival, Marlowe. We already know that Marlowe was Shakespeare's 'provocative agent', in an exchange that was sometimes combative and sometimes comradely.[50] But I think we still have much to learn about a working relationship so close that

---

48 Cf. Black, note to 5.4.67; Ure, note to 5.5.66.

49 A dandyish affectation gone out of style by the time Shakespeare mocked it in *All's Well That Ends Well*.

50 Nicholas Brooke, 'Marlowe as Provocative Agent in Shakespeare's Early Plays', *Shakespeare Survey 14* (1961), pp. 34–44; Brooks, 'Marlowe and the Early Shakespeare'; Muriel Bradbrook, 'Shakespeare's Recollections of Marlowe', *Shakespeare's Styles*, ed. Philip Edwards, Inga-Stina Ewbank, and G. K. Hunter (Cambridge, 1980); Marjorie Garber, 'Marlovian Vision/Shakespearean Revision', *Research Opportunities in Renaissance Drama* 22 (1979), 3–10; James Shapiro, *Rival Playwrights: Marlowe, Jonson, Shakespeare* (New York, 1991), pp. 75–132.

Forker sees it 'approaching symbiosis' (20), particularly if we examine it in the context of *Edward II*, which is a story about symbiosis.[51] Such an examination can cast light not only on these two plays but also on the widespread process of dramatic collaboration on the early modern stage, and on the meanings, unconscious as well as conscious, that collaboration may have had for writers.

In other words, perhaps Shakespeare, like Brecht, chose Marlowe's *Edward II* as a model for his Richard not only to 'improve on' its portrayal of Edward and the pangs of abdication but also to rework its portrayal of Edward and Gaveston. Brecht's overt 'collaboration' with Marlowe foregrounds Edward's friendship with Gaveston. Shakespeare's 'original' play erases Richard's friendships from *Richard II*, perhaps as part of an effort to erase Marlowe. If so, it is interesting that Marlowe's presence remains strong in Shakespeare's play.[52] Richard's death may seem nothing like Edward's – 'Mount, mount, my soul ... / Whilst my gross flesh sinks downward' (5.5.111–12); but his last words recall Faustus' unsuccessful dying effort to 'leap up to my God', before he asks, despairing, 'Who pulls me down?' and cries out in 'erotic self-surrender and horrified revulsion' as he yields to the embrace of his demon lover: 'Ah, Mephistopheles.'[53] Shakespeare's Richard seems to leave behind the erotic violence in Edward's love for Gaveston or Edward's death, but he may have simply sublimated it instead.[54]

---

51 And in the context of *Richard II*, which seems in so many ways to be a bridge for Shakespeare between older Marlovian and newer styles of language, of rhetoric, and of dramaturgy.

52 It has been pointed out that besides *Edward II*, *Tamburlaine* is echoed (and mocked) in 1.1 and 1.3; and that *Doctor Faustus* is quoted in Richard's abdication speech.

53 Wilbur Sanders, *The Dramatist and the Received Idea. Studies in the Plays of Marlowe and Shakespeare* (Cambridge, 1968), p. 242.

54 This essay has benefitted from the comments of Alan Grob, Janet Adelman, and James Lake, each of whom read and responded to early drafts, as well as from questions posed by members of the psychoanalytic seminar at the Shakespeare Association of America (1996) and by audience respondents at the Shakespeare Institute at Stratford (1996).

HAMLET'S EAR

PHILIPPA BERRY

An alienation from the hypocrisy of a courtly style or decorum in language afflicts Hamlet from his first appearance in the play. The courtly airs or 'songs', the 'words of so sweet breath', the 'music vows', with which he wooed Ophelia are no longer part of his idiom, although he will briefly redeploy them to disguise his true state of mind. In Act 1 scene 2, we meet a Hamlet whose abrupt retreat from social intercourse is not only signalled by his mourning dress, but is also articulated through an intensely satiric relationship to language. This scathing view of the world is articulated in all of Hamlet's language, in his soliloquies and monologues as well as in his dialogues with others; it finds its most effective form of expression, however, in his use of wordplay. Indeed, before the final tragic catastrophe Hamlet's role as malcontent and revenger succeeds not so much by action as by his disordering, through punning, of social constructions of identity. The centrality of the pun to the view of earthly mutability and death which Hamlet gradually elaborates in the course of the play is aptly illustrated by the fact that he puns not only on his own death ('The rest is silence'), but also as he finally accomplishes his task of revenge and kills Claudius, asking 'Is thy union here?' as he forces him to drink the wine that Claudius has poisoned with a pearl or 'union'. Yet the chief interest of Hamlet's quibbling lies not in his semantic puns, which play upon words with two or more meanings, like 'rest' or 'union', but in his richly suggestive use of homophonic resemblances between words, in order to expand their significance. Through these linguistic acts of expansion, Hamlet comments upon particular elements of the tragic narrative, augmenting their apparent meaning by interweaving ostensibly disparate themes and motifs into a complex unity.

In contrast to the use of wordplay as the supreme instance of a dialogic courtly wit which celebrates the shared values of an aristocratic group, it is through an ironic use of iteration, and of the pun in particular, that Hamlet's echoic or quibbling discourse is able to enunciate, albeit obliquely, those hidden meanings which are concealed within the polite language of the Danish court. Hamlet condemns and rejects that courtly playing upon him as a phallic pipe or recorder of which he accuses Rosencrantz and Guildenstern:

> You would play upon me, you would seem to know my stops, you would pluck out the heart of my mystery, you would sound me from my lowest note to the top of my compass; and there is much music, excellent voice in this little organ, yet cannot you make it speak. 'Sblood, do you think I am easier to be played on than a pipe? Call me what instrument you will, though you can fret me, you cannot play upon me. (3.2.352–60)

In contrast to this courtly attempt to play upon or 'sound' him, Hamlet's resonant unsettling of courtly language follows a different tune. For his quibbles remind us constantly of Hamlet's familial displacement, as a son and heir whose place in a masculine genealogy of kings is no longer certain. In these puns, as well as in the tropes which are applied to him by others, we find a curious refiguring of Denmark's 'heir' – a word which, significantly, is only evoked through homophony in this play – in relationship to 'th'incorporal air' (3.4.109).

In his magisterial study of *Shakespeare's Pronunciation*, where he aimed to recover many Elizabethan homonyms which are no longer pronounced alike, Helge Kökeritz concluded that hair-heir-here-hare were four words often pronounced similarly in early modern English; in particular, he noted the likely pun on air-heir in *Hamlet*, together with related puns on hair-heir and heir-here from other Shakespearian plays.[1] Through a common interlingual pun, whereby *mollis aer* (Lat.: soft air) was equated with *mulier*, the Latin for woman, the attributes of air were frequently associated with the female sex in the English Renaissance. But although Shakespeare could apply this pun quite conventionally, to female dramatic protagonists such as Imogen and Cleopatra, he also used it to trope the beloved youth of the *Sonnets*; while Imogen is compared to 'tender air' (5.5.234, 5.6.447–53) and Cleopatra, in her dying, is 'as soft as air' (5.2.306), the beautiful youth who is initially exhorted by the poet to 'bear' his father's memory through procreation is also a 'tender heir' (*Sonnets*, 1, 4). Similarly, Hamlet's airy and echoic utterances emphasize his failure to conform to traditional forms of masculine identity and sexuality; in particular, he rejects the implicit association which runs through the play, between kingship and 'earing' as copulation. Yet the association of his 'air' imagery with a nexus of images related to hearing as well as to fertility serves to remind us that a significantly different use of the ear is central to Hamlet's punning activity, which often appears to imply vocal play on 'ear' as well as 'air' in relation to an unspoken 'heir'. Although Kökeritz did not mention 'ear' in his hair-heir-here-hear combination, elsewhere he noted homonymic play on ear-here, while he also observed that John Lyly puns on ear-hair in *Midas* (4.1.174f.).[2] Hamlet's quibbling language substitutes an echoic or airy form of auditory attention for sexual or procreative modes of (h)earing. The motions of air as wind were often associated by the ancients with a ghostly and uncannily repetitive auditor, the nymph Echo; Abraham Fraunce declared that Echo 'is nothing els, but the reverberation and reduplication of the ayre. *Eccho* noteth bragging and vaunting, which being contemned and despised, turneth to a bare voyce, a winde, a blast, a thing of nothing',[3] while in Ben Jonson's *Cynthia's Revels*, first performed in 1600, the same year as *Hamlet*, Mercury asks Echo to:

> Salute me with thy repercussive voice,
> That I may know what caverne of the earth
> Contains thy airy spirit, how or where
> I may direct my speech, that thou mayst hear.[4]

There are certainly puns in Hamlet's soliloquies, yet punning requires a social context in order to be fully effective; it is therefore an apt instrument of the satirist. It is also one of the ways in which a rhetorical emphasis upon the singular fate of the tragic protagonist, as articulated through soliloquy or monologue, can be juxtaposed with a dialogic form of self-

[1] Helgë Kökeritz, *Shakespeare's Pronunciation* (New Haven, 1953), pp. 90–1, 111. Kökeritz observes that air-heir are punned on by Lyly in *Mother Bombie*, 2.2.24–6 and 5.3.13, and are given as homonyms in Charles Butler, *English Grammar* (1634) and R. Hodges, *A Special Help to Orthographie* (1643). He emphasizes that 'no homonymic pun has been admitted here which has not stood the combined test of phonology and context' (pp. 64–5). See also Margreta de Grazia and Peter Stallybrass, 'The materiality of the Shakespearian text', *Shakespeare Quarterly*, 44 (Fall 1993), 3, pp. 255–83, where the wordplay in *Macbeth* on air-hair-heir is discussed.

[2] Kökeritz, *Shakespeare's Pronunciation*, p. 111. See also Stephen Booth's comment on 'hearsay' in Sonnet 21, line 13, in his edition of *Shakespeare's Sonnets* (New Haven, 1978).

[3] Abraham Fraunce, *The Third Part of the Countesse of Pembrokes Yvychurch: entituled, 'Amintas Dale'* (London, 1592), p. 15^{r}.

[4] Ben Jonson, '*Cynthia's Revels*', in *The Complete Plays of Ben Jonson*, ed. G. A. Wilkes, vol. II (Oxford, 1981), 1.1.104–7.

undoing, in a comic discourse which is less focussed on the subjective 'I', and more on the exposure of an illusory social mask. At the same time, as Gregory Ulmer has observed, the pun can often function as a 'puncept', in its formation of new concepts which may hint at another order of knowledge.[5]

Through multiple entendre, unobserved or hidden relationships can be demonstrated, as various homophones reverberate echoically throughout a text. It is above all through his relentless quibbling that Hamlet meditates upon the sexuality of – and within – families. Yet the oblique meanings of his word-play also extend beyond this immediate sphere of familiarity. For Hamlet reintroduces nature, the body and death into the sphere of courtly discourse, reimaging courtly society in terms of an 'overgrowth' within nature, and thereby reassimilating culture into nature. Thus, in a trope used several times in the play, 'rank' as the foul smell and abundant growth of weeds is substituted for social rank: 'things rank and gross in nature / Possess it merely' (1.2.136–7). Similarly, Claudius' kingship is troped as a sexual excess which is also a 'moor' or wilderness, as well as a disturbing racial difference (3.4.66). And in spite of his several misogynistic diatribes, which attribute this degenerative trend in nature to the female body and female sexuality in particular, through his quibbling language Hamlet also tropes himself as having an obscure figurative association with these processes of decay.

In his encounter with his father's ghost, Hamlet is informed of Claudius' twofold poisoning of the ear of Denmark. Claudius has killed Old Hamlet with 'juice of cursèd hebenon', poured 'in the porches of mine ears' (1.5.62–3); furthermore, he has deceived the court as to the nature of the king's death: 'the whole ear of Denmark / Is by a forgèd process of my death / Rankly abused' (1.5.36–8). But Hamlet, the other ear – and other heir – of Denmark, has already begun to hear Claudius' courtly discourse otherwise – or satirically. He is now fully undeceived by his exchange with the airy spirit. In the ghost's imagery of ears there is an implicit quibble upon 'earing' as copulation, since it is through his incestuous marriage, as well as his murderous attack on the royal ear, that Claudius has interrupted the patrilineal transmission of royal power. The usurper's assumed sexual appetite parallels what Hamlet sees as the disorderly disseminating power of nature – with the result that, in Hamlet's eyes, the state of Denmark 'grows to seed', while Claudius is a 'mildewed ear' of corn (3.4.63). It seems, therefore, that the usurper is a chief tare or weed (in Latin, this could sometimes be *aera* as well as the more common *lolium*) in what Hamlet now defines as the 'unweeded garden' of the world; and of course, like Lucianus in *The Murder of Gonzago*, Claudius has literally used 'midnight weeds' to poison or 'blast' (like a strong wind blighting a crop) both Old Hamlet's life and Young Hamlet's inheritance. But while his uncle, as a 'mildewed ear', is associated by Hamlet with the paradox of a degenerative fertility within nature, Hamlet's own wit performs a more oblique and airy form of generation as well as (h)earing. This is inspired not so much by a commitment to the monarchy as the political (h)earing of the state as by a more feminine and aesthetically responsive form of hearing: one which is appropriate to the narration or the performance of tragedy, and which also interprets human suffering as inextricably interwoven with a tragedy within nature.

In Greek tragedy, the role of listener was an important function of the chorus, as the primary auditors and spectators of the tragic events. It is this echoic and choric mode of hearing which is implicitly required by the ghost of Old Hamlet when he describes his murder to his son; like the mythological figure of Echo, Young Hamlet is left to repeat the ghost's final words: 'Now to my word: / It is "Adieu, adieu,

5 Gregory Ulmer, 'The Puncept in Grammatology', in *On Puns: The Foundation of Letters*, ed. Jonathan Culler (Oxford, 1988), pp. 164–90.

remember me"' (1.5.111–12). But this acutely responsive and implicitly feminine mode of hearing is also comparable to that enacted by Dido when she asks Aeneas to tell her of the fall of Troy, for it is Dido's place which Hamlet effectively occupies when in Act 2 he asks the player to give an impromptu performance of Aeneas' tale. And the more feminine faculty of hearing which motivates Hamlet's interest in the drama also appears to involve responsiveness to the mysterious resonance of nature within language; in the last act, he will trope the more discerning members of society as 'the most fanned and winnowed opinions' (5.2.153): in a figure that is probably derived from the winnowing of the soul by wind in the *Aeneid* (6.740), they are like ears of corn which have been separated out from the chaff by the activity of the wind. Similarly, through his ironic quibbling, Hamlet uses his different style of hearing to effect an airy and echoic reordering of the world around him, in a discursive equivalent to winnowing whose spiritual implications are apparent from the traditional affinity of air and wind with spirit as well as breath (from the Latin *spiritus*). A chief result of this reclassification through punning is a reinterpretation of those distorted relations between kin which are integral to the tragedy.

The theme of a kinship which is both rather less than affectionate and also excessive or incestuous is wittily introduced by Hamlet's first paronomasic play on 'kin' and 'kind'. *Adnominatio* or *paronomasia* (or 'prosonomasia', as it was sometimes called in the Renaissance) depends on a slight change, lengthening or transposition of the letters in a word; Henry Peacham defines the trope as 'a certayne declyninge into a contrarye, by a lykelyhoode of letters, eyther added, chaunged, or taken awaye', while George Puttenham describes it as 'a figure by which ye play with a couple of words or names much resembling, and because the one seemes to answere th'other by manner of illusion, and doth, as it were, nick him, I call him the *Nicknamer* chaunged, or taken awaye'.[6]

In response to Claudius' greeting, 'But now, my cousin Hamlet, and my son –', Hamlet murmurs his aside: 'A little more than kin, and less than kind' (1.2.64–5). The quibble aptly suggests the difficulty of finding suitable words to represent Claudius' outrageous transgression of the conventional boundaries of kinship, which is also, Hamlet implies, a subversion of courtly conventions of *gentilité* or kindness. However, Hamlet's subsequent homophonic quibble on 'son', is made to his uncle's face, inspired by Claudius' own indirect pun on son-sun in his query about Hamlet's mourning garb. To Claudius' question: 'How is it that the clouds still hang on you?', Hamlet replies 'Not so, my lord, I am too much i'th' sun' (1.2.66–7). This ironically suggests that whereas another homophone of kin and kind – king – does describe Claudius' situation, through the traditional association of king with sun it is also related to Hamlet's own position, as a son (and heir). The pun spells out more clearly the still unspoken pun on kin and king, allying an excess of kinship (since Hamlet is not Claudius' son, and Claudius has married his brother's wife) with an image of kingship (the sun) that is itself excessive, apparently because its brightness is incompatible with those conventions of mourning dress which (in contrast to Hamlet) the Danish court has signally failed to observe. But beneath its apparent compliment to the king as sun, the quibble also alludes to a potentially unhealthy surplus of sons or heirs; we are reminded that in spite of his mourning attire, as a king's son, Hamlet too has a homophonic affinity with the sun, and that, like Claudius, he too may have an unexpected generative potential.

The peculiar difference of Hamlet's disseminating activity is made clear in his retorts to Gertrude. Her description of dying as

[6] Henry Peacham, *The Garden of Eloquence* (London, 1577), sig. Kii^r; George Puttenham, *The Arte of English Poesie*, eds. G. D. Wilcox and Alice Walker (Cambridge, 1936), pp. 168–9.

'common' is allied by Hamlet's ironic iteration with the 'common' or vulgar usage of 'to die', evoking thereby the commonness of another, sexual, dying; similarly, her question, 'Why seems it so particular with thee?' (1.2.75) is converted by Hamlet into a barbed criticism of the King and Queen's courtly semblance of mourning: 'Seems, madam? Nay, it *is*, I know not "seems"' (1.2.76). This ironic differing of 'seems', which additionally hints at the links between courtly seeming and the spilling of generative seed (from the Latin: *semen*), also anticipates the 'enseamèd bed' that Hamlet will later accuse the Queen of copulating in with Claudius. The rejection by Hamlet of sexual activity is also implied in his subsequent reference to a near-synonym for 'seems', when he tells Gertrude that 'I have that within which passeth show' (1.2.85); later, in his quibbling exchange with Ophelia during the play scene, the sexual meaning of 'show' will be stressed. None the less, it is Hamlet's mocking echoes of courtly language which turn the meaning of 'common' or ordinary words back towards the body and sexuality. He will warn Polonius, in a remark which appears to imply his own erotic intentions towards Ophelia: 'Let her not walk i'th' sun. Conception is a blessing, but not as your daughter may conceive. Friend, look to't' (2.2.186-7). Here the use of a semantic pun, or *antanaclasis*, in which the same word (conception) has two different meanings, clarifies the difference of Hamlet's fertilizing powers from those of his uncle; the nephew's sun-like powers seed a legacy or inheritance which operates above all at the level of signs (from the Greek, *semeion*), in the realm of words and ideas. And while he assists conception, as understanding, in women in particular – for the 'conceits' which are attributed to both Gertrude and Ophelia (3.4.104, 4.5.44) are directly or indirectly inspired by Hamlet – this son also 'conceives' much himself. For him, morbid meditations, or 'conceits' concerning natural and human corruption, are themselves part of a (re)generative process. But if, through his quibble on 'conception', the gendered identity of the heir is effectively called into question, what kind of heir is he?

As *The Murder of Gonzago* is about to be performed, Claudius greets Hamlet with 'How fares our cousin Hamlet?' (3.2.89). Hamlet replies with a triple quibble. Redefining 'fares' in terms of sustenance, he simultaneously converts 'fare' to 'air' by *paronomasia*, and he also quibbles thereby on the unspoken 'heir': 'Excellent, i'faith, of the chameleon's dish. I eat the air, promise-crammed. You cannot feed capons so' (3.2.90–1). Although the word 'heir' is only evoked through homophony in the play, this quibble makes explicit the obscure but important connection which runs through the play, between the dispossessed 'heir' of Denmark and 'air'; at the same time, it presents us with the trope of the displaced heir as a 'chameleon' or shape-shifter who is not, he warns Claudius, as stupid as a castrated cock or 'capon': a bird which allows itself to be overfed for the table. Instead, it seems, Hamlet is mysteriously feeding on himself (as heir/air), in a way which is not only consistent with the mutable identity of the chameleon (a creature which was nourished by air), but which also hints at his affinity with the mysterious singularity of the double-gendered phoenix. And the substance which Hamlet figuratively feeds on is paradoxically full as well as empty, although as 'promise-crammed', its fecundity is associated only with words. Thus while the empty flattery of Claudius to his 'son' is ironically dismissed by Hamlet, his quibble suggests none the less that the airy substance of speech does afford him a curious kind of nourishment, where none might be expected.

This metamorphosis of the heir of Denmark through and in relation to air begins, of course, on the battlements of Elsinore, where, as Hamlet and his companions wait for the ghost to appear, he declares: 'The air bites shrewdly, it is very cold'. To this Horatio replies: 'It is a nipping and an eager air' (1.4.1–2). His words aptly convey the change that has already begun to affect Hamlet, in his assumption of a satiric demeanour, expressed through a mordant or biting wit which is 'eager', or sour. In its later echo by the ghost's reference to the curdling of his blood by Claudius' poison, 'like eager droppings into milk' (1.5.69), this reference to the eager air, ear or heir attributes to Hamlet a property of bitterness which parallels the corrupting effects of Claudius' fratricide. But these images in Act 1 also give a new, auto-erotic dimension to Hamlet's satiric temper. For as he develops a new, biting relationship to the air, as well as to the courtly language (or promises) which fill it, he is also consuming his identity as heir.

In feeding upon himself (as well as others) through his mordant quibbling, Hamlet plays the part of Narcissus as well as Echo. Like the addressee of Shakespeare's *Sonnets*, he can be accused of self-love, or of 'having traffic with thyself alone' (*Sonnets*, 4.9). But in also assuming the implicitly feminine role of the 'tender heir' (as *mollis aer* or *mulier*) who will bear the father's memory (*Sonnets*, 1.4), Hamlet is able to redefine both his father's and his own inheritance verbally or vocally, through his airy conceits. In this respect, his own legacy or inheritance will be twofold: while his 'story' is bequeathed directly to Horatio, who by telling it will preserve his name, it is Fortinbras who will be the ultimate recipient both of that story and of Hamlet's 'dying voice' – which chooses him, perforce, as the future king of Denmark. Significantly, neither man is even a member of Hamlet's kin-group, much less his child. Hamlet thereby refigures inheritance in terms of a phoenix-like succession to other men (and most importantly, to two rather than to one), as a succession which circumvents the generative obligations of patriliny. And this formation of a different bonding 'between men' – a bonding across rather than within families – is effected by the historical reverberations of Hamlet's echoing voice.

When Polonius refers to Hamlet's replies as 'pregnant', he attributes a feminine or fecund character to his quibbling; similarly, the tropes and puns used by Claudius of Hamlet's melancholy or madness figure it as concealing an airy fecundity which is apparently feminine. The prince is twice imaged as a female bird on her nest in late spring or early summer: 'There's something in his soul / O'er which his melancholy sits on brood' (3.1.167–8);

> This is mere madness,
> And thus a while the fit will work on him.
> Anon, as patient as the female dove
> When that her golden couplets are disclosed,
> His silence will sit drooping. (5.1.281–5)

But a more grotesque, and implicitly masculine, version of this differing of gendered models of generation is later proposed by Hamlet himself when, in his remark to Polonius about the dangers of Ophelia walking 'i' the sun', he defines the sun as a breeder of worms or maggots which eat the flesh, and so accelerate the decay of dead matter: 'For if the sun breed maggots in a dead dog, being a good kissing carrion –' (2.2.182–3). Yet in the myth of the phoenix as reported by Pliny (an account which was often cited in the Renaissance), a worm or maggot plays a central part in the bird's solitary work of regeneration through self-consumption: Pliny tells us that 'from its bones and marrow is born first a sort of maggot, and this grows into a chicken'.[7]

In his reflexive relationship to air, therefore, Hamlet has a superficial resemblance to Narcissus as well as Echo. However, several of the images I have mentioned were connected in Renaissance iconography with Hermes or Mercury, a classical deity whose identity was especially marked by paradox and doubleness. This god, whose emblematic creature was a cock, herald of the dawn, and who was frequently depicted with a pipe as well as his more familiar caduceus, combined his role as a divine messenger and god of eloquence with attributes

[7] Pliny, *Natural History*, trans. H. Rackham (London, 1938), vol. 3, x, ii, p. 294.

of trickery, secrecy and concealment; according to Richard Linche in *The Fountaine of Ancient Fiction*: 'Mercurie was often taken for that light of knowledge, & spirit of understanding, which guides men to the true conceavement of darke and enigmaticall sentences'.[8] And Mercury's identification by Macrobius with 'that power [of the sun] from which comes speech' hints at another, solar, aspect of his classical identity, whereby he was associated with the return of fertility to the earth in springtime.[9] The affinity between Mercury and obscure yet meaningful utterances makes it hardly surprising that in *Cynthia's Revels* it is Mercury who temporarily restores the speech of Echo, inviting her to 'strike music from the spheres, / And with thy golden raptures swell our ears' (1.2.63–4). It was this play, in fact, which was the first production of the 'little eyases', or young hawks, whose 'eyrie' was the Blackfriars playhouse: the Children of the Chapel.

Yet Charles Dempsey has recently pointed out, in his reinterpretation of Botticelli's *Primavera*, that it was Mercury as a wind-god (for example, in the *Aeneid*, 4, 223ff.), able to calm harsh winds and storms, and to disperse clouds, who was most explicitly regarded as a god of spring, or *Mercurius Ver*.

> Botticelli shows Mercury dispersing and softening clouds with his upraised caduceus in the *Primavera*, a representation of him that unequivocally identifies him as acting in his archaic persona as a springtime wind god. By this action he ends the season that began with the warming west blowing its regenerative breath over the bare earth, shown as Zephyr and Chloris, and that reaches its fullness in April, the month presided over by Venus.[10]

In the *Primavera*, clusters of seeds swirl about the god's winged sandals, but no act of copulation is associated with this generative process. Instead, Mercury's fertilizing role is implied to supplement rather than complement that of Venus as a goddess of nature. Indeed, although the mythographers are understandably silent on the subject, their curious debates about whether or not Mercury has a beard, together with the emphasis on his youthfulness (in other words, his difference from adult masculinity), created a distinct aura of ambiguity around his sexual identity, as Joseph A. Porter has shown.[11]

The *Primavera* suggests that Mercury enjoys a different and more harmonious relationship with the feminine generative principle within nature from that attributed to figures of masculine generation. In alchemical texts, Mercury likewise emblematized the mysterious changes wrought within nature or matter by a principle of ambiguous gender, sometimes called *Mercurius duplex*; in this literature, 'our Mercury' was analogous to the *spiritus* which was the secret transforming substance within matter, and was variously described as 'divine rain', 'May dew', 'dew of heaven', 'our honey'. Such was its ambivalent character, however, that alchemical Mercury was also identified with that part of matter which, phoenix-like, fed upon itself in order to produce transmutation.[12]

Similarly, Hamlet's puns may indeed articulate a covert but coherent level of meaning, in a Renaissance alchemization of language. While his mercurial messages function to disrupt the fixity of social identities – along with the embassies or utterances of aberrant father figures – they hint too at the existence of a different order, hidden within the visible one. Douglas Brooks-Davies has pointed out that the imagery of Mercury was often appropriated by royalist panegyrics during the Renaissance;[13] yet in Mercury's oblique association with

8 Richard Linche, *The Fountaine of Ancient Fiction* (London, 1599), Ri^{r}–Ri^{v}.

9 Macrobius, *The Saturnalia*, trans. Percival Vaughan Davies (New York, 1969), pp. 114–15.

10 Charles Dempsey, *The Portrayal of Love: Botticelli's 'Primavera' and Humanist Culture at the Time of Lorenzo the Magnificent* (Princeton, 1992), p. 40.

11 See Joseph A. Porter, *Shakespeare's Mercutio: his History and Drama* (Chapel Hill, 1988), pp. 32–53.

12 Charles Nicholl, *The Chemical Theatre* (London, 1980), p. 46.

13 Douglas Brooks-Davies, *The Mercurian Monarch: magical politics from Spenser to Pope* (Manchester, 1983), passim.

Hamlet, what appears to be figured is the enigmatic difference of a son and heir who is identified with 'th'incorporal air' and its movements, and hence with a grotesque form of verbal as well as vernal regeneration – through worms of maggots. In French, worms are *vers*; this not only links spring – *le ver* – with the worm, but could also suggest an additional pun in Hamlet's discourse of worms: on the putrefying activity of *vers* as verse. This serves to remind us that in spite of a nominal affinity, Hamlet never occupies the solid place of the earthly father; instead he is distinguished by a mutability of identity which implicates him in the more sexually ambiguous spheres of nature and spirit, and identifies him especially with the mobility of air or wind. It is noteworthy in this connection that it is the mercurial bird, the cock (whose castrated equivalent – the capon – Hamlet mentions in his ironic remark to Claudius about eating the air), which by its crowing dispels the apparition of the paternal ghost in the first scene of the play, thereby eliciting allusions to the cock's connection with that other son/sun figure, Christ, with whom the *Mercurius* of the alchemists was indeed often equated (1.1.119–46).

Hamlet's satirical rejection of the generative activity – or 'earing' – which would make a son a father has often been dismissed as misogyny; by this move, however, he confirms his separation from that genealogy of fathers upon which a hereditary (in contrast to an elective) model of kingship depends. And curiously, this is a dislocation which Claudius' assumption of the throne has already initiated. Yet through his mercurial and quibbling language 'of darke and enigmaticall sentences' Hamlet accords the final inheritance of all costly or aristocratic breeding to nature, and 'my lady Worm': 'Here's fine revolution, an we had the trick to see't' (5.1.88–9).

SECRECY AND GOSSIP IN *TWELFTH NIGHT*

JOHN KERRIGAN

Renaissance secrecy is no longer quite as secret as it was. Art historians and iconologists have returned to the myths and emblems explored by Panofsky and Edgar Wind, and reassessed (often sceptically) their claims to hermetic wisdom. Thanks to Jonathan Goldberg and Richard Rambuss, we now have a better understanding of the early modern English secretary,[1] and of how his pen could produce, in Lois Potter's phrase, *Secret Rites and Secret Writing*.[2] Not just in popular biographies of Marlowe and Shakespeare,[3] but in such Foucauldian accounts of high culture as John Michael Archer's *Sovereignty and Intelligence*,[4] the world of Renaissance espionage is being analysed afresh. William W. E. Slights has written at useful length about conspiracy, fraud and censorship in middle-period Jonson.[5] And, though the tide of Puttenham studies has now begun to ebb, students of Elizabethan England are still profiting from the work done by Daniel Javitch and Frank Whigham[6] on what *The Arte of English Poesie* calls 'false semblant' or 'the Courtly figure *Allegoria*'[7] – a line of enquiry which leads back to the civilized dissimulation advocated by Castiglione, but also to the politic ruthlessness of 'l'art machiavélien d'être secret'.[8]

These investigations have not advanced in a state of mutual ignorance, but they have, inevitably, suffered from a degree of exclusive specialism. What interests me, on the other hand, is how different modes of concealment operated together. Certainly, I have found it impossible, in thinking about *Twelfth Night*, to separate iconography from secretarial inscription (as when Malvolio unpicks the Lucrece seal of silence on Maria's riddling letter), or to divorce Sebastian's intelligence-gathering, among 'the memorials and the things of fame' in Illyria,[9] from that rhetorical discretion in him which is equally recommended in courtesy

1 Jonathan Goldberg, *Writing Matter: From the Hands of the English Renaissance* (Stanford, Stanford University Press, 1990), Richard Rambuss, *Spenser's Secret Career* (Cambridge, Cambridge University Press, 1993).

2 Lois Potter, *Secret Rites and Secret Writing: Royalist Literature, 1641–1660* (Cambridge, Cambridge University Press, 1989).

3 E.g., Charles Nicholl, *The Reckoning: The Murder of Christopher Marlowe* (London, Cape, 1992), Graham Phillips and Martin Keatman, *The Shakespeare Conspiracy* (London, Century, 1994).

4 John Michael Archer, *Sovereignty and Intelligence: Spying and Court Culture in the English Renaissance* (Stanford, Stanford University Press, 1993).

5 *Ben Jonson and the Art of Secrecy* (Toronto, University of Toronto Press, 1994); for his comments on Shakespeare see pp. 25–30.

6 Daniel Javitch, *Poetry and Courtliness in Renaissance England* (Princeton, Princeton University Press, 1978), Frank Whigham, *Ambition and Privilege: The Social Tropes of Elizabethan Courtesy Theory* (Berkeley, University of California Press, 1984).

7 George Puttenham, *The Arte of English Poesie*, ed. Gladys Doidge Willcock and Alice Walker (Cambridge, Cambridge University Press, 1936), p. 186.

8 Michel Senellart, 'Simuler et dissimuler: l'art machiavélien d'être secret à la Renaissance', paper at 'Le Secret à la Renaissance', Colloque IRIS 1996.

9 *Twelfth Night*, ed. J. M. Lothian and T. W. Craik (London, Methuen, 1975), 3.3.23.

literature.[10] At the same time, *Twelfth Night* pushes one's perception of Renaissance secrecy beyond the usual categories. It makes one return, for instance, to courtesy literature to notice what it says about that irregular but ubiquitous practice, the circulation of secrets as gossip, and to wonder how the gendered speech-patterns which Castiglione and his successors discuss might bear on the reticences and self-concealments involved in the construction of sexual identity.

By gesturing towards social practice, I am, of course, begging questions, and it is worth saying, at once, that Elizabethan London was not, in my view, full of cross-dressed maidens in love with Dukes. There is plainly much to be said against the current historicist tendency to discount the made uniqueness of particular Shakespearian play-scripts for the sake of readily meshing them with circumstantial contexts. Formalist criticism had its drawbacks, but its respect for the artful integrity – for the shifting, secret coherence – of such elusive works as *Twelfth Night* remains, in my view, admirable. On the other hand, there is no doubt that, as Richard Wilson (among others) has shown with *As You Like It*,[11] mature Shakespearian comedy goes much further in internalizing and articulating political conflict than traditional criticism realized. Good productions of *Twelfth Night* – such as John Barton's in 1969 – have always been alert to the tensions which arise between kin-status and the dignity of office (Sir Toby vs. Malvolio), to the insecurity of a figure like Maria, whose social rank is ambiguous, and to the importance, in Illyria, of jewels and cash changing hands. Above all, in this connection, *Twelfth Night* is interested in service. It explores the fraught relations which often held, in early modern households, between employment and eroticism. This dialectic is most active in the Viola-Orsino plot,[12] but it also significantly contributes to the misfortunes of Malvolio. Too often, critics view his gulling as an incidental intrigue. When he asks his mistress, however, in Act 5, 'tell me, in the modesty of honour, / Why you have given me such clear lights of favour' (5.1.334–5), he lands on a complex word which catches his outraged feeling that his preferment (both real and imaginary) cannot have stemmed from nothing in Olivia's heart. The play punishes the steward for believing that the more precisely he obeys his mistress's wishes the more he will deserve her favour (in every sense), even while it allows, in Cesario/Viola's relations with Orsino, a ripening into love of what is erotically problematic in Elizabethan ideas of service.

One way of developing these claims is to make an oblique approach to *Twelfth Night* through the autobiography of Thomas Whythorne: the Tudor poet and musician who was employed in a series of noble households before his death in 1596. Though the memoir which he compiled in the late 1570s lacks great events, it is altogether enthralling because of its attentiveness to social detail, its intricacy of self-criticism and rationalization, and its almost neurotic sensitivity to the role of flirtation, deceit and gossip in the politics of favour. Like Gascoigne's *Adventures of Master F.J.* – a work which probably suggested to Whythorne how his occasional poems could be linked by commentary and narrative – the *book of songs and sonnets, with long discourses set with them* is particularly alive to the use and abuse of secrecy. Thus, as autobiographical writing starts to emerge from the commonplaces which begin the memoir, Whythorne describes a friend who

[10] E.g., James Cleland, *'Ηρω-παιδεία, or The Institution of a Young Noble Man* (1607), Bks v, chs 7–9, and vi ('shewing a young Noble mans Dutie in Travailing') – esp. pp. 258–62, on sight-seeing as gentlemanly espionage (the pursuit of 'manie secrets').

[11] 'Like the Old Robin Hood: *As You Like It* and the Enclosure Riots', *Shakespeare Quarterly*, 43 (1992), 1–19; rpt. as Ch. 3 of his *Will Power: Essays on Shakespearean Authority* (Hemel Hempstead, Harvester Wheatsheaf, 1993).

[12] Cf. Lisa Jardine's excessively darkened judgements, in *Reading Shakespeare Historically* (London, Routledge, 1996), pp. 72–7.

once told a woman 'the very secrets that were hidden in his heart', only for her to 'blaz[e] abroad that which he had told her to keep in secret'.[13] Similarly, the first of many love intrigues in which he played a part involves a girl who wooed him by leaving a note threaded through the strings of his gittern. His typically wary reply praised her for proceeding 'secretly', but gossip made the affair 'known all about the house' and the girl was promptly discharged (pp. 22–3). Throughout his memoir, Whythorne describes situations in which secrecy and dissimulation shadow-box with each other and attempt to evade the tattling which his epigram, 'Of secret things', calls '*blab*' (p. 224).

The episode which bears most interestingly on *Twelfth Night* – though it can only be loosely contextual – comes shortly after the dismissal of the gittern girl, while Whythorne was still at the age which he calls 'adolescency' (p. 11). Like the young Cesario waiting upon Olivia, Whythorne found his way to the household of a beautiful young widow. Even before he accepted a position as her tutor and 'servingman', he was wary of enduring 'the life of a water-spaniel, that must be at commandment to fetch or bring here, or carry there' (p. 28). His resentment mounted when he discovered how manipulative his mistress could be. Whythorne vividly describes the sort of emotional pressure which could be brought to bear on a man whose position as a servant resembled that of a biddable suitor:

> Many times when I was not nigh unto her, although she had appointed me to wait on her cup when she sat at meat, she would bid me come nigher unto her. And therewithal scoffingly she would say to those that were with her, 'I would fain have my man to be in love with me, for then he would not be thus far from me, but would be always at mine elbow.' And then would she sometimes put a piece of good meat and bread on her trencher, and forthwith bid me give her a clean trencher, for the which I should have that of hers with the bread and meat on it.
>
> (p. 29)

The problem for Whythorne, however – as he chooses to remember the situation – was that, while he disliked these coercive games, he had to flirt with a mistress towards whom he was clearly attracted (not least in her exercise of power) because 'open contempt might breed such secret hate in her toward me' (p. 30). Innured, like F. J., to duplicity, and hoping for advancement, he recalls deciding that, 'if she did dissemble, I, to requite her, thought that to dissemble with a dissembler was no dissimulation ... But and if she meant good will indeed, then I was not willing to lose it, because of the commodities that might be gotten by such a one as she, either by marriage or otherwise' (pp. 30–1). As a result, when the widow told him 'how she would have me to apparel myself, as of what stuff, and how she would have it made' (though cross-gartering is not specified), he 'feathered his nest' by accepting money from her to buy clothes and other finery (p. 32). He also wrote to her in secret, and was, like Malvolio, deceived by an encouraging letter which, he later discovered, had been written by her 'waiting gentlewoman' (p. 34). By now, of course, gossip was rife (the attempt at secrecy assured that) – 'our affairs were not so closely handled but they were espied and much talked of in the house' (p. 36) – and the problem of his mistress having to disguise any signs of love which might, in themselves, be dissimulated, added to Whythorne's difficulty in deciding whether she could be won. The 'comical' affair (as he calls it) reached its climax when he appeared before her, not exactly in yellow stockings, but in 'garments of russet colour (the which colour signifieth the wearer thereof to have hope). And one time I did wear hops in my hat also; the which when my mistress had espied, she in a few scoffing words told me that the wearing of hops did but show that I should hope without that which I hoped for' (pp. 40–1). Thanks to his quibbling wit, Whythorne

---

[13] *The Autobiography of Thomas Whythorne: Modern Spelling Edition*, ed. James M. Osborn (London, Oxford University Press, 1962), p. 19.

was able to deflect this rebuff, but his suit thereafter cooled.

If one moves too hastily from this material across to Viola and Malvolio, the contrasts are overwhelming. Where Whythorne describes his affair in such calculating and duplicitous terms that even an impression of mutual vulnerability cannot offset his cynicism, *Twelfth Night* shows Viola concealing what she is to persist in faithful service. Unlike Rosalind, who seems, at least initially, pleased by the experimental scope which men's attire affords, she speaks of frustration and self-division, and the dissembling which her disguise entails is not embraced with relish. Malvolio, rather similarly, is constrained by the habit he adopts. His alacrity in putting on yellow stockings may smack of the self-promotion which infuriates Sir Toby, but his inability to see (as Whythorne instantly would) that he is being made a fool of stems as much from his eagerness to obey Olivia as from ingrown pride. Yet these differences between the memoir and *Twelfth Night* should not distract attention from their shared early modern fascination with the ambiguities of service, and their interest in how secrecy relates to what Cesario calls 'babbling gossip' (1.5.277).

Certainly these issues are prominent in Viola's opening scene. When she questions the Captain about Illyria, he can tell her of the Duke's love for Olivia – that obsession of his 'secret soul' (below, p. 72) – because 'murmur' has put it about. 'What great ones do,' he observes, 'the less will prattle of' (1.2.32–3). Gossip is equally active around the countess's reclusive life. The Captain knows of her resistance to Orsino because, again, of report: '(They say) she hath abjur'd the company / And sight of men' (40–1). Olivia's withdrawal into mourning for the death of her father and brother naturally attracts Viola, because she fears herself equally bereft, and she cries out for a position in her household which she imagines will bring emotional consonance: 'O that I serv'd that lady' (41). Though the motif is merely incipient, the play is beginning its exploration of the knot which ties employment to love. Hence the Captain's reply, 'That were hard to compass, / Because she will admit no kind of suit, / No, not the Duke's' (44–6), where the idea of suing to serve is inextricable from a lover's suit.

In Shakespeare's chief source, Barnabe Riche's novella 'Of Apolonius and Silla', the Captain is a villain whose designs on Silla's virtue are only foiled by tempest and shipwreck. Early audiences of *Twelfth Night* may or may not have recalled this when they saw Viola come on stage with the Captain, but Shakespeare alludes, through the heroine, to the possibility that he might be as he is in Riche:

> There is a fair behaviour in thee, Captain;
> And though that nature with a beauteous wall
> Doth oft close in pollution, yet of thee
> I will believe thou hast a mind that suits
> With this thy fair and outward character.
> I prithee (and I'll pay thee bounteously)
> Conceal me what I am, and be my aid
> For such disguise as haply shall become
> The form of my intent. (47–55)

This is touchingly complex because Viola's youthful moralism about appearances slips into an equally youthful trust, while she raises doubts about dissimulation in the same breath as she proposes concealment. But their deeper interest lies in their showing us how secrets are made: produced through interaction with possible or actual disclosure. For what is only known to yourself cannot be a secret, except in so far as its potential for disclosure anticipates that disclosure, or in so far as you might feel (as Viola/Cesario will later feel) that you are sharing the secret with your self as with another person.

Unlike Silla, Viola does not explicitly disguise herself in men's clothes to avoid sexual predators. While she may share this motive, the scene points towards a practical desire to secure a court position and an impulse to escape from herself. It is as though, by becoming Cesario, she hoped to leave Viola to grieve in secret.

That is, paradoxically, why her suit to serve the Duke can resemble Olivia's immurement. Just as the countess resolves to withdraw into a nun's asexuality, and thus becomes a 'cloistress' (1.1.28), so Viola proposes to be a eunuch – if not for the kingdom of heaven, then at least to sing at court. 'I'll serve this duke', she says:

> Thou shalt present me as an eunuch to him.
> It may be worth thy pains; for I can sing,
> And speak to him in many sorts of music,
> That will allow me very worth his service.
> (55–9)

These lines have baffled editors not least because they seem to go from singing to speech but then return to music. What Viola is saying, however, in a play which is much concerned with that branch of rhetoric which Feste calls *vox* (5.1.295), is that she is not only musically competent but has the flexible *pronunciatio* of a courtier. 'The pleasure of speech,' writes Stefan Guazzo, in Pettie's 1581 translation of *The Civile Conversation,* 'so wel as of Musicke, proceedeth of the chaunge of the voyce, yea ... the change of the voice, like an instrument of divers strings, is verie acceptable, and easeth both the hearer and the speaker'.[14] 'If Nature haue denied you a tunable accent,' James Cleland urges in *Ηρω-παιδεια, or The Institution of a Young Noble Man* (1607), 'studie to amend it by art the best yee maie' (p. 186). Interestingly, when Viola concludes the scene by urging 'silence' on the Captain (61), he sustains her rhetorical concerns by promising to avoid the speech-style which Thomas Whythorne calls '*blab*': 'Be you his eunuch, and your mute I'll be: / When my tongue blabs, then let mine eyes not see' (62–3).

At once the blabbers enter, as Maria, Sir Toby and, a few lines later, Sir Andrew come on stage. Maria is eager for Toby to avoid expulsion from Olivia's household by moderating his behaviour, but when she urges, 'confine yourself within the modest limits of order', he replies: 'I'll confine myself no finer than I am' (1.3.8–10). We have by this point become so accustomed to characters *seeking* confinement – Orsino lying 'canopied with bowers' (1.1.41), the countess's enclosure in mourning – that Toby's quibbling excess, as he sprawls through the play's first prose dialogue, is bound to appeal. As the scene goes on, however, the superb inconsequentiality of Maria's wit, when she toys with Sir Andrew, and his stupefying inability to get a grip on language, test the audience's patience. We feel assailed as well as amused by the prattle and networking chat which conduct books typically chastise by citing Plutarch's *De Garrulitate.* This challenge to the audience mounts. As the RSC director John Caird has noted, it creates problems in production that Sir Toby 'goes on and on and on' during Acts 2 and 3.[15] Even in 1.3, Shakespeare points up the garrulity of networking. Sir Andrew's reputation has reached Maria, for instance, from those she refers to as 'the prudent' and Toby calls 'scoundrels and subtractors' (32–5). Where report is offered sceptically by the Captain, gossip is here the stuff of life.

Anthropological work on gossip has stressed the importance of verbal trivia in maintaining social bonds. Max Gluckman, for instance, argues that scandalous chat draws participants together while serving to exclude others because access to conversation depends on inside knowledge. 'The right to gossip about certain people is', he says, 'a privilege which is only extended to a person when he or she is accepted as a member of a group.'[16] This account can be squared with the way the lighter people network in *Twelfth Night* in opposition

[14] *The Civile Conversation of M. Steeven Guazzo*, tr. George Pettie (Bks I–III) and Barthlomew Young (Bk IV), introd. Sir Edward Sullivan (London, Constable, 1925), 2 vols; I, p. 129.

[15] Bill Alexander, John Barton, John Caird and Terry Hands, *Directors' Shakespeare: Approaches to 'Twelfth Night'*, ed. Michael Billington (London, Nick Hern Books, 1990), p. 22.

[16] 'Gossip and Scandal', *Current Anthropology*, 4 (1963), 307–16, p. 313.

to the aloof Malvolio. But Gluckman's critics are right to insist that gossiping is by no means always collective, and that a group can turn out, once inspected, to be full of conversational partitions.[17] In that sense, the garrulous in *Twelfth Night* form an interestingly fractious set, with Fabian and Feste as satellites, and Sir Toby prepared to bamboozle Andrew with what sounds like friendly chat, in ways which make it easier for him to scorn and reject him in Act 5. But Sir Andrew is not the only one left behind in the conversational flow. Everyone who works on gossip would agree that the morsels of information and rumour which it retails must have some element of obscurity, some secret component worth disclosing, since they would otherwise not be passed on. *Twelfth Night* respects this principle to the point, almost, of defiance, by including material which may well have been written to exclude early audiences from what the play's in-crowd knows, and which certainly excludes us now. Who, for instance, is Mistress Mall, and why should we care about her picture?

In the drinking scene of Act 2, the obscurities of prattling accumulate. What is Sir Toby on about when he says, 'My lady's a Cataian, we are politicians, Malvolio's a Peg-a-Ramsey' (2.3.76–7)? The clown calls this 'admirable fooling' (81), and it does, indeed, resemble the patter of Feste, which rings in Andrew's empty head, and which he now babbles out: 'thou wast in very gracious fooling last night, when thou spok'st of Pigrogromitus, of the Vapians passing the equinoctial of Queubus' (22–4). This replication of proliferating nonsense recalls Plutarch's comparison of gossip to the porch or gallery at Olympia which 'from one voice by sundry reflections and reverberations ... rendered seven ecchoes'. When speech comes 'to the eares of a babbler,' he says, 'it resoundeth again on every side ... insomuch, as a man may well say: That the conducts and passages of their hearing reach not to the braine ... but onely to their tongue.'[18] Babbling of this sort climaxes in the drinking scene for obvious reasons. It hardly needs Plutarch to tell us (though he does so more than once) that drunkenness provokes 'much babling and foolish prattle' (p. 194). What we can misunderstand, historically, is that the folly of babbling was – partly because of Plutarch – so routinely associated with drink that when a commentator such as Thomas Wright seeks to explain garrulity, he gravitates to talk of 'foolery' and ale-house metaphors: 'he that wil poure foorth all he conceiueth, deliuereth dregges with drinke, and as for the most part, presently men apprehend more folly than wisdom, so he that sodainely vttereth all he vnderstandeth, blabeth forth moore froath than good liquor'.[19] This is the mixture of assumptions which Malvolio provocatively ignites when he stalks in and rebukes the drinkers for choosing 'to gabble like tinkers' (88–9).

It should now be clear why the Captain's word 'blab' refers as much to a style of speech as to the betrayal of secrets. Early modern accounts of the psychology and practice of gossip start, as it were, from rhetoric.[20] The blabber was a verbal incontinent, whose itch to gabble whatever was in his mind would lead (as Plutarch warned) to rash disclosure. Avoid making friends, advises Wright, with the

---

17 E.g., Robert Paine, 'What is Gossip About?: An Alternative Hypothesis', *Man*, n.s. 2 (1967), 278–85.

18 'Of Intemperate Speech or Garrulitie', in *The Philosophie, Commonlie Called, The Morals Written by the Learned Philosophy Plutarch of Chæronea*, tr. Philemon Holland (1603), pp. 191–208 (p. 192).

19 *The Passions of the Minde in Generall*, rev. edn (1604), p. 107.

20 Contrast the more recent views surveyed in, e.g., Patricia Meyer Spacks, *Gossip* (1985; Chicago, University of Chicago Press, 1986), ch. 2. For work by social historians on the practice of sixteenth- and seventeenth-century gossip see, e.g., J. A. Sharpe, *Defamation and Sexual Slander in Early Modern England: The Church Courts at York*, Borthwick Papers no. 58 (York: University of York, 1980) and Steve Hindle, 'The Shaming of Margaret Knowsley: Gossip, Gender and the Experience of Authority in Early Modern England', *Continuity and Change*, 9 (1994), 391–419.

'blabbish, and ... indiscreet' because they will not 'keep secret, or conserue thy credit, and so with one breath they blow all away' (pp. 119–20). The corresponding virtue to this vice was called 'discretion' – a word which, symptomatically, has etymological and semantic links with 'secrecy'.[21] Time and again, in conduct books, gentlemen are advised to be discreet. The courtier, Castiglione says, 'shall be no carier about of trifling newes ... He shall be no babbler [but keep] alwayes within his boundes.'[22] In Guazzo, who is almost anti-courtly, at moments, in his mistrust of easy eloquence,[23] there is an equally firm resistance to what Cleland calls 'pratling' and 'Babling' (p. 189). 'Blaze neuer anie mans secret,' Cleland says, 'nor speake of that which discretion commandeth you to conceale, albeit it was not commended to your silence' (p. 190).

This has a gendered aspect, in that, while gentlemen are encouraged discreetly to converse, women are incited to a discretion which can be absolute. It is the anti-feminist Lord Gaspar who maintains, in Castiglione, 'that the verye same rules that are given for the Courtier, serve also for the woman', and the sympathetic Julian[24] who argues that 'in her factions, maners, woordes, gestures and conversation (me thinke) the woman ought to be muche unlike the man' (pp. 215–16). Like the courtier, he argues, women should be 'discreete' and avoid 'babblinge', but they should concentrate, further, on cultivating 'sweetnesse' and reticence (pp. 216–18). English writers were as confident as Guazzo that 'a young man is to be blamed, which will talke like an olde man, and a woman which will speake like a man' (I, p. 169). Nor was it just the fools, including Sir John Daw in *Epicoene*, who believed that '*Silence in woman is like speech in man*.'[25] In *The English Gentlewoman* (1631), Richard Brathwait pushes his praise of 'Discretion' to the point of insisting that 'bashfull silence is an ornament' in women (p. 89). Against the background of a prejudice which assumed (as it still does) that women are more garrulous than men,[26] he writes: 'It suites not with *her* honour, for a *young woman* to be prolocutor. But especially, when either men are in presence, or ancient Matrons, to whom shee owes a ciuill reuerence, it will become her to tip her tongue with silence' (*ibid.*).

In 'The Table' to *The English Gentlewoman*, Brathwait cites the apothegm, '"Violets, *though they grow low and neare the earth, smell sweetest: and* Honour *appeares the fullest of beauty, when she is humblest*"' (††2). As Gerard's *Herball* confirms,[27] the Latin word '*Viola*' was used in Elizabethan England as another name for the violet, a flower which, in general, was associated with modesty. What Cesario inherits from Viola is the discretion which a female upbringing made second nature to gentlewomen. What he gains, as it were, over Viola is permission to speak out – even when men are present. These claims are not in conflict with traditional accounts of the role, but they do, I think, point up the hybridity of Viola's performance. To think about her in relation to courtesy literature is to notice those comical moments when she

21 Cf. Sissela Bok, *Secrets: On the Ethics of Concealment and Revelation* (1982; Oxford, Oxford University Press, 1986), p. 286 n. 7.

22 *The Book of the Courtier*, tr. Sir Thomas Hoby (1561), introd. Walter Raleigh (London, David Nutt, 1900), p. 124.

23 For contexts see, e.g., Daniel Javitch, 'Rival Arts of Conduct in Elizabethan England: Guazzo's *Civile Conversation* and Castiglione's *Courtier*', *Yearbook of Italian Studies*, 1 (1971), 178–98, pp. 188–9.

24 See, e.g., Gaspar's remarkable anticipation, out of Aristotle, of Freud on the castration complex in women, and Julian's reply: 'The seelie poore creatures wish not to be a man to make them more perfect, but to have libertye, and to be ridd of the rule that men have of their owne authoritie chalenged over them' (pp. 226–7).

25 *Epicoene or The Silent Woman*, ed. L. A. Beaurline (London, 1966), 2.3.109.

26 Cf., e.g., Lisa Jardine, *Still Harping on Daughters: Women and Drama in the Age of Shakespeare* (Brighton, Harvester, 1983), ch. 4.

27 John Gerard, *The Herball or Generall Historie of Plantes* (1597), p. 701.

overplays the courtly rhetoric – as when Cesario impresses Sir Andrew (always a bad sign) by praying for the heavens to 'rain odours' on Olivia, or, more oddly, when Andrew surprises us by speaking French, and exchanges such exquisite salutations with Cesario that both are satirically construed.[28] As strikingly, to look at Viola in the light of Guazzo, Cleland and other conduct writers is to recognize the acute importance of discretion in the play.

While describing his affair with the widow, Whythorne glumly notes: 'It is a common matter among servants, ... if any one of them be in favour with their masters or mistresses above the rest, by and by all the rest of the servants will envy him or her, and seek all the means and ways that they can imagine to bring them out of credit' (p. 36). Again, it would be wrong to read too directly from this into *Twelfth Night*. Because critics have neglected the politics of favour, however, they have missed the edginess of Viola's first exchange as Cesario, when s/he comes on stage with Valentine, who was trusted, in I.1, with the task of visiting Olivia, but who is now losing his influence. 'If the Duke continue these favours towards you,' Valentine says, 'you are like to be much advanced: he hath known you but three days, and already you are no stranger.' This could be spoken neutrally, but Cesario's reply indicates that the actor playing Valentine should give his words some salt: 'You either fear his humour, or my negligence, that you call in question the continuance of his love. Is he inconstant, sir, in his favours?' (I.4.1–7). The question is fascinatingly pitched, given the erotic range of 'favour', since the constancy which Cesario hopes for in his master is not one which Viola, who now loves the Duke, would unambiguously welcome – at least in Orsino's relations with Olivia.

One thing is clear immediately, though: Valentine is right to envy Cesario's progress with Orsino. As soon as the Duke appears, his cry is for Cesario, and for the rest to stand 'aloof' (12). Drawing his servant down-stage, no doubt, into the theatre-space which signifies and facilitates intimate conversation, he says:

Cesario,
Thou know'st no less but all: I have unclasp'd
To thee the book even of my secret soul.
Therefore, good youth, address thy gait unto her,
Be not denied access ... (12–16)

In the Italian comedy *Gl'Ingannati* – a probable source for *Twelfth Night* – the Viola-figure says to Clemenzia, when asked why she attends her lover in disguise, 'Do you think a woman in love is unhappy to see her beloved continually, to speak to him, touch him, hear his secrets ...?'[29] Shakespeare's emphasis is more on the intimacies of disclosure than on the content of those 'secrets' which are, in any case, the stuff of Illyrian gossip. This is not a process which can be represented, entirely, through dialogue. It depends on proximity and touch between actors, and on the boy or woman playing Cesario having a demeanour which promises that discretion described in Bacon's 'Of Simulation and Dissimulation': 'the *Secret* Man, heareth many Confessions; For who will open himselfe, to a Blab or a Babler? But if a man be thought *Secret*, it inviteth Discoverie.'[30]

Cesario gains access to Olivia by means of stubborn pertness, but his suit is then advanced because he is a '*Secret* Man'. As Bacon adds, with worldly acumen: 'Mysteries are due to *Secrecy*. Besides (to say Truth) *Nakednesse* is uncomely, as well in Minde, as Body; and it addeth no small Reverence, to Mens Manners, and Actions, if they be not altogether Open' (*ibid.*). If there is a technology of mystery,

28 3.1.86–7, 72–3. On courtly excess in 'Salutation ... complements, false offers, & promises of seruice' see, e.g., Cleland, *Institution*, pp. 176ff.

29 Tr. and excerpted as *The Deceived*, in Geoffrey Bullough (ed.), *Narrative and Dramatic Sources of Shakespeare*, vol. II (London, Routledge and Kegan Paul, 1958), pp. 286–339 (p. 296).

30 *The Essayes or Counsels, Civill and Morall*, ed. Michael Kiernan (Oxford, Clarendon Press, 1985), pp. 20–3 (p. 21).

Cesario exemplifies it. Olivia's veil of mourning cannot but advertise the celebrated beauty it conceals, and she is right (though her modesty is false) to worry about prosaic nakedness when the lacy screen is lifted to reveal 'two lips indifferent red ... two grey eyes, with lids to them' (I.5.250–1). Cesario, whose 'smooth and rubious' lips are so meshed into gender ambiguity that their very nakedness tantalises (I.4.32), has a nature more covert and estranged, which, because of Viola's recessive psychology, is not just disguised by clothes. His embassy goes in stages. At first, he attracts attention by presenting himself as a forward page-boy, seeking to recite a script of compliments,[31] but he intrigues Olivia by modulating into a more inwardly performative role which plays on the comeliness of secrecy while expressing, with a twist of pathos, Viola's sense of being mysterious to herself as she comes to terms with loving the Duke: 'and yet, by the very fangs of malice I swear, I am not that I play' (184–5). Orsino has told his servant to 'unfold the passion of my love' (I.4.24), but, as Cesario quickly discovers, that secret is too open to entice. It is almost an objection to the Duke, for Olivia, that his qualities are manifest and talked of: 'Of great estate, of fresh and stainless youth; / In voices well divulg'd' (I.5.263–4). Cesario, by contrast, has a secret allure – the allure of secrecy; and he uses it to secure a private audience by promising revelation: 'What I am, and what I would, are as secret as maidenhead: to your ears, divinity; to any other's, profanation' (218–20).

These lines are alive with risk. As Georg Simmel has noted, in his classic account of secrecy: 'the secret is surrounded by the possibility and temptation of betrayal; and the external danger of being discovered is interwoven with the internal danger, which is like the fascination of an abyss, of giving oneself away.'[32] Cesario's mention of a 'maidenhead' produces secrecy from what is hidden by anticipating disclosure. He alludes to the 'she' in Cesario, and 'she' alludes to something so essentially intimate that her feelings for Orsino come to mind. Yet the process of tempting Olivia into private conference, of enticing her (and the audience) with intimations of a sexual secret more real than maidenheads merely talked of,[33] goes along with an urge on Viola's part to be done with her intolerable disguise and give herself away by blabbing. For as Simmel adds: 'The secret puts a barrier between men but, at the same time, it creates the tempting challenge to break through it, by gossip or confession – and this challenge accompanies its psychology like a constant overtone' (*ibid.*).

The overtone is most audible, a few lines later, in the willow cabin speech. If I loved you, Cesario tells Olivia, I should

> Make me a willow cabin at your gate,
> And call upon my soul within the house;
> Write loyal cantons of contemned love,
> And sing them loud even in the dead of night;
> Halloo your name to the reverberate hills,
> And make the babbling gossip of the air
> Cry out 'Olivia!' O, you should not rest
> Between the elements of air and earth,
> But you should pity me. (272–80)

The speech is emotionally electric because, by positing herself as Orsino wooing Olivia, Viola is imagining what it would be like to woo the Duke,[34] while seducing Olivia into imagining

---

[31] Compare (but also contrast) lines 169–96 with Mote at *Love's Labour's Lost* 5.2.158–74, addressing the Princess and her ladies.

[32] 'The Secret and the Secret Society', pt IV of *The Sociology of Georg Simmel*, ed. and tr. Kurt H. Wolff (New York, The Free Press, 1950), pp. 307–76 (p. 334).

[33] The effect of elusive enigma was enlarged, no doubt, for early audiences aware of being addressed by a boy (playing a woman playing a boy), especially given medical doubts concerning the existence, in reality, of the hymen: see, e.g., Helkiah Crooke, *Μικροκοσμο-γραφια: A Description of the Whole Body of Man*, 2nd edn (1631), p. 256: 'It hath beene an old question and so continueth to this day, whether there be any certaine markes or notes of virginity in women ...'.

[34] To woo, that is, as Viola (if a woman might be so assertive), rather than compoundly, as in 2.4, where the attraction of Cesario/Viola's eye to 'some favour that it

what it would be like to be wooed by Cesario.[35] But the energy of the utterance, as it moves through double, endstopped lines to the suddenly freed enjambment and exclamatory caesura after 'gossip of the air',[36] also stems from her frustrated impulse to babble out what she is. Given the fact that Shakespeare varied his characters' names from those in the sources, it can hardly be accidental that, if 'the babbling gossip of the air' *did* cry out 'O-liv-ia', the rebounding echoes would reverberate into something very like 'Vi-o-la' – a word which is, for innocent audiences, a secret within the secret until, near the end of the play, Sebastian greets Cesario by saying '"Thrice welcome, drowned Viola"' (5.1.239).

Characterization in mature Shakespeare is angled into complexity by what holds between roles as well as by what is written into them. The lucid symmetries and parallels which shape such early comedies as *Errors* and *Love's Labour's Lost* give way, from *Much Ado* onwards, to a recognizably more mannerist procedure in which analogies are elliptical and overdetermined, and characters who seem unlike can be, in fluctuating ways, related. No case is more extreme, perhaps, than the coupling of Cesario and Malvolio. Yet the resemblances are there. Both gentlemen are upwardly mobile suitors (respectively unwelcome and coerced) of Olivia. In the echoing cluster of names which lies at the heart of the play, 'Malvolio' is more involved with 'Olivia' and 'Viola' than is, for instance, 'Orsino'. And this reflects, perhaps, a similarity rooted in source-material, given that, in 'Of Apolonius and Silla', the Viola-figure is thrown into the dark house reserved, in *Twelfth Night*, for Malvolio, when the Duke gathers, from gossip among servants, that the countess has fallen in love with his man.

It is in their role as servants, however, that the two are most closely aligned. As I noted in relation to Whythorne, both are equally subject to the politics of favour. At first, Malvolio is as successful as Cesario. If Orsino finds it natural to turn to his discreet young servant when thoughts about Olivia well up, Olivia calls for that 'known discreet man', her steward (1.5.95), both in sending Cesario her ring, and, later, in 3.4, when she comes on stage with Maria, but talks, rather, to herself about how to win the Duke's handsome ambassador. 'I speak too loud', she says, checking her own indiscretion: 'Where's Malvolio? He is sad and civil, / And suits well for a servant with my fortunes: / Where is Malvolio?' (4–7). The word 'sad' here does not mean 'gloomy', as in modern English. The steward is grave and close. He can observe the decorum which Puttenham praises when he says that a man should be 'secret and sad' in counsel (p. 292). This quality is defined, of course, against the babbling indiscretion of Sir Toby and his friends. Towards the end of 3.4, Cesario will say that he hates 'babbling drunkenness' (364). It is a trait which

loves' (which riddlingly means the Duke's 'favour' (24–5)), prompts him/her to utter the half-betraying speech about 'concealment', 'My father had a daughter lov'd a man ...' (108–19). Symptomatically, in the exchange which follows, Bacon's observation, 'he that will be *Secret*, must be a *Dissembler*, in some degree. For Men are too cunning, to suffer a Man, to keepe an indifferent carriage ... They will so beset a man with Questions, and draw him on, and picke it out of him' (p. 21) is ratified both by Orsino's leading interrogation ('But died thy sister of her love, my boy?' (120)) and by Cesario/Viola's dissimulation ('I am all the daughters of my father's house, / And all the brothers too' (121–2)), which slurs into poignant honesty, as s/he hopes for Sebastian's survival ('... and yet I know not' (122)), but which remains sufficiently in touch with the deviousness of his/her opening ploy to recall (for instance) the explicitly seductive discretion of F. J. when he woos Dame Elinor with a lute song composed by 'My father's sister's brother's son' (Gascoigne, *The Adventures of Master F.J.*, in Paul Salzman (ed.), *An Anthology of Elizabethan Prose Fiction* (Oxford, Oxford University Press, 1987), pp. 3–81 (p. 28)).

35 For another perspective see John Kerrigan, ed., *Motives of Woe: Shakespeare and 'Female Complaint'. A Critical Anthology* (Oxford, Clarendon Press, 1991), esp. pp. 20–3, 41–5.

36 Folio punctuation mostly conforms to the rhetorical shape of the passage, though, as routinely, it divides the run-on 'air / Cry' with a comma.

Malvolio shares, as we know from his denunciation, in the drinking scene, of those who 'gabble like tinkers' and keep 'uncivil rule' (2.3.89, 122).

To insist that Malvolio feels the same urge as Viola/Cesario to disclose a hidden nature through babbling would be false to the glancing way in which parallels work in *Twelfth Night.* His yellow stockings and forced smile do involve an element of disguise, since they belie his 'sad and civil' self; but they owe more (I shall argue) to adornment, and they cannot be patly compared to the costume which stirs up in Cesario a desire to reveal the Viola in him. Yet the steward is not as indifferent to 'babbling gossip' as he would like the world to suppose. Even before he reads the forged letter, he is fantasizing about Olivia by recalling, 'There is example for't. The Lady of the Strachy married the yeoman of the wardrobe' (2.5.39–40). This snippet from Illyrian gossip columns is every bit as trivially topical, or, more likely, pseudo-topical, as Sir Toby's allusion to Mistress Mall. Indeed the plot against Malvolio can be understood, in early modern terms, as designed to bring out the babbler in the discreet man, by emptying his language. 'My masters, are you mad?', the steward asks the drinkers (2.3.87). When denounced as a madman and locked up, he is not just confined as finely as Sir Toby Belch could wish: his words – once so commanding in the household – are discredited and trivialized, then mocked as empty verbiage. 'Malvolio,' Sir Topas cries, 'thy wits the heavens restore: endeavour thyself to sleep, and leave thy vain bibble babble.'[37]

It is easy to see how the courtesy literature which sheds light on Cesario can also illuminate his double, Sebastian. In the elaborate, even stilted idiom of his first exchanges with Antonio, in the reserve and sturdy valour with which he engages Sir Andrew and Sir Toby, and in his discreet handling of the secret betrothal to Olivia, he conforms with the ideals laid out in such texts as Henry Peacham's *Compleat Gentleman* (1622). The plot against Cesario's more eccentric co-rival, Malvolio, might seem harder to relate to conduct books. In practice, though, even the courtly Castiglione is more tolerant of what Fabian calls 'sportful malice' (5.1.364) than a modern reader might expect. *The Book of the Courtier* describes, indeed, a series of 'Meerie Pranckes' which bear comparison with *Twelfth Night.* In one of them, an unfortunate man is persuaded by his companions that the dark room in which he has been sleeping is illuminated by the – actually, unlit – candles which they carry. Like Sir Topas visiting Malvolio, they cry, with incredulity, 'Say'st thou that house is dark?' (4.2.35) until – lacking the steward's resilience – the poor man is convinced of his blindness, repents his sins and prays to Our Lady of Loreto, whereupon his friends undeceive him (pp. 193–5). Almost as cruel is the tale told by Monsieur Bernarde about the occasion when he fell a-wrestling, in sport, with Cesar Boccadello on the Bridge of Leo. When passers-by made to separate them, Bernarde cried 'Helpe sirs, for this poore gentilman at certein times of the moone is frantike, and see now how he striveth to cast himselfe of the bridge into the river' (p. 197). Cesar was instantly set upon, and the more he struggled and protested, the more apparently justified and inevitable his confinement (like Malvolio's) became.

There are, Castiglione says, 'two kyndes of Meerie Prianckes . . . The one is, whan any man whoever he be, is deceyved wittilie . . . The other, whan a manne layeth (as it were) a nett, and showeth a piece of a bayte so, that a man renneth to be deceyved of himself' (p. 191). The plot against Malvolio is a fine example of this latter, more sophisticated form of joke. It is always surprising, when one returns to the play, to discover just how deeply the steward is mired in fantasies about Olivia *before* he finds the letter. Yet Malvolio does need some enticement to run himself into the net, and Maria's

[37] 4.2.98–100; cf., e.g., the 'jangling bibble babble' of 'praters' in Plutarch's 'Of Intemperate Speech' (p. 193).

letter is well-judged to appeal not only to his ambitions but to his pride in managing secrets. It is relevant, in this regard, that her writing parodies secretaryship – or, as likely, abuses a secretarial office which she has discharged on other occasions – by conducting the sort of covert correspondence with a suitor which such a servant might expect to handle for her lady (as when the devious secretary in Gascoigne writes to F. J. on Elinor's behalf). In a secretary, discretion was essential. Indeed, as Angel Day notes, in *The English Secretary*, 'in respect of such *Secrecie* ... the name was first giuen to be called a *Secretorie*'.[38] Equally integral, however, was the idea of imitative substitution. The secretary, Day reports, will be 'a zealous imitator' of his master, down to the 'forme and maner' of his penmanship.[39] This is the context of Maria's announcement, 'I can write very like my lady your niece; on a forgotten matter we can hardly make distinction of our hands' (2.3.160–2). She is indicating that her letter will not be a forgery so much as a duplicitous secret.

The hermeticism of the missive is compounded, for it is wrapped in mysteries – ornamented by secrets – from the tantalizing address on its outside ('*To the unknown beloved* ...' (2.5.92)), through the seal which closes it up (but which also dis-closes its matter, by hinting that Olivia is the author), into the enigmas of its message:

I may command where I adore;
But silence, like a Lucrece knife,
With bloodless stroke my heart doth gore;
M.O.A.I. doth sway my life. (106–9)

This 'secrete conceit' – to use Puttenham's phrase for the posies and anagrams of amorous courtiers (p. 102)[40] – is a sub-plot version of those riddles which elsewhere in the play (and especially in Cesario/Viola's lines) have an ontological aspect. And it does, more locally, raise the thought that Malvolio's cultivated discretion (his chosen mode of being) is a form of self-advertisement. For the ornate secrecy of the letter is calculated to command attention: it engages in a covert exhibitionism which the steward finds congenial. To that extent it recalls Simmel's insight, that 'although apparently the sociological counter-pole of secrecy, adornment has, in fact, a societal significance with a structure analogous to that of secrecy itself' (p. 338). In other words, the secrecy of the letter has much in common with the yellow stockings, cross-gartering and fixed smile which it encourages its recipient to adopt.

This claim may sound unlikely, but I am encouraged to advance it by the cogency of Simmel's observation that, while man's desire to please may include outward-going kindness, there is also a

> wish for this joy and these 'favors' to flow back to him, in the form of recognition and esteem, ... [B]y means of this pleasing, the individual desires to *distinguish* himself before others, and to be the object of an attention that others do not receive. This may even lead him to the point of wanting to be envied. Pleasing may thus become a means of the will to power: some individuals exhibit a strange contradiction that they need those above whom they elevate themselves by life and deed, for they build their own self-feeling upon the subordinates' realization that they *are* subordinate. (*ibid.*)

Even before he finds the letter, Malvolio's attentiveness to Olivia and his contempt for those like Sir Toby exemplifies a power-seeking desire for 'favours'. His attraction to the countess has less to do with eroticism than with a longing for the unruly, over whom he elevates himself, to become his subordinates: his day-dream about Toby curtsying to him, and

38 *The English Secretary*, rev. edn (1599), pt 2, p. 102.

39 *English Secretary*, pt 2, p. 130; cf. Rambuss, *Spenser's Secret Career*, p. 43.

40 For examples beyond Puttenham (esp. pp. 108–12), see, e.g., [Sir John Mennis], *Recreation for Ingenious Head-peeces* (1654), P5r–Q4r, R3r–4r. On verse composition, more broadly, as 'secret intercommoning' – a compromise formation between self-consuming inwardness and full disclosure (below, p. 79) – see Gascoigne, *Adventures of Master F.J.*, pp. 40–1.

being required to amend his drunkenness, shows that he cannot imagine life in the household (certainly not an agreeable life) without having the lighter people to condescend to. In preparation for the happy day when he will be made Count Malvolio, he distinguishes himself before others by means of a singular discretion (so unlike their collective gabbling) which is actually a form of ostentation. We are not surprised when Maria reports that Malvolio 'has been yonder i' the sun practising behaviour to his own shadow this half hour' (2.5.16–18) because he is that recognizable type: a secret exhibitionist. The invitation to put on yellow stockings, cross-gartered, is, in one sense, ludicrous and improbable, because it contradicts those 'sad and civil' qualities which attract Olivia's praise. But it is hardly surprising that Malvolio takes the bait, because, as Simmel says, 'Adornment is the egoistic element as such' (p. 339), and the strange garb – which the steward claims he already owns, and which he may indeed have worn, at least in fantasy (2.5.166–8) – amplifies and gives expression to his desire for singularity without compromising his attentiveness to Olivia: on the contrary, it is a way of 'pleasing' her.

Simmel goes on to notice that adornment does not express the organic nature of the person adorned, but depends on superfluousness and impersonality. Jewels and precious stones are typical of its highly external relationship with the person, but yellow stockings and cross-garters work to similar effect because they divide up and cut into the wholeness and ease of the body (they obstruct, indeed, Malvolio's circulation (3.4.19–20)). One might compare Simmel's example of new clothes as against old: the former 'are particularly elegant', he says, 'due to their being still "stiff"; they have not yet adjusted to the modifications of the individual body as fully as older clothes have' (p. 341). There is a vein of comedy here, of course, because, as Bergson points out in *Le rire*, laughter is provoked by superimpositions of mechanical rigidity on the organic flow of the body. The ornaments seemingly requested by Olivia, the clothes which Malvolio puts on to mark his new status, are laughable even as – and for precisely the same reason that – they signify advancement. For adornment is a mark of status regardless of the materials used, and Malvolio's attire shares the usual property of adornment in bringing together, or parodying (since Olivia cannot bear yellow), what Simmel calls 'Aesthetic excellence' and the '*sociological* charm of being, by virtue of adornment, a representative of one's group' (p. 343) – with the added delight, in this case, for Malvolio, that, by becoming a count, he will represent the dignity of Olivia's house to the consternation of Sir Toby and his ilk. Beyond that, and underwriting it, is secrecy: the ultimate bait. To assume yellow stockings and be cross-gartered puts Malvolio's discretion on display, without abolishing it, because the new garb allows him, as he thinks, to share a secret with Olivia, to signal an ambition and grasp of courtly intrigue (hence 'I will read politic authors' (2.5.161–2)) which she will understand and appreciate while the drinkers and babblers will not.

That this exhibitionistic secrecy is designed to please Olivia only with the intention of gratifying Malvolio is compatible with the sickness of self-love which she diagnoses when he first comes on stage (1.5.89). From a psychoanalytical perspective, indeed, the yellow stockings are narcissistic fetishes while the cross-gartering looks auto-erotic. This line of enquiry could bear a Lacanian twist, given that the anagrammatic relations which hold between 'Olivia' and 'Malvolio' – pointed up by the disjection of those names ('*M.O.A.I.*') in the letter – register, at the level of the sign, her role in reflecting Malvolio's constitutive desire back on himself. Freudian speculation aside, there is certainly something masturbatory about the steward's complacent cry, as Sir Toby and the rest move in to take the yellow-stockinged madman away: 'Let me enjoy my private' (3.4.90). This recoil into self-pleasuring is not restricted, of course, to the steward. Critics often call Orsino (rather loosely) a narcissist, and his early remark – before Cesario's charms get to work – 'for I myself am best / When least in company' (1.4.37–8) would have suggested to an Elizabethan audience, with its inherited disapproval (to simplify somewhat) of solitariness,[41] a similarly troubling mind-set. The conduct literature is emphatic in its insistence on affective sociality. '*Self-Loue* is the greatest disease of the minde,' according to James Cleland, and it has 'beene the cause of manie *Narcissus* his changing among you Nobles' (p. 241). There is, in other words, an important Renaissance distinction between the socially produced (and socially productive) quality called secrecy and suspect, anti-social solitude.

It is entirely in line with this that Stefan Guazzo celebrates discretion but bends his dialogue towards showing how arguments for civil conversation can persuade his brother, William Guazzo, from abandoning society: 'And now my joye is the greater', William's interlocutor, Anniball Magnocavalli, says at the end, 'that I understande how readie and willinge you are to caste of the obscure and blacke Robe of Solitarinesse, and in liew of that to revest and adorne your selfe with the white and shininge garment of Conversation' (II, p. 215). The danger was, inevitably, that discretion could become exaggerated into self-absorption. Malvolio's anti-social vanity bears out Nashe's observation in *Pierce Penilesse his Supplication to the Divell* (1592): 'Some thinke to be counted rare Politicans and Statesmen, by being solitary: as who would say, I am a wise man, a braue man, *Secreta mea mihi: Frustra sapit, qui sibi non sapit* [My secrets are my own; he is wise in vain who does not know his own business], and there is no man worthy of my companie or friendship.'[42]

Much is now being written about the way Renaissance culture developed modern ideas about privacy by building and exploring the uses of secluded chambers and closets.[43] This emergent mentality is reflected in the appeal which *Twelfth Night* makes to varieties of privy space. Somewhere off-stage Andrew has his 'cubiculo' and Toby his own retreat. But it matters that we should learn of the former by Toby saying, 'We'll call thee at thy cubiculo' and of the latter by his remark (to Feste or Maria) 'Come by and by to my chamber' (3.2.50, 4.2.73–4). The babblers are social in their privacy, where Malvolio seeks to be private even in the open spaces of Olivia's great house. That is why the 'dark room' (3.4.136) – that dramatically overdetermined locale – is such an apt punishment for his pretensions: locked up there he is both cast out of society and thrown in upon himself. He is forced into a solitude which represents, but which is also maliciously designed to induce, asocial derangement. But he is also given a chance – I shall end by suggesting – to reassess the value of what Nashe calls 'companie or friendship'.

I referred, a little earlier, to ontological riddling. What I mean by that is the presence of, and counterpoint between, such claims, in Cesario/Viola's part, as 'I am not that I play' and 'I am not what I am' (1.5.185, 3.1.143). As disguise and confusion mount, even simple indicative statements such as 'I am the man' (when Viola deduces that Olivia has fallen for Cesario) are deceptive, twisting into dubiety and delusion: 'if it be so, as 'tis, / Poor lady, she were better love a dream' (2.2.24–5). 'Nothing that is so, is so', the clown will later quip (4.1.8–9). Sebastian calls this 'folly', but Olivia

41 See Janette Dillon, *Shakespeare and the Solitary Man* (London, Macmillan, 1981), chs 1–2.

42 *The Works of Thomas Nashe*, ed. R. B. McKerrow, corr. by F. P. Wilson (Oxford, Basil Blackwell, 1958), 5 vols, I, pp. 137–245 (p. 169).

43 See, e.g., Orest Ranum, 'The Refuges of Intimacy', in Roger Chartier (ed.), *Passions of the Renaissance*, tr. Arthur Goldhammer (Cambridge, Mass., Harvard University Press, 1989), vol. III of *A History of Private Life*, pp. 207–63, Patricia Fumerton, *Cultural Aesthetics: Renaissance Literature and the Practice of Social Ornament* (Chicago, Chicago University Press, 1991), ch. 2 and Alan Stewart, 'The Early Modern Closet Discovered', *Representations*, 50 (1995), 76–100.

is alert to the instability of so-ness when, a few lines later, she thanks him for agreeing to be ruled by her by saying, quite simply, but, by now, with some perplexity, 'O, say so, and so be' (64). This line of enigmatic quibbling, of instability in the indicative of being, runs all the way through the play to its perhaps redemptive reformulation when Cesario meets Sebastian: 'A natural perspective, that is, and is not!' (5.1.215). It matters to the Malvolio plot because, in his attempt to subvert the steward's sanity, Feste turns such riddling against him. '"That that is, is"', he tells Sir Toby (with the assurance that, by this point, what is is not): 'so I, being Master Parson, am Master Parson; for what is "that" but "that"? and "is" but "is"?' (4.2.15–17).

Malvolio does not doubt that Master Parson is Master Parson, even when Feste presents himself in that guise without disguise – just in a different voice. By the same token, however, he persists in a stubborn belief that 'that' is 'that' and 'is' 'is'. He has a self-centred clarity about what he credits which carries him with some dignity through Feste's peculiar questions about Pythagoras' metempsychosis, and whether the soul of one's grandam might haply inhabit a bird. No audience can entirely warm to Malvolio's self-assurance, unchanged since the letter scene, but his persistent protestations of sanity seem the more admirable as his opponents' pranks become redundantly sadistic. Their cruelty is particularly marked in respect of the motif of 'companie or friendship', because, if the plot to incarcerate Malvolio is justified in so far as it obliges him to confront what it means for a man to be truly solitary, it abandons any claim to the moral high ground when Feste assists the steward by bringing him writing materials and agreeing to take a letter to Olivia, but then suppresses the missive – an event of such moment that Shakespeare underscores it in that otherwise null episode where the clown refuses to divulge the letter's contents to Fabian (5.1.1–6).

I have touched, several times, in this paper, on the social dimension of secrecy, and stressed how it is produced, in the early modern period, out of civil intercourse. It should be clear, in consequence, at this late stage, why 'companie or friendship' is so important in *Twelfth Night*. Obviously, in this play of cross-dressing and variant sexuality, there is an interest in the mergings of heterosexual love with same-sex friendship, and with the friendship in heterosexual love as well as the eroticism of same-sex amity. But secrecy impinges on, and gives rise to, friendship (as in the shaping confidences shared between Sebastian and Antonio) because, although the period knew that – as the cynical commonplace put it – three can keep a secret when two of them are away, it was also aware that not to confide a hidden thing was to go the readiest way to public exposure or self-destruction. In trying to 'keepe love secrete', says Lord Julian in *The Book of the Courtier*, it is bad to be 'over secrete' and better to trust a friend with your feelings so that he can help you conceal what you will otherwise, certainly, betray (pp. 284–5). Recall Duke Charles the Hardy, Bacon advises, in his essay 'Of Frendship', who, because he 'would communicate his Secrets with none', damaged his wits. 'The Parable of *Pythagoras* is darke, but true; *Cor ne edito; Eat not the Heart*. Certainly, if a Man would give it a hard Phrase, Those that want *Frends* to open themselves unto, are Canniballs of their owne *Hearts*.'[44]

Bacon's fable from Pythagoras is not the same as Feste's, but something close to what the clown says can be found in Cleland's *Institution*, where, immediately after explaining why a man's friend should not be 'a great pratler', he enthuses:

> O how much am I bound to Gods bounty amongst al the rest of his benefits towardes me, in sending me such a friend! ... In the very first daie of our meeting ... I found my minde so changed and remooued into the place of his, which before that time was in me. Hitherto I could neuer excogitate

[44] *Essayes*, ed. Kiernan, pp. 80–7 (p. 83).

anie reason why I shoulde loue him, but *Pythagoras* his μετεμψύχωσις, and that hee is another my selfe. (p. 197)

Why is a friend so valuable? Cleland's answer is typical of the period: because he is a person 'in whom I dare better trust, and vnto whom I dare discover the most secret thoughtes of my minde with greater confidence then I am able to keepe them my selfe' (*ibid.*). So the dialogue between Feste and Malvolio about the steward's grandmother and a woodcock is not just random nonsense, and more than an insult to the old lady's intelligence. It contributes to the close texture of *Twelfth Night* a riddling reminder that, notwithstanding the resistance of the self-centred steward, the soul can be said, at least in amity, to migrate from one body to another. This is what Viola/Cesario means when s/he speaks of calling 'upon my soul within the house' (above, p. 73), and what Orsino invokes when he promises the assembled lovers that 'A solemn combination shall be made / Of our dear souls' (5.1.382–3).

Malvolio is often seen as excluded from this finale. In one of the best essays on *Twelfth Night*, Anne Barton stresses the fragmentariness of its ending by pointing out that, like Sir Toby and Sir Andrew, the steward 'comes as a figure of violence and leaves unreconciled'. At the end of *As You Like It*, 'Jaques had walked with dignity out of the new society; Malvolio in effect is flung.'[45] This is largely true. Yet the charmed circle of amity does not actively dismiss Malvolio: if anything, Olivia and Orsino do the opposite, acknowledging, in an echo of his own words, that 'He hath been most notoriously abused' and commanding, 'Pursue him, and entreat him to a peace: / He hath not told us of the captain yet' (5.1.378–80). What Orsino reminds the audience of here is that Malvolio is holding 'in durance', at his own suit, the Captain who arrived with Viola in the third scene of the play. This character, almost forgotten, is now freshly important, because he holds Viola's 'maiden weeds' (272ff., 251ff.). I am not myself persuaded that clothes were so constitutive of identity for Shakespeare's original audience that Cesario cannot become Viola until those very clothes are recovered from the Captain. Even Orsino, piquantly intrigued at being affianced to a boy, only says that 'Cesario' will keep his masculine name until 'in other [unspecified] habits you are seen' (386).[46] Yet the gesture of deferral – as against fragmentation – is unmistakable, and compatible with a denouement which straggles its endings out, from the pre-emptive coupling of Maria and Toby, through the betrothal but delayed marriage of Olivia and Sebastian, to the as-yet-unrealized resolution of the Cesario/Viola-Orsino romance. In that delayed conclusion, space is made for Malvolio, his hold over Viola's weeds confirming what his anagrammatic link with her name implies. These characters belong together. Until the steward is reconciled, comedy will not be consummated. Just how he will be persuaded remains one of the secrets of the play.

---

45 '*As You Like It* and *Twelfth Night*: Shakespeare's "Sense of an Ending"' (1972), rpt. in her *Essays, Mainly Shakespearean* (Cambridge, Cambridge University Press, 1994), pp. 91–112 (p. 110).

46 Contrast Stephen Orgel, *Impersonations: The Performance of Gender in Shakespeare's England* (Cambridge, Cambridge University Press, 1996), p. 104.

SHAKESPEARE REWRITING OVID: OLIVIA'S INTERVIEW WITH VIOLA AND THE NARCISSUS MYTH

A. B. TAYLOR

> The writer is always a rewriter, the problem then being to differentiate and authenticate the rewriting. This is executed not by the addition of something wholly new, but by the dismembering and reconstruction of what has already been written.
>
> (Terence Cave on creative imitation of the classics in the sixteenth century)[1]

When Orsino sends her to Olivia with his latest message of love, Viola sees little hope of success for,

> If she be so abandoned to her sorrow
> As it is spoke, she never will admit me.
>
> (1.4.19–20)

Still grief stricken after nearly a year, the young Countess has only recently announced her intention to continue in mournful seclusion for a further seven years;[2] and it is public knowledge that she has also solemnly forsworn any romantic attachment. And yet it takes only a brief display of obstinacy before Viola is admitted, Olivia explaining that hearing of her spirited responses to Malvolio, she has 'allowed your approach rather to wonder at you than to hear you' (1.5.189–91). She has no interest in the message, then, but the messenger is being entertained because 'he' promises to be a diverting curiosity. Yet if Olivia were still 'so abandoned to her sorrow / As it is spoke', the interview would not take place at all. And even if one ignores the incongruity of a 'fair young man' being admitted to the presence of one who has 'abjured the sight / And company of men' (1.2.36–7), here is a young woman, having just publicly announced that she is shutting herself away from the world to spend the foreseeable future weeping and mourning, ready to avail herself of casual diversion.

The evidence indicates that, although she continues to display all the external trappings, Olivia's grief has run its course, and that by the time the play opens, for all the public pronouncements, she is simply a bored young woman with time on her hands. Like others in Illyria where appearance and reality are constantly confused and 'Nothing that is so, is so' (4.1.8), the young Countess is not what she

---

[1] *The Cornucopian Text: Problems of Writing in the French Renaissance* (Oxford, Clarendon Press, 1979), p. 76. I am indebted in this article, as in so much of my work, to the wise counsel of Michael Quinn of University College, Cardiff.

[2] Shakespeare may have in mind the Bible where seven years is traditionally the period of famine (see, for example, Genesis 41.30). In courtly literature like *The Adventures of F.J.*, seven years is also used to signify 'the flower' of a woman's youth. (Reference is to *The Complete Works of George Gascoigne*, ed. J. W. Cunliffe in 2 vols (Cambridge, Cambridge University Press, 1907), vol. 1, p. 430; and *The Geneva Bible* ed. L. E. Berry (Madison, University of Wisconsin Press, 1969)).

seems. And in a dramatic world where it is not until the anagnorisis that 'the glass seems true' (5.1.263), her appearance as the eternally grieving sister is one more 'untrue' image. It is a reminder, too, that, although she may create the impression of maturity with her presence and the command she exercises over her household, Olivia is still, as E. S. Donno, the New Cambridge editor, has reminded us, 'very young indeed'.[3] Both the public extension of her mourning and her going to the extreme lengths of forswearing all men, for example, smack of the impractical idealism of the young, and also have more than a hint of the histrionics in which even the more sensible young ladies of her age sometimes indulge. But her behaviour goes deeper than youthful whimsy: basically, it stems from a lack of interest in and complete indifference to the outside world and a wish not to be bothered by it. As virginal figures on the fringes of life sometimes do, the elegant young Countess, who is comfortable in her reclusive life-style, sees no reason to emerge into the world and suffer its complications and entanglements. Consequently, in a household where time hangs heavy, the young mistress is yet another victim of the 'lethargy' that afflicts various other members in one form or another. And as she languidly allows her life to drift into sterile emptiness, excuses made earlier when Viola was still at the gate, that Olivia was 'sick' or 'asleep' (1.5.134 and 136), carry far more truth than was intended.

The interview which fundamentally transforms her outlook, 'curing' and 'awakening' her to life, is a key moment in the play. It is also a very remarkable and rare example of the 'language of imitation' in Shakespeare, a reminder that imitation of classical texts could be a rich linguistic resource for sixteenth-century writers. The only comparable imitation in the dramatist's work is Prospero's invocation ('Ye elves of hills, brooks, standing lakes and groves' *The Tempest* 5.1.33ff.) where with superb inventiveness and consummate skill, he closely follows Ovid's Medea speech ('montesque amnesque lacusque / Dique omnes nemorum' *Metamorphoses* vii.197ff.).[4] The interview, too, is based on an Ovidian text, the Narcissus myth which with its confusion of appearance and reality and ambience of lethargy has long been recognized as having relevance to the play.[5] But it is imitation of a different order, a carefully crafted and substantial example of 'creative imitation' of a classical text as it was known and practised in the Renaissance.[6] Accordingly, focusing throughout on *Metamorphoses* iii.339–510, Shakespeare disasssembles Ovid's text and, carefully shaping and adapting its various parts

---

[3] *Twelfth Night* (Cambridge, Cambridge University Press, 1985), p. 8.

[4] Reference is to a standard sixteenth-century edition of Ovid's poem containing the notes of Regius and Micyllus, *Metamorphoseon Pub, Ovidii Nasonis* (Venice, 1545).

[5] For important recent considerations of the Narcissus myth and the play, see D. J. Palmer, '*Twelfth Night* and The Myth of Echo and Narcissus', *Shakespeare Survey 32* (1979), pp. 73–8; William C. Carroll, *The Metamorphoses of Shakespearean Comedy* (New Jersey, Princeton University Press, 1985), pp. 80ff.; and Jonathan Bate, *Shakespeare and Ovid* (Oxford, Clarendon Press, 1993), pp. 148–51. Although the eclectic approach to myth fashionable in the sixteenth-century saw a wide variety of traditions associated with Narcissus, the Elizabethans would know that the myth had particular relevance to Illyria's 'lethargy'. When they first met Ovid's myth in the grammar school, for example, they used Natalis Comes's *Mythologiae*, and while he recounts various other traditions associated with the boy, Comes gives prominence to that identifying him with 'inactivity' and 'sluggishness; ('*torpor*'). (See *Mythologiae*, ed. S. Orgel (London and New York, Garland Publishing Inc., 1976), p. 285r; for the use of Comes in the grammar school, see T. W. Baldwin, *Shakspere's Small Latine and Lesse Greeke* 2 vols. (Urbana, University of Illinois Press, 1944), vol. 1, pp. 421 and 436. In *Narcissus and the Invention of Personal History* (London and New York, Garland Publishing Inc., 1985), where he traces the traditions linked to Narcissus through the ages, Kenneth Knoespel shows the association of the boy with '*torpor*' goes back to Ancient Greece and 'an etymological link between the Greek words narcissus and narcotic' (p. 3)).

[6] On imitation in the Renaissance, see Terence Cave, *The Cornucopian Text* and Thomas Greene, *The Light in Troy: Imitation and Discovery in Renaissance Poetry* (New Haven, Connecticut, Yale University Press, 1982).

to the dramatic circumstances, brilliantly reconstructs it to serve his own purposes.

I

A feature of the myths of the innocents in the *Metamorphoses* who also shun love and languidly turn away from the world is the comparison of their beauty to a work of art. Ovid uses this motif ironically, placing it just as they lose their picturesque composure and their lives are thrown into confusion by the advent of passion. Hermaphroditus, for example, is compared to carved ivory figures or lilies preserved in glass as he enters the waters of Salmacis' pool where his world will be shattered (iv.354–5). And Narcissus is compared to a statue of Parian marble as he lies by the pool and sees the non-existent 'boy' who is to inflame and totally confuse him (iii.418–19). The interview where passion first enters the life of Shakespeare's own beautiful young recluse, throwing her into confusion and inflaming her, too, with ardent desire for a non-existent 'boy', begins with a variation on Ovid's motif and the Narcissus image. At Viola's request, Olivia removes her veil and, as she does, compares herself to a painting: 'we will draw the curtain and show you the picture' (1.5.223). The variation from statue to painting which is more in accord with immediate circumstances, may have been suggested by details of Golding's translation of the Parian marble simile which, as we see below, was in Shakespeare's mind at this point.

Although Olivia's self-comparison is accompanied by a sardonic question, 'Is't not well done?', her words remind us that the young Countess has her share of vanity; they also unintentionally throw into relief the stillness and inertia of her life. And confronted by Olivia's 'picture', Viola, who has had to bear her own share of grief and hardship, and yet remains 'fresh and quick' with love, is provoked into a courteous but not unsympathetic reprimand:

> 'Tis beauty truly *blent*, whose *red and white*
> *Nature's own sweet and cunning hand* laid on.
> Lady, you are the cruell'st she alive
> If you will lead these *graces* to the grave
> And leave the world no copy.
> (1.5.228–32: *italics mine*)

Direct and indirect echoes of Narcissus thread this speech. With its image of the red and white of Olivia's complexion skilfully mixed ('truly blent') as if they were paints, together with the reference moments later to Olivia's lips as 'indifferent red' (236), and the subsequent reference in the speech to physical gifts as 'graces', the first line echoes Golding's translation of the mythical boy lying by the pool 'like an ymage made of Marble stone' (3.523), and gazing upon:

> *the perfect grace*
> Of *white and red indifferently bepainted in his face.*
> (3.529–30: *italics mine*)[7]

'*Nature's own sweet and cunning hand*' is also taken from Golding, but this time from the translator's version of the Pythagorean Sermon where the picture of man's brief span begins when '*Dame Nature*' releases him from the womb at birth with '*conning hand*' (15.240).[8] And this description of the brevity of human life leads directly into the great classical caveat

---

[7] Golding is translating '*decusque / Oris, & in niveo mixtum candore ruborem*' (iii.422–3).
(Reference to Golding is to *The xv Bookes of P. Ovidius Naso, entytuled Metamorphosis, translated oute of Latin into English meeter, by Arthur Golding Gentleman* (London, 1567), ed. W. H. D. Rouse (London, 1904, rpt. Centaur Press, 1961).)

[8] Ovid had written that 'Nature moved cunning hands' ('*Artifices natura manus admovit* ...' xv.218) which Golding translates as 'Dame Nature put too cooning hand' (15.240).
(It is the Christian colouring the Calvinistic Golding repeatedly gave to his translation that explains why Shakespeare chose to recall it rather than the original in Viola's speech. For this recurrent but spasmodic feature of his work, see my analysis of the Pythagorean Sermon in 'Melting Earth and Leaping Bulls: Shakespeare's Ovid and Arthur Golding', *Connotations* 4 (1994/5), 192–206).

on woman's vanity, the haunting image of the aged Helen who, as she awaits 'lingring death':

> when shee saw her aged wrincles in
> A glasse, wept also: musing in herself what men had seen (15.255–6)[9]

Even before his heroine actually begins her polite censure of Olivia for leading 'graces to the grave' in line three of the speech, then, the dramatist's thoughts are on Narcissus, childbirth, vanity, and 'tyme the eater up of things'. And the brief censure when it is delivered, recalls moments involving narcissistic figures from two of Shakespeare's other works. The burden of Viola's argument, and details like leaving the world a 'copy' of one's beauty, recall the repeated appeals to the 'lovely boy' of the *Sonnets*. And also echoing in the background as Viola politely censures Olivia's 'picture', is a far more outspoken rebuke of another figure who also scorned love and involvement, Adonis:

> Fie, lifeless picture, cold and senseless stone,
> Well painted idol, image dull and dead,
> Statue contenting but the eye alone
> (*Venus and Adonis* 211–14)

The context in which Ovid's motif is set, as Shakespeare adapts the first element of the myth, sees a resumption of an old argument between the two great writers. Ovid's comparison of Narcissus' youthful beauty to a work of art stems from his belief that only art had permanence in an ever-changing world;[10] the implication is that if the boy had indeed been a work of art, his beauty would have survived instead of simply wasting away. But Olivia's self-comparison to a painting, and Viola's critical response, show once again how little Shakespeare cared for Ovid's aesthetic creed. Equally concerned for the plight of frail beauty amid the 'wastes of time', his firm view was, as is shown by the *Sonnets*, *Venus and Adonis*, and perhaps most splendidly by the magnificent resurrection of Hermione in *The Winter's Tale*, that it is in 'warm life' that salvation lies, not in any 'poor image' or 'cold stone', or 'curtained' 'oily painting' (see 5.3.35ff.). And through Viola, he is here underscoring his conviction that it is in a child, a living 'copy' of the individual, that beauty survives. What is needed, it is implied, is not a retreat from 'all complexities of mire or blood' into man-made art, but a commitment to life and a meaningful use of God's 'graces'. Having already implicitly reminded Olivia that 'God did all', Viola is arguing that Olivia should not bury her heaven-sent gifts 'in the earth' as the 'slouthful' servant did in the Parable of Talents (see Matthew 25.25 and 26), but use them before it is too late.

The interview now appropriates a second element of the Narcissus myth and probably its most celebrated feature, the catalogue of the boy's beauty. As he gazes into the mirror of his pool, Narcissus surveys his eyes, cheeks, neck, and complexion, Ovid concluding that 'he admires all the things for which he himself was admired' ('*Cunctaque miratur, quibus est mirabilis ipse*' iii.424). And Olivia, who, as we have seen, has her share of vanity, now brushes aside Viola's argument to present a catalogue of her own beautiful features. In contrast to the myth, however, Olivia's catalogue has an immediate air of death about it; fastening on the reference to the 'grave', she 'labels' her beauty as if composing a 'will':

> O sir, I will not be so hard-hearted. I will give out divers schedules of my beauty. It shall be inventoried and every particle and utensil labelled to my will, as *item*, two lips, indifferent red; *item*, two grey eyes, with lids to them; *item*, one neck, one chin, and so forth. (233–7)

To her own mind, she is languidly indulging in

[9] The Latin text reads:
> Flet quoque, ut in speculo rugas adspexit aniles,
> Tyndaris et secum cur sit bis rapta requirit.
> (xv.232–3)

[10] It is Ovid's proud claim at the poem's conclusion, for instance, that his own 'art' ('*opus*') will survive 'the anger of Jove, war, fire, and the ravages of time' ('*Iovis ira . . . ignis . . . ferrum . . . edax vetustas*' xv.871–2).

witty repartee; but it is as she is ironically and ominously 'tombing' her own 'unused beauty', just as the narcissistic boy of *Sonnet 7* threatened to do, that Viola realizes why she cannot love:

> I see you what you are, you are too proud (239)

It is the culmination of the subtextual imagery linking Olivia and Narcissus for, as D. J. Palmer has pointed out in an influential article, it identifies the young Countess with the mythical boy.[11] Narcissus turned away from the world and shunned love because 'his delicate beauty was mixed with unyielding pride' ('*in tenera tam dura superbia forma*' iii.354), and Olivia's 'most radiant, exquisite, and unmatchable beauty' (163) is similarly infected. Hence, like Narcissus, who realized too late that 'plenty has made me poor' ('*inopem me copia fecit*' 466), she, too, to use the words of the *Sonnets*, is making 'a famine where abundance lies' (1.7). Moreover, although she cloaks her vanity in sardonic humour, to this point in the interview, in the elegant, lethargic setting of the household which is her retreat, her eyes, like the boy's in his refined, languid *locus amoenus*, have been on her own image.[12]

II

One now becomes aware of the extent of Shakespeare's imitation of Ovid's myth for at this point Viola becomes Echo to Olivia's Narcissus.[13] Just as Ovid's nymph echoed words of love to the disdainful boy in an attempt to persuade him to love, so does Viola to the disdainful Countess. Initially, when asked how Orsino loves Olivia, she echoes her master; like Echo, 'she reports words she has heard' ('*audita ... verba reportat*' 369). The accents of Orsino's clichéd yet somehow intensely passionate speech sound through as she tells Olivia that her master loves her 'With adorations, fertile tears, / With groans that thunder love, with sighs of fire' (244–5). And then when asked what she would do, becoming even more like Ovid's nymph, she echoes her own frustration in love:

> Make me a willow cabin at your gate
> And call upon my soul within the house,
> Write loyal cantons of contemnèd love,
> And sing them loud even in the dead of night;
> Halloo your name to the reverberate hills,
> And make the babbling gossip of the air
> Cry out 'Olivia!' O, you should not rest
> Between the elements of air and earth
> But you should pity me. (257–65)

As she reveals love as a passionate, urgent power, set 'Between the elements of air and earth' and driving those it afflicts into a restless pursuit of its goal, her message is that of her mythical counterpart – 'let us meet' ('*coeamus*' iii.387).[14] But ironically, like Echo, Viola is only a voice, 'calling', 'singing', 'hallooing', and making the nymph herself, 'the babbling gossip of the air', 'cry out', and the hills 'reverberate' with hopeless love. And the loved one, Olivia, who is pictured as having the absolute power that Echo gave to Narcissus ('*sit tibi copia nostri*'

---

11 '*Twelfth Night* and The Myth of Echo and Narcissus', p. 74.
(It is also evocative that as Olivia emerges as a Narcissus figure, Viola continues: 'But if you were the devil, you are fair' (240). Amid the cluster of traditions associated with the mythical boy, the Elizabethans would have known the medieval associations of Narcissus with the fallen angels who 'by reflecting upon themselves, and admiration of their owne excellency, forgot their dependence upon their creator' (George Sandys, *Ovids Metamorphosis englyshed mythologiz'd and Represented in figures* (London, 1632), p. 106).

12 This lends considerable irony to her statement that she has granted the interview '*to wonder at*' Viola. To this point, in her girlish vanity, it is not Viola that she has 'wondered at' but herself.

13 Her general affinity to Ovid's retiring nymph in the play has been the subject of much discussion: recently, for example, Jonathan Bate considers that in the role of Echo, Viola 'redeems the play' (see *Shakespeare and Ovid*, pp. 149ff.).

14 As Raphael Regius reminds us with his annotation on this word, besides being a request to meet, it also carried a sense of physical desire and meant 'let us lie down together, copulate' ('*Coire ... & convenire & concumbere significat*').

('I am yours to command') iii.392), is like the legendary boy, isolated by pride in a shadowy, world.

At the very beginning of the interview, as they first engage in conversation, Viola and Olivia make reference to the 'divinity' of love, its 'profanation' by the incognoscenti, the lover's suit as 'doctrine' contained in the 'chapters' of his 'bosom', and his insincerity as 'heresy' (1.5.209–19). In polite, aristocratic circles, such pseudo-religious terminology was conventional and gave what were often casual liaisons the appearance of great substance.[15] But Shakespeare is not content with such clichéd romantic language for long and it suddenly deepens into actual religious terminology with 'God doing all' as the Creator and endowing men with 'graces'. A similar depth is imparted to trite, conventional language in Viola's speech where the tormented, sleepless lover, his anguished state symbolized by the willow, serenades his disdainful lady through the night in the hope that she might 'pity' him.[16] But this time cliché is not suddenly transformed; it is infused with genius from the first. However, amid the speech's passionate and beautiful lyricism, there is one particularly arresting phrase, 'my soul within the house'. Apparently sounding a beautiful but merely lyric note, this relates the speech *via* a religious image to the play's central themes of sterility and fruitfulness. It recalls the magnificent Pauline image of the 'soul' within the 'earthly house' of the body from 2 Corinthians 5, an epistle which warns that men should not 'rejoice in the face' (12) and 'live unto themselves' (15) but seek a renewal of their life. In a way that is characteristic of his eristic approach to the Roman poet, Shakespeare is thus both using and going beyond Ovid and continuing to invest his imitation of the latter's pagan myth of physical beauty with profound spiritual undertones.

The speech proves the turning point of the interview. Brief and hypothetical though it is, it has apparently offered Olivia the novel prospect of herself as an object of real desire; and this does more for her than any amount of reasoning has been able to do for suddenly, all opposition forgotten, she falls in love. The irony, of course, is that the feelings expressed in the speech have nothing to do with her; they are no more than an *echo* of Viola's passionate but frustrated love for Orsino.[17] But the end result is that Olivia becomes even more like Narcissus; for her, as for her mythical counterpart, it is now a case of 'a sweet boy beloved in vain' ('*Heu frustra dilecte puer*' iii.500) and of 'gazing insatiably on a beautiful, deceiving form' ('*Spectat inexpleto mendacem lumine formam*' 439).

Ovid had opened the Narcissus myth with a witty parody of the words of the Delphic Oracle in Tiresias' prophecy that the boy would come to maturity '*only if he did not know himself*' ('*si se non noverit*' 348). And Shakespeare, again bridling at negative elements in Ovid, concludes the interview by reversing this opening motif. Hearing Viola, Olivia has at last come to know herself, and finally been awakened to the depths and needs of her own

---

15 The religious language of love in aristocratic affairs can be briefly illustrated by *The Adventures of Master F.J.*: rising early because of his longing for his mistress, for example, F.J. is a 'knight' at 'Morrow Masse' serving his 'Saint with double devotion' (401), and when she later attends his sickbed, his mistress 'bedewed his temples with sweete water' saying 'Good servaunt be whoale' (426–7).

16 Again cf. *The Adventures of F.J.* where the willow is repeatedly used as a symbol of the suffering rejection can bring (see 418 and 421), and where, when his lady disdains him, F.J. writes a poem 'to plead for pitie' (450).

17 It is symptomatic of the general malaise prevailing in the aptly named country of Illyria that a thorough corruption of language takes place. Both Viola's great speeches on love, to Olivia and to Orsino (2.4.110ff.), for example, have an air of duplicity and mendacity. The difference is that her corruption of language tends to have a healing effect; the corruption of words by others – for example, Orsino's strained interpretation of Olivia's rejection of his suit (1.1.32ff.), Malvolio's tortured gloss on Maria's letter (2.5.84ff.) – merely causes reality to recede.

nature. For this Narcissus figure self-knowledge will be the key to the ripeness her Ovidian counterpart never reached. And the process begins as Olivia falls in love with the deceptive form of the 'boy' before her: for her, in contrast to Ovid's Narcissus, the advent of passion does not mark the beginning of a slow decline toward death but of a renewal of her appetite for life. No longer will her richness make her poor, and in a very different sense to the Narcissus of the *Metamorphoses*, Olivia has been brought to the realization that 'what I seek is in myself' ('*Quod cupio, mecum est*' 466). She therefore becomes most like Narcissus in the very moment that she is most unlike him and the lethargic spell is broken. She herself now realizes that she should not 'rest' between 'the elements of air and earth' and, having been confronted by the illusion of love, her life is to resolve into an urgent pursuit of its reality,[18] a pursuit in which, although often frantic and undignified, she is to be refreshingly free from concern for self and able to express the innate richness and generosity of her nature.

Of his own borrowings from classical literature, John Donne wrote, 'If I doe borrow any thing of Antiquitie, besides that I make account that I pay it to posterity, with as much and as good: You shall still finde mee to acknowledge it, and to thanke ... him ... that hath digg'd out treasure for mee.'[19] Shakespeare was of a like mind for he now closes the interview by tacitly and gracefully acknowledging his debt to Ovid and the Narcissus myth as both women closely echo the Latin text. Viola leaves with the wish that Olivia one day endure what her master endures:

> Love make his heart of flint that you shall love,
> And let your fervour, like my master's be
> Placed in contempt. (276–8)

This recalls the prayer to Nemesis of one of Narcissus' suitors who is placed in contempt ('*despectus*' iii.404) – 'So may he love and be reduced to despair' ('*sic amet ipse licet, sic non potiatur amato*' 405). And moments after Viola has left, Olivia declares:

> Methinks I feel this youth's perfections
> With an invisible and subtle stealth
> To creep in at mine eyes. (286–8)

which echoes the moment Narcissus is 'silently overcome by the sight of the beautiful image before him' ('*visae correptus imagine formae*' 416).

From the impact of Erasmus analysing the problems of emulation and the preservation of the writer's own identity when imitating the classics in works such as *Ciceronianus*, right down to the schoolroom where masters like William Kempe instructed boys to imitate 'Tullyes Epistles' 'altered with many varieties at once',[20] creative imitation of specific classical texts was as central to Humanist culture in England as it was elsewhere in sixteenth-century Europe. And as two excellent recent studies remind us, creative imitation was often positively discordant: in his seminal and wide-ranging study of imitation in Renaissance poetry in Europe, Thomas Greene refers to a special category he calls 'dialectical' imitation which is based on an awareness of the 'incompleteness' of the classical subtext;[21] while in his examination of the problems of writing in the French Renaissance, Terence Cave defines all imitation of the classics as 'a kind of intertextual dialogue or conflict'.[22] It is against such a backcloth that Shakespeare's contentious imitation of Ovid's myth should be seen. As he rewrites Ovid's text in a radical fashion, making the self-knowledge motif the conclusion instead of

[18] For a stimulating consideration of Spenser's similar investment of the Narcissus myth with Platonic undertones, see Calvin R. Edwards, 'The Narcissus Myth in Spenser's Poetry', *Studies in Philology* 74 (1977), 63–88.

[19] Prefatory Epistle to 'The Progresse of the Soule', cited by Thomas Greene, *The Light in Troy*, p. 47.

[20] See 'The Method of Schooling' in *The Education of Children in Learning* (London, 1588).

[21] Greene, see pp. 45ff.

[22] Cave, *The Cornucopian Text*, p. 36.

introduction, and rearranging its various parts so that it becomes life-affirming rather than life-denying, one's eye is inevitably taken by the ongoing arguments with his favourite classical poet; but the real importance of this fractious imitation of Ovid is its function within the overall context of the play.

When Viola arrives in Illyria and proposes assuming disguise as Orsino's 'eunuch' (1.2.52), she is doing no more than unwittingly adapt herself to an environment which is sterile and in which 'Nothing that is so, is so.' The tone is set in Illyria by Orsino and Olivia who both seem to be what they are not and who both have adopted barren life-styles. Apparently engaged in society, the one observing the rituals of courtship, the other those of mourning, in reality, both have turned away from the world and retreated into themselves to live a life of self-centred and barren seclusion. Moreover, in their elegant retreats, both are bemused by shadows for like the mythical boy, they dwell, in their different ways, on their own images and reflexions. When the inner sanctum of Olivia's world is penetrated, as we have seen, beneath the dark mourning veil is a beautiful, young victim of arid self-fixation. And Orsino suffers, albeit in a less obvious way, from the same condition. The 'image of the creature / That is beloved' (2.4.18–19) which he spends hours contemplating when 'canopied with bowers', is carefully modelled after his own constant and idealistic nature. It has long been recognized that the noble duke is in love with an idea of love but the extent to which that idea is a subtle projection of his own image has, perhaps, been insufficiently appreciated. And, like the mythical boy in his fascination with this 'shadow' of love, he is careful to preserve his isolation, fearing exposure to the real world would show him what Narcissus secretly knew was true, that 'what you seek is nowhere' ('*quod petis est nusquam*' iii.433).[23] Finally, the play's preoccupation with the theme of narcissism is underscored by the presence in the sub-plot of Malvolio, patently 'sick of self-love' (1.5.86) and periodically retiring to the seclusion of the garden to practise his 'behaviour to his own shadow' (2.5.16). Where the steward is different is that in his case, there is an absence of any sense of rich gifts being wasted; a pastiche of Narcissus, he possesses comparative pride and vanity but is conspicuously lacking in the grace and personal beauty that went some way towards explaining the boy's fascination with himself.

For Orsino and Olivia, the play is a movement from shadow into sunlight, from the confusion of an unreal world where they are 'jaded' by uncertain and deceptive 'images', 'dreams', and 'fancies', into the reality of a 'daylight' world where confusion dissolves and 'appearances seem true'. The action turns on the exposure of their narcissism. As she does with Olivia, Viola holds a mirror up to Orsino, making him aware of his stagnant life-style; the turning point is again a key speech, in this case – 'She sat like patience on a monument' (2.4.114). Consequently, responding to the promptings of love, he, too, awakens to life, dispenses with shadows and emerges into the real world to claim Viola's hand and take his place in the community. For Olivia, exposure and release come, of course, with the interview, the moment when, freed from the confines of the imagination, she begins to change from a proud, vain, self-centred girl into a mature and giving woman. Her progress to reality, which is reflected in a newly discovered sense of time ('The clock upbraids me with the waste of time' 3.1.129), is to culminate in union with Sebastian and the appearance of 'the glorious sun' (4.3.1). For Malvolio the movement of the main plot is reversed; he moves from shadow into darkness, from confusion into madness. The box-tree scene shows his foolishness can only be exposed to

[23] For discussion of Orsino as a Narcissus figure, see D. J. Palmer, '*Twelfth Night* and The Myth of Echo and Narcissus', 74, and my 'Narcissus, Olivia, and a Greek Tradition', *Notes and Queries* 241 (1997), 58–61.

others: he himself is so encased by pride and vanity in his private world that he is totally incapable of realising it. Predictably finding his own image in the 'mirror' of Maria's letter, he just as predictably plunges even deeper into self- fixation and egocentric fantasy. Because of his overweening *philautia* and a spiteful, mean nature that is incapable of love, it is his lot to remain in isolation mocked and driven to madness by uncertain shadows. He stands as a powerful warning against what Orsino and Olivia have escaped: the ultimate consequences of self-centred absorption into 'the world of the imagination' and the mockery and torment that comes with subjection to 'its inconstant shapes'.[24]

[24] In both this play and *A Midsummer Night's Dream*, as Jonathan Bate has pointed out in his admirable study, *Shakespeare and Ovid*, the dramatist is preoccupied with the 'world of the imagination and its inconstant shapes' (see pp. 146ff.).

'VOICE POTENTIAL': LANGUAGE AND SYMBOLIC CAPITAL IN *OTHELLO*

LYNNE MAGNUSSON

Before Brabanzio complains to the Venetian senators of Othello's marriage, Iago warns Othello that 'the magnifico is much beloved, / And hath in his effect a voice potential / As double as the Duke's'. Brabanzio's words will exert power – the power to 'divorce you, / Or put upon you ... restraint or grievance' (1.2.12–15). Their power, however, will depend not upon Brabanzio's rhetorical skill but instead upon his social position – that is, both on his aristocratic status ('magnifico') and on the accumulated credit he has with his auditors ('much beloved'). How his speech is received will depend less on what he says than on the social site from which it is uttered. Othello rebuts Iago's position, but he does not dispute Iago's presupposition that linguistic competence counts for less than rank or otherwise attributed status in this matter of 'voice potential': 'My services which I have done the signory', he responds, 'Shall out-tongue his complaints' (1.2.18–19). In the event, Othello's voice does outweigh Brabanzio's, with an unanticipated element affecting the reception of their discourse and the outcome of the scene: that is, the exigency of the military threat to Cyprus.

In 'The Economics of Linguistic Exchanges', the French sociologist Pierre Bourdieu develops a market analogy to explain how utterances receive their values in particular contexts and how, in turn, the conditions of reception affect discourse production. Giving discourse pragmatics a sociological turn, he asks questions critical to the Senate scene and to other situations in *Othello*: whose speech is it that gets recognized? whose speech is listened to and obeyed? who remains silent? and whose speech fails to gain attention or credit? In Bourdieu's account, language in any situation will be worth what those who speak it are deemed to be worth: its price will depend on the symbolic power relation between the speakers, on their respective levels of 'symbolic capital'.[1] The price a speaker receives for his or her discourse will not, however, be an invariable function of class position or relative status, even in a rigidly hierarchical society. Instead, as Othello's positive reception in the context of the Turkish threat suggests, the price will vary with varying market conditions.

Focusing on a reading of the Senate scene (1.3) and other public situations, in this paper I will sketch out the complex and variable linguistic market that shapes and refigures 'voice potential' in *Othello*. Gender, class, race, necessity, linguistic ingenuity and a number of other competing measures enter into the moment-by-moment relations of symbolic power that affect discourse value – that affect, for example, how Brabanzio's charges against Othello or

[1] 'The Economics of Linguistic Exchanges', *Social Science Information*, 16 (1977), 645–68; p. 648. Much of the material in this essay is recirculated as 'Price Formation and the Anticipation of Profit' in *Language and Symbolic Power*, ed. John B. Thompson (Cambridge, Mass., 1991), pp. 66–89.

Desdemona's request to accompany Othello to Cyprus are heard. This paper will explore not only discourse reception in *Othello*, but also the force within Shakespeare's play of Bourdieu's hypothesis that a person's discourse production is conditioned by anticipatory adjustments to discourse reception. Finally, I will focus on Iago as a rhetorician and argue for a new perspective on Iago's rhetorical performance in terms of his efforts to manipulate the linguistic market in *Othello*.

In enunciating a sociology of speech in opposition to formal linguistics, Bourdieu argues that 'Language is not only an instrument of communication or even of knowledge, but also an instrument of power. A person speaks not only to be understood but also to be believed, obeyed, respected, distinguished.'[2] One main event in Act 1 of *Othello* is the contest of voices between Brabanzio and Othello. What is at issue between them is whose voice will be given credit, whose voice will have power to shape the ensuing course of events. This criterion for evaluating a particular discourse is foregrounded even before Brabanzio and Othello enter the Senate chamber, as the Senators endeavour to digest the news of the Turkish fleets: the Duke observes that 'There is no composition in these news / That gives them *credit*' (1.3.1–2; emphasis added). As the discursive contest between Brabanzio and Othello proceeds, the verbal performance of each speaker receives a summary evaluation from the Duke. Whereas Brabanzio's accusation draws the caution that 'To vouch this is no proof' (106), the Duke responds with approval to Othello's colourful account of wooing Desdemona: 'I think this tale would win my daughter, too' (170). Although the Duke apparently evaluates intrinsic features of the linguistic performance of each speaker, it is situational context, as I have already suggested, more than verbal competence that accounts for Othello's profit and Brabanzio's loss.

The carefully staged entrance of senator and general provides a vivid theatrical emblem for the dynamic variation in relative power. First, the significance of the entrance is prepared by the Duke's order to write 'post-post-haste' (46) to Marcus Luccicos, a character not otherwise identified except by his unavailability at this time of crisis. The verification of his absence heightens the importance of 'the man', in Brabanzio's words, 'this Moor, whom now' the Duke's 'special mandate for the state affairs / Hath hither brought' (71–3). A stage direction signals the arrival of a large group of characters, including '*Brabanzio, Othello, Roderigo, Iago, Cassio, and officers*'. The First Senator announces the arrival selectively, singling out 'Brabanzio and the valiant Moor' (47) and relegating to lesser importance those left unnamed. The structure of the Duke's greeting encapsulates the power dynamic of the situation, articulating the priorities of the moment:

> Valiant Othello, we must straight employ you
> Against the general enemy Ottoman.
> *(To Brabanzio)* I did not see you. Welcome, gentle
> signor.
> We lacked your counsel and your help tonight.
> (48–51)

Othello is greeted first; the need for his military skills accounts for his precedence. Brabanzio is greeted in second place, with the conversational repair work nonetheless signalling a recognition of his claim, based on rank, to first place.

This account of how Othello's voice gains ascendancy within the immediate situation in no way exhausts the complexity of the linguistic market depicted in the Senate scene. Another principal speaker whose voice power is at issue in the scene is Desdemona. Answering the Duke's summons, she speaks first to confirm Othello's account of their courtship and later to make a request of her own, to accompany Othello to the war zone. In both cases her speech wins credit, in the first instance solidifying the Duke's acceptance of the marriage and silencing Brabanzio's complaint and in the

[2] Bourdieu, 'Economics', p. 648.

second instance gaining her permission to go with Othello. In making the request to accompany Othello, Desdemona does show her devotion to Othello, but she also asserts her separate and independent voice, her own claim to have her wish heard even after he has already publicly requested accommodation for her in Venice. Desdemona shows herself by Renaissance standards a bold and self-confident speaker in a setting whose formality and importance would silence most speakers, especially – one might expect – a woman. Her verbal behaviour in the scene and in the play as a whole is not consistent with any simple stereotype of feminine speech, especially not with the Renaissance commonplace concerning silence as woman's eloquence. In her initial appearances in the play, Desdemona is an assured and self-confident speaker. That is not to say that stereotyped gender roles do not come into play here. Consider, for example, Othello's embedded narrative of the courtship as 'mutual' recognition: 'She loved me for the dangers I had passed, / And I loved her that she did pity them' (166–7). What could better exemplify the standard clichés about male and female roles in cross-sex conversation prevalent even today than Othello's account of how he talked and she responded?[3] When Othello told over 'the story of my life' (128), Desdemona 'gave me for my pains a world of sighs'[4] and 'swore in faith 'twas strange, 'twas passing strange, / 'Twas pitiful, 'twas wondrous pitiful' (158–60). And yet, whatever we are to make of the accuracy of Othello's report, such self-effacing speech behaviour is not Desdemona's predominant manner in the play.

Traditional readings of *Othello* have often focused, as I am doing now, on the complex speech patterns of the characters. In such readings, the *raison d'être* for an utterance is the speaker's character, or essential nature. Dramatic language is said to construct character: whereas in life language expresses character, in his plays Shakespeare shapes language to make it seem that language expresses pre-existing character.[5] In this view, the divergence from received stereotypes of female speech evident in Desdemona's self-assured and eloquent public speaking is to be explained as a particularizing and richly complicating mark of her essential character. But in a play so insistently dialogic as *Othello* – a play so intently focused on how one character's conversational contributions shape and direct the words, thoughts, and actions of another – it seems particularly pertinent to argue a different case, to take up Bourdieu's thesis that '[t]he *raison d'être* of a discourse . . . is to be found in the socially defined site from which it is uttered'.[6] Bourdieu's account of the social production of discourse emphasizes anticipatory adjustment, and offers a fruitful way to account for the speech patterns of Desdemona and other characters in *Othello*.

'[O]ne of the most important factors bearing on linguistic production', Bourdieu argues, is 'the anticipation of profit which is durably inscribed in the language habitus, in the form of an anticipatory adjustment (without conscious anticipation) to the objective value of one's discourse.'[7] What one says, how one says it, and

[3] For overviews of research on cross-sex conversations, see Deborah James and Sandra Clarke, 'Women, Men, and Interruptions: A Critical Review' and Deborah James and Janice Drakich, 'Understanding Gender Differences in Amount of Talk: A Critical Review of Research', in *Gender and Conversational Interaction*, ed. Deborah Tannen (New York and Oxford, 1993), pp. 231–80 and 281–312.

[4] Here I quote Q1's 'world of sighs' instead of F's 'world of kisses'. While still a non-verbal response, the Folio's version gives a significantly different turn to Desdemona's portrayal here. If Desdemona is so forward here with her kisses, it is hard to reconcile with Othello's remark later in the speech that he spoke of his love upon a 'hint' (1.3.165) from her. I am grateful to Paul Werstine for drawing my attention to this variant.

[5] Virginia Mason Vaughan notes critics' fascination with language in *Othello* and the general tendency to relate language patterns to essential character in the Introduction to *'Othello': New Perspectives* (London and Toronto, 1991), pp. 14–15.

[6] Bourdieu, 'Economics', p. 657.

[7] *Ibid.*, p. 653.

whether one speaks at all in any given situation is strongly influenced, in this view, by the 'practical expectation ... of receiving a high or low price for one's discourse'.[8] An utterance, then, inscribes an expectation of profit, an estimate of the likelihood that the speaker will be believed, recognized, obeyed. This expectation will not, in most instances, derive solely or even in the main part from an assessment of the immediate social situation; it cannot be entirely accounted for by the immediate relation of speaker to listener. The context of reception which shapes a speaker's linguistic production has a history, and it is that history Bourdieu tries to account for by positing the 'language habitus' of the speaker. That language habitus is a practical memory, built up through the accumulated history of speech contexts in which a speaker has functioned and received recognition or censure. The language habitus is shaped by the history of a person's most sustained social connections, by a person's cumulative dialogue with others.

But let us begin with Desdemona and class. Desdemona does not enter the play as the stereotypical silent and modest woman, but rather as an aristocratic speaker whose discourse is full of the assurance and self-confidence of her class habitus. This can be seen not only in the remarkable ease with which she speaks before the Duke and Senators, but also in the basic facts that she speaks at all and that she initiates speech topics. If we consider how it could be that speech patterns inscribe a speaker's expectation of profit, we need to look not only at the internal constitution of the speeches but also at turn-taking and access to the floor. '[T]he linguist', Bourdieu remarks, 'regards the *conditions for the establishment of communication* as already secured, whereas, in real situations, that is the essential question.'[9] To read the power relations of the scene one needs to observe the access to speech in this formal Senate setting of those who speak. Furthermore, one needs to consider what shapes the silence or non-participation of Roderigo, Cassio, the soldiers – and, most important for the developing action, the silence of Iago. Of course, in a play, considerations apart from those of real life will affect the access of speakers to the floor. The distinction, for example, between major and minor characters within any plot structure will help account for who speaks at length and whose speech is sparing. Nonetheless, one can still reasonably argue that the configuration of speakers Shakespeare represents in the Senate scene primarily reflects the power dynamics of the urgent situation as played out in a formal setting of the kind that regulates speaker access to a very high degree. Desdemona's confidence in her access to the floor, borne out by the Duke's solicitous question – 'What would you, Desdemona?' (247) – suggests a history of access, the history of her class habitus.

This discourse history is also emphatically suggested by Desdemona's conversation with Cassio in 3.3 regarding her commitment to mediate on his behalf with Othello. 'Be thou assured' is the opening phrase and repeated motif of her talk:

Be thou assured, good Cassio, I will do
All my abilities in thy behalf. (1–2)

... *Do not doubt*, Cassio,
But I will have my lord and you again
As friendly as you were. (5–7)

... and *be you well assured*
He shall in strangeness stand no farther off
Than in a politic distance. (11–13)

Do not doubt that. Before Emilia here
I give thee warrant of thy place. *Assure thee* ...
(19–20; emphasis added)

When she moves Cassio's suit to Othello, her whole manner bespeaks this assurance of a ready acquiescence to her request – her repeated insistence that he set a time to see Cassio, her understated persuasion tactics, her assumption that she has a role to play in Othello's public affairs, her low assessment of

8 *Ibid.*, p. 655.
9 *Ibid.*, p. 648.

the speech act risk involved in making the request, and finally her minimizing of her suit:

> Why, this is not a boon.
> 'Tis as I should entreat you wear your gloves,
> Or feed on nourishing dishes, or keep you warm ...
> ... Nay, when I have a suit
> Wherein I mean to touch your love indeed,
> It shall be full of poise and difficult weight,
> And fearful to be granted. (77–83)

This assurance is not simply the naïvety of a new wife about her power to sway a husband she scarcely knows. Desdemona's assurance inscribes the history of her prior speech reception, the ease that marks the dominant classes and exempts them from speech tension, linguistic insecurity, and self censoring. The crisis for Desdemona in this play comes as a surprising alteration in how her speech is received, specifically by Othello. The change in speech reception, it is possible to argue, also makes for a change in Desdemona.

If Desdemona's 'voice potential' in the Senate scene and later bespeaks her class habitus, to what extent can be read a history of voice inscribed in Othello's speech? Othello's long speeches in Act 1 can be distinguished partly by their amplitude, by a high degree of elaboration and embellishment. Characteristic are the nominal and adjectival doublets, in some instances marked by syntactic strangenesses bearing some relation to hendiadys:[10] Othello speaks of 'circumscription and confine' (1.2.27), 'the flinty and steel couch of war' (1.3.229), 'A natural and prompt alacrity' (231), 'such accommodation and besort' (237), being 'free and bounteous to her mind' (265), 'serious and great business' (267), 'speculative and officed instruments' (270), 'all indign and base adversities' (273). In what George Wilson Knight called the 'Othello music', there is, E. A. J. Honigmann has suggested, a complicating note of bombast.[11] It is an eloquence that displays its eloquent performance, not – like Desdemona's – an eloquence that bespeaks its adequacy. Apparently at odds with this high performance speech is Othello's familiar disclaimer:

> Rude am I in my speech,
> And little blessed with the soft phrase of peace,
> ...
> And little of this great world can I speak
> More than pertains to feats of broils and battle.
> And therefore little shall I grace my cause
> In speaking for myself. Yet, by your gracious patience,
> I will a round unvarnished tale deliver
> Of my whole course of love ...
> (1.3.81–2; 86–91)

While I argued earlier that it is not primarily the distinction of Othello's verbal performance that accounts for his voice power in the scene, it is nonetheless untrue that he delivers 'a round', or plain, 'unvarnished tale' (90). Verbal virtuosity, and not plainness, marks his tale. Othello's discourse style, then, blends linguistic insecurity and linguistic effort. Not, as with Desdemona, ease and assurance, but instead some degree of tension characterizes Othello's discourse production. And, by the logic of Bourdieu's hypothesis that discourse production is shaped by anticipated discourse reception, it is not the aristocratic insider who will feel a performance compulsion, an impulse to linguistic overreaching, in the accustomed formality of the senate chamber. Hence we can see how Othello's distinctive speech patterns may have a social motive: a man of great talent without so consistent and homogeneous a history of speech-making and speech reception as the dominant speakers among the Venetians may well overreach in his speech, and a highly formalized, institutionalized setting will increase

[10] On hendiadys in Shakespeare, see George T. Wright, 'Hendiadys and *Hamlet*', *PMLA*, 96 (1981), 168–93.

[11] G. Wilson Knight, 'The *Othello* Music', in *The Wheel of Fire: Interpretations of Shakespearian Tragedy* (Oxford, 1930), pp. 97–119; E. A. J. Honigmann, 'Shakespeare's 'Bombast'', in *Shakespeare's Styles: Essays in Honour of Kenneth Muir*, ed. Philip Edwards, Inga-Stina Ewbank, and G. K. Hunter (Cambridge, 1980), 151–62; pp. 158–9.

the likelihood of speech tension.[12] As Bourdieu argues in his efforts to characterize the speech of aspiring groups, 'the greater the gap between recognition and mastery, the more imperative the need for the self-corrections aimed at ensuring the *revaluing of the linguistic product* by a particularly intensive mobilization of the linguistic resources, and the greater the tension and containment that they demand'.[13] This helps to explain why Othello, as a person of colour and an exotic outsider, might – even without making conscious adjustments – tend to mobilize his verbal resources more fully than Venetian speakers of the dominant group. In language terms, what he does is to try harder.

As we have seen, trying harder to produce well-crafted discourse may not always pay off, since a discourse's value depends on the power relations obtaining in a particular market. Not all the characters in the play respond in the same way to a felt gap between the recognition they commonly receive and their verbal mastery. Consider Iago, who early on in the play registers his perception of a gap between recognition and mastery in the assertion: 'I know my price, I am worth no worse a place' (1.1.11). Iago is keenly aware of a gap between his own considerable skills – including his verbal skills – and the limited advantages that readily come his way through their deployment. This shows in the extreme contempt he expresses for the linguistic accents of other characters – a contempt bound up in his recognition that the limited verbal repertoires of some others nonetheless garner them easy profits that his own greater rhetorical expertise cannot attain. At the start of the play, Iago derides the 'bombast circumstance' (1.1.13) of Othello's talk, but the intensity of his resentment against the speech of others is most strongly illustrated in his reaction to Cassio's conversation with Desdemona upon their arrival in Cyprus. Shakespeare takes great care to draw his audience's attention to the courtier-like politeness of Cassio's speech here and elsewhere. When Iago derogates Cassio's style, delivering sarcastic asides about his gestural and verbal courtesies, he is not, I think, voicing resentment that his lower-class position excludes him from the verbal finesse of a gentlemanly discourse. Iago is a verbal chameleon; he knows how to speak like Cassio. What Iago resents is how easily Cassio's speech gains credit with his auditors, a credit Iago could not earn by employing the same speech patterns. Iago devalues the products of civil conversation not because he cannot replicate them but because he is not socially positioned to receive advantage from them. Cassio, Iago remarks to Roderigo, has 'an eye can stamp and counterfeit advantages' (2.1.243–4). What Iago expresses is a keen awareness that different people can draw different profits from the same discourse – that Cassio's gentlemanly status and good looks make even the very motion of his eyes able to garner an advantage his own finest verbal performance could not attain in situations like the conversation with the aristocratic Desdemona. In *Othello*, Iago is – as many scholars have previously noted – a consummate rhetorician. But he is a rhetorician keenly aware that the prize for best speaker cannot be won with polished verbal skills.

The significant fact about Iago's discourse in the senate scene is that he does not speak. His silence signals his slight chance of profit in that formal public setting. Whether with full consciousness or not, Iago as rhetorician assesses the conditions of the linguistic market in which he operates and chooses tools and timing that will work to gain him profit. Adapting Bourdieu's suggestions, we can generalize that rhetorical

[12] Clearly, with Othello, this linguistic overreaching, with its exotic touches, has become a habit that has itself received a positive reception in various settings (e.g., in Brabanzio's household), thus adding a motive beyond linguistic insecurity for Othello to reproduce the style. Hence, this encoded discourse history may even be consistent with a proud and apparently self-assured delivery in 1.3, but it nonetheless anticipates Othello's susceptibility to Iago's persuasions.

[13] Bourdieu, 'Economics', p. 658.

mastery consists not merely in the capacity for discourse production but also in 'the capacity for appropriation and appreciation; it depends, in other words, on the capacity ... to impose the criteria of appreciation most favourable to [one's] own products'.[14] This helps to explain Iago's preference for private conversational settings, for in the less restricted discourse conditions of talk between friends he can more readily capture the floor and win an appreciation for his speech products.

In the concluding movement of this paper, however, I will concentrate on Iago's rhetorical expertise as exercised within the constraints of public occasions, where he exhibits rhetorical strategies substantially different than in conversation. One of his key strategies for public situations is voice mediation. Where his own voice has little chance of success, Iago appropriates other voices to his use. The play opens with Iago commenting on how he (like a typical Elizabethan suitor) negotiated through mediators for the place, lost to Cassio, as Othello's lieutenant: 'Three great ones of the city, / In personal suit to make me his lieutenant, / Off-capped to him; ... / But he ... / Nonsuits my mediators' (1.1.8–15). But Iago by no means restricts his tactics of voice mediation to this institutionalized form. Act 1, scene 1 also provides, in the role Iago constructs for Roderigo, a characteristic example of how Iago appropriates the credit of an intermediate voice. In the effort to fire Brabanzio up against Othello, Iago uses his own voice in chorus with Roderigo's. To arouse Brabanzio's emotions, Iago – keeping his personal identity obscure – takes on the voice of a 'ruffian[ ]' (1.1.112), a voice from the gutter, whose lewd conceits prompt Brabanzio to ask, 'What profane wretch art thou?' (116). A ruffian's voice has power in public to stir up trouble, but little chance within the verbal economy of the polite Venetian society to elicit belief. Iago therefore deploys the different accent of Roderigo's voice to the end of shaping Brabanzio's belief. Roderigo speaks as a gentleman, and calls upon Brabanzio to 'recognize' his voice ('Most reverend signor, do you know my voice?' [93]). He calls upon Brabanzio not merely to recognize that it is Roderigo who speaks but also to recognize that the speaker's social status guarantees his credit: 'Do not believe / That, from the sense of all civility, / I thus would play and trifle with your reverence' (132–4). Shrewdly calculating his slight chances of gaining such credit through his own voice in making this public disturbance, Iago appropriates to his own purposes the Cassio-like politeness and the matching status of Roderigo's voice. Iago tells the audience of how he makes 'my fool my purse' (1.3.375), but we never actually see Iago spending Roderigo's money. What we see instead is how he deploys the symbolic capital of Roderigo's voice.

Fundamental, then, to Iago's rhetorical mastery is his manipulation of what Bourdieu claims linguists long ignored: social context, understood here as the conditions for speech profit. While many public occasions tend to restrict his own access to speech and his opportunities for speech profit, Iago is what he ironically calls Cassio – 'a finder of occasion' (2.1.242–3). The riotous street scene is his public occasion of choice, the scene in which he most profitably draws speech credit away from others and toward himself. As I have suggested, Bourdieu distinguishes sharply between the communication conditions obtaining in situations of high formality and in situations of lesser formality. In situations of high formality the reproductive role of politeness is most pronounced, scripting in the language of the participants a mutual recognition and acknowledgement of their relative social stations: 'Politeness', as Bourdieu explains it, 'contains a politics, a practical, immediate recognition of social classifications and of hierarchies, between the sexes, the generations, the classes, etc.'[15] In our analysis of the Senate

[14] Bourdieu, *Language and Symbolic Power*, p. 67.

[15] Bourdieu, 'Economics', p. 662.

scene, we have seen how the combination of formal scene and disruptive urgency made for a kind of re-ranking: the urgency of the moment meant that forms of symbolic capital apart from static social rank could more readily take on importance. But the adjustment in power relations was still strictly contained by the formal setting, keeping lesser ranking characters like Iago in their silent – and inferior – places. Lessen the formality and intensify the disruptive urgency of a scene, and Iago can make occasions in which even his speech can prevail over those of higher rank. Provide an outdoor setting, street fighting, darkness – as Iago does both when Cassio is discredited (2.3) and when Roderigo is murdered and Cassio badly hurt (5.1) – and restrictions on speech roles are relaxed or overturned.[16] As the murder scene in 5.1 draws towards its conclusion, Iago himself articulates this principle which has released his speech, at least for a short space of time, from the perpetual obligation to 'recognize' his subordinate relation to others: 'Signor Graziano', he exclaims, pretending only then to make out who his interlocutor is and adjust his language to their prescribed relation: 'I cry your gentle pardon. / These bloody accidents must excuse my manners / That so neglected you' (5.1.95–7). Hence we see that Iago's instruction to Roderigo – 'do you find some occasion to anger Cassio' (2.1.266–7) – is as supreme a rhetorical act as any virtuoso speech of persuasion he makes in the play. It is through this construction of a favourable context that Iago can set up a contest of voices in which he is able to secure the floor ('Honest Iago, that looks dead with grieving, / Speak.' (2.3.170–1)) and to disable the voices of his superiors Cassio and Montano ('I pray you pardon me. I cannot speak.' (182); 'Your officer Iago can inform you, / While I spare speech – which something now offends me' (191–2)). Iago has full scope to elaborate his version of reality at extended length before important people. What he seeks and what he gains is not the hearers' simple belief in the facts as he represents them. What he is after is an enhancement of his 'voice potential', or – in Bourdieu's terms – an accumulation of his symbolic capital, which is registered in the personal approbation of Othello's response: 'I know, Iago, / Thy honesty and love doth mince this matter, / Making it light to Cassio' (2.3.239–41). Furthermore, Iago has engineered the loss of Cassio's lieutenancy with – perhaps more important – the loss of his annoying expectation that he can easily profit from the 'show of courtesy' (2.1.102) characteristic of his discourse: 'I will ask him for my place again. He shall tell me I am a drunkard. Had I as many mouths as Hydra, such an answer would stop them all.' (2.3.296–8). A rhetorician able to understand the mechanisms by which the polite Venetian social order, instantiated in its typical speech situations, stops talented voices and gives credit to the incompetent, Iago manages, if only for a short time,[17] his own correction of the gap between linguistic capital and credit.

In this paper, I have used Bourdieu's economic model for linguistic exchange as a heuristic to explore speech reception and speech production in some public scenes of *Othello*. This enabled, first, an examination of how variable power relations affect discourse reception in a particular setting and, second, an account of how the history of a person's speech reception functions together with immediate context to shape speech production. This

16 Penelope Brown and Stephen C. Levinson, *Politeness: Some Universals in Language Usage*, 2nd edn (Cambridge, 1987), pp. 95–6 and p. 282, make the point that in situations of urgency and desperation, when maximum efficiency of communication is required, the face-redress work of politeness is unnecessary.

17 The rough and improvisatory nature of Iago's rhetoric of situation makes his a particularly high risk performance. In the end he loses control of the play's speech outcomes when he fails to anticipate that circumstances very much like those that gained him speech access and credit – a public disturbance coming as the aftermath of street violence – could contribute to Emilia's speaking out against him and being heard.

reading has allowed me to offer a different perspective on the interrelation Shakespeare represents between character and language than is usual in *Othello* criticism – a perspective that links linguistic performance not to essential character but instead to character as the locus of social and power relations. Bourdieu's economic model for linguistic exchange also provided the foundation for assessing Iago's rhetorical artistry, an artistry founded on manipulating speech context, or the conditions for 'voice potential'.

HOUSEHOLD WORDS: *MACBETH* AND THE FAILURE OF SPECTACLE

LISA HOPKINS

In her epic novel on the life of Macbeth, *King Hereafter*, Dorothy Dunnett suggests that one of the primary reasons for the eventual failure of her hero's kingship is his inability to be perceived as sufficiently charismatic: 'a diverse people in time of hardship need a priest-king. The English know that. Edward is anointed with holy oil: he has the power of healing, they say'.[1] Although Dunnett's Macbeth-figure – an Orkney jarl also known as Thorfinn – is very differently conceived from Shakespeare's, each shares an unfortunate tendency towards the mundane. Most particularly, Shakespeare's hero and his wife both, at certain crucial moments of their lives, strongly favour a low-key, occasionally almost bathetic vocabulary.[2] This aspect of their characterization has been much mocked in the English comic and popular tradition: Bertie Wooster is continually amused by the concept of the cat i' th' adage, and Edmund Crispin's irascible literary detective Gervase Fen, Oxford professor, gives the play very short shrift:

> 'Do!' exclaimed Fen. 'If it were done when 'tis done, then 'twere well it were done quickly.'
>
> 'What is that supposed to mean?'
>
> 'It isn't supposed to mean anything. It's a quotation from our great English dramatist, Shakespeare. I sometimes wonder if Hemings and Condell went off the rails a bit there. It's a vile absurd jingle.'[3]

The point was, perhaps, made most strongly, and most elegantly, by Dr Johnson, fulminating on the 'lowness' of the diction in the 'Come, thick night ...' speech (though he mistakenly attributes this to Macbeth). He castigates the use of 'an epithet now seldom heard but in the stable ... *dun* night may come or go without any other notice than contempt';[4] he rhetorically enquires, 'who, without some relaxation of his gravity, can hear of the avengers of guilt *peeping through a blanket?*'; and he asserts:

> sentiment is weakened by the name of an instrument used by butchers and cooks in the meanest employments; we do not immediately conceive that any crime of importance is to be committed with a *knife*; or who does not, at least, from the long habit of connecting a knife with sordid offices, feel aversion rather than terror?

Coleridge concurred so strongly with Johnson's strictures on the inappropriateness of 'blanket' that he suggested that the reading should actually have been 'blank height' –[5] though the quality of his engagement with the play's language in general is perhaps indicated by his remark that, '[e]xcepting the disgusting passage of the Porter, which I dare pledge myself to

[1] Dorothy Dunnett, *King Hereafter* [1982] (London, 1992), p. 672.

[2] On the relationship between the two characters' diction, see William Shakespeare, *Macbeth*, edited by Nicholas Brooke (Oxford, 1990), introduction, pp. 14–19.

[3] Edmund Crispin, *Holy Disorders* [1946] (Harmondsworth, 1958), p. 136.

[4] From *The Rambler*, no. 168, 26 October 1751.

[5] Samuel Taylor Coleridge, *Shakespearean Criticism*, edited by Thomas Middleton Raysor, 2 vols. (London, 1960), vol. 1, p. 65.

demonstrate an interpolation of the actors, I do not remember in *Macbeth* a single pun or play on words' (pp. 69–70).

Other responses have been less damning and more interested in teasing out the implications of the imagery. Bradley, characteristically, saw it as evidence of characterization, and (correctly attributing the speeches) believed mundanity of diction to be differentially, and deliberately, employed in the play: he suggested that Lady Macbeth 'uses familiar and prosaic illustrations' as an indication of '[t]he literalism of her mind'.[6] More recently, Paul Jorgensen has observed that the use of the banal is not in fact confined to Lady Macbeth, but is still disposed to regard patterns of speech as symptomatic and revelatory of states of mind, commenting of the 'If it were done ...' speech that Macbeth 'is still, as in his talk with Lady Macbeth, relying upon shrinking words like *it* (four uses) and *do* (three uses)';[7] and Coppélia Kahn performs a similar manoeuvre when she offers a sustained and ingenious reading of Macbeth's apparently simple use of the word 'cow'.[8] Even Coleridge was prepared to concede that some at least of the play's language might be suggestively, rather than disturbingly, 'low', commenting on 'the appropriateness of the simile "as breath" in a cold climate',[9] and speculating that 'enkindle you unto the crown' might still further underline the play's concern with childlessness by encoding the suggestions not only of 'kind' and 'kin' but of the 'kindling', or engendering, of rabbits (p. 61).

Perhaps most interesting of all, however, are the observations of Walter Whiter on the supposedly prosaic character of the imagery. Responding silently but unmistakably to Johnson, Whiter observes:

> The word '*knife*' (says Mr Malone) has been objected to, as being connected with the most sordid offices; and therefore unsuitable to the great occasion on which it is employed. But, however mean it may sound to our ears, it was formerly a word of sufficient dignity, and is constantly used by Shakespeare and his contemporaries as synonimous [sic] to *dagger* ... *Blanket* (Mr Malone observes) was certainly the Poet's word, and 'perhaps was suggested to him by the coarse *woollen* curtain of his own Theatre, through which probably, while the house was yet but half lighted, he had himself often *peep'd*.'[10]

The idea that Shakespeare could have 'peep'd' through a *curtain* at a *half-lighted* Globe which he would have called a *house* clearly owes a very great deal more to eighteenth-century awareness of its own theatrical practices than to any historical awareness of what Elizabethan ones had been; but nevertheless I think Whiter, and Malone before him, have grasped something really central to the play here. Whiter goes on to develop his insights further, declaring that 'Nothing is more certain, than that all the images in this celebrated passage are borrowed from the *Stage*' (pp. 63–4) and commenting that '[t]he peculiar and appropriate dress of TRAGEDY personified is a PALL with a KNIFE' (p. 64).

In Whiter's reading, the ostensible 'lowness' of the diction is, with breathtaking ingenuity, completely recuperated in a register which allows the passage to be perceived as a sustained piece of metatheatricality. Other critics have not been slow to see similar links, ranging from Bradley's remark that Macbeth 'is generally said to be a very bad actor'[11] to Malcolm Evans' comment that 'numerous theatrical references emerge on the "bloody stage" (II.iv.930) of Scotland in the course of the play, culminating in Macbeth's speech on "signifying

6 A. C. Bradley, *Shakespearean Tragedy* [1904], (London, 1974), pp. 312 and 311.

7 Paul Jorgensen, 'Macbeth's Soliloquy', from *Our Naked Frailties: Sensational Art and Meaning in 'Macbeth'* [Berkeley, 1971], reprinted in Roy Battenhouse, ed., *Shakespeare's Christian Dimension* (Bloomington, 1994), pp. 481–5; p. 483.

8 Coppélia Kahn, *Man's Estate: Masculine Identity in Shakespeare* (Berkeley, 1981), p. 191.

9 Coleridge, *Shakespearean Criticism*, p. 61.

10 Walter Whiter, 'Specimen of a Commentary on Shakespeare' [1794], reprinted in John Wain, ed., *Macbeth: A Casebook*, pp. 63–76; p. 63.

11 Bradley, *Shakespearean Tragedy*, p. 298.

nothing''.[12] And Christopher Pye combines elements of both these lines of critical approach, that focusing on the mundanity of the play and that focusing on its theatricality, in virtually the same breath: citing 'a foolish thought to say a sorry sight', he comments on 'the spectacular banality of Macbeth's response',[13] but he also calls the play 'the most spectacular of Shakespeare's tragedies. Like Lady Macbeth and like the inquisitive king [James I] who watches her, *Macbeth* is notable for the disquieting visibility of its mysteries' (p. 145). What I want to argue, however, is that the two elements are, precisely, forced apart by the play's structure so that what we see in *Macbeth* is not in fact, in Pye's suggestive phrasing, 'spectacular banality', but a banality which achieves spectacularity only in metaspectacular terms – a concept which I am, I hope, going to be able to clarify.

Dr Johnson's objection to terms like 'knife' and 'blanket' was, in effect, that they were household words, representing a 'low' diction associated with 'sordid offices'. Walter Whiter counters that all these banal-seeming terms have in fact another meaning in another register, in which they are associated not with the home but with the theatre, and that they are thus actually instances of elevated – and technical – terminology by their association with the classical concept of tragedy; the value-system which Whiter is implicitly working with here is clearly signalled by the typography, which italicizes *Stage* and uses upper case for TRAGEDY, PALL, and KNIFE. However, these theatrical meanings are accessible only on the metatheatrical or extradiegetic level: they are there to be perceived by the audience of the play, but not by its characters. We may conceive of the characters in *Macbeth* primarily as actors on a stage, but they, with the notable exception of Macbeth himself towards the end of his career, are presented as representations blind to their own status as representations. When Lady Macbeth speaks of knives and blankets, she, at least, can have no access to any ulterior meaning which casts them as the accoutrements of tragedy: to her, as to Dr Johnson, they are only knives and blankets, though to us, as to Walter Whiter, they may be the appropriate props of the role she plays. Moreover, Lady Macbeth is alone: if she herself does not register the metaphorical force of her words, there is no one else present to do so. This is, in fact, a consistent and striking feature of *Macbeth* as a whole. It may well be, as Christopher Pye terms it, 'the most spectacular of Shakespeare's tragedies', but the elements which are most obviously 'spectacular', the episodes centring on the outlandish appearance and supernatural doings of the Weird Sisters, are (even when they are of undoubtedly Shakespearian origin) consistently staged very much for the benefit of the audience alone, and are never perceived by the majority of the characters. After their initial appearance to Macbeth and Banquo jointly, the Weird Sisters are seen only by Macbeth, and so too is the ghost of Banquo, and Lady Macbeth, for all her apostrophizings and invocations of the supernatural, never has any personal contact with it. Most other characters are even less aware than she of the presence of the diabolical and the paranormal in the play: when Malcolm gives the order for the cutting of the branches, he is adhering to a military requirement for camouflage rather than consciously fulfilling a prophecy, and it is doubtful that Macbeth's half-hints about his 'charmed-life' can convey to Macduff any sense of the extent and nature of his dealings with the Weird Sisters (indeed Macduff can refer to them, collectively, merely as an 'angel' [5.7.44]). In short, Macbeth's subjects are consistently denied any sight of the spectacles of horror that have made the play so theatrically celebrated.

This discrepancy between the experiences of Macbeth's on-stage subjects and his off-stage audience serves to reveal the ways in which

[12] Malcolm Evans, *Signifying Nothing*, second edition (London, 1989), p. 133.

[13] Christopher Pye, *The Regal Phantasm: Shakespeare and the Politics of Spectacle* (London, 1990), p. 150.

Shakespeare's Macbeth shares with Dorothy Dunnett's a vulnerability to the accusation that his kingship is insufficiently charismatic and theatrical. In fact, he and Lady Macbeth are, for all their egregious brutality, in some sense the most domestic of couples, making literal and consistent use of household words. In the theatre, it may be customary to present their relationship as an explosively erotic one,[14] but Nicholas Brooke well observes that 'no play of Shakespeare's makes so little allusion to sex'.[15] The element of familiarity and domesticity is strongly highlighted from the very outset of the play. The Weird Sisters may have beards, live on a heath and vanish into thin air, but their conversation is notably marked by features serving to associate it with the normal concerns of women in the home:[16] they use popular terminology like 'hurly-burly',[17] and they discuss household animals like Greymalkin and Paddock which are, literally, familiar(s). They even talk about the weather. As with their later parodic rituals of food preparation, the alienness of the Weird Sisters is closely inscribed here within degrees of difference and inversion of the normal.

The motif of food preparation, in however distorted a form, is first signalled in the speech of the sergeant who describes the battle, when he relates how Macbeth, fighting Macdonwald, 'unseamed him from the nave to th' chops' (1.2.22). This is the first hint of the Macbeth whom Malcolm will eventually label 'this dead butcher' (5.7.99), and the epithet of butcher is applicable to him both metaphorically and literally, though the elaborate imagery and rhetorical patterning of the sergeant may tend to submerge, for the moment at least, the possibility of a literal reading. His set-piece speech, which deliberately delays the knowledge of success until he has carefully cultivated fears of uncertainty, sits well in Duncan's camp, for Duncan, as we soon learn, is marked precisely by those shows and ceremonies of kingship which will be so notably absent from the court of Macbeth. In marked contrast to the unheralded, unglossed entrance of the Weird Sisters, the sergeant is formally presented to Duncan by Malcolm, who performs a similar function when he announces the arrival of Ross to his father (1.2.45) – surely a ceremonial rather than a factual communication, unless hyper-naturalism desired a short-sighted Duncan here. Duncan, moreover, ends the scene by conferring an honour: Macbeth is to become Thane of Cawdor. The bestowal of favours and titles is a marked feature of Duncan's kingly style, and something which, we see in the closing speech, his son will also practise (could there be here an unusually favourable imaging of James I's notorious open-handedness with knighthoods and other titles?); Shakespeare had already shown in *Richard III* how crucial a tool this could be in retaining support. Macbeth, notably, never does this. There are no nobles of his creation, no henchmen (with the arguable exception of the Murderers) dependent entirely on his continued favour; from the time of the disrupted banquet, he converses only with those conspicuously beneath him, like the doctor, the 'loon', and Young Seyward. Here, as in other areas, there are no outward manifestations of his kingship.

Macbeth can, however, think in terms of the spectacular and the ceremonial. We see this in his first soliloquy:

> (*aside*) Two truths are told
> As happy prologues to the swelling act

[14] This could, I think, be illustrated from many productions, but a recent and striking example was Philip Franks' November, 1994 production at the Crucible Theatre, Sheffield. Lady Macbeth's backless purple dress was so eye-catching that the actress was featured wearing it, in character, in the Sheffield *Star*'s 'wardrobe' section (usually including only real people), sharing her 'seduction tips'.

[15] *Macbeth*, ed. Brooke, introduction, p. 19.

[16] On the element of domesticity in the representation of the Weird Sisters, see also Naomi Conn Liebler, *Shakespeare's Festive Tragedy* (London, 1995), p. 224.

[17] William Shakespeare, *Macbeth*, ed. Brooke, I.1.3. All further quotations will be taken from this edition and reference will be given in the text.

> Of the imperial theme – I thank you gentlemen –
> This supernatural soliciting
> Cannot be ill, cannot be good. (1.3.128–32)

The most marked feature of his language here, however, is the dramatic register shift between his public and private discourses in the early part of the play, before horrid banquetings force disastrously together the arenas of the public and the domestic. To himself, this early Macbeth speaks stirringly, with elaborate metaphors of theatre and performance; but for public consumption, he confines himself to the plain 'I thank you gentlemen', and later apologizes, 'Give me your favour: my dull brain was wrought / With things forgotten' (1.3.150–1). A similar dualism of approach characterizes Lady Macbeth. Alone, she talks of symbolically hoarse ravens; to her servants, she speaks, like a good housewife, of preparation for the king's visit. But perhaps the most marked contrast of this type comes in Macbeth's next soliloquy:

> Go bid thy mistress, when my drink is ready,
> She strike upon the bell. Get thee to bed. *Exit Servant.*
> Is this a dagger which I see before me,
> The handle toward my hand? (2.1.32–5)

The movement from bedtime drinks to imaginary (or supernatural) daggers within the space of two lines tellingly encapsulates the contrast between Macbeth's public and private faces. In public, he is the model of bourgeois marital comfort; but in private, he – and the audience – see strange things. At the same time, though, even Macbeth's inner life displays clear elements of continuity with his outer one, for the dagger of the mind does not only represent the antithesis of the comfort and normality offered by the drink; it also comes from the same world of household objects and food, as is suggested by the lack of any noticeable register shift in the diction, with 'drink' and 'bell' giving place almost seamlessly to 'dagger' and 'hand'. The connection becomes strikingly apparent when Lady Macbeth prefigures the Weird Sisters' parodies of cooking in her preparations for the murder: she makes drinks not only for her husband but for the guards, but she has 'drugged their possets' (2.2.6); and she has 'laid their daggers ready' (2.2.12) not for a meal, but for murder. Her housewifery continues as she soothes her husband's night fears, bids him wear his nightgown (2.2.69), and, above all, adjures him to wash his hands (2.2.45–6) – the domestic ritual that will still be with her in her madness. Her infamous cry of 'What, in our house?' (2.3.89) does not simply strike the bathetic note of her husband's ''Twas a rough night' (2.3.62); it sits perfectly with her public image as 'most kind hostess' (2.1.16). We never see Lady Macbeth out of her own house, and her mental collapse narrows even further the world we perceive her to inhabit, as we are shown her bedchamber. Bradley's comment that '[s]trange and almost ludicrous as the statement may sound, she is, up to her light, a perfect wife'[18] could well have been extended to the argument that she is also, up to her light, a perfect housewife. The Macbeths are, after all, so apparently innocuous that those about them are notably slow to realize the full horror of their behaviour.

Perhaps the most striking example of this emphasis on the discrepancy between the public and private lives of Macbeth, and the simultaneous, paradoxical, imbrication of both in the domestic, comes at the opening of 1.7. The scene is prefaced by an unusually detailed stage direction:

> *Hautboys. Torches.*
> *Enter a sewer and divers servants with dishes and service crossing over the stage.*
> *Then enter Macbeth* (1.7.s.d.)

This is so elaborate that Brooke elevates it to the status of formal 'dumb-show' (see note), a phenomenon without precedent in Shakespearian tragedy except in the deliberately archaic play-within-the-play in *Hamlet,* and although Brooke points out that the episode

[18] Bradley, *Shakespearean Tragedy*, p. 316.

'stresses the evening-time and the obligations of lavish hospitality' it does nothing to advance the narrative. What it does do, however, is make for a particularly startling contrast. Shakespeare brings on stage the whole panoply of the elaborately regulated ritual of the courtly serving of food; he then follows this with the very sequence of repetitive monosyllables which aroused the scorn of Gervase Fen, and which Nicholas Brooke concurs in terming 'notably plain vocabulary'.[19] Superficially, this inverts the contrast between private eloquence and public reticence which characterized Macbeth's earlier soliloquy; but in fact he goes on to launch himself upon one of the most sustained and dense speeches in the play, in the course of which he figures the possibility of murder, and its potential consequences, precisely in terms of food:

This even-handed justice
Commends th'ingredience of our poisoned chalice
To our own lips. (1.7.10–12)

When Lady Macbeth enters, demanding 'He has almost supped: why have you left the chamber?' (1.7.29) we realize that Macbeth has, indeed, been once again neglecting his public image, causing a feast to be disrupted by his failure to attend to it fully, just as he will on the occasion of the appearance of Banquo's ghost. His wife indeed characterizes his dereliction in terms of improper banqueting when she uses the language of drunkenness and surfeit to describe it:

Was the hope drunk
Wherein you dressed yourself? Hath it slept since?
And wakes it now to look so green and pale
At what it did so freely? (1.7.35–8)

Typically, the one attempt at public show that the Macbeths do make revolves round cooking: they hold a ceremonial feast. Just as the murder of Duncan violated codes of hospitality, though, so too do their dinner invitations, since they demand compulsory attendance, a fact twice underlined – 'Fail not our feast' says Macbeth to Banquo (3.1.27), and Lennox lists a precisely similar crime as one of the reasons for Macduff's downfall:

But peace – for from broad words, and 'cause he failed
His presence at the tyrant's feast, I hear
Macduff lives in disgrace. (3.6.21–3)

Nicholas Brooke points out that in Holinshed, 'the quarrel with Macduff involves a complicated story about the building of Forres castle which Shakespeare reduced to refusal of an invitation (command) to dinner';[20] the modification may well have been made not only in the interests of dramatic economy but because of its thematic congruence. The clear suggestion that the Macbeths are a couple at whose dinners attendance must be enforced is a powerful and compact device. It neatly measures the length of the journey they have travelled since, in the first act, Duncan deliberately solicited them as host and 'most kind hostess'. Equally, it reinforces the images both of their customary domesticity and of its rapid disintegration, making theirs a nightmare which, even at its most outlandish, retains that most distinctive quality of what Freudian theory on the uncanny has termed the *unheimlich* by relying for its full horror on the distortion of the traditional comforts of home. It is little wonder that the Lord who converses with Lennox should figure the rule of Macbeth precisely in terms of the subversion of the domestic:

with Him above
To ratify the work – we may again
Give to our tables meat, sleep to our nights,
Free from our feasts and banquets bloody knives.
(4.1.32–6)

Macbeth has not only murdered sleep, he has also perverted the proper consumption of food.

As well as Macduff's decision to boycott it (which in itself ironically recalls Macbeth's earlier failure to attend his own feast, for

[19] *Macbeth*, ed. Brooke, introduction, p. 7.
[20] *Ibid.*

suggestively similar political reasons), the grand banquet is also devastatingly upstaged by its near-homonym Banquo, the name that we might always have guessed would lurk within the word in this instance, who is, suggestively, imaged by Macbeth almost in terms of a distasteful food item: 'Thy bones are marrowless, thy blood is cold' (3.4.95). The disastrous feast is a common enough feature of Renaissance drama, but it is particularly appropriate in the Macbeths' case, especially since the next time we see Macbeth it is at an eerily similar occasion, the brewing of the Weird Sisters' hell stew, with its foul concoction of ingredients, for 'a devil's-banqueting'.[21] As with so much in the play, however, the cause of the occasion's failure is never apparent to the onlookers. Macbeth's language, especially in the early part of the scene, is infuriatingly riddled with deictic phrases intelligible only to the off-stage audience, not to the on-stage one:

> Which of you have done this? (3.4.49)
>
> Thou canst not say I did it – never shake
> Thy gory locks at me. (3.4.50–1)
>
> Ay, and a bold one, that dare look on that
> Which might appal the Devil. (3.4.58–9)
>
> Prithee, see there – behold, look, lo (3.4.69)
>
> Thou hast no speculation in those eyes (3.4.96)
>
> Take any shape but that (3.4.103)

'This', 'it', 'that', 'behold', 'look', 'lo', 'those eyes', and 'any shape but that' can all make sense only in the presence of the referent, but that referent is literally invisible to all others on stage (and it is of course also open to the director similarly to tantalize and titillate the off-stage audience by staging the scene without an actual ghost). Moreover, 'behold', 'look' and 'lo', which Macbeth piles one on top of the other like a demented thesaurus, undo themselves even as they are spoken by their status as near-variants of one another. Their iteration serves only to underline the inadequacy of each on its own: as speech continually glosses itself, with a lack of difference that powerfully reinforces *différance*, we are offered a radical awareness of the slippage between signifier and signified which, even as the deictic is spoken, undermines its ability to show. (Here again, as with the banqueting, we are afforded an ironic prolepsis of the 'show' shortly to be offered by the Weird Sisters).

The whole scene is typical of the experience of Macbeth's subjects: under his rule, they get no visual value for their money. Macbeth himself is a conspicuous example of his regime's radical failure to validate itself through the performance of spectacles of power: even when he becomes aware of his own role-playing, he denigrates acting, characteristically, with his image of the 'poor player' (5.5.24), and when we hear that his title is ill-fitting 'like a giant's robe / Upon a dwarfish thief' (5.2.21–2) the image may well suggest a simple failure to achieve proper costuming for his part. While the spectacle of Banquo's ghost may be one of horror, it is, surely, more frustrating to be so comprehensively denied not only the experience of seeing it, but of hearing any coherent description of it. Certainly the public, performative nature of state punishment at the time would indicate that such sights would be enjoyed, and it is a pleasure that is definitively envisaged as part of Malcolm's regime:

> Then yield thee, coward,
> And live to be the show and gaze o'th' time.
> We'll have thee, as our rarer monsters are,
> Painted upon a pole, and underwrit
> 'Here may you see the tyrant'. (5.7.53–7)

Just as Duncan had made a public show of the execution of Cawdor, with the full Foucauldian apparatus of proper acknowledgement of guilt by the criminal, so the reign of his son will be inaugurated with spectacle: Macbeth's head is publicly produced (5.7.84–5), and the play's last line is an invitation 'to see us crowned at Scone' (5.7.105).

---

[21] G. Wilson Knight, *The Imperial Theme* (Oxford, 1931), p. 138.

The latter actions of Macbeth's own reign have been in marked contrast to this. As he is seen talking not to his generals or lords, but only to his doctor and his armourer, the paradoxical homeliness of the 'butcher' in him becomes ever more apparent. Dismissing the English as 'epicures' (5.3.8), he notably identifies himself with simpler produce. He rails at the servant 'The Devil damn thee black, thou cream-faced loon: / Where got'st thou that goose-look?' (5.3.11–12). 'Cream-faced' functions in obvious opposition to 'black', but a simple 'white' would have done so even more strongly; indeed in this sense 'cream', by failing to act as a clear contrast, undoes itself as constituent part of a trope and stakes a claim for a more literal meaning. Particularly in conjunction with 'goose', 'cream' must surely suggest, however momentarily, the simple farm-food from which Macbeth's own actions have so radically alienated him. The images are appropriate, for he is thinking of his 'land' here (5.3.50), and he again sites it in terms of an economy of ingestion when he asks the Doctor 'What rhubarb, senna, or what purgative drug / Would scour these English hence?' (5.3.54–5). It is such images of evacuation and failure to nourish which lead directly to his peculiarly apposite threat to the messenger who informs him that Birnam wood is moving:

> If thou speak'st false,
> Upon the next tree shall thou hang alive
> Till famine cling thee; if thy speech be sooth,
> I care not if thou dost for me as much.
> (5.5.38–41)

Macbeth counters his enemies' moving wood, with its obvious connotations of renewed fertility and Maying rites, with branches of his own, twice figured as bearing parodic fruit – first the messenger and then himself – which denies life and nourishment rather than celebrating it.

Macbeth's images of a cream-faced, goose-like messenger who hangs like fruit provides the climax to a strain of cannibalistic suggestion throughout the play. Triply interpellating the messenger as foodstuff, he also recapitulates in 'cream' a recurrent play on figures centring on milk and cows. The first example of this comes in Lady Macbeth's invocation, 'Come to my woman's breasts / And take my milk for gall, you murd'ring ministers' (1.5.46–7). This clearly follows from the request to 'unsex me here' (1.5.40), but it may do rather more than simply develop the earlier idea: Janet Adelman suggests that 'perhaps Lady Macbeth is asking the spirits to take her milk *as* gall, to nurse from her breasts and find in her milk their sustaining poison'.[22] If so, she specifically identifies herself as a food-source, a thing to be eaten. This is soon followed by the most striking and most notorious instance of the image, in Lady Macbeth's infamous lines:

> I have given suck, and know
> How tender 'tis to love the babe that milks me;
> I would, while it was smiling in my face,
> Have plucked my nipple from his boneless gums
> And dashed the brains out, had I so sworn
> As you have done to this. (1.7.54–9)

Clearly this picture of monstrous motherhood encodes a terrifying ferocity, accentuated by the rapidity of the change from the emotional range of 'tender' to that of 'dashed'. Equally, though, the aggression it registers is directed not only against the putative 'babe', but also, masochistically, against Lady Macbeth herself. The action of plucking the nipple from the gum would be (as anyone who has breastfed knows) deeply unpleasant; it is more usual to insert one's little finger to prise the infant's gums apart so that the nipple can be released gently and (relatively) painlessly. Perhaps more suggestive, though, is the tacit auto-interpellation of Lady Macbeth here as a thing milked – in essence, a cow. This not only returns to the earlier *motif*; it is also closely echoed, as Coppélia Kahn has shown, by Macbeth's lament that 'it hath cowed my better part of man' (5.7.48).[23] In his final

[22] Janet Adelman, *Suffocating Mothers* (London, 1992), p. 135.

[23] Kahn, *Man's Estate*, p. 191.

dehumanization, Macbeth is unmanned, feminized, and radically identified with his wife, all in one fell swoop; moreover, all this is achieved, neatly, in another of his monosyllabic, literally household words.

This 'cowing' of both Macbeths works in conjunction with other images of cannibalism in the text. Duncan's horses eat each other (2.4.18); prey and predator change places when a falcon is devoured by a 'mousing owl' (2.4.12–13). Like the Weird Sisters' hideous banquet in which parts of babies are eaten, like Macbeth figuring the messenger and his enemies as cream-faced and goose-like, all of these invert conventional categories of eater and eaten, deconstructing boundaries as crucial to civilization as Lévi-Strauss's raw and cooked. In many of them, the thrust, whether covert or overt, is towards imaging humans themselves as, or in terms of, food, as it is also with the 'chops' of Macdonald and with Banquo's 'marrowless' bones;[24] such an undercurrent may even be discernible in Malcolm's assertion that in comparison with himself, the state will esteem Macbeth as a 'lamb' (4.3.54), and it certainly inheres in Macduff's figuring of Macbeth as a 'hell-kite' (4.3.218) and his wife and children as 'chickens and their dam' (4.3.219). All of these offer powerful images of a humanity diminished to either prey or predator, and all of them, again, do so in terms of household words. There is the lamb which could, in other circumstances, be redolent of the pastoral, the chickens which might, but do not, evoke the farmyard, the mousing owl, the geese and the cream which might also belong there,[25] and the chops and bones which could suggest the kitchen. This is, indeed, a plain diction, but its very plainness is what enables it to strike so directly to the deepest fears, and to allow *Macbeth* to root horror in the heart and in the home.

What all these instances of plainness do, however, is work to remove the play from the arena of state affairs and situate the concerns of its main characters, at least, insistently within the realm of the domestic. As such, they doubly indicate the reasons for Macbeth's ultimate failure. The expedience of the use of ceremony in the creation of the royal image, and the seriousness of Macbeth's failure to do so, can perhaps best be appreciated by reinserting the play into the circumstances of its production. Jonathan Goldberg suggests that 'the text of *Macbeth* that we have derives from a court performance'.[26] He also argues that the dramaturgy of the play is profoundly affected by the traditions of court theatre: 'we can come closer to the source of *Macbeth* if we look at the Jonsonian masque that stands somewhere behind the masquelike movement that the play ultimately takes' (p. 254). He suggests, as others have done, that the obvious comparator is Jonson's *The Masque of Queens*, termed by its author 'a spectacle of strangeness',[27] which features an antimasque of twelve witches who boast that they have 'Kill'd an infant, to have his fat' (p. 78). Goldberg terms Jonson's play a 'spectacle of state';[28] Pye uses the same phrase when he argues that 'Macbeth's "rapture" aligns the play with spectacles of state.'[29] But within *Macbeth*, it is not only that the Weird Sisters perform a purely private cabaret; there are no spectacles of state at all. Though the play itself may function as one for its off-stage audience, the experience of the court to which the play is represented will be radically different from the experience of the court which is represented within it. Goldberg suggests of

24 *OED* cites the first use of 'chop' as a cut of meat as occurring in 1461, in the Paston Letters.

25 This element would have been even more pronounced when the Cat appeared in the Middleton-authored revisions, which Brooke prints.

26 Jonathan Goldberg, 'Speculations: *Macbeth* and Source', in *Shakespeare Reproduced*, edited by Jean E. Howard and Marion F. O'Connor (London, 1987), 242–64; p. 251.

27 Ben Jonson, *The Masque of Queens*, in *Jacobean and Caroline Masques*, Vol. 1, edited by Richard Dutton (Nottingham, 1981), p. 71.

28 Goldberg, 'Speculation', p. 260.

29 Pye, *The Regal Phantasm*, p. 156.

James and Macbeth that 'one king slides into the other' (p. 251), but however true this may be of the rulers, the very act of staging the play performatively undoes any likeness between the self-presentational strategies of the two regimes.

There may indeed, though, be one pertinent point of similarity between the inhabitants of the stage-play world and those of the court which views it. Though we are carefully reminded that James is descended from Macbeth's enemy, Banquo, and has no blood-link with his tyrannical predecessor, the play may perhaps be seen as encoding subtle comment on James's own attitude towards the use of spectacle. Alan Sinfield notes the particular relevance of touching for the King's Evil to the world of the play: 'James himself knew that this was a superstitious practice, and he refused to undertake it until his advisers persuaded him that it would strengthen his claim to the throne in the public eye.'[30] It might also be worth noting that the title of Jonson's *Masque of Queens* overtly declares its affiliation with Queen Anne of Denmark – well known for her passion for the theatre – rather than with the King himself.[31] Were James a sufficiently attentive viewer, he might perhaps draw conclusions from *Macbeth* about the proper use of theatrical display which might lead him to find his own behaviour wanting – except that to do so would probably demand from him a cognitive shift as radical as that which might enable the characters in the play to become aware of their own imbrication in theatricality. If the play can indeed be read as offering such a commentary on the appropriate use of the spectacular, it would then be harking back directly to the didacticism of the morality play, a genre with which the porter scene has already connected it; and in addition to this artistic self-reflexivity, it would also be remarking on the domestic politics of the royal household itself, and pointing up the extent to which, though the language of the home may be plain in diction, it may be complex indeed in terms of resonance and register.

---

30 Alan Sinfield, '*Macbeth*: History, Ideology and Intellectuals', in *Critical Quarterly*, 28 1:2 (Spring, Summer, 1986), 63–77, reprinted in *New Historicism and Renaissance Drama*, edited by Richard Wilson and Richard Dutton (Harlow, 1992), 167–80; p. 172.

31 Suggestively, *Sophonisba*, another play with which *Macbeth* is occasionally compared, also focuses on a queen. (Kenneth Muir comments on the comparison in his introduction to the Arden edition [London, 1951], introduction, p. xxii.)

ERRING AND STRAYING LIKE LOST SHEEP: *THE WINTER'S TALE* AND *THE COMEDY OF ERRORS*

BRIAN GIBBONS

It was while looking at double meanings in *The Winter's Tale* that I unexpectedly found myself being reminded of *The Comedy of Errors*; and what I took to be a side-track rapidly developed into the argument set down here. Close comparison of these two plays, obviously different in tone and widely separated in date, is unusual, yet when compared each play becomes a kind of commentary on the other's mode, and throws into particular relief a certain quality of bold extravagance combined with a certain elusiveness, as when more is meant than meets the ear.

Viewed from the perspective of *The Comedy of Errors*, one feature of *The Winter's Tale* stands out – a concern with twins, as a challenge to the idea of the self and a challenge to the exclusive union of man and wife. Together with this common concern are similar dramatic aims – although, due to the general development in Shakespeare's art, these may be less evident – focused on the dividing of an audience's attention so that an episode can be understood from two opposite points of view simultaneously: a whole plot can have a double meaning apparent to an audience but not to the characters, and the narrative can generate whole orders of subsidiary double meanings. Moreover, reversing the process and viewing *The Comedy of Errors* from the perspective of *The Winter's Tale* brings out, in the early play, an already fully fledged mastery of high-intensity equivocal design which yokes together opposites to teasing effect, the fully absorbed inheritance of More and Erasmus.

In *The Comedy of Errors*, the Syracusian Antipholus, in his first scene, likens himself, seeking his lost twin, to a drop of water

> That in the ocean seeks another drop,
> Who, falling there to find his fellow forth
> (Unseen, inquisitive), confounds himself.
> (1.2.36–8)

This speech is all the more poignant in retrospect since it marks his last moment of sanity before the entry of the wrong Dromio plunges him deeper and deeper into an ocean of confusion, until he fears he is among

> Dark-working sorcerers that change the mind,
> Soul-killing witches that deform the body
> (1.2.99–100)

In Shakespeare's main source, Plautus's *Menaechmi*, the image of the drop of water is used to signify identical likeness only,[1] but in *The Comedy of Errors* there are further aspects: a drop being soluble, transparent and volatile, can be understood as a metaphor for the Christian soul (as in Marvell's 'Upon a Drop of Dew'), and for the interinanimation of two souls; but these same qualities of transparency and volatility are also associated, ironically, with the

[1] See Robert Miola, *Shakespeare and Classical Comedy* (Oxford, 1994), p. 27. I am grateful to Robert Miola for his helpful comments on an earlier version of this essay, and to Inge Leimberg, the editor of *Connotations*, for prompting me to work on word-play in *The Winter's Tale* and publishing 'Doubles and Likenesses-with-difference: *the Comedy of Errors* and *the Winter's Tale*' in Vol. 6 (1996/7).

opposite, mental instability and loss of identity in madness.

In a later episode the wife, Adriana, fearing her husband is being unfaithful, suddenly comes upon him. She passionately appeals to him to uphold the ideals of marriage as spiritual union:

> For know, my love, as easy mayst thou fall
> A drop of water in the breaking gulf,
> And take unmingled thence that drop again,
> Without addition or diminishing,
> As take from me thyself and not me too.
>
> (2.2.125–9)

The audience, knowing that this is not her husband but his twin, will not respond with full sympathy to her speech – they will be more interested in its effect on the bewildered Antipholus of Syracuse. He does his best to respond clearly and formally:

> Plead you to me, fair dame? I know you not:
>
> (2.2.147)

but the situation gives this simple utterance two opposite meanings: the audience can see that it is perfectly reasonable – since he is a stranger – but it is equally clear that to Adriana it must appear to be frightening evidence of a sudden change in her husband – it is either calculated cruelty or madness. Moreover, Adriana's simile of the drop of water will have another significance to this Antipholus – one she cannot be aware of – because (as we have noted) in the earlier scene he has already used it to refer to himself. Her unwitting echo may not only disconcert him, it may even strike him as uncanny. The play's audience, unlike Antipholus, will find the effect of the echo amusing, but like him, they may also feel the echo uncanny: a darker tone which colours the atmosphere from this moment on.

As the play unfolds, Adriana's assertion of indivisible union with her husband is belied by her suspicion that he is unfaithful, by the audience's observation of his temper and of his relations with the courtesan, and by the remarks of the Abbess about jealous wives; so that the ultimate issue is the crisis in the marriage, something not caused, but only precipitated, by the arrival of the twin. Thus resonant double meanings are focused in Adriana's passionate question:

> How comes it now, my husband, O, how comes it,
> That thou art then estranged from thyself?
>
> (2.2.119–20)

Act 1 Scene 2 of *The Winter's Tale* likewise concerns a married couple, Leontes the husband having a (spiritual) twin brother, then being struck suddenly by mistaken jealousy, the wife Hermione apparently virtuous but, victim of a compromising situation, exposed to his madness and vindictive rage, amid accusations of witchcraft and conspiracy. Shakespeare in *The Winter's Tale* manipulates the audience's perception so that they see events in a double sense: the husband is a tyrant but at the same time a victim, he is a tragic figure and at the same time as grotesque as Antipholus of Ephesus in pursuit of Dr Pinch.

Shakespeare contrives a highly indirect exposition in 1.1 of *The Winter's Tale*, the blatant discrepancies between surface and depth in the speeches of the courtiers setting the tone for a general doubleness and difficulty in the play's discourse. So when Camillo in 1.1.21 observes 'Sicilia cannot show himself overkind to Bohemia' he means 'however strong the expression, it cannot exceed his feelings of love', but could also mean 'he must not show that his feeling for Polixenes goes too far' and 'he tries but fails to keep up the appearance of love'. Camillo remarks of the two kings 'They were trained together in their childhood' (22–3), and he will not let go of the image of the boys' intertwined arms: they 'shook hands, as over a vast, and embraced, as it were, from the ends of opposed winds' (30–1). Here courtly hyperbole, as it seems, too abruptly magnifies, with the effect of distortion and painful strain – and *vast* can refer to a great stretch of time as well as space. The stress on vastness of scale seems apparently to be a function of courtly rhetorical style, to accentuate the positive (as is the negative construction), but it will soon enough take on an opposite meaning, as untimely storms both emotional and actual cause destruction. And the onset of these storms will be in Leontes' sudden obsessive attention to visible on-stage actions of Hermione and Polixenes – joining hands, putting an arm round a waist, embracing. In the first scene Camillo's elaborate courtly paradox 'embraced, as it were, from the ends of opposed winds' (1.1.30–1) is so absurd one might suspect Shakespeare of a sly pun on Puttenham's term for hyperbole, which is 'the over-reacher' – and yet embracing 'from the ends of opposed winds' will retrospectively seem to be a surprisingly cogent summary of the whole tale: easily overlooked, yet actually encapsulating the entire tragicomedy, which unites contraries in a manner that easily outdoes anything in Donne.

The play's opening scene, though very brief, is full of oblique allusions, by two courtiers, to the shared childhood of their respective kings: 'They were train'd together in their childhoods; and there rooted betwixt them then such an affection, which cannot choose but branch now' (1.1.22–4). Implicit in this superficially effusive exchange of courtly compliment are some telling points: in the childhood of the kings there was determinism: education ('training') interacted with Nature's laws (producing the growth of root and branch), and the divine is behind both of these. The negative construction 'cannot choose' has the function of further emphasis on determinism, but it does not wholly efface the association of 'branch'[2] with choice. Here the language employs the consistent decorum of Pastoral, allowing us (but not requiring us) to decode it in Christian terms: it is Christianity that teaches that in due time comes man's adulthood, marked by acquisition of a divinely given capacity to exercise free will.

Polixenes stresses the idea of childhood as freedom *from* choice, and consequently blissful: that is how it was with himself and Leontes:

> We were as twinn'd lambs that did frisk i' th' sun,
> And bleat the one at th'other. What we chang'd
> Was innocence for innocence, we knew not
> The doctrine of ill-doing, nor dream'd
> That any did. (1.2.67–71)

The two lambs were identical, as was their discourse, the exchange of innocence for innocence (appropriately so, out of the mouths of babes and sucklings). Though they were two, he says, there was no sense of individuation nor self-division; but when consciousness of change came (in dream as well as waking) it was because their 'weak spirits' were 'reared with stronger blood' and this had the direct consequence of sin.

> Had we pursu'd that life,
> And our weak spirits ne'er been higher rear'd
> With stronger blood, we should have answer'd heaven
> Boldly, 'Not guilty'; (1.2.71–4)

This usage of 'blood' is complicated: taken with 'reared' it can literally apply to the human child's progression from being milk-fed (like lambs) to a red-meat diet; and while 'blood' is, positively, the full vigour of life, its negative connotation (according to 'the doctrine of ill-

[2] In her study *Shakespeare's Wordplay* (London, 1957), M. M. Mahood pointed to the ambiguity of the word 'branch' in *The Winter's Tale* and used it and other examples to suggest the complex verbal patterning of the text. In her wake, Richard Proudfoot, 'Verbal reminiscence and the two-part structure of *The Winter's Tale*', *Shakespeare Survey 29* (1976), pp. 67–78, went on to add instances of verbal patterning between the two halves of the play, but noted 'What the verbal links seem to invite is rather a toying with such associations than any attempt to use them as the basis for a systematic exegesis' (69). Proudfoot also suggested some possible doubling of parts which, in stage performance, might extend audience awareness of this two-part structure. My own approach assumes that Shakespeare writes in the Renaissance spirit of *serio ludere* as it is manifest in Erasmus and More, and that the double patterns are the basis for a consciously paradoxical exegesis; on this see also Andrew Gurr, 'The bear, the statue, and hysteria in *The Winter's Tale*', *Shakespeare Quarterly* 34 (1983) 420–5, or Brian Gibbons, *Shakespeare and Multiplicity* (Cambridge, 1993), 73–4, and chapter 8 generally.

doing', Original Sin) is as the seat of animal or sensual appetite, lust and anger. Given the royal status of the boys, the sense of 'blood' meaning family and lineage is present; and in the Bible 'blood' often refers to blood shed in sacrifice, and this strengthens the typological association of the lamb with Christ, the redemptive power of innocence sacrificed.

If there is a more pervasive biblical influence in the play than the idea of the Garden of Eden it is (as in *The Comedy of Errors*) that of St Paul, in the Epistles. The idea that in childhood one is filled with the milk of innocence and this is only changed by one's being given a new diet, recalls Paul in Hebrews 5.13–14: 'For every one that useth milke, is unexpert of the word of righteousness, for he is a babe. But strong meate belongeth to them that are perfect, even those which by reason of use, have their wits exercised to discerne both good and evill.' Polixenes implies that with adulthood inevitably comes sin, specifically sexual sin, something from which they would have been protected by remaining children and sharing childhood affection. It should be noticed how firmly this identifies the adult world of the court with sexual guilt and contrasts it to the child's world of natural innocence, though at the same time implying that it is according to Nature that a child develops from a state of innocence to guilt; and this leaves the door ajar, so to speak, for the Freudian interpretation of childhood.

The stage action of 1.2 involves an audience in assessing the manner, the signals of voice, face and body, of the three figures who at first seem undivided in affection – and the two kings may, in stage performance, be made very similar in appearance.[3] Yet the kings' continuing sense of being twins (both are prone to childhood reminiscences) means that Hermione is aware of being subtly excluded, while she is no less aware that, in sharing things with one, she is in a way also sharing with the other: she must find it difficult to distinguish between them in her manner. Her relation to Polixenes will naturally be a close one yet it must not break – and must not be believed to break – the taboos; although among people of royal rank, manner may permit itself some privileged largesse readily susceptible to misreading.

Shakespeare complicates the interpretation of body-language by drawing attention to Hermione's state of advanced pregnancy. This might be supposed to guarantee her a degree of sexual immunity: but while it may allow her a more relaxed closeness to Polixenes, it may involve a slight sexual distancing from her husband Leontes, which could naturally produce tension. Furthermore Polixenes' wife, although briefly referred to in 1.2, is absent,

---

[3] In the theatre a decision must be made as to how far, if at all, the behaviour of Hermione and Polixenes makes Leontes' interpretation plausible. In the production of 1910 at New York the two kings were made to look extraordinarily similar, with identical neat, black Italianate beards and similar furred gowns and crowns. In 1.2 Hermione took the hand of Leontes as she spoke the line 'The one for ever earn'd a royal husband' (1.2.107) and she turned to Polixenes with the next line, 'Th'other for some while a friend', and took his hand. Moving away, she sat by Polixenes and read his hand, their heads very close together (there is a photograph of this in Dennis Bartholomeusz, *'The Winter's Tale' in Performance in England and America 1611–1976* (Cambridge, 1982), p. 139). When Leontes spoke the lines 'To your own bents dispose you; you'll be found, / Be you beneath the sky' (1.2.179–80) Polixenes placed a shawl on Hermione's shoulders as they moved towards the garden. Such a close reading of the dialogue's explicit and implicit stage directions maintains a lifeline to the non-scenic theatre of the Elizabethans; nevertheless there is still a range of emphasis to choose from – Hermione and Polixenes may be shown to display no more than friendly good manners, and in that case Leontes' commentary will seem certainly wrong, sheer delusion. Such an interpretation accords less well with the highly detailed texture of the dialogue, and departs from Shakespeare's precedent as I have described it in *The Comedy of Errors*. It is moreover (the crucial point) far less interesting dramatically than one where Hermione and Polixenes *do* show affection which *could* plausibly be misinterpreted – as in the production of 1910 in New York, or of 1960 by Wood (Bartholomeusz p. 209), or more recently, Peter Hall – see Irving Wardle's review in *The Times*, 20 May 1988, or Roger Warren, *Staging Shakespeare's Late Plays* (Oxford, 1990).

and this gives visual emphasis to an exclusive triangular relationship. As the action unfolds attention is concentrated on the way each of the three adults is divided in turn from the remaining pair; and then for Leontes there is a further stage of alienation triggered by the presence of his two offspring, the unborn child as significant as the boy Mamillius. Thus Hermione finds herself in this scene dividing her attention between the two kings, showing affection in different ways to both, and provoking equivocal responses from each. Polixenes is divided between an obligation to go home and requests that he stay. To Leontes the sense of sharing affection with these two is suddenly supplanted by the sense of division as decisive as that in a theatre between spectator and actors. He turns from Hermione, carrying the unborn child, to his boy Mamillius, as if they constituted another choice, rather than mirroring his self-division: the unborn child's survival as a *branch* of a family, though Leontes tries to kill it, will lead to the growth of a whole new narrative from Act 3 forwards.

Leontes' compulsive criminal impulses are very sudden, to judge by the shocked reaction of his wife and friend, but an audience, being privy to Leontes' soliloquies, can interpret the outburst in terms of the many detailed hints of its origins, both social and psychological. It is all the more remarkable, then, that in the play's action so much credence is also given to the influence of supernatural powers, in the form of Pagan oracles and prophetic dreams, while the role and language of Paulina is resonant with Christian allusions. She is an effectual exorcist, unlike Dr Pinch.

In *The Comedy of Errors* the changes Shakespeare makes to his main source, Plautus, emphasize the pathos of human capacity for error and man's subjection to the power of Fortune. The doubling of masters *and* servants results in situations in which innocent actions appear guilty; the fact of identical twins puts in question the very idea of Nature, as well as the human quest for self-knowledge. Shakespeare ensures that the audience knows more of the situation than the characters do (except for the very last revelation), which increases the impression that the characters are victims, thereby producing effects both ridiculous and pathetic. In 2.2.110–46 the wife Adriana declares her belief in the sanctity of marriage as a spiritual union, she and her husband being 'undividable, incorporate' (she is echoing Ephesians 5. 31, the passage explicitly cited in the Marriage Service). The audience is aware – though she is not – that her husband has an identical twin, and that it is to this man, a complete stranger, that she is declaring herself indissolubly knit. The metaphysical paradox that man and wife are one flesh is thus (ironically) confronted by the physical paradox that man and brother are identically the same. The longing for reunion that one twin feels for the other is contrasted with the frustration both husband and wife feel within the bonds of marriage, and these contrasting emotions are transformed by a final restoration and reconciliation, precipitated by the Syracusians' sudden surprise discovery of a priory, a Christian refuge from persecution (5.1.37). We remind ourselves that Shakespeare is deliberately adapting Plautus: first his *Menaechmi*, changing the setting from Epi*damn*um (nobody, says a character in Plautus, leaves the town 'sine damno') to Ephesus, associated with St Paul; and secondly *Amphitruo*, in which the equivalents of the Syracusian Antipholus and Dromio are gods taking mortal shapes. A close Elizabethan analogue is Gascoigne's comedy of mistakes, *Supposes* (dated 1566). Shakespeare, we note, preferred the word 'errors', which unlike 'supposes' has Christian resonances; and he certainly uses his opening scene to give emphatic stress to the Romance element, which as T. S. Dorsch[4] says, presents the Egeon family journey from three aspects, 'a human quest, a surrender to chance, and a knowing or unknowing pil-

[4] T. S. Dorsch, ed. *The Comedy of Errors*, The New Cambridge Shakespeare (Cambridge, 1988), 1.1.132–4 n.

grimage'. But how far are such associations subdued as the action gets under way?

It is tempting to suppose that an alert Elizabethan spectator might have heard a Christian resonance in the title's reference to 'errors'. One might object 'What else are comedies made of?' – but then one should consider the power of those phrases learned by heart and repeated in the General Confession at Morning Prayer (1559): 'We have erred and strayed from thy ways, lyke loste shepe. We have folowed to muche the devyces and desyres of our own heartes. Wee have offended agaynst thy holy lawes. We have lefte undone those thinges which we oughte to have done, and we have done those thinges which we ought not to have done, and there is no health in us . . .' It seems altogether characteristic, given the exuberant fantasy apparent in the writing of this play, to suppose the dramatist saw the ironic application of these phrases – erring and straying from the way, the devices and desires of the heart – to the comic tradition of Plautus, and how by adapting Plautus he might put together the hilarious absurdity of farce with the divine comedy of the Christian dispensation, playing always on the edge of the lawful.

Elizabethan censorship was anxious about the controversial potential of religious allusion in plays, and forbade the direct presentation of religious ceremonies on the stage. Having decided to present the Dr Pinch exorcism episode, it would be only prudent to choose an exaggeratedly farcical mode; but the very extremity of outright slapstick treatment of Christian rite might seem to present its own risk – and this only the most obvious instance of a general feature of *The Comedy of Errors*, one that orthodox critical and stage interpretation has not found easy to account for: its paradoxical representation of events in simultaneous but contradictory terms, as both hilarious and spiritually serious.

The ministrations of Dr Pinch can be seen to be serious in so far as Antipholus is believed by his wife to be genuinely possessed by Satan, and (at another level) as constituting fitting punishment, however unintended, for his behaviour as a husband, but at the same time the ceremony is an obvious parody, absurd. The audience sees why Dr Pinch in turn, in the opinion of Antipholus, deserves what he gets, being bound, his beard set on fire, and then doused with puddled mire. As this is revenge, it is more violent; as it is a parody of a parody, it exaggerates by completely inverting the ceremony; but as it is a breaking of taboos, it is dangerous. The act of binding alludes to the Christian apocalypse itself, most obviously to Revelations 20, 1: 'And I sawe an Angel come downe from heaven, having the key of the bottomlesse pit, and a great chaine in his hand. And he tooke the Dragon, that old serpent, which is the devill and Satanas, and bound him a thousand yeres.' In view of censorship, it is to the playwright's and actors' advantage if Pinch is accused of being a mountebank, a 'doting wizard' – the very opposite (of course) of a priest; the difficulty is that once irony and its kin parody are admitted, the subversive consequences are not precisely calculable – as the reactions to famous ironic works of Erasmus and More confirm.[5]

As a background specifically to the binding, imprisonment and break-out of the Ephesian Antipholus and Dromio, Arthur Kinney[6] cites the Miracle plays of the Harrowing of Hell. The words of Paul – Ephesians 6, 11–17 in particular – are alluded to when the Syracusian pair, in the matching episode (4.4.143.ff), defend themselves with drawn swords.[7] The Abbess (5.1.68.ff), rebuking Adriana, refers to the duty of wives to submit to their husbands (thereby recalling Ephesians as cited in the

[5] See, for instance, Douglas Duncan, *Ben Jonson and the Lucianic Tradition* (Cambridge, 1979), 1–97.

[6] Arthur Kinney, 'Shakespeare's *The Comedy of Errors* and the Nature of Kinds', *SP* 1988, 29–52.

[7] Noted by Dorsch, *The Comedy of Errors*, Appendix 2, p. 113.

Marriage Service) and, climactically, recognizing her long-lost husband in Egeon, she makes an excellent conceit:

> Whoever bound him, I will loose his bonds.
> (5.1.340)

That is, in removing his prisoner's bonds she reclaims him to the bonds of marriage. She being an Abbess, and this the final moment of the play, where joy prevails, we can take this optimistically, as referring to the Christian ideal of service as perfect freedom. Yet this conceit focuses the interesting question of the play of irony between the Christian, the Plautine and Romance dimensions here.

An assessment of the dramatic mode of *The Comedy of Errors* needs to take full measure of a sense of humour as profound, or as Lucianic, as we may suspect of a playwright with an interest in Sir Thomas More. I want to suggest that it would be consistent with that Renaissance tradition of serious joking to sustain to the end the element of provocation in *The Comedy of Errors*. After all, look at the way Shakespeare begins the play: what else can we think but that he is provoking us, and means us to realize it? (See below, p. 121).

It is my argument that the dramaturgy of *The Comedy of Errors* divides an audience's attention so that episodes can be understood from two points of view simultaneously, and that, bearing in mind the tradition of Erasmus and *The Praise of Folly*, this is no diffusion of its dramatic and intellectual force. Take for example 3.2 where Luciana appeals to her brother-in-law Antipholus to be kinder to his wife: even if he does not love her, she says, at least he could conceal it: if he must commit adultery, then 'do it by stealth', 'Be secret-false',

> Look sweet, speak fair, become disloyalty;
> Apparel vice like virtue's harbinger;
> (3.2.11–12)

Unfortunately she does not realize this is the wrong twin brother, who while being confused by much of what she says, reacts eagerly to her beauty:

> Sing, Siren, for thyself, and I will dote
> (3.2.47)

The woman's struggle is with a morally complex dilemma, and her advice attempts to be morally adult; her appeal is made emotionally and is understandably anxious; but the man is simply enraptured by her at first sight. The situation, we may say, subverts her. As for him, he attempts polite formality while seized by intense emotion. The more open his confessions to Luciana, the more cunningly immoral he must appear to her to be, whereas her effect on him makes him so excited he takes a step clearly too hasty, in offering to marry her (and Christian marriage, says the service for Holy Matrimony in the Book of Common Prayer, 'is commended of Sainct Paule to bee honourable . . . and therefore is not to bee enterprised, not taken in hand unadvisedly, lyghtly or wantonly, to satisfie mennes carnall lustes and appetites . . . but reverentlie, discretely, advisedly, soberly, and in the feare of God'). It must therefore seem providence in the guise of error that Dromio should then enter to regale him with the horror-story of the kitchen-wench. This persuades Antipholus that Luciana is an enchantress who

> Hath almost made me traitor to myself.
> (3.2.162)

That is to say, however fantastic and hilarious the comedy may become, the mode is never insulated from serious considerations; indeed the humour actually arises from the serious human experience which is kept steadily before the audience and is never obscured, and this maintains in equipoise a kind of double design corresponding to the worldly and spiritual discourses of which the play is composed.

As a general background to incidents in the play, Arthur Kinney has suggested not only the Epistles of St Paul and Anglican Liturgy and the Homilies but the Miracle cycles, and he concludes that *The Comedy of Errors*, although Shakespeare's shortest play, 'moves all the way from the Nativity to the Last Judgement'.[8] Schematically speaking, agreed; yet this is not, surely, quite how it works: what is crucial is the manner of representation. We need to try to take the fullest measure of the figure of paradox which presides in the design and writing of this play, since it is paradox in its most metaphysical profundity which characterizes the teaching of the presiding Christian genius behind the text, St Paul. If – as I maintain – the play's whole design is, like its individual episodes, double, then it is to be read from two opposite points of view, Plautine and Elizabethan, simultaneously; it is to be read *both* as kaleidoscope of errors through which the human spirit grows *and* as providential pilgrimage. Furthermore, even in terms of the specific Christian code, if *The Comedy of Errors* is to be considered a providential pilgrimage that moves from a nativity to a last judgement, then it must also, simultaneously, be seen as the *reverse*. In the Pauline–Christian terms of rebirth ('It is sowen a naturall body, it riseth a spirituall body', 1 Corinthians 15, 44) – it moves *from* a last judgement *to* a nativity. Only here the paradoxical, ludic structure results in no double meaning: instead it doubly augments the positive, and this is the same pattern which is glimpsed in the Abbess's last and most far-fetched conceit:

> After so long grief, such nativity. (5.1.407)

Here then is theatre simultaneously profane yet holy, profound yet full of nonsense.

Structurally *The Winter's Tale* is a double action divided by Time the Chorus. Part 1, the movement from court to country and from kings to shepherds, is reversed in part 2, a movement from country to court and from shepherds to kings, as in a diptych or pair of hinged mirrors: and this double pattern is repeated in other terms, the repetition in the two parts of stories, characters, events, motifs and even individual words composing patterns of likeness-with-difference, of conceits which are far-fetched over a gap between Sicily and Bohemia, winter and spring, tragedy and comedy. The double design is echoed in the smallest verbal links between the two halves of the play, as with the single word *hook*, used by Leontes gloating at the prospect of seizing Hermione: 'she / I can hook to me' (2.3.7), and by Polixenes rebuking Florizel: 'Thou a sceptre's heir, / That thus affects a sheep-hook' (4.4.419–420): or the single word *slip*, used by Perdita in 4.4.100 to mean 'a twig, sprig or small shoot taken from a plant or tree for purposes of grafting or planting' (*OED* sb 2.1) but earlier used in another sense, 'sin', by her mother playfully ('slipp'd', 1.2.85) and by her father savagely ('slippery', 1.2.273). The patterns of likeness-with-difference in this play often begin in language and are realized later in stage images: as in the throw-away jocular remark of Autolycus about the Old Shepherd's fate: 'Some say he shall be ston'd; but that fate is too soft for him, say I.' (4.4.778–9). This collocation *stoned/soft* bizarrely anticipates the description of the Old Shepherd weeping 'like a weather-bitten conduit of many kings' reigns' (5.2.55–6), a statue-image that reverses Autolycus' *stoned/soft* opposition, and which though in travesty-form, anticipates the words of the 'marble-breasted' Leontes before the statue of Hermione – 'does not the stone rebuke me / For being more stone than it?' (5.3.37–8) and the reverse transformation of Perdita as the spectators see her, rapt in admiration, 'Standing like stone' beside the statue of Hermione (5.3.42).

In *The Winter's Tale* 1.2 there is stress on subtle divisions between the three figures Leontes, Hermione and Polixenes, even before Leontes begins to lose control. An intricate reflection of 1.2 is presented by 5.1 where, instead of Hermione and Polixenes it is this

---

[8] Kinney, 'Shakespeare's *The Comedy of Errors*', p. 50. Kinney argues that the play's mode is analogous to the medieval drama's mixture of farce and piety as seen in *Secunda Pastorum*.

time the youthful Perdita and Florizel who confront Leontes, and who remind him of what his rage has deprived him of:

> I might have look'd upon my queen's full eyes,
> Have taken treasure from her lips (5.1.53–4)

The baby girl present though not yet born in 1.2, and there disowned by him, is here in 5.1 grown up: Perdita, first freed and enfranchized from her father's rage, then subject to rage from Florizel's father, is now again with her own father, Leontes, and yet again unintentionally provoking him, though this time to opposite effect – he confesses that while he gazes at her it is Hermione he is reminded of.

The first sight of Florizel is also a source of wonder, reminding Leontes vividly of the Polixenes he loved in youth:

> Your mother was most true to wedlock, Prince,
> For she did print your royal father off,
> Conceiving you. (5.1.124–6)

This also recalls the moment in 1.2.122 when Leontes found comfort in his own son Mamillius, saw the likeness to himself, that in fact the boy's nose was 'a copy out o'mine'. There is another echo here, more interesting because more teasing. Paulina had insisted that it was Leontes' features that the new-born baby reprinted:

> Behold, my lords,
> Although the print be little, the whole matter
> And copy of the father – eye, nose, lip;
> The trick of's frown, his forehead . . .
> (2.3.98–101)

Perhaps no one in real life is on oath when first showing a father his new-born child, certainly not Paulina. Nevertheless, this insistence on precise details of facial likeness is striking. In 5.1 the baby girl which Paulina had so strongly urged to be a copy of Leontes, is now aged sixteen a copy of Hermione. So the loving pair Perdita and Florizel are the offspring of the 'twinn'd lambs' Leontes and Polixenes. They represent a lawful reconciliation of the triangular relationship Leontes – Hermione – Polixenes but also, they stand for Leontes' two lost children, his baby daughter and Mamillius. That is to say, Perdita and Florizel, as they stand before Leontes, are copies, doubles, for five remembered figures from the past: his wife, his best friend, himself, his son, his daughter. Those were the very figures which tortured his alienated mind at the beginning of the play.

Paulina, concerned to awaken loving associations in Leontes' mind, reminds him that Florizel was born in the very same hour as Mamillius; but this to an audience is surprising news – it seems to invite the speculation that, in the form of a son-in-law, Leontes' lost son is redeemed – but also, more obscurely, that the twinning of the fathers was replicated in the sons. But reviving the memory of Mamillius only revives grief: the fantasy of complete wish-fulfilment is denied, loss is to be permanent, including loss of innocence and twinship.

The emphasis on the likeness of Mamillius and Perdita may be supported, in stage performance, by the same actor doubling the roles; what cannot be done plausibly (though it has been tried), and should not be done thematically, is for one actor to double the roles of Perdita and Hermione. There must be likeness-with-difference between them. Florizel and Perdita are like their parents, but if they were to be exchangeably identical to them, the implication of growth and change and loss would be absent: but the new generation has its own branching. What is here made unmistakably explicit, in *The Winter's Tale*, helps us to recognize a parallel though only implicit ambivalence in the ending of *The Comedy of Errors*.

The question of the meaning of the double in *The Comedy of Errors* is distilled finally in stage images which seem visually, conclusively, identical in their doubleness. At the climax the entrance of the Abbess unwittingly brings the two long-separated pairs of twins together. A sense of incredulity combines with deep satisfaction and light-headedness all round: Antipholus wonders 'If this be not a dream I see and hear' (5.1.377), but for his brother the preceding action, which the audience know to be entirely explicable as error, has been rather one of nightmare, in which the people he knows best have acted like strangers or treated him insolently or declared him a victim of witchcraft and satanic possession and insanity.

Astonishment, therefore, but also a powerful undertow of awe and fear, are palpable as the Duke sees the twins together: 'which is the natural man, / And which the spirit?' (5.1.334–5) Their reunion results in the restoration to the Abbess of her sons, and then of her husband, rescued from the gallows in the nick of time. The Abbess, anticipating the manner of *The Winter's Tale*, employs a remarkable 'overreacher' in describing this extreme separation as a pregnancy of thirty-three years now astonishingly delivered: 'After so long grief, such nativity' (407). Dromio jests to his twin: 'Methinks you are my glass and not my brother' (418), the reunion of the two pairs of twins constituting a supreme moment of happiness. As the moment passes a discerning spectator may see opening up for each twin the inevitability of further branching – likenesses-*with*-difference – as Antipholus of Syracuse contemplates union with Luciana, and Antipholus of Ephesus union again with his wife Adriana, acknowledging – perhaps – their mutual errors of selfishness and self-deception.

The question of the double is resolved in the single figure, the Abbess-mother, combining opposites: she has been both long-lost and always present (though hidden), she is both priestess and wife, she is both holy and natural. *The Winter's Tale*, too, presents a climactic reunion centred on the mother and charged with wonder, yet in contrast to *The Comedy of Errors* it deliberately heightens the sense of discrepancy and incommensurability – indeed it makes clear how much must remain unredeemable (as if the ghost of Pandosto the suicide were half-acknowledged); and this is a vital difference from *The Comedy of Errors*. In the final scene of *The Winter's Tale* Florizel is not identical to, but only like, Polixenes, a likeness-with-difference. This separates him from the symbolic role of reflecting the past, of exact duplication and repetition. This is not to be the world of Beckett's *Play*. Perdita is emphatically identified with Hermione but then decisively separated from her, precisely at the point where the statue is seen (like old Aegeon in *The Comedy of Errors*) to have marks of 'time's deformed hand' upon it. Hermione returns so much altered, unlike what she was (and Perdita shows what she was like) but truly like her present self, that is, alive to a revived Leontes: revived, but like Leontes, old, and with not long to live.

In this moment, as the statue of Hermione moves, Shakespeare subjects the idea of playing to extreme pressure. Edgar Wind has discussed the Elizabethan naturalization of the Renaissance tradition of *serio ludere*, 'experiments in metaphor, semi-magical exercises which would solemnly entertain and astonish the beholder'. These serious games consisted in 'finding within common experience an unusual object endowed with the kind of contradictory attributes which are difficult to imagine united in the deity'.[9] Wind makes the point that the Renaissance thought a baffling account, patently incomplete, should be given, 'so that the reader may be induced to figure out the concealed part for himself' (Wind, p. 234). There is a serious modification I would add to this argument: it is in the nature of irony that there can be no certainty about the significance of the act of concealing in itself; no certainty of the priority of what is openly expressed over what is concealed and alluded to; no certainty, given that there is allusion, about when its full extent has been recognized. Interpretation in such cases is ultimately, as Paulina firmly declares, a matter of faith.

[9] Edgar Wind, *Pagan Mysteries in the Renaissance* (London, 1958, rev. edn. 1967), 222–35.

HERE A GAP OF SIXTEEN OR THIRTY-THREE YEARS

The structural pattern of *The Comedy of Errors* is simple in itself, Shakespeare relies on repetition with variation to achieve the effect of complexity. In *The Winter's Tale* the patterning, both verbal and structural, is much more complex, so that many critics have objected to its seeming excess. In my view this is a misunderstanding of its mode, which comparison with *The Comedy of Errors* can help clarify; and comparing the treatment of time in the two plays may confirm Shakespeare's fidelity to the rhetorical mode of *serio ludere* even when, in *The Winter's Tale*, writing an outright tragicomedy.

The disorientation of the spectator (and the would-be interpreter) are the very first things Shakespeare concentrates on in *The Comedy of Errors*, and in its first scene. The opening lines sound like the end of a play, as a long court hearing concludes with a judgement: Egeon declares

> Proceed, Solinus, to procure my fall,
> And by the doom of death end woes and all.

The impression that the case has been heard at some length seems confirmed by the Duke's response:

> Merchant of Syracusa, plead no more.

and by Egeon's answer, which repeats the stress on a long process terminating:

> Yet this my comfort, when your words are done,
> My woes end likewise with the evening sun.

The Duke brings matters to a close with perfunctory courtesy:

> Well, Syracusian, say in brief...

Only with an effort can Egeon manage a reply at all: he sounds worn out:

> A heavier task could not have been impos'd
> Than I to speak my griefs unspeakable
> (1.1.31–2)

So, a wordless valediction and finis? What happened to the rest of the play? The spectators, put off-balance in this way, are disconcerted again when the apparently exhausted Egeon embarks buoyantly on his story with the leisured amplitude of someone who has all the time in the world. He proceeds for an unhesitating sixty-four lines, then briefly pauses – 'O let me say no more' – but only for rhetorical effect, while the Duke, having before enjoined brevity, is now egging him on:

> Nay, forward, old man, do not break off so
> (1.1.96)

Twenty-two lines later, Egeon's narrative still shows no sign of arriving at the present; meanwhile the Duke is settling down for a story he clearly feels is only just getting into its stride – 'Do me the favour to dilate at full' (122). That it should be just at this point that Egeon runs out of steam (he can only manage fifteen lines more) is a further droll Shakespearian touch.

The opening situation (as the final lines also remind us) virtually constitutes a Beckett opening: 'Nothing to be done.' The scene begins with a conclusion, a judgement, then follows this with a retrospective narration. In performance this is likely to feel recklessly prolonged, yet in another sense, given that it presents an absurdly foreshortened account of a long complicated story, it is recklessly hasty.

We should note an additional contradiction. The story was sufficiently far-fetched before Shakespeare got hold of it, and by the time he had finished it achieves a very zenith of improbability; but the chosen decorum for its telling in this scene – unvarying solemnity of tone and heavy pathos – puts all the stress on the opposite sense of sheer inevitability.

Egeon's long woe crowned by sudden wonder points to the play's general concern with the comic possibilities of delay and haste. In the two hours traffic of the stage *The Comedy of Errors* shows thirty-three years[10] concentrated in one day. It proceeds by a dizzying interweaving of fast- and slow-paced action as well as of wildly contrasting time-scales; and, related to this, it plays with the effects of time, especially of delay and haste: time as it instils patience or provokes exasperation, and, more existentially still, pace and timing as fateful determinants. In this play it is the pace at which experience is encountered that determines whether it can be absorbed coherently or induces confusion and terror, and it is timing which keeps the family missing one another until they finally collide.

Attitudes to delay are telling in their variety. The Merchant requires payment on the nail, and summons the Law; Adriana, waiting for Antipholus to come home, is agitated; Luciana, just waiting around (for the right man), tries to be stoical; the Abbess gets on with her duty, serving God, but when the right time comes she seizes her chance. Egeon must wait passively all day, since the Duke has delayed the execution until sunset. Above all, both Antipholus of Syracuse and Antipholus of Ephesus have repeatedly to spend time waiting about for their respective Dromios; but whereas Egeon remains patient, waiting without incident until the very end, his sons throughout the action are prone to impatience and are subjected to a bewildering variety of surprises, whether of miraculous-seeming gratification or acute frustration. To them a series of sudden, apparently unrelated events occur, seemingly existential, arbitrary: for instance Antipholus of Syracuse receives the unexpected hospitality of Adriana, Antipholus of Ephesus finds his door inexplicably shut against him; yet their extremely opposed reactions to what they think disorder only enhance the spectator's sense of symmetry in the dramatic design.

In *The Winter's Tale* first of all, the *negation* of time is identified with happiness: an idea Polixenes touches on early in 1.2 when he says his small son 'makes a July's day short as December', preventing thoughts that 'would thick my blood' (1.2.171). Associated with this is the idea of natural law as expressed in the time taken by its proceedings, and the trouble caused by Nature's erratic timing, by its delay or haste: so in Nature too-forward young buds may be killed by late wintry storms, and a gardener's pruning aids growth, but only when the time is right.

The first words of Polixenes assert that he has *delayed* his return to his duty and his family during nine months. Leontes stresses that he chose Hermione for love (he makes no reference to dynastic considerations); and Hermione exercised her right of choice too – but Leontes recalls that 'three crabbed months soured themselves to death' while she delayed her choice. To Leontes in his jealousy, memory of Hermione's *three months* delay suddenly suggests a suspicious link to Polixenes, whose first words are of *nine months*. For Leontes, rashly jumping to conclusions and burning with impatience for revenge, *haste*, just as much as *delay*, can be a sign in others of guilt: in 1.2 Leontes obsessively supposes lustful Hermione and Polixenes driven to frantic impatience,

> wishing clocks more swift?
> Hours, minutes? noon, midnight?
> (1.2.289–90)

whereas Hermione good-humouredly teases Polixenes about when the due time came for him to experience temptation (1.2.75–86).

Shakespeare goes on to play obliquely with

[10] Thirty-three years: the Abbess has the last word on the matter, though her husband (admittedly overwrought) says twenty-three years – eighteen plus five – in 1.1 while in 5.1 (again overwrought) he changes five to seven. In any case a great length of time. Shakespeare perhaps also intends, ironically, to recall Sidney's mocking description of how Elizabethan dramatists handled time: 'she is got with child, delivered of a fair boy; he is lost, groweth a man, falls in love, and is ready to get another child; and all this in two hours space: which, how absurd it is in sense, even sense may imagine, and Art hath taught ...' (E. D. Jones ed., Sidney, *An Apology for Poetry* in *English Critical Essays XVI–XVIII Centuries* (Oxford, 1922), p. 45.

the idea of delay and haste in relation to Nature's measure of time, when Hermione's son Mamillius, surprisingly, shows a marked forwardness, a precociousness, in banter of a sexual kind with the court ladies in 2.1. In 2.3 the audience learns that Perdita's own birth was brought on by Leontes' rage: Hermione consequently was delivered 'something before her time' (2.2.23). The second half of the play will open in 3.3 with the Old Shepherd's remark that youth is a prolonged wait for adulthood – a kind of delay in the life-cycle – producing nothing but impulsive disruption, 'getting wenches with child, wronging the ancientry, stealing, fighting' (3.3.61–3). In 4.4 stress falls on the forwardness – the precociousness – of youthful Florizel as well as of young Perdita, and how this exposes them to a father's wrath. Perdita, unaware of her own past history, or her dead brother's, or of the present threat posed by Polixenes, dwells on the vulnerability of the very young to premature death, of young maids like flowers that risk a too-hasty appearance in early Spring 'before the swallow dares', or like pale primroses

> That die unmarried, ere they can behold
> Bright Phoebus in his strength (4.4.123–4)

When Polixenes does unmask in rage to disrupt the proceedings, Florizel, undismayed, declares himself 'delay'd'

> But nothing alt'red; What I was, I am;
> More straining on for plucking back.
> (4.4.464–5)

And here, we may notice, the motif of delay / haste having been by now made familiar, is given a new twist: and it is ingeniously varied again in the case of the Old Shepherd who, having successfully delayed death well beyond the traditional life-span of the Bible, three score and ten years, fears he is now to be all too hastily cut off:

> a man of fourscore three,
> That thought to fill his grave in quiet; yea,
> To die upon the bed my father died.
> (4.4.453–5)

The play ends with a final wry twist to this motif of time stretched by delay or compressed by haste, of time suspended in dream or illusion contrasted to time measured by the beat of the pulse. In the play's last moment Leontes looks back on its events and concludes that everybody present has 'perform'd' a 'part' in 'this wide gap of time'. His word 'gap' signifies a measurable extent of time, between then and now, but also a sheer blank, a nothing. To Leontes it is almost as if time had been suspended while they performed a dream-like comedy of errors, and now they are awake again.

But is there a third possible meaning, more metaphysical? May the 'wide gap of time' be *the span of life*, after which they are freed from time? Then the idea of childish happiness freed from time, which Polixenes describes in 1.2.67–71, would be transfigured into the apocalyptic terms of Paul (1 Corinthians 15, 51–3): 'Beholde, I shew you a mystery. We shall not all sleepe, but we shall all be changed, In a moment, in the twinckling of an eye, at the last trumpe; (for the trumpe shall blowe) and the dead shall rise incorruptible, and we shall be changed'. This also, in a further sense, is to be free from time: and such a triple-meaning seems wholly appropriate, viewed from *The Comedy of Errors*.

THE 'SHAKESPEARIAN GAP' IN FRENCH[1]

JEAN-MICHEL DEPRATS

Major literary works are characterized by a seeming paradox. They call for translation and resist translation. As no translation can circumscribe or exhaust them, their infinite richness and resonance fuels an endless desire for translation. But as creativity is essentially and intimately linked in them to the poetic potentialities of one specific language – the poet's native tongue – they also defy and baffle translation. My intention is to map the world of untranslatability for a French translator of Shakespeare, suggesting eventually that close attention to the theatrical dimension of a play, to its rhetorical and imaginary economy, without necessarily reducing the losses in poetic gloss, enables the translator to stick closely to the original language in all its physical reality, its palpable materiality.

Jakobson contends that poetry, governed as it is by paronomasia – by the relationship between the phonemic and the semantic unit as in a pun – is, by definition, untranslatable.[2] Here, the welding of matter and form is so close that no dissociation is admissible. But attacks on the translation of poetry are simply the barbed edge of the general assertion that no language can be translated without fundamental loss. Every translation of a linguistic sign is, at some level, a 'creative transposition'. Because all human speech consists of arbitrarily selected but intensely conventionalized signals, meaning can never be wholly separated from expressive form. Even the most purely ostensive, apparently neutral terms are embedded in linguistic particularity, in an intricate mould of cultural-historical habits. The postulate of untranslatability is founded on the conviction, formal and pragmatic, that there can be no true symmetry, no adequate mirroring, between two different semantic systems. The vital energies, the luminosity and pressure of the original text have not only been diminished by translation; they have been made tawdry. Somehow, the process of entropy is one of active corruption. As Nabokov puts it in his poem 'On translating *Eugene Onegin*':

> What is translation? On a platter
> A poet's pale and glaring head,
> A parrot's screech, a monkey's chatter,
> And profanation of the dead.[3]

As soon as one defines translation as 'grasping a meaning', the fact that meaning is inseparable from the literal layer of speech immediately denies the legitimacy of that process. Translators, writers and readers have always experienced that. The conquering process of translation cannot be carried on without a certain feeling of violence, inadequacy and

[1] The phrase is George Steiner's in *After Babel, Aspects of Language and Translation* (Oxford University Press, 1975), p. 366.

[2] 'On Linguistic Aspects of Translation' in Reuben A. Brower (ed.), *On Translation* (New York, Oxford University Press, Galaxy Books no. 175), 1959, pp. 232–9.

[3] 'On translating Eugen Onegin', *The Portable Nabokov*, Page Stegner ed., (Penguin Books, 1977, [Viking Press, 1968]) (From *New Yorker* and *Poems*, 1955), p. 531.

betrayal. Steiner is right to talk of the sadness that always accompanies the experience of translation.[4] There is always a certain element of pain, not only that of the translator, but, if I may say so, of the translated text – that is, of the meaning cut off from the letter.

Jacques Derrida describes this beautifully: 'The verbal body cannot be translated. Dropping that body is the essential energy of translation.'[5] But what has been dropped, the body of the text, takes its revenge. Translation finds out to its cost that the meaning and the signifier can be dissociated and cannot. In that sense, untranslatability is the life of speech. If in a text, the letter and the meaning are tightly linked, translation can only be a betrayal, even if this kind of betrayal is necessary for cultural exchange and communication in general. But the miracle is never complete. Each translation falls short. At best, translation can come close to the demands of the original, but there can be no total circumscription.

How can the musical softness of a line such as: 'How sweet the moonlight sleeps upon this bank' be translated into French – or into any other language – in which the 'sweet/sleep' assonance is lost and where the long drawn-out sounds do not exist? Sounds do not translate, and thus translation comes up against the different phonetic structures of languages. The gist of a poem is its harmony, its music. Rhythm, metrics, rhyme are the mainsprings and elements of this harmony. Leaving them out, leaving out any single one of them, results in flattening out the original text.

André Gide, who translated *Hamlet* and *Antony and Cleopatra*, wrote that 'though there is no writer who deserves translation more than Shakespeare, he is without doubt the most difficult playwright to translate. In no other case is translation more likely to disfigure the original text'.[6] Along with its ascending rhythm inverted in the last foot, the musical lightness, fluidity and expressiveness of the first line of *Twelfth Night*: 'If music be the food of love, play on' relies on its verbal structure: nine words, among which only one has more than one syllable. It is impossible to express all this in French in an equally short way. The fundamental difficulty of translating Shakespeare into French lies first in this difference of proportion, of volume, between languages. French takes more place, it simply uses more words or longer words.

The goal of translation, as far as poetry is concerned, is not only to communicate a meaning. It is also to reproduce an object, its rhythm, form and volume. French translations of Shakespeare thus appear too slow, too laboured. In Shakespeare, the images overlap and cascade over one another. The translator would like to keep such density, but in the effort to preserve it, is often led to expand into a whole sentence the metaphor which, in the English text, is contained in a single word. All the poetic movement in this verbal intricacy is in translation like a broken spring.

This is not only a question of rhetorical economy or of sensory impact. The systematized use of monosyllables may at times be connected with overall patterns of meaning, as in the cauldron scene in *Macbeth* in which the witches' atomized language – words reduced to their shortest possible length – is the linguistic image of their metaphysical design of chaos and destruction. Just as the heterogeneous bits and scraps thrown into the brew – parts of vegetable and animal bodies torn from their organic wholes – reflect their satanic attempts to undermine the unity of macrocosm and microcosm.

Shorter words being of Saxon origin, longer words of Latin root, Shakespeare constantly plays on two linguistic planes available to him, two registers which he can at will contrast and combine. The pathos of Othello's predicament in the 'It is the cause, it is the cause' speech, his

4 Steiner, *After Babel*, pp. 269, 293.

5 *L'Ecriture et la différence* (Paris, Seuil, 1967), p. 312 (my translation).

6 Foreword to the 1959 Pléiade edition of Shakespeare's works (Paris, Gallimard), p. IX (my translation).

self-deception, his desperate attempt to impose on his contemplated murder the meaning of a sacrifice done in the name of justice, are to a large extent brought home by the opposition between simple, concrete monosyllabic words of Saxon origin ('Put out the light and then put out the light ...') and more resonant, more sophisticated longer words of Latin origin ('monumental alabaster'; 'pattern of excelling nature'; 'Promethean'; 'relume' etc. ...). This dramatic effect is suppressed in a translation into a homogeneous romance language.

Another source of reduction in translation is linked to Shakespeare's linguistic lavishness. Faced with the lexical inventiveness of Shakespeare's language, the translator feels cramped in his/her own clothes. Creating neologisms to render words of Shakespearian coinage is seldom possible. Modern French no longer has the plasticity which made possible Rabelais' and Montaigne's verbal inventions. In any case, the lexical narrowness of French entails a loss, which is not only linguistic and semantic but historical and dramatic. Shylock and Antonio's first encounter in *The Merchant of Venice* revolves around the question of interest or, rather, in historical terms, of usury. Significantly, neither Antonio nor Shylock uses the word 'usury', they play on at least five periphrases: usance/usances, thrift, interest, excess, advantage.[7] This strategy of circumlocution, this linguistic beating about the bush characterizes the antagonists' behaviour in this scene. In French, the translator has only three terms available: *intérêt, profit, usure,* the last one being precisely the only word the protagonists do not utter or refuse to utter.

Polysemy, ambivalence, amphibology confront the translator with even more insurmountable hurdles than synonymy. Shakespeare delighted in the many different meanings which could be compacted into a word or a phrase. More than any of his contemporaries, he was fond of puns and witticisms, word games, elaborate conceits. He relied upon his ear and common usage and the associative logic of a language which had not yet been disciplined by neo-classical rules. Such linguistic practice obviously baffles translation. How can we satisfactorily translate a line like 'My poor fool is hanged' in *King Lear,* when any translation by a term of pity and endearment misses the reference to the Fool? Elizabethan speech is surrounded by an aura of evocation – for which Gide proposes the term *harmoniques* – generally recalcitrant to the bias towards precision, towards definite nomination, in French. Often the sense of the original is indeterminate; native English speakers, scholars of Shakespeare and Elizabethan usage offer widely divergent interpretations. What is the French translator to make of *Antony and Cleopatra* 5.1.52: 'A poor Egyptian yet ...' in which 'yet' can mean 'however', 'still', 'so far', 'from now on', 'again', 'besides', etc. ... or might, by a change in punctuation, be attached to the clause following: 'yet the queen my mistress ...'? How can he translate Macbeth's 'She might have died hereafter' where 'hereafter' doesn't mean 'later', but, according to John Middleton Murry, 'in a different mode of time than that in which Macbeth is imprisoned now'?[8] It is probably a part of Shakespeare's strategy, and of the strategy of spoken drama as such, to allow indecision, to let different possibilities of meaning 'hover' around the principal axis. But the translator must choose or inflate into explicative paraphrase; and the French translator is induced, by the grain of his/her language and mental habits, to make his/her choice damagingly exact. When you have to translate, you either choose a precise meaning and lose the complexity of the line, and the ambiguity of the word, or you decide upon a more complex analytical rendering – and then use more words.

---

7 Strangely enough, the list does not include the term 'use' so often employed in the Sonnets in its financial meaning.

8 *Shakespeare* (London, Jonathan Cape [1936] 1955), p. 335.

Then, there is the excruciating and often insoluble problem of the puns. The translation of Feste's 'I live by the church' in which 'by' alternately means 'near' and 'through' leads to a far-fetched verbal game and to very clumsy quibbling in French. Sonnets 135, 136 and 143 which involve elaborate punning on will (wishes, carnal desire, one or more persons named Will[9]) are almost untranslatable. Jean Fuzier maintains the same word (Désir) throughout,[10] Jean-François Peyret refers to 'le *William*' throughout.[11] However ingenious the solution chosen may be, the translated text inevitably has a narrower scope than the original and functions differently. Any translation of *Love's Labour's Lost* is bound to sound clearer than its English counterpart. One may wonder, in this particular case, whether the spectator is not better off with a translation. In her Riverside introduction to the play, Anne Barton notes that '*Love's Labour's Lost* is perhaps the most relentlessly Elizabethan of all Shakespeare's plays. Filled with wordgames, elaborate conceits, parodies of spoken and written styles and obscure topical allusions, it continually requires – and baffles – scholarly explanation. Nothing can ever make most of the puns and witticisms of *Love's Labour's Lost* seem contemporary again.' She later emphasizes 'the inaccessibility of much of the dialogue'. In translation, if much of the ingenuity and complexity of Shakespeare's quibbling is subdued, the linguistic energy can be revitalized and the play communicates its freshness and brilliance more efficiently. Highfalutin or scholarly puns can be replaced by more immediate and intelligible ones.

The case of *Love's Labour's Lost* enables us to perceive that aspect of translation which Goethe praised as rejuvenation (*Verjüngung*), regeneration (*Auffrischung*).[12] It places the question of translation in its dialectic dimension of remoteness and closeness. Translation, almost always presented in terms of loss, can also be at times thought of in terms of gain and opportunity. Peter Brook has often insisted on the hindrance caused by Shakespeare's archaic terms and obscure phrases to the direct flux of communication between actor and audience. As far as Shakespearian performance is concerned, he has often vindicated his theatrical adventure in France and in French at the Bouffes du Nord on the ground that a translated text, more contemporary, enabled him to stage Shakespeare anew. No one would deny that the distance between Shakespeare's text and modern English speaking audiences is constantly increasing. Contemporary British audiences find Shakespeare's language, in its use of unfamiliar words and turns of phrase, difficult to grasp. Modern ears are not trained to catch the tricks of assonance, dissonance, changing stresses within the verse line, alliteration and punning rhymes. To some extent, defective though it be, translation, when practised as creative transposition, may remove some of the barriers to understanding and make Shakespeare sound more immediate, more contemporary.

This is of course a general statement which applies only to the overall effect of translation. As far as polysemy is concerned, there is no denying that, in specific occurrences, the non-coincidence of semantic and phonetic structures in different languages entails an impoverishment of the functioning of the text in translation. Effects of irony and perspective can be erased. In *Timon of Athens*, an Athenian Lord says about Timon in the first scene:

> no meed but he repays
> Sevenfold above itself; no gift to him
> But breeds the giver a return exceeding
> All use of quittance. (280–3)

[9] Quibbling on 'will' usually also implies the meaning 'testament' and 'will-power'.

[10] Pléiade edition pp. 130 and 133.

[11] *Quarante Sonnets de Shakespeare traduits par Jean-François Peyret pour servir à la scène*, Série Les Belles Infidèles (Actes-Sud, 1990), pp. 72–3.

[12] Antoine Berman, *L'épreuve de l'étranger.* Culture et traduction dans l'Allemagne romantique (Paris, Gallimard, 1984), p. 105.

'Quittance' here does not only mean 'receipt', it also or rather simultaneously implies in Shakespeare's English 'what is due in return': gratitude. Thus, the word plays on two registers: financial and moral. The same can be said of 'use' which means both 'usual practice' and 'interest'. 'Use of quittance' can be analysed as meaning either 'rates of interest one must repay' or 'gratitude required by custom'. Thus, the line functions both ways: it depicts Timon, whose bounty goes far beyond customary good manners, but is also self-revealing about the Lord who speaks it by telling us that, contrary to Timon, he never forgets his financial interest. 'All use of quittance' is not an obscure phrase, it's double keyed language. Thus, it is not meaning but formulation which baffles translation as the text is not ambiguous but ambivalent. The two parallel meanings are clear and relevant. Neither should be given pride of place or chosen in isolation but translation cannot preserve the two.

For me, as a translator, the main requirement is to preserve the performability of the text.[13] Translating Shakespeare for the stage forces one to give the actors precise material to work with. Thus, in a way, you translate *theatre* rather than simply *for* the theatre, a phrase which suggests that you are adapting something for an external goal. In that respect, literary translations, meant for the eye but not the ear, preclude an essential dimension of the text.

A Shakespeare play is, above all, a text written for mouths, lungs and human breath. Translating it for the stage invites us then to write a language which is both oral and gestic, full of power and life, in which the properties of the verb become acting material. Thus André Gide's version of *Hamlet* (1.2.76): 'Apparence? Eh! non, Madame. Réalité. Qu'ai-je affaire avec le "paraître"?'[14] is obviously more 'oral', and conveys greater energy than does Yves Bonnefoy's translation: 'Qui me semble, madame? Oh non, qui est! Je ne sais pas ce que sembler signifie!'[15] The translator must take into account the physical demands of the actor, and ensure that the verbal fabric is supported by the actions of the body and the modulations of the voice. The reason Shakespeare's plays constitute such precious dramatic material is that they possess that specific quality which defines them as texts for the theatre, they are fraught with suggestions concerning the actor's bearing on stage. Shakespeare's texts are entirely geared towards performance. Written by an actor for actors, a play by Shakespeare is a theatre script in which the word order, the rhythms and the images imply certain gestures, where the sensory characteristics of the words are an instrument for the player. The translator's task is to preserve the theatricality and the rhythm embedded in the original text. Preserving the oral and sonorous impact requires a translation which is more concerned with movement and rhythm than with intellectual understanding. If we are to avoid drawn-out explanations which weaken the taut dramatic structure, the translation must be clear, resolute, kinetic and concise, and must have considerable verbal economy. Sticking closely to the construction of the original text, trying to keep the same word order and (as far as we can) the same number of words as there are in English, does not mean attempting to create an impossible imitation. It simply means trying to preserve the dramatic impetus and vocal energy of the original play. Shakespeare wrote for the stage, and the spectator, borne along by the swiftness of both word and action, is more sensitive to form than to content. The perception of rhythms and sounds takes precedence over intellectual comprehension. Or rather, the latter can only come about by way of the former. If we emphasize tenor over vehicle, and favour

13 A longer version of these remarks has been published in *Shakespeare and France*, ed. Holger Klein and Jean-Marie Maguin, *Shakespeare Yearbook*, vol. 5, 1994 (The Edwin Mellen Press, Lewiston, 1995), pp. 345–58.

14 *Hamlet*, translated by André Gide, Pléiade, vol. 2, p. 620.

15 *Hamlet*, Folio no. 1069 (Paris, Gallimard, 1978), p. 39.

the denotative use of a language to the detriment of its music and movement, we only contribute to making a translation difficult to perform. The demand for theatricality and attention to the poetics of the text are requirements which, far from being contradictory, in fact intersect, or even go hand in hand with one another. So the first aim of any translation written for performance is to preserve the play's vocal energy.

Theatricality does not imply orality alone. Shakespeare's plays are also dramatic in the sense that they call for stage action. By means of precise indications of gesture and movement, or through implicit suggestions of physical bearing, they have the capacity to set the body in motion. Language has a body, not only in the metaphorical sense. There is, indeed, a gestic quality of the poetic word. In a dramatic text, the actors' movements are present within the verbal fabric itself in the form of hints to guide the actions of the body. Without giving stage directions – which are rather infrequent in Shakespeare's plays – the spoken text sets up, describes or suggests actions.[16] Every dramatic text demands to be brought to life by the player's body, voice and action. The word pronounced on stage must be deciphered or decoded by the actor's body if it is to be understood by the spectator. That it should be uttered is not enough; the entire body must participate in the act of speaking. And the language of Shakespeare possesses this 'physicality' to the highest degree.

Brecht tells us that: 'A language is gestic when it indicates the exact standpoint adopted by the speaker toward others. The phrase "Pluck out thy right eye if it offend thee" is from a gestic point of view less rich than the phrase "If thy right eye offend thee, pluck it out." In the latter, the eye is shown first, then comes the first part of the phrase, which clearly contains the *gestus* of the conjecture, and finally the second part, like an ambush, a liberating piece of advice'.[17]

At the end of his speech about the death of kings, Richard II stresses the fact that a king is as mortal as his subjects, and concludes:

> ... Subjected thus,
> How can you say to me I am a king?
> (*Richard II*, 3.2.172–3)

The literal translation:

> ... ainsi assujetti,
> Comment pouvez-vous me dire que je suis roi?

is certainly more gestic, and contains a more precise indication of how the actor should deliver it, than does that of Pierre Leyris:

> Qu'avez-vous à me dire, esclave comme je suis,
> que je suis roi?[18]

Although this translation is borne by the rhythm of oratory, it is governed by the logic and poetics of written language. Leyris makes no difference between two *gestus* which are clearly separate in the original text. In the former version, on the other hand, the presence of the word *assujetti* suspended at the end of the line, the upholding of the anacoluthon and the syntactical twist, together with the rapid projection of this paradoxical royalty, give the player more analytical and more precise acting material.

What Brecht calls *gestus*[19] when he writes about gestic language includes the physical bearing of the actor, his/her stance in relation to his/her fellow actors, but also his/her mental attitude vis-à-vis his/her lines and the theatrical

[16] On the question of language-implied or explicitly stated directions concerning gesture and movement, see Jörg Hasler, *Shakespeare's Theatrical Notation: The Comedies* (Bern: Francke, 1974).

[17] Bertolt Brecht, 'Schriften 2' in *Werke*, vol. 22-1 (Frankfurt, Suhrkamp, 1993), p. 329 (my translation).

[18] *Œuvres complètes de Shakespeare*, vol. 4 (Paris, Club Français du Livre, 1958), p. 121.

[19] For the importance of this notion for the study of the language of theatre, see Michael P. Hamburger, 'Gestus and the Popular Theatre', *Science and Society*, vol. XLI no. 2, New York, Spring 1977, in which the author analyses the popular roots of Shakespeare's gestic language and pinpoints the 'gestic inadequacies' of the Schlegel–Tieck translation.

situation he/she is in. In a dramatic text meant for performance, as Shakespeare's are, all the properties perceptible in the verse, above and beyond its denotative value, are part of the *gestus*, and hold great significance for the actor. All the formal elements of the text: its stylistics, rhythm, phrasing, syntactical breaks, redundancies and repetitions, metric structures and prosodic patterns, are part of the *gestus*. No dramatic text is as rich in suggestions as to the vocal and corporal approach the actor must adopt. Through rhythms, images and prosody, Shakespeare suggests physical movement and directs the actor's voice and body. Antony, expressing his rage following the rout of his fleet, employs what J. L. Styan also terms 'gestic poetry';[20] that is to say poetry which sets the body in motion:

The shirt of Nessus is upon me. Teach me,
Alcides, thou mine ancestor, thy rage.
Let me lodge Lichas on the horns o'th' moon,
And with those hands that grasped the heaviest club
Subdue my worthiest self.

(*Antony and Cleopatra*, 4.13.43–7)

All the properties perceptible in this verse: alliterations (hushing sounds and sibilants in the first two lines), the melodic curve (rising in the third line, falling in the last two), the auditory texture (heavy sounds in the last two lines), translate physical movement. Antony writhes in pain under the effect of an imaginary burning sensation (lines 1 and 2). He raises his arms to the heavens as though to free himself of his mental and physical torture (line 3), and his arms fall again (lines 4 and 5) as if under the weight of Hercules' club. There is therefore a virtual inscription of movement in the body of the language that the translator must, of course, take into account.

To take into account that dimension of the performance is not damaging to the imaginative lavishness or the poetic structure of the original. On the contrary, it implies trying to preserve the particularities of its writing, because, for example, the abundance of metaphors has a theatrical function – that of increasing the tension of speech and the energy of diction. The plays' vigour and dramatic force originate in a virtually ceaseless flow of powerful words, thoughts and images which form constellations and radiate outwards in all directions. Pointing out this construction is acknowledging from the outset the difference between the logic of the French sentence, which is based on linear development, and the prismatic nature of the Shakespearian one. The French sentence can only be fully understood when we reach its end. The Shakespearian sentence opposes this logic in every way. Shakespeare constructed his text so that actor and spectator may be bound together by a constant flow of words. If this dramatic force is to be retained in translation, one is obliged to do at least some violence to the 'genius' of the French language and its common usage. In its 'classical' definition and practice, French has to meet criteria such as clarity, logic and ease of expression. It is no doubt appropriate to modify these principles when translating Shakespeare. If the text's dynamic force is to be preserved, one cannot take a metaphor contained within one word and develop it into an entire phrase. When one seeks to untangle webs of images, logic is satisfied but at the cost of the poetic and dramatic flow. A mixed metaphor is better than a prolonged explanation of the original. André Gide said that he preferred to sacrifice the meaning of a phrase to its cipher. Perhaps we should add that when translating Shakespeare into French, one should be trying less to manipulate the existing forms and usual turns of phrase than attempting to create new ones. And this to serve the demands of the original language rather than those of the language we are translating into. The long history of Shakespearian translation can perhaps be summed up by this series of blows dealt out to Cartesian logic and its avatars. Since the classical era, the

[20] *Shakespeare's Stagecraft* (Cambridge, Cambridge University Press, 1967), p. 53.

French language has evolved in such a way as to allow the establishing of forms which were not originally organic but are becoming so. Translation doubtless has an important role to play in this evolution. Nowadays we no longer risk barbarism or an attack on the genius of the French language if we translate:

When, spite of cormorant devouring time,
Th'endeavour of this present breath may buy
That honour which shall bate his scythe's keen edge
(*Love's Labour's Lost*, 1.1.4–6)

by:

Contre le Temps vorace cormoran
Puisse aujourd'hui l'effort de notre souffle acheter
Cet honneur qui mordra le tranchant acéré de sa faux

whereas François-Victor Hugo felt obliged to explain:

En dépit du temps, ce cormoran qui dévore tout,
nous pouvons, par un effort de cette éphémère
existence, conquérir un honneur qui émoussera
le tranchant acéré de sa faux[21]

Shakespeare does translate into French, probably better than Racine translates into English. There are lines in Racine of pure verbal magic[22] as there are in Shakespeare, of course;[23] but in Racine, they are isolated gems of poetry, whereas in Shakespeare, we have to deal with gestic poetry, poetry in action, which has an undeniable concreteness. The sensory implication of the words uttered gives body, in the literal meaning of that word, to the elusive abruptness and wide sweep of Shakespeare's images.

The problems of Shakespearian translation must not be thought of in terms of isolated words or lines, but in terms of the whole dramatic poem. Either the translated work is a poem as well, or else it is merely an explanatory and introductory paraphrase meant to decipher a complex text – and not to offer an imaginative and performable script.

There are always losses, passages which have a narrower scope than the original, but there can be successful inventions which make up for those losses. In French, Yves Bonnefoy's phrase: 'le tumulte de vivre' is a beautiful recreation of 'this mortal coil' in Hamlet's 'When we have shuffled off this mortal coil.' Of course, only one meaning for coil has been translated, that of 'turmoil', leaving out the quibble upon 'coil', the winding of a rope.[24] But translation implies choices and, in French, the phrase is a strong creative transposition.

The argument that each translation falls short is facile. No human product is perfect. No duplication, even of materials that are essentially labelled as identical, will turn out a total facsimile. Minute differences and asymmetries will always persist. To dismiss the validity of translation because it is not always possible, and never perfect, is absurd. Translation, in brief, is desirable and possible. We always have translated between languages, since the beginning of human history. The defence of translation in general starts with the immense advantage of abundant, vulgar fact. How can we go about our business, if the thing was not inherently feasible? Translation is 'impossible'. But so is all absolute concordance between thought and speech. Somehow the 'impossible' is overcome at every moment in human affairs.

The truth is that the translator experiences at the same time the urge to translate and the impossibility of translation.

To quote George Steiner again:

The translator has taken too much – he has padded,

---

21 Shakespeare, Pléiade, vol. 1, p. 1081.

22 Think of 'Dans l'orient désert quel fut donc mon ennui' or 'Que le jour recommence et que le jour finisse / Sans que jamais Titus puisse voir Bérénice' (*Titus et Bérénice*).

23 Among many others that any translation inevitably disfigures: 'Parting is such sweet sorrow / That I shall say good night till it be tomorrow', *Romeo and Juliet* 2.2.184–5.

24 During the 1994 Shakespeare conference seminar on translation in Stratford, I learned that, apparently, the Danish word 'virvar' can translate both meanings. Happy Danes!

enbroidered, 'read into' – or too little – he has skimped, elided, cut out awkward corners [...] Unquestionably there is a dimension of loss, of breakage [...] But the residue is also, and decisively, positive. The work translated is enhanced. This is so on a number of fairly obvious levels. Being methodical, penetrative, analytic, enumerative, the process of translation, like all modes of focused understanding, will detail, illumine and generally body forth its object [...] The motion of transfer and paraphrase enlarges the stature of the original. Historically, in terms of cultural context, of the public it can reach, the latter is left more prestigious [...] There can be no doubt that echo enriches, that it is more than shadow and inert simulacrum [...] The mirror not only reflects but also generates light.[25]

Of course 'some translations edge us away from the canvas, others bring us up close'. Such closeness is, of course, what every translator aims for – and tries to reach, humbly but with persistence.

[25] Steiner, *After Babel*, pp. 300–1.

READING THE EARLY MODERN TEXT

MARION TROUSDALE

> Never again will a single story be told as though it were the only one.
>
> John Berger[1]

In what follows I examine multiple jurisdictions first in the context of Shakespeare's language, both literary and material, and then in early modern social formations. My sense is that language and social formation form a continuum. But at the end I leave the question open to invite others to intervene.

In the 1984 MLA session on Shakespeare and the New Criticism the late Joel Fineman, while claiming to distance himself both from Foucauldian and Derridean modes of analysis, staked out territory that he would later develop at large in *The Perjured Eye*.[2] His stated intention in this initial reconnaissance missile was to show the ways in which, and I quote Fineman, 'Shakespearean subjectivity governs, for strictly formal reasons, the literature of personality from its beginning in the early modern period through its end in twentieth-century Modernism.'[3] This subjectivity he saw as inhering in the larger rhetorical strategies of Shakespeare's two narrative poems as well as in his sonnets, and also in the particular detail of the individual rhetorical figures that make up the poems' collective style. I am not interested here in Shakespearian subjectivity either in its early modern or postmodern configurations, though I will return near the end of this paper to the question of character as suggested by the material texts. My initial concern is rather with the formal reasons Fineman selects and, in particular, his extended analysis of a rhetorical figure that occurs at the beginning of Shakespeare's *Rape of Lucrece*. I see Fineman's reading as symptomatic of one of the ways we have of talking about Shakespeare and his language. I shall raise some questions about the implications Fineman chooses to draw from this formal analysis in order to probe ideas of signification that we attach to the early texts. Let me begin with the rhetorical figure that is the focus of Fineman's concern.

His paper is ominously titled 'The Temporality of Rape' and the figure that bears the burden of Fineman's provocative argument is syneciosis, Puttenham's 'cross-coupler'.[4]

Cross-coupler is one of several figures in Puttenham which involve differing kinds of repetition. Puttenham includes these figures

---

[1] Quoted by Michael Ondaatje at the beginning of *In the Skin of a Lion* (London, Secker and Warburg, 1987).

[2] Joel Fineman, *Shakespeare's Perjured Eye: The Invention of Poetic Subjectivity in the Sonnets* (Berkeley, The University of California Press, 1986).

[3] Joel Fineman, 'The Temporality of Rape', a paper delivered at the meetings of The Modern Language Association in December, 1984.

[4] George Puttenham, *The Arte of English Poesie*, ed. Gladys Doidge Willcock and Alice Walker (Cambridge, Cambridge University Press, 1936), p. 206.

among the rhetorical figures which both please the ear and stir the mind. In anaphora the beginning of a sentence is repeated; in antistrophe it is the ending which is recursive and the conjunction of the two creates symploche or 'figure of replie'. In anadiplosis the repetition links the end of one verse with the beginning of another, and epanalepsis occurs when the same word both begins and ends a verse, a figure Puttenham labels the echo sound or the slow return. The cross-coupler comes after all of these and is described as a figure which takes two contrary words and ties them, Puttenham writes, 'as it were in a paire of couples, and so makes them agree like good fellowes as I saw once in Fraunce a wolfe coupled with a mastiffe, and a foxe with a hound'. Puttenham's example, which he draws from his own not very distinguished verse, uses Petrarchan oxymoron: 'Thus for your sake I dayly dye, / And do but seeme to liue in deede / Thus is my blisse but miserie, / My lucre losse without your meede /.'[5] The cross-coupling here links bliss with misery and life with death.

In *Lucrece*, Fineman notes, near the beginning of the poem, Shakespeare's use of cross-coupling to portray Tarquin's indecision: 'Away he steals, with open list'ning ear, / Full of foul hope and full of fond mistrust, / Both which as servitors to the unjust / So cross him with their opposite persuasion / That now he vows a league, and now invasion' (283–7). What we see here, as Fineman points out, as in Puttenham's own example, are two coupled oxymorons. *Hope* in what it suggests is the opposite of *foul*, even as *mistrust* betrays the trust suggested by the *fond* of affection. And in our judgement of Tarquin's anticipated act, hope has a negative moral value and mistrust a positive one. The usual connotations within the semantic fields, in other words, are reversed to create the suggestion of a chiasmus in which mistrust and hope change places, the one acquiring the moral valency of the other. Fineman sees in this chiasmus the rhetorical pattern of the poem which, he argues – and it is this phrase of Fineman's I wish to press – 'mimetically figures the rape'. In other words the syntax itself mimetically copies Lucrece's resistance when she sees Tarquin. 'The poem,' Fineman writes, 'projects the details of the rape onto a description of Tarquin's progress towards Lucrece's bedroom.'

Three obstacles bar Tarquin's progress toward Lucrece – a series of locked doors, the wind which blows out his torch and Lucrece's glove 'wherein her needle sticks' which Tarquin picks up only to have his finger pricked. As the material world 'conspires to retard the rape', so the initial impediments that Shakespeare describes heighten Tarquin's desire, and thus in yet another instance of chiasmus, instead of impeding him, spur him on. As Tarquin says, 'these lets attend the time, / Like little frosts that sometime threat the spring / To add a more rejoicing to the prime, / And give the sneapèd birds more cause to sing' (330–3). Fineman draws from this phrase two amazing conclusions: 'that the cross-coupler as Shakespeare employs it is not a neutral trope; it is instead the trope of a specific desire . . . the tropological structure and expression of an eros whose *contrapposto* energy simulates the action of a rape'.[6] His second, even more startling conclusion is that the logic of 'let' – 'these lets attend the time, / Like little frosts that sometime threat the spring' – links Lucrece to Tarquin and makes Lucrece responsible for her own rape by virtue of the energetic and energizing resistance that she offers to it. The inevitable conclusion has to be that if Lucrece had not resisted, she would not have been raped.

My concern in this paper is not with feminist revisions of a Derridean reading for which 'chauvinistic' is too pale a word, but rather with early modern notation. I start with Fineman because of the challenging ways in which he

[5] George Puttenham, *The Arte of English Poesie*, pp. 198–207.

[6] Fineman, 'The Temporality of Rape'.

argues that consciously figured language is literally mimetic – imitating in its rhetorical patterns what he calls the *res* or stuff of the poem – actions within the fictional construct presumed real. To place two phrases – 'foul hope' and 'fond mistrust' – in tandem in such a way as to bring about a sense opposite to that of normal usage, in other words, figurally copies the erotic effect of Lucrece's resistance on Tarquin's lust. He makes this argument in part because of the repetition in the poem of the word 'let'. As I have said, Shakespeare has Tarquin use it to characterize the impediments Tarquin meets on his way to Lucrece's bedroom – 'these lets attend the time, / Like little frosts that sometime threat the spring'; but Tarquin also uses it in response to Lucrece's entreaties. 'Have done . . . my uncontrollèd tide / Turns not, but swells the higher by this let. / Small lights are soon blown out; huge fires abide, / And with the wind in greater fury fret' (645–8).

I want to look a little more closely here at what is being compared to what. Obviously to Fineman the fact that Lucrece's resistance stimulates Tarquin's desire suggests a chiasmus similar to both fond hope and foul mistrust, and to the impediments that bar Tarquin's progress through the house and at the same time spur him on. If Tarquin's desire is spurred on and indeed enabled by the impediments placed in his way, then to bar is to aid. That which seeks to prevent the action in Fineman's reading instead becomes the agency of the action. Fineman goes beyond that observation to set up an equation which says in effect that the essence of the rape is the resistance of the victim which spurs it on, and that the metaphorical resistance which Shakespeare attributes to the inanimate objects in Tarquin's path, insofar as they are said to resist, thereby imitates the action of the rape. In both instances to impede is to aid. If we pin this even more closely to the actual words, then we have to add that to use the word *let* in two places in the poem is to attribute to the victim in the second instance the agency attributed to the material impediments of the first, and it is not simply that rhetorically these two incidents share a common place. Fineman sees in repetition an enabling of the self-similar, a form of identity.

One can argue that hindrance heightens desire in both instances, but I am uncomfortable with Fineman's strategy because Shakespeare makes those instances distinct. The 'lets' of Tarquin's approach are equated with the pleasure that comes from delay – 'to add a more rejoicing to the prime'. The *let* incurred from Lucrece's resistance is described as an increase of lust – 'my uncontrollèd tide / Turns not, but swells the higher by this let. / Small lights are soon blown out; huge fires abide, / And with the wind in greater fury fret' (645–8). These two 'lets' appear to me then to have different causes with different effects. A word is repeated and its meaning slightly changed. In Fineman's reading the distinction between cause and effect is erased, as is the distinction between heightened-because-delayed pleasure, and increased-because-delayed lust. To Fineman all resistance looks alike.

I see in Fineman's discussion a kind of essentializing of verbal patterns which I think characterizes much of our reading of the early modern. Early modern notation like early modern social formations is almost never single-voiced, almost never unequivocal, almost never in any sense a thing. The chiasmic structures, far from duplicating the rape, probe the nuances of the social values that enable it. Rather than being self-similar, as Fineman suggests, the cross-couplings, as Puttenham points out, are figures of thought that stir the mind. In *Lucrece* to trace their recursive patterns is to ponder in some detail Elizabethan anxieties as they reveal themselves in the rhetorical exploration of the nature of Tarquin's deed.

We see the chiasmic structure of the poem in the first instance in the way in which Shakespeare treats the actual rape. Tarquin's load of lust through that action is transferred from Tarquin to Lucrece. 'She bears the load of lust he left behind, / And he the burden of a guilty mind' (734–5). In a similar crossover Lucrece's death is meant to transfer her shame from herself to the man responsible for it. 'Mine honour be the knife's that makes my wound; / My shame be his that did my fame confound;' (1201–2). Such a double counterchange, used here as a figure of thought, shifts the taint from the guilty to the innocent, from the perpetrator to his victim and then reinscribes the shame by moving it from the victim back to the perpetrator. The satisfaction of Tarquin's lust which is the source of his shame becomes the shame of Lucrece in a movement which suggests much more than the kind of cross-coupling we see in 'foul hope' and 'fond mistrust'. The kinds of value placed upon the perpetrator and his victim are momentarily reversed, or to use that Derridean word that runs as a subtext through Fineman's discussion, invaginated or turned inside out.

Obviously the act of rape lies at the centre of the action of the poem. But the chiasmic structure that I have just described is only the efficient cause of an earlier counterchange in which Shakespeare effects an exchange not between perpetrator and victim but within the perpetrator himself. Tarquin, we are told early in the poem, is made captive by Lucrece's beauty, and this beauty Shakespeare characterizes as both physical and moral. In pursuit of the moral beauty that has made him captive, Tarquin destroys that which he seeks, and he destroys it through his possession of it. 'Besides, his soul's fair temple is defaced,' we are told, 'To whose weak ruins muster troops of cares / To ask the spotted princess how she fares' (719–21). Tarquin, in the poet's words, is 'a captive victor that has lost in gain' (730). Here counterchange, as it doubles back on itself, becomes paradox and it is around this central paradox, in which effect doubles back on cause so as to negate it, that Shakespeare develops the argument of his poem.

Questions about the nature of honour lie at the centre of this argument. This is most obvious at the point at which the actions of Tarquin cross in the form of a chiasmus the actions of Lucrece. Lucrece, in resisting Tarquin's advances, is persuaded finally by his threat to kill her and then put a slave in bed with her, claiming afterwards to have killed her when he found her in an act of adultery. We are led to believe that it is the threat of such defamation of character that leads her to yield. The rape, in other words, which deprives her of her honour as it deprives her of her chastity, is itself achieved by means of a threat to her public honour. She loses her honour for the sake of her honour. And it is concern with that honour, honour again as reputation, that Lucrece appeals to when she destroys that vessel that Tarquin has desecrated.

Chaucer's Lucrece kills herself refusing Tarquin forgiveness and arranging her clothes as she dies to be sure that her feet are covered, 'so wel she lovede clennesse and eke trouthe'.[7] In Ovid as in Livy[8] she refuses to grant to herself the pardon that Collatine grants her. Painter changed it slightly: 'As for my part, though I cleare my selfe of the offence, my body shall feele the punishment: for no unchast or ill woman, shall hereafter impute no dishonest act to Lucrece.'[9] Shakespeare makes Lucrece's act an act which she commits solely for the sake of honour, both hers and Collatine's. 'Poor hand,' she asks when she decides on suicide, 'why quiver'st thou at this decree? / Honour thyself to rid me of this shame, / For if I die, my honour lives in thee' (1030–2). Later that honour becomes attached by Lucrece to the actual knife and defined by the fame the act

[7] *The Legende of Good Women*, in Geoffrey Bullough, *Narrative and Dramatic Sources of Shakespeare* (London, Routledge and Kegan Paul, 1957), vol. 1, p. 188, line 1860.

[8] T. Livius, *The Romane Historie*, trans. Philemon Holland (London, 1600), p. 41. Ovid, *Fasti*, trans. John Gower (1640) in Bullough, *Narrative and Dramatic Sources*, vol. 1, p. 195, line 110.

[9] William Painter, *The Second Novell*, Bullough, *Narrative and Dramatic Sources*, vol. 1, p. 198.

will bring her. 'For in my death I murder shameful scorn: / My shame so dead, mine honour is new born' (1189–90). The complicit nature of that honour Shakespeare makes explicit in Lucrece's own words. Lucrece's honour belongs to Collatine and is part of Collatine's honour, so that in stealing her honour, Tarquin has stolen Collatine's as well. 'If, Collatine, thine honour lay in me, / From me by strong assault it is bereft' (834–5). Yet it was because of Collatine's honour that Tarquin was entertained as a guest. 'Yet am I guilty of thy honour's wrack; / Yet for thy honour did I entertain him. / Coming from thee, I could not put him back, / For it had been dishonour to disdain him' (841–4). Collatine is thus robbed of his honour through the very act of sustaining that honour, even as Lucrece, in submitting to Tarquin to save her reputation and hence her honour, loses that very honour that she sought through fear to save.

Fineman sees such inside-out rhetorical devices as characteristic of both of Shakespeare's narrative poems and suggests that 'Shakespeare tries to energize his experimental efforts at erotic epyllion by seeing what happens when antithetical arguments are cross-coupled with each other.'[10] But I think that Shakespeare's use of cross-coupling is more complicated and indeed more radical than that.

This paper is not meant to be a reading of *Lucrece*. I want only to argue that the two instances which Fineman makes univocal or single-voiced are multiple in their conceptual resonance and that the cross-couplings which Fineman posits as contradictions are not contradictions but contraries. If we return to Puttenham's example, we can see that his own verse, in its linking of 'bliss' with 'misery' and 'live' with 'die', attaches words in a way in which Puttenham when he talks of a wolf coupled with a mastiff and a fox with a hound, does not. A fox and a hound are pursued and pursuer, victim and perpetrator, contraries perhaps, but not contradictions. In certain senses they are related as Abraham Fraunce in *Lawyer's Logic* describes them: 'Contraries bee such opposites whereof eyther one is onely opposite to one, or one to two, but more to the one of them, than to the other', and he adds, 'they bee Relatiues or repugnant. Relatiues are contraries whereof the one is so opposed to the other, as yet there may bee in other respects a mutuall consent and reciprocall relation between them.'[11] The reciprocal relationship that exists between a mastiff and a wolf or between a fox and a hound is not unlike the relationship that exists between the honour of Lucrece and the honour of Tarquin, a relationship Shakespeare develops through the strategic positioning of the word *honour* in the poem.

The honour that Lucrece claims through her death is only superficially the same honour that Tarquin pursues through his lust, and if anything the honour of Collatine which allows Tarquin to be entertained by Collatine's wife is an honour created through the trust of respect which alone makes possible the trust of social exchange. It is this social exchange which Tarquin violates in a travesty of true friendship, and the exchange that occurs in the rape, among other things, is an exchange by means of which differing kinds of honour are both distinguished from and reverberate against differing kinds of shame. Beyond that, in a quite terrifying way, honour itself as a viable social value is subverted by every possible means. In order to make alike that which is similar Fineman conflates. He changes that which is similar but distinct into that which is self-similar and the same.

Is this then, as Fineman claims, the beginning of the modern age? In order to explore that

10 'The Temporality of Rape'.

11 Abraham Fraunce, *The Lawiers Logike, exemplifying the praecepts of Logike by the practise of the Common Lawe* (London, 1588) f. 48 [H4]. See also *Of Mariage and Wiuing* (n. 34 below), D1: 'Amongst likenesse of things, there is no necessitie that the similitude should hold in euery point, but rather that it chaungeth and turneth for the most part amongst those of diuers kindes, according vnto some conformitie or proportion of the same.'

question while extending the discussion of our readings of the early modern that I started above, I want to turn now to the material text. In a series of brilliant essays which have appeared over the last decade Randall McLeod, who himself is variously named, has drawn our attention to the ways in which the problematic characteristics of Shakespeare's material text suggest a language at once richer and more accountable than eighteenth-century editors were prone to believe. Examining the material text of Sonnet 111, for instance – 'For my sake doe you wish fortune chide' – and focusing on the crux in the opening line, 'doe you *wish* fortune chide',[12] McLeod argues that the accepted emendation first used by Gildon in 1709 and subsequently by Capell and Malone – 'do you *with* Fortune chide' – has no authority.[13] He does this in the first instance bibliographically by demonstrating the authority of the Q1 reading used as well by Benson in 1640. Part of that argument involves the consideration of a so-called '"muscular error", that is, an error made by the compositor by reaching into the wrong compartment of the case when setting or distributing [type]'. He then goes on to demonstrate the intelligibility of the text as it stands. 'Wish', as McLeod describes it, is a three-sort word, with two of its letters, long s and h, tied and printed by a single type. 'With', on the other hand, is a four-sort word with no ligatures. As McLeod remarks, 'it is strange but true that this simplest of physical facts, ligation, completely undercuts the only rationale editors have ever used to justify their emendations in Sonnet 111, that *wish* – as they print it – is an obvious typo'.[14] The other part of his argument in his discussion of this sonnet demonstrates the syntactical intelligibility of *wish*. McLeod's ensuing analysis shows that the crux in Sonnet 111, *wish*, is not only accepted usage in the period, but in the sonnet is used to equivocate at least among three different kinds of sentence – assertive, interrogative, and imperative, and between transitive and intransitive verbs. And, he adds, 'this does not take into account the alleged interpretation of *chide* as a transitive verb with ellipsis of the object *me*. Whether we read goddesse in apposition to fortune multiplies the ambiguity further, as does the uncertainty of whether *chide* is an infinitive or subjunctive.' 'I do not see that there is any criterion that serves to decide among these ambiguities of construction in Q1,' McLeod adds, 'and the best course seems to be to countenance them all'.[15] I see this multi-layered, multi-voiced ambiguity as characteristic of early modern notation, and particularly characteristic of Shakespeare. Complex as it is, Fineman's reading does not admit of this kind of textual richness. Rather it cordons off the rhetorical figures by making them self-similar to the action of the rape. The early text, as McLeod shows us, suggests a more problematic if richer mix, and I use this one essay of McLeod to suggest some of the ways in which the early modern in its material notation as in its rhetorical figures is not in any sense modern, is almost never single-voiced. But I think in another of McLeod's essays, and one that is better known, we see McLeod reading much as Fineman reads.

In this essay notation again becomes single-voiced. McLeod starts with Pope's praise of Shakespeare's characterization and goes on to look at speech tags, particularly in *All's Well* where the Countess is referred to severally, and in terms of modern print representation, inconsistently, as Mother, Countess, Old Countess, Lady, and Old Lady. His conclusion on the basis of this evidence of the early text is that our sense of the unity of Shakespeare's characters has been invented by editors who have regularized the speech tags in accordance with modern convention beginning with Pope.[16]

---

12 'Un-Emending Shakespeare's Sonnet 111', *Studies in English Literature*, 21 (1981), 75–96.

13 'Un-Emending Shakespeare's Sonnet 111', 82–6. Quotation 82–3.

14 *Ibid.*, 92–3.

15 *Ibid.*, 92–6.

16 '"The very names of the Persons": Editing and the Invention of Dramatick Character', *Staging the*

McLeod's multiple essays at constructing readings of early texts on the basis of the material evidence of the text are part of a much broader attack on the principles of editing inherited from the eighteenth century, and their argument is that early modern and post-modern, far from being joined teleologically, as egg to chicken or parent to child, are aliens from different planets whose attempts at co-habitation can never be more than that – attempts. The early modern in its inconsistent spellings, its overlapping jurisdictions, its persistent and ubiquitous disuniformity, its dedicated and covert deviance in the face of regulation cannot be accurately represented by the now standardized conventions of print culture, and in an essay written in celebration of the work of McLeod, Margreta de Grazia and Peter Stallybrass suggest that in four different areas – the single work, the discrete word, the unified character, and the autonomous author – because of the changes in notation which signal changes in conceptual modes, the early modern cannot be accurately represented and, in fact, cannot be known.[17] I do not know that it can, but it is the argument of my reading of *Lucrece* as well as that which is to follow that it can at least be known in part. To move from a rhetorical analysis of *Lucrece* to a discussion of the early material text is to move from literary readings to questions about Renaissance notation and it is these questions which ultimately concern me here.

Renaissance notation was obviously not self-similar in the ways in which modern notation is. As McLeod himself observes, we cannot read their codes in terms of our codes because our codes result from an undoing of theirs. Yet McLeod himself does this very thing in his discussion of the inconsistent speech tags Shakespeare uses to refer to his characters, and it is revealing to watch how McLeod does this. A sense of unified character, he claims, in a Shakespearian play, is established by consistency of signifier. The Countess, in other words, must always be referred to as Countess, not as Mother, Countess, Old Countess, Lady, Old Lady.

It is important to notice that this is not a question about whether or not character, as portrayed on the stage, is unified. This is a question again about language and reference in the early modern period, and in this regard the reading of Mcleod is obviously vulnerable. To dispute an idea of character on the basis of speech tags is, to begin with, to treat early modern notation as though it were modern notation. The self-identical character names that we are accustomed to in modern texts are equated with an idea of stable character on stage. In a similar fashion it follows that inconsistency in naming means inconsistency in character. This is, of course, to equate the signifier with the signified, which we saw happening in Fineman, and beyond that, in the wake of Fineman, as it were, reference is not distinguished from the material shape of the words. The language itself, in other words, is essentialized, and the distinctions being made by means of different speech tags confused with the identity of the person to whom they refer.

'For any member of the audience who knew Marseilles', Albert Braunmuller points out in a discussion of early spelling, 'The early texts' spelling and the actors' pronunciation conveyed information: for those who did not know Marseilles, no spelling, no pronunciation, could convey that information.'[18] The uses of Cor, Cori, Corio, Coriol are designations of a

---

Renaissance: Reinterpretations of Elizabethan and Jacobean Drama, ed. David Scott Kastan and Peter Stallybrass (London, Routledge, 1991), pp. 88–96.

[17] 'The Materiality of the Shakespearean Text', *Shakespeare Quarterly*, 14 (1993), 255–83. 'Even if we could convince ourselves that we had an "original" or "unedited" text, we would have established not its existence but rather the persistence of the epistemological categories that make us believe in its existence', p. 257.

[18] A. R. Braunmuller, '"How fare is't to Soris" or where was Mr. Hobbs when Charles II Died', in *Textual Formations and Reformations*, ed. Laurie Maguire and Thomas L. Berger (Newark, Delaware, University of Delaware Press, forthcoming).

particular human being, and on stage of a particular actor, and it is only if we identify standardization of spelling with the creation of the modern subject and the concomitant concept of unified character that a variety of character ascriptions in an age in which there is no fixed orthography, can be thought to signify an idea of instability in the character so designated. In a similar fashion de Grazia and Stallybrass remark that because *King Lear* is referred to as 'The True Chronicle History' in both the 1608 and the 1619 quartos and called a tragedy in the 1623 Folio, even the genre of the play is mutable.[19] 'Any name which you give,' Hermogenes says to Socrates in *Cratylus* 'is the right one, and if you change that and give another, the new name is as correct as the old.'[20] Whoever the guardian of Helen is, she is as the speech tags suggest, Mother, Countess, Old Countess, Lady, and Old Lady. The signifieds are differing kinds of material print representation. The reference of all of them is the same.

I see in both of these readings traces of a failure to separate signifier from signified, a failure to recognize the existence of multiple jurisdictions in the early modern, a failure to distinguish what is generic from what is particular, a failure to distinguish what is common from what is distinct.

And yet it is not hard to understand how the conceptual fields of the early modern can thwart our most concerted efforts to unlock their codes. The accessibility of the culture itself is daunting. If we look just at printing, for instance, which I think in its complexities defeated the best efforts of Greg and McKerrow, we cannot easily unravel either the processes of textual formation or the texts that resulted from them. Overlapping and at times contested jurisdictions seem to be the order of the day.

In the case of the King James Bible, the new translation was authorized by the King at the Hampton Court Conference in 1604, but the printers themselves both were and were not appointed by the King. Richard Jugge had been authorized in 1575 by Stationers' Court to print the Bible in Quarto, while the printing of the Bible in Folio was left open to any member of the Stationers' Company. Christopher Barker, however, had a royal monopoly on the printing of acts of Parliament and on official proclamations (by the Queen). He was then in some sense the designated royal printer, and James's Bible was in some sense the Royal Bible. Barker secured the signatures of seven members of the Privy Council to a petition that he alone should publish all Bibles. So for a period of time there were two authorized printers of the King James Bible. The conflicting jurisdictions were acknowledged by the Stationers' Company whose Court made a provision that was meant to accommodate the authority of both printers while recognizing the authority of the monarch. The Court ruled that should Barker be commanded by the Queen or other persons of high office to print any English testament or any English Bible in Quarto, he would tell Richard Jugge and that Jugge quietly would both print it and sell it at his own expense.[21]

Christopher Barker himself provides us with another instance of the intimidating complexity of social formations. Barker, as we have seen, had a royal monopoly on the printing of acts of parliament. He was, in fact, a Draper, and we know from the work of Gerald Johnson that in May of 1600, some twelve Drapers, which is to say freemen of the Drapers' Company, but who worked as publishers and booksellers, were 'translated' to use the language of record, to the company of the Stationers against the express desires of the Drapers' Company. The Drapers argued that custom of the City gave their freemen the right to engage in the trade of a

[19] 'The Materiality of the Shakespearean Text', p. 259.

[20] *The Dialogues of Plato*, trans. B. Jowett (Oxford, Clarendon, 1953), vol. 3, p. 42.

[21] M. H. Black, 'The Printed Bible', *The Cambridge History of the Bible*, Vol. 3: *The West From the Reformation to the Present Day*, ed. F. L. Greenslade (Cambridge, Cambridge University Press, 1963), pp. 408–75.

different guild, which it did. But as early as 1583 a Commission appointed to advise the Privy Council on printing had told them 'not to suffer the multitude of printers to be increased by men of other companies, pretending by the general liberty of the city'. To complicate matters more, the book-selling Drapers who took apprentices trained them as Stationers and then freed them as Drapers.[22]

A similar pattern of overlapping jurisdictions with porous boundaries – and obviously the word pattern is fraught with risks – seems to emerge if we look at the relationship between print and manuscript culture in the period. In a brilliant discussion of the transmigrations of the play and its text, Barbara Mowat[23] reminds us that far from the linear progression from manuscripts to performance to print that we like to imagine in the narratives we write, play texts transmigrated in many diverse ways – from printed book to performance, in the instance of the *Lear* and *Pericles* performed at Gowthwaite Hall in Yorkshire in 1609 and according to the testimonies of the actors, performed from the printed quartos;[24] from printed book to manuscript in the instance of the Dering manuscript of Shakespeare's *Henry IV* which appears to have been copied from the printed quartos of *1 Henry IV* and *2 Henry IV* for the purpose of a 1622 performance, though the performance seems not to have taken place.[25] Again from print to manuscript in the instance of the seventeenth-century manuscript of *Julius Caesar* in the Folger that appears to have derived from the text of the Second Folio. That appears also to have been done for a performance.[26]

I cannot yet begin to grasp the complexities of these overlapping and competing jurisdictions, even more complex legally with regard to property, particularly in the borough of Southwark as David Johnston has shown.[27] And I know that I am doing the period a disservice in dumping a hodgepodge of cultural artifacts into one box, in doing, in effect, what I have accused Fineman of doing in his reading of *Lucrece*. So let me end somewhere near where I started by trying to suggest one or two ways in which I think the early modern made their own kinds of distinctions, distinctions different in kind from our own.

Stephen Orgel, using work by Richard Helgerson,[28] points out that what came to be known as Saxton's maps were originally known as Secford's maps because it was Secford as Master of Requests who had asked the cartographer to make the maps for the Queen. And in 1577 Saxton was himself granted a monopoly on the publication and sale of his maps, though only for ten years.[29] Certainly this is an instance of multiple jurisdictions, but we can see that those jurisdictions are distinct. Contrary to our own sense of outright ownership which for the purposes of this argument I would describe as univocal – if this is my book, it is not your book – what we see in the instance of Saxton's maps is that the same thing belongs to different

[22] Gerald D. Johnson, 'The Stationers Versus the Drapers: Control of the Press in the Late Sixteenth Century', *The Library*, 6th Series, 10 (1988), 1–17.

[23] Barbara A. Mowat, 'The Theatre and Literary Culture', *The New History of Early English Drama*, ed. John Cox and David Scott Kastan (New York, Columbia University Press, 1997), pp. 390–416.

[24] C. J. Sisson, 'Shakespeare Quartos as Prompt-Copies with Some Account of Cholmeley's Players and A New Shakespeare Allusion', *Review of English Studies*, 18 (1942), 129–43, particularly 135.

[25] George Walton Williams and Gwynne Blakemore Evans, eds., *The History of King Henry the Fourth, as revised by Sir Edward Dering, Bart.* (Charlottesville, University of Virginia, for the Folger Library, 1974), x–xi. Cited by Barbara Mowat, 'Literary Culture'.

[26] G. Blakemore Evans, 'Shakespeare's *Julius Caesar* – a Seventeenth-century Manuscript', *Journal of English and German Philology*, 51 (1942), 401–17. Cited by Barbara Mowat, 'Literary Culture'.

[27] David J. Johnson, *Southwark and the City* (Oxford, Oxford University Press, 1969).

[28] Richard Helgerson, *Forms of Nationhood: The Elizabethan Writing of England* (Chicago, University of Chicago Press, 1992), pp. 107–8.

[29] Stephen Orgel, 'Elizabeth Surveyed', delivered at the Folger Institute weekend workshop *Court and Culture during the Reign of Elizabeth I: The Last Decade*, 5 October 1992.

persons according to their different ways of holding it. The multiple jurisdictions that I see as characteristic of the early modern and which can be read as a kind of fluid indeterminacy both in relation to language and in relation to cultural formations appear on closer scrutiny not to be indeterminate. The final cause of the maps and the final owner is the Queen. But Secford is the efficient cause, and Secford is acting for the Queen. In Saxton's ten-year monopoly to publish the maps, Saxton himself is granted a warrant not by the person who asked to have the maps made and who is praised by both Holinshed and Harrison for doing so,[30] but by the person for whom the maps were made, the Queen. We can see similar distinctions being made in the middle of the next century by Thomas Hobbes. Writing in *Leviathan* 'Of Persons, Authors, and things Personated' he says:

> Of Persons Artificiall, some have their words and actions Owned by those whom they represent. And then the Person is the Actor, and he that owneth his words and actions, is the AUTHOR: In which case the Actor acteth by Authority. For that which in speaking of goods and possessions, is called an Owner, and in latine Dominus ... speaking of Actions is called an Author. And as the Right of possession is called Dominion; so the Right of doing any Action is called Authority and sometimes warrant. So that by Authority, is alwayes understood a Right of doing any act: and done by Authority, done by Commission or Licence from him whose right it is.[31]

Here again the same thing belongs to different persons according to their different ways of holding it.

Let me return for a moment to the example of genre. Stephen Orgel a very long time ago, writing about J. C. Scaliger's *Poetics* which was first published in 1561, described it as a filing system and observed that works were characteristically filed under a number of headings.[32] So if *Lear* is referred to as 'The True Chronicle History' in the quartos and as tragedy in the 1623 Folio there is at least something similar going on, and *Lear* is not the only play with differing generic designations. *Troilus and Cressida* is described in the 1609 preface as being as witty as the best comedy in Terence or Plautus but is included in the tragedies in the Folio.[33] To me this phenomenon is explained by Aristotle near the beginning of *The Poetics* when he points out that imitation can be described in terms of medium, the objects imitated, or the manner in which the imitation is done and goes on to add that Sophocles can be seen as an imitator of the same kind as Homer for both imitate higher types of character, but that from another point of view he is the same kind of imitator as Aristophanes for both imitate persons acting and doing. Here the same work receives different classifications according to which aspect of the work is used for the classification. To Scaliger the *Oresteia* was both comic and tragic. *King Lear* in terms of the material being imitated is a true chronicle history, in terms of the fate of the King it is a tragedy. The point is a name is not a thing, the signifier is not the signified, genre is not identity, at least not in this system. What I am arguing, had I the wit and means and time to do it, is that systems of notation that seem fluid and decentered to us, are probably only fluid and decentered in terms of our conceptual systems. They are coming rather from a different system which is to say from a different place.

'Ajax was valiant after one fashion,' the author of *Mariage and Wiuing* writes in 1599, 'and Achilles after an other; neither was that wisdome of Nestor, that which was in Vlisses:

30 'The great charges and notable enterprise of that worthy gentleman, Master Thomas Secford in procuring the charts of the several provances of this realm to be set forth', in Helgerson, *Forms of Nationhood*, p. 108.

31 Chapter XVI. This passage was pointed out to me by Amy Stackhouse.

32 'Shakespeare and the Kinds of Drama', *Critical Inquiry* 6 (1979), pp. 113–16. His most recent discussion of genre in the Renaissance is in his edition of *The Winter's Tale* (Oxford, Oxford University Press, 1996), pp. 2–6.

33 Orgel, *The Winter's Tale*, p. 3.

nor that prudence of Agesilaus, the selfsame that Cato had.'[34] Is *Mariage and Wiuing* using a system of notation different in kind from *Lucrece*? Are Saxton's maps commissioned by Secford for the Queen analogous to the different speech tags used for the Countess in *All's Well*? Are the differing speech tags comparable in their way to the different kinds of honour in *Lucrece*? My argument, I suspect, is a kind of cross-coupling, a strategy, as I have noted above, that takes two contrary texts and ties them, as it were, in a pair of couples and so makes them agree like good fellows such as Puttenham saw in France, a wolf attached to a mastiff, a fox attached to a hound. Is it made up of contradictions or are the two parts only contraries? Among the conflicting jurisdictions of our ever more dispersed postmodern readings, Lucrece will have to remain in part responsible for her own rape.

[34] *Of Mariage and Wiuing. An Excellent, pleasant, and Philosophicall Controuersie, between the two famous Tassi now liuing, the one Hercules the Philosopher, the other, Torquato the Poet.* Done into English, by R. T. Gentleman (London, Thomas Creede, 1599), 13v.

SHAKESPEARE AND THE METAMORPHOSIS OF THE PENTAMETER

KENNETH MUIR

Many years ago I attended a conference at Providence, RI, at which the main speaker was O. B. Hardison Jr, then the Director of the Folger Shakespeare Library. He demonstrated that in the sixteenth century all the critics agreed that the iambic pentameter was the most colloquial form of verse, 'nearest prose'. (I had inadvertently, or subconsciously, echoed Dryden's phrase that described the rhymed couplets he had used in *Religio Laici*[1]). Although Hardison admitted that dramatic verse was a special case, he gave the impression, which he afterwards modified, that the actors ought to speak the verse as colloquially as possible. Some of the old actors, when I first came to the theatre, declaimed the most prosaic passages as pompously as they knew how. But there are verse passages that are not at all prosaic. I doubt whether any good actor, remembering Marlowe's mighty line and the mightier line of Shakespeare's tragedies, could be persuaded to be what Hamlet called 'tame'.

Some directors, indeed, have done their best to make the actor speak the lines as prose. In a production of *Antony and Cleopatra* a few years ago, my brother, who appeared mainly on television, was shocked to discover that the whole text had been re-typed as prose. Another relation of mine, Miriam Adams, playing the *Woman Killed with Kindness*, with Robert Donat as her lover, told me that the kind husband was played by a successful West End actor, who had never before ventured to perform in an Elizabethan play. So, when he found his wife in the arms of her lover, the actor had to tackle Heywood's most famous lines:

O God, O God, that it were possible
To undo things done, to call back yesterday;
That Time could turn up his swift sandy glass,
To untell the days, and to redeem the hours;
[. . .] that I might take her
As spotless as an angel in my arms.
(sc. 13.52–5, 61–2).[2]

The actor spoke the lines as though he were in a West End play, expressing his vexation at mislaying a favourite tobacco-pouch. The result could have been foreseen. The audience, who had been brought up on the old Mermaid dramatists, roared with laughter.

When I graduated, every serious study of the chronology of the plays and most editions contained tables of metrical tests; now they are virtually ignored. I am not concerned with the validity or otherwise of such statistics, but merely with the facts. In the first twelve of Shakespeare's plays there are an average of around three light and weak endings per play. In the last five unaided plays (excluding e.g. *Pericles* and *The Two Noble Kinsmen*) there are no less than five hundred of such endings,

[1] 'And this unpolish'd, rugged Verse, I chose; / As fittest for Discourse, and nearest Prose'. *The Works of John Dryden*, ed. by H. T. Swedenberg Jr and others, 20 vols. (London, 1972), vol. 2, p. 122.

[2] Thomas Heywood, *A Woman Killed With Kindness* (Manchester, 1961, repr. 1970), p. 74.

averaging one hundred per play.[3] These provide a problem for actors and actresses, and they generally solve it in the same way – by attaching the endings to the beginning of the following lines; as when Cleopatra, for example, speaking of the shame of being taken to Rome in Caesar's triumph, declares:

> [. . .] Mechanic slaves
> With greasy aprons, rules, and hammers
> Shall | Uplift us to the view.
>
> (*Antony and Cleopatra* 5.2.205–7)

Similarly the actor playing Leontes transfers the weak ending to the next line:

> And his pond fished by his next neighbour,
> By | Sir Smile, his neighbour.
>
> (*The Winter's Tale* 1.2.196–7)

Miranda in the second scene of *The Tempest* has one light and one weak ending in the same sentence. The actress perforce transfers both.

> Had I been any god of power,
> I would | Have sunk the sea within the earth,
> Or ere | It should the good ship so have swallowed and
> The fraughting souls within her.
>
> (*The Tempest* 1.2.10–13)

This is one of the metrical characteristics of the later plays of Shakespeare. There are many others. One is the frequent use of internal rhyme. It seems almost as though the poet was haunted by the ghosts of assassinated couplets. An extreme case, perhaps a unique case, is Edgar's soliloquy when he decides to escape pursuit by disguising himself as a Bedlam Beggar. The Bastard has had a soliloquy which goes down well with the audience, and several other speeches in verse. Edgar has been confined to prose and he seems at first to be a fall-guy or stooge. But Shakespeare knows that he is to end up as an heroic champion to the next king, so it is important that his first verse shall be a step towards his rehabilitation:

> [. . .] I heard myself proclaimed,
> And by the happy hollow of a tree
> Escaped the hunt. No port is free, no place
> That guard and most unusual vigilance
> Does not attend my taking. Whiles I may scape
> I will preserve myself, and am bethought
> To take the basest and most poorest shape
> That ever penury in contempt of man
> Brought near to beast. My face I'll grime with filth,
> Blanket my loins, elf all my hairs in knots,
> And with presented nakedness outface
> The winds and persecutions of the sky.
> The country gives me proof and precedent
> Of Bedlam beggars who with roaring voices
> Strike in their numbed and mortifièd arms
> Pins, wooden pricks, nails, sprigs of rosemary,
> And with this horrible object from low farms,
> Poor pelting villages, sheep-cotes and mills
> Sometime with lunatic bans, sometime with prayers
> Enforce their charity. 'Poor Tuelygod, Poor Tom.'
> That's something yet. Edgar I nothing am.
>
> (*King Lear* 2.2.164–84)

In this speech of twenty-one lines, there are a number of straightforward rhymes, either in the adjacent lines: 'tree'/'free', or separated by a single line: 'scape'/'shape', 'arms'/'farms'. Others are widely separated: 'bethought'/ 'brought' (3); 'place'/'face'/'outface' (6,8); 'hairs'/'prayers' (9); 'myself'/'elf' (4); 'grime'/ 'sometime' (10). In addition, there are numerous words ending in '-y': 'penury', 'charity', 'rosemary' and echoes of parts of previous words: 'taking'/'take', 'presented'/ 'precedent'; and one or two imperfect rhymes: 'knots'/'cotes'. The rich internal harmonies will be apparent, assisted as they are by subtle alliteration, and echoes of 'basest', 'poorest' in 'beast' and of 'man' in 'bans' and 'blanket' and the sounds of 'nails', 'mills' and 'whiles'.

The speech is remarkable in other ways. We are transported a thousand years from the legendary past to the problems of Elizabethan England so that some of Shakespeare's admirers might well have exclaimed over their tankards, 'Shakespeare is our contemporary.' In the next

[3] E. K. Chambers, *William Shakespeare: A Study of Facts and Problems*, 2 vols. (Oxford, 1930), vol. 2, p. 401.

act we find ourselves in the world of Harsnett's bogus demoniacs and exorcisms and the birth of Lear's realization that he had taken too little care of the poor.

George Wright, in what is incomparably the best book on the subject, *Shakespeare's Metrical Art*, has demonstrated with sensitive brilliance that the poet's deviations from regular iambic pentameters are not a matter for apology or excuse, but the very means by which he triumphed. Wright has some illuminating pages on the counterpoint set up between the metrical beat, enormously varied as he has proved it to be, and the rhythms of ordinary speech:

> Such verse requires to be equally attentive to the claims of the line and the claims of the sentence. We take for granted the syllable-and-stress requirements of the line [...] but this verse makes us aware of the different kind of order [...] not easily described, but known to every competent speaker of English.[4]

This I believe to be true, and if I attempt to insert some qualifications, it may well be that I am only spelling out what Professor Wright regarded as obvious, and my alternative proposal is not meant to deny the general truth of his.

Shakespeare, as we have seen, used in his last eight plays, with increasing frequency, weak and light endings. Many actors, faced with lines ending in 'and', 'in', 'or' and 'but', ignore the line endings and speak the lines as clumsy prose. The best, however, do not. Judi Dench (as Hermione), Gielgud (as Leontes), and Ashcroft and Redgrave as Innogen, for example, all contrived to retain the underlying sense of verse without the sacrifice of natural speech. In the third scene of *Cymbeline*, Innogen tells Pisanio how she would have gazed after the ship that was taking her husband into exile.

> I would have broke mine eye-strings, cracked them, but
> To look upon him till the diminution
> Of space had pointed him sharp as my needle;
> Nay, followed him till he had melted from
> The smallness of a gnat to air, and then
> Have turned mine eye and wept.
> (*Cymbeline* 1.3.17–22)

The lines in their impetuosity and regality are characteristic of one speaker. They help to establish what is later called 'the tune of Innogen'. We can just hear the underlying metrical beat and could be persuaded that Innogen's sentence is exactly what she would say.

How the lines should be delivered may be seen from the method employed by Ashcroft and Redgrave. It consists in holding the audience in suspense until the end of the speech, in convincing them that despite apparent discordances, all will come right in the end, come right at the very moment when the sense is completed. The musical analogy seems inescapable. The audience looks forward to a resolution and is duly satisfied by it. What I am suggesting is that Shakespeare in his late plays occasionally, and sometimes in his most beautiful passages is no longer thinking in pentameters, pentametrically we might say, but in longer units, speeches or paragraphs. Such a suggestion would get round the difficulty felt by many auditors that they do not actually hear the metrical beat.

Professor Wright does not discuss Innogen's speech, but he analyses speeches by Florizel and Perdita in the Bohemian scenes. He rightly stresses the absence of grandiose phrasing and their conformity with the pastoral mode. He finds in them an equilibrium between the claims of the metre and sentence. Here again I wonder if Shakespeare had not deserted the line as a unit, and I would emphasize the satisfaction of the listener when the discords are resolved.

When Perdita turns from her general flower distribution to her private offering to her lover (concealed partly by including him among the young of both sexes) she has an uninterrupted sentence which covers fourteen lines of verse.

> O *Proserpina*,
> For the Flowers now, that (frighted) thou let'st fall
> From *Dysses* Waggon: Daffodils,
> That come before the Swallow dares, and take

[4] George T. Wright, *Shakespeare's Metrical Art* (London, 1988), p. 222.

The windes of March with beauty: Violets (dim,
But sweeter than the lids of *Iuno's* eyes,
Or *Cytherea's* breath) pale Prime-roses,
That dye unmarried, ere they can behold
Bright *Phoebus* in his strength (a Maladie
Most incident to Maids:) bold Oxlips, and
The Crowne Imperiall: Lillies of all kinds,
(The flowre-de-Luce being one.) O, these I lacke,
To make you Garlands of) and my sweet friend,
To strew him o're, and ore.
(*The Winter's Tale* (from the 1623 folio), 4.4.1930–43)

Shakespeare never forgets that Perdita is a real princess as well as the mistress for the year of the sheep-shearing feast. He was probably looking forward to the marriage of the adored Princess Elizabeth, and certainly when the play was revived in 1613 it marked that occasion. Some of the best of Shakespeare's later poetry – in *Cymbeline* and *The Winter's Tale* – was spoken by young actors and the poet was right to trust them. In our own day we have heard choir boys, with thoughts beyond the reaches of their souls, triumphing in Handel's *Messiah*.

While Shakespeare was collaborating with Fletcher, his colleague was already contributing to the disintegration of the pentameter. The fact that different compositors could print the same speeches, and even whole plays, either as prose or verse is one indication of this. We should not assume that Shakespeare by his occasional substitution of a larger unit for the pentameter was assisting in its disintegration. As George Wright says, the verse used in Prospero's renunciation of magic showed that 'his staff was not yet broken and buried, his book not yet drowned'.[5] Shakespeare remained a writer of plays conceived as dramatic poems. He doubtless assumed that his fellows and the best of his followers shared his artistic aims – the aims of the dead shepherd, Marlowe, modified to suit the Jacobean play.

[5] Wright, p. 228.

REREADING ILLUSTRATIONS OF THE ENGLISH STAGE

JOHN H. ASTINGTON

Playing fast and loose with graphic evidence from the English Renaissance is at least as prevalent, on a statistical basis, as doing so with literary or documentary historical material – pictures, it seems to be felt, offer a wide field for speculative ingenuity. So in September 1995 Eric Sams took up a whole page of the *TLS* with the claim that the Swan drawing shows a performance of *Hamlet*, and in 1992 the editors of *Theatre Notebook* saw fit to publish an article by Evert Sprinchorn in which a woodcut from *The Three Lords and Ladies of London* is used to support a theory about 'passing over the stage'.[1] Sprinchorn either did not know or did not care that in the 1920s Alfred Pollard identified this picture as originating from a non-theatrical book published twenty-one years before the play, and the readers for the journal apparently shared his ignorance or indifference.

A distinctly casual attitude to the status of illustrations as artefacts with a precise historical and cultural context has led, for example, to the widespread use of the Lawrence Johnson engraving of Tamburlaine as a representation of Edward Alleyn, a misconception I have attacked elsewhere,[2] or to the acceptance of the Scottowe drawing of Tarlton as the standard icon of that actor, a mistake about which I will have something to say here. In this century two serious attempts have been made to examine categories of visual evidence with some care and rigour: in his *Bibliography* W. W. Greg included reproductions of most of the illustrated material in dramatic texts, and rather more than ten years ago R. A. Foakes took a wider scope in assembling a variety of visual evidence in his anthology *Illustrations of the English Stage 1580–1642*. This has proved to be a particularly stimulating collection for my own research, and turned me towards more serious thought about theatre pictures from the period; much of what I have to say in this paper corrects or supplements both detail and theoretical approach in the book, but I want to begin by making plain my gratitude to it.

Foakes's introduction calls for more detailed attention to the evidence of illustrations, simultaneously pointing out the provisional nature of his own survey, which may, he suggests, 'turn out to be incomplete'.[3] In some ways, however, the book is a victim of its comprehensive ambition. The first section, for example, is called 'Maps and panoramas'. There is no question that this is not an exhaustive collection of the very many views of London showing the Globe, say, published throughout Europe in the seventeenth century, variously copying Visscher and Hollar. Such a catalogue might be culturally interesting, and would be enormous, but wouldn't have much to tell theatre historians. So a certain kind of completeness is exchanged

[1] Evert Sprinchorn, 'An Intermediate Stage Level in the Elizabethan Theatre', *Theatre Notebook*, 46 (1992), 73–94.

[2] 'The "Unrecorded Portrait" of Edward Alleyn', *Shakespeare Quarterly*, 44 (1993), 73–86.

[3] R. A. Foakes, *Illustrations of the English Stage 1580–1642* (Stanford, 1985), p. xvii.

for a selection of historically prior material, based on scholarly assessments of the status of such material. Yet even this selection includes views which derive from other views, and at least one (no. 20) which seems entirely valueless as independent evidence. If William Marshall's 1643 view of London is worth consideration, then so is a great deal of other material not included in the collection.

The basis of categories and boundaries both for selection and for discussion of material remains in question throughout the book, particularly in the sections having to do with published illustrations, where Foakes distinguishes between woodcuts and engravings 'relating to the stage' and those 'having no reference to the stage'. The problem here is that woodblocks and engravings relate far more closely to artists and craftsmen connected with the publishing industry than to the stage, and asking other questions about them may provide more answers than interrogating them as theatrical evidence first and foremost. Who made them, who printed them, who published them, and in each case what other artefacts did these men produce at about the same time? Very often such approaches will produce a good deal of information which bears on the picture in question, as I found in examining the plate for *The Wits*.[4] Pictures in Elizabethan and Stuart books were frequently recycled – I shall address this problem below – and were also published in cheaper formats, as ballads and broadsides.

Foakes's index reflects his relative lack of interest in the makers of the images he reproduces. His captions to the first section of the book give (most of) the engravers of the plates, but he ignores signed or assignable work thereafter. William Marshall is not to be found in the index, though he made three plates reproduced in the book;[5] Thomas Cecil's name is trimmed from the image of no. 74, the frontispiece to Gomersall's *Sforza*; the plates to Robert Fludd's *Microcosmi Historia* (no. 67) were made by the famous pair of Theodore de Bry and Matthew Merian the Elder.[6] The enormously different contexts of the images in the book require more attention than they seem to receive. William Marshall, a prolific engraver who also produced pictures of Fletcher, Shakespeare, and other dramatists, theatrical imagery on various title-pages, including one to an edition of Terence, and the famous hand signals in Bulwer's two books (assuming we might think these have some possible theatrical connections) seems worth some wider consideration as an artist with a significant visual vocabulary.

In the remainder of this essay I will address a number of theoretical problems which underlie the study of theatrical illustrations from the sixteenth and seventeenth centuries, through specific discussion of items in the Foakes collection which seem to me in need of adjustment or correction. I shall begin with illustrations in playbooks, about which Foakes seems to me to make certain questionable assumptions. It seems fair to assume that when an illustration represents a recognizable scene or episode from a play, as do those, for example, on the title-pages to the 1615 edition of *The Spanish Tragedy* (no. 44), the 1619 edition of *The Maid's Tragedy* (no. 50), or the 1625 editions of *A Game at Chess* (no. 54), then some kind of attempt is being made to represent the action of the dramatic text, although even at this stage of reading the picture we can make wrong assumptions, as I shall suggest below. Why particular episodes are chosen, who directed their composition, and what relationship such pictures might bear to the play as

---

4 '*The Wits* Illustration, 1662', *Theatre Notebook*, 47 (1993), 122–40.

5 Marshall is undoubtedly the engraver of the strange frontispiece plate to *The Rebellion of Naples* (1649; no. 77), which is signed 'M' at bottom left – a detail not visible in Foakes's cropped photograph. Such a form of his signature is perhaps unique; it is not recorded in M. Corbett and M. Norton's standard reference, *Engraving in England in the Sixteenth and Seventeenth Centuries. Part III. The Reign of Charles I* (Cambridge, 1964).

6 See J. Godwin, *Robert Fludd* (London, 1979).

1 Woodcut figures, Thomas Hill, *The Contemplation of Mankind*, 1571.

acted are all questions which are not easily answered.[7]

The first item in Foakes's section C (illustrations relating to the stage in printed texts of plays), rather unfortunately, is Marlowe's *Tamburlaine*, in the editions of 1590 and 1597 (no. 37). Foakes reproduces the Lawrence Johnson engraving of Tamburlaine from 1603, which does not relate to the stage and is not from a play text, but also the two woodcuts of half-length male and female figures printed in *Tamburlaine* in the 1590s. Foakes is rightly sceptical about these stiff generic figures, but he could have been more so. In 1973 Fredson Bowers, assisted by John Crow, had found out that the publisher of *Tamburlaine*, Richard Jones, had previously published the male woodcut figure in 1587, as a decoration to *A Short Admonition of Warning, Upon the detestable Treason, etc.*[8] It was therefore unlikely to be related to the stage when it was published in a play text three years later. More recently Ruth Luborsky, in her comprehensive examination of all Elizabethan published illustrations, has discovered that both the *Tamburlaine* woodcuts derive from a book on physiognomy published in 1571, Thomas Hill's *The contemplation of mankind* (*STC* 13482).[9] That

7 See my discussions of such matters in the context of the illustrated editions of Middleton's plays, in 'Visual Texts: Middleton and Prints', *Thomas Middleton and Early Modern Textual Culture*, ed. Gary Taylor (Oxford, forthcoming).

8 *Christopher Marlowe. The Complete Works*, vol. 1 (Cambridge, 1973), p. 73.

9 R. Luborsky and E. Ingram, *A Guide to English Illustrated Books 1536–1603*, forthcoming. I am grateful to Ms. Luborsky for communicating her knowledge of the *Tamburlaine* woodcuts to me privately.

publication provides an amusing illustration of the semiotic mobility of generic images, since the female figure is used three times in three different contexts, and with quite different 'meaning' – she stands in one place for the lascivious woman, and in another for the modest and honest one (see illustration 1). In any event, she was more than twenty-five years old when she appeared as a putative Zenocrate. The common thread between the four publications is the publisher Richard Jones. He acquired the copy to *The contemplation* in 1579 (although there is no extant copy with his imprint) and hence the set of woodblocks which illustrated it, which he then used to decorate other publications, including the *Tamburlaine* quartos. The figures have absolutely no connection with the stage, and are useless as theatrical evidence.

In 1618 there appeared a third edition of *Jack Drum's Entertainment* (no. 48); this reissue of an old play is decorated with a generic woodcut figure on the title-page. Foakes includes it in his category 'relating to the stage', and notes that it appears in ballads after 1618. But it had already appeared as a ballad decoration in 1615 (*STC* 16864a.1; see illustration 2), and hence can't be claimed as having any connection with the stage. Foakes speculates that the military figure relates to the comic Frenchman in the play, creating a 'general impression of flamboyance'. I agree with the characterization, but the figure is German, not French. The feathered hat, slashed clothing, baggy breeches, large codpiece, and bristling weaponry are all conventions of the popular and common sixteenth-century prints of landsknechts, from one of which this woodblock was no doubt copied.[10] Figures in such costumes had certainly been seen at least in English court entertainments in the previous century: costumes for 'launceknightes' and 'Almanes' – probably the same group of maskers – were made by the Revels office for Christmas 1549.[11] Outlandish flamboyance was probably the effect desired on that occasion also, and it seems to me quite likely that the Revels designers worked from imported German prints. There seems little reason to connect such a visual convention with *Jack Drum*; on the title-page we are observing the rough and ready tendency of publishers and printers to add generic and approximate decoration where they felt it was required.

The cases of the 1630 edition of *Friar Bacon and Friar Bungay* (no. 55), and the 1655 edition of *The Merry Devil of Edmonton* (no. 63), suggest other kinds of problem. (Of these the *Bacon* woodcut is by far the better known, the 'brazen head' detail having been adopted as a logo of the Records of Early English Drama series.) In both instances, as Foakes eventually makes clear in his commentary, although not in the dates of his head titles, the woodcuts were first published elsewhere, and are respectively three and twenty-four years older than the books in which they appear. In what ways, then, can they be said to relate to the stage? They originally appeared in prose versions of the stories of the two plays, and hence they do illustrate incidents from those stories – was the illustrator thinking of the incidents as dramatized, however? This is evidently a large question, and we should be asking it not only about these two pictures, which technically do not belong in the category in which Foakes has placed them, but about other woodcuts in later editions of plays the subjects of which were also treated in other genres, notably the ballad. I have the famous *Doctor Faustus* picture (no. 46) particularly in mind. First printed on the title-page of the first issue of the B text (1616), it was published by John Wright, a prolific producer of ballads. A ballad on the Faustus legend had been in existence since 1589, when it was published by the same Richard Jones who was

[10] See J. R. Hale, *Artists and Warfare in the Renaissance* (New Haven, 1990), Chapter 2, 'The Germanic Image of the Soldier'.

[11] A. Feuillerat, *Documents Relating to the Revels at Court in the Time of King Edward VI and Queen Mary* (Louvain, 1914), pp. 42–3.

econd part of the Louers gift,

to the ſame tune.

Edmund.

Deare ſweet would you ioyne,
Your loue vnto mine,
My loue ſhould for euer ſtand ſure,
Or to end the ſtrife
Wouldſt thou be my wife,
Like Turtles we both would indure:
There ſhould not procéede
No bad word nor déede,
That ſhould haue the power to grieue thée,
We'le liue till we dye
Moſt merily,
Thou knowſt not what I haue to giue thée.

Priſilly.

Since nothing can ſhift,
Say what is the gift,
That you vpon me would beſtow,
And if I doe finde
It contenteth my minde,
Then more of my loue you ſhall know,
That guift will me moue,
To like as I loue,
There quickly repeat it to me,
And heere I proteſt,
My heart ſhall reſt,
Thou and I ſtraight will agrée.

Edmund.

Then if you'le agrée,
To marry with me,
Ile make thée a Joynter by the yeare:
And ſet downe profound
fiue hundred pound,
And all for the loue of my deare:
What a woman can craue,
Be ſure to haue,
And if that thou durſt to beleeue me,
'Tis a gift moſt rare,
To a mayden ſo faire,
Loe this is the gift I will giue thee.

Priſilly.

This gift is of force
To make your recorſe,
The eaſier to my bed,
No longer lets tarrie,
But ſtraight let vs marry,
And then take my mayden-head:
No longer I can
Liue without a man,
Then pray thee ſweet hart beleeue me,
Ile loue thee ſtill,
If with a good will,
This prettie guift thou wilt giue me.

Edmund.

Then ſweeting pray come,
I long till 'tis donne,
To Church let vs hie vs with ſpeed,
I can when I liſt,
Procure a blinde Prieſt,
Which for vs ſhall doe this ſame deed,

Priſi. Then ſweet let vs goe,
We muſt not be ſlow,
If euer you meane to win me,
But thinke vpon this,
That you doe not miſſe,
This ſame pretie gift to giue me,

Author.

Away then they went,
And fulfil'd there intent,
Vnto their great comfort and ioy,
Fortie weekes being paſt
This young wife at the laſt,
Did bring her young husband a boy,
Heauen ſend all young wiues,
To lead honeſt liues,
And husbands to liue with them kinde:
May wiues ſtriue to pleaſe,
All ſuch husbands as theſe
That are of ſo honeſt a minde.

Printed at London for Iohn Trundle, and are to be ſolde at his ſhop in Barbican.

2 Ballad illustrations, 1615.

responsible for the texts of *Tamburlaine*, and it seems not entirely unlikely to me that the *Faustus* woodcut might have begun life as a ballad illustration rather than having been made with the stage play specifically in mind; it was certainly doing duty as a ballad picture in 1628 (on the Doctor Lamb scandal) between appearing in the fourth and fifth reprints of the B text.[12] Were its origin a ballad decoration we would have to place firm constraints on our reading of the woodcut as evidence of, say, Alleyn's costume, or of the staging of 1.2 of the play, as has been done in the past.[13] Illustrations may have had more employment than the accident of surviving publications might lead us to think – particularly, ephemera from the period have perished in statistically large proportions. The possibly significant intersection of interests of publishers and booksellers who consistently dealt in both ballads and playbooks – John Trundle, George Purslowe, the Wrights, for example – seems worth further thought and research.[14]

A clear case of the resurrection of ballad woodblocks may be observed in the illustrated title-page of the pamphlet *The Stage-Players Complaint*, from 1641. This item (no. 69) Foakes places in his category D (Miscellaneous illustrations connected with the stage), but the woodcut figures printed with this text are not remotely connected with the stage, despite the implicit claim that they represent the comedians Andrew Cane and Timothy Reed, whose names appear above them. They are stock figures which had long been used to decorate ballads when they appeared in this publication. Foakes calls the left-hand print a 'dancing figure', but he actually began life, in 1610, as the assassin Ravaillac in a broadside on the murder of Henri IV of France (*STC* 13137; see illustration 3a). Subsequently his dagger was broken or cut away, and he appeared in ballad after ballad as a stock decoration. The larger right-hand figure on the *Complaint* page is at least as old as 1618, when it was printed in a ballad (illustration 3b). These pictures have nothing to tell us about the two Caroline actors who supposedly conduct the 'pleasant dialogue' of the book.

It is apparent that we should check our assumptions about how illustrative material was used by Elizabethan and Stuart publishers and printers. If we cannot confidently claim 'theatrical' meaning for woodblocks used as factotums or stock decoration, neither should we too easily dismiss the cultural significance of decorated dramatic texts which seem not to have much direct connection with contemporary playhouse stages. Foakes's category E – called 'Illustrations in play-texts having no reference to the stage' – seems to me to create a boundary of the wrong kind, as well as an inaccurate one, as preceding examples have shown. A number of related cases will make this point clearer. Two editions of the play *The Valiant Welshman* (1615 and 1662) are the subject of Foakes's item 72, and seem to receive rather short shrift: both had illustrated frontispieces, but Foakes gives only one reproduction, a (rather cropped) photograph of the 1662 woodcut, which is not identified as such – the uninitiated reader does not know quite what he or she is looking at. The two woodcuts are in fact similar, although different in style and pose: they both show mounted equestrian military figures in armour. Neither evidently has much to do with the play, and presumably the 1662 block was chosen from old stock to approximate to the original woodcut, which had disappeared over the intervening years, and it is to that extent the less important of the two prints. But as a generic decoration a mounted hero is a perfectly explicable choice for a title featuring the words 'valiant' and 'man'

[12] See Tessa Watt, *Cheap Print and Popular Piety* (Cambridge, 1992), pp. 123–4.

[13] Martin Wiggins has pointed out to me that in *The Knave of Clubs* (1609) Samuel Rowlandson speaks of Alleyn playing Faustus in 'a surplice/ with a cross upon his breast', and not in the robes of a secular doctor as shown in the woodcut.

[14] See 'Visual Texts'.

The lamentabe complaint of Fraunce, for the death of the late King Henry the 4. who was lately murdred by one Fraunces Rauilacke, borne in the towne of Ang[illegible]lem, shewing the manner of his death, and of the election and Proclayming of the new King, Lewis the 13. of that name, being a childe of 9. yeeres of age. To a new tune

FRaunce that is so famous,
and late in ioyes abounded,
May now lament the losse of him:
that mischiefe hath confounded.
Their thrice renowned King,
that Souldier braue and bolde,
In peace and wars so well belou'de
lyes clad in earthly molde.
All Kingdomes come and mourne,
for this same sad mischaunce:
For wee haue lost our Countries King,
and flower of famous fraunce.

The bloudy hand that wrought,
and hart that gaue consent:
Now makes more eies in France to weep:
then euer did lament.
More sig[illegible] [illegible] robes was neuer heard,
then be in Fraunce this day,
For euery one now mourning sits:
this pleasant month of May.
No ioye, no hearts delight,
but death and bloudy deedes,
In euery Coast of famous Fraunce:
much griefe and sorrow breedes.

In May the thirteenth day,
it pleased this royall King:
To make his Wife a Crowned Queene,
which was a princely thing
Who then in Triumph rode
along fayre Paris streets,
Whom all the Lordes & peeres of Fraunce
in ioyfull manner greetes.
And all the streetes along,
whereas the Queene did ride.
Were like the walles of Paradice,
bedeckt on euery side:

The royall King himselfe,
the Dolphin his young sonne:
The lordly Prelates of that land,
and Barrons many one.
With all the states of Fraunce:
there honored Henries Queene,
More stately triumphes neuer was,
within that Countrie seene.
But soone thiese glories vanish't,
for death put in his hand,
And in lesse time then forty houres
made Fraunce a wofull land.

This noble King god wot,
supposing all good friends:
The following day for pleasures sake:
a iorney foorth intends.
Wherein his Coach he rides,
some of his lordes with him,
Along renowned Paris streetes,
being then deckt out most trim.
The people cryed with ioy:
God saue our Royall King,
The presence of your Maiestie:
reioycing loue doth bring.

The People throng'd so fast,
about him in the streetes,
That hardly he could passe along:
such numbers did he meete.
Amongst so many friends,
a Judas hand there was,
That turnd the cheerefull flower of france
to fading withered grasse,
Two Coatches by hard chaunce.
his graces Passage stayde,
A time wherein his gentle life,
by murder was betrayde.
The Traytour [illegible] three times,
before had mist his ayme,
And could not in his royall bloud:
his cursed fingers stayne.
Now desperatly thrust foorth:
vnto his coatches side,
And gaue him there, 2 mortall wounds,
by which, the King soone dyed,
A cursed knife it was,
which did this bloudy deede,
But ten times cursed be the cause,
that did this mischiefe breed.

The wounded King cryed out,
then with a fainting breath:
Oh, saue his life till hee reueale,
the plotters of my death.
The Traytour being stayed,
was is offence bereauen,
That presently for this vilde deede:
he thought to purchase heauen.
Some led this villaine thence,
and some, the King conuayde:
Vnto his Pallace mournfully,
in bloudy Robes arrayde.

A natiue frenchman borne,
this wretch is knowne to be:
Bred in the Towne of Angolsem,
a Courtier in degree.
Fraunces Rauilliacke nam'de,
in passed time a Feyer,
Maynteyned long about this court,
to accomplish his desire.
But who the causers be:
and chiefest in this crime,
By wisedome of the peeres of Fraunce:
wilbe found out in time.

Meane while the villanes teeth,
are pulde out euery one:
Least he should bite cleane out his tongue,
and so no trueth be showen,
His nayles likewise pincht off,
least he should teare it out,
And speachles thus should lose his life:
and no wayes cleare this doubt
But let vs speake againe,
of this the bleeding King,
Who entring at his pallace gate:
death broke his life heart string.

Euen in a Bishops Armes,
he yeelded vp his breath,
And said I dye true Christian King,
sweete lordes reuenge my death.
His Queene, his sonne, and peeres,
with wringing handes made mone,
And sayde, if God be not our friende,
our states be ouerthrowne.
The heauiest day in Fraunce,
this is that euer was seene,
His death now makes an orphant Prince,
and eke a widdowed Queene.

Yet wisedome so preuailde,
amongst the lordes of Fraunce,
That by the gracious helpe of God,
they salued this mischaunce.
The next day in the morne:
fower Cardinalls of estate,
And Princes of the Kings owne bloud,
this busines did debate.
To establish loue and peace:
within this mournefull land,
They there proclaym'd the Dolphin King
in Paris out of hand.

A childe of nine yeeres olde,
being true and lawfull heyre,
The onely hope the Kingdome hath,
to rid them from all feare.
Up to his fathers throne,
the Dolphin straight was led,
In Purple Robes most gorgeously:
with sumptuous Jewells spread.
Whome, in the peoples hearts,
did moue such present ioy,
That euery one in gladsome sort,
did cry viva, le roy.

Yea euery one doth pray,
now dwelling in the land,
That like his father he may proue,
an Impe of Mars his band.
But three such dayes in Fraunce,
no age hath euer knowne,
Where present ioy gayn'd sudden woe,
yet woe to ioy is growne.
One day a Crowned Queene,
the next a murdred King,
The third a Prince in ioy proclaymde,
a setled peace to bring.

But God defend each Land,
from such a suddaine chaunce,
As lately hath befalne the King,
of fayre renowned Fraunce.

FINIS.

At London printed for William Barley, and are to be sould at his shop in Gratious Streete 1610.

3a Woodcuts from broadside ballad, 1610.

+ A new Song of a Young mans opinion, of the difference betweene good and bad Women.
To apleaſant new tune,

Shall I wreſtling in diſpaire,
Dye becauſe a womans faire,
Shall my cheekes looke pale with care,
Cauſe anothers roſie are:
Be ſhe fairer then the day.
Or the flowry meads in May:
If ſhe thinke not well of me,
What care I how faire ſhe be.

Shall my fooliſh heart be pinde,
Be cauſe I ſee a Woman kinde,
Or a well diſpoſed nature,
Joyned with a comely feature,
Be ſhe meeker kinder then,
The Turtle Doue or pellican:
If ſhe be not ſuch to me,
What care I how kind ſhe be,

Shall a womans goodneſſe moue,
Me to periſh for her loue,
Or her worthy merites knowne,
Make me quite forget mine owne,
Be ſhe with that goodneſſe bleſt,
As may merit name of beſt,
If ſhe be not ſuch to me,
What care I how good ſhe be,

Be ſhe good or kinde or faire,
I will neuer more diſpaire,
If ſhe loue me this beleeue,
I will dye ere ſhe ſhall grieue,

If ſhe ſlight me when I woe,
I will ſcorne and let her goe.
If ſhe be not fit for me,
What care I for whome ſhe be.

Shall a Woman ſweet of voyce,
Make my fooliſh heart reioyce:
Or the pleaſures of her tongue,
Be the meanes to doe me wrong:
If ſhe had the ſweetes of minde,
Aboue the pitch of women kinde,
If ſhe be not ſo to me,.
What care I how ſweet ſhe be.

Shall a Woman truely wiſe
Draw amazement from mine eyes,
Wondring that from ſuch a Creature
Wiſdome thus ſhould come by nature
And comprehend the beſt of thinges
That from ẏ well of wiſdome ſprings:
If ſhe be not ſuch to me,
What care I how wiſe ſhe be.

Shall Cupid ſet my heart on fire,
To ſee a womans chaſt deſire,
And no fond perſwaſions moue,
A chang vnto her mayden loue,
With purity of vertue grac't,
To make her more in liuing chaſt:
Yet if ſhe be not ſuch to me,
What care I how chaſt ſhe be.

Shall all the ſweetes that doe belong,
Vnto a beauty faire and young,
Vpon a womans forehead ſhine,
To make a Creature moſt deuine,
When on her cheeks ẏ youthfull bloud,
In prime of May begins to bud,
Yet if ſhe not ſuch to me,
What care I how young ſhe be,

Then if ſhe be young or chaſt,
Or with the beſt of Women plac't,
And of my loue will not thinke ſtrange
No life ſhall be ere I will change:
But if regardles I her finde.
Farewell falſe loue Ile change my (mind
Then is ſhe not ſo fit for me,
As I deſire my loue ſhould be.

FINIS.

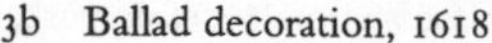

3b Ballad decoration, 1618.

4a Equestrian figure, Jost Amman, *Kunstbüchlein*, 1599.

4b Frontispiece to *The Valiant Welshman*, 1615.

(although perhaps not 'Welsh', given standard Jacobean jokes), and the block matches the play far better than does the stock figure chosen to decorate *Jack Drum*, for example. As it happens, the 1615 *Welshman* block was also copied from a German source: it is a very close reversed copy of a print from Jost Amman's *Kunstbüchlein* (1599; see illustrations 4a and b).[15] We have no evidence that it was printed anywhere else before appearing in this text, and hence it may have been commissioned for it – the play received some attention from the publisher and printer to make it a visually attractive product, and one of the chief functions of title-page or frontispiece decorations was to attract the eye in bookshops. It may seem difficult to assert that generic figures were specifically commissioned given that so many publications from the period have been lost, and perhaps such status isn't particularly important, as it evidently is when a woodcut or engraving depicts an event or a dramatic moment. But what is the boundary between the generic figure, chosen for approximate decorative qualities, and the figure which represents a specific character from, in this context, a play?

One clear example of the patently non-referential figure may be seen on the title-page of *Englishmen for my Money*, 1616 (no. 73). Foakes is right that the generic woodcut of a woman in Elizabethan costume which appears in this text has no connection with the play, or with the stage; it had appeared in the previous year in a similar position on the title-page of Swetnam's *Arraignment of Women* (*STC* 23534: illustration 5). The block simply signifies 'woman', and it was subsequently used in numerous ballads. But why, for example, should the similarly generic woodblock printed on the title-page of *The Fair Maid of the West*

[15] Jost Amman (1539–91) was one of the most famous south-German illustrators of the later sixteenth century. The equestrian figure copied in *Welshman* was first printed in *Artliche vnnd Kunstreiche Figurn zu der Reutterey* (1584).

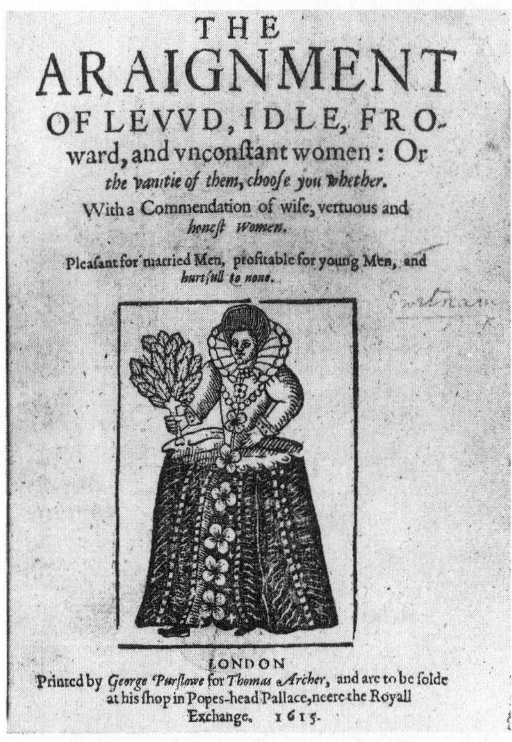
THE
ARAIGNMENT
OF LEVVD, IDLE, FRO-
ward, and vnconſtant women: Or
the vanitie of them, chooſe you whether.
With a Commendation of wiſe, vertuous and
honeſt Women.
Pleaſant for married Men, profitable for young Men, and
hurtfull to none.

LONDON
Printed by *George Purſlowe* for *Thomas Archer*, and are to be ſolde
at his ſhop in Popes-head Pallace, neere the Royall
Exchange. 1615.

5 Title-page, *The Arraignment of ... Women*, 1615.

(1631; Foakes no. 57), have a different significance? Foakes places it in the 'relating to the stage' category, and treats the figure as if it represented Bess Bridges in costume, but I think he is mistaken on both counts. As far as I have been able to discover this little woodblock was not published before it appeared in the playbook. In that it resembles the *Welshman* print. After 1631, it appears constantly in ballads; in that it resembles the *Englishmen* print. To find some other use of 'Bess Bridges' before 1631 might nail things down, but would not alter the evident fact that this block was made not with the remotest reference to the stage, but to serve as a printer's decoration for use ad hoc in various contexts. Other woodblocks in Foakes's category C might be understood in this light. How closely related to the stage, per se, are the conventional representations of Queen Elizabeth with which Nathaniel Butter decorated the various editions of *If You Know not Me, You Know Nobody* (no. 38), or the similarly conventional woodcut of Henry VIII which the same publisher used on the title-page of *When You See Me, You Know Me* (no. 42)? They would serve very well in other contexts as visual decoration. Probably the actors did make an attempt to copy the costumes and poses of the two famous monarchs, but do the woodcuts refer to actors' portrayals, or to the icons that the actors would also have copied? The latter seems generally more likely. A third publication of Butter which appeared between the first edition of *If You Know not Me* (1605) and *When You See Me* (1613), George Wilkins's *The Painful Adventures of Pericles Prince of Tyre* (1608), demonstrates that the theatre could influence illustrations which appeared in non-theatrical publications. The title-page woodcut representation of John Gower, in medieval costume, standing by a table with an open book on it, has no connection with Wilkins's prose version of the Pericles legend, in which the poet is not mentioned. The picture is evidently exploiting the contemporary popularity of the King's Men's play at the Globe, and one might claim, as Gary Taylor has done, that it shows how the part of Gower was costumed.[16] As far as published illustrations are concerned, the border between the theatrical and the non-theatrical could be crossed in both directions.

Two items which certainly do not seem to belong in a selective anthology with a theatrical focus are both interregnum publications which re-use earlier woodcuts from non-dramatic sources, and hence on two counts are unlikely to tell us anything about the stage before 1642. These are *The Jovial Crew*, from 1651 (no. 78), a satiric 'dialogue' which reprints a woodcut specifically made for a

[16] See *William Shakespeare. The Complete Works*, ed. Stanley Wells and Gary Taylor (Oxford, 1986), p. 1167; illustrations 10 and 11.

non-dramatic publication in 1647,[17] and the 1658 edition of the short entertainment *Wine, Beer, Ale and Tobacco* (no. 79) with its reprint of a woodcut which had first appeared in a ballad in 1629 (*STC* 19239; illustration 6), and which has no theatrical significance.

To turn from printed pictures to contemporary drawings and sketches is to enter yet more puzzling territory. Two of the most reproduced icons in modern books about the Shakespearian stage are the Swan drawing and the sketch of a scene from *Titus Andronicus*, both of which are in many ways notorious enigmas, as baffling as they are informative. I have no new light to shed on their dark corners, but would like to comment on another Elizabethan drawing popular in modern reproduction, John Scottowe's representation of Richard Tarlton (no. 23). Foakes discusses this as the first item in his rather miscellaneous category B (drawings, plans and vignettes relating to the stage).[18] The Scottowe drawing has never been properly interrogated by theatre historians. Foakes repeats old 'truths' about this picture, so popular with modern art editors,[19] although the scholarly means to question those assumptions were in print when he wrote. The general line is that the drawing has some prior status, and that because it is a drawing it has more connection with the living man (a very Romantic attitude). Chambers said that the evidently related woodcut, surviving today in late imprints of *Tarlton's Jests* (1613 and 1638), was based on the drawing, and Foakes follows him.[20] Chambers was probably not the first to make this assertion, which he is likely to have inherited from his Victorian predecessors, but I have not tracked this error, as I take it to be, to its lair. Foakes gives no reproduction of the woodcut print, evidently considering it to be of minor importance.

It is an easy matter, once in London, to call up Harleian MS 3885 and have a look at it. One is delivered a very handsome cased folio book which turns out to be an elaborately produced volume of scripts, with manuscript figural decorations in the medieval tradition, and arranged as an alphabet, with one large capital letter on the recto of each vellum page. The media are ink and wash, with light gilded decoration here and there; the colour is sombre, and all the dynamics are in the lines. The figure of Tarlton is contained within the letter T. The book was evidently made with great care, if not always with great art, probably for presentation to someone important and with money, some of which the maker hoped would flow his way. That important someone probably then locked the book in a study or library, where it was seen by few people before it passed to a more public domain, and the Tarlton figure began to be reproduced in nineteenth-century books. As a modern touchstone of Elizabethan stage illustration it has become detached from its context, and hence misunderstood and misinterpreted.

Scottowe was a provincial writing master of French origin who worked and died in Norwich (in 1607); his book was probably made for some member of the local gentry, and presumably passed at least the first century of its life in East Anglia. How could it have been available to a London craftsman wanting to

[17] See *A Catalogue of Prints and Drawings in the British Museum* (London, 1870), pp. 385, 444–5. 'This woodcut was before used for the tract called "Grand Plutoes Progresse", &c "Sept 2" 1647' (p. 444). In the 1647 tract the print is accompanied by ten lines of verse explaining the illustration, quoted in op. cit., p. 385.

[18] The title-pages of the second edition of *Roxana* (1632) and *Messalina* (1640), for example, are placed here, giving them an emphatic status they probably do not deserve. Since they're stage illustrations in published plays, why don't they belong in category C? – another boundary problem. But more of all this below.

[19] The drawing is reproduced, for example, in *The Riverside Shakespeare* (Boston, 1974), *The Revels History of Drama in English, Volume 3* (London, 1975), *The Cambridge Companion to English Renaissance Drama* (Cambridge, 1990), and *The Oxford Illustrated History of the Theatre* (Oxford, 1995); it is used as a dust-jacket decoration for William Ingram's book *The Business of Playing* (Ithaca, 1992).

[20] E. K. Chambers, *The Elizabethan Stage*, 4 vols. (Oxford, 1923): vol. 2, p. 344.

A good throw for three Maiden-heads.

Some ſay that mayden-heads are of high price,
But here are three maids that haue loſt theirs at dice.

To the Tune, Of Ouer and Vnder.

Three maides did make a meeting,
With one young man of late,
Where they had ſuch a greeting,
As paſſes Peg and Kate.
They talke of many matters,
Not fitting to be told :
Alſo they dranke ſtrong waters,
To heat their ſtomacks cold.
and when they had,
drunke with the Lad,
Untill they were merry all :
betweene them three,
they did agree,
Into diſcourſe to fall.

Concerning husbands getting,
The queſtion did ariſe,
And each of them their fitting,
Some reaſon did deuiſe.
One was a milkemaid bonny,
The other Ile not name,
And ſhee did get much mony,
By ſelling of the ſame,
her name is Ione,
as is well knowne,
I hope tis no offence :
to tell what they,
did on that day,
Before they went from thence.

They all did loue this young man
And each for him did ſtriue,
It ſeemes he was a ſtrong man,
That could his worke contriue.
Now which of them ſhould haue him,
They neither of them knew,
But each of them did craue him,
As her owne proper due.
now meeting,
and greeting,
As maids and young men uſe;
with them he dranke,
his money was franke,
Indeed hee could not chuſe.

And either of them telling,
Her mind in full to him,
Meane while the reſt were filling;
Their cupps up to ye brim.
Becauſe in either of them,
It ſeemes he had a ſhare,
Unleſſe he meant to ſcoffe them,
He now muſt chooſe his ware.
and therefore they,
without delay,
Being on the merry pinne :
with good aduice,
did throw the dice,
Who ſhould the young man win.

The young man was contented,
And ſo the dice were brought.
The maids that this inuented,
Their leſſons were well taught :
For the youngman all luſted,
And by this fine deuice,
They ſeuerally all truſted,
To win him by the dice.
but harke now,
and marke now,
The manner of their play :
in their behalfe,
I know youle laugh,
Before you goe away.

6 Ballad illustration, 1629.

make a woodblock of Tarlton? Evidently it wasn't, and Chambers has the story the wrong way round. The modern authority on Scottowe is the manuscript scholar Janet Backhouse.[21] She believes that the book was made in the early 1590s, in the years immediately following Tarlton's death in 1588: the picture is not, then, 'from the life'. She also thinks that Scottowe was not very happy at drawing human figures, and in one demonstrable instance he traced or pricked a figure from a print in a book. Her opinion of the Tarlton figure is that 'The Scottowe portrait probably came from a woodcut circulating soon after his death, perhaps as the decoration of a broadsheet.'[22] We know that cheap printed pictures of Tarlton were produced in this period. In his play *The Three Lords and Three Ladies of London*, published in 1590, Tarlton's colleague from the Queen's Men, Robert Wilson, brings on to the stage a ballad-seller, who holds up Tarlton's picture while he speaks in his praise. This stage property is likely to have been the real thing, and the ballads were probably for sale outside the playhouse after the performance. The image held up on a London stage late in the fifteen eighties is probably the same one Scottowe copied from a ballad bought from a travelling vendor.

There is a close relationship between the Scottowe drawing and the woodcut published on the title-page of *Tarlton's Jests* (illustration 7). Both show a standing male figure moving to the right, with head and shoulders turned towards the observer. The figure wears a moustache, with curly hair emerging from a cap, and he is playing on a pipe (steadied by the left hand) and tabor (drumstick in the right hand). The figure wears a simple belted doublet, with a purse on the left hip, and plain long breeches, with a large phallic codpiece appearing above the tabor; plain-looking pumps (called 'sturtups' in the verses accompanying the drawing) are worn on the feet. The resemblances are so close as to preclude coincidence: either one image as copied from the other – and given what I say

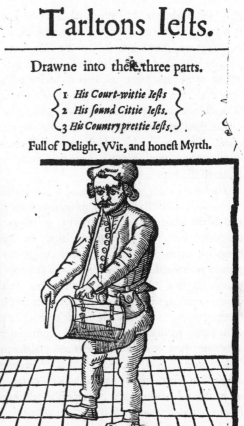

Tarltons Ieſts.

Drawne into theſe three parts.

1 *His Court-wittie Ieſts*
2 *His ſound Cittie Ieſts.*
3 *His Country prettie Ieſts.*

Full of Delight, Wit, and honeſt Myrth.

LONDON,
Printed for *Iohn Budge*, and are to be ſold at his ſhop, at the great South doore of Paules. 1613.

7 Title-page, *Tarlton's Jests*, 1613.

above, the woodcut is the source – or both were copied from some third icon, now lost. But the case is fairly strong for the *Tarlton's Jests* woodcut being the original print, made at some time after late 1588. The woodblock printed in 1613 was evidently not new: the frame has now been broken at the top left, and damaged at bottom left (see illustration 7). The book in which it appeared was first mentioned in the Stationers' Register in 1600, so the block may have been at least thirteen years old, but the

21 See *John Scottowe's Alphabet Books* (London, 1974).
22 *Ibid.*, p. 13.

Jests was already by 1600 into its 'Second Part'. It seems not inconceivable that the block used in 1613 may have been, like the 'Zenocrate' picture, already twenty-five years old, and that it had previously been used to illustrate ballads about Tarlton, one of which Scottowe copied. Woodblocks were made to last, and usually succumbed to woodworm, not the printing press. This particular block was still being employed as late as 1663, when it was used again to illustrate a ballad.[23]

There are clear grounds, then, for regarding the woodcut of Tarlton, so unfashionably stiff and plain when compared to the drawing, as the prior image; it is certainly likely to have been the picture of the legendary comic actor which memorialized him for large numbers of people in the fifty years following his death. The cultural significance of the two pictures has been reversed, it seems, by modern historians, who prefer to disseminate an icon produced for a private, élite context in an antiquated format – a representation, moreover, that changes its original in ways that are probably accidental and inept but which create a considerably different figure of the famous performer.

The Scottowe Tarlton is dwarfish, rounded, and cuddly – a distinctly child-like fool. He has a very large head in proportion to the rest of his body, and the odd angle made by head, neck, and left shoulder has led at least one modern commentator to call him a hunchback.[24] Peter Thomson's re-imagination of Tarlton's performance is of a player who traded on physical oddness and ugliness, and while there are many stories of Tarlton's mugging and weird facial contortions it seems to me that these may have been produced professionally rather than by Dame Nature. Certainly the woodcut shows a quite different figure, although once again not drawn with any great skill. This Tarlton is erect rather than stooped, long-bodied rather than short, and comically lugubrious rather than winsome; altogether he looks a tougher nut than the figure in Scottowe's picture, and a more likely version of the athlete who became a Master of Fence.

Those who choose the Scottowe drawing to speculate about Tarlton's appearance or performance should be advised about how the picture probably was made. It evidently was not directly traced or pricked from the woodcut as printed in *Tarltons Jests*: the Scottowe figure is 142 mm high, the woodcut figure 98 mm high. The significance of this difference, I think, is that Scottowe began the composition of his page with the defining outline of his capital T, and then sought to fill the loop with the Tarlton figure, discovering that the woodcut was too small at actual size to be transferred directly to the space. Accordingly Scottowe began to copy it freehand, beginning with the head, but discovering as he went on that his scale was too large, and hence shrinking the rest of the figure to fit it in.[25] The Tarlton in the Scottowe drawing is a copy which has been rearranged to fit within a decorative scheme. It has very little reliability as a representation of the actor, and in any survey of contemporary illustrations it should be given secondary status. The rough, vernacular woodcut print is to be preferred as the prior representation, and as the image widely disseminated in the late Elizabethan and Stuart periods. Both pictures, however, are posthumous, and neither is attempting a naturalistic portrait.

Other problems of dating bedevil the interpretation of perhaps the clearest contemporary

---

23 See *A Wonder of Wonders*, reproduced with commentary in *The Pack of Autolycus*, ed. H. E. Rollins (Cambridge, Mass., 1927), pp. 114–21.

24 Peter Thomson, *Shakespeare's Professional Career* (Cambridge, 1992), pp. 101–4. Thomson repeats the observation in commentary on a reproduction of the drawing in *The Oxford Illustrated History of the Theatre*, ed. J. R. Brown (Oxford, 1995), p. 190.

25 The considerable rearrangement made by Scottowe, and the resultant effect of the completed figure, may be appreciated by considering that the relative proportions in height of head, body and legs are in the woodcut 19 per cent, 27 per cent, and 54 per cent; in the drawing 27 per cent, 27 per cent, and 46 per cent.

graphic conception of a playhouse, the Inigo Jones drawings which Foakes identifies as 'probably relating to the Cockpit in Drury Lane' (no. 29). In doing so he adopts the case urged by John Orrell in the pages of this journal in 1977, and subsequently in *The Theatres of Inigo Jones and John Webb* (1985). Such a connection remains a speculative one, at best. The date of the drawings is in some doubt, and Graham Barlow's research into the history of the Cockpit site indicates that a building of the size and shape shown in the Worcester College drawings would have been very difficult to accommodate there.[26] Most commentators have received Orrell's hypothesis as interesting but unproven, and until further supporting evidence can be produced to strengthen the case commentary on the drawings should note that they remain, as D. F. Rowan first dubbed them, a 'theatre project'. The modern project to realize the drawings in a building, as part of the Bankside Globe complex, does not claim that the theatre will represent the Cockpit in Drury Lane; rather the building will be called the Inigo Jones theatre.

Recovering a certain amount of evidence about the early stage can and should result in re-interpretation of other related evidence, but it is all too easy to let a few grains of weight tip the beam too far in one direction or the other. The uncovering of the Rose foundations, evidently, was a watershed in modern interpretation of Elizabethan theatres and theatrical culture. At the time of the excavations I was engaged in research on the little stage scenes shown on the title-pages of the plays *Roxana* (no. 31) and *Messalina* (no. 34), which have in their time been used as support for that outdated historians' invention, the 'inner stage'. My mistrust of what they show had to be reconsidered once the plain testimony of the Rose foundations was clear: both the Rose stages were of exactly the same plan as those shown in the seventeenth-century engravings – a platform with sides tapering to a downstage front narrower than the upstage edge of the acting area. And although the engraver of the later *Messalina* plate was demonstrably copying the work of the man who had made the *Roxana* picture it is of more than passing interest that he was also the author of a play which had had a successful run at the Salisbury Court playhouse, where *Messalina* was staged at about the same time. The picture itself remains suspect, I think, as the depiction of a specific place in reliable detail, but the strong circumstantial connection of its maker, Thomas Rawlins, the author of the play, Nathaniel Richards, and the Salisbury Court playhouse as used by Prince Charles's Men between 1631 and 1634 should give us sufficient confidence to interpret this little representation of a playhouse stage in a rather different manner henceforth.[27]

In the preface to his collection Foakes predicted that new graphic evidence would turn up from time to time, and so indeed it has since 1985. Four years later Alan Nelson drew attention to another graphic decoration in a text connected with a play, *The Prologue and Epilogue to a Comedie*, a pamphlet containing speeches from Abraham Cowley's *The Guardian*, which was acted at Trinity College, Cambridge before Prince Charles in March 1642.[28] In the short Royalist tract published the same year (Wing C6683A) a small framed woodcut appears between the printed Prologue and the Epilogue (Sig. A2v; see illustration 8a). It shows a standing male figure half-turned to the right, in dark clothes – doublet, breeches, and a cloak folded over the left arm. The man is bare-

[26] See J. Orrell, *The Theatres of Inigo Jones and John Webb* (Cambridge, 1985), p. 195, note 11; Graham Barlow, 'Wenceslas Hollar and Christopher Beeston's Phoenix Theatre in Drury Lane', *Theatre Research International*, 13 (1988), 30–44.

[27] See my articles 'The Origins of the *Roxana* and *Messallina* Illustrations', *Shakespeare Survey 43* (1990), 149–69; 'The *Messalina* Stage and Salisbury Court Plays', *Theatre Journal*, 43 (1991), 141–56.

[28] *Records of Early English Drama: Cambridge*, 2 vols. (Toronto, 1989); vol. 1, pp. 700–1; vol. 2, pp. 884–5, 995, 1041.

headed, with shoulder-length hair in Caroline fashion; he wears a beard. He carries a hat in his left hand, and he wears boots with spurs. His extended right arm and hand hold out a piece of paper with writing on it.

It seems that we might have in this picture an indication of the kind of dress worn by actors delivering formal prologues and epilogues to plays. One interesting detail is that the hat has been removed in deference to the audience – in the case of the first performance of *The Guardian* a royal audience. The text of the speech (apparently) is being carried, though not being consulted. Various references in London plays, from the late sixteenth century onwards, to the black cloak worn by the prologue, are collected and cited by Chambers,[29] and it would seem that the woodcut shows that the academic theatre at Cambridge copied and continued the practice of the professional troupes. Can we then accept this woodcut as new evidence of theatrical practice in the pre-Restoration theatre?

Alas, no. Once again, the publisher of this book took only part of a larger older woodcut, made for the pamphlet *Canterbvrie Pilgrimage* in 1641 (Wing C459), in which the 'prologue' character is approaching a left foreground half-length representation of Archbishop Laud, whom he addresses in a speech ribbon, admonishing him to 'REDE AND CONSIDAR' the proffered letter, petition, or writ (illustration 8b). The figure is not simply a messenger, but an active agent of political dissent and accusation, 'Shewing the Glory of Reformation, above Prelaticall Tyranny', as the title-page has it: Laud was under arrest by the time this picture was published, in March 1641. So the hand-held text proves not – originally – to have been a prologue, and the deference of the figure in its original setting has an ironical edge. The entire woodcut was printed twice more in other publications during 1641 before, evidently, the block was cut in half.[30] The right-hand half, the 'prologue', has also had the speech ribbon cut away, to leave a stock figure

8a Woodcut figure, *The Prologue and Epilogue to a Comedie*, 1642.

suitable for decoration in roughly appropriate places – as in the 1642 pamphlet. It may be observed that either a thin fillet of wood has been tacked to the left edge or a type rule set against it, to give the effect of the closed frame of a complete woodblock. Once again this print must be dismissed as theatrical evidence, although its evidence of publishers' practices is instructive.

29 Chambers, *Elizabethan Stage*, vol. 2, p. 547.

30 See *Catalogue of Prints and Drawings in the British Museum* (London, 1870), pp. 138, 146, 158, 164. The other two tracts are *An Exact Copy of a Letter . . .* (Wing A2) and *A Conspiracie of the Twelve Bishops* (Wing C5934). My photograph of the print is taken from the latter.

8b Woodcut decoration, *A Conspiracy of the Twelve Bishops*, 1641.

Other new evidence raises questions about the boundaries of the Foakes anthology. In a later volume designed to be a medieval companion to the Foakes book, for example, Clifford Davidson included not only the famous photograph by Andrew Fulgoni of the Rose foundations in 1989, but also photographs and later drawings and plans of buildings where plays are known to have been produced.[31] Such a wider scope reveals that Foakes's biases of selection are metropolitan, and directed towards permanent theatre buildings. 'The English Stage 1580–1642' has been defined in an unduly restricted fashion, and the visual evidence for widespread theatrical activity outside the London playhouses could be expanded commensurately.

In 1990 I discovered in the collections of the College of Arms a seventeenth-century plan of the Great Chamber at Whitehall, and reported it the following year.[32] The document is a heraldic memo recording the ceremony at a formal meal on Twelfth Night 1601, and although it has no primary theatrical significance it is a contemporary representation of a place in which many plays were staged, with which Shakespeare and his fellow actors must have been familiar, and about which we have hitherto known very little. It offers more precise information to do with the use of physical space than do most of the pictorial woodcuts in plays with regard to staging. It

31 *Illustrations of the Stage and Acting in England to 1580* (Kalamazoo, Mich., 1991).

32 'A Drawing of the Great Chamber at Whitehall in 1601', *REED Newsletter*, 16, 1 (1991), 6–11.

shows where the queen was placed at a diplomatic dinner, and hence the 'high' end of the room, where she undoubtedly also sat to watch plays. It shows there were only two doors to the room – one for general access and one leading to the royal suite. Evidence of such an important playing place is of considerable significance, and there is more similar evidence. Foakes does not exclude the court from consideration, but the only pictures included are those of purpose-built theatres. It seems important to me to recognize that many places at the court (and elsewhere) functioned as playing places occasionally, and their form and layout were represented in contemporary drawings and maps, as were those of the playhouses. So a useful addition might be those parts of Wyngaerde's drawings of the royal palaces at Richmond, Hampton Court, Whitehall, and Greenwich which show the great halls at those four palaces, together with other, later representations of halls, banqueting houses, and other chambers with theatrical significance. There are engravings from the 1630s which illustrate the interiors at St James's palace, another theatrical site, and which can be shown to be not proportionally realistic because they can be compared with the surviving building, or photographs and plans of it; the same exercise can be followed at Hampton Court. Thus one might usefully interrogate the reliability of early representations, or examine their stylistic characteristics. In any event, there are at least as many interesting and significant pictures of court buildings as there are of the commercial playhouses.

But to consider court places is only one step in a general widening of the material bearing on theatrical culture in England between 1580 and 1640. 'The English Stage' included activity from Carlisle to Dover, and more than a few of the buildings used for theatrical events survive, and have been recorded in drawings, plans, and photographs from the sixteenth century to the present, as have others not extant.[33] Like court buildings, all of them had other uses, but a proper understanding of early modern theatrical conditions can only be arrived at by including them in one's survey. A comparative examination of the plans of great houses known to have patronized visiting players, for example, might yield significant results. A strictly historically defined collection, like Foakes's, would include only contemporary representations of such places, and there may not be a great deal of interesting material of this kind from before 1640. One would have to test the truth of that guess by first assembling the material.

If we are going either to make new sense of familiar theatrical pictures from the pre-Restoration period or possibly to discover significant new material, a great deal of work remains to be done, most of it having no direct bearing on the theatre of the period. No amount of concentrated thought about *Hamlet*, or even *A Chaste Maid in Cheapside*, is going to tell us more about the Swan drawing, but we do need to know about the contexts in which pictures were made, and about the assumptions which governed their making and their viewing, which must have been different from our own. Chiefly we need more systematically organized information which will allow us to read the contextual sense of pictures more intelligently.

A larger view is needed, in a number of different directions. The very miscellaneous collection of graphic material brought together in the Foakes book has as its common denominator 'English Stage', but almost every item can and should be placed in other categories: to consider the representation of the Swan in the

33 Surveys of the staging of early theatre in specific cities, for example, have been undertaken by Alan Nelson – *Early Cambridge Theatres* (Cambridge, 1994) – and Don Rowan – 'The Players and Playing Places of Norwich', *The Development of Shakespeare's Theater*, ed. J. H. Astington (New York, 1992), pp. 77–94. For a review of playing places country wide, see Alan Somerset's recent article, '"How Chances it They Travel?" Provincial Touring, Playing Places, and the King's Men', *Shakespeare Survey 47* (1994), pp. 45–60.

context of Johannes de Witt's and Aernout van Buchell's other drawings and sketches seems to me precisely the kind of enquiry we should pursue.[34] The imperatives – or the whims – of the London publishing industry should also be interrogated. Why was it that certain plays received illustrative decoration? – were pictures recalling fame on the stage or attempting to stimulate interest in a possibly cold product?[35] Was the decoration of plays regarded as substantially different from that appearing in other published material? – if not, should we not be attempting to understand 'theatrical' pictures in playbooks within the general conventions covering all illustrated books in the period? Does the relative sophistication of the medium (woodcut, engraving, etching) or the execution of the image indicate a certain 'target' market? And so on.[36]

We should find out all we can about the work of the artists and craftsmen who produced the images, with the aim of understanding their visual style and modes of representation. For woodcuts, anonymously produced, this is a rather limited enterprise, but it is still worth gathering contextual groupings, by book, by publisher/printer, and by decade, within which individual images may be read. For engravers, who generally signed their work, the standard reference work, by A. M. Hind, is out of date and incomplete, and we need more monographs, catalogues raisonnés, and studies of such figures as the printseller Peter Stent;[37] in all such works we need access to numerous well-printed photographic reproductions of graphic images.

As we widen our understanding of the ways in which visual artists worked, national boundaries become less and less meaningful. The printing press was at least as internationally significant in its production of images as of texts; the former circulated without the barrier of language, and were quickly copied and imitated elsewhere. Foreign prints were circulating in England by the end of the fifteenth century, and many artists of all kinds working in England from at least that time onwards were foreign-born and foreign-trained – in Italy, Germany, and the Low Countries in particular. As I have suggested, representations in the period Foakes surveys are frequently composed with reference to other representations – copying them, alluding to them, adapting them. Such visual allusiveness was particularly dependent on prints; artists either kept their own collections or used the stock of the printsellers or booksellers for whom they worked. A careful study of the iconography of given images – from the roughest woodcut to the most finished engraving – seems to me essential to work in this area.

As regards the theatre, then, any visual images of stages, actors, and playing places, of whatever kind, published as mechanically reproduced prints anywhere in Europe between 1580 and 1640, might have influenced the visual imagination of both illustrators and viewers in England regarding pictures of English theatrical subjects. In other words generic reference within a picture might have been felt to be as important as specific reference, and a given picture might have included elements of both (as may the Swan drawing, for example). A wide-ranging study of theatrical iconography in the Renaissance – once again with many illustrations – could usefully reposition our modern assumptions about the

[34] See Johan Gerritsen, 'De Witt, Van Buchell, the Swan and the Globe: Some Notes', *Essays in Honour of Kristian Smidt*, ed. P. Bilton (Oslo, 1986). Gerritsen suggests that there may be more de Witt manuscript material to be found, among which may be versions of the Swan sketch.

[35] One related question of interest is why the famous King's Men plays of Beaumont and Fletcher all were printed as decorated quartos in 1619–20, while the first edition of *Othello*, an equally famous and spectacular play, was published in 1622 by Thomas Walkley (who had produced the illustrated *A King and No King* in 1619) with a mere decorative device at the centre of the title-page.

[36] See 'Visual Texts', cited above, n. 7.

[37] Alexander Globe, *Peter Stent, London Printseller c. 1642–1665* (Vancouver, 1985).

referential significance of pictures in the period, and help us redraw categorical boundaries (how might we be able to tell, for example, when a graphic representation is attempting specific, local realism?) If graphic material from the sixteenth and seventeenth centuries is not simply incidental and external, as it is frequently treated in modern books, then it deserves serious examination in its own terms. Only after such examination can we ask if it has anything to tell our histories of the theatre.

And it may be that it does *not* have a great deal to tell. There are, it seems to me, very few representations in this period which are closely connected to the stage, and the most reliable are diagrams and plans rather than sketches. The others can be grouped in various categories, as Foakes does, but the effect is pseudo-scientific. An omnium gatherum, for example, of all decorations in printed dramatic texts (Greg style) is probably of more use than attempting classifications based on prior assumptions. Descriptive analysis of this kind of material seems altogether more useful – single figure as against 'scenic' cuts, alignment (horizontal or upright rectangles, square cuts, unframed figures), measurements, comments on relative sophistication of style (representation of anatomy, depth of field, perspective) – and insists on its status as a medium with formal limits and conventions. Hence one might place 'theatrical' pictures within a cultural field which is likely to enable one to read them better, but which does not take one any closer to contemporary theatrical conditions, to which they are sometimes taken to be a guide. The recognition that many of them are not should not lead to an equally naive dismissal of their significance. We are still learning the representative language of pictures of all kinds from the sixteenth and seventeenth centuries. As we become more articulate I hope and expect that we will be able to speak more clearly about how illustrations represent the contemporary theatre.

NIETZSCHE'S *HAMLET*

PETER HOLBROOK

> It was not until the nineteenth century, whose speculative genius is a sort of living Hamlet, that the tragedy of Hamlet could find such wondering readers.
>
> Emerson, 'Shakespeare; or, the Poet'

> [W]hoever would become light and a bird must love himself . . . only man is a grave burden for himself! That is because he carries on his shoulders too much that is alien to him. Like a camel, he kneels down and lets himself be well loaded. Especially the strong, reverent spirit that would bear much: he loads too many *alien* grave words and values on himself, and then life seems a desert to him.
>
> Nietzsche, *Thus Spoke Zarathustra*

> I don't want to be confounded with others – not even by myself.
>
> Nietzsche, *Ecce Homo: How One Becomes What One Is*

Nietzsche's thinking about *Hamlet* goes beyond the brilliant, glancing remarks in *The Birth of Tragedy* and is bound up with the deepest themes of his philosophy. His ideas, moreover, have influenced twentieth-century criticism of the play, especially that which is troubled by the Ghost and which may even find something positive in Hamlet's not immediately setting to work and dispatching Claudius. This essay attempts to explore some of the ways *Hamlet* mattered to Nietzsche. Like Coleridge, and many others who have identified with Shakespeare's Prince, Nietzsche seems to have used *Hamlet* to interpret his own life. And his views on revenge, I will argue, illuminate a central issue of the play.[1]

[1] Nietzsche's remarks on *Hamlet* occur in sections 7 and 17 of *The Birth of Tragedy*. For a discussion, see Philip Edwards, ed. *Hamlet* (Cambridge, 1985), pp. 34–5, 45. The epigraphs to my essay come from: 'Shakespeare; or, the Poet' in the *Oxford Authors* selection of Emerson's writings, ed. Richard Poirier (Oxford, 1990), p. 335; *Thus Spoke Zarathustra* in *The Portable Nietzsche*, trans. and ed. Walter Kaufmann (Harmondsworth, 1978), pp. 304, 305; *Ecce Homo: How One Becomes What One Is* in *Basic Writings of Nietzsche*, trans. and ed. Walter Kaufmann (1966; repr. New York, 1992), p. 715. The latter collection also contains *The Birth of Tragedy*; *Beyond Good and Evil: Prelude to a Philosophy of the Future*; *On The Genealogy of Morals: A Polemic*. Paul N. Siegel

Nietzsche was both appalled and inspired by the modern age. On the one hand, he recognized that the critical, sceptical, scientific spirit of modernity was necessary if old illusions were to be overthrown and new values created. In *On the Genealogy of Morals*, he wrote: 'If a temple is to be erected *a temple must be destroyed*: that is the law ...'[2] On the other hand, the recognition that the old truths were lies could produce despair. Nietzsche's view of modernity, then, was ambivalent. Like the concept of nihilism, with which it is often associated in his writing, modernity can display boldness and strength or sickness and life-weariness. There is the nihilism which is the capacity to live without illusions and to create one's own values. There is priestly, or philosophical, nihilism, which has for millennia devalued the earth in favour of an otherworldly Ideal, and seduced human beings into a desire for death. Modern nihilism, then, like many categories in Nietzsche's thought, is a positive and negative phenomenon.[3] Those who have tapped the old idols with a hammer and found them to be hollow may be inspired to affirm new values. Equally, however, they may be led to 'the radical repudiation of value, meaning, and desirability ...'[4] The modern era, the twilight of the idols, is both an end to the long day of European idealism and, Nietzsche fervently hopes, the first glimmer of some new dawn.

Shakespeare occupied an important place in Nietzsche's attitude to modernity. Like his hero Emerson, Nietzsche thought of him as the poet of modernity (Emerson said that Shakespeare 'wrote the text of modern life').[5] He seems to have regarded Shakespeare as both a symptom of the modern age and one of its diagnosticians. Nietzsche – who saw himself as both a product of modern decadence and its sternest critic – may have found *himself* prefigured in Shakespeare. He certainly, I argue, found his situation prefigured in Hamlet's. The autobiography, *Ecce Homo: How One Becomes What One Is*, which he was writing weeks before his collapse into madness, is shaped by his meditations on *Hamlet*.

Nietzsche finds in Shakespeare both beginnings and ends: pictures of the human types he wants to promote and those he wishes to discourage. While a schoolboy he wrote in a letter to his sister Elisabeth that Shakespeare 'presents you with so many strong men – rough, hard, powerful, iron-willed. It is in men like these that our age is so poor.'[6] In *Ecce Homo*, he wrote: 'When I seek my ultimate formula for *Shakespeare*, I always find only this: he conceived of the type of Caesar. That sort of thing cannot be guessed: one either is it, or one is not. The great poet dips *only* from his own reality ...'[7] Shakespeare's interest in portraying actual 'types', such as Caesar, taken from the real historical world, is another point in his favour. It distinguishes him from the philosophers, whose 'Egyptianism' – their tendency to study phenomena, including morality, unhistorically, to traffic only in 'conceptual

---

discusses critics 'who do not regard Hamlet's revenge as a moral duty' in '"Hamlet, Revenge!": The Uses and Abuses of Historical Criticism', *Shakespeare Survey 45* (1992), p. 18. The most brilliant and notorious Nietzschean commentator on the play is G. Wilson Knight, who condemned Hamlet as a 'soul ... sick to death' and defended Claudius. See 'The Embassy of Death: an Essay on *Hamlet*' (1930) and '*Hamlet* Reconsidered' (1947) in *The Wheel of Fire: Interpretations of Shakespearean Tragedy with Three New Essays* (London, 1962); the quotation is from 'Embassy of Death', p. 20. Knight later acknowledged the similarities between his interpretation and that in *The Birth of Tragedy* ('Embassy of Death', p. 46). *Christ and Nietzsche: An Essay in Poetic Wisdom*, on politics, religion, poetry and almost everything else, appeared in London in 1948.

2 *Genealogy of Morals*, p. 531.

3 Nietzsche typically identifies 'a strong ... and weak version of the same phenomenon': Henry Staten, *Nietzsche's Voice* (Ithaca, 1990), p. 147.

4 *The Will to Power*, ed. Walter Kaufmann, trans. Walter Kaufmann and R. J. Hollingdale (New York, 1968), p. 7.

5 Emerson, p. 338.

6 Quoted in Ronald Hayman, *Nietzsche: A Critical Life* (London, 1980), pp. 43–4.

7 *Ecce Homo*, p. 702.

mummies' – Nietzsche deplored.[8] Shakespeare's fascination with 'the revolution of the times'[9] makes him an historical dramatist, thus an ally of Nietzsche's in his campaign against idealism. And modernity, it could be argued, thought of as the nihilism that succeeds upon the passing of the old certainties, is central to *Hamlet*, with its questioning, sophisticated humanist hero and his heroic, awesomely archaic and absolutist father.

Modernity is Nietzsche's problem. The old idols – God and morality – are hollow. What will stand in their place? Zarathustra is a transitional figure, appearing in the time of those 'suffering of *the great nausea*, for whom the old god has died and for whom no new god lies as yet in cradle and swaddling clothes . . .'[10] The collapse of the old truths through scientific critique has produced in the moderns stasis and will-lessness: 'modern man', writes Nietzsche, is the one who 'sighs', saying 'I know not which way to turn; I am everything that knows not which way to turn.'[11] Nietzsche addresses himself to this destructive nihilism. In a letter of 1887 he wrote: 'I have still not despaired of finding the way out, the hole that will lead us to "something."'[12] In *Ecce Homo* he claims that:

> The psychological problem in the type of Zarathustra is how he that says No and *does* No to an unheard-of degree, to everything to which one has so far said Yes, can nevertheless be the opposite of a No-saying spirit; how the spirit who bears the heaviest fate, a fatality of a task, can nevertheless be the lightest and most transcendent – Zarathustra is a dancer – how he that has the hardest, most terrible insight into reality, that has thought the 'most abysmal idea', nevertheless does not consider it an objection to existence, not even to its eternal recurrence – but rather one reason more for being himself the eternal Yes to all things . . .[13]

Nietzsche describes himself here. He has himself in mind again when, in *The Genealogy of Morals*, he imagines a resolution of 'this decaying, self-doubting present' in the form of a 'man of the future, who will redeem us not only from the hitherto reigning ideal but also from that which was bound to grow out of it, the great nausea, the will to nothingness, nihilism . . . this Antichrist and antinihilist; this victor over God and nothingness – *he must come one day*. –'[14]

In *Twilight of the Idols*, Nietzsche writes: 'Formula of my happiness: a Yes, a No, a straight line, a *goal* . . .'[15] But modern people are incapable of such unity of purpose. A passage in *Beyond Good and Evil* declares:

> In an age of disintegration that mixes races indiscriminately, human beings have in their bodies the heritage of multiple origins, that is, opposite, and often not merely opposite, drives and value standards that fight each other and rarely permit each other any rest. Such human beings of late cultures and refracted lights will on the average be weaker human beings: their most profound desire is that the war they *are* should come to an end.[16]

The modern lacks character, is 'physiological self-contradiction'.[17] The type of this chaotic modern non-person is Rousseau, whom Nietzsche loathed and feared as a forerunner of the ordinary, democratic man of the future: 'this first modern man, idealist, and *canaille* in *one* person . . . sick with unbridled vanity and unbridled self-contempt'.[18] Yet – like so many since the Romantic era – when Nietzsche thinks of modern man he also has in mind Hamlet. And where he simply detests Rousseau, as an irredeemably degenerate figure, he

[8] *Twilight of the Idols, or How to Philosophize with a Hammer*, trans. R. J. Hollingdale (London, 1990), p. 45. This book includes Hollingdale's translation of Nietzsche's *The Anti-Christ*.

[9] *2 Henry IV*, 3.1.46. Shakespeare quotations are from Peter Alexander's edition of the *Complete Works* (London, 1951).

[10] *Thus Spoke Zarathustra*, p. 409.

[11] *The Anti-Christ*, p. 127.

[12] Quoted in Hayman, p. 313.

[13] *Ecce Homo*, p. 762.

[14] *Genealogy of Morals*, p. 532.

[15] *Twilight of the Idols*, p. 37.

[16] *Beyond Good and Evil*, p. 301.

[17] *Twilight of the Idols*, p. 107.

[18] *Ibid.*, p. 113.

finds in Hamlet – as in himself – signs of ascent and descent, health and decadence. He is drawn to Hamlet, seeing in him many of the decadent modern tendencies described in the passages just quoted – the self-doubt, 'the great nausea', the conflicting 'drives and value standards', the despairing search for rest from this conflict in death ('their most profound desire is that the war they *are* should come to an end') – but also the eventual overcoming of modern nihilism. Consequently, Hamlet – the figure Emerson found essentially modern – helps Nietzsche understand, and (as I shall argue) affirm, his own life.

What contrasts in Nietzsche's mind with modernity and the pitiful non-personalities it throws up, mere bundles of ill-sorted drives and affects, is the Renaissance.[19] This age is central to his thinking, because it proved that personality was still possible – even after the catastrophe of Christianity, which, as the most cunning slave-rebellion ever devised, had taught the powerful to despise themselves and prepared the way for the triumph of the herd, those whom Zarathustra describes as 'sitting still in a swamp' and whose proudest boast is 'We bite no one and avoid those who want to bite ...'[20] Nietzsche feared that immorality was dying out, that humanity was perishing of its small virtues. The Renaissance, especially as interpreted by Jacob Burckhardt, Nietzsche's friend and colleague at the University of Basel, is for him the last age of character – and, therefore, of evil, for the notion that there is one morality to which all should conform is precisely that which depresses individuality.[21] Burckhardt wrote that 'The fundamental vice of [the Italian character in the Renaissance] was at the same time a condition of its greatness – namely, excessive individualism ... If, therefore, egoism in its wider as well as in its narrower sense is the root and fountain of all evil, the more highly developed Italian was for this reason more inclined to wickedness than the member of other nations of that time.'[22] This was Nietzsche's view. He rages against the Germans, remembering how Luther, that 'calamity of a monk ... did Europe out of the harvest, the meaning, of the last *great* age, the age of the Renaissance', by subverting the rebirth of immorality under the Borgias.[23] Zarathustra will not prescribe: 'I am a law only for my kind, I am no law for all.'[24] The only goal proper for everyone (though not achievable by all) is: 'Become who you are!'[25] Becoming who you are is antimoral: as Zarathustra says, 'Man is hard to discover – hardest of all for himself ... He, however, has discovered himself who says, "This is *my* good and evil"; with that he has reduced to silence the mole and dwarf who say, "Good for all, evil for all." '[26] Just as Christ's disciples often misunderstood Him, Zarathustra's followers do not comprehend his teaching: ' "This is *my* way; where is yours?" – thus I answered those who asked me "the way." For *the* way – that does not exist.'[27] Morality is replaced by art, goodness by style – and the Renaissance is pre-eminently the age of style. 'Ages', Nietzsche writes, 'are to be assessed according to their *positive forces* – and by this assessment the age of the Renaissance, so prodigal and so fateful, appears as the last *great* age, and we, we moderns ... appear as a *weak* age ... the chasm between man and man, class and class, the multiplicity of types, the will to be oneself, to stand out – that which I call *pathos of distance* – characterizes every *strong* age'.[28] He pays tribute to Rome and Venice,

19 And Greece. On Nietzsche's esteem for the Renaissance, see Walter Kaufmann, *Nietzsche: Philosopher, Psychologist, AntiChrist* (Princeton, 1968), p. 320.

20 *Thus Spoke Zarathustra*, p. 207.

21 See Kaufmann, *Nietzsche*, p. 308.

22 *The Civilization of the Renaissance in Italy*, trans. S. C. G. Middlemore (New York, 1958), vol. 2, p. 442.

23 *Ecce Homo*, p. 776.

24 *Thus Spoke Zarathustra*, p. 397.

25 *Ibid.*, p. 351.

26 *Ibid.*, p. 306.

27 *Ibid.*, p. 307.

28 *Twilight of the Idols*, p. 102.

'those great forcing-houses for strong human beings'.[29]

The one absolute in Nietzsche's thought is the self. One must give one's life its signature, become a person rather than 'a rendezvous of personalities'.[30] As Alexander Nehamas has recently shown, Nietzsche's approach to the problem of selfhood, the central issue in his thought, is fundamentally aesthetic.[31] '*One thing is needful*', Nietzsche says in *The Gay Science*: 'To "give style" to one's character – a great and rare art! It is practised by those who survey all the strengths and weaknesses of their nature and then fit them into an artistic plan until every one of them appears as art and reason and even the weaknesses delight the eye . . . It will be the strong and domineering natures that enjoy their finest gaiety in such constraint and perfection under a law of their own.'[32] In a note in *The Will to Power*, he defines evil as 'exaggeration, disharmony, disproportion'.[33] Will to Power, Nehamas has argued, is thus partly a psychological, partly a hermeneutical, concept: on the one hand the giving of form to one's life by organizing the drives and affects; on the other, the ability to look at that life in such a way as to find in it meaning and pattern. To see oneself in this way is, according to Zarathustra, to make it possible to love oneself – which is the natural disposition of the aristocrat and 'of all arts the subtlest, the most cunning, the ultimate, and the most patient'.[34] The mark of the modern man, however, to the extent that he is a chaos of impulses, is nausea and self-disgust. But '*The noble soul has reverence for itself*'.[35]

There is no ideal personality – no particular arrangement of drives that defines 'noble'. Each must find the structure that works best. What Nietzsche most admires is the greatest amount of complex organization in a human being: the more of such *organized* complexity, the more personality. A person is like a city; a non-person, a mob. This view demoralizes Plato's political metaphor for the self in the *Republic*. Plato regarded a healthy human being as one whose rational part controlled the other parts. It does not concern Nietzsche which part dominates, so long as *one* does. It is, accordingly (as Nehamas points out) impossible to say exactly the sort of person Nietzsche esteems.[36] All that can be said is that he admires *persons*, that is, not the non-persons most human beings, especially moderns, riven by conflicting value standards, are.

Nietzsche's attitude to Shakespeare is complex. He is a great poet who portrays admirable human types. Yet, rather in the manner of Voltaire, Nietzsche sometimes disapproves of him as a wild modern genius, an 'amazing Spanish-Moorish-Saxon synthesis of tastes',[37] whose works offend against classical sobriety. Shakespeare's oeuvre does not add up to a personality. However, despite these strictures, Shakespeare's plays often lie behind Nietzsche's thoughts on the problem of character. In *The Will to Power* he observes that 'the highest man would have the greatest multiplicity of drives, in the relatively greatest strength that can be endured. Indeed, where the plant "man" shows himself strongest one finds instincts that conflict powerfully (e.g., in Shakespeare), but are controlled.'[38] Nietzsche summed up this ideal of extreme yet integrated complexity in the slogan 'the Roman Caesar

---

29 *Ibid.*, p. 104.

30 *The Will to Power*, p. 522.

31 *Nietzsche: Life as Literature* (Cambridge, Mass., 1985). Nietzsche relies 'on artistic models for understanding the world and life and for evaluating people and actions' (p. 39). I am indebted to Nehamas's book throughout.

32 *The Gay Science*, trans. Walter Kaufmann (New York, 1974), p. 232.

33 *The Will to Power*, p. 29.

34 *Thus Spoke Zarathustra*, p. 305.

35 *Beyond Good and Evil*, p. 418.

36 '[J]ust as there is no single type of great artist or great artwork, there also is no type of life that is in itself to be commended or damned' (Nehamas, p. 229). The preoccupation with self-fashioning that Nehamas finds in Nietzsche Wilson Knight extended to Shakespeare: the 'life-work' of both Nietzsche and Shakespeare 'may be discussed . . . in terms of "self-realization"' ('*Hamlet* Reconsidered', p. 325n).

37 *Beyond Good and Evil*, p. 342.

38 *The Will to Power*, p. 507.

with Christ's soul'.[39] The ideal is the man who creates out of inner conflict a unique self. In *Hamlet*, I suggest, Nietzsche finds a compelling example of the creation of such a self.

Hamlet informs many of Nietzsche's meditations on subjectivity, modernity, and nihilism. His Hamlet is a modern. He exemplifies the opportunities and risks facing Nietzsche and the best of his contemporaries, that is, all those who might become free spirits – nihilists in the good sense – or who might fall into the despair resulting from the destruction of old truths. In *Ecce Homo* Nietzsche draws upon Hamlet to understand his own life and the lives of other moderns.

In *The Birth of Tragedy*, Nietzsche argued against the notion that *Hamlet* is a tragedy of reflection. The play is actually about the cost of knowledge of reality:

> [T]he Dionysian man resembles Hamlet: both have once looked truly into the essence of things, they have *gained knowledge*, and nausea inhibits action; for their action could not change anything in the eternal nature of things; they feel it to be ridiculous or humiliating that they should be asked to set right a world that is out of joint. Knowledge kills action; action requires the veils of illusion: that is the doctrine of Hamlet, not that cheap wisdom of Jack the Dreamer who reflects too much and, as it were, from an excess of possibilities does not get around to action. Not reflection, no – true knowledge, an insight into the horrible truth, outweighs any motive for action . . .[40]

This passage, from Nietzsche's first book, anticipates that from *Ecce Homo* quoted above, in which he imagines the person who has the 'most terrible insight into reality', but who finds that merely 'one reason more for being himself the eternal Yes to all things'. Like Hamlet, Nietzsche, the modern philosopher, has seen through lies. 'I was the first', he says in *Ecce Homo*, 'to *discover* the truth by being the first to experience lies as lies – smelling them out. – My genius is in my nostrils.'[41] For Nietzsche, to see through the pious frauds of religion or the convenient fictions of metaphysics is to see the chaos at the bottom of things, 'the horrible truth'. Bad nihilism – (the seduction to nothingness, the belief that nothing is worth more than anything else and that therefore all willing is pointless – is accordingly Hamlet's (and Nietzsche's) specific temptation as moderns: '*Nausea* at man', he writes in *Ecce Homo*, 'is my danger'.[42] Yet, as *Ecce Homo* makes plain, Nietzsche does not believe himself to have succumbed to nihilism. Nor – and here he differs from many interpreters, including those like Wilson Knight who are indebted to him – does he see Hamlet as succumbing.[43]

---

39 Quoted in Kaufmann, *Nietzsche*, p. 316.

40 *Birth of Tragedy*, p. 60.

41 *Ecce Homo*, p. 782. Hamlet's love of truth and 'aversion from all that is false' has long been noted: see Edward Dowden, *Shakspere, His Mind and Art* (3rd edn, London, n.d.), p. 151. For G. R. Hibbard, ed. *Hamlet* (Oxford, 1987), the hero's 'concern for truth' is 'total' and he 'is powered . . . by his consuming urge to know and to understand' (p. 63). Like Nietzsche's Dionysian man, Knight's Hamlet 'has seen through all things, including himself, to the foulness within' ('Embassy of Death', p. 25).

42 *Ecce Homo*, p. 787.

43 Many critics feel the Ghost is an evil tempter, for example John Vyvyan in *The Shakespearean Ethic* (London, 1959), p. 31. Nietzsche (I am arguing) would agree – though not, obviously, on Christian grounds. But Nietzsche does not, it seems to me, regard Hamlet as giving in to the Ghost's temptation. Many commentators do, however. L. C. Knights sees Hamlet as tempted 'to gaze with fascinated horror at an abyss of evil': 'An Approach to *Hamlet*' (1960) in '*Hamlet*' *and Other Essays* (Cambridge, 1979), p. 37. (Knights's argument recalls the epigram in *Beyond Good and Evil*: 'when you look long into an abyss, the abyss also looks into you', p. 279.) Hamlet's 'inability to affirm' (p. 80) is linked to the Ghost's contamination of his mind: 'Hamlet . . . cannot break out of the closed circle of loathing and self-contempt, so that his nature is "subdued to what it works in, like the dyer's hand"' (pp. 80–1). The interpretation is not unlike Wilson Knight's: Hamlet's 'disease, or vision, is primarily one of negation' ('The Embassy of Death', p. 42). For Eleanor Prosser the Ghost is a hellish spirit whose cry of vengeance is a temptation Hamlet does not yield to: 'Hamlet is guilty of manslaughter, not premeditated murder . . . He adminis-

The antidote to a self-destructive reaction to the 'horrible truth', it emerges, is becoming what one is. In *Ecce Homo* Nietzsche asserts: 'I contradict as has never been contradicted before and am nevertheless the opposite of a No-saying spirit'.[44] What Nietzsche says Yes to in *Ecce Homo* – which sports such chapter titles as 'Why I Am So Clever' and 'Why I Write Such Good Books' – is himself.

Like Hamlet, Nietzsche in his autobiography is full of irony, mockery, provocation, malice, wit, playfulness, madness, buffoonery – 'Perhaps I am a buffoon', he declares.[45] His readers are in the position of Hamlet's interlocutors (perhaps even Polonius's): we often do not know whether to take him seriously or not. The madcap quality of *Ecce Homo* recalls Hamlet's antic disposition. Yet, like the Prince's clowning, Nietzsche's masks suffering: as he says in the book, 'I know no more heart-rending reading than Shakespeare: what must a man have suffered to have such a need of being a buffoon!'[46] Nietzsche's isolation, appallingly acute in his later years, also links him to Hamlet, that 'loneliest of heroes', as Philip Edwards has described him.[47] In a discarded draft for the chapter entitled 'The Case of Wagner', he wrote: 'I am *solitude* become man';[48] he is amused yet pained by 'the absurd silence under which [his name] lies buried . . .'[49] Like Hamlet, he is not understood. Yet also like Hamlet he seems not to want to be. The buffoonery wards off prying misunderstanders; as he had said in *Beyond Good and Evil*, 'Whatever is profound loves masks . . .'[50] Indeed, *not* being understood is virtually what guarantees the existence of an unusually deep and rich inner life that cannot be plumbed by shallow inquirers: it is here with Nietzsche and his readers as it is with Hamlet and Gertrude and Claudius, or Rosencrantz and Guildenstern.[51] Like the cosmopolitan Prince in Claudius's rather boorish court, Nietzsche is an outsider among his own people: 'I was *condemned* to Germans.'[52] And like Hamlet again, who is more at home in Wittenberg than Elsinore, Nietzsche is happiest abroad: 'As an *artist* one has no home in Europe, except Paris . . .'[53] His aestheticism and '*délicatesse*'[54] bring to mind

ters the deathblow instinctively . . . [I]n the gravedigger's metaphor, Hamlet did not go to the water. The water came to him': *Hamlet and Revenge*, 2nd edn (Stanford, 1971), pp. 237–8. Thus Hamlet has (to use a Nietzschean phrase) overcome himself, or 'won the battle within' (p. 239). The reading closest to the Nietzschean one I am developing here is Harold Goddard's, in volume one of *The Meaning of Shakespeare* (1951; repr. Chicago, 1961). The essential conflict is in Hamlet's breast, between 'loyalty to his father and the desire to grow unto himself'; the paternal command is 'morally wrong'; thus 'Hamlet's delay . . . does him credit' (p. 341). Not only wicked, the Ghost's command is alien to Hamlet's true nature: 'his soul abhors' it (p. 356) and cries out 'Do not obey your father' (p. 360). The 'delay is a perpetual shifting of ground in an attempt to get away from the Ghost' (p. 354), to live up to 'the highest duty of any man', which is 'to be true to the divinity within him, to remain faithful to his creative gift' (p. 360). However, 'in the end the Ghost has his way' (p. 354). Hamlet surrenders his will (p. 359) and becomes an instrument of his father's: 'the fourth and fifth acts exhibit Hamlet's gradual engulfment under the ancestral tide' (p. 374). Hamlet was 'tempted by hell – and fell' (p. 382). Neither of Goddard's two citations of Nietzsche in this volume are connected to *Hamlet*, but overall his interpretation is informed by Nietzsche's conviction that the task of life is to become what one is. My suggestion is simply that Nietzsche's *Hamlet* is not as pessimistic as Goddard's.

44 *Ecce Homo*, p. 783.

45 *Ibid.*, p. 782.

46 *Ibid.*, p. 702. The philosopher suffers from the knowledge that the world is chaos: 'Is Hamlet *understood*? Not doubt, *certainty* is what drives one insane. – But one must be profound, an abyss, a philosopher to feel that way. – We are all *afraid* of truth.' (*Ibid.*)

47 In his edition, p. 58.

48 *Ecce Homo*, p. 799.

49 *Ibid.*, p. 780.

50 *Beyond Good and Evil*, p. 240.

51 Hamlet's insistence upon his inscrutability, for example in his mockery of Rosencrantz and Guildenstern's attempt to pluck out the heart of his mystery (3.2.357), has made him virtually the literary embodiment of subjectivity in the West. Nietzsche too insists upon the depth and range of his inner life – 'the multiplicity of inward states is exceptionally large in my case' (*Ecce Homo*, p. 721) – thus recalling the unfathomable Hamlet.

52 *Ecce Homo*, p. 705.

53 *Ibid.*, p. 704.

54 *Ibid.*

Hamlet's connoisseurship and sensibility. He has Hamlet's aristocratic '*hauteur*'.[55] These disparate connections merely point to the extent to which Hamlet pervades the book. The more important link is that in *Ecce Homo* Hamlet represents for Nietzsche the strenuous achievement of a rich modern subjectivity, one which is imperilled, like all modern selves, but ultimately triumphant.[56]

The importance of Shakespeare's play for Nietzsche is simply that despite Hamlet's modernity there is no more intensely realized figure in literature than he. Indeed, the play is about subjectivity, 'that within which passes show' (1.2.85), in a more explicit way than almost any other literary work. It is this predominantly *personal* quality of Hamlet that makes him so important for Nietzsche, since it is his view that the fundamental task for a human being is to 'become what one is' – but for moderns this is especially difficult. As Nehamas interprets Nietzsche, the self, the unification of the drives and affects, 'is not something given but something achieved, not a beginning but a goal'.[57] But how achieve a self when one is riven by incompatible values (say those of an heroic warrior culture and Renaissance humanism) or when one is so demoralized by 'the horrible truth' about the world that life itself seems pointless? Yet the creation of a self is what Nietzsche finds in Hamlet.

In *Ecce Homo* Nietzsche writes about his 'art of style': 'To communicate a state, an inward tension of pathos, by means of signs, including the tempo of these signs – that is the meaning of every style; and considering that the multiplicity of inward states is exceptionally large in my case, I have many stylistic possibilities – the most multifarious art of style that has ever been at the disposal of one man.'[58] This, of course, is one of Hamlet's claims upon our interest: that his is one of the most various, protean styles – of speech, behaviour, outlook – and yet that he virtually signifies personality in literature. In the autobiography, Nietzsche presents it as his obligation to declare his identity:

> Seeing that before long I must confront humanity with the most difficult demand ever made of it, it seems indispensable to me to say *who I am*. Really, one should know it, for I have not left myself 'without testimony'. But the disproportion between the greatness of my task and the *smallness* of my contemporaries has found expression in the fact that one has neither heard nor even seen me. I live on my own credit; it is perhaps a mere prejudice that I live.
>
> I only need to speak with one of the 'educated' . . . and I am convinced that I do *not* live.
>
> Under these circumstances I have a duty against which my habits, even more the pride of my instincts, revolt at bottom – namely, to say: *Hear me! For I am such and such a person. Above all, do not mistake me for someone else.*[59]

Not to be mistaken for another – nor, even more crucially, to mistake oneself. The importance of *Hamlet* to Nietzsche is now clear: it lies in its picture of besieged subjectivity, which Nietzsche took as paradigmatic for moderns. Hamlet is confronted by a figure of over-

55 Hibbard, p. 54. Nietzsche claimed descent from Polish nobility.

56 Cf. G. K. Hunter, for whom the play is also a drama of selfhood: Hamlet 'is . . . caught between two equally impossible courses: to give in to the ghost's command, reverberating out of that region where truth is never less than absolute (and so lose control that way), or to give in to the world of social and political truth, meaning expediency . . . both would be equally destructive of his individual life': 'The Heroism of Hamlet' (1963) in *Dramatic Identities and Cultural Tradition: Studies in Shakespeare and His Contemporaries* (Liverpool, 1978), p. 246. The play shows Hamlet's struggle 'to create the sense of meaning in his action out of himself' (p. 246); it develops 'a version of heroism which depends less upon acting or even knowing than upon *being*' (p. 247). This heroism is intensely personal: 'Hamlet cannot, without loss of his kind of heroism, be absorbed into a framework of meaning outside himself' – which explains why Shakespeare does not (in the tradition of revenge plays) have the Ghost appear at the end, for 'the point of the denouement [is] not that the ghost is satisfied, but that Hamlet has fulfilled his destiny' (p. 248).

57 Nehemas, p. 182.

58 *Ecce Homo*, p. 721.

59 *Ibid.*, p. 673.

whelmingly powerful subjectivity and the command, 'Remember me'. As if to point up Hamlet's blameworthy passivity, Fortinbras and Laertes are vigorously active on behalf of their fathers. By contrast, for much of the play Hamlet appears to be one of the men Zarathustra describes: 'the men of great longing, of great nausea, of great disgust ...'[60] Yet Nietzsche, I think (and all readers and spectators who admire Hamlet implicitly agree with him here) interprets Hamlet's *not* acting in accordance with his father's command as the true beginning of style in his character – of becoming what one is. Zarathustra's remark that 'whoever heeds commands does not heed *himself*' is relevant.[61] To the extent that Hamlet remembers his father he forgets himself:

Remember thee!
Ay, thou poor ghost, whiles memory holds a seat
In this distracted globe. Remember thee!
Yea, from the table of my memory
I'll wipe away all trivial fond records,
All saws of books, all forms, all pressures past
That youth and observation copied there,
And thy commandment all alone shall live
Within the book and volume of my brain,
Unmix'd with baser matter. (I.5.95–104)

To Nietzsche, such willed self-erasure is horrifying.

In *The Genealogy of Morals*, Nietzsche, anticipating Freud, asserts the importance to psychic health of what he calls 'active forgetfulness, which is like a door-keeper, a preserver of psychic order, repose, and etiquette ...' There can, he says, 'be no happiness, no cheerfulness, no hope, no pride, no *present*, without forgetfulness. The man in whom this apparatus of repression is damaged and ceases to function properly may be compared (and more than merely compared) with a dyspeptic – he cannot "have done" with anything.'[62] This observation again has Hamlet in the background – the Hamlet who vows never to forget his father, who dwells incessantly on 'the horrible truth'. But in Act v of the play, in the graveyard, the command 'Remember me' has faded in intensity for the hero. The past is dead – old bones merely. Now for Nietzsche, as I have said, the problem of life is to find one's task – and, above all, not to mistake another's task for one's own: 'The best are lacking when egoism begins to be lacking.'[63] In *Beyond Good and Evil* he points out with dismay the sceptical weakness of will of the modern scientific scholar, the '*objective* spirit'[64] who is

> a passageway and reflection of strange forms and events even to himself. He recollects 'himself' only with an effort and often mistakenly; he easily confuses himself with others, he errs about his own needs and is in this respect alone unsubtle and slovenly.[65]

This figure, who typifies modern depersonalization, is, says Nietzsche, only 'an instrument ... but in himself, nothing'.[66] The discussion of the modern scholar-scientist occurs in section 207 of *Beyond Good and Evil*. It is in the next section that Nietzsche mentions the scholar Hamlet, associating him with 'the gentle, fair, lulling poppy of skepticism'.[67] This bad scepticism, he writes,

> is the most spiritual expression of a certain complex physiological condition that in ordinary language is called nervous exhaustion and sickliness; it always develops when races or classes that have long been separated are crossed suddenly and decisively. In the new generation that, as it were, has inherited in its blood diverse standards and values, everything is unrest, disturbance, doubt, attempt; the best forces have an inhibiting effect, the very virtues do not allow each other to grow and become strong; balance, a center of gravity, and perpendicular poise are lacking in body and soul. But what becomes sickest and degenerates most in such hybrids is the *will*: they no longer know independence of decisions

60 *Thus Spoke Zarathustra*, p. 395.
61 *Ibid.*, p. 312.
62 *Genealogy of Morals*, p. 494.
63 *Twilight of the Idols*, p. 98.
64 *Beyond Good and Evil*, p. 316.
65 *Ibid.*, p. 317.
66 *Ibid.*, p. 318.
67 *Ibid.*, p. 319.

and the intrepid sense of pleasure in willing – they doubt the 'freedom of the will' even in their dreams.

Our Europe of today, being the arena of an absurdly sudden attempt at a radical mixture of classes, and *hence* races, is therefore skeptical in all its heights and depths – sometimes with that mobile skepticism which leaps impatiently and lasciviously from branch to branch, sometimes dismal like a cloud overcharged with question marks – and often mortally sick of its will. Paralysis of the will: where today does one not find this cripple sitting?[68]

In this passage, and in the other passages diagnosing the 'European sickness'[69] that I have quoted from *Beyond Good and Evil*, we see an interpretation of Hamlet: a dangerously self-forgetful figure, a mere 'instrument' or 'passageway' for another; a sceptic, unable to believe anything ('a cloud overcharged with question marks'), one for whom 'everything is unrest ... doubt'; whose will is paralysed; whose very virtues 'have an inhibiting effect'; who is a member of that 'new generation that ... has inherited in its blood diverse standards and values' (the modern humanist who feels bound to obey an archaic and 'imperious demand from outside', as John Holloway puts it).[70] Nietzsche's description of the self-divided and incoherent modern non-person is, I am suggesting, informed by *Hamlet* – but with this qualification, that Nietzsche, like everyone else, recognizes Hamlet as one of the great personalities of literature. (The psychological analysis of modernity is, of course, another link back to the play. Psychology, wrote Nietzsche in *Beyond Good and Evil*, is 'the queen of the sciences ... the path to the fundamental problems'.[71] *Hamlet*, the psychological play *par excellence*, is for Nietzsche a central document for the evaluation of modernity.)

Hamlet suffers from the European sickness. But this is not the whole story of Nietzsche's relation to Hamlet. It cannot explain his close identification with him in *Ecce Homo*. There Nietzsche declares that the four essays known as the 'Untimely Ones' prove that he is 'no Jack the Dreamer',[72] a phrase recalling his criticism of the dreamy, delicate, ineffective Hamlet of Goethe and Coleridge.[73] On the contrary, Nietzsche points out, he 'take[s] pleasure in fencing', and boasts that he is 'dangerously quick at the draw'.[74] Hamlet, too, we remember, was a fencer: since Laertes went into France he had been in continual practice. As one of the most richly individual characters in literature, he shows a way out of the destructive type of nihilism: he is not a shadowy, passive figure, but capable of attack. As with A. C. Bradley (and many another reader or spectator) so for Nietzsche 'the apparent failure of Hamlet's life is not the ultimate truth concerning him'. I turn now to these positive, creative, enabling aspects of Nietzsche's Hamlet.[75]

---

68 *Ibid.*, p. 320.

69 *Ibid.*

70 *The Story of the Night: Studies in Shakespeare's Major Tragedies* (London, 1961), p. 29.

71 *Beyond Good and Evil*, p. 222.

72 *Ecce Homo*, p. 732.

73 On this Romantic Hamlet, see R. A. Foakes, 'The Reception of *Hamlet*', *Shakespeare Survey 45* (1992), pp. 1–13.

74 *Ecce Homo*, p. 732.

75 See *Shakespearean Tragedy: 'Hamlet', 'Othello', 'King Lear', 'Macbeth'* (1904; repr. New York, 1983), p. 147. Bradley's comment goes deep into the paradox of tragic joy, or the ability to affirm in the face of suffering. Hibbard (correctly in my view) observes that the story of *Hamlet* is not merely depressing but 'comes over to us as an intensely exciting, significant, and positive experience' (p.29). But what did Nietzsche think of actual suffering, his own or that of others, outside of art? Michael Tanner makes it clear that Nietzsche refused 'to give pain an automatically negative role in life': *Nietzsche* (Oxford, 1994), p. 17; see p. 27. Death itself may not be an evil but a constituent part of greatness and triumph: 'it is of the very essence of the rich spirit to squander itself carelessly, without petty caution'; the Renaissance was 'lavishly squandering and fatal' (Nietzsche quoted in Staten, pp. 137, 136). In *Daybreak: Thoughts on the Prejudices of Morality*, trans. R. J. Hollingdale (Cambridge, 1982), Nietzsche wrote that if a hero, for example Macbeth, 'perishes by his passion this precisely is the sharpest spice in the hot draught of this joy' (p. 140); Staten discusses this passage on p. 138. Critics finding triumph in Hamlet's end include Prosser, p. 240 (he 'has fought his way out of Hell');

When one recalls the desperate life of its author, the most moving and striking thing about *Ecce Homo* is the gratitude suffusing it:

> On this perfect day, when everything is ripening and not only the grape turns brown, the eye of the sun just fell upon my life: I looked back, I looked forward, and never saw so many and such good things at once. It was not for nothing that I buried my forty-fourth year today; I had the *right* to bury it; whatever was life in it has been saved, is immortal. The first book of the *Revaluation of All Values*, the *Songs of Zarathustra*, the *Twilight of the Idols*, my attempt to philosophize with a hammer – all presents of this year, indeed of its last quarter! *How could I fail to be grateful to my whole life?* – and so I tell my life to myself.[76]

The euphoria of *Ecce Homo* expresses Nietzsche's philosophy of tragic joy. The ripe, autumnal voice captures his 'formula for greatness in a human being': '*amor fati*: that one wants nothing to be different, not forward, not backward, not in all eternity. Not merely bear what is necessary ... but *love* it.'[77] 'Was *that* life?' Zarathustra wishes to say to death; 'Well then! Once more!'[78] This attitude – in affect so oddly resembling Christian faith in God's will – grows out of self-love. If one loves oneself, one wants nothing different about oneself – and, therefore, one wants one's life (with all its evils and misfortunes), just as it is and has been. In this state of mind, one's past appears as desirable and necessary – nothing should be different about my life – *could* be different if it is to be my life. Hamlet, I suggest, for Nietzsche finally represents the nihilism – borne out of Dionysian insight into the chaotic nature of the world – that overcomes itself in a calm and insouciant mood of self-affirmation. Everyone notices that Hamlet has changed when he returns from his aborted trip to England with Rosencrantz and Guildenstern. Bradley noticed 'a consciousness of power' (though he wondered whether it was greater than that displayed after the 'Murder of Gonzago').[79] There is a new equanimity. Equally, however, there is nothing obviously better about Hamlet's situation: in fact, with the death of Ophelia, things are worse than ever.[80] It is this Hamlet, the Hamlet of the graveyard, whom Nietzsche seems to have in mind in the chapter in *Ecce Homo* entitled 'Why I Write Such Good Books'. Here he describes what his readers require in order fully to enter the 'noble and delicate world' of his writings.[81] 'Every frailty of the soul', he says, 'excludes one once and for all, even every kind of dyspepsia ... even more, any cowardice, uncleanliness, secret vengefulness in the entrails ... One must never have spared oneself, one must have acquired hardness as a habit to be cheerful and in good spirits in the midst of nothing but hard truths.'[82] Here seems to be the Hamlet of Act 5: a hero less devoured by bitterness,[83] calmer, with more gravity and more cheerfulness, even in the midst of the hardest truths (death and the corruptibility of the body that mock every human hierarchy and value – 'the noble dust of Alexander ... stopping a bung-hole'), more – to use the language of an individualistic, self-actualizing culture in part created by Nietzsche – 'centred'. It is not that Hamlet has abandoned the cynicism (*realism* Nietzsche would call it)

Irving Ribner, *Patterns in Shakespearian Tragedy* (1960; repr. London, 1964): 'By submission to the will of God, Hamlet attains his victory' (p. 82); Harold Wilson, *On the Design of Shakespearian Tragedy* (Toronto, 1957): 'in the act of submission' to divine law Hamlet 'triumphs' (p. 46); and Dowden: 'The last moments of Hamlet's life are well spent, and for energy and foresight ... the noblest moments of his existence' (p. 160). The contrary view is strongly stated by Edwards: 'There is no doubt of the extent of Hamlet's failure' (p.58); he 'made a mess of what he was trying to do' (p. 60).

76 *Ecce Homo*, p. 677.

77 *Ibid.*, p. 714.

78 *Thus Spoke Zarathustra*, p. 430.

79 *Shakespearean Tragedy*, p. 121.

80 Cf. Lars Engle, *Shakespearean Pragmatism: Market of his Time* (Chicago, 1993), p. 71: 'Hamlet's mysterious change of feeling toward the end of the play is *like* the acceptance and loss of intensity felt at the end of successful therapy. Objective bad relations remain ... but their subjective intensity is lessened.'

81 *Ecce Homo*, p. 719.

82 *Ibid.*, p. 720.

83 See Prosser, p. 236.

that he maintained in the face of his mother's weakness and his uncle's treachery; nor, for all its high-spiritedness, is *Ecce Homo* soft in this sense. But what is missing is the despair, along with the all-consuming vengefulness and hatred (including self-hatred) that has indicated the intensity of Hamlet's ties to his father, and which – from a Nietzschean viewpoint – has simply diverted him from *himself*.

In other words, and *pace* Wilson Knight, for whom Hamlet never 'rise[s] beyond what Nietzsche calls "the avenging mind," '[84] in Act 5 Hamlet is freed from *ressentiment*. *Ressentiment* is an ignoble, reactive and secondary, disposition. The slave resents the master; the noble soul knows only self-love. 'For *that man be delivered from revenge*, that is for me the bridge to the highest hope, and a rainbow after long storms.'[85] The extent to which this central theme of Nietzsche's – *ressentiment*, and deliverance from it – has been formed around the figure of Hamlet becomes clear in his discussion, in the chapter of *Ecce Homo* entitled 'Why I Am So Wise', of '*Russian fatalism*'.[86] It arises as part of his review of the dreadful illnesses that have plagued his life. Nothing in *Ecce Homo* is more expressive of its mood of absolute affirmation – self-affirmation – in the face of suffering than its author's extraordinary gratitude to his sickness: since everything in his life has made him what he is, and since he esteems himself, none of it is subtractable. Thus *even his sickness has been a blessing* – it has, for example, given him his extraordinary sensitivity to signs of sickness in individuals and cultures, and thus made him a psychologist: 'Need I say . . . that in questions of decadence I am *experienced*? . . . I have a subtler sense of smell for the signs of ascent and decline than any other human being before me . . . I know both, I am both.'[87] His illness is the source of his greatest gift to humanity, the revaluation of all values, which is founded on the psychological discovery that morality is hostile to life. Nietzsche's immoralism, it turns out, is a system of hygiene: 'I turned my will to health, to *life*, into a philosophy.'[88] Thus has he freed himself from the ignoble desire to be different from what he is: his life, as interpreted to himself, is beautiful and meaningful, the sickness necessary because it taught him the value of health and thus made him the first Dionysian, non-pessimistic, non-life-slandering '*tragic philosopher*'[89] – he who 'has thought the "most abysmal idea", [yet] . . . does not consider it an objection to existence'. Nietzsche has proven by his own experience what he asserted in *Twilight of the Idols*: 'What does not kill me makes me stronger.'[90]

Nietzsche's sickness has shown him the great danger of *ressentiment*: desire for revenge is symptomatic of and encourages morbidity. It is, then, precisely Hamlet's sickness that makes him of interest: the play shows that curing oneself may involve the most drastic inactivity (actually strenuous self-preservation). 'The sick person', Nietzsche writes in a long passage that must be quoted in full,

> cannot get rid of anything . . . cannot get over anything . . . – everything hurts. Men and things obtrude too closely; experiences strike one too deeply; memory becomes a festering wound. Sickness itself *is* a kind of *ressentiment*.
>
> Against all this the sick person has only one great remedy: I call it *Russian fatalism*, that fatalism without revolt which is exemplified by a Russian soldier who, finding a campaign too strenuous, finally lies down in the snow . . .
>
> Because one would use oneself up too quickly if one reacted in *any* way, one does not react at all any more: this is the logic. Nothing burns one up faster than the affects of *ressentiment*. Anger, pathological vulnerability, impotent lust for revenge, thirst for revenge, poison-mixing in any sense – no reaction could be more disadvantageous for the exhausted: such affects involve a rapid consumption of nervous energy, a pathological increase of harmful excretions

84 '*Hamlet* Reconsidered', p. 315.
85 *Thus Spoke Zarathustra*, p. 211.
86 *Ecce Homo*, p. 686.
87 *Ibid.*, pp. 679, 678.
88 *Ibid.*, p. 680.
89 *Ibid.*, p. 729.
90 *Twilight of the Idols*, p. 33.

– for example, of the gall bladder into the stomach. *Ressentiment* is what is forbidden *par excellence* for the sick – it is their specific evil – unfortunately also their most natural inclination . . .

Born of weakness, *ressentiment* is most harmful for the weak themselves. Conversely, given a rich nature, it is a *superfluous* feeling; mastering this feeling is virtually what proves riches. Whoever knows how seriously my philosophy has pursued the fight against vengefulness and rancor . . . will understand why I am making such a point of my own behaviour, my *instinctive sureness* in practice. During periods of decadence I forbade myself such feelings as harmful; as soon as my vitality was rich and proud enough again, I forbade myself such feelings as *beneath* me. I displayed the 'Russian fatalism' I mentioned by tenaciously clinging for years to all but intolerable situations, places, apartments, and society, merely because they happened to be given by accident: it was better than changing them, than *feeling* that they could be changed – than rebelling against them.

Any attempt to disturb me in this fatalism, to awaken me by force, used to annoy me mortally – and it actually was mortally dangerous every time.

Accepting oneself as if fated, not wishing oneself 'different' – that is in such cases *great reason* itself.[91]

Behind this passage, as behind Nietzsche's whole diagnosis of the reactive, uncreative modern soul, lies a reading of *Hamlet.* Nietzsche, I am suggesting, sees Hamlet as having by the end of the play freed himself from such reactivity: memory is no longer 'a festering wound'; the dyspeptic rage and self-loathing and 'impotent lust for revenge' have dissipated. Hamlet's fatalism feels like a restoration of himself to himself; the ease and integration of Hamlet towards the end of the play attest to some such change. His passivity, from Nietzsche's viewpoint, has proven itself an unconscious, subtle form of self-conservation – an act of self-mastery, of becoming what one is by not confusing oneself with another, of 'instinctive' self-healing. His fatalism evinces a new self-love and self-acceptance. Zarathustra had said 'he who cannot obey himself is commanded. That is the nature of the living.'[92] In *Twilight of the Idols* Nietzsche defined decadence in a way that sums up the temptation of Hamlet confronted by the Ghost's awful command: 'weakness of will, more precisely the inability *not* to react to a stimulus, is itself merely another form of degeneration'.[93] The definition is repeated in *Ecce Homo,* in a discussion of pity, Zarathustra's specific 'temptation': pity is decadent because it is almost always 'a particular case of being incapable of resisting stimuli'.[94] Hamlet's filial pity for his murdered father's Ghost is his great danger.[95] The challenge of life is to create oneself, to define one's task, to give oneself one's law; but this requires conserving oneself: it is precisely *not* to have one's task or law defined *for* one. That is why it is essential, in Nietzsche's opinion, not to be enthralled to any kind of idol – '*idols* (my word for "ideals")', he wrote in *Ecce Homo.*[96] The problem with idols is that they are given one from outside: they take one away from oneself. Hamlet, for most of the play, is enthralled to just such an idol-ideal: his father. Idols, for Nietzsche, teach self-hatred; freeing oneself from them is the first stage of the noble, difficult art of learning to love oneself.

By the end of the play, Hamlet seems to have acquired that freedom from rancour, vengefulness, and *ressentiment* that for Nietzsche is essential for personality and the core of his philosophy. There is an augmentation in the sense of power, an unblocking and flowing away of anger and frustration. In the last Act, for example in the killing of Claudius, Hamlet seems to be acting on his own account rather than as the mere avenging instrument of his father: the killing seems his, qualitatively different from what it would have been, for

---

91 *Ecce Homo*, pp. 686–7.

92 *Thus Spoke Zarathustra*, p. 226.

93 *Twilight of the Idols*, p. 53.

94 *Ecce Homo*, p. 684.

95 Cf. Knight: 'pity enlists Hamlet not in the cause of life, but of death' ('Embassy of Death', p. 45).

96 *Ecce Homo*, p. 674.

example, had Hamlet, the good son, dispatched Claudius in cold blood when he happened upon him at prayer. For Nietzsche, Hamlet's lack of premeditation virtually ensures that the killing is his deed.[97] A remark in *Twilight of the Idols* is apposite to Hamlet's new-found naturalness and integration. Nietzsche writes that 'disintegregation of will ... virtually define[s] the *bad*. Everything *good* is instinct – and consequently easy, necessary, free. Effort is an objection, the *god* is typically distinguished from the hero (in my language: *light* feet are the first attribute of divinity).'[98] In *Zarathustra* he wrote: 'the devil is the spirit of gravity'.[99] The lightness, unentangledness, freedom – humour even – that attends Hamlet in the final Act is bound up with the abandonment of self-hatred, a change connected with the gradual forgetting of the command 'Remember me' and the call for vengeance. In *The Gay Science* Nietzsche asked: '*What is the seal of liberation?*', and answered: 'No longer being ashamed in front of oneself.'[100] Hamlet is no longer ashamed of himself at the end of the play.[101]

Hamlet appears, moreover, to have begun to see his life in the way Nietzsche understood his: as fated, affirmable, redeemable. 'Accepting oneself as if fated, not wishing oneself "different" – that is ... *great reason* itself.' This is the tragic Dionysian wisdom of Zarathustra, which justifies the past: 'to turn every "it was" into a "thus I willed it" – that alone should I call redemption'.[102] In *Ecce Homo*, Nietzsche describes this attitude as '*severe* self-love'[103]: Hamlet acquires something like it at the end. Nietzsche, intending himself, describes in *Ecce Homo* the person '*who has turned out well*'. Behind this figure can be glimpsed Hamlet, whose sickness, like Nietzsche's, has turned out to be a stage on the path to health:

> A typically morbid being cannot become healthy, much less make itself healthy. For a typically healthy person, conversely, being sick can even become an energetic *stimulus* for life, for living *more*. This, in fact, is how that long period of sickness appears to me *now*: as it were, I discovered life anew, including myself; I tasted all good and even little things, as others cannot easily taste them – I turned my will to health, to *life*, into a philosophy.
>
> For it should be noted: it was during the years of my lowest vitality that I *ceased* to be a pessimist; the instinct of self-restoration *forbade* me a philosophy of poverty and discouragement.
>
> What is it, fundamentally, that allows us to recognize *who has turned out well*? That a well-turned-out person pleases our senses, that he is carved from wood that is hard, delicate, and at the same time smells good. He has a taste only for what is good for him; his pleasure, his delight cease where the measure of what is good for him is transgressed. He guesses what remedies avail against what is harmful; he exploits bad accidents to his advantage; what does not kill him makes him stronger. Instinctively, he collects from everything he sees, hears, lives through, *his* sum; he is a principle of selection, he discards much. He is always in his own company, whether he associates with books, human beings, or landscapes: he honors by *choosing*, by *admitting*, by *trusting*. He reacts slowly to all kinds of stimuli, with that slowness which long caution and deliberate pride have bred in him: he examines the stimulus that approaches him, he is far from meeting it halfway. He believes neither in 'misfortune' nor in 'guilt': he comes to terms with himself, with others; he knows how to *forget* – he is strong enough; hence everything *must* turn out for his best.[104]

Certainly not everything in this will remind us of Shakespeare's *Hamlet*. Nonetheless, in this picture of the sickness that cures itself and of the nature that turns accident into necessity,

97 For Hunter, the play by its end is Hamlet's. Claudius may have engineered the duel, 'but it is Hamlet who has taken control of it and made it his own' (p. 250).

98 *Twilight of the Idols*, p. 59.

99 *Thus Spoke Zarathustra*, p. 219.

100 *The Gay Science*, p. 220.

101 Cf. Knight: Hamlet 'has accepted ... himself' by this point ('*Hamlet* Reconsidered', p. 322). Bradley observes that at his death Hamlet 'forgives Laertes [and] we hear ... no word of lamentation or self-reproach' (p. 124).

102 Zarathustra's assertion is quoted in *Ecce Homo*, pp. 764–5.

103 *Ecco Homo*, p. 788.

104 *Ibid.*, pp. 680–1.

Nietzsche has, I think, described *his* Hamlet: the man who in spite of everything has *turned out well.* In doing so he has described himself.[105] In Hamlet Nietzsche found a hero who finally achieves the 'active forgetfulness' essential for 'psychic order', and who helps explain his own life, which has meant the progressive detachment of himself from those people and places and tasks that took him away from himself, and yet which were, in the end, justified in so far as they made him what he is. 'Not to remain stuck to a person – not even the most loved – every person is a prison ... One must know how *to conserve oneself*: the hardest test of independence.'[106] In Hamlet, Nietzsche found his most desired self-image: the modern affirming tragic philosopher, he who has seen through the fictions of the world to the bitter truth of its chaos and meaninglessness yet who in spite of that does not succumb to nihilism. This is the man who 'has thought the "most abysmal idea," [yet] ... does not consider it an objection to existence'; the man who 'says No ... to an unheard-of degree' but is 'the opposite of a No-saying spirit'. The tragic philosopher loves himself, and so affirms the world, all that has made him what he is. He conserves himself, works his way free from idol-ideals, all those beliefs (for example, in a father) that devalue his life. Hamlet saves himself by forgetting an otherworldly and charismatic call to self-destruction – to dedicate his life to a task not his.[107]

What has changed is Hamlet's understanding: instead of a series of disasters his life has begun to cohere for him into a meaningful pattern. By the end it is a story that can be told, that he asks Horatio to tell. A story is order and form, not chaos. There is the appeal to Providence – it is discernible 'in the fall of a sparrow' (5.2.212). It is given to Horatio to articulate a meaning out of the play's events:

So shall you hear
Of carnal, bloody, and unnatural acts;
Of accidental judgments, casual slaughters;
Of deaths put on by cunning and forc'd cause;
And, in this upshot, purposes mistook
Fall'n on th'inventors' heads ... (5.2.372–7)

Nonetheless the sense of chaotic meaningless waste and 'havoc' (5.2.356) is overwhelming. The stage awash with corpses; Hamlet himself dead; what story can be salvaged from it all?

For Nietzsche it has to do with Hamlet's reluctance to have his task given him, for his life to lack its signature and become another's (his father's in his case). Hamlet has avoided having his life take on the style of another; he has refused to play the stereotyped role – Telemachus, Orestes, Pyrrhus – of the faithful avenging son.[108] Yet everything has been pressing him to play this role, including, in his weaker moments, himself. It has been by *not* reacting to a great stimulus that he has achieved a self. He has had to overcome himself – his deepest promptings as well as those of heaven and hell (2.2.580) – in order to become what he is.

From Nietzsche's perspective, Hamlet has achieved towards the end of the play *amor fati*: the sense that everything in his life is justified, is necessary to who he is. Paradoxically for the philosopher who proclaimed himself Anti-Christ, the psychology of love of fate is not easily distinguishable from the faith in Providence that Hamlet expresses in the last Act: it issues in the same calm and joyful fortitude, the

105 'Ultimately, nobody can get more out of things, including books, than he already knows' (*Ecce Homo*, p. 717).

106 *Beyond Good and Evil*, p. 242.

107 Bradley observed that for much of the play 'Hamlet, so far from analyzing his duty ... *forgets* it' (p. 108).

108 Cf. Engle, p. 73: 'Hamlet ... eludes the scripted ... mode of violent activity which the Ghost enjoins and which Fortinbras and Laertes exemplify.' That the play was about 'the world-old conflict between father and son, between the younger and the older generation' was Ernest Jones's view in *Hamlet and Oedipus* (London, 1949). He quotes Freud: 'The detachment of the growing individual from the authority of the parents is one of the most necessary, but also one of the most painful, achievements of developments' (pp. 75, 76).

same ability to affirm in the face of suffering, the same sense of meaning in catastrophe. This is, of course, the triumphal perspective of *Ecce Homo*: 'From this point of view even the *blunders* of life have their own meaning and value – the occasional side roads and wrong roads, the delays, "modesties", seriousness wasted on tasks that are remote from *the* task.'[109] Objectively, perhaps, Hamlet's life *is* a failure. Superficially – or, at least, from a non-Nietzschean perspective – how much more successful a life is that of Fortinbras! Nietzsche's life was also outwardly a failure: a lonely, sick man writing unread books. Inwardly, however, seen from the point of view of self-affirmation, the lives of both Hamlet and Nietzsche are meaningful *because* highly individualized. Fortinbras is barely distinguishable from his father, indeed his purposes *are* his father's. By contrast, Hamlet's life turns out to be *his* story, not someone else's or an ill-assorted mix of stories. Everything in it – '*blunders* ... side roads and wrong roads, ... delays, "modesties", seriousness wasted on tasks ... remote from *the* task' – is essential. It had to be that way in order for Hamlet to be what he is – and since he esteems himself, why should he want it other? That is what Nietzsche would call will to power, the perspective that makes life worth living. It is the view that overcomes nihilism, which is the peril Hamlet faces in the play: the sense that his life has no order, is an unweeded garden, a conviction which leads to longing for death. Hamlet is, it could be said, like Nietzsche, an expert in decadence – but also in health; in his case, as in Nietzsche's, sickness issues in the *affirmation* of a self. What matters is that Horatio report him and his cause aright, that he tell his story, that he be justified. Nietzsche too closes his life with the impulse towards autobiography and justification: '*How could I fail*', he asks in his last book, '*to be grateful to my whole life?* – and so I tell my life to myself'. Thus does Nietzsche read *Hamlet* as the overcoming of bad destructive nihilism – the specific peril of modernity.

---

[109] *Ecce Homo*, p. 710.

Thanks to Graham Bradshaw, Hugh Craig, A. D. Nuttall and Bob Pile for comments and suggestions.

'STRANGE AND WOONDERFULL SYGHTS': *THE TEMPEST* AND THE DISCOURSES OF MONSTROSITY

MARK THORNTON BURNETT

On the seventeenth of July, 1583, the town chronicler of Shrewsbury recorded in his diary an extraordinary event, an Elizabethan 'freak show':

> cam to the towne ... one Iohn Taylor ... a marchant of loondoon and free of the coompany of fyshmoongers there who ... brought ... with hym strange and woonderfull syghts that ys to saye a dead childe in a coffyn which had ij heades and ... ij bake boanes. More a lyve sheep beinge a tupp the which had ... ij foondementes vnder hys tayle, also ij pyssells and ij paire of codds ... and yf the partee which keapt hym wold aske hym and saye be thosse people welcoom he wold lyft vp hys foorefoote and Crye heighe, heighe, heighe ... And also more a glasse artyfycially made beinge but ij candells therin and a chayne with ij faces or pycturs which wolld represent inwardly to the sight of the beholders soondrye candells, chaynes facys, Iuells and other things myraculously ...[1]

The chronicler's breathless narrative offers a powerful registration of some of the period's deepest fears and aspirations. In early modern England, 'monsters', defined in a 1634 translation of a medical treatise by Ambroise Paré as '*things ... brought forth contrary to the common decree and order of nature*', occupied vexed places in popular culture and scientific debate.[2] Monstrous births were quickly versified in ballads, while fairs with monster booths drew holiday crowds.[3] As monsters appealed to the amusement of the fairground populace, so did they tax the minds of the period's most established philosophers and authorities. Attempting to determine how monsters might have been generated, Paré included 'the glory of God', 'mens wickednesse', 'abundance of seed', 'deficient' seed, 'the force ... of imagination' and 'the craft ... of the divell' in his catalogue of chief ingredients.[4] It is an index of the fascination monsters exercised that he should have produced a text in which divine intervention, biological complication, intellectual speculation and supernatural visitation are all countenanced as valid interpretative frameworks.

In this paper I shall concentrate on Shakespeare's *The Tempest* (1610–11), taking as a point of departure its preoccupation with questions of monstrosity and portentous occurrence. In realizing 'natural' and 'unnatural' phenomena as signs to be read and deciphered, the play reveals charged connections with contemporary wonder books in which monsters and prodigies are an area of vigorous enquiry. The discourses of monstrosity in the play, however,

1 J. Alan B. Somerset, ed., *Records of Early English Drama: Shropshire*, 2 vols. (Toronto, Buffalo and London, University of Toronto Press, 1994), vol. 1, p. 237.

2 Ambroise Paré, *The workes of that famous chirugion* (London, 1634; STC 19189), p. 961.

3 Henry Fitzgeffrey, *Satyres: and satyricall epigram's* (London, 1617; STC 10945), sigs. A7^{v}–A8^{r}. For exhibitions of monsters in the period, see Katharine Park and Lorraine J. Daston, 'Unnatural Conceptions: The Study of Monsters in Sixteenth- and Seventeenth-Century France and England', *Past and Present*, 92, August (1981), pp. 20–54; Somerset, ed., *Shropshire*, vol. 1, pp. 219, 221, 226.

4 Paré, *The workes*, pp. 962–3.

are neither stable nor consistent. Several monstrous *topoi* interweave and contradict: monsters blur with wonders, and Prospero is as much a monster as the servants and spirits of his magic kingdom. In the English Renaissance, a number of discursivities shaped monstrous constructions, illuminating points of contemporary debate as well as the evolving philosophy of a more 'rational' establishment. If *The Tempest* is a work deeply implicated in the colonial endeavour, then, it is also one concerned with peculiarly English habits and institutions. Like John Taylor's marvellous glass and the monster pamphlets themselves, the drama can finally be viewed as a mirror, which deflects audiences away from monstrosity abroad and back towards the local, domestic forms that it may always inhabit.[5]

I

If the theatre is the institution with which *The Tempest* is most commonly compared, the fairground would seem to be an equally striking component of its dramatic design. The spirits' performances, for instance, have charged local meanings and associations, such as Ariel's willingness 'to fly, / To swim, to dive into the fire, to ride / On the curled clouds', like a circus acrobat.[6] The number of references to puppets makes clear that such acts, which played within striking distance of the monster booths, formed only one part of a multitude of entertainments crowded together on a single site: it was at the fair, Henry Farley observed in 1621, that Londoners could enjoy 'a strange out-landish Fowle . . . a Gyants bone . . . a Puppit play . . . A Woman dancing on a Rope . . . a Iuglers cheats, / A Tumbler shewing cunning feats'.[7] In the play, puppets are evoked in allusions to the 'living drollery' (3.3.21) of the spirits and the 'demi-puppets' (5.1.36) Prospero commands, while the fair lies behind Caliban's refrain, ''Ban, 'Ban, Ca-Caliban / Has a new master – get a new man! / Freedom, high-day!' (2.2.179–81): on holidays (high-days or hire-days), servants attended hiring fairs to look for new employment.[8]

Part of the complex effect of *The Tempest* is to suggest at one and the same time the fair and the ethnographic claims that, in a later, vulgarized form, it came to represent. For Prospero is less the showman than the Renaissance collector and, in giving shape to his performative dimension, the play allows him to slip between a range of very different entertainment categories. While still Duke of Milan, Prospero amasses books; in exile, he collects daughters, memories, courtiers, spirits and natural forces.

---

5 The association of the monstrous races, monstrous births and Africa was proverbial. See Henry Miller, *God the protector of Israel* (London, 1641; Wing M2060A), p. 18; Sebastian Munster, *Cosmographiae universalis lib. VI* (Basileae: apud Henrichum Petri, 1554), p. 1151. Wonder and monster books often advertised themselves as instructive mirrors; see William Averell, *A wonderfull and straunge newes* (London, 1583; STC 982.5), sig. Avi^{r}. For an excellent local reading of *The Tempest*, see Douglas Bruster, 'Local *Tempest*: Shakespeare and the work of the early modern playhouse', *Journal of Medieval and Renaissance Studies*, 25 (1995), 33–53.

6 William Shakespeare, *The Tempest*, ed. Stephen Orgel (Oxford and New York, Oxford University Press, 1990), 1.2.190–2. All further references appear in the text.

7 Henry Farley, *St. Paules-Church her bill for the parliament* (London, 1621; STC 10690), sigs. E4^{r-v}. See also Ben Jonson's parody of *The Tempest* in *Bartholomew Fair* (1614), ed. E. A. Horsman (Manchester, Manchester University Press, 1979): 'If there be never a servant-monster i' the Fair, who can help it? he says; nor a nest of antics? He is loth to make Nature afraid in his plays, like those that beget *Tales, Tempests*, and such like drolleries' (Induction, 128–32).

Barbara A. Mowat has recently argued that Prospero 'belongs more to the mundane world of the streetcorner "art-Magician" or "Jugler" (these are Reginald Scot's terms for Houdini-type illusionists) than to the arcane, terrifying Hermetic or demonic spheres . . . Performing magicians . . . played on street corners, in "Fayres and Markets", in provinces, and in London theatres' ('Prospero, Agrippa, and Hocus Pocus', *English Literary Renaissance*, 11 (1981), 297–8).

8 See Michael Roberts, '"Waiting upon Chance": English Hiring Fairs and their Meanings from the 14th to the 20th Century', *Journal of Historical Sociology*, 1, June (1988), 119–60.

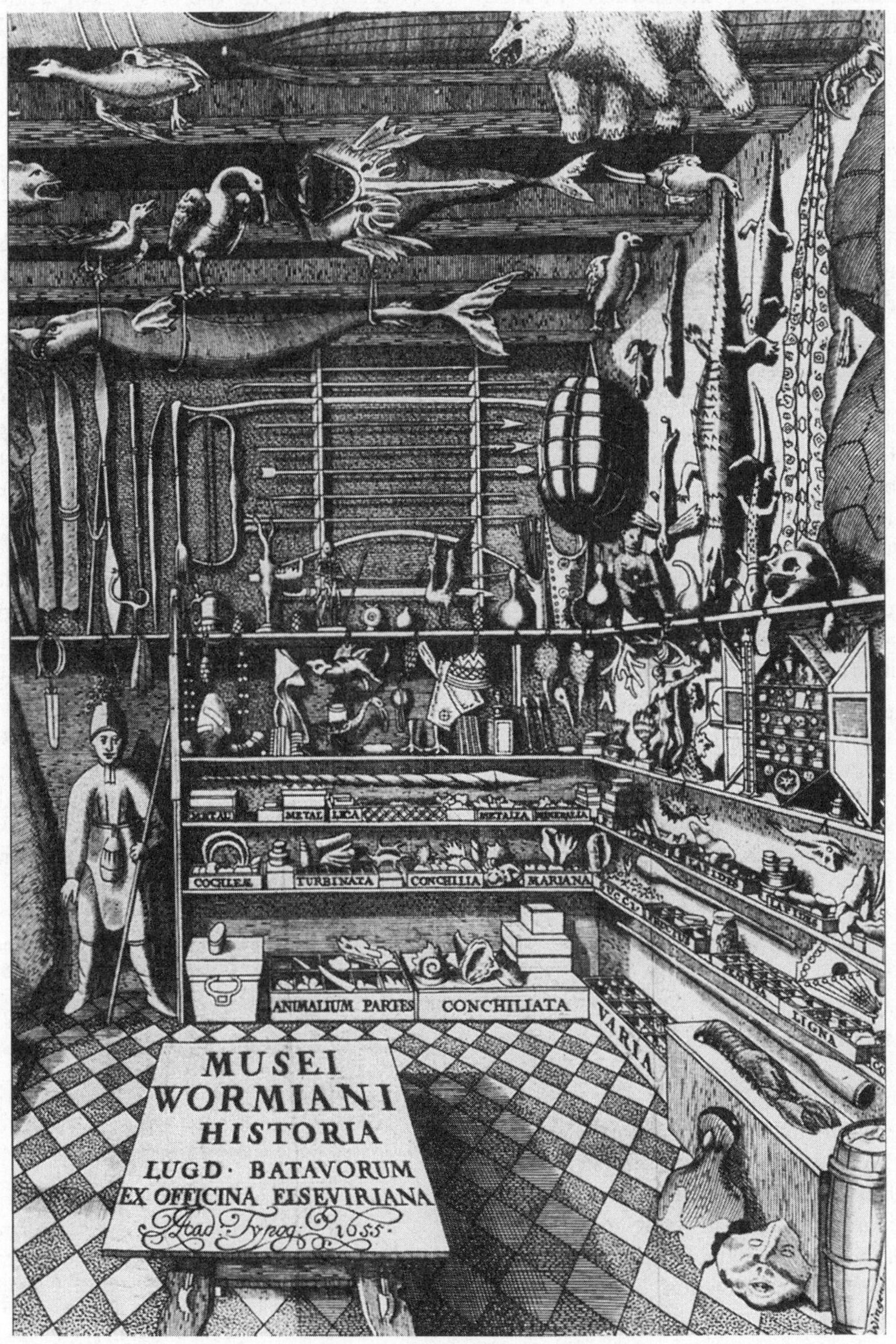

9 Ole Worm, *Museum wormianum, seu Historia Rariorum* (Lugdunum Batavorum, 1655), p. ii.

'Be collected' (1.2.13), he instructs Miranda, arranging the shards of her past as he reflects upon his dedication to the 'study' of the 'liberal arts' (1.2.73–4), and the 'volumes' given to him by Gonzalo from 'mine own library' (1.2.167). Prospero's 'cell', in fact, might be seen as an oblique version of the 'cabinet of curiosities', the assembly of bizarre artefacts, monstrous aberrations and miscellanea that was to grow into the museum of the eighteenth and nineteenth centuries (illustration 9).[9]

II

We find the fair and the museum hinted at more forcibly in the scenes with Caliban, which bring into play rival explanations for the generation of monstrous creatures. At Trinculo's entrance, a process of defining and displacing is quickly initiated. The jester likens the cloud to 'a foul bombard that would shed his liquor' (2.2.21) and, seeing Caliban, cannot decide if he is a 'man or a fish' (2.2.24):

> A strange fish! Were I in England now, as once I was, and had but this fish painted, not a holiday-fool there but would give a piece of silver. There would this monster make a man – any strange beast there makes a man. When they will not give a doit to relieve a lame beggar, they will lay out ten to see a dead Indian. Legged like a man, and his fins like arms! Warm, o' my troth! I do now let loose my opinion, hold it no longer: this is no fish, but an islander, that hath lately suffered by a thunderbolt.
>
> (2.2.26–35)

Employing the techniques of the ballad, in which a picture of the monstrous birth or 'strange fish' is followed by a textual commentary, Trinculo runs through various categories to fix Caliban in the world he has left (illustrations 10 and 11).[10] The speech enacts a colonial defamiliarization: Caliban is re-presented in terms of the domestic, and Trinculo, imagining a fresh fairground attraction, plays a comic ethnographer conducting a bizarre autopsy experiment. In a final twist, moreover, he creeps under the gabardine, highlighting the attraction of the monstrous, the creation of a new form with two sets of members, and the possibility that 'man' and 'monster' may soon become indistinguishable.

In contrast, Stephano's experience of Caliban leads him to a more elaborate attitude towards exotic anatomies. Initially his interpretative mode, which recalls fairground jugglers, parodies Prospero's earlier arguments: 'What's the matter? Have we devils here? Do you put tricks upon's with savages and men of Ind?' (2.2.56–7). But popular instincts rapidly take over from the lure of supernatural enquiry. In assuming that the form beneath the gabardine has 'four legs' (2.2.58–9) but only one head, Stephano regards Caliban as a conjoined twin – a type of *eusomphalien pygopage* or *syncephalus ectopagus* – and the monster's stakes accordingly rise in the commodity market (illustrations 12a and 12b).[11] Now, rather than being part of a sideshow, Caliban will be exhibited to 'any emperor that ever trod on neat's-leather' (2.2.67–8), and the ambitions of the drunken butler begin to take on magnificent proportions.

In his essays, first published in English in 1600, Montaigne describes a '*monstrous Childe*' who was 'Vnder his paps . . . fastned and joyned to an other childe, but had no head, and . . . the conduite of his body stopped, the rest whole'.[12]

---

[9] See Oliver Impey and Arthur MacGregor, eds., *The Origins of Museums: The Cabinet of Curiosities in Sixteenth- and Seventeenth-Century Europe* (Oxford, Clarendon, 1987); Susan M. Pearce, *On Collecting: An Investigation into Collecting in the European Tradition* (London and New York, Routledge, 1995).

[10] For accounts of strange and monstrous fish in wonder books, medical works and ballads, see Pierre Boaistuau, *Certaine secrete wonders of nature* (London, 1569; STC 3164.5), fos. 47ʳ–54ʳ; Paré, *The workes*, pp. 1002, 1007; Hyder E. Rollins, ed., *A Pepysian Garland: Black-Letter Broadside Ballads of the Years 1595–1639* (Cambridge, Mass., Harvard University Press, 1971), pp. 440–1.

[11] These terms are taken from Ambroise Paré, *On Monsters and Marvels*, ed. Janis L. Pallister (Chicago and London, University of Chicago Press, 1982), pp. 177–80.

[12] Michel de Montaigne, *The essayes or morall, politike and millitarie discourses* (London, 1600; STC 18041), p. 409.

The forme and shape of a Monstrous Child/borne at Maydstone in Kent, the.xxiiij.of October. 1568.

1568

As ye this shape abhorre
In body for to haue:

So flee such Vices farre
As might the soule depraue

In Gods power
all flesh stands,
As the clay in the
Potters hands.

To fashion euen
as he wyll,
In good shape
or in yll.

AT Maydstone in Kent there was one Marget Mere, Daughter to Richard Mere of the sayd Towne of Maydstone, who being vnmaryed, played the naughty packe, and was gotten with childe, being deliuered of the same childe the.xxiiij.daye of October last past, in the yeare of our Lord.1568.at.vij.of the clocke in the after noone of the same day being Sonday. Which child being a man child, had first the mouth slitted on the right side like a Libardes mouth, terrible to beholde, the left arme lyng vpon the brest, fast therto ioyned, hauing as it were stumps on the handes, the left leg growing vpward toward the head, and the ryght leg bending toward the left leg, the foote therof growing into the buttocke of the sayd left leg. In the middest of the backe there was a broade lump of flesh in fashion lyke a Rose, in the myddest whereof was a hole, which voyded like an Issue. Thys sayd Childe was borne alyue, and lyued.xxiiij.houres, and then departed this lyfe. Which may be a terrour aswell to all such workers of filthynes & iniquity, as to those vngodly liuers. Who (if in them any feare of God be) may mooue them to repentance and amendement of lyfe, which God for Christes sake graunt both to them and vs. Amen. Witnesses hereof were these, William Plomer, John Squier Glasier, John Sadler Goldsmith, besides diuers other credible persons both men and women.

A warnyng to England.

This monstrous shape to thee England
Playn shewes thy monstrous vice.
If thou ech part wylt vnderstand,
And take thereby aduice.

For waying first the gaspyng mouth,
It doth full well declare:
What rauine and oppression doth
Is vsed wyth greedy care.

For, for the backe, and gorging paunch,
To lyue in wealth and ease:
Such toylmen take that none may staunch
Their greedy minde, nor please.

For in such sort, their mouthes they infect,
With lying othes, and slaightes:
Blasphemiug God, and Prince reiect,
As they were brutish beastes.

Their filthy talke, and poysoned speech,
Disfigures so the mouth:
That som wold think ther stood ẏ breech
Such filth it breatheth forth.

The hands which haue no fingers right
But stumps fit for no vse:
Doth well set forth the idle plight,
Which we in these daies chuse.

For rich and poore, for age and youth,
Eche one would labour flye:
Few seekes to do the deedes of truth,
To helpe others thereby.

The leg so clyming to the head,
What meaneth it but this?
That some do seeke not to be lead,
But for to leade amis.

And as this makes it most monstrous,
For foote to clyme to head:
So those Subiects be most vicious,
That refuse to be lead.

The hinder part doth shew vs playne,
Our close and hidden vice,
Which doth behind vs run amayne,
In vyle and shameful wyse.

Wherefore to ech in England now,
Let this Monster them teach:
To mend the monstrous life they show,
Least endles death them reach.

Imprinted at London by
John Awdeley, dwellyng in little
Britain streete without Aldersgate.
The.xxiij.of December.

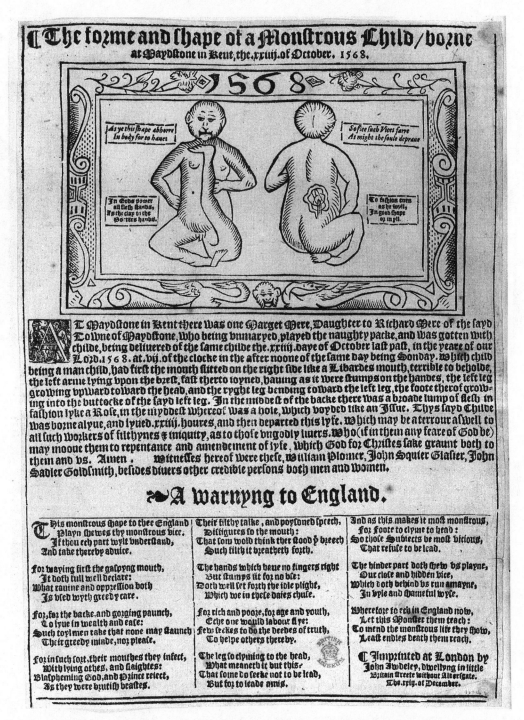

10 *The forme and shape of a monstrous child* (London, 1568; STC 17194).

¶ A Moste true and marueilous straunge wonder, the lyke hath seldom ben seene, of. XVII. Monstrous fisshes, taken in Suffolke, at Downam brydge, within a myle of Ipswiche. The .XI. daye of October. In the yeare of our Lorde God. M.D.LX.VIII.

Nowe you shall vnderstande, that the begynners first Venterers to take these fishes, was Nycholas Gibbins, and Jhon Carnaby, with theyr men: after came John Baker, and Robert Haulley wt theyr men, being all Saylers & Shipmen dwelling in Ipswiche, with other, besydes manye of the countrey ther about, whyche when they harde of it, came thyther to helpe, and see the taking of them.

¶ Also, of these .xvii. fysshes, there was a male, and a female, that was more howge and monstrous then the other .xv. For the least of these .ii. fisshes, were .xxvii. foote longe: and as bigge in the middle eche of them, as .iii. Buttes of Malmezie, and of a marueylous great strength, as it is well knowen to dyuers in Ipswich & other places, beside those men aboue named. For they tyed one of these fysshes to a boat, to brynge hit to Ipswich wharfe, and being so tied to the boat, swam awaye wyth the boat & all the men that weare in it, toward the sea a maruaylous swyft pace, for all that they could do: this was when the tyde came in, for they had made prouision before, whẽ the water was loo, to tie great roapes about theyr tayles and finnes with small boates, and by such meanes as they could. (And as I sayd before) the tyde commyng in & the fyshe hauinge water, swam away with the boat so fast toward the sea, that if ther had not byn rescue of other boates and such vessels as they had thear, that boat and all they in it, had ben lost and vtterlie cast away. But as God wold haue it, by the helpe of thother boates or vessels, tieng the fishe also. Brought him by force to a conuenient place, and tied him fast to a tree with strong Cable roapes, and so vsyng theym one by one, founde meanes to brynge theim to Ipswych wharfe. Wher they were layd with great labour and trouble, besyde breaking of theyr wyndlace & a great Cable roape, wyth halyng them vp, they weare of suche maruaylous greatnes, strength and wayght. Som of them laye vpon the wharfe .ii. dayes and a nyght before they weare dead, and yet they strooke them wyth Axes & other weapons to kyll them. The ryuer wherin they weare taken was coloured red, wt the blood that issued from theyr woundes, whyle they weare a takyng, ye water beinge so deepe that a Hoy might well ryde thear in. Thear was also .iii. Butchers a hole day cutting out one of these fysshes, and as manye to carye it awaye with hand barows to the town ware house, and the Butchers were fayne to put on bootes to stand in to cut it out, it was so deepe & full of garbyge: this fishe was a mans heyght in thicknes, from the top of the backe to the bone: and his bones as harde as stones, that the Butchers mard al theyr Axes they occupied a bout them. The other .xv. fisshes were .xxiiii. foote longe, and som of them, xxi. foote, and byg accordingto theyr length. But the .ii. biggest, male and female, was .xxvii. foote long, and as byg in the middle as .iii. Buttes of malmsie. Hauinge a round snout. His mouth wyde, gapinge aboue a yeard broad. And had xliiii. teeth, one beinge wayed & waith a pound & a halfe, viii. inches & a half long, and aboue .vi. inches in compas about, yet none of the biggest. Also a great long tung, a marueylous byg head, & is a yeard betweene the eies. Upon theyr heds were holes, as big that a man might put in both his fistes at once, out of the which they did spoute a great quantitie of water whyle they were a takinge, that they had almoste drownd .ii. boates men and all, with spoutynge of water: for the water wold assende vppwarde from the fisshes, as hie as any house, and so fall doun & weet all them that were within theyr reache moste cruellie. Also they were white beneath the eyes a hand broad, theyr eies blacke, and no bigger then the eyes of a Calfe. Theyr backes as blacke as ynke, so smoth & bryght ye one myght haue seene his face on it, as in a dim Glasse. Theyr bellies as whyte as mylke. And vpon their backes they had eche of them one great blacke Fin growing, and sum of them were a yeard and a halfe long, verie thycke, & strong, and .ii. great blacke ones vnderneath the fore part of his bellye. Also the male, one of the .ii. biggest had a yerde, that when it was out, was more then .iii. quarters of a yearde long, and as byg toward his bodye as a mans arme sleeue & all, by the elboe. His tayle was .iii. yeardes long, and .ii. yerdes broad verye thycke & blacke, & wonderfull stronge: for .x. tall men stood vppon his tayle, & he liftng his tayle vp, ouer threw theym all. Also when he had lifted vp his tayle it was of such monstrous waight strength, and bygnes, that when it fell the verye grund wold rynge, and shake therwith. Thys fyshe was cut out in peeces, and geuen away to diuers in the towne that did eate of it, and was verye good meate, eyther rosted or bakt, (so much of it as was kept sweete) and the meate of them bakt tasted lyke red Deere. And as they cut it out it was wayed by peeces, so that the verye boddye of this one fishe, wayed .LII. hondred the bare carckas, besyde many lytle peecis that was geuen away vnwaied to crauers that stood by, & besydes a Carte loade of garbyge that came oute of his bellye, so that all to gether was a boue threescore hondred and od.

If the men of Ipswych had knowne so muche betyme whyle they were sweete, as they haue sence, they might haue made .ii. C. marcke more of them then is now made. But now they bee barreld vpp to make Oyle of, and will not bee sold for a great peece of monney.

¶ And this you maye see, the perfect and true discripcion, of these straunge fishes, wherin is to be noted, the straung and marueylous handye workes of the Lord, blessed be God in all his giftes, & holye in all his workes, the Lordes name bee praysed, in them, and for them, for euer and euer. So be it.

Quod. Timothie Granger.

Imprynted at London in Fleetestreate, at the signe of S. John Euangelist by Thomas Colwell.

11 Timothy Granger, *A moste true and marueilous straunge wonder* (London, 1568; STC 12186).

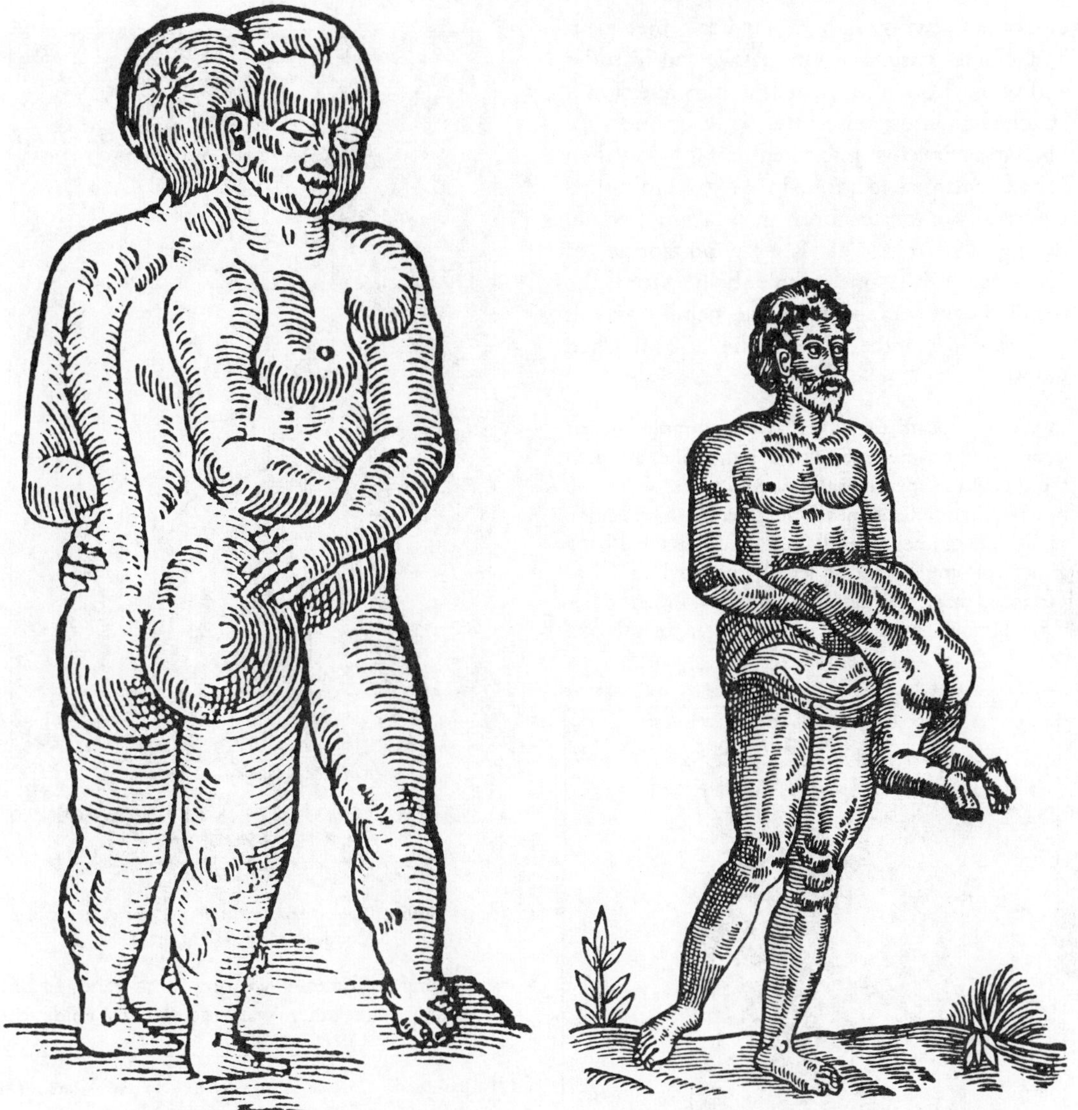

12 a and b Ambroise Paré, *The workes of that famous chirugion* (London, 1634; STC 19189), pp. 965, 967.

It may have been that Shakespeare, who certainly consulted Montaigne in his composition of *The Tempest*, found in this passage one prompt for Caliban's fluctuating condition and changing appearance. More pressing influences, I would suggest, are to be found in popular attitudes towards conjoined twins, as Stephano's increasingly frustrated approximations indicate. Once Caliban–Trinculo has spoken with both voices, Stephano's tune alters:

> Four legs and two voices; a most delicate monster! His forward voice now is to speak well of his friend, his backward voice is to utter foul speeches and to detract. (2.2.85–7)

This assessment of the passive–active nature of

conjoined twins has a medical precedent and chimes curiously with passages in histories and wonder books, in which writers question if attached children possess two souls or one.[13] In his chronicles, first published in 1577 and then in an enlarged edition in 1587, Holinshed describes a 'monster' born in Northumberland during the reign of King Constantine of Scotland. With 'one whole bellie from the nauill downe ... and from the nauill vpwards ... diuided into two bodies', Holinshed states:

> so did it appeare there was two contrarie wils or desires in the same, euer lusting contrarilie, as when the one did sleepe, the other would wake; when the one required to haue meat, the other passed for none at all. Oftentimes would they chide and brall togither, insomuch that at length they fell so far at variance, that they did beat and rent either other verie pitifullie with their nailes. At length the one with long sickenesse wearing away and finallie deceassing, the other was not able to abide the

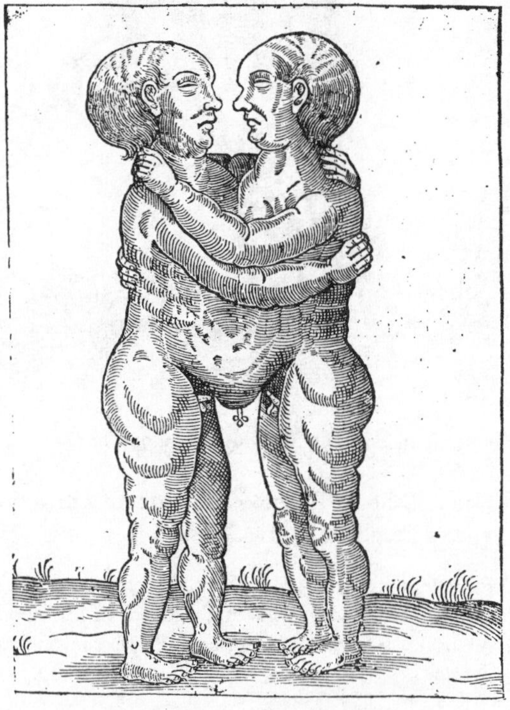

13 Thomas Bedford, *A true and certaine relation of a strange-birth* (London, 1635; STC 1791), frontispiece.

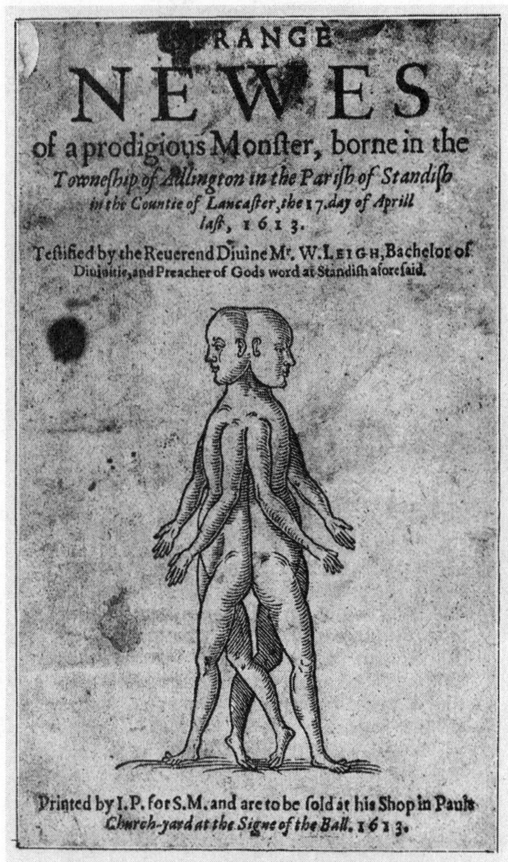

...RANGE
NEWES
of a prodigious Monster, borne in the
Towneship of Adlington in the Parish of Standish
in the Countie of Lancaster, the 17. day of Aprill
last, 1613.
Testified by the Reuerend Diuine Mr. W. Leigh, Bachelor of Diuinitie, and Preacher of Gods word at Standish aforesaid.

Printed by I.P. for S.M. and are to be sold at his Shop in Pauls *Church-yard at the Signe of the Ball.* 1613.

14 William Leigh, *Strange newes of a prodigious monster* (London, 1613; STC 15428).

[13] Boaistuau, *Certaine secrete wonders*, fo. 36^{r}; Paré, *The workes*, p. 966; Park and Daston, 'Unnatural Conceptions', 22.

In a recent BBC documentary, it was stated of the conjoined twins, Dao and Duan: 'one twin – Dao – is smaller and weaker than her sister. Even though they share a third leg, Duan appears to have more control over it. Wherever Duan wants to go, Dao must follow.' Following a successful separation operation, '[Dao's] personality is just as strong now as Duan's. She has independence, which she never had before. She talks back to Duan, which she never did before – she was always the one that was quiet and let Duan dominate.' See *Horizon: 'Siamese Twins'* (London, Broadcasting Support Services, 1995), pp. 5, 19.

greeuous smell of the dead carcase, but immediatlie after died also.[14]

For Stephano, however, recognizing that the gabardine creature – with two heads, a type of *spondylodymus*, *ischiopagus* or *dicephalus dipus dibrachius* – is a living body (rather than a dead carcass) necessitates drastic action (illustrations 13 and 14).[15] The efforts of the jester and the butler to define the monster culminate in Stephano playing midwife to a grotesque delivery, which is also linked to an evacuation of waste. 'I'll pull thee by the lesser legs – if any be Trinculo's legs, these are they . . . Thou art very Trinculo indeed! How cam'st thou to be the siege of this mooncalf? Can he vent Trinculos?' (2.2.98–102). Parodying Prospero's earlier acts of revelation and his predilection for summoning things into existence, Stephano discovers Trinculo, casting Caliban as a monster and a mother that gives birth to 'matter' (2.2.56) – the three terms are locked in a bizarre, triadic relationship. The conjoined twins are surgically separated; Caliban and Trinculo stand again as autonomous; but the strange and threatening properties of the monster remain undiminished.

Ultimately, however, the monstrous in *The Tempest* ranges far beyond a single character or several scenes. In some senses, the play is primarily concerned with 'disability' and 'imperfection' in all of their manifestations. The courtiers 'mar [the] labour' (1.1.13) of the sailors; Ariel claims that the shipwrecked party has arrived without a 'blemish' (1.2.218); and Ferdinand refused earlier offers of marriage because of 'some defect' (3.1.44) in the 'women' (3.1.43) to whom he was introduced. Behind these details lies an apprehension about the exact consequences of heterosexual intercourse. Birth can never be mentioned in the play without the possibility of complicating factors. In particular, Prospero broods obsessively on 'that which breeds' (3.1.76) between the lovers, as his warning to Ferdinand indicates:

If thou dost break her virgin-knot before
All sanctimonious ceremonies may
With full and holy rite be ministered,
No sweet aspersion shall the heavens let fall
To make this contract grow; but barren hate,
Sour-eyed disdain, and discord shall bestrew
The union of your bed with weeds so loathly
That you shall hate it both. (4.1.15–22)

Curiously for the Renaissance, a period in which high infant mortality constantly endangered the patrilineal system, Prospero wishes for quality not quantity of issue. While the prevailing metaphors in his speech are horticultural – parasitic vegetation will foul the paradisial garden – the spectre of the monstrous birth and another Caliban (who has already threatened to people the island with his own kind) is the dominant idea, one consequence of sexual incontinence. As Ferdinand's reply makes clear, moreover (he also hopes for 'fair' (4.1.24) children), the desire for perfect progeny is shared by potential grandfather and son-in-law alike. Judging from *The Tempest* as a whole, it would appear that the overriding imperative is less the representation of monstrosity than the terror of reproduction itself.

III

As several critics have observed, Prospero's wish to be self-sufficient has a gendered dimension, which shows itself in anxious constructions of women and the contaminating powers they are thought to exercise. Stephen Orgel writes: Prospero's wife 'is missing as a character, but [he], several times explicitly, presents himself as incorporating the wife, acting as both father and mother'.[16] What has not received

---

[14] Raphael Holinshed, *Holinshed's Chronicles of England, Scotland and Ireland*, 6 vols. (London, Johnson, 1807–8), vol. V, p. 228.

[15] The terms are from Paré, *On Monsters and Marvels*, ed. Pallister, pp. 177–80.

[16] Stephen Orgel, 'Prospero's Wife', in Margaret W. Ferguson, Maureen Quilligan and Nancy J. Vickers, eds., *Rewriting the Renaissance: The Discourses of Sexual*

notice is the extent to which the play, as a consequence of the banishment of maternal properties, favours acts of parthenogenesis. Notably it is the unregenerate who seem to want to fashion forms according to their own imperatives. Most feared by Prospero is Antonio's part in having 'new created / The creatures that were mine ... or changed 'em' (1.2.81–2), and even Sebastian recognizes the ability: 'The setting of thine eye and cheek proclaim / A matter from thee, and a birth, indeed, / Which throes thee much to yield' (2.1.227–9). And conspiracy and treason, hatched by Antonio parthenogenetically, have indeed a monstrous shape.

Equally overlooked in critical assessments have been the precise connections between parthenogenesis, the monstrous birth and the artist. The single author's work is invariably figured as a monstrous delivery. In the *Arcadia*, first completed in 1580, Sir Philip Sidney states that if his 'idle work ... though in itself it have deformities ... had not been in some way delivered, [it] would have grown a monster', a perception which informs a similar remark in his *An Apology for Poetry* (1580–1); the poet, he writes, 'lifted up with the vigour of his own invention, [delights] ... in making things either better than Nature bringeth forth, or, quite anew, forms such as never were in Nature, as the Heroes, Demigods, Cyclops, Chimeras, Furies, and such like'.[17] Such relations between monstrous progeny and artistic production are at the heart of *The Tempest*'s aesthetic. Giving birth to Ariel from a tree (1.2.292–3) permits Prospero to demonstrate his 'art' (1.2.291) and to use the spirit for tasks of an essentially theatrical nature. With Ariel's aid he produces from the heavens the masque of Ceres, Iris and Juno, who join in harmony to banish famine (4.1.116–17), a prodigious token sent by God as a judgement.[18] Prospero's parturition of wonders is more sharply observed still. As a 'wondered father and a wife' (4.1.123), Prospero '*discovers*' Ferdinand and Miranda at chess by pulling aside a curtain, adding, 'I will requite you with as good a thing, / At least bring forth a wonder to content ye / As much as me my dukedom' (5.1.169–71). Between Sycorax, the witch who brings forth monsters, and Prospero, the magician who brings forth wonders, there may be little room for manoeuvre.

In delivering Ariel from his sylvan hysteria, Prospero avails himself of the opportunity to use the spirit for providential purposes. Ariel's transformation into the monstrous creatures of myth and legend enables the magician to bring the courtiers to a semblance of repentance. The central stages map his efforts to produce in his enemies a spiritual change as dramatic as his spirits' prodigious performances. With the villains Prospero's schemes fail to achieve even a measure of success. For instance, when Antonio's plot is foiled by Ariel, he explains away his behaviour with the ruse of a noise, which implies that the ultimate monstrosities are his own dissimulations: ''twas a din to fright a monster's ear, / To make an earthquake' (2.1.312–13). The 'monstrous shape' (3.3.31) of

---

Difference in Early Modern Europe (Chicago and London, University of Chicago Press, 1986), p. 54. See also Janet Adelman, *Suffocating Mothers: Fantasies of Maternal Origin in Shakespeare's Plays, 'Hamlet' to 'The Tempest'* (New York and London, Routledge, 1992), p. 237; Anny Crunelle-Vanrigh, '"Unmixed with baser 'mater'": Le monstre et la matrice', in Claude Peltrault, ed., *Shakespeare 'La Tempête: Etudes Critiques* (Besançon, Université de Franche-Comté, 1994), pp. 99, 109.

17 Sir Philip Sidney, *The Countess of Pembroke's Arcadia (The Old Arcadia)*, ed. Katherine Duncan-Jones (Oxford and New York, Oxford University Press, 1994), p. 3; Sir Philip Sidney, *An Apology for Poetry*, ed. Geoffrey Shepherd (Manchester, Manchester University Press, 1973), p. 100. In an unpublished paper, 'Masculine Parturition and the Generation of Monstrous Prodigies', William E. Engel suggests that the idea of the author's parthenogenesis leading to monstrous births may derive from Montaigne's essays. I am grateful to Professor Engel for sending me a copy of his paper.

18 Charles Fitz-Geffrey, *The curse of corne-horders: with the blessing of seasonable selling* (London, 1631; STC 10938), p. 31; Samuel Hieron, *A helpe unto devotion* (London, 1608; STC 13406.3), p. 207; Ludwig Lavater, *Three christian sermons, of famine and dearth of victuals* (London, 1596; STC 15322), sig. A4^r.

the spirits similarly makes little impression on Sebastian, who only sees in them justification for hackneyed fantasies: 'Now I will believe / That there are unicorns; that in Arabia / There is one tree, the phoenix' throne, one phoenix / At this hour reigning there' (3.3.21–4). But with the rest of the company Prospero's art reaps greater rewards. Appalled by the warnings of Ariel as a harpy (a mythical creature described in a 1626 dictionary as one of a group of 'Monstrous devouring birds'), Alonso laments the death of his son: 'O, it is monstrous, monstrous! / Methought the billows spoke and told me of it, / The winds did sing it to me ... and the thunder' (3.3.95–7).[19] The exclamations of the King of Naples offer a final demonstration of the magician's strategic powers. Like Sidney's artist, Prospero produces prodigies which inspire wonder and threaten terrible developments. Having appropriated the maternal function, he forces his captives to read their landscape, and to discover in its strange operations corroboration of a monstrous interior or hope for a miraculous recovery.

IV

For the majority of early seventeenth-century spectators, wonders in the air, such as Ariel's prodigious pyrotechnic displays before the mariners and the courtiers, had a key role to play in scriptural tradition and exegesis. Almost all extraordinary phenomena were regarded as tokens of the far more disturbing judgements that were to accompany the end of the world, the apocalypse. As a devotional work of 1610 detailed:

> the Sun shall be turned into darknesse, and the Moone into blood, and the starres shall fall from heauen, the aire shal be full of whirle winds, stormes, correscations, flashing meteors, and thunders: the earth with fearefull tremblings, and swallowing Gulfes: the flouds of the sea shall swell so high, as if they would ouerflow the whole world ... an Archangel shall ... giue a signe to all that are dead, to rise againe, and to come to Gods iudgement.[20]

Eclipses and, not surprisingly, monstrous births were invoked as additional indications of the time of great reckoning, and it was in *Revelation* that they were granted their most forceful realization.[21] With its multiple monstrous forms, such as plagues and seven-headed beasts, *Revelation,* the discovery of God's word, takes us back to the monster's etymological derivations. In Latin, '*monstro*' means 'To show ... demonstrate ... expound, [and] reveal'; a '*monstrum*' is a 'portent, prodigy, [or] sign'; and '*moneo*' translates as 'to give warning of, presage'.[22] Many of these meanings are at work in Renaissance uses of the discourses of monstrosity, and lie behind the warnings threatened in the vision of Saint John the divine, which also takes us forward to the apocalyptic concerns of *The Tempest.*

By 1610–11, when *The Tempest* was composed, millenarian ideas had lost none of their Elizabethan popular appeal. In addition to enlisting the obvious apocalyptic sign of the tempest, the play invests with contemporary meanings Prospero's appeal to an army of spirits to come to his assistance:

> I have bedimmed
> The noontide sun, called forth the mutinous winds,
> And 'twixt the green sea and the azured vault
> Set roaring war; to the dread rattling thunder
> Have I given fire, and rifted Jove's stout oak
> With his own bolt; the strong-based promontory
> Have I made shake, and by the spurs plucked up
> The pine and cedar. Graves at my command

19 Henry Cockeram, *The English dictionarie* (London, 1626; STC 5462), sig. T4^{v}.

20 Thomas Tymme, *A silver watch-bell* (London, 1610; STC 24424), pp. 48, 51, 54, 56.

21 *Gods handy-worke in wonders* (London, 1615; STC 11926), sigs. B1^{v}–B2^{r}; *A true relation of the French kinge his goode successe* (London, 1592; STC 13147), sig. B3^{r}. For scriptural antecedents, see Lloyd E. Berry, ed., *The Geneva Bible: A facsimile of the 1560 edition* (Madison, Milwaukee and London, University of Wisconsin Press, 1969), New Testament, *Revelation* (VI.12–14), fos. 116^{v}, (VIII.5, 7, 10, 12), 117^{r}, (XVI.21), 120^{r}.

22 P. G. W. Glare, ed., *Oxford Latin Dictionary*, 2 vols. (Oxford: Clarendon, 1983), vol. II, pp. 1130–1.

Have waked their sleepers, oped, and let 'em forth
By my so potent art. (5.1.41–50)

It has long been recognized that the passage derives from Medea's incantation in Golding's 1567 translation of Ovid's *Metamorphoses*, but more apposite would appear to be its apocalyptic dimensions – the eclipses, thunder and lightning, earthquakes and revelation of the graves' contents.[23] As earlier dramatic representations indicate, moreover, Prospero's sentiments have a recognizable precedent: the speech illuminates the specific events of its historical moment and gains energy from an established theatrical lineage.[24]

As the 'revels' (4.1.148) end and Prospero's 'pageant' (4.1.155) dissolves, we are once again reminded of the arresting connections between popular entertainment and divine judgement. To 'reveal' is etymologically related to the old French, *révéler* (to revolt, make a din and make merry), from which are derived the verb, to 'revel', and the noun, 'revel', a parish fair.[25] In the final scene the play's prevailing metaphors are deployed in innovative combinations – Prospero discovers himself and passes judgement on the assembled courtiers. But Prospero is fallible, and his strange remark – 'this thing of darkness I / Acknowledge mine' (5.1.275–6) – expresses several tendencies – an attraction to the monstrous, which entails a twin-like dependency. Dependency is certainly the hallmark of his epilogue:

Now 'tis true
I must be here confined by you,
Or sent to Naples . . .
release me from my bands
With the help of your good hands . . .
Now I want
Spirits to enforce, art to enchant;
And my ending is despair
Unless I be relieved by prayer . . .
(5.1.321–3, 327–8, 331–4)

The main idea is of being freed from a cage: presenting himself as a kind of limbless wonder, Prospero is finally twinned to the audience, on whom he depends for favourable judgement. In requesting release and relief, Prospero is also asking for deliverance – it is only through being monstrously reborn, with the theatre's spectators as a parthenogenetic parent, that the magician can become the actor and abandon the part, that he can clarify the already blurring perimeters of a dissolving playworld. The performance concluded, Prospero, finally more of a monster than a showman, solicits applause.

V

As we approach another millennium, it is sobering to contemplate the very different inflections that are now placed on monstrous phenomena and apocalyptic possibilities. If Shakespeare does enjoy a prophetic ability, then it resides in his glimpses into the remarkable power of technology. Prospero's magical ambitions have their counterpart in the modern conquest of space. Indeed, with so much of the world available to the eye of the scientist, monsters have been relocated to areas which lie outside an earthly perimeter. In Prospero's destruction of books, moreover, are the seeds of another apocalyptic tendency for, in this theoretical climate, the author is dead, the future of the book is in jeopardy, and text has been superseded by hypertext.

The 'freak show' of the late nineteenth and early twentieth centuries is no more, only surviving in a handful of 'museum pieces' still

[23] Arthur Golding, *Ovid's 'Metamorphoses'*, ed. W. H. D. Rouse (London, De La More Press, 1904), Book VII, lines 244–89.

[24] See William Shakespeare, *Hamlet*, ed. Harold Jenkins (London and New York, Methuen, 1987), 1.1.116–18, 120, 123; John Marston, *The Malcontent*, ed. George K. Hunter (Manchester, Manchester University Press, 1975), 2.5.128, 130–1.

[25] J. A. Simpson and E. S. C. Weiner, eds., *The Oxford English Dictionary*, 20 vols. (Oxford, Clarendon, 1989), vol. XIII, pp. 811–12.

HEATH'S VIEW

'Roll up! Roll up! See the only schoolboy with no A-levels'

15 'Heath's View'.

on tour in American carnivals.[26] But the logic and discourse with which it was associated are still alive. In the tabloid newspapers of the summer of 1995, for instance, the 'monster' is the schoolboy who has failed his A-Levels, as a cartoon in *The Mail on Sunday* reveals (illustration 15).[27] The academic manifestations of the monstrous aside, and our own status as hawkers of intellectual progeny, the technological dimensions of the question require further comment. In the twentieth century technology is such that monstrosity can either be created or destroyed. The biological effects of global war are still fresh in the imagination. Cases of children with microcephaly increased dramatically following the nuclear bomb dropped on Nagasaki; Dioxin, contained in 'Agent Orange', which was used in Vietnam, has been linked to the malformation of infants' limbs; and babies have been born without ears or spleen to Gulf War veterans.[28] There may be little finally separating Prospero's tempest and the mushroom cloud of the holocaust. The world of wonders captured in the miraculous glass of John Taylor, the Elizabethan Shrewsbury showman, has now dissolved. But we continue to discover in the past reflections of our own anxieties, and look to Shakespeare for revelations of mysteries and demonstrations of things to come.[29]

---

[26] Robert Bogdan, *Freak Show: Presenting Human Oddities for Amusement and Profit* (Chicago and London, University of Chicago Press, 1988), passim; Randy Johnson, Jim Secreto and Teddy Varndell, *Freaks, Geeks and Strange Girls: Sideshow Banners of the Great American Midway* (Honolulu, Hardy Marks, 1996), p. 15; 'Your Place or Mine?', BBC Radio 4, 26 June 1996.

[27] Joe Murphy, 'Shephard orders exam pass probe', *The Mail on Sunday*, 20 August (1995), p. 15.

[28] John Pilger, 'Nam now', *The Guardian Weekend*, 22 April (1995), p. 21; Sean Ryan, 'Disabled baby "is Gulf war victim"', *The Sunday Times*, 20 November (1994), p. 13; Alice Stewart, 'Children of a lesser god', *The Times Higher*, 11 August (1995), p. 19.

[29] I am grateful to the following for their helpful and trenchant comments on earlier drafts of this paper: John Archer, Emily Bartels, Crystal Bartolovich, Doug Bruster, Brian Caraher, Fran Dolan, Neil Kenny and Laura Lunger Knoppers.

SHAKESPEARE PERFORMANCES IN ENGLAND 1996

ROBERT SMALLWOOD

The most eagerly awaited event of the Shakespearian theatrical year, or, perhaps, of the decade, was the first production at the new Globe theatre. The 'Prologue Season', at what still described itself as a building site, but which presented a virtually complete auditorium and what is expected to be the final form of the stage in temporary construction, offered a production of *The Two Gentlemen of Verona.* Perhaps a little surprisingly, the Globe's Artistic Director, Mark Rylance, had ceded the responsibility of inaugural direction to Jack Shepherd, though he nevertheless exercised considerable influence on proceedings from the role of Proteus. It was an event that one approached with enormous expectations and overflowing goodwill and it was a terrible disappointment.

The issues raised by that disappointment are fundamental not only to the existence and purpose of the reconstructed Globe but to the whole enterprise of Shakespeare production in the 1990s. Why had *The Two Gentlemen of Verona* been chosen, one wondered. The programme provided no clues, offering only a cast list. Presumably the play's presence near the top of most putative chronological lists of Shakespeare's plays made it seem an appropriate opening choice for the new theatre; it is also comparatively unfamiliar in performance, which removes some of the pressure for directorial innovation; and its limited but varied cast of older generation, clowns, and lovers, with no role dominant (except it be that of Crab) offers a good range of opportunities for a small company. All these may seem plausible reasons for doing a play. What the production demonstrated beyond doubt is that they are not reasons good enough: unless a production demonstrates from within itself its reason for existing, unless there is some sense of why this director needed to do this play at this time, the result, be the performing space never so new and never so authentic, will be essentially hollow. How fervently one tried to quell such sentiments and give the new enterprise the benefit of the doubt, but how insistently they reasserted themselves.

Another fundamental truth reaffirmed by this production is that good acting has more to do with theatrical pleasure than the spaces in which we might be lucky enough to find it. There was, sadly, little good acting to be seen here, even the most interesting performance on view, and the only one to demonstrate real command of the space – Mark Rylance's Proteus – having largely been sacrificed to gratifying the audience's puerile eagerness to hiss and boo its stagy villainy. The grimaces and shruggings, the ostentatious stealth and overplayed wickedness, came straight from the world of pantomime and elicited identical audience reactions. (It was important to keep firmly at bay the thought that it might all be preparation for the definitive Iago.) For the rest, the cast appeared overwhelmed by the vastness of the arena in which they were playing.

And vast indeed it seemed. The scholarship that has gone into this reconstruction makes it

16 Mark Rylance as Proteus, *The Two Gentlemen of Verona*, directed by Jack Shepherd, Shakespeare's Globe Prologue Season, 1996.

17 Lennie James as Valentine, *The Two Gentlemen of Verona*, directed by Jack Shepherd, Shakespeare's Globe Prologue Season, 1996.

difficult not to believe that the Globe stage really *was* like this, but in this production there was certainly something about its large and uncompromising rectangularity that doomed to futility the efforts of actors rushing about to make it appear populated. The stage flooring, apparently a mixture of hay and sand, helped them not a jot and seemed a poor approximation to the rushes strewn on oak boards that authenticity would presumably demand; and for all one's efforts to resist literal-mindedness, such a floor could not but signal 'outdoors' to all sorts of scenes that required one to imagine 'indoors'. It was, presumably, just a result of the temporary nature of the playing area, but, for all that, something that one eagerly looks forward to not seeing again. Nor did the costumes do anything to help the actors fill the space. Bravely eschewing the doublets and hose and farthingales one might have predicted – no doubt in a determined effort to avoid the 'theme park' danger that lurks round every corner for an enterprise such as this – the performers were dressed in jeans, t-shirts, trainers, nylon suits, straw hats, baseball caps, sunglasses. For Julia there was an orange mini-skirt and little orange pumps, for Sylvia a white trouser-suit. The aim was understandable, but the ultimate effect, sadly, was of thin, mean, rather Lowryesque little figures, their attempts to fill the energy-devouring stage made all the more forlorn by the low-key costumes. That sense was exacerbated by the absence of the attention-focusing lighting to which we are so habituated, and by the studied economy with larger properties, which were limited to the odd chair or two and from time to time a table. All of this, in an ideal world, should have thrown our attention on to the acting and the story, but the poverty of the former only made the thinness of the latter more apparent than it need be. Jim Bywater tried hard, in a music-hall comedian style, with the soliloquies of Lance, but succeeded only in vulgarizing their wistful charm; Anastasia Hille's Sylvia had a certain elegance but little sense of the witty intelligence discoverable in the role; Matthew Scurfield's Duke was a gesturing windbag; Stephanie Roth rode roughshod over all the poignant vulnerability of Julia's love, turning her into a squawking, gesticulating teenager; and Lennie James offered us Valentine as merely goofy. It was left to Mark Rylance to provide the only interesting performance of the evening, a Proteus much troubled by the sense of his own guilt, laboriously working out his plots for betraying his friend, failing to convince even himself in his attempts at self-justification. Had it not been for its hammy inability to resist provoking those boos and hisses, this would have been an intelligent performance, with something to say about the role and the play. It was also audible throughout – which was far from true of the rest, Julia above all, though one's attempts to hear were not, I suspect, much helped by the constant need to retune between British and American accents. Apart from Rylance's performance the production seemed devoid of ideas, unless one was supposed to regard as 'ideas' such gratuities as Sir Thurio appearing for one scene in swimming drawers and making as if to dive from the stage, or the sudden, unexplained appearance of a prostitute in red leather in one of the four eye-catchingly empty upper bays (the little band occupied the fifth and central one), or the outlaws, inexplicably, as deformed Waterloo Bridge beggars on crutches and little trolleys.

The ending of *The Two Gentlemen of Verona* is notoriously difficult, but David Thacker's production a few years ago proved that its problems are not insuperable. Here the difficulties seemed hardly to have been considered and the scene became simply unbelievable, with the audience laughing (at such moments as the discovery of Julia from her boy's disguise) at the expense of the story rather than in sympathy with it. There was a fine black mongrel of a Crab, and there was Proteus, but otherwise there was nothing here to make one think again about this play, or seriously to suggest much thought about it by director or actors. It has to be recorded, however, that the audience (at least on the evening I was there) had a hugely good time, shouting their approval and disapproval as at a Punch and Judy show. With more productions like this the new Globe will no doubt prove a major popular success; but, then, theme parks and Disneylands are major popular successes. If the new Globe theatre is going to tell us anything interesting about Shakespeare's plays it is going to have to take itself much more seriously than this. The space now exists – and bravo for all the hard work and all the faith that made it possible - but the space is nothing unless at least as much intellectual effort and ingenuity as created it goes into extracting theatrical benefit from it. But it was only a 'Prologue Season' after all; next year, surely, there will be a different tale to tell.

From a production very short of ideas one turns to one that had, perhaps, too many. In a year with few major Shakespeare productions in Britain, even the Royal Shakespeare Company offered only what it called a 'mini season' in Stratford, a six-month programme from April to early October which enabled the company to shift its ten months in Stratford from the traditional April to January period to a new November to August pattern. The season opened with Steven Pimlott's production of *As You Like It* on the main stage. It was played in a box set, designed by Ashley Martin-Davies, of ribbed and shiny metal, empty apart from ornate armchairs in the court scenes and unchanging for Arden except for the addition of long metal poles, flown in in varying numbers and perfectly believable as tree trunks if one was so disposed, even taking on a strange beauty in certain lighting states. A metal shutter with a slit entrance created a smaller downstage playing area for the scenes in Oliver's orchard and for the scene (1.3) of Rosalind's confession to Celia of her love for Orlando, their *déshabillé* intimacy shockingly invaded by Duke Frederick and his followers with their swords drawn. Within this determinedly non-realistic space the costumes were ornately and defiantly Elizabethan, Rosalind's anxiety at being seen by Orlando in her doublet and hose reflecting for once the simple truth. She even arrived in Arden with a hefty spear in hand, perfectly adequate, to the non-expert eye, to deal with most boars. The basic simplicity of the set allowed the play to alternate between the court and Arden, as the text requires, rather than, as so many productions do, moving up the discovery of the girls' flight (2.2) and the interrogation of Oliver (3.1) to form a single court sequence followed by a big transformation to Arden. The benefit to the rhythm and tension of the play was significant, as was the sense provided by the basic sameness of the set that court and forest were really one, their differences deriving from the responses of their inhabitants rather than from any inherent characteristics. Indeed, the move from court to country seemed a distinct change for the worse as we encountered Robert Demeger's exiled Duke in a howling snowstorm preaching the benefits of the 'life exempt from public haunt' to a bunch of bored and disbelieving followers huddled in blankets. He kicked off his boots to prove his fortitude, flinched as his bare feet touched the snow, then clicked his fingers to order one of the underlings to put the boots back on again. This sense that social and economic power structures tend to survive exile was latent throughout. At the forest dinner table there were wooden cups for everyone except the Duke, who had a silver goblet; the girls were frightfully keen on getting their 'jewels and . . . wealth together' as they fled the court and Corin was humbly aware of their financial status as the purchase of the sheep-cote was discussed; and in the final scene, as the return to court was planned, the Duke's reminder that rewards would be to everyone 'according to the measure of their states' again insisted on the old hierarchies.

The harshness of this Arden claimed a notable victim – possibly a theatrical first. Carried in by Orlando from collapse in the evening's most hostile snowstorm, Adam lay at the end of the ducal table wrapped in blankets and with attentive forest lords trying in vain to feed him. The Duke walked across to him at the end of the scene, remarked cheerily 'Support him by the arm', and escorted Orlando (unaware of his servant's condition) from the stage. Whether the remark derived from myopia or from the Duke's habitual sense of indifference to the lower orders it was impossible to say, but either way the rest of us could see perfectly well that the old man was well past support of any kind. As the Duke and Orlando strode off arm in arm Adam breathed his last and the first half of the comedy ended (generically a little dubiously) with his death. It was a solemn, surprising, and above all directorial interval effect. For the second half of the evening there was a huge mound of earth, daffodils strewn over it, upstage centre; nobody behaved as it if was anyone's grave – and it was, indeed, large enough to have contained a horse or two – but as Silvius and Touchstone, Orlando and Ganymede, ran round and over it, one could not but think of poor old Adam gently recycling below.

Such thoughts did nothing, however, to dampen the infectious energy of the second half of the play. The last return to court found Colum Convey's Duke Frederick, tetchy, goggle-eyed, and highly neurotic from the start, in the last stages of psychopathic dementia, having Oliver drowned in a little tin bath as he interrogated him about his brother. There was something about this last stage in a journey towards breakdown that made the final news of

18 Rachel Joyce as Celia, Liam Cunningham as Orlando, Niamh Cusack as Rosalind, *As You Like It*, 3.2, directed by Steven Pimlott, RSC, 1996.

his entering a monastery oddly plausible. (The production was a little like that, trying hard to explain things that the play leaves contentedly unexplained.) Then we were back to Arden and to the wooing scenes between Liam Cunningham's excellent Orlando – amiable, more mature than the text really supports but, perhaps because of that, with a manly dignity that the role too often lacks and for once, therefore, seeming worthy of Rosalind's love – and Niamh Cusack's splendidly vital, unselfconsciously sexy, intelligent, and touchingly vulnerable Rosalind. She gave him a quick little kiss on 'I do take thee, Orlando, for my husband' (4.1.128), which disconcerted him, and there was another kiss, longer, passionate, and mutual on 'as if thou wert indeed my Rosalind' (4.1.182), which worried Orlando deeply, for there was (rightly, of course) no sense whatever that he had seen through the disguise. 'If this be so, why blame you me to love you' (5.2.100), he demanded, with deeply felt seriousness in his last scene with Ganymede, and the question seemed a culmination of the production's pervasive interest in love in all its sexual variousness, from the cousin princesses in each others' arms in Act 1, Scene 3, the gentleness of their affection in the sharpest contrast to Charles the Wrestler's cheap little smirk on 'never two ladies loved as they do' (1.1.105), to Orlando and Oliver's kiss of reconciliation lying exactly where their future wives had lain so much earlier in the play, and encompassing on the way the girlish crush of Phebe on Ganymede and the complexities of Orlando's feelings for his disguised lover. This was a subtle

19 Doreen Andrew as Hymen, Liam Cunningham as Orlando, Niamh Cusack as Rosalind, Robert Demeger as Duke Senior, *As You Like It*, 5.4, directed by Steven Pimlott, RSC, 1996.

and sensitive treatment of the play's exploration of love, brotherly, sisterly, heterosexual, and homosexual.

There were other good things too: a genuinely funny, trenchantly intelligent Touchstone from David Tennant, a red-suited, cap-and-bells court jester like an illustration from an old Complete Works, valiantly getting laughs on the lines and bursting with lustful energy for Susannah Elliott-Knight's buoyantly responsive Audrey; an only slightly exaggerated partnership of Victoria Hamilton's pert and swanky little Phebe and Joseph Fiennes's besotted, long-haired Silvius, nuzzling round her in wide-eyed, lap-dog devotion; a crisply spoken, hatchet-faced, gravely sententious Jaques from John Woodvine, tartly demanding, as Orlando worked hard at carving Rosalind's name some three feet up on a tree-trunk, 'What *stature* is she of' (3.2.261); and a sharp, poised Celia from Rachel Joyce, as interested in Orlando on first meeting as her cousin, but beaten in the race for his attention by the need to maintain a princess's dignity, bewildered and lonely in the forest as Rosalind's commitment was directed elsewhere, and falling in love a little desperately, one felt, but not unconvincingly, with Sebastian Harcombe's oddly intense Oliver as their eyes met over Rosalind's swoon.

The most remarkable event of the evening was the appearance of Hymen. 'Enter Hymen' is the Folio direction, and Pimlott had decided to take the idea of theophany literally: no Corin dressed up for this production, and to revive Adam for the role would have been altogether too remarkable. Instead there entered the stage from the stalls a middle-aged, grey-haired woman in a black Marks and Spencer trouser-suit, who must have seemed to many in the audience to be a member of the front-of-house staff who had wandered accidentally into the performance until, in a homely northern accent, she spoke the blessings on the lovers. As ever with this production, there was no doubting the directorial thought that had gone into the moment: if gods come from outside the play's everyday world, what better than to bring into this Elizabethan-costumed piece a figure from the twentieth century? If a theatre performance takes its imaginative power from the audience's willingness to believe in the fiction, from where else should the figure of ultimate power come but from the audience? If this is a play about love and marriage dominated by a young woman in love, how better to end it than with the loving blessing of a woman who may be supposed to have experienced love, marriage, motherhood, and grand-motherhood? Intellectually it all made perfect sense; theatrically it was a flop for the utterly basic reason that it cut the magic cord of belief, jolting us into a moment of panic that something had gone wrong and that we were about to be – the ultimate theatrical horror – terribly embarrassed by an intrusion from outside the world of the play. It was immensely interesting, thoughtful, and thought-provoking, but, in the end, quintessentially bathetic, and it was followed by another moment in which directorial thoughtfulness seemed to be working overtime. As Jaques stalked haughtily from the marriage scene, Touchstone, the other Shakespearian anti-romantic invention among the play's characters, presented him with a skull: everyone else, after all, had a companion, so why should not the Yorick of the play present its ageing Hamlet with material to extend his contemplations beyond the seventh age? And once again intellectual ingenuity seemed somehow to outweigh theatrical usefulness. But how graceless to be ungrateful for thoughtfulness, especially after lamenting its absence at the Globe.

Freshness of directorial thought was strongly evident also in the next piece of work at the Royal Shakespeare Theatre. Tim Albery's first production at Stratford was a remarkably courageous (or foolhardy) example of jumping in at the deep end: to tackle *Macbeth* on the main stage was to rush in where many a director more experienced at Stratford had failed. Whether Albery followed them in failure was very much a matter of opinion – particularly among the main newspaper reviewers, who either loved or loathed this production but did not, on the whole, offer much by way of intermediate reaction. This was an austere, uncompromising production, played altogether without music (a great RSC rarity) on a bleak and hostile set, designed by Stewart Laing, that had something of the quality of a laboratory experiment box. A steep front ramp swept asymmetrically up from stage left to right, with a great trench backed by a series of little box-like platforms behind it, vaguely suggesting the moat and battlements of a castle. It was possible (just) to step or hop from one battlement to the next, as the drunken porter (hilariously) and the sleep-walking Lady Macbeth (frighteningly) were to prove. Beyond that, a tiny, steeply raked playing area with dour, brown-papered walls and four plain, brown, aluminium-handled doors boxed and cramped the action into a claustrophobic space with no suggestion of anything beyond. To go through one of those doors was to cease to exist; to be on the stage was to be the object of minute experimental observation. Chairs, and the table for the banquet, were of the most basic design; there was no throne for Macbeth to sit on, no crown for him to wear, no cauldron for the witches. It was, in a sense, an attempt to provide the intensity of studio Shakespeare in a fifteen-hundred seat theatre, to force our concentration solely on to the behaviour and words of the suffering human beings in front of us.

The men's costumes were military, mostly grey-blue and nondescript, suggesting a late nineteenth-century army, perhaps Prussian,

20 Roger Allam as Macbeth, Brid Brennan as Lady Macbeth, *Macbeth*, 2.2, directed by Tim Albery, RSC, 1996.

though Macbeth seemed more naval, both in his shade of blue and in the rings at his cuffs, while about the blue worn by Robert Demeger's droopy-moustached Ross there was a not altogether happy suggestion of the RAF. Lady Macbeth and Lady Macduff, on the other hand, seemed vaguely medieval, in simple, straight dresses (Lady Macbeth's steel blue, Lady Macduff's paler), more or less covered by long black smocks. Their attire was inevitably reminiscent of the witches who opened the production standing statuesque on the battlements in long black dresses, not without a certain elegance as they stood tall and slender, swords hanging from their waists, fair hair braided, each with a little blond beard, intoning their lines in a way that suggested external control. Thus they appeared throughout: graceful, brooding presences, always lingering to watch the scenes that followed theirs, offering little sense of possessing power themselves, but allowing the audience to suppose, if they wished, that they spoke their words, so deliberately and bleakly, at some other, powerful bidding.

Roger Allam presented a Macbeth powerless to resist the idea of killing Duncan from the moment he became Thane of Cawdor, but quite incapable of achieving it without his wife's support. That cliché of most recent productions of *Macbeth*, an element of sexual blackmail in Lady Macbeth's power over her husband, was almost completely absent. There was a close, strong embrace between them on first meeting, but its physicality expressed interdependence, mutual need, rather than sensuality. It was from the words 'dearest partner of greatness' that Brid Brennan's Lady

Macbeth, a tiny, Celtic waif, drew most strength as she read his letter, the very strength that he lacked, the strength of purpose that makes it possible to act before thinking. He learned it immediately she had coaxed and cajoled him through the first murder, nursing him like a child in her arms as he sat crumpled and fearful, trying to escape from the temptation of proceeding 'further in this business'. But when he had learned her lesson he needed her no more – except silently to blame her for making him do what he had all along wanted to do. 'Let every man be master of his time / Till seven' (3.1.40), he said coldly, and she stood there, pathetically unaware that the order included her. 'We will keep ourself till supper-time *alone*', he snapped and at last she got the message and Ross escorted her, humiliated, from the stage: 'Naught's had, all's spent'. At the end of the banquet scene he undid and let down her hair in what seemed about to develop into a moment of sexual tenderness, but his fondling of her tresses was distant, contemptuous, almost brutal. He moved away, only his vast and looming shadow touching hers, tiny and fading, their bodies apart, their exits separate, their relationship dead. In her sleep-walking scene she was neurotically active, fingers twitching as she frantically struck matches in the absence of the traditional candle, jumping precariously along the battlements. Her crisp and practical orders and instructions to him betrayed the yearning to regain her old dominance over him, but the convulsive sobs that punctuated them showed she knew she would never do so, a realization that led, unsurprisingly, to suicide. At the centre of her sad and complicated relationship with Macbeth was his obsession with their childlessness. As he thought of pity 'like a naked, new-born babe', he held out his arms, staring at their emptiness. At her 'I have given suck' he put his hands to his head, shielding himself from the horribly familiar accusation of failure to father another child to compensate for the one they had lost. As he talked with Banquo and Fleance in Act 2, scene 1 his arm was around the boy's shoulder, the gesture of fatherly protectiveness deeply disturbing. And for the last of the witches' visions (the earlier ones, not very effectively, were projections on a screen) seven look-alike Fleances, each with a little blond beard like the witches', drifted about the stage, bewildering and torturing him with their boyishness. Macbeth even came on at the end of the Macduff murder scene to pick up the dead boy's head by the hair, not just, one felt, to check his identity, but to indulge his need to see dead children. 'His wife, his *babes* ...', he had earlier said, with chilling intent. For in his destruction of young life this Macbeth had apparently found some way of compensating for his own inability to beget it; the act of murder had displaced the act of procreation.

It was a production that never allowed one to relax – except, perhaps, in the most outrageously, if uncomfortably, funny Porter scene for some time. Adrian Schiller's frail, thin-faced little Irish Porter, his leg in a calliper, his suit too small, tottered precariously from battlement to battlement, trying in vain to light a cigarette, dropping first one, then another, then the whole packet, down the trench, until finally, inevitably, in the middle of his befuddled excuses for slowness to Macduff and Lennox, he disappeared the way the cigarettes had gone. And as the thanes stared down after him, he reappeared nonchalantly upstage of them, the cigarettes obviously rescued, for one glowed defiantly between his lips as he continued his discourse on the effects of alcohol. He reappeared later, hobbling on to warn Lady Macduff of approaching danger, and then as the cream-faced loon, a frail, crippled, terrified representative of the lower orders in Macbeth's brutal world. Ascending rapidly from those lower orders was Andrew Hesker's Seyton, in cheaply cut, wide-shouldered lounge suit, tinted spectacles, and black leather gloves, the trusted lieutenant detained by Macbeth when everyone, even Lady Macbeth, had been dismissed till seven at night, joining the murderers

21 Adrian Schiller as the Porter, *Macbeth*, 2.3, directed by Tim Albery, RSC, 1996.

of Banquo (to their visible consternation) with suave authority, kicking the corpse into the moat and then striding confidently, matter-of-factly, into the banquet to report to Macbeth. When this deeply disquieting figure brought the news that 'the queen, my lord, is dead', the idea flashed across one's mind that he might have arranged for that – her tendency to give away secrets during her nightly wanderings being so dangerous – such was the quiet, efficient brutality the figure evinced.

Dominating the production and setting its tone was Roger Allam's remarkable Macbeth, a performance as far as it is possible to get from an heroic-romantic version of the title role. Allam's is a voice impressive in its grace and range, and his response to Shakespearian verse is never other than thoughtful and intelligent. He met the witches' initial greeting with a cheerful laugh, shared in soldierly comradeship with Banquo, but that confidence was utterly and irrevocably shattered by the 'Cawdor' greeting a few moments later, inducing an urgency and tenseness that left him only when he reached the emotional and spiritual wasteland that he so vividly presented in the play's final stages. That journey was charted in his speaking, from the easy, bantering tone of the beginning; through the clipped, tense, brittle delivery which took him through the first murder; to the sneering, weary bitterness at the end of the banquet scene as he sat, strongly sidelit, at the end of the empty table, pouring whisky into a glass, staring at it with glazed, unseeing eyes as it overflowed onto table and floor while he contemplated his next visit to the witches; and finally to the measured, uncompromising enunciation of the last monologues, the words of a man looking unflinchingly at a bleak and lifeless inner landscape, the attempt to deaden all feeling apparently successful until the harrowing protest against the void, the great cry of pain and despair that he let out as he betrayed what 'weighs upon the heart'. At the end of 'tomorrow, and tomorrow . . .' he allowed himself a pause, a long moment of stillness, as he sat staring blankly into that pitiless chasm, and then, spoken precisely, with chill finality and entirely without self-pity, as the darkness was embraced, came the words 'signifying nothing'. There was a grim sort of intellectual satisfaction in observing this highly intelligent man as he himself observed his own spiritual destruction, but no inviting us in to share the emotional journey; the production was much too austere for that, and the progress to annihilation all the more remorseless therefor.

Macbeth's end was very terrible. The claustrophobic interior set was replaced for the final stages by a backcloth depicting a vast, blazing landscape (a battlefield, or an inner emotional hell, as one wished to perceive it), with Macbeth on the highest part of the stage seeming to dominate it until he heard the news of the 'moving grove', which provoked the immediate, frantic decision to flee the castle – 'Arm, arm, and *out*' – and set off that same piercing electric alarm bell that had accompanied the discovery of Duncan's corpse. But still he dominated the stage, looming huge and brutal before us, convinced of his own invincibility, the bell maddening in its intensity, then ceasing abruptly on the word 'ripped' as Macduff described his own birth. In the sudden, shocking silence one watched Macbeth's body go limp as the strength ebbed out of him. His hands had been cut during the fight and he held them up, staring, mesmerized by the blood, the moment of his return from killing Duncan precisely recaptured; then slowly he turned to Macduff and pulled him, Macduff's dagger drawn, against his body. His corpse lay stretched across the forestage as Sebastian Harcombe's Malcolm, seemingly traumatized by the brutalities of the battle (and, indeed, by the rest of his experiences in the play) spoke the final lines in a bleak, comfortless monotone.

A spare and thought-provoking *Macbeth* that offered little visual help to its audiences was followed on Stratford's main stage by a *Troilus and Cressida* that, in Ian Judge's usual effusively pictorial style, flaunted its images before us. This was the first main-stage *Troilus and Cressida* for more than a decade and it was determined boldly to fill the space. Stretching the full depth of the stage, from proscenium arch to rear wall, John Gunter's set presented a huge section of the walls of Troy in battered and crumpled steel, patched up with corrugated iron and rubble and spattered with blood, louring over the great corridor of stage that remained. For the Greek scenes suggestions of tents were set up in this space, that of Achilles alongside the great violin-shaped shield that hung on the proscenium arch, stage left, opposite the Trojan wall. And behind this massive confrontational symmetry was a threatening sunset sky, its fierce streak of red hinting, perhaps, at the conflagration that would end the story. For the scenes within Troy, sections of the wall were slid across the stage to suggest spaces within rather than outside the city. There was an upper level (on the wall) from which Cressida and her uncle watched the returning Trojan warriors (1.2) and downstage centre a flight of steps led below the stage. For certain scenes detail was added to a set already by far the most realistic of the season: a shower-room upstage left into which the disarmed and disrobed Trojan warriors proceeded for their communal ablutions, like a football team after the match; a Turkish bath below stage from which a naked Paris and Helen ascended to be wrapped in towels for their sleazy, tired little romp on a chaise longue during Pandarus's song; a long banquet table for the Trojan council scene with golden chairs and drinking vessels based on ancient Greek models.

Costumes were less precise: for the non-combatants, long lightly-flowing robes, basically classical but with a hint of the Japanese, the Trojans' paler and fresher than the Greeks'; and for the battle scenes (and the Hector/Ajax duel) often remarkably little: some leather upper-body armour here and there but mostly just black leather thongs, so that in certain scenes what must have amounted collectively to a hundredweight or two of buttock was on view. Since a good many hefty and dangerous-looking swords and spears were being flashed around to provide distinctly realistic stage effects, it was impossible not to wonder why their users had gone to such trouble to expose the maximum area of vulnerable flesh to their threat. Idle musings, no doubt, but they did provide an answer to the always puzzling question of why Hector should pursue the man in golden armour: sheer necessity, the desire to protect his naked vulnerability, were the perfectly understandable motives. But in answering one question one was only confronted by another, more difficult one: why has only one person in the entire Trojan war had the sense to think of wearing armour?

A certain lack of seriousness about the production is not entirely reprehensible, for the production failed to be entirely serious about the play. It made its intentions clear in the Prologue. Richard McCabe's Thersites bounded down the stage to offer the speech to us, and the undermining process began almost immediately: 'and *that's* the quarrel', he said with a disbelieving interrogative lilt that implied, as clearly as could be, 'you've got to be joking'; the rest of the speech derided the entire enterprise with the cynical contempt that one responds to from the Thersites of the last act, but which, confronting one thus energetically in the Prologue, closed down too many options too early. And for all the best efforts of a fine actor (which McCabe is) the role of Thersites never really recovered from this prematurity, for after it the audience hardly needed him to lure them into cynicism.

Not that they would have needed much luring, even if someone else had given the Prologue, for the blatant sham, the hollow bluster, of the Greek generals was gross and palpable, from Edward de Souza's self-satisfied bullfrog of an Agamemnon through to Richard Dillane's blond hunk of a Diomedes. Towering above them all was a fine Ulysses from Philip Voss, splendidly shaping his two great set pieces (on Degree and on Time) with that mixture of vocal elegance, rhythmic sensitivity, and intellectual clarity that one has come to expect from him. And he was greatly assisted by some admirably intense listening from his interlocutors. The astute political alertness of Ulysses was revealed in such precise details as the look of utter disbelief he registered when Agamemnon agreed to Calchas's request to exchange Antenor for Cressida and one was aware of the calculating brain of the 'old dog fox' constantly at work in the acidity of so many of his comments and the determined patience of his efforts to lure back into the fray Philip Quast's Achilles. Handsome, physically impressive, besotted with his young fair-haired Patroclus and naively proud of the contours of his own body, Quast's Achilles even went so far as to flash his nakedness at Hector before the latter's scrap with Ajax.

But if 'camp' was the word that frequently suggested itself for the dwellers in the Grecian tents, it had to be resisted, for one needed it much more urgently for the astonishing Pandarus of Clive Francis. With vocal intonations not unaffected by memories of Frankie Howerd and Kenneth Williams, a tiered black wig with little hanging curls, heavy facial make-up and frequently replenished lipstick, high chopines, and a costume that managed (disconcertingly) to set one thinking simultaneously of Nanki-Poo and Widow Twankey, he swayed and writhed and minced his way through his pandering, making it perfectly clear that he would be delighted to supply Cressida's place in Troilus's bed if she continued to delay. On the morning after his niece had denied him that privilege his attention was obsessively focused on the young man, the question 'hast not slept

22 Joseph Fiennes as Troilus, Clive Francis as Pandarus, Victoria Hamilton as Cressida, *Troilus and Cressida*, 3.2, directed by Ian Judge, RSC, 1996.

tonight?' addressed directly to Troilus's private parts. And yet there remained just sufficient edge in the performance to leave a touch of doubt about whether all the kowtowing to 'Prince Troilus', all the simpering and coyness around him, might just possibly be as much inspired by his being a prince as by his being a beautiful young man. Joseph Fiennes's Troilus agreed to play Pandarus's flirting games while he needed him for access to Cressida, but flung him to the ground when he tried to wreathe himself into the lovers' embraces in the dawn farewell scene, and spurned and kicked him as he attempted (in 5.3) to piece together Cressida's letter. His 'whoreson tisick' had reduced him to a decrepit, half naked figure crawling downstage towards us for the epilogue. Ash pale, his body oozing sores, his voice reduced to a painful rasp, he croaked the bequest of his diseases to us as he descended the downstage centre steps to that below-stage area that the play's first audiences would have called 'Hell'. In early tellings of the tale Cressida's story ends in leprosy; in Shakespeare's version it is the sixteenth century's new terror disease of syphilis that is wished upon the auditors; here it was to our own decade's equivalent taboo illness, Aids, that the production's final image alluded.

And where, in this world of decadence and disease, did the production place the lovers? They were played young, naive, vulnerable, and shallow. Joseph Fiennes tempered Troilus's idealism with a broad streak of self-pity, the tremulous quality of his voice, though touching (in moderation) at moments of high emotion, was overused and over-indulged, so that he

23 Philip Quast as Achilles, Louis Hilyer as Hector, with the Myrmidons, *Troilus and Cressida*, 5.8, directed by Ian Judge, RSC, 1996.

gave the impression of being constantly on the verge of bursting into tears at the exquisite beauty and pain of his own feelings. And yet, though he was much inclined to whine at Cressida's initial inaccessibility and to howl at her later perfidy, at the news of her exchange for Antenor his uncomplaining compliance seemed even calmer than it usually does. Victoria Hamilton's Cressida, pert and sexy, her clothes all chosen to give maximum emphasis to her femininity, enjoyed her little scene of bawdy banter with her uncle, jumped up and down in glee as she watched the returning warriors prepare for the shower room (even finding it necessary to cool herself with a fan – though perhaps she was just teasing Pandarus), embraced Troilus in the orchard scene, moved away from him, came back to his arms, in a way that, through instinct or design, imparted the maximum urgent energy to their exit to the bedroom.

Her arrival in the Greek camp was a remarkable scene. When he had presented her for Troilus's visual delectation in the orchard, Pandarus had whisked off the veil that covered her face. Pushing her through the gate in the great wall of Troy, Diomedes stripped off the stole that covered her bare shoulders and upper breast. There she stood in a pale lemon, highly revealing dress, riveting the gaze of every man in the Greek army. The kisses of Agamemnon and Nestor were coldly received; that of Achilles interested her more; and the two from Patroclus clearly aroused her, her leg wrapping itself around him in a way that Ulysses registered and which fed directly into his cold and savage denunciation of her as a daughter of the game. The quarto and Folio texts were followed here and Cressida remained on stage for that denunciation, taking it straight in the face and glaring defiantly back at him, apparently on the verge of a reply but deciding against it, trying not to reveal any sense of humiliation but not quite succeeding in hiding the damage it was doing to her – a painful, powerful piece of theatre.

For her final scene with Diomedes her red dress was even more exaggeratedly revealing than any she had worn before – impossible not to reflect on the thinking that went into her packing – and her arousal of his desires by alternating passionate embraces, her legs twining round him, with sudden self-distancing, even more blatant. What the performance was not blatant about, however, was her own inclinations and intentions. The kissing scene with the generals had never threatened the near gang rape that it has in some recent productions; she had, indeed, appeared to be in control until that destructive diatribe from Ulysses. Here with Diomedes her sexual interest in him seemed obvious, yet her reluctance was also clear, the teasing of him with the pledge an expression of her own indecision. When he had gone her 'Troilus, farewell' encapsulated this vacillation: 'Troilus' was wailed out in a grief-stricken dying fall; 'farewell' followed in a crisp, matter-of-fact, dismissive tone. Was this a wonderful expression of Cressida's dilemma or an indecisive production trying to have its cake and eat it? The answer will no doubt depend on whether one thinks it the task of a production of *Troilus and Cressida* to offer a coherent explanation for Cressida's behaviour. This one, clearly, did not.

Left alone with a Ulysses whose admiration for Troilus was strongly emphasized in Philip Voss's performance and which had evinced itself in provision of considerable physical support and comfort during the overhearing scene, Fiennes's Troilus took the long speech of reaction in a slow build-up from quiet, disbelieving attempts to control emotion to full, voice-cracking crescendo. It was an impressive piece of speaking, though more technically dextrous than emotionally involving, a quality that seemed true of the presentation of the lovers throughout. Even Thersites lacked the power that he usually has in this scene, no doubt because his hiding place was below stage level on the downstage centre steps, his asides during the scene offered as little jack-in-the-box interjections, though his sniffing disgustingly at the kerchief which Cressida had let fall was an appropriately disturbing accompaniment to his verdict on what had passed.

The battle scenes were staged with all the technical aplomb and vivid pictorialism one would expect in an Ian Judge production, with great swirling entrances and balletic movements, combatants carried on shoulder high, spears flashing, naked flesh gleaming against the blood red sky. We saw (unprompted by the text) Hector kill the unarmed Patroclus; we saw Achilles discover the corpse and cradle it lovingly in his arms before inciting his masked Myrmidons to revenge, their spears impaling Hector like a stuck pig before lifting him on high; and we saw Troilus lashing about him in cynical and brutal savagery, leading the dead march of exhausted fighters to Troy in a state of grim hopelessness, and kicking at Pandarus as he crawled across his path on his way to bequeath us his diseases. There was more than sound and fury in the production (there was much to look at too) and to dismiss it as signifying nothing would be deeply unfair, for it contained some fine performances and some impressive images and scenes. But as a theatrical experience it failed to achieve overall coherence, mainly because it seemed more intent on embellishing and decorating the parts than on providing an overview of the whole.

Tim Supple's version of *The Comedy of Errors*, which opened (prior to a national and international tour) at The Other Place in Stratford in June came from a world of Shakespeare production altogether different from Ian Judge's. Curious, therefore, that this was the first time the RSC had offered the play since Judge's own main-stage production in 1990, when one actor played both Antipholuses and one both Dromios, creating an evening of slick and brilliant theatrical razzmatazz in which the romance of the play's ending was entirely destroyed by the need to resolve (through the use of doppelgängers) the technical problems created by the doubling. Supple's reading of the piece was infinitely simpler. It presented the play in an unchanging set (designed by Robert Innes Hopkins) of a brick floor backed by a wall with central double doors, a window with a grille, and a bell in a niche above – the simplest of suggestions of a sunlit square in Greece or Turkey. As one entered the theatre one encountered an elderly man dressed in a dirty, ragged cloak and chained to a grid in the centre of the floor, alternately slumped in despair or pacing in anguish and frustration to the limit of his chain. The sound of breaking waves could be heard in the distance, and as 7.30 approached the music that would accompany the production began faintly, hauntingly on that Turkish equivalent of the lute, the *'ud*; then the bell rang sharply, the old man stood up, and, accompanied by a gaoler carrying a great sword and a blindfold, in strode Leo Wringer's crisply dapper Solinus, a black man in a white, high-buttoned military suit, a whiff of Caribbean dictatorship about him, to order, not without a touch of contempt, 'Merchant of Syracusa, plead no more.'

The opening dialogue made clear the principles upon which the rest of the production would be based. It was straightforward, sharply focused, and attentive to the language, and it neither sought, nor needed, to extract from Aegeon's narrative any cheap laughter at the succession of unhappy coincidences that had befallen him. The power of the story was conveyed to us partly by the simplicity with which Christopher Saul's Aegeon told it, but more by the intensity of the listening from Solinus, who was transfixed by what he heard, his attitude changing from the terse and official to the personal and committed as the account progressed. There was no padding, no pantomime pauses and double-takes, just a grief-worn old man telling of his journeyings to despair, punctuated by sad and sympathetic sounds from the little collection of middle eastern instruments – *'ud, zarb, balafan, sitar*, with a violin and female singer – that brought a quality of eeriness, of strangeness and mystery, to the play. The use of music to underscore Shakespearian dialogue so often has the depressing effect of putting a generalized emotional wash over everything that the success of Adrian Lee's accompaniment here is worth remark. It derived partly from its spareness, and from the unfamiliar quality of instrumental sounds, but chiefly from the fact that musicians and actors had rehearsed together from the start, language and sound growing into organic unity. Only once, at the end, did the music intrude. The intensity of the play's conclusion was so fully conveyed to the audience that we needed to make our contribution to the event, to make the play and the space ours, through applause, long before the singer had concluded her valedictory vocalizing. It was an odd failure of judgement on the part of a director who otherwise conveyed his respect and affection for the play with unstinted tact.

He costumed the production in modern dress, the Antipholuses in pale linen suits and suede shoes, their similarity carried most tellingly in identical curly brown hair-styles and jutting little beards. Their Dromios both wore baggy black shorts and t-shirts, but it was Duke Vincentio's formula for blurring identity, shaven heads, that most effectively persuaded us into believing in the confusions. Adriana, in an elegant modern suit with a boldly slit skirt, contrasted sharply with her sister Luciana, modest to the point of austerity (if not dowdiness) in long-skirted grey. And for once the Courtesan (Maeve Larkin) and Dr Pinch (Leo Wringer) remained within the realms of credibility, her red high-heeled shoes being the principal, rather innocently transparent, signal of her professional status, while he, in shiny black tight-fitting suit and black hat, and brandishing a Bible (or book of spells), combined a sense of the evangelical preacher from the southern United States with a hint of the voodoo magician in a way that was both witty and disturbing.

There have, no doubt, been productions of *The Comedy of Errors* in which the central scenes of mistaken identity were more boisterously farcical. Not that the big set pieces – the visiting Antipholus's bewildered response to Adriana's recriminatory tirade, his Dromio's fear of sexual possession by the kitchen maid, the increasing pace and panic of the final arrest and asylum sequence – were not splendidly funny. But they were played against a strong sense of the deeper issues being explored in the play. The complaints of Sarah Cameron's brittle, ill-at-ease Adriana derived from genuine and painful bewilderment and hurt at the loss of her husband's love. Thusitha Jayasundera brought to Luciana a quiet, self-contained intelligence, an apparently knowing caution about emotional commitment and the 'troubles of the marriage-bed' (2.1.27), that gave the role a stillness and depth that contrasted tellingly with the rawness of her sister's anxieties and vulnerabilities. To her brother-in-law's ardent wooing she responded with a firm and dignified, though wistful, rejection. His hopeful eagerness for a kiss, which she seemed about to allow but at the last moment rejected, left her with tears in her eyes – for her sister, but also for herself and for him. Even at the end, the impediments gone, she remained cautious and thoughtful, the feminist conscience of the play, uncertain about commitment. Robert Bowman's Antipholus of Syracuse responded to the blandishments of Ephesus with a beautifully poised mixture of innocent delight and wary bafflement. His distrust (aided by the plaintive, otherworldly music, reinforcing his suspicions of magic and witchcraft) could be seen gradually developing into frightened uncertainty about the stability of his own identity ('If everyone knows us and we know none ...' (3.2.160)), forcing him into close alliance with his Dromio (Dan Milne) in a relationship that was always, and quite rightly, more trusting, and fonder, than that of their twins. His voice, lighter than his Ephesian brother's and with a faint crack to it, gave him a gentle, hesitant, slightly fey quality, very different from his twin's solid, four-square bass. Simon Coates's Antipholus of Ephesus found all the harshness of the part, his resentments fierce, his anger towards his wife bitter and self-righteous, his rage with his Dromio (Eric Mallett) hard and unamused. Funny noises from the band's percussion more or less persuaded us to laugh at his brother's slapstick attacks on *his* Dromio, but the energy with which the Ephesian Antipholus hit his servant made that impossible, the audience's mounting distaste on several occasions seeming to shame the band into silence as the blows rained down.

The production, then, treated the play with deep respect and with a thoughtful, affectionate delight in the story it had to tell. The effect of all this was most marked, and most welcome, at the play's ending. Aemilia – who last time at Stratford, in a hat like a double lampshade, had been the last in a succession of absurd caricatures – was here, in Ursula Jones's performance, a figure of quiet dignity and gentle authority, costumed simply in a nun's habit. The revelations that accompanied her arrival had a feeling of the miraculous about them, giving to the reunions something of a sacred quality. From here, it was clear, the route to the restoration of Sebastian to Viola, of Marina to Pericles, of Hermione to Leontes, was straight and direct. The ending was not, however, all unalloyed joy – any more than it is in those later plays. The wonder and delight had a touch of muted uncertainty, of hesitation about daring to believe, that gave them a profound seriousness. Much was still to be understood, much to be forgiven. Precisely what had happened between brother and sister-in-law at Adriana's dinner? He had certainly appeared after it in a state of bemused exhaustion and now, at the end, its

24 Eric Mallett as Dromio of Ephesus, Maeve Larkin as the Courtesan, Leo Wringer as Dr Pinch, Simon Coates as Antipholus of Ephesus, Gary Oliver as Balthasar, Thomas Fisher as the Guard, Thusitha Jayasundera as Luciana, and Sarah Cameron as Adriana, *The Comedy of Errors*, 4.4, directed by Tim Supple, RSC, 1996.

memory cast its little shadow over the long-yearned-for reunion with his brother. And how much did Adriana deserve the Abbess's energetic telling off that left her publicly humiliated, the Courtesan sniggering in the background? Precisely how culpable was the Ephesian Antipholus's friendship with the Courtesan? Adriana winced and glared at him as he thanked her rival for his 'good cheer'; he registered his wife's pain and revealed his own embarrassment and shame. Theirs had been the first embrace in the reunion sequence, the long stare of uncertain wonder between the brothers broken by Antipholus of Ephesus's energetic 'No, I say nay to that' (5.1.372) as Adriana was about to repeat her dinnertime confusion between them. He held her in his arms tentatively, awkwardly; these two, one knew, had a lot of bridges to mend. The two pairs of brothers finally achieved their embraces after Aegeon's unfastened chains had clattered to the floor, an event that followed hard upon the Goldsmith's last little moment of fuss about *his* chain. Then, and most movingly, those two elegantly dressed young men in turn took their ragged, exhausted father, just rescued from death's door, in their arms and Aemilia began her final speech of blessing, receiving the embraces of her sons as she declared her heavy burden finally delivered. The verbal benedictions done, she blessed everyone manually as they knelt in front of her before making their exits to the gossips' feast: the Duke, benevolent and eager; Aegeon returning her long, hesitant gaze before going in, without an embrace – thirty-three years of separation, and a nun's habit, clearly requiring a great deal more thought on both sides; Adriana compelled, in spite of protest, to accompany the Courtesan; Luciana, silent through the scene, once moving close to Antipholus of Syracuse but forced away again by the pressure of the scene's events and now departing alone; an unwilling Balthazar, his financial obsessions and sartorial vulgarity strongly suggesting that abbeys are unfamiliar territory; and Aegeon's erstwhile guard, respectfully removing his cap and leaving his sword at the door – an exquisitely detailed and thoughtful sequence of exits. The two pairs of twins were thus left to face the future, Antipholus of Ephesus much less certain that he regarded it with enthusiasm than his brother – for he'd not been searching for anyone, anywhere, and life for him had been just fine until this appalling day. He watched his brother kiss his servant Dromio on the lips, a kiss that rendered thanks for loyalty and patience and friendship through years of wandering, but also marked the end of all that; for, now that it was no longer to be just the two of them, things would never be quite the same again. The Ephesian Dromio watched that kiss too and seemed to will his master to perceive the need for symmetry. His Antipholus did, indeed, think about the possibility for a moment or two; but there was no way that he could change so quickly – or that this director would be tempted along so sentimental a road. Perceiving the unkissed Dromio's disappointment, Antipholus of Syracuse rescued the situation by instructing his servant to 'Embrace thy brother there', a piece of sensitivity to the text that was typical of so much in the production. And so the two shaven-headed, bare-kneed sufferers of the play's blows and buffets, real and metaphorical, were left alone to discover from each other, with poignant hopefulness, that after all they were sweet-faced youths, and to scurry off, hand in hand, after the rest. And it was all done in precisely two hours, without fuss and without self-indulgence, by constant alertness and sensitivity to the play's language and delight in the wonders of the story it has to tell. A pity we weren't allowed to applaud it quite as soon as we wanted to.

25 Eric Mallett as Dromio of Ephesus and Dan Milne as Dromio of Syracuse, *The Comedy of Errors*, 5.1, directed by Tim Supple, RSC, 1996.

The year's most significant staging of a history play, and the latest 1996 production to find space in this review, was the English Touring Company's version of both parts of *Henry IV*, directed by Stephen Unwin. It opened in October at the Lyceum, Crewe at the beginning of a national tour scheduled to take it on to the Old Vic in the spring of 1997. Its simple, unfussy box set of dark oak panels was the work of Pamela Howard (described in the programme as 'Scenographer' rather than designer) and it served well for both court and tavern; an extra half-width panelled wall flown in at centre stage effectively provided greater intimacy, while the flying out of the back wall created the outdoors – a starlit sky for Gadshill

26 Gary Waldhorn as Henry IV, *Henry IV, Part 1*, 1.1, directed by Stephen Unwin, English Touring Theatre, 1996.

and Wales, a seashore for the Northumbrian scenes, apple trees in autumnal sunshine for Gloucestershire. If 'scenographers' provide working spaces for actors that are unobtrusively effective and atmospherically suggestive, which this was, they are certainly to be encouraged. Costumes, equally unfussy, were 'timeless Elizabethan' throughout, the King mostly in black, Falstaff mostly in red, Hal variable but finishing part II in a startlingly white, high-buttoned suit of the kind favoured by the late Mr Nehru.

The production's main *raison d'être* was to present Timothy West and his son Sam as Falstaff and Hal, casting designed, presumably, with more than just box office in mind, since the prince's relationship with father and with surrogate father may be said to drive the play. There were intelligent and interesting performances from both of them, but whether, in the end, we learned anything new about Hal's paternal relationships is a question. Sam West's Hal, tall and slender, with curly golden hair and finely chiselled features, was never less than elegant – and he never intended to be. His sense of utter certainty about his separateness from his Eastcheap companions was very striking. Not that he didn't enjoy himself in the tavern; there was much genuine pleasure in the meetings with Falstaff, their stomach-bumping greeting technique obviously the product of long practice, but the ultimate aloofness, the certainty that he could never truly relax into this world, were always part of his conscious, not subconscious, awareness. He began the first soliloquy – 'I know you all' – as a simple, wholly familiar, almost tired, statement of fact, becoming intellectually involved in the expression of newly arriving ideas only as he warmed to the notion of achieving extra credit for reformation. 'I do . . . I *will*', he said to Falstaff at the end of the play-acting, and the second verb, uttered calmly and with quietly matter-of-fact precision as he removed the cushion from his head to return to his own persona and looked Falstaff straight in the eye, came as no surprise to either of them, though Falstaff flinched as he was forced publicly to acknowledge its unequivocal message. With Gary Waldhorn's old, bald-headed, melancholy Henry IV, austere almost to the point of grimness, Hal was dutiful, listening intently in the part I interview to the measured and inexorable tones of those irrefutable accusations, his answer deriving from that listening, not something he'd arrived with, ready prepared. But the relationship remained cold, even in the death-bed scene, the yearning for filial affection, brought out by some recent Henrys, not breaking surface – or, perhaps more accurately, not being allowed to break surface – in Waldhorn's intelligently spoken, sad, but in the end rather distancing portrait of self-recrimination and loneliness.

Nor was the emotional heart of the piece to be found in Timothy West's Falstaff, at least not consistently. This was a constantly engaging and inventive performance, full of illuminating choices and deft touches, technically astute, rarely less than interesting and entertaining; but somehow real power and revelation eluded it, for in the final analysis it lacked danger. If the Hal/Falstaff relationship is to work at full throttle one must surely be conscious of the twin threats of the absolute ruthlessness of Falstaff's pursuit of self-interest and the desperate vulnerability to which his emotional commitment to Hal exposes him – the good old duo of pity and fear, in fact. Timothy West gave us a highly intelligent, engagingly self-aware old aristocrat, patronizingly contemptuous of those from lower social origins, conscious of, and pleased with, his own verbal dexterity and observant of his own performance, sharp, astute, and ultimately detached. Hal's rejection of him was not really shattering for him, or for us. We knew it was coming all along, and we knew, too, that Hal knew it was coming. It was calmly spoken, Hal looking, after the first sentence, to the Lord Chief Justice for approval (and with a strong suggestion of 'I told you I would'). He walked over

27 Timothy West as Falstaff and Samuel West as Prince Hal, *Henry IV, Part 1*, 1.2, directed by Stephen Unwin, English Touring Theatre, 1996.

to Falstaff at 'Make less thy body hence', the two men standing, apparently quite calmly, looking each other straight in the face. There was no great sense of pain for Hal in the moment, and as he moved back into the procession, no sense either that Falstaff had been irrecoverably humiliated or emotionally destroyed by the blow. He might, indeed, have genuinely believed that he would be 'sent for soon, at night'; and about Prince John's and the Lord Chief Justice's approval of the King's 'fair' proceeding there seemed no sense of vindictive triumph, no hidden irony. One came away from the scene with a strong sense of depths left unplumbed.

But there were revelations too in Timothy West's performance, and elsewhere in the production. 'Well, 'tis no matter', he said casually, 'honour pricks me on', and wandered off the stage; two seconds later he boomeranged back on again: 'But how if honour prick me off when I come on?', and the force of the conjunction, and the pressure of the interrogative, were all the more urgent, and funny, for the little exit. 'If I had a thousand sons', he said as he sat on his little camp stool admiring, with a connoisseur's eye, the colour of the sherris-sack in the glass his page had just filled from the barrel which it was his principal duty to carry round the battlefield. And at the mention of sons he patted the boy affectionately, and wistfully, on the head, looking into space. The little rueful shrug he gave to Coleville of the Dale as Prince John ordered Coleville off to execution spoke volumes about Falstaff's attitude to Prince John, about his fellow feeling for Coleville, about his sense of responsibility for placing him in the position he was, and about his own temperamental disinclination to find the energy to do anything about any of these things. There was genuine joy and real triumph when Falstaff hit upon the perfect lie in the big part I tavern scene: the idea that he had known it was Hal all along came to him in a flash of inspiration following the blankness and near panic at first produced by the Prince's challenge and it was greeted with a huge burst of laughter and with applause led by Hal. The contrast at the equivalent moment in the part II tavern scene was well pointed, Falstaff's floundering arrival at the excuse of dispraising Hal before the wicked producing only lukewarm laughter and absolutely no applause.

Eighteen actors performed the play's two parts, most of them taking several roles. Performances were generally at least adequate, often much more than that, particular pleasures being Ian Flintoff's steely Lord Chief Justice, fiercely earnest and splendidly humourless, and Mary Macleod's round-faced, white-capped Mistress Quickly, looking all plainness and Puritanism, as if she'd just stepped in from a Dutch painting to scatter her *double-entendres* so lavishly. There was one major disappointment, and one gem. Patterson Joseph, splendid in part II in the thankless part of Pistol, with accents from several continents to match the range of his theatrical allusions, failed to find anything beyond wild energy in Hotspur, the epitaph from his widow seeming to have little to do with the hollowness of the ranting, gesticulating, and often simply absurd figure we had seen. And then there was Joseph O'Conor's wonderful Shallow. He had already made more of Northumberland than one can reasonably expect, threatening much greater danger to Henry through his impressive stillness in his part I scene than ever his son did in rushing madly round the stage; and in part II, as his daughter-in-law's recriminations for his desertion of her husband hit home, he seemed physically to dwindle and sink into his chair, hiding his face as shame and grief ebbed the strength and the ability to face the world out of him – of course he had to go and hide in Scotland. O'Conor's Shallow was a wonderfully sunny figure, with none of the grasping querulousness that David Bradley (perfectly legitimately too) found in the part at Stratford a few years ago. In battered straw hat and old green jacket he exuded innocent pleasure in the world and in his own way of life, a beam of self-satisfied goodwill (slightly reminiscent of Mr Godfrey in *Dad's Army*) illuminating his face as he twinkled and blinked and peered, and forgot, his way through his transactions with Sir John. His verbal articulation was a little whistly through the teeth, slightly soggy about the gums, as though he'd neglected to put in his lower set of dentures. He wore little half spectacles to check the role of recruits and laughed a wonderfully wheezy laugh at all Falstaff's witticisms about them. When he remembered his performance as Sir Dagonet in Arthur's show he drifted away into memories so distant, and yet so vivid, that he was lost to the present world and stood transfixed. 'And is old Double dead?', he repeated disbelievingly, and pulled back on an imaginary bow, watching the arrow in its flight, little whistles charting its progress. And as it failed to reach the target we'd rather expected, and flew on and on, out of imaginary sight, and he gave it a little wave of farewell, his old eyes blinking into the distance, one realized that the arrow and its shooter had become one, and the personal goodbye to the remarkable bowman had been said and his own unavoidable journey contemplated: 'Death, as the psalmist saith, is certain.' This was a magical performance.

And it was part of an admirable production, sensible and clear in its overall direction, intelligent and thoughtful in nearly all its choices, an ideal introduction to the play for anyone coming to it for the first time. But for all its clarity, and for all that it was often touching and funny, it was rarely surprising and only in the few moments I have isolated (above all in Joseph O'Conor's Shallow) did it really extend one's awareness of the play and make one think about it differently from before. And it thus raised the question of the kind of audience at which directors of Shakespeare productions (at the Globe, at Stratford, or on tour) should be aiming. And the answer, it has to be admitted, is probably not at anyone likely to be invited to write a review for *Shakespeare Survey* – which is more or less where this essay started.

PROFESSIONAL SHAKESPEARE PRODUCTIONS IN THE BRITISH ISLES, JANUARY–DECEMBER 1995

compiled by

NIKY RATHBONE

Most of the productions listed are by professional or semi-professional companies. Information is mainly taken from newspaper reviews held in the Birmingham Shakespeare Library. There were an exceptional number of productions of *Macbeth*, many reflecting the civil war in Bosnia. By contrast, only one professional production of *King Lear* was recorded.

ALL'S WELL THAT ENDS WELL

The Nuffield Theatre, Southampton: November 1995
Director: Patrick Sandford
Designer: Farnsworth
A modern dress production.

ANTONY AND CLEOPATRA

Moving Theatre Company
The Riverside Studios, Hammersmith, British and European tour: April 1995
Director/Cleopatra: Vanessa Redgrave
Re-cast during the tour. Also performed in Wormwood Scrubs Prison.

Northern Broadsides, tour: November 1995–
Director/Antony: Barry Rutter
Designer: Jessica Worral

AS YOU LIKE IT

Cheek by Jowl, tour continues.
See *Shakespeare Survey 48*.

The Midsommer Actors, Arundel Festival and tour: June 1995–
A walkabout production, touring open air venues. The native inhabitants of the Forest of Arden were presented as Native American Indians.

Tamara Theatre at the Dudley Shakespeare Festival, Dudley Castle: summer 1995
Director: Robert Leach
Rosalind: Sonia Ritter
Tamara are a new theatre company, and intend to perform Shakespeare annually at Dudley Castle.

Scapegoat Theatre Company, Norwich, tour of open air sites around Norwich: June 1995

Stafford Shakespeare Company, Stafford Castle: July 1995
Director: Rob Swinton
Set in 18th century pre-Revolutionary France, and performed by a mixed amateur and professional cast.

Hot Air Productions, The Oxford Shakespeare Festival: July 1995

A and BC Theatre: August 1995
Director: Gregory Thompson
The change of location from Court to Forest was effected by costume changes, signalling that essentially they were the same place.

THE COMEDY OF ERRORS

Third Party Theatre, tour of the UK and Lebanon: February 1995–
Director: Ben Benison

Lincoln Shakespeare Company, The Lawn, Lincoln: March 1995
Director: Simon Hollingworth

The Duke's Playhouse, open air promenade production in Williamson Park, Lancaster: June 1995–
Director: Han Duijvendak
Antipholus of Syracuse was presented as defensive in character, his twin as aggressive.

Oddsocks, in association with Chester Gateway Theatre, touring as the Pembroke Players, Chester Playhouse and open air venues: May 1995–
Director: Ellie Mackenzie
Presented as fast, funny spectacle, with jugglers, fire-eaters and stilt-walkers.

Wondrous Light at the Edinburgh Fringe: August 1995
Director: A. Anderson
Presented as a black and white Twenties film, bursting into colour just before the final unravelling of the plot.

CORIOLANUS

The RSC at the Barbican, London. Transfer from Stratford. See *Shakespeare Survey 49*.

West Yorkshire Playhouse: May 1995
Director/Coriolanus: Steven Berkoff
Presented on a black and white set, the production evoked images of European Fascism. Mime was used effectively, particularly for battle scenes, and the text was cut.

CYMBELINE

The Tabard Theatre, Chiswick: November 1995
Director: David Evans Rees
An all-male cast.

HAMLET

The Wolsey Theatre, Ipswich: February 1995
Director: Antony Tucker
Set in northern Europe in the late nineteenth century.

The New Victoria Theatre, Stoke on Trent: March 1995
Director: Peter Cheesman

The Almeida Theatre Company at Hackney Empire, London; European and American tour: April 1995–
Director: Jonathan Kent
Designer: Peter J. Davidson
Hamlet: Ralph Fiennes
See *Shakespeare Survey 49*.

The Royal National Theatre in Brixton Prison: April 1995
Organized by the Education Department, with the prisoners taking roles as extras.

Friction Theatre, tour: May 1995–
Director: Mark Swatkins
Designers: Karen Moore and Susannah Towne
Set in the early eighties. Yorick's ghost became one of the gravediggers.

Heartbreak Productions, Leamington, tour of heritage sites, with *Romeo and Juliet* June 1995–
Director: Ben Crocker
The company presented themselves as strolling players in Elizabethan costume.

Full Circle, Jersey at the Edinburgh Festival Fringe: August 1995
Set in a Victorian mental institution.

Shenandoah Shakespeare Express (USA), tour: August 1995–
Director: Ralph Alan Cohen

The Belgrade Theatre, Coventry: September 1995
Director: Simon Usher
Hamlet: Adrian Scarborough

Theatre Babel, the MacRobert Arts Centre, Stirling, Tramway, Glasgow and tour, with *Romeo and Juliet*: September 1995–
Director: Peter McAllister
A modern setting.

Mappa Mundi at the Sherman Theatre, Cardiff and tour: October 1995–
Director: Rob Lane
Played as a thriller film set in the Elizabethan period.

Second Age at the Riverbank Theatre, Dublin: October 1995
Director: Brian de Salvo
Designer: Bryan O'Donoghue
Played in the round.

Traffic of the Stage, tour with *A Midsummer Night's Dream*: October 1995–

The Royal Lyceum, Edinburgh: November 1995
Director: Kenny Ireland
Designer: Robin Don
Music: Matthew Scott

Adaptations

Fortinbras gets drunk, by Janusz Głoewacki
Timepiece Productions at the Polish Theatre, Hammersmith: February 1995
Director: Nina Marc
A black comedy, presented as a Norwegian plot to seize the throne of Denmark.

Hamlet, adapted by George Dillon
Vital Theatre at the Komedia Theatre, Brighton: and summer tour: March 1995
A humorous adaptation for a small cast.

Hamlet II, Prince of Jutland by Cargill Thompson
Our Theatre Company, Manchester, Edinburgh Festival Fringe: August 1995
A monologue performed by Rik Forrest, which corrected the historical inaccuracies in the play.

Hamlet by Arthur Smith
Edinburgh Fringe Festival: September 1995
A forty-minute humorous adaptation.

Hamlet
An adaptation for six actors.
Right Angle Productions at the Brixton Shaw Theatre, London: November 1995–
Director: Nicholas Pegg
Hamlet seeks solace in theatricality and illusion after his father's death.

HENRY IV

BBC2 TV 28 October 1995
Director: John Caird
Falstaff: David Calder
Henry IV: Ronald Pickup
Prince Hal: Jonathan Firth
A conflation of Parts I and II, with some lines from *Henry V*.

HENRY V

The RSC at the Barbican Theatre, London, 1995
Transfer from Stratford. See *Shakespeare Survey 49*.

Adaptations

Henry V, Lion of England
One-man show written and directed by Nick Hennegan, at the Studio Theatre, Waterside, Stratford. Adapted and produced by Ray Rosenberg in association with Maverick Theatre and the Birmingham Stage Company. Starring Michael Shaw.

Henry V: After Agincourt by Peter Mottley
Roy Heather in a touring one man show: November 1995
Agincourt and Henry seen from Pistol's viewpoint.

HENRY VI

Henry VI: the Battle for the Throne
RSC tour continues. See *Shakespeare Survey 49*.

JULIUS CAESAR

The RSC at the Royal Shakespeare Theatre, Stratford: June 1995–
Director: Sir Peter Hall
Designer: John Gunter
Music: Guy Woolfenden
Caesar: Christopher Benjamin
Brutus: John Nettles
Antony: Hugh Quarshie
See *Shakespeare Survey 49*.

Wales Actors' Company, tour of Welsh open air sites: August 1995–
Director: Ruth Garnault

KING LEAR

West Yorkshire Playhouse and Hackney Empire, London: November 1995–
Director: Jude Kelly
Designer: Paul Andrews
Lear: Warren Mitchell

Adaptations

Lear's Fool by David Henry Wilson
Michael Friend Productions, the Jermyn Street Theatre, London: February 1995
Played with *The Tragedy of Lady Macbeth.*
Director: Michael Friend
Designer: David Myerscough-Jones

LOVE'S LABOUR'S LOST

The Festival Theatre, Edinburgh: March 1995
Director: Ian Judge
An Oxbridge college setting.
See *Shakespeare Survey 48*.

MACBETH

The Octagon Theatre, Bolton: February 1995
Director: Lawrence Till
Designer: Richard Foxton
A production reminiscent of the film *Pulp Fiction*, set in gangland Manchester. The witches, played by men, doubled as murderers and the Porter.

Journeyman Productions at the New End Theatre, London: February 1995–
Director: Kate Brooke
Designer: Dan Jones
A modern dress production. The witches played as nymphettes, doubled as servants, courtiers and the Porter, pervading the action.

Traffic of the Stage, tour: March 1995–
Revival of the 1990–1991 production. See *Shakespeare Survey 46*.

Kicking Bardom, Croydon, schools tour: March 1995
Director: Mark Helyar
Designer: Gerry Livesey
Set in the present day. The production was accompanied by schools workshops.

Factotum Theatre Company, West Sussex, tour of open air sites: June 1995–
Director: William Gilbert

Theatre Adrift and Greenwich Theatre Studio Company, London: August 1995
Director: Mark Feakins
Set during the eighteenth century Jacobite Rebellion.

Tokyo Shakespeare Company, Edinburgh Festival: August 1995
Much of the text was replaced by kabuki mime

in this bilingual production. Only the final act was played in full, with selected highlights from the earlier acts.

Edinburgh Arts Theatre, Edinburgh Festival Fringe: August 1995
This amateur production is included for the interest of extracts from *Macbeth* in Scots, in Robin Lorimer's translation, played after some performances.

Zip Theatre and Open Door, Wolverhampton; tour: September 1995–
A mainly black cast in a production with references to both modern Africa and ancient Scotland.

Birmingham Repertory Theatre: September 1995
Director: Bill Alexander
Designer: Ruari Murchison
Macbeth: Jeffery Kissoon
A production set on the battlefields of modern Europe.

English Touring Theatre, Crewe, co-production with the Lyric Theatre, Hammersmith: September 1995
Director: Stephen Unwin
Designer: Franzisk Wilcken
Music: Corin Buckeridge

Phoebus Cart at Greenwich Theatre, London and tour: September 1995
Director/Macbeth: Mark Rylance
Designer: Jenny Tiramani
Music: Claire van Kampen
Set in a world of contemporary alternative religious cults. The Porter took on multiple roles as Third Murderer and Messenger to Lady Macduff. Young Macduff returned as a ghost proclaiming the movement of Birnam Wood.

Tricycle, London Borough of Brent: October 1995
Director: Nicholas Kent
Designer: Christine Marfleet
Set on a metal-shrouded stage, and reflecting the Bosnian civil war.

The Crucible, Sheffield: November 1995
Director: Philip Franks
Designer: Gideon Davey
Repeated use was made of the chorus *Dies Irae*.

Liverpool Everyman Theatre: September–October 1995
Director: Peter Rowe
Music: Rick Jukes
The production made considerable use of video, and again reflected the Bosnian civil war.

Adaptations

Macbeth
Classworks Theatre Company, Cambridge: January 1995
A cast of six touring schools.

An Gaisgeach, The Hero by Ike Isaksen
Invisible Bouncers, Inverness at Aberdeen University Festival of one-act plays, and Scottish tour: March 1995
Producer: Alasdair McDonald
In Gaelic, Doric, an Aberdeenshire dialect, and English. A rehabilitation of Macbeth based on historical fact.

The Tragedy of Lady Macbeth by David Henry Wilson
Michael Friend Productions at the Jermyn Street Theatre, London: February 1995
Played as a double bill with *Lear's Fool*, giving a new perspective on the tragedies.

The Amazon Macbeth
The Actors' Theatre at The Nightingale pub theatre, Brighton: May 1995
Director: Nicholas Young
Set in South America.

MEASURE FOR MEASURE

The RSC at the Barbican Theatre, London
Transfer from Stratford. See *Shakespeare Survey 49*.

Show of Strength Theatre at the Hen and Chicken, Bristol: January 1995
Director: Andrew Hilton
Designer: James Helps
What You Will Theatre Company, tour of small London venues: March 1995
Playing the unrehearsed First Folio text, to simulate the conditions under which Shakespeare's company supposedly worked.

Adaptations

Measure for Measure, adapted by Kelvin Goodspeed
Generation Dance Theatre at the Finsborough, London Fringe Theatre: February 1995
A brief adaptation, with dancers representing the inner emotions of the characters.

Groping for Trout in a Peculiar River by Stephen Jameson
Sturdy Beggars Theatre Company at the BAC, Battersea, London
A re-evaluation of the monarchy, British politics and Shakespeare.

THE MERCHANT OF VENICE

The Royal Lyceum, Edinburgh: August 1995
Translator: Elisabeth Plessen
Director: Peter Zadek
Designer: Wilfried Minks
Shylock: Gert Voss
Portia: Eva Mattes
Played in German with English surtitles. The production reflected Zadek's childhood experience of 1930s Berlin, though it was set in the modern world of banking. Shylock was represented as apparently interchangeable with Antonio. First performed, Vienna, 1988.

THE MERRY WIVES OF WINDSOR

The Olivier Theatre, Royal National Theatre, London: January 1995–
Director: Terry Hands
Designer: Timothy O'Brien
Music: Guy Woolfenden
Falstaff: Denis Quilley
See *Shakespeare Survey 49*.

Illyria Theatre Company, tour of open air sites, with *A Midsummer Night's Dream*: June 1995–

A MIDSUMMER NIGHT'S DREAM

The RSC at the Barbican Theatre, London
Transfer from Stratford. See *Shakespeare Survey 49*.

Compass Theatre Company
Tour continues. See *Shakespeare Survey 49*.

Tilt Theatre Company, tour of London and Cornwall: February 1995–
Director: Sue Colverd

Breach of the Peace at the Bridewell, London: April 1995
Director: Carol Metcalfe
Played in the round, in imitation of a circus, and opening with a trapeze act by Circus Space.

Classic Theatre Company, The New End Theatre, London: May 1995
Director: Michael Cabot
Set in 1930s clubland, with Puck as a sardonic, sequined Master of Ceremonies, Oberon as northern nouveau riche and Hippolyta popping valium tablets.

The New Shakespeare Company at the Regent's Park Open Air Theatre, London: June 1995–
Director: John Doyle
Designer: James Merifield
Puck: Toyah Willcox
An Edwardian setting.

Illyria Theatre Company, tour of open air sites, with *The Merry Wives of Windsor*: June 1995–

Theatre Set Up, international tour: June 1995–
Director: Wendy McPhee
Set in the 1890s with Mendelssohn's music played on a dulcimer and Beerbohm Tree fairies.

OpenHand Productions, Cambridge College gardens: July 1995

The Ninagawa Company at Plymouth Pavilions and Newcastle Playhouse: July 1995
Director: Yukio Ninagawa
Designer: Tsukasa Nakagoshi
In Japanese. A production influenced by Noh theatre, but with elements representing modern life.

The Northcott Theatre, Exeter, open air production in Rougemount Castle grounds: July 1995
Director: John Durnin

Hot Air Productions: Cambridge College gardens: July 1995

Hot Air Productions, Oxford College gardens: July 1995
Two distinct productions, running simultaneously in Oxford and Cambridge.

Theatre Unbound, Leeds Shakespeare Festival and tour with *Twelfth Night*: August 1995–
Director: Robert Williamson
Billed as the first Leeds Shakespeare Festival. Theatre Unbound are a company of fifteen professional actors.

Soho Drama Group, London, in association with Kent Shakespeare Project, tour of open air sites: August 1995–
Director: Lake Dixon
Six professionals, taking two roles each, and changing gender each time they switched from mortal to fairy roles. Amateurs were used as extras.

Traffic of the Stage, tour with *Hamlet*: October 1995–

The Octagon Theatre, Bolton: October 1995
Director: Ian Forrest
Designer: Richard Foxton
A modern dress production with the fairies in Edwardian bathing costumes.

Adaptations

If We Shadows
Insomniac Productions and Dancehouse Theatre, London. Tour continues. See *Shakespeare Survey 49*.

If We Shadows
The Custard Factory, Birmingham and tour: February 1995
Director: Joanna Reed
The young lovers are forced to act out their roles in a distorted fairy tale.

A Midsummer Night's Dream
Unicorn Arts Theatre, London tour: September 1995
An abridged version for schools and young audiences.

A Midsummer Night's Dream
Humberside Theatre in Education, tour of schools in Hull and Humberside: October 1995–
Director: John Hazlett
Three performers playing selected scenes.

The Fairy Queen
London Coliseum: October 1995
Directors: Robert Israel and Danya Ramicova
A new adaptation of Purcell's opera.

MUCH ADO ABOUT NOTHING

Hysterica Passio Theatre Company at Southwark Playhouse. April 1995
Director: James Menzies-Kitchin
Women were cast in many male roles.

Lincoln Shakespeare Company at the Bishop's Old Palace, Lincoln and short local tour: July 1995.

Albion Shakespeare Company, Norwich, tour of open air venues near London, with *Richard III*: July 1995–
Director/Benedict: John Hales

Hot Air Productions, Oxford College Gardens: July 1995

OpenHand Productions, Cambridge College gardens: September 1995–

OTHELLO

Hot Air Productions, Oxford College Gardens: July 1995

Wooden O Productions, The Bridewell Theatre, London: October 1995
Director: Christopher Geelan
Designer: Briget Kimak

The Watermill Theatre, Newbury: October 1995
Director: Edward Hall
Designer: Georgia Sion
Played in an intimate space, with a minimal set.

Harrogate Theatre: November 1995
Director: Andrew Manley
Othello, played by a white actor, was blacked up on stage. The production was intended as a study in racial perceptions.

RICHARD II

The Cottesloe Theatre, Royal National Theatre, London: June 1995–
Director: Deborah Warner
Designer: Hildegard Bechtler
Richard: Fiona Shaw
See *Shakespeare Survey 49*.

RICHARD III

Derby Playhouse: February 1995
Director: Mark Clements
Designer: Steven Richardson
A popular modern production, revived November 1995, with cast changes.

The New Shakespeare Company, Regent's Park Open Air Theatre: May 1995–
Director: Brian Cox
Designer: Tanya McCallin
Richard: Jasper Britton
Played as grand guignol comedy, using video projection screens for the murder scenes.

Ludlow Castle: June 1995
Director: Val May
The throne was placed high on the set, with the murders taking place in a killing room below.

Albion Shakespeare company, Norwich, tour of open air sites around London, with *Much Ado About Nothing*: July 1995
Director: John Hales
A traditional production with lavish costumes.

Freestage Theatre, Byelorussia at the Demarco Foundation, Edinburgh Fringe Festival: August 1995
Director: Valery Mazynsky
The production drew parallels between Byelorussia and mediaeval England.

The RSC at the Royal Shakespeare Theatre, Stratford: September 1995–
Director: Stephen Pimlott
Designer: Tobias Hoheisel
Music: Jason Carr
Richard: David Troughton

ROMEO AND JULIET

Sound and Fury at the Duke of Cambridge, London: January 1995
Director: Alex Chisholm

A circus setting, a male Nurse, and a female Friar Lawrence.

West Yorkshire Playhouse and the Lyric Theatre, Hammersmith: February 1995–
Director: Neil Bartlett
Romeo: Stuart Bunce
Juliet: Emily Woof
A modern dress production, played on an almost bare stage dominated by a bed.

The Sherman Theatre, Cardiff and Welsh tour: February 1995–
Director: Glen Watford
Designer: Claire Lyth
A black and white set, and an unusually youthful Lady Capulet and Nurse.

Actions and Words at Jackson's Lane Theatre, London: March 1995
Director: David Beaton

Second Age at the Riverbank Theatre, Dublin: February 1995
Director: Jim Cullerton

Katch 22, tour: February 1995
Performed by a young theatre company, who aim to stage the classics.

The RSC at the Royal Shakespeare Theatre, Stratford: April 1995–
Director: Adrian Noble
Designer: Kendra Ullyart
Romeo: Zubin Varla
Juliet: Lucy Whybrow
See *Shakespeare Survey 49*.

Hot Air Productions, Cambridge College gardens: July 1995–

Theatre Babel, Glasgow tour of Scotland, with *Hamlet*: September 1995–
Director: Maggie Kinloch
The production also toured in 1994 with *Twelfth Night*.

The Byre Theatre, St. Andrews: October 1995
Director: Ken Alexander

Contact Theatre, the University Theatre, Manchester: October 1995
Director: Irina Brown
Designer: Andrew Wood
A simple, futuristic set, based on the wheel of fortune.

Adaptations

Romeo and Juliet
Solent People's Theatre, tour: February 1995
Director: Mollie Guilfoyle
A very cut version, set in Belfast, and incorporating modern Irish poetry.

Romeo and Juliet Get Laid
Rebellious Subjects, London tour: April 1995
Director/Narrator/Romeo: Andrew Saltman
A thirty minute bawdy comedy played by an all-male cast.

Romeo and Juliet
Ophaboom Theatre Company, tour: May 1995
A comic adaptation based on Commedia dell'Arte.

Roméo et Juliette
Nada Theatre, Edinburgh Festival Fringe: August 1995
The adaptation revolved around the balcony scene, with the set transforming from bed to tomb to balcony, to re-stage the lovers' original encounter.

THE TAMING OF THE SHREW

Mappa Mundi, tour continues. See *Shakespeare Survey 49*.

The RSC at the Royal Shakespeare Theatre, Stratford: April 1995–
Director: Gale Edwards
Designer: Russell Craig

Music: Stephen Warbeck
Katherine: Josie Lawrence
Petruchio/Sly: Michael Siberry
See *Shakespeare Survey 49*.

Leicester Haymarket: April 1995–
Director: Mihai Maniutiu
Designer: Doina Levinta
Katherine: Josette Simon

THE TEMPEST

The European Theatre Group at the ADC, Cambridge: January 1995
In the last three hours of Prospero's life, he sorts through the fragments of memory searching for peace.

Box Hedge Theatre Company, tour of open air venues: June 1995–
Director: Katie Milledge
Designer: David Farley

OpenHand Productions, Cambridge College gardens: July 1995
Included a spectacular masque.

Shenandoah Shakespeare Express, Edinburgh Festival Fringe: August 1995
Director: Jim Waren
A fast-moving, imaginative production.

Performance Exchange, Edinburgh Festival Fringe: September 1995
Director/Designer: Risah Atah
Daniel Foley in a one-man version which attempted to fuse Western and Eastern theatrical techniques.

Nottingham Playhouse, Theatre Clwyd and Hebbel Theatre, Berlin, joint production British and European tour: September 1995–
Director: Silviu Purcarete
Designer: Jose Manuel Melo
Music: Vasile Sirli
A stark, haunting production, set in a madhouse, with Ariel represented by a chorus of aged violinists, and all the characters apparently the products of Prospero's deranged mind.

Kaos Theatre, the Brewery Arts Centre, Cirencester and tour: September 1995–
Director: Xavier Leret
A combination of Indian dance and Commedia dell'Arte.

Crew of Patches Theatre Company, Deal and Dover castles: November 1995

Adaptations

The Tempest
The Royal National Theatre, tour: January 1995–. An adaptation for schools, played by six actors.

Storm in a Teacup
Intimate Exchange Theatre Company, tour: February 1995
An adaptation for young people.

Foul Conspiracy
The Rhoda McGaw Theatre, Woking: February 1995

Caliban on Thursday, an adaptation from the novel by John Ginger
Electric Company at the Festival Club, Edinburgh Festival Fringe: August 1995
Director: Mary Considine
Played alternately with *The Tempest*.

The Tempest
Movingstage Marionette Company production on the Theatre Barge, London: 1995
Revival of the 1987 production.

TITUS ANDRONICUS

The Market Theatre of Johannesburg at the West Yorkshire Playhouse Courtyard Theatre,

Leeds and the Cottesloe Royal National Theatre, London: July 1995
Director: Gregory Doran
Designer: Nadya Cohen
Titus Andronicus: Antony Sher
Set in modern Africa.

TROILUS AND CRESSIDA

The London Theatre Base at the Diorama Theatre, Camden Town, London: September 1995

TWELFTH NIGHT

The RSC at the Barbican Theatre, London. Transfer from Stratford. See *Shakespeare Survey 49*.

The Library Theatre, Manchester: February 1995
Director: Chris Honer
Designer: Michael Pavelka
Music: Chris Jordan
Set in the Jazz Age Twenties.

Nottingham Playhouse: February 1995–
Director: David Pountney
Designers: Huntley/Muir
Music: John Harle
Set on an island paradise in the present day.

The Belgrade Theatre, Coventry: March 1995
Director: Rumu Sen-Gupta

Oracle Productions at the Wimbledon Theatre and tour: March 1995–
Director/Malvolio: Peter Benedict
Designer: James Hendry
Music: William Hetherington
Many of the cast were drawn from well-known TV dramas. The production was played as a film in the making.

Hot Air Productions, Cambridge College gardens; Oxford and Cambridge Shakespeare Festival: July 1995

Theatre Unbound, the Leeds Shakespeare Festival and tour with *A Midsummer Night's Dream*: July 1995
Director: David Cottis
Festival Director/Feste: Robert Williamson
A professional company, advertised as producing the first Leeds Shakespeare Festival.

York Theatre Royal: October 1995
Director: John Doyle
Designer: James Merifield
Music: Catherine Jayes
A Victorian Christmas setting inspired by Tissot.

The Oxford Stage Company, Oxford Playhouse and tour: October 1995–
Director: John Retallack
Music: David Brett

The Mercury Theatre, Colchester: November 1995
Director: Pat Trueman
A surrealist production, opening with an acrobatic display.

THE WINTER'S TALE

The Royal Theatre, Northampton: October 1995
Director: Dilys Hamlett
Designer: Ray Lett
A traditional production.

The Library Theatre, Manchester: November 1995
Director: Chris Honer
Designer: Paul Kondres
A modern dress production.

THE SONNETS AND POEMS

The Rape of Lucrece
A and BC Theatre Company tour of London fringe venues: February 1995–
Director: Gregory Thompson
A small group production derived from theatre

workshops, linking the poem to Shakespeare's major tragedies.

Venus and Adonis
The Actors' Touring Company with the Hairy Marys; tour: February 1995–
Director: Nick Philippou
Designer: Stewart Laing

Venus and Adonis
The Young Vic Company, the Young Vic, London: February 1995
Adapted and directed by: Mark Rylance
Music: Claire van Kampen
Designer: Jenny Tiramani

MISCELLANEOUS

Bardathon
Lincoln Shakespeare Company: June 1995
Non-stop rehearsed readings of all the plays, done with props and costumes.

Dark Lady of the Sonnets
Etcetera Theatre, Camden, London: January 1995–
The Lady: Matthew Scott

My Son Will
The Waterside Theatre, Stratford: spring 1995
One man show by Colin George, concerning Shakespeare's father and their relationship.

Sawn Off Shakespeare
Torsion Theatre, tour: April 1995
Brief, comic adaptations of *Hamlet, Macbeth* and *Romeo and Juliet.*

THE YEAR'S CONTRIBUTIONS TO SHAKESPEARE STUDIES

1. CRITICAL STUDIES

reviewed by JANETTE DILLON

Note: publication details of writings reviewed appear at the end of each article.

GENERAL

Surprisingly perhaps, three of the best books this year recycle earlier material. Patricia Parker's *Shakespeare from the Margins*, Louis Montrose's *The Purpose of Playing* and Lisa Jardine's *Reading Shakespeare Historically* all contain much that is familiar from published essays by these critics, yet succeed in creating integrated and exciting new wholes. All insist too on the necessity for historicism while simultaneously displaying an impulse to distance themselves from the early 1980s thrust of New Historicism. Patricia Parker's book primarily concentrates on language, but from a perspective which is carefully tuned to the historical resonances of both individual words and discursive contexts. Her book comprises a set of wonderfully subtle and detailed explorations of particular verbal matrices within Shakespeare's plays, revealing more forcefully than any general argument could that there is no language free of ideology. As her title indicates, part of her project is to pay serious attention to plays hitherto marginalized in the study of Shakespeare, and her approach really opens up some relatively under-explored plays as well as the familiar ones. A further aspect of her title is its application to her method, which is often to begin with an apparently marginal or inconsequential quotation. In chapter 6, for example, she starts from the point of Parolles' advice to Bertram in *All's Well That Ends Well* to 'take a more dilated farewell' and works outwards from there towards a learned and wide-ranging study of the figure of increase. Her best work is quite simply dazzling, and demonstrates how much work remains to be done on the cultural specificity of language.

Louis Montrose's book is in two parts: a general account of theatrical conditions in Shakespeare's time and a discussion of *A Midsummer Night's Dream*. The first part is a concise and masterly synthesis (with full and proper acknowledgement to E. K. Chambers) of the most important primary materials for the study of the Elizabethan theatre. Statutes, proclamations, letters, all familiar to scholars of the period, are cited, and sometimes quoted at some length, in a way that makes their significance clear and accessible to the reader coming to this material for the first time. Long footnotes, to which my gut-response is initially hostile, justify themselves here by their comparable conciseness and their useful separation of secondary scholarship from the primary materials. They regularly provide helpful bibliographical guides and brief summaries of the critical debate in particular specialist areas, and the student reader thus stands to gain from the book in this respect as well as for its clear outline of the conditions of playing. The publishers have made matters easier too by supplying footnotes on the page. (One wonders why Chicago, also Parker's publisher, couldn't have offered her and her readers the same service.) The second part, on *A Midsummer Night's Dream*, builds on and expands Montrose's earlier well-known essay of 1983 with a slightly different emphasis, as Montrose himself points out, on Elizabethan discourses of gender rather than of erotic desire. As in the first part, the contextualizing of the analysis within current critical discourses is full and explicit and the arguments lucidly and elegantly constructed.

Jardine reproduces a decade's work in terms of a powerful and committed argument for the necessity of historicist analysis and brings a freshness to the project by engaging critically with her own history as well as with the discipline of historicism. She demonstrates a willingness to revise in two senses: she bothers to reshape some of her earlier essays for this book; and she constructively disagrees with much of it in the present context. Part of the pleasure of reading her work is the way the active engagement of the writing stimulates a similarly active response, even when one of disagreement, in the reader. Her return, via a chapter on *Twelfth Night*, to the arguments on gender of her earlier book, *Still Harping on Daughters* (1983; 2nd edn 1989), is a good example of this kind of writing. Two previously unpublished chapters, on *King Lear* and *The Jew of Malta*, are especially fascinating, though not all chapters are so focused. A rather dull chapter on *The Changeling* seems out of place, and the volume concludes with a rather slight and disappointing piece on *Hamlet* (also the subject of an earlier chapter). The penultimate chapter, which uses the myth of Penelope unpicking her tapestry as a way of thinking about the task of scholars of women's history, and is much more characteristic of Jardine at her best both in the challenge of its polemic and in its generosity to other scholars, would have made a more fitting conclusion.

Though Parker, Montrose and Jardine are at the forefront of current theoretical work, all write clear, jargon-free prose using only those terms which have become indispensable to certain kinds of theoretical understanding. Their clarity may be appreciated by setting their books next to Eric Mallin's *Inscribing the Time.* Mallin looks at three plays, *Troilus and Cressida*, *Hamlet* and *Twelfth Night*, with a view to analysing how they negotiate their historical moment. The book, published in a New Historicist series, pays the customary homage to Foucault and lacks the critical distance insisted on by the three writers above. The theoretical introduction is useful in many respects, arguing carefully for the ways in which 'context' is both necessary and unstable. On the other hand, many of the features which are set to become an irritant as the book proceeds are already in place here: the overcomplicated vocabulary, the excessive length, the argument from analogy and, more worryingly, the presentation of a pleasing metaphor as though it had logical force. The nature of the book's historicism is also disturbing, since Mallin seems to exploit the perception that history is not a fixed quantity as an excuse for distorting it to his own ends. More than half of the book is taken up with two chapters on *Hamlet* which hinge on arguments that necessitate dating the play after James's accession. Mallin's strategy is simple: he chooses the second Quarto (printed 1604) as his text and makes the date of its printing the crucial one. Mallin, who often seeks to pre-empt criticism, notes here that to some critics his argument 'will smack of historical implausibility'. He's right.

Pauline Kiernan's book, *Shakespeare's Theory of Drama*, addresses a very simple question: 'Why did Shakespeare write *drama*?' It maintains an elegant simplicity in its mode of address throughout, despite producing some very sophisticated analyses. This a groundbreaking book, the kind it is hard to believe hasn't already been written. Kiernan identifies a curious reluctance on the part of critics 'to explore the possibility that Shakespeare might have developed a theory of drama'. Her book attempts to remedy that omission by proposing that he did, and that it is notable for its rejection of the mimetic aesthetic we typically associate with Renaissance theorists such as Sidney. In place of imitation, she argues, Shakespeare valued 'presence'; his insistence on working in a medium that 'privileges the living human body' is the logical corollary of his rejection of an aesthetic that freezes nature into rhetorical tropes. This deceptively simple argument results in some stunning rereadings of both poems and plays. Kiernan writes about the Ovidian shapes of Shakespeare's poetry in a way that sheds genuinely new light and persuasively revises some classic moments in the art and nature debate through close, even literal-minded, attention to what is actually said. Her reading of the masque in *The Tempest* and Prospero's comment on it ('Our revels now are ended' etc.), a speech virtually fossilized by criticism into a metaphorical comment on life in general, should be required reading for students.

David Beauregard's understanding of Shakespeare's 'poetic' in *Virtue's Own Feature* could scarcely be more different from Kiernan's. He has no doubt that Shakespeare is working according to a model derived from Sidney and is undisturbed by any distinction between plays and poetry; indeed he routinely refers to Shakespeare as a 'poet'. For Beauregard the plays are texts to be read, and to be read via an intellectual tradition to which Shakespeare's relative lack of education is no bar. 'A first-rate mind', Beauregard tells us, could comprehend Aristotle and St Thomas whether or not the possessor had read them directly. His readings of plays are reductive and over-schematic, and the refusal to think about performance leads to some strange emphases. Hamlet's speech to the players, for example, though returned to as a central point of reference, is not considered at all in terms of the different kinds of acting prevalent on the Elizabethan stage, but offered as crucial evidence for Shakespeare's 'remarkable familiarity with Aristotelian–Thomistic ethical categories'. And keeping theatre out means too that the didactic poetic supposedly informing the plays never has to confront the anti-theatrical lobby of the period which attacked the drama precisely for its corrupting qualities. Beauregard's project is clear, if old-fashioned: he reads for unity. Ambiguity and exploration are dirty words here. 'If the plays are approached as vehicles for raising questions and posing problems without providing the answers and solutions such questions and problems imply', Beauregard argues, we are left with 'an incomplete and failed corpus'.

A book more productively shaped by its refusal of current critical trends is Philip Davis's *Sudden Shakespeare*. Davis's strength is in the close analysis of short extracts; and though in a single sentence he dismisses politically oriented criticism without further argument as 'bleak' and 'damaging', his textual criticism is at least enriched by a literary historical context provided by the examination of parallels with contemporary writers such as Hooker, Bruno, Campanella and, above all, Montaigne. Davis is interested in how those writers explore the nature of human consciousness and demonstrates especially well how the numerous parallels between Montaigne and Shakespeare expose not merely borrowing or similarity in their thinking but important differences between their ways of conceiving selves. The first chapter is particularly stimulating and original: starting with the sonnets, Davis shows very specifically how the creation of pattern and tension worked out in the placing of syntax and rhyme in individual lines is a technique that in dramatic form does the work of producing our sense of thought in action. As with Beauregard, however, performance seems to obtrude itself as the acid test. The attempt in chapter 4 to separate performance from other considerations seems misguided in terms of the nature of this study, and simply goes over similar ground to other chapters but without the tightness of focus which is the strength of chapters 1 and 2. Here some rather hollow remarks and a tendency towards bardolatry replace the active and energetic analysis which makes the first part of the book so stimulating to read.

John Russell Brown's *William Shakespeare: Writing for Performance* is, as its title suggests, unlike the previous two books in its emphasis on the need to consider the plays as performed pieces, but it shares their resistance to the enemy Theory, who is here ignored rather than attacked. Brown's approach is dominated by an interest in character which owes as much to Stanislavski as to liberal humanism. Each chapter draws on a number of passages from different plays, though a marked fondness for *Richard II* emerges overall. The best chapter is the last, where Brown abandons character and language for story and plot and draws attention to some of the things Shakespeare was *not* doing or trying to do. Brown's strengths are his experience and his enthusiasm: he has the capacity to make his readers think in detail about how a particular section of text might make meanings in performance, and his quotations from twentieth-century actors, if anecdotal, are often thought-provoking.

René Fortin's essays (published as *Gaining upon Certainty*), like Davis's book, demonstrate that not everything written before the advent of 'theory', or in opposition to it, is uttered from a position of unthinking liberal humanism or operates on the crass assumption that dramatic characters are indistinguishable from real people. The editors single out 'Desolation and the Better Life' as perhaps Fortin's best essay on Shakespeare, and this is indeed a perceptive piece on the significance of what Fortin refers to as the 'two voices' of Shakespearian tragedy, the heroic and the 'kenotic', the ways respectively of self-assertion and selfless patience. Other pieces are more original in their approach than this one, however. The early 'Allegory and Genre in *Othello*' is a thoughtful study of the interrelation between the allegorical and naturalistic elements of the play. Its conclusion, like several of Fortin's conclusions here, tends towards a somewhat sentimentalized rhetoric, but the body of the essay offers a clear and concise account of how the play refuses coherent genre.

Gordon Williams's *Shakespeare, Sex and the Print Revolution* is full of information and lively discussion, but has more to say about Shakespeare and sex than about the print revolution, which, though regularly invoked as a context, is scarcely pursued as a motivating argument. Part I includes some broad perspectives and is particularly good on censorship, but Part II, having made the unexceptional and unexceptionable point that classical stories were made more widely accessible through print, goes on to compare Shakespeare's adaptations of those stories with the versions available to him with barely a reference to print. (Eccentrically, too, there is no reference anywhere to Elizabeth Eisenstein's important work on printing.) Hence, when Williams begins his introduction to Part III, it is like taking up a different book. And here, where Williams does concentrate more pointedly on the print revolution, there is a marked tendency to collapse the concept of printed culture with that of written culture, together with a failure to give adequate consideration to manuscript culture (or to the very special and different status of printed playtexts, a topic which surfaces only belatedly in the conclusion). The book maps out important territory for scholars to consider, but leaves much work to be done.

The authority of the written word is a topic also taken up by *Reading and Writing in Shakespeare*, edited by David Bergeron. As in Lisa Jardine's book, there is a sense that Shakespeare is something of a constraining focus here, and that the more apt subject, if the publisher could have been persuaded of it, was the subject of reading and writing in Renaissance dramatic texts. Robert Knapp's concluding essay, which sets out to make reference to all the contributions, a project that can scarcely avoid a certain laboured quality, nevertheless formulates a useful binary between what he calls the 'Cabbalistic' and the 'Baconian' Shakespeare (an opposition, broadly speaking, between the plays as self-sufficient authorities unto themselves and as objects of a quasi-scientific inquiry). Both these Shakespeares, he argues, 'result finally from an irreducible difference between two realms that perpetually interact in and as it were around the plays: the realm of custom and performance, within which provisional authority is possible, though fleeting, and the realm of ... the "fixed text," which ultimately subverts all merely local knowledge and authority, while nowhere itself (except through the medium of institutions) embodying or representing any identifiable authority'. This is an important distinction, and it is a pity that so few contributors actually confront it. The essays by Douglas Lanier and Martin Elsky posing questions about text, authorship and readership are the most interesting, but neither gives much attention to the difference between performed and printed status.

Cross-culturalism emerges as a dominant interest in a good deal of work published this year. Cultural exchange is the theme of *Shakespeare Survey 48*, and translation study, noted as a thriving area of work by David Lindley in last year's equivalent of this review, offers one route into this area. Inga-Stina Ewbank examines a German dictionary to show how far language has already been appropriated in various ways before translation even begins. Geoffrey Hartman's 1993 Weimar lecture, 'Shakespeare and the Ethical Question', published in English translation this year, speaks for a particularly resonant cultural moment, addressing the German Shakespeare Society at the point of the rejoining of its Eastern and Western groups. Hartman's starting point is a question aimed at the familiar assumptions of eighteenth- and nineteenth-century criticism: if Shakespeare's work is so close to nature as virtually to 'be' nature itself, how can we ask what its ethical position is?

Further translated work offers a range of cross-cultural perspectives. Jean-Pierre Maquerlot, in *Shakespeare and the Mannerist Tradition*, uses mannerism as a framework for analysing a group of Shakespeare's plays (*Julius Caesar, Hamlet, Troilus and Cressida, All's Well* and *Measure for Measure*). Some good, brief formulations of the mannerist perspective point the way towards illuminating approaches to the plays ('everything attracts the eye, nothing arrests it'; 'a Mannerist work always has a streak of narcissism about it, as if much of the enjoyment comes from detecting the irony of the message'), but the term is occasionally in danger of collapsing into something like the mere awareness of artifice or eschewing of emotional engagement. Maquerlot's reading is nevertheless an enriching one, though there seems to me to be no good argument for singling out these plays alone as reflecting the concerns he identifies. Nor is this the first time that mannerist features have been identified in Shakespeare's plays, and the book might have profited from a more extended recognition of and engagement with predecessors such as Cyrus Hoy and Patrick Cruttwell, together with more recognition of critical work produced over the last fifteen years.

Michele Marrapodi's collection of conference papers, *Il Mondo Italiano del Teatro Inglese del Rinascimento*, is an oddly fragmented and underedited volume, which never seems to make up its mind about its published status. Only six papers, of very differing length and levels of formality, are included, and the collection ends with a round table discussion asking questions about and making reference to numerous papers not included. All the papers have footnotes, and the round table questions and answers are tidied up into continuous prose, yet elsewhere it pretends to lay claim to something like the character of a transcript, including every opportunity for mutual back-slapping between the delegates. This comes across as *faux-naif*, an endless reminder of what a 'marvellous, and marvellously good' conference we missed. We even hear the thanks to the Dean of the Faculty and the Conference secretary. As the last words of the book have it, 'Thank you'.

Vikram Chopra's collection, *Shakespeare: Varied Perspectives*, also registers a certain unevenness in its mix of papers. Though many of the contributors here retain a universalizing perspective on Shakespeare, others, notably Jyotsna Singh, building on the work of Ania Loomba, comment on the damage such a perspective has done. Howard Felperin, in an important piece on 'Historicizing Bardolatry', argues that the transcendentalization of Shakespeare's plays is inextricably linked with their historicization in a necessary 'cultural dialectic': it was the effect of Malone's historicizing labours, culminating in the weight of annotation provided in the Third Variorum edition, that necessitated Coleridge's need to find a way of reading Shakespeare that could surmount the barrier represented by precisely such annotation. 'At a certain level', Felperin argues, 'the historical text must always offer itself, and be received, as timeless and universal textuality even as it remains at another level remote and specific historicity – *if it is to be interpreted at all.*'

As Patricia Parker's work demonstrates, one of the areas where much detailed historicizing work remains to be done is that of vocabulary. David Hillman's thought-provoking essay on 'discretion' as a word much abused and resorted to at the end of the sixteenth century, 'Puttenham, Shakespeare, and the Abuse of Rhetoric', is a welcome contribution to this enterprise. Hillman points out Puttenham's self-confessed 'difficultie' with the word, and proceeds to demonstrate how it is called into use to separate social and mental categories and made to endorse the reliability of those who have it and to highlight the untrustworthiness of those who don't.

Pictures as well as words figure among this year's topics, and John Astington's 'Three Shakespearean Prints' reminds us that Shakespeare and his audience were dependent on graphic as well as verbal culture for their sense of the familiar. Astington does not claim the prints he examines as direct sources for Shakespeare, though his title and sub-headings rather misleadingly seem to imply such a relationship. Two of the three parallels are well taken (though the parallel between the graveyard scene of *Hamlet* and the tradition of the dance of death could be illustrated from any number of visual sources); but Mercutio's famous remark that 'the bawdy hand of the dial is now upon the prick of noon' scarcely needs the scholarly documentation of a visual tradition to suggest its currency. Hands on pricks must surely have been familiar via a less mediated form of experience.

Theatre and theory also elicit general essays. Robert Weimann, in 'Thresholds to Memory and Commodity in Shakespeare's Endings', discusses Shakespeare's endings as mediating between the world of representation and that of the spectators, drawing attention to their function of transferring authority to the audience; James Forse, in 'After 1603 Theatre is spelled – JAMES', mounts a persuasive argument for seeing James I as adopting a deliberate strategy of appropriation with regard to the public stage; and Richard Levin, in 'Negative Evidence', launches another attack on current critical methodologies, this time with particular animus against Marxism and Freudianism.

COMEDIES

Michael Mangan's *Preface to Shakespeare's Comedies* is the companion volume to his useful 1991 *Preface* to the tragedies, and treads a careful line between overlap and new material. Overlap is in fact small, so that although the reference section in the later book retains the same categories (short biographies, further reading and the London theatres), there are differences within them. The only disadvantage of this is that future readers will need to be aware, for example, that for a concise, yet detailed overview of 'Shakespeare's England' and the contemporary London theatres, they will need to turn to *A Preface to Shakespeare's Tragedies*. This is not to say that the 'prefatory' material of the new book is less relevant; it is simply more specific to the subject of comedy, offering a wide-ranging and informative view of some 'Contexts of Comedy'. Readings of the plays are lively and well-directed towards a student audience.

Several volumes in the Theory in Practice series, also designed for undergraduates, have now started appearing on individual Shakespeare plays. The format invites four critics each to outline a particular theory of their choice and to show how it works in practice on the text in question; and the four explorations are framed by the editor's attempt to contextualize them, both through a summary of their approach and through questions on their pieces, as well as via a general Introduction and Endpiece. On the whole the format is successful, though there is, unavoidably perhaps, some disparity between the levels of address in different essays. Howard Felperin's opening essay in Nigel Wood's volume on *The Tempest*, one of the first two volumes to appear on Shakespeare (six have come out altogether over the period of this review), makes few concessions to students new to theory (a readership invited by the format), but sets an admirable, if challenging, example. Felperin wrestles with Frederick Jameson's question about how a text that fulfils an ideological function can also embody a Utopian impulse and looks at the interaction and overlap between Marxist and idealist ways of thinking. John Turner's reading of the play through the approaches to fairytale and myth of Bettelheim and Malinowski is also acute and enabling, making space for attention to the play's compelling insistence on the power of story as well as to its scepticism towards this literally spellbinding power.

The volume on *Measure for Measure* is less successful overall, despite a strong piece by Richard Wilson reading the play through the lens of Foucault's work and a long essay by Nicholas Radel raising some crucial theoretical questions in relation to feminism. Radel presents a clear account of his chosen critic (Patrocinio P. Schweickart), the methodology in question and its application to *Measure for Measure*, and the essay is as meticulous on the play as on theoretical issues. Radel does not claim to solve all the problems he raises; his real strength lies in the clarity and detail with which he makes visible the *process* of thinking through theoretical problems in relation to the play.

An incipient dilution of the project is apparent in the volume on *The Merchant of Venice*, where three out of four contributors are doing something rather different from what the series first seemed to promote. John Drakakis's approach, as Wood's headnote admits, 'draws on several associated perceptions'; Karen Newman uses her own earlier work as the point of reference (though the theoretical perspective might be argued to be that of the exchange paradigm explored by Marcel Mauss and Lévi-Strauss); and Scott Wilson happily acknowledges that 'heterology', which he takes from Georges Bataille as the ground of his approach, is not a literary theory. Only Graham Holderness takes a particular essay, Marx's 'On the Jewish Question', and shows how it can offer a productive way of reading the play. This is not to say that the volume does not contain interesting work, simply that its coherence within the terms of the series is dubious.

The Merchant of Venice also receives consideration from Lynn Enterline in *The Tears of Narcissus*. Since this book offers a long introduction outlining what it proposes to do, I may well be at risk of simplifying its project in this short space. It is emphatically not a thematic study of either the Narcissus trope or the topics of melancholy or masculinity, but rather an exploration of the apparent necessity of relationship between figures of self-reflection and figures of loss. In a study ranging over the works of Tasso, Marvell, Shakespeare and Webster, two Shakespeare plays are the subject of chapter 4: *The Comedy of Errors* and *The Merchant of Venice*. Enterline leans heavily on psychoanalytic theory, especially the work of Lacan, in order to raise questions about subjectivity, sexual identity and literary form. Despite occasionally knotted and abstract writing, the book offers interesting and illuminating readings of the texts it selects, though I find it less persuasive on Shakespeare than on Marvell or *The Duchess of Malfi* and, surprisingly, less persuasive on *Merchant* than on *Errors*. Antonio's inexplicable sadness at the opening of *Merchant* would seem at first sight to offer more fruitful ground than *Errors* for this kind of interpretation, but Enterline's reading here collapses into a rather laboured exposition of the supposed pun on 'dam'/'damn', which is forced into an argument concerning the production of gendered identity and value. Nevertheless, there is much that is good in the book as a whole, even if the tantalizingly brief reading of 'The Phoenix and the Turtle' suggests that Shakespeare's poetry might have been more receptive to this kind of study than the plays turn out to be.

Mark Breitenberg's study of *Anxious Masculinity in Early Modern England* overlaps with Enterline's book in its concerns. Like Enterline, Breitenberg is interested in the conjunction of masculinity and loss, but Breitenberg is keen to maintain the framework of Elizabethan humours theory alongside a Lacanian psychoanalytic perspective. His basic thesis is that male subjectivity is premised upon unfulfilled desire, and that the satisfaction of desire must therefore mark 'the death of a subjectivity that knows itself as desire'. The thesis is plausible, but more persuasive in relation to some texts than others: Burton, for example, proves more rewarding than Bacon. As far as Shakespearian texts go, Breitenberg, like Enterline, is more interested in Shakespeare's comic and lyric writing than in tragedy or history, though *Othello* figures briefly in a chapter which is more generally focused on jealousy. Separate chapters are devoted to *The Rape of Lucrece* and *Love's Labour's Lost*. The historicist argument about male subjectivity, however, tends to veer towards the commonplace observation that desire is fuelled by inaccessibility, particularly in the discussion of *Love's Labour's Lost*, and is in danger of collapsing into mere truism.

I have to admit to finding Mark Stavig's book on *Romeo and Juliet* and *A Midsummer Night's Dream* virtually unreadable. The introduction pulls its punches to such an extent that a real subject fails to emerge. It is clear from the title, *The Forms of Things Unknown: Renaissance Metaphor in 'Romeo and Juliet' and 'A Midsummer Night's Dream'*, that the topic is metaphor; but the attempt to locate the approach to metaphor seems to consist of paying brief lip-service to various critical methodologies without dismissing any. Individual chapters are structured around a chart of concentric circles provided on the first full recto page, with a key indicating how to read abbreviations in the text (UL = upper left, UC = upper centre etc.). The rest of the chapter then proceeds to formulate sentences like this one on *Romeo and Juliet*: 'The swords that should be used by a community of people acting with dignity and wisdom UR to preserve the peace UC have instead become "neighbor-stained" (1.1.82) with blood LR'. The usefulness of the charts is questionable; the act of reading the chapters via the charts simply not worth the candle.

Margo Hendricks's more thought-provoking study of the *Dream*, '"Obscured by dreams": Race, Empire, and Shakespeare's *A Midsummer Night's Dream*', focuses on the way a particular production of the play in 1991 exploited the Indian boy as an erotic and ornamental object, thereby demonstrating 'the fantasy of a silent, accepting native who neither speaks nor resists'. From there Hendricks goes on to ask the question why Shakespeare's Indian boy had to be Indian. The answer is complex and involves a wide-ranging examination of early modern narratives constructing India as both an imaginary and a geographical reality. His presence in the play, she argues, embodies '*mestizaje*' (mixedness) and constitutes 'an ideological fissure producing a problematic dichotomy between race as genealogy and race as ethnicity or physical appearance'.

The theme of cultural appropriation is again evident in Thomas Moisan's 'Interlinear Trysting and "household stuff": the Latin Lesson and the Domestication of Learning in *The Taming of the Shrew*', which ranges over a number of other issues too, from the value of learning to the representation of gender. Natasha Korda's 'Household Kates: Domesticating Commodities in *The Taming of the Shrew*' is more difficult, but also more rewarding. Taking as her starting-point Petruccio's own wordplay on Kates/'cates' (bought provisions, usually more dainty than those produced at home), Korda situates Petruccio's taming strategies within the context of the changing commodity form emergent in the early modern period.

The only piece I have come across on *Twelfth Night* this year is also one of the year's most rewarding essays on any of the comedies. This is Keir Elam's 'The Fertile Eunuch: *Twelfth Night*, Early Modern Intercourse, and the Fruits of Castration', an extended assessment of the centrality of the eunuch trope to comedy. Though only traces of this history survive in Shakespeare's *Twelfth Night*, Elam presents a wonderfully rich and detailed examination of how the threat of castration regularly produces the same familiar plot-elements of twinship and crossdressing in new and unfamiliar combinations.

The last plays dominate two book-length studies, T. G. Bishop's *Shakespeare and the Theatre of Wonder* and Maurice Hunt's *Shakespeare's Labored Art*. Bishop takes three plays for study: *The Comedy of Errors* (where Bishop's work overlaps interestingly with Enterline's), *Pericles* and *The Winter's Tale*. There is excellent material in this study, especially on the two late plays. The long final chapter on *The Winter's Tale* justifies its length in asking and offering answers to probing questions about the play. Bishop underlines the centrality of Mamillius and brings out the importance of both story-telling and what he calls the play's awareness of the 'stakes *for* theatre' (Bishop's emphasis) inherent in its setting of 'versions of theatre' against one another. My main reservation is that the whole critical project set out in chapter 1, where the author analyses the theoretical stances towards wonder adopted by Plato, Aristotle and Longinus, is barely necessary to the work of the book. Few references to it crop up after chapter 1, and the conclusion, which does not mention it at all, concludes (rightly, in my view) that the 'Shakespearean practice of wonder ... is underpinned by little aesthetic theory articulated anywhere in the period'. Despite, or perhaps because of, its lack of relation to the book's self-proclaimed theoretical underpinning, the conclusion offers a brief, but powerfully suggestive, explanation of Shakespeare's lack of interest in masque as a self-sufficient form.

The opening chapter of Hunt's book, examining attitudes to work in Shakespeare's lifetime, looks promising and offers shrewd insights (for example, the perception that King James's view of monarchy was making Parliament feel like dispossessed labourers, and the tying of this perception to the more familiar one of the notorious, parasitic idleness of James's courtiers). Disappointingly, however, it dwindles into a theme-based study without an argument. The writing suggests a methodology spurred by technology: the book reads as though Hunt has run computer searches on the words of his subtitle, 'stir' and 'work', together with appropriate synonyms like 'tempest' and 'labour', and given us little more than the raw data in published form. Though such searches are undeniably useful starting points (and the author may not of course have worked in this way at all), the data have to be collected with questions in mind. One cannot substitute for real questions a mere stylistic emphasis on the chosen words, such as frequently emerges in passages of Hunt's writing that demonstrate the strain of showing the relevance of this research.

This is a pity, since the subject looks like a fruitful one that might have produced a nuanced and detailed account of the interaction between a specific aspect of Jacobean culture and the possible meanings of Shakespeare's late plays.

Several essays in *Shakespeare Survey* examine *The Tempest* from the perspective of cultural exchange; and Arthur Kinney's 'Revisiting *The Tempest*' highlights Rosier's 1605 pamphlet on the new world and a sermon on the story of Jonah by Henry Smith, reminding us that the contexts for the play are wider and more various than the rather single-minded attention of critics to Strachey's letter would suggest.

TRAGEDIES

Naomi Conn Liebler's *Shakespeare's Festive Tragedy* has the look and assurance of a book set to make its mark on Shakespeare studies. Its aim, as the title's reference to C. L. Barber's work suggests, is to extend the examination of the role of ritual to the tragedies, and some interesting readings of the plays result. Happily, too, this book does not single out the 'big four' for special treatment, but considers *Julius Caesar*, *Titus Andronicus* and a range of other tragedies with as much seriousness as *Lear*, *Hamlet* and *Macbeth*, while omitting *Othello* altogether. Yet the book does not quite live up to the inflated claims of its blurb. Neither the extension of the festive theme to the tragedies nor the incorporation of anthropological work is as original as its publicity suggests: François Laroque's *Shakespeare's Festive World* (1991) was not restricted as to genre, and anthropology has been a visible element in both performance theory and New Historicism for some time. More seriously, the book also falls short of the claims made for it by bundling too many theories together, and it is unclear whether the focus on ritual is on ritual as an element within dramatic content or as an aspect of dramatic form. The attempt to bring together Aristotle, Brecht and Artaud in chapter 2, for example, effaces important distinctions between these theorists by describing them all as sharing the view that theatre 'shak[es] people up and disturb[s] their complacencies'. A specific example of how too many theories spoil the broth may be cited from Liebler's reading of *Coriolanus* within the double matrix of the mummers' play of St George and Turner's theory of liminality. Here is how she moves, in tortured prose, from Turner through Derrida and Aristotle to St George: 'The boundary-transgressive ambiguity characteristic of both liminality and the Derridean *pharmakon*, as well as the Aristotelian precept for difference within similarity, can be seen in the hero-monster identification, while the "incorporation" occurs in George's victory and distribution of largesse.' Yet it would be unfair to suggest that the book is predominantly badly written. Despite a problematic mixing of theoretical frameworks throughout, Liebler often writes acutely on both plays and theories, suggesting new perspectives.

John Kerrigan's *Revenge Tragedy: Aeschylus to Armageddon* is wide-ranging and learned, full of fascinating detail and comparative analysis. Kerrigan considers topics as diverse as how the possible shapes of revenge interact with those of detective fiction, or how Maria Callas, famous in the role of Medea, uses her position as *diva* to take certain kinds of revenge on her public. Several chapters include discussion of Shakespeare. Kerrigan writes revealingly on various plays, but the best of these chapters is probably the one devoted to 'Shakespeare and the Comic Strain', which concentrates not so much on Shakespeare's comedies as on the comic impulse inherent in his revenge tragedies (and is also particularly suggestive on the role of Balurdo in Marston's *Antonio's Revenge*). The book is in the main elegantly and clearly written, though occasional rhetorical flourishes substitute for clarity: 'A revenge plot undoes modernity, establishing a "regeneration of time" (Eliade's phrase) in the space before history starts.' It sounds great; but what does it mean?

Some good work is reprinted in a new

collection of essays on *Shakespearean Tragedy and Gender*, edited by Shirley Nelson Garner and Madelon Sprengnether, but the organization of the volume as a whole is disappointing. Given the historicizing perspective of both the introduction (which situates 1980, when two important anthologies of feminist work appeared at the same time as Greenblatt's *Renaissance Self-Fashioning*, as a landmark year) and the concluding essays (which present autobiographical narratives by Shirley Garner and Gayle Greene, locating their own interest in Shakespeare within the changing emphasis of the academy from the 1950s to the 1990s), it is a pity that this anthology bypasses the potential critical narrative underpinning its own selection. Only four out of twelve pieces, excluding the introduction, are here published for the first time, and the earliest, Janet Adelman's essay on fantasies of maternal power in *Macbeth*, dates from 1985. Even Gayle Greene's concluding narrative, here entitled 'Leaving Shakespeare', is excerpted from a longer piece first published in 1991. Though an argument can be made for reprinting good work, including Neely's piece on madness and Kahn's on *Timon*, the refusal to organize these earlier pieces alongside new work in a way that tries to situate them within the perspective of developing feminism insisted on in the introduction signals an opportunity missed. Simply erasing the difference between new and reprinted work suggests a commercial rather than an academic project, and yet another publisher looking for a safe seller quickly assembled.

Geoffrey Miles's book, *Shakespeare and the Constant Romans*, begins by providing a useful summary of Stoic principles, looking at Cicero, Seneca and neo-Stoicism, especially in the work of Montaigne. The account is well-written, balanced and careful, though Miles is ultimately more informative and persuasive on Stoicism than on the plays (which occupy less than half the book). The argument Miles wants to make – that the ending of *Antony and Cleopatra* is 'more liberating' than those of the other two Roman plays – is spoiled, as he admits, by the standard dating, which places *Coriolanus* later than *Antony and Cleopatra*. Though Miles is to be commended for admitting this, the last page is a dangerous place to do it. It does work against his argument about what Shakespeare was doing and leaves the project of *Coriolanus* difficult to explain.

Antony and Cleopatra is one of two tragedies to receive the Theory in Practice treatment discussed above. Both volumes (the other is on *Hamlet*) are surprisingly slim compared with those on the comedies, and the general introductory material is much less helpful. The introduction to *Antony and Cleopatra* is laconic in the extreme at under eight pages, while the *Hamlet* introduction wastes too much space fending off attacks on 'theory' and whining about the failure of the *TLS* to give the series 'serious' space. This new degree of embattlement about the project is unhelpful. Of the two volumes, the one on *Antony and Cleopatra* is livelier and more challenging. Unusually, three of its four essays are by women, and the essays by Dympna Callaghan and Mary Hamer using the theoretical approaches respectively of Gayatri Spivack and Luce Irigaray examine the play within productively different feminist frameworks, interestingly juxtaposed. Both describe the work of their chosen critic with clarity and enthusiasm and write with a strong sense of polemic. Though I would resist some of Hamer's arguments regarding the play, I found her direct and confrontational style pleasurably different from most academic writing.

The essays in the *Hamlet* volume, like those on *The Merchant of Venice*, seem to register some discomfort with the format, given their somewhat oblique relation to theoretical issues. Sharon Ouditt openly states her intention to do something different from the general expectation of the series format and offers instead an account and critique of three feminist approaches. Nigel Wheale, writing on Lacan, again offers a critique rather than an application, so that his subject is more Lacan then *Hamlet*. Mark Thornton Burnett, using the figure of the trickster as a way into the play, does not identify a central critical text and could scarcely be said to be applying an accepted theoretical approach, as the multiple focus of Nigel Wood's preamble to his essay indicates; and Peter Holland, like Oudítt and Wheale, offers a critique of Raymond Williams's work on drama in performance rather than a straight 'application'. All these essays offer interesting and productive approaches to the material, but seem to be fighting the focus and format of the volume. It is a pity, too, that the format does not allow contributors to take up overlap with each other. Holland, in exploring Williams's failure to theorize the dramatic performance as fully distinct from the dramatic text, clearly signals the need for further work in establishing this as a proper area for theoretical investigation, while Wheale encounters the same absence of theorization in exploring Lacan's inability to deal with performance, rightly noting that 'rigorous performance criticism is even now a strangely underdeveloped branch of drama studies'; yet there is nowhere for the two to take this up with each other, nor do the editors take it up in their framing pieces.

Hamlet in Japan, edited by Yoshiko Uéno, returns us to the issue of cross-culturalism, and several contributors concentrate on Japanese mediations of *Hamlet*, in either textual or dramatic form. Takeshi Murakami provides a useful chronological overview of Shakespeare and *Hamlet* in Japan; Hiroshi Izubuchi collects rewritings of *Hamlet*, notes the dominance of the novel form in these rewritings and speculates on why Japanese writers are so interested in the father/son relationship and so apparently uninterested in the question of legitimate succession. Kazuko Matsuoka surveys Tokyo productions, pointing out the astounding number (seventeen in 1990) following the staging of Bergman's *Hamlet* there. Adrian Pinnington provides a fascinating account of a Japanese Noh adaptation, staged in English. The first two parts of the book group essays respectively on the history and ideas of Shakespeare's age and on representations of Ophelia and Gertrude. I found two of the pieces by younger Japanese scholars particularly interesting: Shoichiro Kawai's essay on imagination, a carefully researched contribution to dismantling, or at least complicating, the old binary of reason and passion, and Tetsuya Motohashi's piece on writing and playing space in the play. The latter is flawed by a misunderstanding of the specific and contradictory meanings of the term 'liberty' in sixteenth-century London (a misunderstanding fuelled by the carelessness of some of the critics to whose work the piece is indebted), and the writing is marked in places by cultivated difficulty, but the informing argument, that the play is structured around a polarity between the free space of play (and the players) and the restrictive authoritarianism of writing, is important and suggestive.

Two eloquent warnings against the dangerous anachronism of reading Shakespeare's plays as from within a realist aesthetic, 'The Case Against Hamlet' by Alistair Fowler (the British Academy Shakespeare Lecture for 1995) and 'Soliloquies and Wages in the Age of Emergent Consciousness' by Margreta de Grazia, take *Hamlet* as their test case. Both argue that the soliloquies resist being read as documents of a continuous inner life. For Fowler, this is because they deliberately incorporate multiple perspectives, while for de Grazia it is because they may speak with a voice which is detached from the individual speaker. Both, from different angles, note the potential importance of carrying or reading a book on stage and both explore the notion of Hamlet as Everyman rather than a particularized individual. The battle against realist reading is one that seems to need endless replaying in order to combat the still powerfully naturalized status of the realist aesthetic.

Othello is also prominent this year. Garner and Sprengnether's collection includes a special section on the play, and Chopra's collection includes three essays on it. Margo Hendricks's piece, published for the first time in the former anthology, seeks to show that 'Venice is a crucial yet often critically neglected racial persona in *Othello*', and this emphasis on Venice is also shared by Mark Matheson, who argues in 'Venetian Culture and the Politics of *Othello*' for the political importance of the Venetian republic to the play. (Similarly indicative of this emerging shared interest is the prominence of Venice in both Wood's introduction to his collection on *The Merchant of Venice* and Drakakis's essay for that collection.)

Emilia's obedience also emerges as a shared topic of interest: it figures in Hendricks's piece on Venice as a neglected player, and is the subject of Tom Flanigan's concise exploration of the different obediences of the play's two wives, Desdemona and Emilia, within the context of contemporary discourses inveighing against violent husbands but also recommending wifely submission. On a different tack, Martha Widmayer compares the two men whom Desdemona loves, Brabanzio and Othello, arguing for their similarity and for a tragedy that emerges out of the paradigm of a woman who marries a man like her father.

King Lear is the subject of less attention. J. G. Saunders, in '"Apparent Perversities": Text and Subtext in the Construction of the Role of Edgar in Brook's Film of *King Lear*', argues that Brook's interpretation was more interventionist than has been recognized. Charles Spinosa's 'The name and all th'addition': *King Lear*'s Opening Scene and the Common-Law Use' begins well, assembling important material on the transition in Shakespeare's time from possession to 'use' in landholding, and mounting a detailed case concerning the implications of these matters for identity. In the course of a long essay, however, Spinosa seems to lose direction and to revert disappointingly to older, untheorized formulations (Cordelia and Kent as having 'inwardness', Goneril and Regan as 'innocent of character') that seem to float free of the opening analysis of landholding.

Philip Armstrong's piece on 'Cartography and the Gaze in Shakespearean Tragedy and History' starts from a point similar to the area of interest so well covered in John Gillies's recent book, *Shakespeare and the Geography of Difference* (1994), and takes its examples from a number of different plays, concluding that theatre and cartography develop along a parallel trajectory towards a single mapping gaze.

HISTORIES

Robert Shaughnessy's book on *Representing Shakespeare* takes a brisk and lively look at twenty-five years in the life of the Royal Shakespeare Company (1963–88) and examines how its representations of Shakespeare's history plays over that period can be made to speak of the England in which they find themselves at the moment of representation. Shaughnessy's briskness, while preventing the book from becoming too bogged down in the details of production, is inevitably somewhat sketchy and allusive in its account of England in the period under discussion, and occasionally over-schematic in its equations, but the overall effect is of a coherent position confidently argued. The book's structure, however, conceals any easy access to a chronologically developing England from the 1960s to the 1980s in favour of a more topic-based approach. It must be acknowledged, too, that there is a paradox at the heart of a project which concerns itself with mediation but simultaneously seeks to efface another form of mediation central to its own workings: its reliance on second-hand material for its own sense of the productions it describes. I assume Shaughnessy has not personally seen them all and is relying on reviews and published interviews with directors for his accounts of what the productions were like, but he nowhere says so or confronts this problematic. Shaughnessy writes well, without jargon, weaving together description and quotations in a readable way, yet it is precisely the seamlessness of the job that produces the desire for some acknowledgement of and reflection on the seams.

Paola Pugliatti's *Shakespeare the Historian* is clearly written and organized. The broad argument for what Pugliatti calls, following Michael Hattaway, 'perspectivism' ('a dramatic cross-examination from differing points of view, embodied in different dramatic styles, of the issues raised and events enacted on the stage') is not new, but Pugliatti properly acknowledges the work of both earlier and contemporary critics in this area, and often highlights differences of approach within the broad spectrum. She has a firm grasp on her material, from plays and Tudor chronicles to Shakespeare criticism, and a facility for citing exactly apposite, and sometimes unfamiliar, quotations from sixteenth-century writers. Part I situates the subject within the current academy with admirable conciseness, and several brief chapters provide a clear outline of the aims and methods of Tudor historians as against the less sequential and more problem-oriented approach of Shakespeare's history plays. This part also offers suggestive comments on the 'reality effects' of the theatrical medium and the importance of the issue of verisimilitude to Renaissance theories of both history and poetry. Longer chapters in part II on how individual history plays problematize political issues go over well-trodden ground with a freshness of approach that combines close examination of sources, useful engagements with other critics and constant illumination of the plays. Part III ranges across the history plays by subject, looking at 'thresholds and margins'. This is among the most over-explored areas of Elizabethan drama in recent criticism, yet Pugliatti manages to keep this part of the study sufficiently firmly anchored in relevant detail to prevent it becoming yet another theoretical application of a tired category. Her accounts of the functioning of local government or the Elizabethan militia, for example, provide a thickness of description which helps to locate the issues discussed in a material world.

Another Theory in Practice collection addresses itself to *Henry IV Parts One and Two*. Here the essay by Peter Womack stands out as a model of good practice for the series' declared aims. Womack uses Walter Benjamin's work on seventeenth-century German tragic drama to construct an approach to the *Henry IV* plays which is packed but beautifully clear. He applies the techniques of what Brecht came to name 'epic theatre' to the plays, suggesting that critical approaches insistent on unity are asking the wrong questions. Womack demonstrates from a number of angles, ranging from incompatible time-frames to the character of Falstaff, that the plays are designed to foreground precisely the arbitrary imposition of design, and are hence resistant to a notion of design that would seek to naturalize its presence. Nowhere is the precision of Womack's argument more forcefully shown than in his responses to Nigel Wood's questions. Other pieces demonstrate the problem of pitching the arguments at comparable level. McDonald's explanation of Bakhtin's work seems to address a considerably less well-informed student than Goldberg's essay, which, though it begins with a clear and succinct account of critical work theorizing sexuality, becomes difficult to make sense of once it moves on to the plays. Nigel Wood's questions, together with Goldberg's correction of his mistaken assumptions, seem to indicate that he too had difficulty with this piece.

In 'The Emperor's New Body?' David Norbrook looks closely at the current canonical status of Ernst Kantorowicz's book on the king's two bodies, with its reading of *Richard II* as the tragedy resulting from division between the two. Those involved in the Essex rebellion, as Norbrook points out, must have read the play very differently. Looking back over Kantorowicz's career and his early book on Frederick II, Norbrook establishes that his reading of the play is 'rooted in a long tradition of counter-revolutionary discourse', and that critics who cite him as an authority are thereby implicitly endorsing a set of views from which they might otherwise wish to distance themselves. Furthermore, Norbrook argues, the theory of the two bodies was far from being as central to early modern political discourse as Kantorowicz and his subsequent cult status might lead us to believe.

David Womersley's essay asking 'Why is Falstaff Fat?' is less frivolous than it might sound. Womersley links Falstaff's size with a passage in Foxe's *Acts and Monuments* where Foxe responds to Nicholas Harpsfield's attack on Sir John Oldcastle by satirically suggesting that he might have depicted him as 'some grandpanch Epicure of this world'. Womersley doesn't explicitly claim the passage as a source, nor does he argue for Shakespeare as a crypto-Catholic; instead he proceeds to an illuminating exploration of the different chronicle accounts of Henry V, and ends by arguing that Shakespeare's fat Falstaff is 'the corollary, not of any Catholic sympathies on Shakespeare's part, but of the playwright's intention to unify political and spiritual authority in the person of Henry'.

Three further essays look specifically at *Henry V*: 'Holy War in *Henry V*' by Steven Marx, 'Princes, Pirates, and Pigs' by Janet M. Spencer and 'Wars of Memory in *Henry V*' by Jonathan Baldo. All three are concerned with war and its justification by the monarch. Marx looks at links with the depiction of holy war in the bible. Spencer constructs the tale of Alexander the Great's encounter with the pirate Dionides as an emblem of the tension between royal prerogative and the attempt to impose legal restraint on the crown, arguing that it occasionally served 'to speak a dangerous knowledge about the origins of power'. Baldo, focusing on the recent, painful loss of Calais and the fact that Ireland was, for the first twenty-five years of Elizabeth's reign, and for the first time since 1066, the only overseas territory in England's possession, argues that the collective memory on which nationhood is built is as important for what it needs to forget as for what it needs to remember. The play, he argues, 'quietly subverts Henry's rhetoric of remembrance by building a case for Henry and his nation's debt to forgetting'.

Tom McAlindon's 'Pilgrims of Grace: *Henry IV* Historicized' examines how *Henry IV* (both plays) is 'shaped by ideas of grace and rebuke'. Placing it in the context of Tudor rebellions from the Pilgrimage of Grace onwards, McAlindon offers a rich exploration of the play within the larger set of associated ideas around pilgrimage, crusade and reformation. Gordon McMullan, in 'Shakespeare and the End of History', considers the insistent concern with truth in *Henry VIII* (alternatively titled, of course, *All is True*), arguing that the play 'is best viewed as a complex and unsettling meditation on the "end of history", simultaneously promoting and denying the possibility of truth at a moment of cultural crisis within which the word "Truth" held very specific sectarian resonances'.

POEMS

I am aware of little in the way of separate publications on the poetry this year, though good work on the poems is contained in some of the general books reviewed above (notably Kiernan and Davis). Two essays look at the influence of Golding's Ovid on Shakespeare's imagery, though the focus is on the plays, and both are particularly interested in images of melting. Kerri Thomsen, in 'Ovidian References in Hamlet's First Soliloquy', writes on the transformation of the nymph Cyane, a figure that 'melts, thaws and resolves itself as a result of overwhelming sorrow', as a source for Hamlet's first soliloquy; while the focus of Anthony Taylor's study is evident in his title, 'Melting Earth and Leaping Bulls: Shakespeare's Ovid and Arthur Golding'. Stephen J. Carter's 'Lucrece's Gaze' takes a Lacanian perspective and considers the spatial metaphorizing of gender, concentrating on Lucrece's viewing of the wall painting of Troy's defeat. In this act of viewing, Carter argues, 'she constructs herself as a rhetorical, gendered Other, whom she then projects back into herself as subject', becoming a 'newly sighted' space. I'm not convinced.

WORKS REVIEWED

Armstrong, Philip. 'Spheres of Influence: Cartography and the Gaze in Shakespearean Tragedy and History'. *Shakespeare Studies*, 23 (1995), 39–70.

Astington, John. 'Three Shakespearean Prints'. *Shakespeare Quarterly*, 47 (1996), 178–89.

Baldo, Jonathan. 'Wars of Memory in *Henry V*'. *Shakespeare Quarterly*, 47 (1996), 132–59.

Beauregard, David N. *Virtue's Own Feature: Shakespeare and the Virtue Ethics Tradition*. Newark and London: University of Delaware Press, Associated University Presses: 1995.

Bergeron, David M., ed. *Reading and Writing in Shakespeare*. Newark and London: University of Delaware Press, Associated University Presses: 1996.

Bishop, T. G. *Shakespeare and the Theatre of Wonder*. Cambridge Studies in Renaissance Literature and Culture 9. Cambridge: Cambridge University Press, 1996.

Breitenberg, Mark. *Anxious Masculinity in Early Modern England*. Cambridge Studies in Renaissance Literature and Culture 10. Cambridge: Cambridge University Press, 1996.

Brown, John Russell. *William Shakespeare: Writing for Performance*. Basingstoke and London: Macmillan, 1996.

Carter, Stephen J. 'Lucrece's Gaze'. *Shakespeare Studies*, 23 (1995), 210–24.

Chopra, Vikram, ed. *Shakespeare: Varied Perspectives*. Delhi: B.R. Publishing Corporation, 1996.

Davis, Philip. *Sudden Shakespeare: The Shaping of Shakespeare's Creative Thought*. London: Athlone Press, 1996.

De Grazia, Margreta. 'Soliloquies and Wages in the Age of Emergent Consciousness'. *Textual Practice*, 9 (1995), 67–97.

Elam, Keir. 'The Fertile Eunuch: *Twelfth Night*, Early Modern Intercourse, and the Fruits of Castration'. *Shakespeare Quarterly*, 47 (1996), 1–36.

Enterline, Lynn. *The Tears of Narcissus: Melancholia and Masculinity in Early Modern Writing*. Stanford: Stanford University Press, 1995.

Ewbank, Inga-Stina. 'Shakespeare Translation as Cultural Exchange'. *Shakespeare Survey 48* (1995), 1–12.

Flanigan, Tom. 'Domestic Violence and Wifely Submission in *Othello*'. *Shakespeare and Renaissance Association of West Virginia*, 18 (1995), 104–17.

Forse, James H. 'After 1603 Theatre is spelled – JAMES: The 'Royalization'' of the Theatres as a Facet of Attempts by James I to Put His New Kingdom ''in good order'' '. *Shakespeare and Renaissance Association of West Virginia*, 18 (1995), 41–74.

Fortin, René. *Gaining upon Certainty: Selected Literary Criticism*. Ed. Brian Barbour and Rodney Delasanta. Providence, Rhode Island: Providence College Press, 1995.

Fowler, Alistair. 'The Case Against Hamlet', *Times Literary Supplement* (22 December 1995).

Garner, Shirley Nelson and Madelon Sprengnether, eds. *Shakespearean Tragedy and Gender*. Bloomington and Indianapolis: Indiana University Press, 1996.

Hartman, Geoffrey. 'Shakespeare and the Ethical Question', *English Literary History*, 63 (1996), 1–23.

Hendricks, Margo. ' ''Obscured by dreams'': Race, Empire, and Shakespeare's *A Midsummer Night's Dream*'. *Shakespeare Quarterly*, 47 (1996), 37–60.

Hillman, David. 'Puttenham, Shakespeare, and the Abuse of Rhetoric'. *Studies in English Literature*, 36 (1996), 73–90.

Hunt, Maurice. *Shakespeare's Labored Art: Stir, Work, and the late Plays*. Studies in Shakespeare, 3. New York etc.: Peter Lang, 1995.

Jardine, Lisa. *Reading Shakespeare Historically*. London and New York: Routledge, 1996.

Kerrigan, John. *Revenge Tragedy: Aeschylus to Armageddon*. Oxford: Clarendon Press, 1996.

Kiernan, Pauline. *Shakespeare's Theory of Drama*. Cambridge: Cambridge University Press, 1996.

Kinney, Arthur. 'Revisiting *The Tempest*'. *Modern Philology*, 93 (1995), 161–77.

Korda, Natasha. 'Household Kates: Domesticating Commodities in *The Taming of the Shrew*'. *Shakespeare Quarterly*, 47 (1996), 103–31.

Levin, Richard. 'Negative Evidence'. *Studies in Philology*, 92 (1995), 383–410.

Liebler, Naomi Conn. *Shakespeare's Festive Tragedy: The Ritual Foundations of Genre*. London and New York: Routledge, 1995.

Mallin, Eric S. *Inscribing the Time: Shakespeare and the End of Elizabethan England*. Berkeley, Los Angeles and London: University of California Press, 1995.

Mangan, Michael. *A Preface to Shakespeare's Comedies 1594–1603*. London and New York: Longman, 1996.

Maquerlot, Jean-Pierre. *Shakespeare and the Mannerist Tradition: A Reading of Five Problem Plays*. Cambridge: Cambridge University Press, 1995.

Marrapodi, Michele, ed. *Il Mondo Italiano del Teatro Inglese del Rinascimento: Relazioni Culturali e intertestualità*. Palermo: Flaccovio Editore, 1995.

Marx, Steven. 'Holy War in *Henry V*'. *Shakespeare Survey 48* (1995), 85–98.

Matheson, Mark. 'Venetian Culture and the Politics of *Othello*'. *Shakespeare Survey 48* (1995), 123–34.

McAlindon, Tom. 'Pilgrims of Grace: *Henry IV* Historicized'. *Shakespeare Survey 48* (1995), 69–84.

McMullan, Gordon. 'Shakespeare and the End of History'. *Essays and Studies*, 48 (1995), 16–37.

Miles, Geoffrey. *Shakespeare and the Constant Romans*. Oxford English Monographs. Oxford: Clarendon Press, 1996.

Moisan, Thomas. 'Interlinear Trysting and "household stuff": The Latin Lesson and the Domestication of Learning in *The Taming of the Shrew*'. *Shakespeare Studies*, 23 (1995), 100–19.

Montrose, Louis. *The Purpose of Playing: Shakespeare and the Cultural Politics of the Elizabethan Theatre*. Chicago and London: University of Chicago Press, 1996.

Norbrook, David. 'The Emperor's New Body? *Richard II*, Ernst Kantorowicz, and the Politics of Shakespeare Criticism'. *Textual Practice*, 10 (1996), 329–57.

Parker, Patricia. *Shakespeare from the Margins: Language, Culture, Context*. Chicago and London: University of Chicago Press, 1996.

Pugliatti, Paola. *Shakespeare the Historian*. London and Basingstoke: Macmillan; New York: St Martin's Press, 1996.

Saunders, J. G. '"Apparent Perversities": Text and Subtext in the Construction of the Role of Edgar in Brook's Film of *King Lear*'. *Review of English Studies*, 47 (1996), 317–30.

Shaughnessy, Robert. *Representing Shakespeare: England, History and the RSC*. Hemel Hempstead: Harvester Wheatsheaf, 1994.

Smith, Peter J. and Nigel Wood, ed. *Hamlet*. Theory in Practice. Buckingham and Philadelphia: Open University Press, 1996.

Spencer, Janet M. 'Princes, Pirates, and Pigs: Criminalizing Wars of Conquest in *Henry V*'. *Shakespeare Quarterly*, 47 (1996), 160–77.

Spinosa, Charles. '"The name and all th'addition": *King Lear*'s Opening Scene and the Common-Law Use', *Shakespeare Studies*, 23 (1995), 146–86.

Stavig, Mark. *The Forms of Things Unknown: Renaissance Metaphor in Romeo and Juliet and A Midsummer Night's Dream*. Duquesne Studies: Language and Literature Series, 20, Pittsburgh: Duquesne University Press, 1995.

Taylor, Anthony Brian. 'Melting Earth and Leaping Bulls: Shakespeare's Ovid and Arthur Golding'. *Connotations*, 4 (1994–5), 192–206.

Thomsen, Kerri Lynne. 'Ovidian References in Hamlet's First Soliloquy', *English Language Notes*, 33 (1995), 19–23.

Uéno, Yoshiko. *Hamlet and Japan*. New York: AMS Press, 1995.

Weimann, Robert. 'Thresholds to Memory and Commodity in Shakespeare's Endings'. *Representations*, 53 (1996), 1–20.

Widmayer, Martha. 'Brabantio and Othello'. *English Studies*, 77 (1996), 113–76.

Williams, Gordon. *Shakespeare, Sex and the Print Revolution*. London and Atlantic Highlands, N.J.: Athlone, 1996.

Womersley, David. 'Why is Falstaff Fat?'. *Review of English Studies*, 47 (1996), 1–22.

Wood, Nigel, ed.. *Antony and Cleopatra*. Theory in Practice. Buckingham and Philadelphia: Open University Press, 1996.

Henry IV Parts One and Two. Theory in Practice. Buckingham and Philadelphia: Open University Press, 1995.

The Tempest. Theory in Practice. Buckingham and Philadelphia: Open University Press, 1995.

Measure for Measure. Theory in Practice. Buckingham and Philadelphia: Open University Press, 1996.

The Merchant of Venice. Theory in Practice. Buckingham and Philadelphia: Open University Press, 1996.

2. SHAKESPEARE'S LIFE, TIMES, AND STAGE

reviewed by MARK THORNTON BURNETT

In the twenty-fifth anniversary edition of *English Literary Renaissance*, 'The State of Renaissance Studies' is the chosen topic. Together, the finely crafted essays throw considerable light upon the concerns of scholars working in the field today; at the same time, they suggest new critical directions for future generations. Almost all of the contributors acknowledge that 'Renaissance Studies' is now a necessarily pluralized and interdisciplinary domain of enquiry. Some (Jonathan Crewe, for example) begin by confronting the difficulties inherent in terms such as 'English', 'Literary' and 'Renaissance'. Others (Stanley Fish, A. C. Hamilton, Lisa Jardine and Kathleen E. McLuskie) discuss the territory shared by 'literature' and 'history', and they are complemented by David Bevington, Katharine Eisaman Maus and Raymond B. Waddington, who explore the differences between critics of opposed ideological orientations. In her contribution, Lynda Boose applies these observations, arguing for a return to archival scholarship as part of the recovery of the woman's voice. Two contributors (Annabel Patterson and Anne Lake Prescott) single out examples of 'good' and 'bad' literary and historical interpretative practice, while a third, Leah S. Marcus, maintains that the computer has had a profound impact on the study of a period dominated by the print revolution.

The *English Literary Renaissance* anniversary issue makes an important statement. It offers contrasting readings of a variety of scholarly activities, and identifies a number of needs and requirements, hopes and recommendations. In addition, it asks, sometimes coincidentally, several far-reaching questions. How possible is it to recover the past? What texts might be privileged? In what ways should literary canons be confined or extended? What is the relationship between contextual pressures and early modern literary representations? How best can the theatrical performance be critically appreciated? Does Shakespeare possess an inherent appeal, or is he of interest only in terms of multiple cultural appropriations? In the current list of titles in Renaissance and Shakespearian studies, these questions occupy a prominent place.

EDITORIAL ENDEAVOURS

As the volume of recent editions of Renaissance texts attests, the editorial tradition is in an active phase of its development. Canonical works continue to surface, and less well-known materials are making their first commercial appearance. There are even studies of individual editorial undertakings. Among these is Peter Martin's absorbing *Edmond Malone, Shakespearean Scholar: A Literary Biography*. As the first editor to search systematically in the Stratford records and to attempt to establish an authenticated chronology for Shakespeare's plays, Malone was an influential figure. Having tracked down crucial documentation in manuscript repositories in Britain, the Netherlands and the States, Martin writes a full and lively history of Malone's career, describing his relations with other literary personalities as well as his monumental editorial projects. It is not entirely clear which of the 'modern estimates' (p. 34) for the order of composition of Shakespeare's plays Martin accepts, and he is mistaken to suggest that Malone's is the 'only record' (p. 126) of Sir Henry Herbert's Office-Book, but this remains an elegant and a worthwhile study, and further work on Shakespeare and the eighteenth century will be in its debt.

As far as editions themselves are concerned, several are devoted to canonical authors. A much larger number, however, concentrates on writers who are only just beginning to receive scholarly attention. In the former category, Brian Nellist has produced a welcome paperback edition of Thomas Lodge's *Rosalynd*, one of the 'source' texts for *As You Like It*. The points of contact between the play and the prose romance are set out in the introduction, and there is a useful bibliography. Less successful is Roma Gill's volume on *The Jew of Malta* for the ongoing Oxford University Press edition of Marlowe's complete plays. The introduction is wanting in several respects. Its main contents were published in the 1970s in the journal, *Scientia*, but this is never acknowledged. Recent scholarship on the play is barely mentioned, and questions about composition methods, the naming of characters and playhouse conditions are left unanswered. 'There are no known ... antecedents for the main events of [the] plot' (p. ix), Gill comments, but this statement neglects to consider the influence of such dramas as *The Play of the Sacrament* (*c.* 1460), *Respublica* (1553) and *The Three Ladies of London* (1584), all of which, it has been suggested elsewhere, have a bearing on Marlowe's creation. Although detailed and substantial, the notes are full of errors. 'Gabrieli' is transcribed as 'Gabriele'; a 1990 edition of *Sir Thomas More* has 1989 as its date of publication (p. 109); 'Lodowick' appears as 'Lodowick' and 'Lodowicke' (p. 112) simultaneously; and editions, page references, line numbers and publishers are inconsistently identified. The bibliography offers an incomplete list of previous editions; muddles the title even of one of Gill's own co-edited essay collections; and misses out or confuses single and double quotation marks. From a fine Marlovian scholar, this is a disappointing performance.

More attractive, arguably, are those collections which assemble less familiar materials, sometimes for the first time. David Cressy and Lori Anne Ferrell have co-edited a first-rate anthology, *Religion and Society in Early Modern England: A Sourcebook*. Compiled by social historians for student use, it covers such areas as the break from Rome, the rise of puritanism and the place of religious ceremonies. Extracts are taken variously from diocesan act books, catechisms and episcopal correspondence. I was particularly pleased to find part of Rose Hickman's memoir of Protestant life under Mary printed (pp. 29–32), for this significant document by a woman came to light only as recently as 1982. If Cressy and Ferrell are judiciously selective, N. W. Bawcutt, in his *The Control and Censorship of Caroline Drama: The Records of Sir Henry Herbert, Master of the Revels 1623–73*, is magnificently comprehensive. Accompanied by a weighty introduction, the volume prints the known material relating to Herbert in addition to fresh information culled from play licences, the Lord Chamberlain's papers, lawsuits, and provincial records. The result is a breath-taking array of professional theatrical activity, enlivened by references to the titles of over thirty new plays, making a total of seventy-nine new entries. One or two items, such as 'Dr Taylor's' Elizabethan chronicle about Shrewsbury and the 1642 pamphlet, *Bartholomew Fayre*, could have brought the section on 'Sights and Shows' (pp. 76–87) into a sharper focus. This does nothing to detract from Bawcutt's achievement, however, and, as he himself indicates (p. 16), it is only a matter of regret that so many of Herbert's papers have perished.

In volumes such as *The Control and Censorship of Caroline Drama*, the dark corners of the early-modern playhouse are illuminated. This is also the case with two play collections recently published by Manchester University Press. On the negative side, Anthony Parr's *Three Renaissance Travel Plays* suffers from a reluctance clearly to identify the authors of the three plays which form the bulk of the edition (*The Travels of the Three English Brothers*, *The Sea Voyage* and *The Antipodes*) and occasionally misaligns its speech-headings. On the positive side, which makes a more lasting impression, the volume furnishes a subtle introduction to three interrelated dramatic productions, and is richly argumentative in its materialist interpretations. The dynamics of class, gender and sexuality are remote from Paul Merchant's edition of *Thomas Heywood: Three Marriage Plays* (*The Wise-woman of Hogsdon*, *The English Traveller* and *The Captives*), which might frustrate some readers. Instead, Merchant provides a sensible if slightly old-fashioned overview of Heywood's *oeuvre*, setting the plays in their dramatic contexts and speculating about early performances. Both editions have much to offer the general student as well as the scholarly specialist, and it is a pity that they are available only in an expensive hardback format.

It is not so much plays by less frequently studied dramatists as texts by and about women that appear to be attracting the greatest interest, however, at least to judge from Routledge's current publishing programme. Three collections are illustrative of these central critical tendencies. The first, *Shakespeare, Aphra Behn and the Canon*, edited by W. R. Owens and Lizbeth Goodman, is the least impressive. The editors read a number of Shakespearian plays in relation to contemporary contexts and modern performances while also printing and commenting upon Aphra Behn's drama, *The Rover*. Overall, the contextual sections are less polished than the performative discussions, but even these are adversely affected by the directive tone of the prose: phrases such as 'I would say that' (p. 153) and 'perhaps you felt, as I do' (p. 162) tend to interfere with the flow of the argument. The stills from films of *Henry V* are helpful, although authorial comments are once again distracting. The Olivier and Branagh versions respectively are repeatedly and diagrammatically characterised as 'up-beat' and 'sombre' (pp. 58, 65, 66, 75).

Two narrower anthologies explore with a greater effectiveness the intersections between canon formation and Renaissance women's writing, and feature materials which will be of invaluable use in a classroom context. Kate Aughterson's *Renaissance Woman: Constructions of Femininity in England* is divided into nine sections: theology, physiology, conduct, sexuality and motherhood, politics and law, education, work, writing and speaking, and proto-feminisms. The collection is particularly strong in mapping the intricacies of medical thought in the period, and is to be applauded in that it places as much stress upon women's own voices as upon masculine discourses. I had only two niggling criticisms. Extracts from diaries are not included, and it would be helpful to know how many of the early printed texts which Aughterson cites are available in modern facsimiles. With a more carefully defined agenda still, S. P. Cerasano and Marion Wynne-Davies' *Renaissance Drama by Women: Texts and Documents* investigates the extent to which women participated in the theatrical culture of the period, attending to their status as writers, translators, performers and spectators. Concise introductions to the particular selections establish their provenance; there is a wide-ranging 'Documents' section; and an indenture between Edward Alleyn and Marie Bryan (pp. 174–5) demonstrates the involvement of women in the shareholding activities of the professional theatres. All of this is to the editors' credit. Just occasionally, some matters required further clarification. The packaging of the volume suggests that Elizabeth I actually translated Seneca's *Hercules Oetaeus* (pp. vii, 7) whereas, in fact (as the prefatory material to the play on pp. 10–11 suggests), her hand in the work cannot be firmly established. More generally, the volume hesitates to identify which theatres women may have attended, and declines to speculate about the precise class location of those women who formed part of contemporary audiences. Apart from these shortcomings, *Renaissance Drama by Women* stands as a well-informed synthesis of current knowledge, a vigorous intervention in and reformulation of early-modern theatrical practice.

TEXTS AND CONTEXTS

From the previous paragraphs, it should be clear that the will to edit and anthologize is the companion of the need to contextualize. In recent criticism, a sensitivity to the interplay of social and economic forces consorts with a nuanced appreciation of the nature of censorship, of the ideologies of gender, and of the constraints and possibilities of the theatrical institution. Taken as a whole, the books under review in this essay reveal a parallel urge to understand medieval and Renaissance texts through a consideration of their determining contexts – literary influences, social anxieties, gendered expectations and racial assumptions.

Increasing numbers of scholars are looking to medieval dramatic traditions and philosophical explorations in order to chart the continuities between the Renaissance and earlier historical periods. While only partly located in the Renaissance, Meg Twycross' edited book, *Festive Drama*, a collection of papers from the sixth conference of the International Society for the Study of Medieval Theatre, is an example of this critical development. Not surprisingly for a volume which features the work of twenty-four different contributors, the standard tends to vary, although there are invigorating archival pieces by Malcolm Jones on the Towneley plays, by David Mills on the Midsummer Show at Chester, and by James Stokes on the Wells Shows of 1607. What is lacking in *Festive Drama* is any sustained theoretical enquiry, a remarkable omission considering the popularity of recent work on folk humour and carnival licence. Mikhail Bakhtin makes a late and isolated entry on p. 278 in an endnote to an essay on the figure of the old Czech apothecary. Between medieval and Renaissance scholars, therefore, a yawning divide may still loom, despite attempts to bring their activities into a fruitful partnership. From a similar mould is the authored volume by Carol Falvo Heffernan, *The Melancholy Muse: Chaucer, Shakespeare and Early Medicine*. The virtue of the book lies in its painstaking elaboration of points of contact between medical theory and literary representations, and in its suggestion that André Du Laurens' 1599 treatise on sight may have been a 'source' for *Hamlet* (pp. 129–31). The book's failing centres on its decision to view melancholy as a historical constant and to reflect subjectively upon Shakespeare's own temperament. Heffernan is adept at drawing parallels between Chaucer and Shakespeare's melancholy constructions, but she generally resists pushing her findings to innovative conclusions.

The more intriguing volumes would seem to be those that, while recognizing continuities between historical periods, elect to treat medieval and Renaissance texts as essentially separate entities. In itself this is a powerful indication of the difficulties scholars encounter when attempting to establish a common ground for their work. The eighth volume of *Medieval and Renaissance Drama in England*, edited by Leeds Barroll, chooses not to trace broad historical trajectories; rather, it favours discrete studies of individual playtexts, a policy which is generally productive. One or two contributions are a shade obscure, but Sally-Beth MacLean's meticulous essay on festive liturgy in the Thames Valley and Margaret E. Owens' revealing discussion of juggling motifs in *Doctor Faustus* are particularly recommended. The book review section is leisurely and trenchant: the reviewers have taken time to consider their chosen volumes, and this lends the journal an edge over others in the field. In a similarly eclectic vein, Jean-Marie Maguin and Michèle Willems' co-edited collection, *French Essays on Shakespeare and his Contemporaries: 'What would France with us?'*, explores late medieval and English Renaissance theatre, concentrating on questions of historiography, poetics, iconography and translation. Very few younger scholars are included, which perhaps explains the volume's avoidance of current theoretical issues; nevertheless, there are stimulating and original pieces by Francis Guinle, M. T. Jones-Davies, Richard Marienstras and Yves Peyré, and François Laroque's study of the semantic crisis of *All's Well that Ends Well* is most persuasive. There is a large number of misprints – 'Wichkam' for 'Wickham' (p. 79), 'C. K.

Hunter' for 'G. K. Hunter' (p. 188), 'Tinculo' for 'Trinculo' (p. 297) and, unexpectedly, 'Frençaise' for 'Française' (p. 189) – and the index is not always reliable.

By far the largest number of recent authored studies, however, understands context in terms of contemporary influences. Rather than exploring medieval literary and cultural traditions, these books draw upon social anxieties and ideological formations in the sixteenth and seventeenth centuries to contextualize their arguments. Three books focus upon the drama, reading it as an articulation of wider cultural preoccupations – political conflicts, power contests and epistemological uncertainties. T. H. Howard-Hill's *Middleton's 'Vulgar Pasquin': Essays on 'A Game at Chess'* is a splendid, broadly based study, which displays a range of scholarly and critical skills. It discusses *A Game at Chess* as an allegory and a satire, and is continually alive to issues of performance, publication and critical reputation. Particularly authoritative are the chapters devoted to the six manuscript versions of the play and their differing claims to authenticity. A much wider spectrum of theatrical activity is discussed in Clifford Ronan's *'Antike Roman': Power Symbology and the Roman Play in Early Modern England, 1585–1635*. The metaphor of 'Rome' was deployed in many Renaissance plays, and Ronan addresses it in relation to 'antique' contrasts between civility and barbarity, and imperial sovereignty and bloody violence. There are moments when Ronan's points tend to disappear beneath a welter of examples (he considers forty-four dramas), a problem exacerbated by the athleticism with which he leaps between productions from very different historical periods. Its difficulties aside, this is a vibrant, articulate work, and the appended calendrical list of extant Roman plays will be a frequently used resource.

With a similar enthusiasm, Frank Whigham argues for the social embeddedness of the theatre in his *Seizures of the Will in Early Modern English Drama*, a book with several merits. Questions about rank, gender, service and kin are characteristic of the drama, Whigham maintains, and they amount to a struggle to achieve personal identity. Arresting connections are developed between five plays while ensuring that local observations are richly detailed: the chapter on *Arden of Faversham*, a play concerned with the 'Dissolution' (p. 63), is of a high order. But this is also a book with which there is much to quarrel. Firstly, the prose style is ungainly, full, as it is, of such convolutions as 'interdependent cathexes' (p. 5), 'impacted nodes of social pain' (p. 22) and 'the homophobia of the Egyptian miasma' (p. 162). Secondly, the discussion of service suffers from overstatement. It is Whigham's contention that 'master–servant ... relations' were being replaced by the 'cash-nexus' (p. 13) in the period, but this cannot have applied to all service structures, and certainly not to the institution of apprenticeship, which survived relatively intact well into the eighteenth and even nineteenth centuries. Elsewhere in the book, Whigham passes over specific debates about service in contemporary moral treatises and conduct books to rely upon the comments of modern historians. The use of recent authorities is only to be expected, of course; however, it is misleading to cite Ann Kussmaul's work on servants in husbandry (p. 88) in order to generalize about service in general. *Seizures of the Will* is bound to attract admirers; it will also have its fair share of detractors.

For a smaller group of scholars, the drama is of less interest than related literary forms. Although partly touching upon the theatre, several critical studies are concerned to highlight the ideological force of poetry and prose, and the contextual pressures that shaped these genres' imaginative constructions. Jonathan Sawday's *The Body Emblazoned: Dissection and the Human Body in Renaissance Culture* is a magisterial meditation on the links between poetry and the eroticism of the contemporary anatomy theatre, combining historical discussion, literary analysis and scientific investigation. Thomas Carew, John Donne and Andrew

Marvell are assessed, among others, and there are pertinent considerations of medical illustrations. The book is a model of how interdisciplinary work can be successfully conducted. To such an achievement there can be only minor objections. Cabinets of curiosities could have been examined as precursors to the scientific revolution, and the drama, in which representations of anatomy and performance are surely central, receives only a passing treatment.

Other critics wrestle with the question of a text's relationship to its contexts by engaging with the prose of the period. Discussions of poetry occupy some chapters of Richard Dutton's *Ben Jonson: Authority: Criticism*, but the book is equally directed towards epistles, prefaces and conversations – the prosaic forms that Jonson enlisted to define himself over and above his contemporaries and his classical past. In exploiting these modes of writing, Jonson played a key part in establishing the respectability of literary criticism and the profession of 'letters' for subsequent generations. *Ben Jonson: Authority: Criticism* is a sterling and learned work, in which the phenomenon of the 'author', the demands of patronage, the power of stage authority, and the role of criticism in an expanding metropolitan culture are all excitingly interpreted. In its elaboration of the relations between power and print, Dutton's book invites comparison with Wayne A. Rebhorn's *The Emperor of Men's Minds: Literature and the Renaissance Discourse of Rhetoric*, a subtle enquiry into rhetoricians' participation in contemporary debates about political authority, social mobility, gender and the body. Once again, poetry and the drama are not wholly relegated, for Rebhorn provides some provocative, rhetorically inflected appraisals of Herbert's 'The Method' (pp. 120–1) and Jonson's *The Alchemist* (pp. 247–50, 253). But the book is mostly taken up with English, French and Italian rhetorical prose tracts, whose figures of phallic aggression are viewed as expressions of political contest or ambition. Rebhorn's is an important counter-thesis to the ways in which rhetoric is usually explicated, only slightly marred by an unwillingness to integrate the discussions of the trickster and the 'grotesque' body, and by a regrettable lineation error (p. 176).

Yet the majority of contextual studies range across genres, privileging neither an author nor a particular literary mode. Two recent titles are relevant. Opposing the application of previously formulated theoretical readings is one of the objectives of Richard Strier's *Resistant Structures: Particularity, Radicalism, and Renaissance Texts*. Arguing that texts should be allowed to speak for themselves, Strier is the champion of the obvious and the particular, and develops his theme through a series of lucid and insightful chapters on Donne, Herbert and Shakespeare. As the book unfolds, Strier takes to task a variety of critics, reserving much of his energy for confrontations with 'Deconstruction' and 'New Historicism'. *Resistant Structures* is too sophisticated to advocate a return to a kind of informed 'New Criticism', although it is a little apprehensive about stating what its theoretical battles finally prove. Still, this is a bold and urgent book, and one courageous enough to acknowledge that its argument sometimes slips into those modes of criticism that it would ostensibly resist. Similarly sweeping in its generic coverage is William C. Carroll's *Fat King, Lean Beggar: Representations of Poverty in the Age of Shakespeare*. As a highly accomplished study of the discursive construction of the beggar and the vagabond, and of the lawlessness associated with the type, it is difficult to fault. Nevertheless, Carroll misses the point that the 'monstrous' body of the beggar is dangerous because of its capacity to shape the conceiving imaginations of pregnant women (p. 51), and sometimes confuses apprentices in employment with those 'masterless men' who contributed to social unrest in late sixteenth-century London (pp. 140–57). With the exception of these reservations, I have only praise for Carroll's sensitive adjudication between the claims of legal discourses, pamphlets and the theatre, for his thorough social and demographic research, and for his detailed recovery of a site of pervasive cultural anxiety.

As Carroll's book suggests, context is often equated with an 'other', a subversive or deviant type that throws into disarray established hierarchies. Political authority is viewed as dependent upon, if not defined by, oppositional forces, which are located at the margins of contemporary social life. In this connection, the remaining contextual studies, which deal variously with representations of women, witchcraft and race, are cases in point. For early modern writers, the 'other' was invariably gendered, a fact borne out by recent evaluations of the contaminating powers women were believed to exercise. In *The Trials of Frances Howard: Fact and Fiction at the Court of King James*, now available in paperback, David Lindley sets out to revise the image of Frances Howard as a criminal personality. To this end, he presents a well-combed selection of literary and historical contexts to suggest that the familiar version of Howard's story is based upon flawed, subjective accounts, and that literary representations of her career also contributed to the impression of her moral fallibility. The result is a compelling volume, which, although refusing to restore Howard to innocence, alerts us to the manipulative power of the narrative of history. The woman who conspired to murder was, it was thought, possessed by demonic forces, as Deborah Willis' *Malevolent Nurture: Witch-Hunting and Maternal Power in Early Modern England* eloquently attests. Willis' thesis is that women as well as men were active in witch-hunting, and that fantasies about the mother were determining factors in the numbers of cases brought to trial. These are intriguing and critical distinctions, and they allow Willis to elaborate perceptive readings of James I's fascination with witches and of plays such as *Macbeth* and *Richard III*. Once or twice, I felt that Willis tended to blur the overlap between the 'village' and the 'aristocratic' construction of the witch, and areas of cross-fertilization between pamphlets and plays are not always precisely recognized. Furthermore, some pamphlets, such as *The Wonderful Discoverie of the Witchcrafts of Margaret and Phillip Flower* (1619), the title page of which appears on the book's cover, are arguably preoccupied with witches who are single women and daughters as well as mothers. The value of *Malevolent Nurture* is not affected by these oversights, however, and the book represents a simultaneously ground-breaking and sobering addition to existing knowledge.

If the witch was a locus of anxiety, peoples of other races constituted an even more threatening prospect. Perhaps the most original of the contextual studies are those that investigate representations of the racially 'other', and the geographical enterprises that brought them into prominence. Kim F. Hall's *Things of Darkness: Economies of Race and Gender in Early Modern England* ties allusions to blackness in Renaissance texts with imperialism, sexual politics and the evolution of a white, male identity. On some isolated points of detail, Hall might be challenged. For instance, Sir John Mandeville's views on Africa were not unique, and other writers reproduced similar descriptions of the 'disjointed' races in their accounts of India, Scythia and even the Americas (p. 26). One might also suggest that the trope of the 'disjointed' races persisted into the seventeenth century: it was not necessarily replaced by more complex figurations (p.28). But at the level of general argumentation, *Things of Darkness* is excellent. Although the book is illuminating throughout, its most powerful chapters probe the political implications of polarities of light and dark in the sonnet, and reflections upon gender and property embodied in black servant portraiture. To discussions of colour imagery, *Things of Darkness* introduces a set of vital and unprecedented subtexts. While Mary C. Fuller's *Voyages in Print: English Travel to America, 1576–1624* does not exactly aim to elucidate the construction of the racially 'other', it is nevertheless important as a considered and penetrating study of the travel narratives that exacerbated white, European anxieties. Demystifying the early history of America as a period of glorious expansion, Fuller surveys journals, promotional tracts and theoretical discourses to argue that the early modern 'voyager' was less concerned with heroism than the need to recuperate failure. Accordingly, Fuller suggests that deferral and regret dictate Sir Walter Ralegh's representation of the Guiana expeditions, and that John Smith rewrote his history of Virginia to accommodate fantasies of female benevolence and patronage. *Voyages in Print* is a salutary and cogent revisionist work, which successfully unhinges several shibboleths of cultural opinion, although some readers may feel that it plays down the material benefits which the 'old' world derived from the 'new'.

Pride of place among these recent titles must go to James Shapiro's *Shakespeare and the Jews*, a magnificent investigation into the prevailing myths about Jewish identity that circulated in the English Renaissance. Formidably researched and historically sensitive, the book ranges widely across confessions of faith, sermons and political tracts in its elaboration of the ways in which Jewish questions answered to English preoccupations. The centrepiece of the book is *The Merchant of Venice*, a play that is read variously as a debate about circumcision (pp. 121–6) and as a reflection of late Elizabethan popular xenophobia (pp. 180–9). *En route* to his central arguments, Shapiro is able to account for the imperatives governing much 'New Historicist' criticism (pp. 86–8), and to prompt us to reconsider our own national and cultural loyalties. *Shakespeare and the Jews* is a wonderful fusion of theory and scholarship, a cultural event of monumental stature.

THEATRICAL PERFORMANCES

It is an index of a shift in critical focus that the 'play in performance' seems to be in decline as a field of enquiry. The contributors to the anniversary issue of *English Literary Renaissance* hardly mention work dedicated to the theatrical experience, while context in recent studies is very rarely interpreted as process that takes place within the walls of the playhouse. A consideration of current titles, however, suggests that performance-centred approaches have not died: they are merely reconstituting themselves to suit new historical, synthetic and even postmodern imperatives.

A smaller group of books selects the nature of the early modern theatrical performance as the object of attention. Andrew Gurr chooses not to examine the mechanics of stage business in his invaluable *The Shakespearian Playing Companies*, but he does provide a superb history of theatrical company development from the 1560s to 1642, which includes accounts of the impresarios and stars, a register of travelling performances and an appreciation of different repertory traditions. Only in his comments on the stability of London's urban economy, which recent historical work by K. J. Lindley and Roger B. Manning would complicate, can Gurr be queried. Otherwise, the study is a rich evocation of performative activity – play times, theatrical closures, financial management, licensing practices and royal patronage. It will surpass the earlier collections edited by G. E. Bentley and E. K. Chambers in the currency of its findings and the incisive authority of its interpretations. Confined to a narrower area is Peter Walls' *Music in the English Courtly Masque, 1604–1640*, the more concentrated focus of which serves only to emphasize its importance. Attending to musical elements in masques performed at Whitehall, at the Inns of Court and in great houses, Walls discusses such matters as the division of the composer's responsibilities, the steps of particular dances, and the differences between public and private playing occasions. The technical analysis of a number of songs is a notable feature – Walls is a choral conductor and practising baroque violinist. *Music in the English Courtly Masque* is, then, a work of considerable distinction. Some sections allow room for improvement without, however, compromising the integrity of the book as a whole. The date, 1613, cannot be firmly tied to *The Tempest* (p. 75), since an earlier version of the play may have existed; it is possible that Walls confuses the 'London Museum' (p.190) for the British Library; and the description of the 'Ashby' masque (pp. 284–6, 328) would have benefited from James Knowles' recent article on the entertainment's provenance.

More commonly, the 'play in performance' is addressed from early modern and modern perspectives at one and the same time, as the continuing 'Shakespeare in Performance' series, published by Manchester University Press, so successfully proves. Some titles are now appearing in paperback, which is a welcome development. One such is Bernice W. Kliman's volume on *Macbeth*, a survey of thirteen major versions of the play on stage and screen. *Macbeth* Kliman regards as an experiment in 'unity of focus' (p. 1), a view which she elaborates in chapters on Sir William Davenant, David Garrick and Glen Byam Shaw's productions. The discussion is nimble and discerning, particularly in the sections on Roman Polanski's politically motivated 1971 film interpretation and Trevor Nunn's claustrophobic realization of the play at The Other Place in 1976. Margaret Shewring's volume on *King Richard II* is, likewise, a clear and balanced narrative of the play's fortunes in the theatre. Dramatic features and possibilities are outlined before specific productions are considered in terms of their particular thematic perspectives. Throughout Shewring is responsive to questions of staging and the placing of characters, never more so than in the penultimate chapter on *King Richard II* on the European stage. Unfortunately, typographical discrepancies and omissions sometimes mar the book's attractive presentation: 'Merick' (p. 24), the steward of the Earl of Essex, should appear as 'Meyrick'; I was confused as to 'see below, pp. 00–00' (p. 58); and the Lambarde document of 1601 (pp. 191–2) lacks a source of reference.

Bulkier and more expansive, Anthony B. Dawson's volume on *Hamlet* for the 'Shakespeare in Performance' series sets new standards for performance-centred cultural criticism. For Dawson, productions of *Hamlet* have mirrored changing definitions of selfhood. Assessments of particular stage presentations – from Henry Irving's emotional interpretation to Jonathan Pryce's supernaturally-inspired rendition of the character – are powerful illustrations of this central thesis. It is not to be wondered at, perhaps, that Dawson writes most confidently about more recent productions, such as Franco Zeffirelli's film version, which is considered in the light of the 'gaze' and the Hollywood 'blockbuster'. Contextually precise, textually detailed and refreshingly polemical, the *Hamlet* volume is a work to admire, even if some realizations, such as the BBC television version with Derek Jacobi (pp. 214–23), are not related to their earlier Edinburgh Festival and London run manifestations.

But tracing the points of contact between the early modern performance and its modern counterpart is not an exercise limited to single-authored volumes. It is as evident in essay collections, which demonstrate with varying successes the continuing validity of performative approaches. James C. Bulman's edited volume, *Shakespeare, Theory, and Performance*, assembles eleven contributors to underscore the multiplicity of possibilities available for theorizing the 'performance' phenomenon. All of the essays manage to spark off valuable reflections, although Juliet Dusinberre's piece on the 'boy actor' and Douglas Lanier's study of *Prospero's Books* are superior in quality and inventiveness. More accessible is *Shakespeare: An Illustrated Stage History*, edited by Jonathan Bate and Russell Jackson. Put together in honour of Stanley Wells, the volume provides a set of energetic and sumptuously illustrated essays on the beginnings of the Elizabethan playhouse, the excavations of the Rose, the fortunes of the King's Men, Shakespearian productions in the eighteenth and nineteenth centuries, and the proliferation of forms of theatrical enterprise in the twentieth-century repertory. It is a handsome, pointed and expressive critical undertaking, and a distinguished synthesis of current opinion. For me, the most forceful contribution was Russell Jackson's 'Shakespeare in Opposition: From the 1950s to the 1990s', in which the work of the Cheek by Jowl company and other theatrical groups is thoughtfully reviewed. It will be interesting to see if their example is followed in future projects, and in parts of the country outside a more familiar south-of-England environment.

As theatrical activity continues to gain in diversity and volume, so too does criticism increasingly concern itself with the play in relation to its modern performative contexts. Only a very recent history of theatrical production would appear to be of interest to a growing number of scholars. Work illustrative of this development, however, generally promises more than it actually delivers. Albert Hunt and Geoffrey Reeves' *Directors in Perspective: Peter Brook* is a helpful overview of the director's intellectual curiosity, of the eclectic range of his professional work, and of his seminal productions, such as the 1970 *A Midsummer Night's Dream*. But the book is impoverished by the failure to provide any discussion of Peter Brook's personal history (it is obvious that he did not collaborate with the authors) and by the inclusion of long, often unidentified quotations. It is also difficult to disentangle published interviews in the text from those not yet in print. Comparably unsatisfactory is H. R. Coursen's *Shakespeare in Production: Whose History?*. Presenting itself as a 'New Historicist' work (which it is not), the book proceeds through a series of appreciations of relatively recent Shakespearian production moments, such as the 1936 film version of *Romeo and Juliet* and versions of *The Comedy of Errors* on television. Coursen never arrives at the social and political readings hinted at in the introduction, substituting instead personal responses in conjunction with the judgements of popular reviewers. The result is that sometimes acute perceptions are dragged down by a fashionable but inappropriate theoretical overlay. Equally troubling are the numerous bibliographical errors, such as 'Tannenhouse' for 'Tennenhouse' (pp. 222, 274 and 286), and the misspelling of the names of two of the author's hosts in the acknowledgements.

Altogether more professionally appealing is Michael Mullin's *Design by Motley*, a sprightly book about Elizabeth Montgomery, Margaret Harris and Sophia Harris, who, under the name of 'Motley', designed over three hundred theatrical productions from 1932 onwards. Mullin has the advantage of involvement in the 'Motley Collection' at the University of Illinois at Urbana-Champaign, a resource which he draws upon to fine effect in his discussion of the 'new stagecraft' of the Motley collective. His study is a fascinating compendium of photographs, designs and sketches, which is accompanied by an interpretative narrative account. It represents a unique record of a pivotal moment in modern theatrical history.

SHAKESPEARIAN APPROPRIATIONS

It is, in fact, with broadly based 'performances' that the future of Renaissance and Shakespearian texts is assured. But 'performances' do not only connote the activity that takes place within the theatre. As a number of recent studies suggests, Shakespeare, in particular, can be apprehended through rewritings and appropriations of his most canonically entrenched productions. The relationship between Shakespeare and contemporary culture is a phenomenon that few of the contributors to the anniversary issue of *English Literary Renaissance* address; however, a substantial body of work establishes that the dramatist is now a familiar cultural property in films and festivals, and at sites of political and post-colonial contest.

Several studies engage with these developments by discussing Shakespeare's place in other performative idioms, such as film and even the puppet theatre. Peter Drexler and Lawrence

Guntner's *Negotiations with Hal: Multi-Media Perceptions of (Shakespeare's) Henry the Fifth* is concerned mostly with the fortunes of *Henry V* on screen. Three of the essays make positive contributions: Lawrence Guntner's piece on the connections between Shakespearian films and German Expressionism, Sabine Thürwächter's consideration of Kenneth Branagh's *Henry V* in the light of Renaissance sculpture, and Martina Stelter's exploration of the film's investment in imagery of martial conflict. The remaining essays are rather limited, and suffer from a refusal to dwell upon the political white-washing for which Branagh has recently been criticized. Of greater interest is Susan Young's *Shakespeare Manipulated: The Use of the Dramatic Works of Shakespeare in 'teatro di figura' in Italy*. This fascinating book looks at the popularity of Shakespeare in the Italian theatre of *marionette*, *burattini* and *pupi*, surveying some seventy productions from the eighteenth century onwards. Readers expecting to find a semiotic analysis of puppets, or a reconstruction of English and Italian Renaissance puppet practices, will be disappointed. Those interested in discovering a catalogue of little-known Italian puppet plays, and in enjoying adaptations of Shakespearian texts intended for puppet performances in 1881 and 1906, will be transported.

Neither of the above studies is concerned to highlight the political and sexual dimensions of the appropriation of the Shakespearian text. It is therefore welcome to come across two recent books, which go a considerable way towards filling these crucial omissions. Kate Chedgzoy's *Shakespeare's Queer Children: Sexual Politics and Contemporary Culture* introduces 'Shakespeare' as a space where conflicting desires – aesthetic, social and erotic – can be enacted, explored and transformed. In the chapters that ensue, Chedgzoy accordingly turns her attention to such cultural productions as Angela Carter's *Wise Children* (an interrogation of the nuclear family), the film, *My Own Private Idaho* (a critique of Shakespearian father figures) and Derek Jarman's *Edward II* (a meditation on art, sexuality and identity). The argumentation in the book is exact; the observations are sharp; and the material is clearly developed; but, at times, the prose shows signs of having been rushed, and several chapters end abruptly without adequate conclusions. Less cogent is Xiao Yang Zhang's *Shakespeare in China: A Comparative Study of Two Traditions and Cultures*, a discussion of the interactions between Shakespeare's plays and Chinese culture. Although the book is presented within a 'New Historicist' paradigm, this does not answer to its eventual effect. The theoretical appurtenances are few, and discussions of 'love and marriage' (p. 46), and phrases such as 'Shakespearean ... comedy ... set up for humanity brilliant and lofty social ideals' (pp. 60–1), tend to grate against the materialist framework. Zhang's book, in fact, is a humanist enquiry striving to become a political intervention. But this is an incomplete picture. *Shakespeare in China* will be the starting-point for further explorations: an essential list of Shakespearian productions in China is provided; the section on operatic adaptations is thought-provoking; and there are scattered and enlightening remarks about pedagogy (p. 192) and intellectual dissidence (p. 177).

To appreciate the Shakespearian text in its most powerful political incarnation, it would seem to be to other cultures, and to post-colonial situations, that we need to turn. That is the conclusion of two studies devoted to the late nineteenth- and early twentieth-century exportation of Shakespeare to what was then the 'British Empire'. Harish Trivedi's *Colonial Transactions: English Literature and India*, although touching upon a range of writers from T. S. Eliot to Edward Thompson, includes one chapter on 'Shakespeare' in relation to Indian contexts. Trivedi's gift is his ability to detail the two-way exchanges between English representations of the 'other' and Indian responses to an imperial culture. His book's contribution is to establish that the colonial process can never be broken down into the binaries of 'conquest' and 'dominance'. More ambitious in scope is

David Johnson's *Shakespeare and South Africa*, an impressive study of the teaching and criticism of Shakespeare in South Africa from the nineteenth century to the present. Only occasionally is this a book about Shakespearian performances, such as in references to the repertory of early nineteenth-century Cape Town theatres (p. 36). Instead, it is an astute and generously documented cultural history of South African literary educational policies, which draws upon examination papers, reports and newspaper essays. Editions of Shakespeare in South Africa are discussed, as are the practices of the civil service and the reputation of such plays as *The Tempest*: particularly arresting in Johnson's account is his elaboration of perceived links between Caliban, the 'Kaffirs' and the 'Hottentot' (p. 20). It is with these various and ongoing appropriations of his plays that Shakespeare will continue to serve as a repository of conservative and contested cultural meanings, and therein part of his fate resides. This final selection of books demonstrates with a commanding eloquence the current 'state' of Renaissance and Shakespearian 'studies', and offers timely reminders of what our scholarly endeavours were, are and may yet still become.

WORKS REVIEWED

Aughterson, Kate, ed. *Renaissance Woman: Constructions of Femininity in England*. London and New York: Routledge, 1995.

Barroll, Leeds, ed. *Medieval and Renaissance Drama in England*. Vol. VIII. Madison and Teaneck: Fairleigh Dickinson University Press/London: Associated University Presses, 1996.

Bate, Jonathan, and Russell Jackson, eds. *Shakespeare: An Illustrated Stage History*. Oxford: Oxford University Press, 1996.

Bawcutt, N. W., ed. and introd. *The Control and Censorship of Caroline Drama: The Records of Sir Henry Herbert, Master of the Revels 1623–73*. Oxford: Clarendon Press, 1996.

Bulman, James C., ed. *Shakespeare, Theory, and Performance*. London and New York: Routledge, 1996.

Carroll, William C. *Fat King, Lean Beggar: Representations of Poverty in the Age of Shakespeare*. Ithaca and London: Cornell University Press, 1996.

Cerasano, S. P., and Marion Wynne-Davies, eds. *Renaissance Drama by Women: Texts and Documents*. London and New York: Routledge, 1996.

Chedgzoy, Kate. *Shakespeare's Queer Children: Sexual Politics and Contemporary Culture*. Manchester and New York: Manchester University Press, 1995.

Coursen, H. R. *Shakespeare in Production: Whose History?* Athens: Ohio University Press, 1996.

Cressy, David, and Lori Anne Ferrell, eds. *Religion and Society in Early Modern England: A Sourcebook*. London and New York: Routledge, 1996.

Dawson, Anthony. *Shakespeare in Performance: 'Hamlet'*. Manchester and New York: Manchester University Press, 1995.

Drexler, Peter, and Lawrence Guntner, eds. *Negotiations with Hal: Multi-Media Perceptions of (Shakespeare's) Henry the Fifth*. Braunschweig: Technische Universität Braunschweig, 1995.

Dutton, Richard. *Ben Jonson: Authority: Criticism*. Basingstoke: Macmillan, 1996.

Fuller, Mary C. *Voyages in Print: English Travel to America, 1576–1624*. Cambridge: Cambridge University Press, 1995.

Gurr, Andrew. *The Shakespearian Playing Companies*. Oxford: Clarendon Press, 1996.

Hall, Kim F. *Things of Darkness: Economies of Race and Gender in Early Modern England*. Ithaca and London: Cornell University Press, 1995.

Heffernan, Carol Falvo. *The Melancholy Muse: Chaucer, Shakespeare and Early Medicine*. Pittsburgh: Duquesne University Press, 1995.

Heywood, Thomas. *Thomas Heywood: Three Marriage Plays*. Ed. by Paul Merchant. Manchester and New York: Manchester University Press, 1996.

Howard-Hill, T. H. *Middleton's 'Vulgar Pasquin': Essays on 'A Game at Chess'*. Newark: University of Delaware Press/London: Associated University Presses, 1995.

Hunt, Albert, and Geoffrey Reeves. *Directors in Perspective: Peter Brook*. Cambridge: Cambridge University Press, 1995.

Johnson, David. *Shakespeare and South Africa*. Oxford: Clarendon Press, 1996.

Kinney, Arthur F., ed. *English Literary Renaissance*. Vol. XV, no. 3. Amherst: University of Massachusetts Press, 1995.

Kliman, Bernice W. *Shakespeare in Performance: 'Macbeth'*. Manchester and New York: Manchester University Press, 1995.

Lindley, David. *The Trials of Frances Howard: Fact and Fiction at the Court of King James*. London and New York: Routledge, 1996.

Lodge, Thomas. *Rosalynd*. Ed. by Brian Nellist. Keele: Ryburn Publishing, 1995.

Maguin, Jean-Marie, and Michèle Willems, eds. *French Essays on Shakespeare and his Contemporaries: 'What would France with us'?*. Newark: University of Delaware Press/London: Associated University Presses, 1995.

Marlowe, Christopher. *The Complete Works of Christopher Marlowe: 'The Jew of Malta'*. Vol. IV. Ed. by Roma Gill. Oxford: Clarendon Press, 1995.

Martin, Peter. *Edmond Malone, Shakespearean Scholar: A Literary Biography*. Cambridge: Cambridge University Press, 1995.

Mullin, Michael. *Design by Motley*. Foreword by Sir John Gielgud. Newark: University of Delaware Press/London: Associated University Presses, 1996.

Owens, W. R., and Lizbeth Goodman, eds. *Shakespeare, Aphra Behn and the Canon*. London and New York: Routledge/The Open University, 1996.

Parr, Anthony, ed. *Three Renaissance Travel Plays*. Manchester and New York: Manchester University Press, 1995.

Rebhorn, Wayne A. *The Emperor of Men's Minds: Literature and the Renaissance Discourse of Rhetoric*. Ithaca and London: Cornell University Press, 1995.

Ronan, Clifford. *'Antike Roman': Power Symbology and the Roman Play in Early Modern England, 1585–1635*. Athens and London: University of Georgia Press, 1995.

Sawday, Jonathan. *The Body Emblazoned: Dissection and the Human Body in Renaissance Culture*. London and New York: Routledge, 1995.

Shapiro, James. *Shakespeare and the Jews*. New York: Columbia University Press, 1996.

Shewring, Margaret. *Shakespeare in Performance: 'King Richard II'*. Manchester and New York: Manchester University Press, 1996.

Strier, Richard. *Resistant Structures: Particularity, Radicalism, and Renaissance Texts*. Berkeley, Los Angeles and London: University of California Press, 1995.

Trivedi, Harish. *Colonial Transactions: English Literature and India*. Manchester and New York: Manchester University Press, 1995.

Twycross, Meg, ed. *Festive Drama: Papers from the Sixth Triennial Colloquium of the International Society for the Study of Medieval Theatre, Lancaster, 13–19 July, 1989*. Cambridge: D. S. Brewer, 1996.

Walls, Peter. *Music in the English Courtly Masque, 1604–1640*. Oxford: Clarendon Press, 1996.

Whigham, Frank. *Seizures of the Will in Early Modern English Drama*. Cambridge: Cambridge University Press, 1996.

Willis, Deborah. *Malevolent Nurture: Witch-Hunting and Maternal Power in Early Modern England*. Ithaca and London: Cornell University Press, 1995.

Young, Susan. *Shakespeare Manipulated: The Use of the Dramatic Works of Shakespeare in 'teatro di figura' in Italy*. Madison and Teaneck: Fairleigh Dickinson University Press/London: Associated University Presses, 1996.

Zhang, Xiao Yang. *Shakespeare in China: A Comparative Study of Two Traditions and Cultures*. Newark: University of Delaware Press/London: Associated University Presses, 1996.

THE YEAR'S CONTRIBUTIONS TO SHAKESPEARE STUDIES

3. EDITIONS AND TEXTUAL STUDIES

reviewed by JOHN JOWETT

EDITIONS

Stephen Orgel's Oxford Shakespeare edition of *The Winter's Tale* is a pleasure to read. His introduction shows critical sophistication and a commitment to historical scholarship that both delights and instructs.[1] In a play as editorially straightforward as *The Winter's Tale* Orgel can afford to treat the text conservatively. He is often stoutly resistant to editorial 'improvement' of what he calls 'Shakespeare's sense', and his textual discussion affirms that 'the complexity and obscurity of the verse can only be authorial' (p. 83).[2] The claim in itself sounds transparent and straightforward, but the position of the author within editorial configurations of the text continues to be debated in many of the studies reviewed below.

Orgel edits undeflected by these theoretical complications, elegantly interweaving text and commentary, commentary and introduction. In just one case Orgel makes a strikingly innovative change to the text where a commentary note might have been more diplomatic. A couple of lines before Antigonus exits pursued by a bear we read the bracketed direction '*Storm, with a sound of dogs barking and hunting horns*' (3.3.55). Here Orgel's strong sense of *Winter's Tale* as a precursor of *The Tempest* seems to spill over into the text. The call for a storm, or, as the Mariner anticipated some lines before, 'loud weather', is, admittedly, a constructive addition. Dogs and horns, however, are doubtful. Their justification lies partly in a literal reading of the Shepherd's reference a few lines later to 'these boiled-brains of nineteen and two-and-twenty' who 'hunt this weather', and partly on reading Antigonus' response to whatever he sees or hears, 'This is the chase', to mean that the bear is being hunted. Shakespeare does not elsewhere use 'chase' to mean a hunted animal. The conjunction of 'chase', 'I am gone for ever' and '*pursued*' points consistently to Antigonus seeing himself as the hunted creature. But why '*the* chase', as if Antigonus were expecting the event? Perhaps because he is expecting it. The Mariner gave him a double admonition, ''tis like to be loud weather. / Besides, this place is famous for the creatures / Of prey that keep upon't' (3.3.10–12). Antigonus, having found his dream prophetic, now finds these warnings prophetic too. The savage clamour of loud weather arrives, and the creature of prey, perhaps roaring savagely, enters on cue.

In annotating the text Orgel recognizes the sometimes bewildering complexity of the play's language, repeatedly suggesting that such complexity might intentionally lie beyond coherent paraphrase. This seems an entirely serious twist to the more usual view of the author as the principle of semantic thrift. Occasionally I suspect Orgel of thrift too. In commenting on the Clown's line 'Will they wear their plackets where they should bear their faces' (4.4.242), he notes *placket* as meaning petticoat, pocket-slit, and vagina, but the word also has relevance as a variant of *placard* and might pun on law-Latin *placet*, 'it pleases'. When he glosses this line as 'will they reveal what they should keep hidden?', the paradoxes that wearing is

[1] Despite the occasional coercive 'must be seen in this context' (p. 48), 'one context within which Paulina's statue must be viewed' (p. 56), and Orgel's comment on Hermione and Leontes' separation, 'In the culture at large, husbands and wives often lived apart for long periods' (pp. 78–9), which approaches self-parody.

[2] This editorial reliance on the author does not in Orgel's case spring from anything like innocence. Compare 'We know nothing about Shakespeare's original text' (Orgel, 'What is a Text?', *Research Opportunities in Renaissance Drama*, 24 (1981), 3–6, p. 6.

revealing and bearing is hiding slip away; he does not establish that to bear a face can mean, presumably, to maintain a discreet countenance, and he does not mention that the notion of being bare-faced is present by a piece of word-play that threatens to undo the ostensible meaning. Similarly, with Polixenes' assertion of 'an art / That nature makes' (4.4.91–2), which might at least hypothetically mean 'an art that makes nature' rather than 'an art that is made by nature', Orgel lets the sleeping dog of syntactic ambiguity lie. Occasionally the commentary is more profligate; his note on the passage where Perdita gives flowers blossoms into a catalogue of flower catalogues from Theocritus to Milton. This is, nonetheless, a mostly judicious and well-balanced commentary, much less cluttered than J. H. Pafford's Arden 2, and probably the best currently available on the play.

And the best critical introduction too. Orgel's strong sense of the play's linguistic opacity is his starting point and the key to much that he has to say. Complexity of language and contortions of the audience's understanding make the play a mystery, and Orgel relates artistic illusionism to the mysteries of state. The play challenges James I's own 'deepest convictions about the independence, indeed sanctity, of the royal judgement', though Orgel imagines James finding comfort in reading the play as showing 'that however bad a king may be, he is still the king' (p. 15).

Coleridge is invoked to vindicate 'Shakespeare's psychological acuity' in showing Leontes' outburst of jealousy (p. 18); compared with *Othello* the play is both realistic and modern in showing 'the compulsiveness of paranoid behaviour', which Orgel relates variously to 'the self-generating and autonomous nature of consciousness itself' (p. 19), to the fantasy of dangerously interchangeable twinned lambs, 'two versions of the same psyche' (p. 25), and to misogyny as 'the cultural currency of the age' (p. 27): thus to Leontes' mind of and in itself, to the homosocial relationship, and to Jacobean society at large. As Leontes doesn't say, 'It is the effect': Orgel shows how the motive is known in and only in Leontes' convoluted and untrustworthy language, which shows traces of all these putative causes. It is characteristic for the play to confound knowledge and fantasy (p. 28), nowhere more so than in Hermione's trial. Orgel, taking his cue from *All Is True* (the title is highly relevant to his discussion), compares the trials of Hermione and Anne Boleyn. Elizabeth's and Perdita's proclaimed bastardy was illegal, 'a pure creation of the royal will' (p. 31) – though Leontes' reversal on hearing of Mamillius' death is itself illogical, 'nothing to do with a return to rationality' (p. 32).

Problems of judgement and interpretation beset the pastoral world too, as Antigonus' dream on landing in Bohemia shows (p. 39). Pastoral is ushered in as a world of black comedy, danger, and death, and, although Orgel shows a fine sense of the 'extraordinary expressive range' of Perdita's catalogue of flowers, he dwells particularly on the hint of violent male sexual behaviour in her mention of Prosperina: it is 'through acts of sexual violence against women' that 'the world is filled with flowers and poetry' (p. 45). Pastoral offers no escape from royal fury.

A fascinating section on Autolycus refers to recent studies of masterless men and glances back at the 'literature of cozenage and vagabondage', some of which, like the play's source, was by Greene. Orgel sees Autolycus as 'the figure in this play closest to the playwright' (p. 52), though he recognizes the claim of Paulina and indeed contrasts the two figures valuably: Apollonian Paulina 'keeps the secret of her redemptive witchcraft to herself', whereas 'we are placed in collusion' with Mercurial Autolycus (p. 53). In this respect, it may be added, the play revises the lofty rejection of Mercury in the motto to *Venus and Adonis*, probably written in response to the demeaning attack on Shakespeare as a Mercurial literary thief in *Greene's Groatsworth of Wit*: '*Vilia miretur vulgus; mihi flavus Apollo / Pocula Castalia plena ministret aqua*' – though, as Autolycus is excluded from the sight that cannot be spoken of, is a passive auditor of the account of it in 5.2, and is absent in the final scene where Paulina has the last dramaturgical word, his form of playmaking is finally superseded.

Queen Elizabeth returns into view when Orgel relates Paulina's imaginary statue to King James's reconciliatory and memorializing statues of his predecessor on the English throne and his mother Queen Mary. Orgel recognizes that the virtuous magic that transforms the past is related to religious transcendence, but he places stronger emphasis on its occult properties. Magic is, as in *The Tempest*, 'an erotic control mechanism' (p. 60); moreover, 'The conjuror's art is the art of the theatre' (p. 61). For this reason, Orgel pays firmly selective attention to the theatrical history of the play by pursuing a single detail, the representation of Hermione in the final scene. Orgel's own reading of the play's ending is firmly anti-sentimental: 'For modern audiences, the reunion of husband and wife is the essential element in the dénouement, but this may well be an anachronistic reaction' (pp. 77–8); 'The tragic loss that Perdita represents is ... the loss of an heir' (p. 79). Not everyone's historical imagination will leap these hurdles, not least because the dynastic outcome is settled offstage before the final scene, and because the final scene is focused on emotive and sensory effect. There is, indeed, an emotional bareness to Orgel's account where he fends off responses that would endorse a patriarchal reading. Perhaps such an edition is what is needed, and certainly Orgel's elegant introduction is replete with intellectual riches.

In Appendices the edition prints Simon Forman's eye-witness account, the entire text of *Pandosto*, and musical settings of the songs and 'The Satyrs' Masque' played and danced at 4.4.337. I noted one serious error in the text ('sit you' for 'you sit', 2.1.22) and an unrecorded relineation (2.3.59: two lines in F).

Modern editions of the Sonnets are predominantly exercises in commentary. The introduction to G. Blakemore Evans's New Cambridge edition, written by Anthony Hecht, runs to less than twenty-four pages, whilst Evans's commentary, though double-columned and printed in a smaller type-face, extends to over twice the page-count of the text. Hecht's introduction begins by declaring the Sonnets 'a compact and attractive *vade mecum*' for young lovers (p. 1). Something of what he means can be gleaned from his account of Sonnet 35, which 'hovers among alternatives, all of them anguishing, delicate in its manoeuvring, tense in its anxiety not to place too much blame on the beloved, but unable to conceal the torment from which the poem sprang' (p. 5). The immediate claim is that the poems relate directly to emotional experience; 'I have known both heterosexual and homosexual instances of this kind of devotion', he assures us on p. 3. But then there is literary form, a topic Hecht introduces with what seems to be a touch of weariness: 'It may be as well at this point to say something about ...' (p. 5). Hecht usefully draws a distinction between rhyme-scheme and ideational form, pointing out that a sonnet with 'Shakespearean' rhyme-scheme can be 'decisively Petrarchan' in its rhetorical structure (p. 9). What I find missing from this part of his account is a sense of tension between formal and rhetorical structures. And indeed of tension within the rhetorical structure, in that the 'decisively Petrarchan' Sonnet 18 reinforces the final couplet by beginning a new sentence (in the edited text the sole full-stop appears after line 12) and by beginning both of the final lines with 'So long ...'. Hecht obscures this part of his essay with commentary that has little to do with sonnet form, throwing in, for example, William Empson's famous comments on l. 4 of Sonnet 73. That there should be a lack of purposeful direction when structural matters are addressed shows that Hecht's prose might itself learn something from the poetry he is discussing. What runs through the whole of this rather disorganized account is a sincere concern with tonality and emotional truth. The contextual information is thin, and there is little attention to the areas of thematic interest so successfully addressed in John Kerrigan's New Penguin edition of 1986.

Evans's text is reliably and sensitively edited. Except in that he retains, where possible, Q's parentheses, his claim to preserve the 'often fluid rhetorical movement' of the original punctuation need not be taken too literally, for a modern logicality predominates. Modernization of spelling is conservative, though a few forms left unmodernized in Evans's Riverside Shakespeare edition (1974) are now altered. In the collation, regularizations of acceptable and unambiguous Jacobean spellings are routinely recorded as emendations of the text. In cases where the note does not concern emendation, capitalization, or punctuation, and where the modernization is not ambiguous as it is with a form such as 'weare', the explanation '*variant form*' is added – or so I surmise, for the system at work here is not transparent.

Forms such as 'every where' are routinely printed as two words, though Q's 'my selfe' is almost always merged to a single word. An exception is made for:

> As easy might I from my self depart
> As from my soul (Sonnet 109, lines 3–4).

But elsewhere Evans reads:

> Me from myself thy cruel eye hath taken,
> And my next self thou harder hast engrossed:
> (Sonnet 133, lines 5–6).

Whereas the separation in the first example is noted and attributed to Q, the merging in Sonnet 133, as elsewhere, occurs without note. Yet it is precisely here, where the original reading actively impinges on critical discussion, that a collation-line averaging about seven notes per sonnet might be expected to help. Similarly, the recording of relatively minor details of punctuation creates a misleading impression that the reader has been given everything of note. In Sonnet 98 the insertion of an apostrophe in Q's 'Lillies' is recorded as an emendation originated by Capell, but in the previous Sonnet 97 three apostrophes appear silently. The opening of Sonnet 24 is printed:

> Mine eye hath played the painter and hath stelled
> Thy beauty's form in table of my heart;

Q reads:

> Mine eye hath play'd the painter and hath steeld,
> Thy beauties forme in table of my heart,

Setting aside the crux 'steeld', it might appear from Q that the second line begins a new clause with 'forme' as a verb. In Evans's edition we are told that 'stelled' is an emendation of 'steeld', but not of other changes that have silently created an environment conducive towards the emended transitive verb. Such quibbles might be multiplied; they point as a whole to the difficulty in keeping under self-consistent control a collation that apparently pays close attention to sub-substantive details.

I can stay with Sonnet 24 as a test-case for the commentary, for the poem presents undeniable challenges to the commentator as regards both tone and meaning. Evans provides short headnotes to many of the Sonnets; in them he is prepared to discuss questions of tone and even to risk evaluative judgement. In this instance we read that the poem 'is generally considered one of the most mechanically conceited and imitative of the sonnets; Mahood (p. 93) describes it as "pure Bosch" (perhaps 'pure bosh' might be even more accurate).' Even an editor can afford to abandon hagiography once in a while, but I feel wary of this dismissal of Shakespeare's writing precisely at the point where the language lies outside its usual register. The notes that follow do full justice to the sonnet's artifice. That for l. 4 makes use of elaborate serial and parallel sets of parentheses in a way that is too characteristic of this commentary, but it is dedicated in explicating complex meaning. But, at a first reading at least, Evans's account of l. 8, 'That hath his windows glazèd with thine eyes', offers little clarification of what is one of the more difficult lines in

Shakespeare: 'Which (= 'bosom's shop') has its ('his') windows (i.e. the poet's eyes) glassed over ('glazèd', i.e. as a protection) with your eyes'. This is, I think, accurate as far as it goes, but is unhappily literal; I find myself trying to keep at bay images of domestic double glazing and industrial goggles. Most readers probably need telling more about the underlying literary conceits and Shakespeare's paradoxical attenuation of them. Only then are they likely to discover how the image makes complex play both between what is within and what is outside the poet's body, and between a representation and an emotional reality. Not quite Bosch, though there is a question of style and an Empsonian reading would welcome the suggestion of a body with windows in its chest. Nor quite bosh, as behind the arbitrary playfulness is a serious meditation on art. Instead, perhaps, Donne outdone. The poem needs a different kind of concentration and patience from many of the other Shakespeare sonnets; it is not to be disrelished too quickly.

Kerrigan's commentary deals with these lines more satisfactorily, and remains in other respects too my preferred edition. Evans has extra detail that will be helpful to some readers and adds some fresh illumination; his commentary typically has more notes per sonnet; it is probably longer and more active in evaluation, comparison, and cross-reference. Evans follows Kerrigan in supplying an appendix on manuscript versions and readings. A final point in Kerrigan's favour is his inclusion of the poem published in the same 1609 book as the Sonnets, 'A Lover's Complaint'. Kerrigan's argument that the Sonnets and 'A Lover's Complaint' make an artistically structured entity is partly admitted by Evans when he accepts the likelihood that Shakespeare 'was revising and ordering the Sonnets and adding *A Lover's Complaint*' at the same time (pp. 281–2). On the face of it, the narrative poem should be included, and Evans does not explain its absence.

SHAKESPEARE WITHOUT THE AUTHOR

Barbara Mowat has written a significant article on 'The Problem of Shakespeare's Text(s)' that attempts to pick up some of the ideas emerging through the 'New Textualism' and apply them to the practicalities of editing. There is no questioning the centrality of the problems Mowat confronts to the present situation of the Shakespeare editor. Whether they can be satisfactorily resolved is another matter.

Mowat justly notes that if Shakespeare's manuscripts were found they would probably present editors with textual problems as perplexing as those of the printed texts. In a critical climate that rejects 'the larger single voice that was for so long heard as Shakespeare's own' (p. 35) editors can and should break away from the engrained habit of invoking that lost manuscript in order to affiliate text with author. This perspective has informed her own and Paul Werstine's editorial decision-making for the Folger Shakespeare Library series.[3] She does not offer a fully convincing account of authorless editing, but rather a revelation of some of its challenges and possibilities. Mowat catches W. W. Greg sounding distinctly over-confident in correspondence with Dover Wilson as to the precise features of a manuscript such as would give rise to a suspected error in *The Merchant of Venice* 5.1.49–50, though Greg does confine himself to the word 'conjecture' (Wilson's Cambridge edition (1926), pp. 106–7). In inferring that the mechanics of transmission can be ignored, Mowat pinpoints the disutility of textual theory to editing. An editor contemplating an emendation needs to consider not only whether the emended reading is preferable but also whether the error is plausible. The objective, neither to establish a definitive account of the manuscript nor to justify otherwise unjustifiable emendations, is rather to help

[3] No editions in the series have been submitted for review.

keep the editorial process reasonably convincing and self-consistent. Though the principle has been most clearly articulated by Greg,[4] it is fundamental to editing, not only editing practised under the New Bibliography.

When considering the line in *Romeo and Juliet* 'I will raise her statue in pure gold' (5.3.298), Mowat and Werstine decided in a spirit of conservatism to the copy to break with editorial tradition and restore the verb to Q2's 'ray', meaning 'array' (p. 43). Actually, Q2 reads 'raie'; the misquotation exaggerates the difference between the form and the emendation of it, which is confined to a single letter.[5] In other respects too Mowat's account here is not as reliable as it might be. The 'break' with editorial tradition is not decisive, because Richard Hosley in his 1954 Yale edition accepted Q2's reading on the same basis as did Mowat and Werstine. Of greater importance, 'raise' was not 'taken by eighteenth-century editors from the jumbled first quarto edition' as Mowat claims, but appears in Q4 and F almost simultaneously.[6] Q1 reads 'erect' which, as a synonym for 'raise', offers qualified support for that reading. 'Raise' is the only reading of the three to triangulate with both others (with 'raie' phonically and graphically, with 'erect' semantically).[7] Mowat is justified in defending 'raie', but the collateral readings cannot be brushed aside.

Mowat is not opposed to emendation *per se*, so the challenge lies precisely in finding a satisfactory basis on which to emend without invoking the manuscript Shakespeare wrote. Editorial policy as she articulates it is that one follows a chosen copy-text but 'adds or substitutes variants or emendations only in specific circumstances' (p. 43), which the editor spells out. Unless these circumstances are severely limited, that is potentially a far more permissive formulation than McKerrow or Greg would have tolerated. One circumstance she discusses introduces a particularly uncircumscribed freedom: cases where 'the weight of the familiarity of the line as we have inherited it from the editorial tradition became the deciding factor'. The examples are F *Hamlet*'s 'Gertrude' where Q2 has 'Gertrard', and Q1 *Othello*'s reading '... did love ...' as compared with F's 'That I love the Moor to live with him'. Why might not the criterion be extended to apply equally, say, to the editorial conflation of *King Lear* or *Hamlet*? It is a dangerous Joker in the pack, partly because it could vindicate any of so many non-copy readings, partly because it conflicts so decisively with the main end in view, to stick to a particular early printed text 'as closely as is feasible' (p. 43), and partly because

---

4 '... that no emendation can or ought to be considered *in vacuo*, but that criticism must always proceed in relation to what we know, or surmise, respecting the history of the text' ('Principles of Emendation in Shakespeare', in *Proceedings of the British Academy*, 14 (1928); reprinted in *Aspects of Shakespeare* (1933), p. 133).

5 The quotation is perhaps just silently modernized, but some other quotations are in original spellings and the procedure is irregular.

6 George Walton Williams dates the printing of Q4 'before November 1622' ('The Printer and the Date of *Romeo and Juliet* Q4', in *Studies in Bibliography*, 18 (1965), 253–4). In F, the Histories were evidently completed by the end of the first quarter of 1623 (Charlton Hinman, *The Printing and Proof-Reading of the First Folio of Shakespeare*, 2 vols. (1963), vol. 2, p. 524), so *Romeo and Juliet* was set later in that year. As John Smethwicke was both publisher of Q4 and a member of the Folio syndicate, it seems likely that the emendation in both editions is non-coincidental.

7 In fairness to 'raie', it should be pointed out that Q4 was, according to Williams, printed with reference to Q1 (see his 1964 edition of the play, pp. xi–xii); it is therefore at least possible that 'raie' was corrected to 'raise' through reference to Q1 'erect', and that Q1 here came to influence F. Compare Q4's and F's shared alteration of '*Capels* are' to '*Capulets*' at 3.1.2. What complicates matters still further is S. W. Reid's persuasive suggestion that the copy for F was lightly annotated with reference to a theatrical manuscript or through knowledge of performance ('The Editing of Folio *Romeo and Juliet*', *Studies in Bibliography*, 35 (1982), 43–66), which opens up the alternative possibility that 'raise' is an authoritative correction (which is not necessarily to say that 'raie' is an error). The relation between the collateral readings will always be relevant for establishing the parameters of editorial decisions.

there is no way of determining which of the conflicting principles will prevail. For instance, familiarity from the received text might have been but was not applied to the 'famous line' about Juliet's statue.

In Mowat's formulation the 'Shakespeare' constructed by editors replaces the retired dead-author Shakespeare who wrote plays in the 1590s and 1600s. The need to call on some notion of 'Shakespeare' to justify departing from the copy-text is real, but this partial reversion to the *textus receptus* threatens to enable tactical but sentimental deference to tradition in a spirit of theoretical conflict with, and practical disregard of, what Shakespeare might have written.[8] In contrast, Mowat and Werstine's own introductions in the Folger series use formulations such as (in *Othello*, 1993) 'Shakespeare's Language', 'Shakespeare's *Othello*', 'In *Othello*, Shakespeare creates ...' with conspicuous liberality. The tables have truly turned when the editor as textualist is far more embarrassed to name Shakespeare than the editor as critic.

Werstine's own views on the status of widely variant printed texts were expressed in a sophisticated essay 'The Textual Mystery of *Hamlet*' (*Shakespeare Quarterly*, 39 (1988), 1–26). A reductive summary of Werstine's position would be that he valorizes Q2 and F as independent and mutually 'alien' forms whilst repudiating the view that their differences can all be defined as authorial. He agrees with G. R. Hibbard in his 1988 Oxford Shakespeare edition (pp. 14–28) that the editorial *Hamlet* produces some of the mysteries of Hamlet the character by over-determining his motives. Todd S. Gilman's '*Hamlet* among the Revisionists' mounts a brave critique of the 'revisionists' that concentrates most of its energy on opposing Werstine. That 'Q2 is true too' (p. 80) is a view that will be supported by many revisionists, not least Werstine, but Gilman is surely mistaken in arguing that if both texts are 'true' then a combination of them is best of all. He is right to find that Werstine makes too much of Q2's and F's apparent failures to be totally consistent with any summary characterization of them. But I am not persuaded that Werstine commits the same reduction of polysemous versions to single lines of meaning that he himself detects in Philip Edwards in his 1985 Cambridge edition. Werstine's point is that he consistently avoids the originatory frame of reference: 'To claim that such patterns must originate with Shakespeare is to abolish the distinction between history and aesthetics' (p. 24). Gilman finds such disclaimers contradictory and evasive. There is some truth in the latter charge if one seeks in Werstine's article a basis for editing *Hamlet*, but Werstine's stance in this paper was more magisterial.

Graham Holderness and his collaborators have published widely on the topic of Shakespeare and textual theory. They seem, indeed, locked into a hermeneutic circle that runs this particular author over every time it steams round the track, clocking up the publications as it goes. Holderness, Bryan Loughrey, and Andrew Murphy in 'Shakespeare and Textual Theory' celebrate the trajectory of the term 'materialism' from the 'crude' sense in which it applies to New Bibliography to a 'sophisticated' Marxist theory, their own. This theory enables them to correct the reader of his or her supposed illusion that a printed book has the same 'physical identity' and the same 'relationship to the general process of production' as a theatrical manuscript, and to assert as though for the first time that the printed text is 'primary evidence'. HLM take particular issue with Margreta de Grazia and Peter Stallybrass's article 'The Materiality of the Shakespearean Text' (*Shakespeare Quarterly*, 44 (1993), 255–83), which they characterize as 'poststructuralist

[8] I describe the logic of the position rather than Mowat's point of view or her editorial practice. For example, when she describes Q2 *Romeo and Juliet* as 'the only authoritative text' (p. 43) I suspect a residual acknowledgement that it is relatively close to what Shakespeare wrote. (But compare Halio, as reviewed below, on Q1.)

bibliographical materialism'. There is a contradiction, they claim, between de Grazia and Stallybrass's insistence on the text as a physical object in its own right and the text as an object that bears witness to its relationship with the world in which it appeared.

HLM attack de Grazia and Stallybrass by misreading them. The latter call for consideration of Shakespeare 'in relation to ... the historical contingencies of textual production', these are manifested in the book as 'traces', and de Grazia and Stallybrass complicate the crude axes of synchrony and diachrony in their tellingly enigmatic figure of the absorptive surface of paper. None of this remotely corresponds with either HLM's paraphrase 'open window' (p. 102) or with their suggestion that the book as a textual object in de Grazia and Stallybrass's account can simply disappear. This comes close to contestation by parody. But the wedge has been inserted, the axes are rising, and de Grazia and Stallybrass are pressed onto the wrong one.

HLM themselves advance a notion of historicity that isolates the text from contingency: its '*identity*' lies in its '*original* character as a commodity' and its '*self-differentiation* from the process of production and exchange' (my emphases), as if a text were author of itself and knew no other kin. To change metaphor, history as they invoke it seems to be a still and transparent water at the bottom of which lie preciously autonomous artefacts. To change metaphor again, the textualist's job is, in the vanguardist words of their associate Andrew Spong, to 'place a cordon around each version of each text'.[9] And so, in the practice, or non-practice, of this 'materialist bibliography' even the tokenistically recognized circumstances of printing and circulation as a commodity can be almost entirely ignored. Marx would surely have been astonished.[10]

Whereas Mowat and Werstine seek to edit without reference to the author, Holderness is opposed to emending at all. Yet his edition of Quarto *King Lear* in the Shakespearean Originals series is a heavily mediated presentation of the text even as it strains for authenticity. Even the inelegantly full standard form of the play's title used throughout the introduction, '*M. William Shak-speare: his true chronicle historie of the life and death of King Lear and his three daughters*', rejects the Quarto's continuation describing the Gloucester–Edgar story, thus promoting the main plot and silencing the subplot. The edition's running title offers a convenient reduction of the title-page to '*Chronicle Historie of King Lear and His three Daughters*'.[11] This, or at least the further reduction on the rear cover to 'KING LEAR AND HIS THREE DAUGHTERS', is an illuminating new short title for the play. It does not, however, have the slightest validity. Holderness alleges that the short title *The History of King Lear* was 'invented by the Oxford editors' (p. 25),[12] but he is wrong. The play's running title in Q is, quite simply, '*The Historie of King Lear*'.[13] Holderness's alteration of it is a conspicuous falsification – conspicuous, at least, to those able to consult the document that the edition supposedly represents. Whether or not one likes the generic emphasis in distinguishing between *The History of King Lear* and *The Tragedy of King Lear* is beside the point; these

[9] Andrew Spong, 'Bad Habits, "Bad" Quartos, and the Myth of Origin in the Editing of Shakespeare', *New Theatre Quarterly*, 45 (1996), 65–70, p. 68.

[10] Marx himself examined paper-making: see Karl Marx, *Capital*, trans. Eden and Cedar Paul (1930; revised single-vol. edn., 1974), p. 403. On the effacement of the process of production, compare Marx on the commodity under capitalism and 'the magic of money': 'The intermediate steps of the process vanish in the result, and leave not a trace behind' (pp. 68–9).

[11] In ceasing to be 'True', Q is better distinguished, and needfully, from the source play, referred to as '*The True Chronicle Historie of King Leir*' or, on p. 36, '*The True Chronicle Historie of King Lear*'.

[12] See also Holderness and Naomi Carter, 'The King's Two Bodies: Text and Genre in *King Lear*', *English*, 45 (1996), 1–31.

[13] The entry in the Stationers' Register and the Quarto head-title also refer to the play as the 'Historie of King Lear'.

are the 'textualized' short titles for both versions.

Holderness is thus willing to ignore the document on which he bases his text if it resists his critical perspective.[14] When he does so he abandons the whole point of the series, which is its commitment to minimal editorial interference. Yet the initial claim to minimal interference rests on an attenuated sense of what the text was in the first place. The physical document is abstracted to a string of electronic letter-forms reproducible in modern typography – and no more. Paper, binding, ink, the physical impression of metal type, page layout, catchwords, running-titles, irregular spacing, all disappear; in Holderness's text of *Lear*, Q's marginal stage directions are presented as footnotes. Nor does the materiality lie, if it hypothetically could do, in the letter-forms themselves, because (for instance) two distinct ways of printing 's' are represented as one, and ligatures are routinely resolved as separate letters. If materiality lies not in the printed letters but in the words as signs, it is not clear why the series is committed to printing letter sequences that do not constitute words. My disquiet here is not with the project of presenting affordable editions of specific printed editions in original spelling, nor, at its most fundamental, with weaknesses in execution. At issue is the series's claim to a unique probity founded on sound theoretical credentials. In its practice the material text is crucified to resurrect Materiality and send it to heaven, the flesh made word.

Most of the Shakespearian Originals editors under review have found it productive to look behind the printed text to the manuscript, and even occasionally behind the manuscript to Shakespeare, or have situated one or more texts in relation to postulated early readers, or have compared their copy editions with a collateral text (a task few early modern readers can be supposed to have undertaken), or have considered the text in relation to later performance practices. There is a welcome variety here that reflects both the nature of the texts in question and the diversity of their editors' approaches.

Andrew Murphy opens his account of Q1 *Othello* by citing Thomas L. Berger's description of Q2 (1630) as 'probably the first consistently conflated text of any Shakespearian play' ('The Second Quarto of *Othello* and the Question of Textual "Authority"', in *Analytic and Enumerative Bibliography*, NS, 2 (1988), 141–59, p. 145). Berger is right to show how the procedures of so-called 'modern' editing edge perilously close to Shakespeare's own time, but there is even earlier conflation. I refer particularly to the Folio editors, though the practice goes back further still; the very earliest second edition of a Shakespeare play, Cuthbert Burby's 1599 *Romeo and Juliet*, was itself a conflated text.[15] The distinction between early modern printed books as discrete textualizations and modern editions as bastardized conflations is seriously misleading from the start. Q1 *Othello*, of course, has interest and value in its own right, and Murphy describes that interest and value in a compact piece of advocacy. He rather glosses over some demanding textual problems in Q, and there is hesitation on whether to base his discussion as a whole on the theory of authorial revision or the theory of 'discrete textualization'.

Cedric Watts, in his edition of Q1 *Romeo and Juliet*, shows a better sense of the document than most other editors in the series. Watts reproduces the printer's ornaments throughout the text (though a single exemplar of the bar ornament has been duplicated rather than reproducing each set of blocks). The presence of ornaments makes it all the more desirable to see something even more like the original. For example, only one of the two printers inserted mid-text ornaments, and there is an important

[14] In a similar spirit, plays in the series originally published as by Shakespeare are usually presented on the edition title page as though anonymous. (*Lear* is an exception.)

[15] Though Q2 was predominantly set from manuscript copy, a section was set from Q1. See also n. 7 above.

correlation between John Danter's recourse to larger type, which Watts doesn't reproduce, and Edward Allde's recourse to ornaments. In Watts's edition the ornamental bars that obtrusively and repeatedly interrupt what he calls the 'fluid momentum' of the text remain puzzling, despite a brief account of them in a footnote (n. 10, pp. 21–2). It is impossible to tell even roughly where the change of printers occurred.

The Shakespearean Originals under review include two texts that regularly provide editors with their copy. Annabel Patterson describes Q1 *Merchant of Venice* as 'a very fine text ... possibly printed directly from the holograph' (pp. 32–3) and Laurie E. Osborne calls Folio *Twelfth Night* 'an unusually clean text' (p. 14). There is no need for special pleading as to theatrical or literary quality. What, then, is the appropriate focus for an introduction in this series? *Merchant* has, according to Patterson, 'sufficient philosophical self-identity to satisfy the idealist – the believer in definitive texts which can fully represent autonomous acts of creation [are there such?] – along with some very interesting signs of historical contingency and fossilised evidence of the materiality of printing' (pp. 13–14). She notes the hyperbolic misinformation on the Quarto title-page about Shylock's 'extreame crueltie' in actually 'cutting a iust pound' of flesh from the merchant's chest. There are other losses in standard modernized texts: the stereotyping prefix 'Jewe' becomes 'Shylock'; 'Launcelet' is no longer a lancelet or little knife but rather an irrelevantly Arthurian 'Lancelot',[16] and his patronymic 'Jobbe' is turned from a comic Judaic Job to a hunchback Italianate '*Gobbo*'.

At the heart of Patterson's account is a double-barrelled question, 'Was the Quarto intended to be bought and read as an anti-Semitic play? Or was it intended to be *purchased* as an anti-Semitic play, but one that could lure some of its readers into a more nuanced and anxious position?' (p. 21). These queries are partly rhetorical because unanswerable, especially as one's answer might depend on whether one regards the author, the theatre company, or the publisher as the intending agent. The speech-prefixes, with their alternation between forms for 'Shylock' and 'Jew', are identified by Patterson as authorial, but they are unlikely to be intentional discriminations directed at the Quarto's readers. Though one would wish otherwise, it is scarcely possible to seize eagerly on the second question and answer 'yes'. Patterson contributes some interesting discussion of the subsequent quartos of 1619, 1637, and 1652; the latter is related to the philo-Semitic movement that culminated in the Whitehall Conference of 1656. Unfortunately the 1652 text was not editorially altered from its Caroline copy. It is useful to be reminded that meaning can depend on the situation of the reader, though the relevance to the *First* Quarto is tangential at least.

Osborne looks at the typographical features of Folio *Twelfth Night* and a history of performance that she believes is embedded in it. Reiterating a standard critique of modernization, she notes that it resolves 'I' as either 'I' or 'aye', or a question mark as either a question mark or an exclamation mark, imposing a fixity that the original did not possess. She relishes the ambiguities opened up by the seventeenth-century printing of 'your selfe' and other reflexives as two words, unlike Evans. Developing the theme of subjectivity, she considers the implications for character-identity in F's running together without quotation marks of quoted speech with a character's own speech. As regards the performance history, Osborne's thesis is that 'minor and major indications of revision' reveal no less than 'a host of possible alternative versions for the comedy' (p. 26).[17]

[16] The same convincing correction of the standard modernization is made by Barbara Mowat and Paul Werstine in their Folger edition (1992).

[17] There can scarcely have been a 'host' of actual revised revivals before 1623. For a study of the alterations in an extant playbook that seems to have been through at least two revivals, see William B. Long, '"A bed / for woodstock": A Warning for the Unwary', *Medieval and Renaissance Drama*, 2 (1985), 91–118.

For example, Viola's assertion that she 'can sing' has, as Osborne points out, stimulated stagings with singing Violas who have displaced Feste. Osborne's inference that a singing Viola is part of the pre-1623 performance tradition has a long pedigree that should be cautionary in itself, running towards Osborne as it does from F. G. Fleay via John Dover Wilson. The hypothesis is rejected sensibly by Robert K. Turner in 'The Text of *Twelfth Night*' (*Shakespeare Quarterly*, 26 (1975), 128–38), an article Osborne unconvincingly attempts to refute. To Turner the singing Viola is amongst 'vestiges of ideas never pursued' (p. 133), and there is 'little reason to think that the F1 text of *TN* is one revised after the original production' (p.137). Probably, then, performers and textual critics alike translated an unrealized possibility into a re-created text. As there might have been interplay between the ideas of more recent textual critics and those of more recent performers, it would be especially risky to assume that they had independent intuitions of a pre-1623 theatrical actuality. Turner's seems a preferable narrative to the one Osborne proposes, not because it rests on a fantasy of textual stability, but because it responds to the textual evidence with greater efficiency. And that is to be valued.

Karen Bjelland's 'The Cultural Value of Analytic Bibliography and Textual Criticism: The Case of *Troilus and Cressida*' unleashes an undisciplined stream of rhetoric that is simultaneously restricted and verbose in diction, aggressive in tone, bizarrely inaccurate for a socio-historical approach in its central assumption that Shakespeare was a member of the 'Jacobean aristocracy', illogical in its conduct, and shameless in its pretension to grandeur. A sample of her project is this: 'By diffusing the traditional concentration upon an author's roster of "elite sources," a reconstruction of the potential contexts governing the "epistemological core" of these [Quarto/Folio] variants, and any temporal shifts from one context to another with respect to a given verbal pair, could then be effected along with a reassessment of why editors have chosen one variant as opposed to another in eclectically produced texts. Once done, this will also lead to a subsequent redefining of what constitutes literacy with respect to the audience ...' (pp. 282–3). She manages this investigation without actually referring to a single non-élite text. If there is virtue in her appeal to bibliographers to extend the social and cultural basis of their investigations, it is undermined by the fragmentary and inconclusive nature of her own examples.

Critical Survey has brought out a lively volume given over largely to 'Textual Shakespeare', edited by Graham Holderness and Andrew Murphy. It happily transcends the dogmatism of the editors' theory as expounded in their *Critical Practice* article. Some articles usefully address matters of general editorial and textual theory,[18] but I shall confine my present comments to those that address Shakespeare.

The most substantial and entertaining contribution to the issue, and indeed the finest piece of textual criticism presently under review, comes from Claudia Nimbus, who investigates Hanmer's edition of Shakespeare as Mrs Siddons marked it up for her public recitals of *King John*. In this study Mrs Siddons as adapter assumes some characteristics of the author, though Nimbus reminds us that the theatrical and editorial traditions that precede Siddons's own reshaping had also been busily engaged in some pre-authorship of her performance script. Nimbus describes how a passage relegated to the foot of the page in Pope's and Hanmer's editions was mis-sequenced when worked back into the performance text. The reordered text became an established part of a theatrical tradition that Siddons inherited from Kemble. Nimbus builds, through an analysis of markings, folds, and a pinned-in slip of paper, towards an 'apocalyptic rendering of Mrs Siddons' Book'

[18] See also G. Thomas Tanselle, 'Textual Instability and Editorial Idealism', *Studies in Bibliography*, 49 (1996), 1–60.

(p. 283) in which she reconstructs the entire text of the play as Siddons would have recited it. Nimbus shows how Siddons transposed part of 3.4 to follow 4.3, so providing a strong close to a recital that centred entirely on the role of Constance. A final mystery is revealed in the notes on contributors, where the nimbus disperses to reveal Claudia as McLeod.

In the same volume, Steven Urkowitz inveighs against the conflation of textual details from the Quarto *First Part of the Contention* and Folio 2 *Henry VI*. His paper transforms into a call for jaunty magazine-format editions of Shakespeare with 'space for treats' that open up new possibilities for thinking about the text. Urkowitz obviously believes that a more extensive amount of textual discussion than is customary can be a source of intellectual provocation and enjoyment if it is attractively packaged. He wishes to introduce 'a collaborative, generative model of playing and playmaking' (p. 297). It would have been helpful for Urkowitz to have complemented his critique of current editorial solemnities by providing a sample of an edition such as he proposes. Laurie E. Osborne's contribution 'Shattuck and Kemble: Intermingling editing in facsimile' points to the variety of material assembled under the heading 'promptbooks' in Charles Shattuck's *John Philip Kemble Promptbooks* collection; as a critique of facsimile editing its focus is well represented in its title. Sasha Roberts, like Nimbus and Osborne, examines specific Shakespeare editions as they were read, but her concern is with the early modern literary reader of seventeenth-century texts. This is an important emergent area of study, though, as the evidence is somewhat fragmentary, so too can be the account of it. Roberts finds one kind of focus by concentrating on women readers. She expands on Paul Morgan's important study of 'Frances Wolfreston and "Hor Bouks"' (*The Library*, VI, 11 (1989), 197–219), and notes a number of women readers of the Shakespeare First Folio whose names are inscribed in various Folger copies. The article concludes with a salutary reminder that for early modern readers it was the particular book in the hand that counted, not the work as constituted in modern editions. She observes that 'The implications of this for notions of textual authority and authenticity have only just begun to be addressed' (p. 305).

Indeed: there was Shakespeare as read, which includes, for example, Benson's wilfully eccentric 1640 edition of Shakespeare's (and others') *Poems*, and there was Shakespeare as performed, which includes adaptation by Middleton and various anons. Multiplicity is merrier, but begs the question that arises from human limitation: which less is more?

REVISION AND MEMORY

There are oceans of blue water between the post-Foucauldian textualists and John Jones.[19] His *Shakespeare at Work* is an extrapolation from the field of textual study and editing into the field of criticism, exploring Shakespeare's creativity through the unique window on his mind that is afforded, Jones believes, by the process of textual revision. There are numerous references showing the author's acceptance of and reliance on the Oxford Shakespeare of 1986 and the various studies that informed that edition. Indeed, for textual scholars who uphold the view that Shakespeare was a conscious and self-improving artist, Jones's blithe endorsement of their theories will cause both gratification and alarm. Hypotheses harden into provisional facts, and the textual data that suggest revision fortify a view of Shakespeare that is only one of many possible interpretative applications of those data.

Jones considers a number of works, play by play, devoting major chapters to *Hamlet* and *King Lear*. Except when writing of *Troilus and*

[19] My accounts of Jones's book and E. A. J. Honigmann's *The Texts of 'Othello' and Shakespearian Revision* below are largely based on my review 'The milk of the word', *TLS*, 23 August 1996, pp. 13–14.

Cressida, a play he unjustly detests, his book is crammed with praise. A single example will illustrate the scope and limitation of his approach. The 1623 Folio text of *Othello* adds to Othello's final exchange with Desdemona before smothering her 'a little aside' that has no equivalent in the 1622 Quarto that reads, 'Being done, there is no pawse.' Jones comments that Shakespeare in the passage

> was expressing the weirdness of normal psychology ... We have come to know Othello, and because his psychology, unlike Iago's, is normal, the familiarity has a second sense to it: we know the man and we know human nature ... But it would be hard to imagine anything of greater delicacy than the pitching of Othello's added line ... he [the playgoer] does sense the very subtle obscurity, the internal shifting and instability, that haunt the apparently blunt statement of the man of action. (p. 240)

A refined critical sensitivity is here generously and communicatively at work, relating local detail to the play's largest concerns. It bears witness to an old-fashioned sensibility that the potent alliance of textualist perspective and critical acumen should serve such an emphatically 'essentialist' vision of Shakespeare. Today, it seems that Jones is playing a dangerous critical game when he uses the Folio variant to urge that Shakespeare's motivation is discernible, that Shakespeare aimed to make the playgoer, presumably male, recognize his consanguinity with the wife-murderer and accept such aberrant behaviour as normal. One might see, instead, a dissociation between audience and character. The line in question might represent two, three, or more incompatible and half-realized thoughts riveted together to make up an illogical but effective armour against respite. Its overloaded but unformed meanings call out for the very pause that Othello rules out. The audience is empowered to accuse Othello, even as the audience sees Othello repressing the ability to accuse himself. So the added line does not necessarily give sympathetic amplitude to Othello's strange normality. A textual alteration such as this adds to the text and the interpretative possibilities that constitute 'Shakespeare' but provides no shortcut to the man's soul.

Jones's assumption that textual variants in the plays he discusses are authorial variants is itself being placed under pressure, sometimes more successfully than others. In the Oxford Shakespeare, plays recognized as having been revised by Shakespeare such as *Hamlet*, *Troilus and Cressida*, and *Othello* are edited on the basis of the revised text. Although only one text is presented, the editing recognizes two distinct versions. It continues to provoke and disconcert critics that, if only on account of printing-house errors, the version does not perfectly coincide with the printed text that represents it.

Phebe Jensen's 'The Textual Politics of *Troilus and Cressida*' mounts a strong challenge to Taylor's editing of the play. Here we are once again in that fertile but unstable territory where a theoretically aware textual criticism meets the practicalities of editing. Jensen reads Taylor's '*Troilus and Cressida*: Bibliography, Performance, and Interpretation' (*Shakespeare Studies*, 15 (1982), 99–136) from back to front, claiming that the 'Interpretation' that appears as Taylor's coda actually determines the direction of his textual investigations. Taylor, she claims, has an agenda, which is to stabilize a generically unstable text as a tragedy. And there is a sense in which this is so. Having outlined his textual hypothesis and defined putative 'Inns of Court' and 'Globe' versions of *Troilus*,[20] Taylor gives a clear endorsement of the latter as the text that represents Shakespeare's reconsidered and therefore improved view of the play. It does not necessarily follow that a revision is an improvement, and if the two texts were to correspond with two distinct venues in the way he suggests, if the revision is indeed a reorientation of the play from one audience to another,

[20] The latter is testified by an assertion on the first setting of the Quarto title page that the play had been acted at the Globe, but this is ambiguous evidence as the words were removed when the title-page was reset and the epistle to the reader introduced.

the principle of observing the author's final intentions need not apply. It is an irony of the debate that the two-venue theory Jensen rejects throws a particular lifeline to Q, the version she favours. The effect of Taylor's conclusion is nevertheless to promote, over a viable but subtly discredited alternative, a text that has the theatrical imprimatur of Globe, the textual imprimatur of Folio, and the generic imprimatur of Tragedy.

Taylor notes that F introduces a new version of Troilus' 'Hence, broken lackey' dismissal of Pandarus at the end of the play after his 'words, mere words' speech in 5.3. The repetition as it stands in F is impossible, and so Taylor urges that the new version in 5.3 must be designed to replace the original one in 5.6 that is common to Q and F. Further, as the original lines lead into Pandarus' 'epilogue' speech, the main end in view in the Folio revision was to get rid of this conclusion to the play and supply Pandarus and Troilus with a new, earlier parting.

What is unusual in Taylor's editing of *Troilus* is not that a passage has been excised to resolve a duplication, but that Taylor has moved away from eclectic conflation and based his text on F as representing Shakespeare's revision of the play and accepted the consequences of that stance. Jensen's case is that the two-venue theory is too insecure to permit such a radical alteration of F in a Folio-based edition. There is truth in this, for the sequence of events remains conjectural, and in particular there is no need to assume that Pandarus' 'here' in the Epilogue must allude to a legal environment. Too much, indeed, hangs on that reinterpretable adverb. Emendations of F are available that don't depend on tying 'here' to an Inn of Court, and it is a weakness of Jensen's article that she does not seem aware of them. Nor does she note that E. A. J. Honigmann advanced a critique of Taylor that in some respects anticipates her own, though she refers to his article ('The Date and Revision of *Troilus and Cressida*', in *Textual Criticism and Literary Interpretation*, ed. Jerome McGann (1985), 38–54), nor that Taylor himself consequently lost faith in a two-venue theory that saw the 'epilogue' as an Inns of Court speech inappropriate to a Globe setting.[21] In the general editors' joint 're-view' of the Oxford Shakespeare, Stanley Wells and Taylor proposed instead transposing Pandarus' final speech to 5.3.[22] Edward Capell long ago found another emendation, unconsidered, I think, by recent editors;[23] it seems bibliographically plausible and entirely effective from a performance point of view. The duplication in 5.3 is taken as a misinterpreted cue to move the letter-tearing passage to the end of the play. In Capell's text Cressida is brought back into view right at the very end, represented in the letter; his reconstructed final scene echoes the first scene in which Troilus confesses to Pandarus that he is 'mad / In Cressid's love'. These two solutions both conflict with the supposition that the revisions were made as the play switched to the Globe, for they retain the allegedly Inns-of-Court material.

An editor can scarcely accept F as control text for being the later, more 'finished', and more 'theatrical' text and yet avoid doing anything about the duplication it contains. Reversion to the text from which F is departing is scarcely a credible option, and the credible established options are all radical. Jensen's case, for all its trenchant detail of argumentation, comes down at its most conclusive to the simple point that in

21 'There has always been something unsatisfactory about the hypothesis that *Troilus* was written specifically for an Inns of Court audience' (Stanley Wells and Gary Taylor, with John Jowett and William Montgomery, *William Shakespeare: A Textual Companion* (1987), p. 438).

22 Stanley Wells and Gary Taylor, 'The Oxford Shakespeare Re-Viewed by the General Editors', *Analytic and Enumerative Bibliography*, NS, 4 (1990), 6–20, pp. 14–15. They attribute the solution to Wilbur Sanders.

23 Roger Apfelbaum drew my attention to Capell's reading, in his doctoral dissertation '"Author's Pen or Actor's Voice": A Performance History of Editorial Problems in *Troilus and Cressida*' (University of Birmingham, 1996), pp. 208–9. Capell was following a conjecture by George Steevens.

Q and F there are 'two differently authoritative texts' (p. 421). Her postmodern critical predisposition leads her to prefer the anti-tragic closure found in the Epilogue, and her insistence on the 'equal authority' of Q seems to concede belatedly that there must be consequences for the Epilogue in adopting F. For Taylor the choice of control text was not simply one of critical taste. He was bound by an editorial approach that runs through the entire Oxford edition to prefer the revised text that stands closer to performance.[24] It is Jensen, more than Taylor, who must finally be suspected of allowing critical predisposition to drive the textual perspective, even though it is Taylor who has recognized the vulnerability of his own argument.

E. A. J. Honigmann's major study, *The Texts of 'Othello' and Shakespearian Revision*, is a detailed investigation of the Quarto and Folio texts as a preliminary to his Arden 3 edition. It carries with it important implications for our understanding of Shakespearian revision beyond the immediate case of *Othello*. Honigmann insists that the editor of *Othello* – and by implication of other supposedly revised plays – should select between variants on the basis that they have many different causes, revision being just one of them. By his view, two-text editing lends a spurious acceptability to readings that are most likely to be textual errors. Even in the case of *Lear*, he notes that 'the relationship of revision to corruption, a crucial question, has not so far been dealt with satisfactorily'. *Othello* by general agreement cannot have been revised as extensively or as transformatively as *Lear*. It is usually accepted too that both Quarto and Folio have suffered in the process of copying by scribes. Are there two *Othellos* or one? Should we indeed, as Jones does, embrace the premise of Shakespeare as a bi-textual author?

Honigmann carefully accepts that Shakespeare made changes to the play that account for a significant number of variants between Quarto and Folio *Othello*, and that these two printed texts are indirectly based on two differing authorial manuscripts. But so much difference between the texts must be explained in terms of corruption in one text or the other that it becomes misleading to speak of Quarto and Folio as two authorial versions of the play. Where Jones breezily finds the marks of genius gleaming everywhere, Honigmann persistently throws the coarser fish and the smaller fry out of the authorial net. He inveighs against the revision theory at its most vulnerable point when he claims that the evidence, such as it is, indicates that the longer passages found in the Folio but not the Quarto result from cutting in the pre-Quarto manuscript. Accordingly, there cannot be a single line of development from pre-revision Quarto copy to revised Folio copy, as each must be seen as an independently adapted version of the play. Perhaps the strongest case Honigmann adduces is Desdemona's 'Willow Song', which, though anticipated in the Quarto, is apparently not sung. But Shakespeare was not actually writing the song, for it was a well-known ballad, and it is surely possible that the dash after 'that Song to night / Will not goe from my mind' is authorial shorthand for 'She sings'. Honigmann again finds Q post-excision rather than pre-revision at 1.1.119–35: when Q later has Brabanzio accuse Roderigo of deceiving him, it bears witness that the Folio-only lines in which Roderigo told him about Desdemona's elopement must have stood in the original text. Here economy of hypothesis would indeed favour a cut. Another alleged cut in Q (4.3.101–4) is evidenced by the strong interlinking between the Folio-only passage and its continuation, though I cannot see why Shakespeare might not in revising have made a strong join. All in all, the evidence from the Folio-only passages is less decisive than Honigmann would claim.

Honigmann's conclusion that the Quarto has

[24] His policy is unsettled by Honigmann's theory that the revised play was suppressed from public performance, but it would still be possible to maintain that F is the more performance-oriented text.

suffered a series of cuts would matter less if it were Shakespeare who might have been responsible for them, but the emphasis Honigmann places on the ineptitude and contingency is designed to show that the Quarto is 'theatrical' in the bad sense that it is not conformable with anything Shakespeare would have perpetrated or would voluntarily have allowed. The Quarto prompts further doubts. Honigmann connects this text with other King's Men plays printed in 1619–25, suggesting that the publisher Thomas Walkley and the printer Nicholas Okes 'arouse misgivings as to their professional dealings at the very time when they produced the Quarto version of *Othello*'. Here the discussion depends on some astutely observed if sometimes tangential pieces of evidence, and, as Honigmann recognizes, there is a danger in allowing the character of the text to be defamed by association.

The Folio too is deficient, and Honigmann gives substance and life to a major stage in its transmission by identifying the scribe who prepared the Folio copy as the scrivener Ralph Crane. Crane is known to have prepared a number of extant manuscripts of plays by Thomas Middleton and John Fletcher, and is thought also to have supplied the printer with manuscript copy for several other Shakespeare Folio plays. A number of distinctive and indeed quirky habits of spelling and punctuation show through into the printed texts. Honigmann's demonstration of these traits in *Othello* is argued with impressive care, and an accumulation of significant detail makes the case convincing.

In some ways, it is reassuring to know that the erstwhile unknown scribe is probably Crane. Although he tidied up the presentation of his texts, he can scarcely have been responsible for the more striking differences between the Quarto and Folio. Crane comes into view in assessing alternatives such as 'has'/'hath', 'to haue'/'t'haue', 'ashore'/'on Shore'. But Honigmann's identification of Crane only helps to confirm that the more important substantive variants were not initiated by this scribe: readings that impinge much more directly on the literary and theatrical qualities of the text such as 'vtmost pleasure'/'very quality', 'ascerbe as the'/'bitter as', 'banning'/'foaming', 'her Sex'/ 'their Wiues', or added fragments such as Iago's wonderful exclamation 'Bless'd pudding', or, for that matter 'Being done, there is no pawse'. Honigmann does not emphasize what T. H. Howard-Hill, the leading scholar of Crane, calls his 'scrupulous attention to textual details' ('Shakespeare's Earliest Editor, Ralph Crane', in *Shakespeare Survey 44* (1992), 113–29, p. 120), and he draws limited attention to some important areas where his new hypotheses leave the author as strong a candidate for rewording the text as before.

Nevertheless, the Crane theory, like much else in the book, provides an editor with more finely tuned critical instruments for coping with the mass and range of variants in *Othello*. In doing so, it lends plausibility and finesse to the techniques of editing based on delicate negotiation between conflicting texts regarded as imperfect witnesses to Shakespeare's lost manuscripts. Honigmann's book has a quiet but persistent polemical dimension that becomes emphatic towards the end. He upholds the editor's responsibility to conflate; he rejects Quarto and Folio as distinct authorial entities. As Honigmann knows, 'conflationist' and 'revisionist' approaches do not exclude each other. Any editorial approach to *Othello* that recognizes the need to emend error is bound to engage in a degree of conflation. The question is, which theory prevails where the textual variant alone provides no adequate self-explanation? The Oxford Shakespeare *Textual Companion* signals literally hundreds of 'readings most likely to have been affected by revision' (p. 478), but its procedures are nevertheless committed to identifying and eliminating where possible the interventions of both Quarto and Folio scribes. Honigmann offers to move back very considerably the boundary between authorial and non-authorial, and so to alter the presumption where there is no obvious way of deciding. To be sure, as more variants are diagnosed as non-authorial, it makes less sense to allow the mass of more trivial variants the privilege of mutual coexistence under the umbrella of authorial revision; and where a revisionist might advocate or assume that Shakespeare at different times envisaged both an Indian and a Judean throwing away a pearl at 5.2.356, by Honigmann's rationale '*Indian*' is the textual pearl and '*Iudean*' is textually base.

When Honigmann refers to the 'milk of the word', he makes a revealing allusion to 1 Peter 2:2 that puts the uncontaminated authorial word immediately at odds with the theatrical process. His terms affirm that there is much at stake in the haths and the hases. The alternative to conflation is, we are told, 'to achieve a small good at the cost of an all-corroding evil'. Honigmann finds it unacceptable to affiliate, for the purposes of editing, with either of *Othello*'s deeply perjured witnesses. It is the anti-conflationist's relatively uncritical willingness to do so that disturbs him. Yet in editing there are no Tables of the Law. Conceptual models of the literary process and the boundaries between art and error are constructed and without predetermination. As we have seen, the author is no longer the sole and axiomatic regulator of the editorial procedure. In a world where there are many possible editorial objectives, there are many possible textual outcomes, and so the editor can end up colluding with the diversity and indefinitude of the original documents. Honigmann's best-known book on editorial matters, *The Stability of Shakespeare's Text* (1965), describes the instability of the Shakespearian textual condition in terms that have become widely accepted, positing authorial revision, theatrical adjustment and scribal infidelity as some of the destabilizing ingredients. For Honigmann, the Shakespeare editor's aim and responsibility must be to give fixed authorial form to the edited text. A castle built on sand? Perhaps so, but Honigmann digs deep foundations, and those lines from St Peter are a haunting reminder of a textual faith many have lost.

Sidney Thomas, defending 'The Integrity of *King Lear*', find elements of faith in the revision theory, which he describes as a 'new orthodoxy'. Taking Halio's Folio-based edition as a summary statement of revisionist thought, he argues that many of the Quarto readings defended by the revisionists are in fact demonstrable errors, some of them almost certainly mishearings. He may be right to argue that in 'She is her selfe and dowre' the 'and' should read 'a', as in F (the correction is accepted in the Oxford *Complete Works* but not by René Weis in his 1993 parallel text edition), or that in 'with accent teares', 'accent' should be corrected to F's 'cadent'. Such readings do not, however, undermine the revision theory very far in that it has always been accepted by revisionists that Q is an imperfect text. Thomas seeks to restore memorial error as a primary cause of textual variation in Q. This would be much more damaging, but the reading Thomas offers as the best example is better explained otherwise: 'my rackles' for 'miracles' need be no more than a compositorial spacing error within a recognized spelling of the word. Something more than a catalogue of debatable errors and probable errors of debatable provenance is needed to reinstate Q as a 'bad quarto', an explanation even Greg found doubtful.

Joseph A. Dane in '"Which is the Iustice, Which is the Theefe": Variants of Transposition in the Text(s) of *King Lear*' challenges revisionism by arguing that transpositions in *King Lear* can be explained on the basis that they were 'produced at press'. They are 'perfectly consistent with the notion of ordinary copying processes', though Dane does not adduce examples in print set from known copy to demonstrate this point, and he might have had difficulty in finding examples that compare with the more complex *Lear* variants he discusses. His proposal that it was a printing-house corrector who wrote 'Change places' in the 'handy-dandy' passage to signal a transposition is scarcely credible without some evidence that a corrector would depart from the usual conventions designed precisely to avoid confusion between the instruction to correct and the reading required.

Clearly the highly variant Shakespeare texts display something more than would be expected of a scribe such as Crane or a printing-house corrector. Revision and memorial reconstruction are two numbers in a restricted repertoire of possible explanations for persistent verbal and structural alteration. Laurie E. Maguire's *Shakespearean Suspect Texts* is a full-length and suitably sceptical study of the latter, addressing the canon of allegedly 'bad' quartos, Shakespearian and non-Shakespearian alike. The first half of the book reviews the context. There is an astute and sometimes witty chapter on the rise of the New Bibliography, tracing the central role of the memorial transmission theory in sustaining its typology of texts. Maguire points out that the movement's empiricist outlook was well suited to technical bibliography but foundered when it came to textual criticism; here subjective value-judgements inevitably lay at the heart of the foundationary classifications, and Maguire comments that, however great his skills in other areas, Greg for one was not a good critic. Her book is hugely well-informed on the career of Greg; other major proponents of memorial reconstruction such as A. W. Pollard, Harry R. Hoppe, and G. I. Duthie are dealt with more briefly, and perhaps Hoppe in particular, as a critic who, like Maguire, attempted to analyse and categorize the evidence itself, might have deserved fuller treatment.

Maguire proceeds to survey the evidence for reported texts and to consider the traits of memorial transmission. Some of her central examples of memorial transmission are less secure than she allows. In comparing the ballad Mrs Brown of Falkirk recited orally in 1800 with the transcript she later supplied, Maguire assumes that the written version is a textually stable base text and that memorial error is the only explanation for variation. One wonders whether some of the supposedly memorial readings might derive instead from a variant tradition and testify to the instability of the genre rather than the shortcomings of her personal memory. In reviewing commonplace books Maguire focuses on the fragments from *1 Henry IV* in British Library MS Add. 64078. Although it is a reasonable supposition that the compiler was remembering the play on stage, some measure of scepticism needs admitting even here. A copy of Thomas Middleton's *Two New Plays* (1657; British Library, 162. d. 28) has a spare leaf inscribed with lines culled from the two plays, and, although there are differences between the techniques of this annotator and the compiler from *1 Henry IV*, there are similarities too. Two lines from *Women, Beware Women*, 'It is but begging two or three year sooner, / And stay with her continually' (1.3.19–20), are the basis for the annotation: 'Tis but betting 3 or 4 yrs further & have her'. Here in eleven words are confusion between verse and prose, an ametrical naturalization of idiom (It is/Tis), numerical exaggeration, a substitution of an equivalent word that is actually destructive of the original meaning (sooner/further), and reductive paraphrase. If such a rendition were found in a commonplace book of the 1620s, it would surely be proclaimed as a text based on memory of performance. Yet in this case the transcriber simply must have been depending on the very book into which he was writing. It is a cautionary instance of the vagaries of scribal transmission in a situation where the base text was undeniably available.

Maguire's examination of actors' lines from the BBC Shakespeare videos similarly but much more certainly adduces illustrations of memorial error that can be explained otherwise. Her examples supposedly of actors' errors in the video of *Richard III* derive in fact from discrepancies between Q1 and F, and not from memory failure on the part of the BBC actors. The actors must have referred to a different script from the printed BBC text: probably Honigmann's New Penguin edition (1968), which accepts more Quarto readings than most of its counterparts. The irony is that the bulk of variants in *Richard III* has itself often been ascribed to memorial transmission. Maguire's use of Quarto readings to demonstrate memorial error on the part of modern actors is here a textbook example of contaminated evidence.

These comments of Maguire's chapter on 'Memory' recapitulate some of her own criticism of the New Bibliographers. As she puts it, 'Clearly something is wrong with a textual approach which can cite the same evidence in support of different assumptions' (p. 153). To some extent at least the problem is endemic to the material rather than the methodology. Although written transcription attempts to eliminate the effects of memory, the text inevitably passes through the mind as it is copied and traces of memory are always present in the outcome. Moreover, memory and other forms of transmission share in a conscious or unconscious desire to reform the text. Contamination is everywhere, and it should be no surprise that strictly diagnostic testing is hard to obtain.

Maguire nevertheless attempts to develop diagnostic tests, approaching the generally Shakespearian two-text (or three-text) plays by examining the suspect one 'as if no parallel text existed'. The reason is that 'This puts the Shakespearean suspect texts on an equal footing with the non-Shakespearean, and facilitates contextual understanding' (p. 155). The unstated effect in accordance with her wider aims is to break the study from the bind of what she has previously called 'teleological assumptions' (p. 153), for it is indeed hard to exercise the comparative method without presupposing some elements of a stemmatic relationship. Although there is methodological coherence in setting aside two-text comparison in order to correlate one-text and multiple-text plays, it does not follow that comparison as a tool for textual evaluation need be excluded permanently.

Maguire explains her method thus: 'Without making prejudgements as to origin, and temporarily abandoning the word "symptom", I list and examine the key features of suspect texts, separately and collectively, to ascertain what they might be symptoms of' (p. 153). This entails two processes of critical judgement. The first is to determine what in a text constitutes a 'key feature'; this rather vague concept depends, presumably, on a background notion of the normative that would challenge elaboration. Maguire's second critical process is to determine which features have symptomatic value; here there is an under-explored assumption about irregularities in transmission that might compete with memory in giving rise to 'symptoms'.

If Maguire's language of symptoms and diagnosis conceals the less than empirical dimensions of her study, it reveals a familiar set of assumptions: MR, like MS, is a disease, memorial texts are distinct from specimens in good health. After carefully assessing the symptomatic value of 'key features', Maguire tabulates them for each suspect text and at the foot of the table for each text reaches her diagnosis. The shift from the pre-diagnostic list to the post-diagnostic verdict ('Not MR', 'Possibly MR', etc.) is disturbingly abrupt, almost as though Maguire's study of Greg warned her of the dangers of saying too much. A fuller exposition would have revealed the critical, non-empirical basis of the verdict. This is not to say that Maguire misinterprets her tabulated symptoms. On the whole she seems to evaluate the features in a way that is coherent and consistent with the procedure she has set up. To that extent I trust her judgement. But it would be better if such trust were not demanded.

Maguire assumes that an absence of the features that point distinctively to memorial reconstruction is a sufficient basis on which to declare that a text is in fact not a memorial reconstruction. Her 'Not MR' really means

'Not demonstrated as MR'. But if negative evidence does not lead to a reliable negative diagnosis, future scholars will need to attach considerable weight to Maguire's few positive and qualified identifications of memorial reconstruction: *The Famous Victories of Henry V*, 'Probably MR, at least in the first half'; *Hamlet* Q1, 'Possibly MR, but if so, a very good one'; *A Knack to Know a Knave*, 'Possibly MR'; *The Massacre at Paris*, 'MR'; *Merry Wives* Q, 'Probably MR'; *The Taming of A Shrew*, 'Part MR (most notably in taming plot)'. And that is all. Are there the makings of a plausible new grouping here? Not in terms of performance company, nor stationers. It may perhaps be significant that the dates of publication cluster around 1594 and 1602–3. Yet my impression remains that this list makes little sense as a self-contained set. By acknowledging memorial reconstruction as a process that emanates from up to five different theatre companies but only one company more than once, and never the same stationer in the same capacity,[25] Maguire raises as many questions as she set out to answer. Questions are also raised as to how, if not by memorial transmission, the suspect texts acquired their 'key features'. Her book is still, despite the criticisms I have offered, a ground-breaking and disciplined study in textual criticism. It establishes a new bedrock. For others the silts and sediments.

ROMEO AND JULIET

Two pieces in Jay L. Halio's collection of essays on *Romeo and Juliet* concern the text. Alan C. Dessen considers how far the stage directions in Q1 can be taken to coincide with the staging requirements of Q2. He finds that some have 'possible interpretative significance unique to Q1'. He notes, for example, that at the end of 2.2 Romeo is given no exit in Q1 and in 2.3 he has no entrance; the implication is that when the Friar enters, in Q1 but not Q2 Romeo remains on another part of the stage. (One wonders whether Romeo's possible presence on stage in Q1 during the Friar's speech 'The gray ey'd morne' has anything to do with Romeo being given a first version of this speech before the Friar's version in Q2.) Dessen goes on to suggest that Q1 invites parallel staging of this episode where the Friar enters to Romeo, Juliet's entry to the Friar's cell in 4.1, and the Apothecary's entry to Romeo in 5.1. A portable property such as a basket might have been used by both the Friar and the Apothecary in order to establish a linkage. Yet it is striking in Dessen's account just how much of the Q1 theatrical vocabulary is fully compatible with Q2 – which is not to say that in such cases we can be confident that a Q2-based performance text would always have actually demanded the staging details as they are stipulated in the altered text.

But can we be sure that there would have been a 'long' performance text? Halio's own contribution to the volume challenges the memorial reconstruction theory as it has been applied to Q1. He notes that the supposed characteristics of memorial reconstruction are to be found (locally) in Q2 also, and that Q1 actually avoids symptoms such as textual garbling. He argues instead for 'usually careful' abridgement (p. 128); the alterations 'make good dramatic sense' (p. 132) and are metrically acceptable. More contentiously, he proposes Shakespeare as reviser and at least part stage adapter, and infers that Q1 represents the standard performance text. A passage excepted from Shakespearian authorship is Q1's version of Juliet meeting Friar Laurence in 2.6, but Halio defends reworked lines such as the lamentation episode in 4.5 and Paris' commemoration of Juliet in 5.3 as Shakespeare's. It is

[25] Thomas Creede was publisher of *Famous Victories* and printer of *Merry Wives*. Nicholas Ling was co-publisher of *Hamlet* and in 1607 temporary copy-holder of *A Shrew*. James Roberts entered *Hamlet* in the Stationers' Register and was possibly printer of *Knack to Know a Knave*. Thus where a stationer's name recurs, it does so in a different capacity.

surely more plausible that if a second hand adapted a passage relating to Juliet in 2.6, this same hand may account for other alterations, again relating to Juliet, in Q1's versions of 4.5 and 5.3.

What might be put on a more objective footing is that the elaborately articulated stage directions in Q1 are in their vocabulary and phrasing both uncharacteristic of Shakespeare and characteristic of Henry Chettle, Sidney Thomas's candidate for authorship of the non-Shakespearian verse ('Henry Chettle and the First Quarto of *Romeo and Juliet*', in *Review of English Studies*, NS, 1 (1950), 8–16). Jeffrey Kahan has affirmed Chettle's hand by drawing attention to the formula 'Enter [name(s)]', followed by 'and', followed by a verb inflected '-eth'. As the parallels he cites come from *The Death of Robert Earl of Huntingdon* a strict interpretation of them would be that the hand in *Romeo* could be Chettle's or Anthony Munday's, though Kahan might have noted an example in Chettle's *Hoffman* that suggests that the habit was either shared or unique to Chettle: '*Enter as many as may be spar'd, with lights, and make a lane kneeling while Martha the Dutchesse like a mourner with her traine passeth through*'.[26] A second revising hand, most plausibly Chettle's, seems more prevalent in Q1 than Halio admits. This point needs to be put together with a more contextual issue. The pattern of heavy adaptation and, in particular, drastic shortening that is found in Q1 corresponds better with the other 'bad' quarto texts than with the Folio texts printed, as far as we understand, with reference to theatrical manuscripts. Implicit in Halio's account is that we need to adopt more flexible assumptions about the 'standard' performance style of Shakespeare's plays. This might prove a valuable insight, yet few would be prepared to argue that Q1 *Hamlet* represents the standard playbook, and it still seems to me that Q1 *Romeo* has stronger affinities with Q1 *Hamlet* than with Folio *Hamlet*.

AUTHORSHIP STUDIES

I am not reviewing the controversy over the 'Funeral Elegy' on William Peter,[27] as the case for authorship depends on research that apparently has not been published in full. Indeed it is a striking aspect of the debate that some notable scholars seem to have accepted that Shakespeare wrote the poem on the basis of partial and mediated presentations of evidence. That authorship study can lead to an intemperate taking of positions can be seen in M. W. A. Smith's defence of his own earlier critique of T. Merriam over the authorship of *Edmund Ironside*. Smith himself is wholly temperate. In the course of his response, he draws attention to the serious issue of interdisciplinary communication. Stylometrics depends on statistical analysis and speaks a language entirely foreign to most literary scholars. How is the student of Shakespeare to know what to believe, what to disbelieve?

Fortunately the authorship investigations of MacD. P. Jackson have never been opaque to common sense. His 'Stage Directions and Speech Headings in Act 1 of *Titus Andronicus* Q (1594): Shakespeare or Peele?' argues convincingly that Act 1 and probably two other scenes of *Titus* were written by George Peele. Jackson establishes that the wording of stage directions in Act 1 has distinctively unShakespearian features that are well exampled in plays by Peele. He adds this finding to the already considerable evidence for Peele's hand in a 'Part A' defined as 1.1, 2.1, and 4.1. Peele would have written the opening of the play, for 1.1 and 2.1 are a single uninterrupted sequence, and the opening of the counter action. Jackson adds

26 Henry Chettle, *The Tragedy of Hoffman, 1631* (Malone Society Reprints, 1951, for 1950), lines 1682–4.

27 See Stanley Wells, 'In memory of Master William Peter', *TLS*, 26 January 1996, p. 28; Richard Abrams, 'In defence of W.S.', *TLS*, 9 February 1996, pp. 25–7; Stanley Wells, 'Shakespeare and the Funeral Elegy', *TLS*, 16 February 1996, p. 17; Brian Vickers, 'Whose thumbprints?', *TLS*, 8 March 1996, pp. 16–18.

further weight to the case for Peele by pointing out disparities in the frequency of occurrence of 'and' and 'with' that are consistent with a Shakespeare/Peele distribution of labour, and notes a Peele trick of style that recurs conspicuously in Act 1, the formula preposition, possessive pronoun, monosyllabic noun placed at the end of a line, as in 'of my right', 'with your swords'. He recognizes the argument that Shakespeare might have been imitating Peele, but points out the improbability that such an imitation would be manifested in so many distinct traits whilst being confined to certain sections of the play. The Peelean stage directions are particularly hard to explain with reference to conscious imitation.

Brian Boyd ('Common Words in *Titus Andronicus*: The Presence of Peele') adds further weight to the case for Peele's hand. Looking back on Jackson's and earlier studies, he summarizes the sheer variety and weight of internal evidence that has been adduced in favour of Peele in Jackson's Part A. Boyd's contribution is to identify key words favoured by Peele that recur more often in Part A than in Part B: for example, seventeen times more frequently in the case of *honour*. The result is, at worst, 'a sludgy soup of repetition and rehashed abstraction' (p. 303). Like Jackson, Boyd finds Peele's presence more clearly marked in 1.1 than 2.1 and 4.1. More speculatively, Boyd suggests that in *The Battle of Alcazar* Peele's introduction of the 'superfluous' son of the black villain Muly Mahamet and the 'bloody banquet' of the dumb show in Act 4 both reflect Peele's response to Shakespeare's part in their collaborative work. In contrast, the case for Peele's hand in *Titus* does not depend on a particular order of composition. Boyd shows that even 2.1, the least clearly Peelean scene in Part A, conforms to a Peele pattern of a 'Manet' direction followed by an 'emphatically Marlovian' soliloquy (p. 307). If one had to choose in the light of these new contributions between identifing *Titus* as by Shakespeare or by Shakespeare and Peele, the latter would be much the safer bet.

AN ASSORTMENT

Anthony James West continues his work towards a new census of First Folios by addressing a question that might have seemed superfluous, 'How Many First Folios Does the Folger Hold?' As West explains, the question arises because there is a problem in defining what constitutes a countable copy. Particularly at issue are the three sets identified by Peter Blayney as the Burgundy, Red, and Green sets. The sewn and folded or bound volumes that make up each of these sets consist of between one and three plays each, 'more than one play whenever one play ends on the recto and the next starts on the verso'. In the unbound Burgundy set are thirty-one complete plays; the leaves are 89 per cent from a single copy. The others, though bound, are less complete, are compiled from different copies, and contain facsimile leaves. West recognizes that the Red and Green sets have a questionable entitlement to be regarded as copies, but pragmatically decides to give these assemblages the benefit of the doubt. Thus the answer to the question is that the Folger holds eighty-two Folio copies.

Dorothea Kehler's 'The First Quarto of *Hamlet*: Reforming Widow Gertred' is a perceptive if sometimes speculative account of Q1 *Hamlet*'s Gertred as a woman inscribed within Catholic notions of widowhood. Meek, pious, and tractable though she is as compared with her Q2 and F counterparts, her remarriage in itself 'casts her as a lusty widow' (p. 404). Kehler suggests that the 'else-where' of the performance locations mentioned on the title-page might have been places 'where ideas about the sacred nature of celibacy lingered longest', such as the north of England.

Amongst the various notes in the 1995 *Notes and Queries*, that by R. J. C. Watt considers in his usual temperate and persuasive way Antonio's puzzling 'It is that anything now' in *Merchant of Venice* 1.1.113. Watt proposes the emendation 'It is that in anything now', a reading that deserves consideration by editors.

David Farley-Hills offers to illuminate the hobby-horse crux at *Hamlet* 3.2.128–9 by comparing a passage in *Eastward Ho!* (3.2.42–51). He usefully sees a suggestion of an innocent childhood toy forgotten in favour of adult sexual activity combined with a reference to that activity itself. Penelope Hicks indicates a limit to the applicability of Theobald's historical scholarship. Theobald was right in saying that in Shakespeare's day Lear was unidiomatic in describing how Goneril 'Lookt blacke' upon him, but Hicks posits that nevertheless Shakespeare was not beyond inventing such a phrase himself. Noel R. Blincoe considers *Two Noble Kinsmen* 1.3.79: 'This rehearsall / (Which fury-innocent wots well) comes in / Like old importments bastard'. He defends 'fury-innocent' as meaning a person innocent of fury. The reading remains almost intolerably strained (it would work better if the text read 'The' instead of 'Which'). As it depends on a contrast between the girls' childhood love and the men's fury-corrupted love, there is surely a further difficulty in that the men's fury has not yet erupted.

Those who consider that editing and textual studies are turned in on their own assumptions might care to look at Herbert Ramsay's desktop-published editions of Shakespeare's plays. As the work was undertaken before Ramsay's death in 1968, the scholarship is inevitably dated. Ramsay takes a heavily normative and standardized view of Shakespearian prosody and grammar, and on this basis identifies extensive scribal corruption. Ramsay's theories are unlikely to find widespread acceptance, but some of his readings may be of interest to future scholars.

The first volume of the new Cambridge edition of John Webster's works deserves mention as a monumental achievement in its own right. This is an exhaustive edition that brings together the old-spelling text with full apparatus favoured by Greg and Bowers and an attention to the theatrical dimension as pioneered in the New Penguin and Oxford editions. The Cambridge edition is a mix of 'definitive' and provisional: a remarkably comprehensive edition for here and now, but one whose critical and theatrical cut-off point may make it less durable than other monuments of New Bibliographical editorial enterprise. Indeed, even textural work moves on as can be seen in Martin Wiggins's 'Notes on Editing Webster' (*Notes and Queries* 240 (1995), 369–77). F. L. Lucas's edition nevertheless looks set to be retired.

TO CONCLUDE

In contrasting Mowat and Werstine's articles with their editions, I pointed to a gap between textualist criticism and editing. This gap perhaps extends to Orgel, and certainly extends beyond the practices of these three major scholars. A few years ago textual studies needed freeing from the end of editing; now the two seem in danger of losing touch entirely. The philosophers who contemplate the word are averse to changing it. What they resist, a sense of process, seems necessary to meaningful editing, and in that process one cannot help but discover Shakespeare, a name no-one had honestly forgotten. 'What difference does it make who is speaking?' We hear a thousand voices in the question, but, not only to editors, it makes every difference that amongst them we hear Michel Foucault, it makes every difference that amongst them we hear Samuel Beckett.[28]

WORKS REVIEWED

Bjelland, Karen T. 'The Cultural Value of Analytic Bibliography and Textual Criticism: The Case of *Troilus and Cressida*', *TEXT*, 7 (1994), 273–95.

Blincoe, Noel R. '"Fury-Innocent" as Used in *The Two Noble Kinsmen*', *Notes and Queries*, 240 (1995), 337–8.

Boyd, Brian. 'Common Words in *Titus Andronicus*: The Presence of Peele'. *Notes and Queries*, 240 (1995), 300–7.

[28] Compare Gary Taylor's wilful appropriation of Foucault in 'What is an Author [not]?', *Critical Survey*, 7 (1995), 241–55.

Dane, Joseph A. '"Which is the Iustice, Which is the Theefe": Variants of Transposition in the Text(s) of *King Lear*'. *Notes and Queries*, 240 (1995), 322–7.

Dessen, Alan C. 'QI *Romeo and Juliet* and Elizabethan Theatrical Vocabulary'. *Shakespeare's 'Romeo and Juliet'* (see Halio, below), 107–22.

AN EXCELLENT CONCEITED TRAGEDIE OF *Romeo and Juliet*. Ed. by Cedric Watts, Shakespearean Originals. Hemel Hempstead: Prentice Hall, 1995.

Farley-Hills, David. 'A *Hamlet* Crux'. *Notes and Queries*, 240 (1995), 319–20.

Gilman, Todd S. '"Why seems it so particular with thee?": *Hamlet* among the Revisionists'. *Hamlet Studies*, 17 (1995), 78–93.

Halio, Jay L. 'Handy-Dandy: QI/Q2 *Romeo and Juliet*'. In *Shakespeare's 'Romeo and Juliet': Texts, Contexts, and Interpretation*. Ed. by Halio. Newark: University of Delaware Press and London: Associated University Presses, 1995, 123–50.

Hicks, Penelope. 'Did Goneril Look "Black", "Back", or "Blank" upon Her Father?' *Notes and Queries*, 240 (1995), 322.

Holderness, Graham, Bryan Loughrey, and Andrew Murphy. '"What's the matter?": Shakespeare and Textual Theory'. *Textual Practice*, 9 (1995), 93–119.

Honigmann, E. A. J. *The Texts of 'Othello' and Shakespearian Revision*. London and New York: Routledge, 1996.

Jackson, MacD. P. 'Stage Directions and Speech Headings in Act 1 of *Titus Andronicus* Q (1594): Shakespeare or Peele?'. *Studies in Bibliography*, 49 (1996), 134–48.

Jensen, Phebe. 'The Textual Politics of *Troilus and Cressida*'. *Shakespeare Quarterly*, 46 (1995), 414–23.

Jones, John. *Shakespeare at Work*. Oxford: Clarendon, 1995.

Kahan, Jeffrey. 'Henry Chettle's *Romeo* QI and *The Death of Robert Earl of Huntingdon*'. *Notes and Queries*, 241 (1996), 155–6.

Kehler, Dorothea. 'The First Quarto of *Hamlet*: Reforming Widow Gertred'. *Shakespeare Quarterly*, 46 (1995), 398–413.

Maguire, Laurie E. *Shakespearean Suspect Texts: The 'Bad' Quartos and their Contexts*. Cambridge: Cambridge University Press, 1996.

THE MOST EXCELLENT HISTORIE OF *The Merchant of Venice*. Ed. by Annabel Patterson, Shakespearean Originals. Hemel Hempstead: Prentice Hall, 1995.

Mowat, Barbara A. 'The Problem of Shakespeare's Text(s)'. *Shakespeare Jahrbuch*, 132 (1996), 26–43.

Nimbus, Claudia. 'An Evening without M[rs] Siddons'. *Critical Survey*, 7 (1995), 256–91.

Osborne, Laurie E. 'Shattuck and Kemble: Intermingling Editing in Facsimile'. *Critical Survey*, 7 (1995), 307–18.

Roberts, Sasha. 'Reading the Shakespearean Text in Early Modern England'. *Critical Survey*, 7 (1995), 299–306.

Shakespeare, William. *The Down-Under Shakespeare (Anthony and Cleopatra, Coriolanus, Macbeth, Othello, Richard II, The Tempest)*, ed. by Herbert Ramsay. Totara North, New Zealand: F. W. Ramsay, 1996.

Shakespeare, William. *The Sonnets*. Ed. by G. Blakemore Evans, with an Introduction by Anthony Hecht, The New Cambridge Shakespeare. Cambridge: Cambridge University Press, 1996.

Shakespeare, William. *The Winter's Tale*. Ed. by Stephen Orgel, The Oxford Shakespeare. Oxford: Clarendon, 1996.

Shak-speare, M. William. HIS *True Chronicle Historie of the life and death of King LEAR and his three Daughters*. Ed. by Graham Holderness, Shakespearean Originals. Hemel Hempstead: Prentice Hall, 1995.

Smith, M. W. A. '*Edmund Ironside*: Scholarship Versus Propaganda'. *Notes and Queries*, 240 (1995), 294–9.

Thomas, Sidney. 'The Integrity of *King Lear*'. *Modern Language Review*, 90 (1995), 572–84.

THE TRAGŒDY OF *Othello, the Moore of Venice*. Ed. by Andrew Murphy, Shakespearean Originals. Hemel Hempstead: Prentice Hall, 1995.

Twelfe Night, Or what you will. Ed. by Laurie E. Osborne, Shakespearean Originals. Hemel Hempstead: Prentice Hall, 1995.

Urkowitz, Stephen. '"Brother, can you spare a Paradigm?": Textual Generosity and the Printing of Shakespeare's Multiple-Text Plays by Contemporary Editors'. *Critical Survey*, 7 (1995), 292–8.

Watt, R. J. C. 'Commendable Silence: A Crux in *The Merchant of Venice*.' *Notes and Queries*, 240 (1995), 316–17.

Webster, John. *Works*. Vol. 1, *The White Devil, The Duchess of Malfi*. Ed. by David Gunby, David Carnegie, and Antony Hammond. Cambridge: Cambridge University Press, 1995.

West, Anthony James. 'How Many First Folios does the Folger Hold?' *Shakespeare Quarterly*, 47 (1996), 190–4.

BOOKS RECEIVED

This list includes all books received between September 1995 and September 1996 which are not reviewed in this volume of *Shakespeare Survey*. The appearance of a book in this list does not preclude its review in a subsequent volume.

Campbell, Patrick, ed. *Analysing Performance: A Critical Reader*. Manchester and New York: Manchester University Press, 1996.

Candido, Joseph, ed. *Shakespeare: The Critical Tradition: 'King John'*. London and Atlantic Highlands, NJ: Athlone, 1996.

Dolan, Frances E., ed. *'The Taming of the Shrew': Texts and Contexts*. Boston and New York: Bedford Books of St Martin's Press, 1996.

Erskine-Hill, Howard. *Poetry and the Realm of Politics: Shakespeare to Dryden*. Oxford: Clarendon Press, 1996.

Holderness, Graham, Bryan Loughrey and Andrew Murphy. *Shakespeare: The Roman Plays*. Longman Critical Readers. London and New York: Longman, 1996.

Huffman, Clifford Chalmers, ed. *'Love's Labor's Lost', 'A Midsummer Night's Dream', and 'The Merchant of Venice': An Annotated Bibliography of Shakespeare Studies, 1888–1994*. Binghamton, NY: Medieval and Renaissance Texts and Studies, 1995.

Kerr, Heather, Robin Eaden and Madge Mitton. *Shakespeare: World Views*. Newark and London: University of Delaware Press, Associated University Presses, 1996.

Murray, Peter B. *Shakespeare's Imagined Persons: The Psychology of Role-Playing and Acting*. Basingstoke: Macmillan, 1996.

Ousby, Ian, ed. *Cambridge Paperback Guide to Literature in English*. Cambridge: Cambridge University Press, 1996.

Schlueter, June, ed. *'The Two Gentlemen of Verona': Critical Essays*. New York and London: Garland, 1996.

Shakespeare, William. *Oeuvres Complètes: Tragédies*. Ed. by Michel Grivelet and Gilles Monsarrat, 2 vols. Paris: Robert Lafford, 1995.

Stanton, Sarah, and Martin Banham, eds. *Cambridge Paperback Guide to Theatre*. Cambridge: Cambridge University Press, 1996.

INDEX

The index does not include titles of books referred to in the review articles. These books are listed alphabetically by author at the end of the articles.

Play titles in the chapter by John Astington are not included.

INDEX

INDEX

INDEX

INDEX

INDEX

INDEX